Exam 70-272: Supporting Users and Troubleshooting Desktop Applications on a Microsoft Windows XP Operating System

Objective	Chapter	Lesson
1. Configuring and Troubleshooting Applications		
1.1. Configure and troubleshoot Office applications.		
1.1.1. Answer end-user questions related to configuring Office applications.	6	1–4
	7	1–3
1.1.2. Set application compatibility settings.	6	1
1.1.3. Troubleshoot application installation problems.	6	1 and 2
1.1.4. Configure and troubleshoot e-mail account settings.	4	1, 3, 4
1.2. Configure and troubleshoot Internet Explorer.	5	2, 3
1.3. Configure and troubleshoot Outlook Express.		
1.3.1. Answer end-user questions related to configuring Outlook Express.	4	1–5
1.3.2. Configure and troubleshoot newsreader account settings.	4	2
1.3.3. Configure and troubleshoot e-mail account settings.	4	1, 3, 4
1.4. Configure the operating system to support applications.		
1.4.1. Answer end-user questions related to configuring the operating system to support an application.	3	1–4
1.4.2. Configure and troubleshoot file system access and file permission problems on multiboot computers.	11	2
1.4.3. Configure access to applications on multiuser computers.	11	1
1.4.4. Configure and troubleshoot application access on a multiple user client computer.	11	1
2. Resolving Issues Related to Usability		
2.1. Resolve issues related to Office application support features. Tasks include configuring Office applications and interpreting error messages.	7	1–3, 5
2.2. Resolve issues related to Internet Explorer support features. Tasks include configuring Internet Explorer and interpreting error messages.	5	3
2.3. Resolve issues related to Outlook Express features. Tasks include configuring Outlook Express and interpreting error messages.	4	4
	7	4
2.4. Resolve issues related to operating system features. Tasks include configuring operating system features and interpreting error messages.	3	1–5
3. Resolving Issues Related to Application Customization		
3.1. Resolve issues related to customizing an Office application.		
3.1.1. Answer end-user questions related to customizing Office applications.	6	3
3.1.2. Customize toolbars.	6	3
3.1.3. Configure proofing tools.	6	4
3.1.4. Manage Outlook data, including configuring, importing, and exporting data, and repairing corrupted data.	4	3
3.1.5. Personalize Office features.	6	3
3.2. Resolve issues related to customizing Internet Explorer.	5	2
3.3. Resolve issues related to customizing Outlook Express.	4	5

Objective	Chapter	Lesson
3.4. Resolve issues related to customizing the operating system to support applications.		
3.4.1. Answer end-user questions related to customizing the operating system to support an application.	3	1–5
3.4.2. Customize the Start menu and taskbar.	3	1
3.4.3. Customize regional settings.	3	2
3.4.4. Customize fonts.	7	3
3.4.5. Customize folder settings.	3	3
4. Configuring and Troubleshooting Connectivity for Applications		
4.1. Identify and troubleshoot name resolution problems. Indications of such problems include application errors.	8	4
4.2. Identify and troubleshoot network adapter configuration problems. Indications of such problems include application errors.	8	1, 2
4.3. Identify and troubleshoot LAN and Routing and Remote Access configuration problems. Indications of such problems include application errors.	8	2, 3
4.4. Identify and troubleshoot network connectivity problems caused by the firewall configuration. Indications of such problems include application errors.	10	2
4.5. Identify and troubleshoot problems with locally attached devices. Indications of such problems include application errors.	12	1–2
5. Configuring Application Security		
5.1. Identify and troubleshoot problems related to security permissions.		
5.1.1. Answer end-user questions related to application security settings.	9	1–4
5.1.2. Troubleshoot access to local resources.	9	1–2
5.1.3. Troubleshoot access to network resources.	9	1–2
5.1.4. Troubleshoot insufficient user permissions and rights.	9	1–4
5.2. Identify and respond to security incidents.		
5.2.1. Answer end-user questions related to security incidents.	10	1–4
5.2.2. Identify a virus attack.	10	3
5.2.3. Apply critical updates.	10	1
5.3. Manage application security settings.	4	1, 5
	5	2
	6	3
	7	1–3

Microsoft®

MCDST Self-Paced Training Kit (Exam 70-272):

Supporting Users and Troubleshooting Desktop Applications on Microsoft® Windows® XP, Second Edition

Walter Glenn
Tony Northrup

PUBLISHED BY
Microsoft Press
A Division of Microsoft Corporation
One Microsoft Way
Redmond, Washington 98052-6399

Library of Congress Control Number 2005932155

Printed and bound in the United States of America.

1 2 3 4 5 6 7 8 9   QWT   8 7 6 5

Distributed in Canada by H.B. Fenn and Company Ltd. A CIP catalogue record for this book is available from the British Library.

Microsoft Press books are available through booksellers and distributors worldwide. For further information about international editions, contact your local Microsoft Corporation office or contact Microsoft Press International directly at fax (425) 936-7329. Visit our Web site at www.microsoft.com/mspress. Send comments to tkinput@microsoft.com.

Acquisitions Editor: Ken Jones
Project Editor: Karen Szall

Body Part No. X11-46495

For my kids, Liam and Maya

-Walter

For Sam

-Tony

Contents at a Glance

Practices

Tables

Troubleshooting Labs

Case Scenario Exercises

Contents

2   Resolving a Service Call   2-1

3   **Troubleshooting the Operating System**   **3-1**

System Requirements

Acknowledgments

No matter how good a roll we are on in writing a book, when it comes time to write this page, we always find ourselves a little at a loss for words. Putting a book like this together takes a lot of work from a lot of people. We are always somewhat amazed when the flurry of research, e-mails, writing, rewriting, and proofreading are finished and then, suddenly, there's a book in your hands.

We're even more amazed when a project this size rolls along smoothly from start to finish, but that's exactly what happened thanks to the great folks at Microsoft Press. We'd like to thank everyone who helped out with this book during its various stages. Maureen Zimmerman, our development editor, worked hard to coordinate the project and make sure that the book was published on schedule. Karen Szall, our project editor, did a wonderful job providing feedback and making sure the book was of the highest quality. Bob Hogan, our technical editor, pored over every detail and made sure we actually knew what we were talking about. We'd also like to thank Martin DelRe for his valuable guidance.

Thanks also go to Greg Winston, who developed the MiniDir Exchange Server simulation tool, and to Daniel Akins, who wrote the defrag.vbs script for running Disk Defragmenter automatically so that it can be scheduled. Both of these tools are included on the book's CD.

Finally, as always, we'd like to thank Neil Salkind and everyone else at StudioB for helping put this project together.

—Walter Glenn and Tony Northrup

About This Book

Welcome to *MCDST Self-Paced Training Kit (Exam 70-272): Supporting Users and Troubleshooting Desktop Applications on Microsoft® Windows® XP*, Second Edition. This book teaches you how to resolve end-user requests for configuring and troubleshooting desktop applications running Microsoft Windows XP Home Edition or Windows XP Professional Edition, Service Pack 2 (SP2).

You will learn how to talk to end users about problems, isolate and troubleshoot problems, and then propose and document solutions. This book focuses on the following:

■ Installing, configuring, and troubleshooting Microsoft Office Professional Edition 2003, including Microsoft Word, Microsoft Excel, Microsoft PowerPoint, and Microsoft Outlook

■ Configuring and troubleshooting Microsoft Internet Explorer

■ Creating e-mail and newsgroup accounts in, configuring, and troubleshooting Outlook Express

■ Configuring the Windows XP desktop environment to support running various applications

Note For more information about becoming a Microsoft Certified Professional (MCP) or Microsoft Certified Desktop Support Technician (MCDST), see the section titled "The Microsoft Certified Professional Program" later in this introduction.

Intended Audience

This book was developed for information technology (IT) professionals who plan to take the related Microsoft Certified Professional exam 70-272, "Supporting Users and Troubleshooting Desktop Applications on a Microsoft Windows XP Operating System," and for IT professionals who run Windows XP Professional in a corporate or small-business environment or Windows XP Home Edition in a home environment.

Note Exam skills are subject to change without prior notice and at the sole discretion of Microsoft.

Prerequisites

This training kit requires that students meet the following prerequisites:

- Have a basic understanding of the Windows XP operating system
- Have a basic understanding of Internet Explorer 6
- Have a basic understanding of Outlook Express
- Have a basic understanding of Office applications

About the CD-ROM

This book includes a companion CD-ROM, which contains a variety of informational aids to complement the book content:

- The Readiness Review Suite Powered by MeasureUp. This suite of practice tests and objective reviews contains questions of varying degrees of complexity and offers multiple testing modes. You can assess your understanding of the concepts presented in this book and use the results to develop a learning plan that meets your needs.

- An electronic version of this book (eBook). For information about using the eBook, see the "The eBook" section later in this introduction.

- Tools and sample documents used in some of the Practices throughout the book.

- An eBook of the *Microsoft Encyclopedia of Networking*, Second Edition, and the *Microsoft Encyclopedia of Security*, which provide complete and up-to-date reference materials for networking and security.

Two additional CD-ROMs contain evaluation edition software for your use. One contains a 30-day evaluation edition of Microsoft Office Professional Edition 2003. The other contains a 120-day evaluation edition of Microsoft Windows XP Professional Edition with Service Pack 2.

> **Caution**   The evaluation edition software that is provided with this training kit is not the full retail product and is provided only for the purposes of training and evaluation. Microsoft Technical Support does not support evaluation editions.

For additional support information regarding this book and the CD-ROM (including answers to commonly asked questions about installation and use), visit the Microsoft Press Technical Support website at *http://www.microsoft.com/learning/support/*. You can also e-mail tkinput@microsoft.com or send a letter to Microsoft Press, Attention: *MCDST Self-Paced Training Kit (Exam 70-272): Supporting Users and Troubleshooting*

Desktop Applications on Microsoft® Windows® XP, Second Edition, Editor, One Microsoft Way, Redmond, WA 98052-6399.

Features of This Book

This book has two parts. Use Part 1 to learn at your own pace and to practice what you've learned with practical exercises. Part 2 contains questions and answers you can use to test yourself on what you've learned.

Part 1: Learn at Your Own Pace

Each chapter identifies the exam objectives covered within the chapter, provides an overview of why the topics matter by identifying how the information is applied in the real world, and lists any prerequisites that must be met to complete the lessons presented in the chapter.

The chapters are divided into lessons. Lessons contain practices that include one or more hands-on exercises. These exercises give you an opportunity to use the skills being presented or to explore the part of the application being described.

After the lessons, you are given an opportunity to apply what you've learned in a case scenario exercise. In this exercise, you work through a multi-step solution for a realistic case scenario. You are also given an opportunity to work through a troubleshooting lab that explores difficulties you might encounter on the job when applying what you've learned.

Each chapter ends with a short summary of key concepts and a short section summarizing key topics and listing key terms you need to know before taking the exam.

> **Real World   Helpful Information**
> You will find sidebars like this one that contain related information you might find helpful. "Real World" sidebars contain specific information gained through the experience of IT professionals just like you.

Part 2: Prepare for the Exam

Part 2 helps to familiarize you with the types of questions you will encounter on the MCP exam. By reviewing the objectives and sample questions, you can focus on the specific skills you need to improve on before taking the exam.

See Also   For a complete list of MCP exams and their related objectives, go to *http://www.microsoft.com/learning/mcp/*.

Part 2 is organized by the exam's objectives. Each chapter covers one of the primary groups of objectives, referred to as *Objective Domains*. Each chapter lists the tested skills you need to master to answer the exam questions, and it includes a list of further readings to help you improve your ability to perform the tasks or skills specified by the objectives.

Within each Objective Domain, you will find the related objectives that are covered on the exam. Each objective provides you with several practice exam questions. The answers are accompanied by explanations of each correct and incorrect answer.

Note   These questions are also available on the companion CD as a practice test.

Informational Notes

Several types of reader aids appear throughout the training kit.

- **Tip** contains methods of performing a task more quickly or in a not-so-obvious way.

- **Important** contains information that is essential to completing a task.

- **Note** contains supplemental information.

- **Caution** contains valuable information about possible loss of data; be sure to read this information carefully.

- **Warning** contains critical information about possible physical injury; be sure to read this information carefully.

- **See Also** contains references to other sources of information.

- **Planning** contains hints and useful information that should help you to plan the implementation.

- **On the CD** points you to supplementary information or files you need that are on the companion CD.

- **Security Alert** highlights information you need to know to maximize security in your work environment.

- **Exam Tip** flags information you should know before taking the certification exam.

- **Off the Record** contains practical advice about the real-world implications of information presented in the lesson.

Notational Conventions

The following conventions are used throughout this book:

- Characters or commands that you type appear in **bold** type.

- *Italic* in syntax statements indicates placeholders for variable information. *Italic* is also used for book titles.

- Names of files and folders appear in Title caps, except when you are to type them directly. Unless otherwise indicated, you can use all lowercase letters when you type a file name in a dialog box or at a command prompt.

- File name extensions appear in all uppercase.

- Acronyms appear in all uppercase.

- `Monospace` type represents code samples, examples of screen text, or entries that you might type at a command prompt or in initialization files.

- Square brackets [ ] are used in syntax statements to enclose optional items. For example, [filename] in command syntax indicates that you can choose to type a file name with the command. Type only the information within the brackets, not the brackets themselves.

- Braces { } are used in syntax statements to enclose required items. Type only the information within the braces, not the braces themselves.

Keyboard Conventions

- A plus sign (+) between two key names means that you must press those keys at the same time. For example, "Press ALT+TAB" means that you hold down ALT while you press TAB.

- A comma (,) between two or more key names means that you must press each of the keys consecutively, not together. For example, "Press ALT, F, X" means that you press and release each key in sequence. "Press ALT+W, L" means that you first press ALT and W at the same time, and then release them and press L.

Getting Started

This training kit contains hands-on exercises to help you learn about supporting applications in Windows XP SP2. Use this section to prepare your self-paced training environment.

Software Requirements

The following software is required to complete the procedures in this training kit. A 30-day evaluation edition of Microsoft Office Professional Edition 2003 is included on CD-ROM as well as a 120-day evaluation edition of Microsoft Windows XP Professional Edition with Service Pack 2.

- Windows XP Professional Edition with SP2
- Microsoft Office Professional Edition 2003 (which you will install in Chapter 6, if you do not already have it installed)

Hardware Requirements

To follow the practices in this book, it is recommended that you use a computer that is not your primary workstation, because you will be called on to make changes to the operating system and application configuration. The computer you use must have the following minimum configuration. All hardware should be on the Microsoft Windows XP SP2 Hardware Compatibility List.

- Personal computer with a 233 MHz or higher processor; Intel Pentium/Celeron family, AMD K6/Athlon/Duron family, or compatible processor recommended
- 128 MB of RAM or greater
- 1.8 GB of available hard disk space; optional installation files cache requires an additional 300 MB of hard disk space
- CD-ROM drive or DVD-ROM drive
- Super VGA (800 x 600) or higher resolution monitor
- Keyboard and Microsoft Mouse, Microsoft IntelliMouse, or compatible pointing device
- Internet connection

Setup Instructions

Set up your computer according to the manufacturer's instructions.

Caution   If your computer is part of a larger network, you *must* verify with your network administrator that the computer name, domain name, and other information that is used in configuring Windows XP in Chapters 8 and 9 do not conflict with network operations. If they do conflict, ask your network administrator to provide alternative values and use those values throughout all of the exercises in this book. You should also ask your network administrator whether it is acceptable to perform the practices concerning updating Windows and using antivirus software in Chapter 10.

The Readiness Review Suite

The CD-ROM includes a practice test made up of 300 sample exam questions and an objective-by-objective review with an additional 125 questions. Use these tools to reinforce your learning and to identify any areas in which you need to gain more experience before taking the exam.

▶ **To Install the Practice Test and Objective Review**

1. Insert the companion CD-ROM into your CD-ROM drive.

Note   If AutoRun is disabled on your machine, refer to the Readme.txt file on the CD-ROM.

2. Click Readiness Review Suite on the user interface menu.

Practice files

The \Tools folder on the companion CD contains practice files that you need to complete the hands-on exercises. These files are organized by chapter.

The eBook

The CD-ROM includes an electronic version of the training kit. The eBook is in portable document format (PDF) and can be viewed using Adobe Acrobat Reader.

▶ **To Use the eBook**

1. Insert the companion CD-ROM into your CD-ROM drive.

Note   If AutoRun is disabled on your machine, refer to the Readme.txt file on the CD-ROM.

2. Click eBook on the user interface menu. You can also review any of the other eBooks that are provided for your use.

The Microsoft Certified Professional Program

The Microsoft Certified Professional (MCP) program provides the best method to prove your command of current Microsoft products and technologies. The exams and corresponding certifications are developed to validate your mastery of critical competencies as you design and develop, or implement and support, solutions with Microsoft products and technologies. Computer professionals who become Microsoft certified are recognized as experts and are sought after industry-wide. Certification brings a variety of benefits to the individual and to employers and organizations.

See Also   For a full list of MCP benefits, go to *http://www.microsoft.com/learning/itpro/ default.asp.*

Certifications

The Microsoft Certified Professional program offers multiple certifications, based on specific areas of technical expertise:

- *Microsoft Certified Professional (MCP).* Demonstrated in-depth knowledge of at least one Microsoft Windows operating system or architecturally significant platform. An MCP is qualified to implement a Microsoft product or technology as part of a business solution for an organization.

- *Microsoft Certified Desktop Support Technician (MCDST).* Individuals who support end users and troubleshoot desktop environments running the Windows operating system.

- *Microsoft Certified Solution Developer (MCSD).* Professional developers qualified to analyze, design, and develop enterprise business solutions with Microsoft development tools and technologies including the Microsoft .NET Framework.

- *Microsoft Certified Application Developer (MCAD).* Professional developers qualified to develop, test, deploy, and maintain powerful applications using Microsoft tools and technologies including Microsoft Visual Studio .NET and XML Web services.

- *Microsoft Certified Systems Engineer (MCSE).* Qualified to effectively analyze the business requirements and design and implement the infrastructure for business solutions based on the Microsoft Windows and Microsoft Windows Server 2003 operating systems.

- *Microsoft Certified Systems Administrator (MCSA).* Individuals with the skills to manage and troubleshoot existing network and system environments based on the Microsoft Windows and Windows Server 2003 operating systems.

- *Microsoft Certified Database Administrator (MCDBA)*. Individuals who design, implement, and administer Microsoft SQL Server databases.

- *Microsoft Certified Trainer (MCT)*. Instructionally and technically qualified to deliver Microsoft Official Curriculum through a Microsoft Certified Technical Education Center (CTEC).

Requirements for Becoming a Microsoft Certified Professional

The certification requirements differ for each certification and are specific to the products and job functions addressed by the certification.

To become a Microsoft Certified Professional, you must pass rigorous certification exams that provide a valid and reliable measure of technical proficiency and expertise. These exams are designed to test your expertise and ability to perform a role or task with a product, and are developed with the input of professionals in the industry. Questions in the exams reflect how Microsoft products are used in actual organizations, giving them "real-world" relevance.

- Microsoft Certified Professional (MCP) candidates are required to pass one current Microsoft certification exam. Candidates can pass additional Microsoft certification exams to further qualify their skills with other Microsoft products, development tools, or desktop applications.

- Microsoft Certified Solution Developers (MCSDs) are required to pass three core exams and one elective exam. (MCSD for Microsoft .NET candidates are required to pass four core exams and one elective.)

- Microsoft Certified Application Developers (MCADs) are required to pass two core exams and one elective exam in an area of specialization.

- Microsoft Certified Systems Engineers (MCSEs) are required to pass five core exams and two elective exams.

- Microsoft Certified Systems Administrators (MCSAs) are required to pass three core exams and one elective exam that provide a valid and reliable measure of technical proficiency and expertise.

- Microsoft Certified Desktop Support Technicians (MCDSTs) are required to pass two core exams that provide a valid and reliable measure of technical proficiency and expertise.

- Microsoft Certified Database Administrators (MCDBAs) are required to pass three core exams and one elective exam that provide a valid and reliable measure of technical proficiency and expertise.

- Microsoft Certified Trainers (MCTs) are required to meet instructional and technical requirements specific to each Microsoft Official Curriculum course they are certified to deliver. The MCT program requires ongoing training to meet the requirements for the annual renewal of certification. For more information about becoming a Microsoft Certified Trainer, visit *http://www.microsoft.com/traincert/ mcp/mct/* or contact a regional service center near you.

Technical Support

Every effort has been made to ensure the accuracy of this book and the contents of the companion disc. If you have comments, questions, or ideas regarding this book or the companion disc, please send them to Microsoft Press using either of the following methods:

E-mail:	tkinput@microsoft.com
Postal Mail:	Microsoft Press
	Attn: *MCDST Self-Paced Training Kit (Exam 70–272): Supporting Users and Troubleshooting Desktop Applications on Microsoft® Windows® XP,* Second Edition, Editor
	One Microsoft Way
	Redmond, WA 98052-6399

For additional support information regarding this book and the CD-ROM (including answers to commonly asked questions about installation and use), visit the Microsoft Press Technical Support website at *http://www.microsoft.com/learning/support/ books/*. To connect directly to the Microsoft Knowledge Base and enter a query, visit *http://support.microsoft.com/search/*. For support information regarding Microsoft software, visit *http://support.microsoft.com*.

Evaluation Edition Software Support

The evaluation edition software that is provided with this book is not the full retail product and is provided only for the purposes of training and evaluation. Microsoft Technical Support does not support evaluation editions.

Caution   The evaluation edition software that is included with this book should not be used on a primary work computer. For online support information relating to the full version of Microsoft Office Professional Edition 2003 and Microsoft Windows XP Professional Edition SP2 that *might* also apply to the evaluation edition, visit *http://support.microsoft.com/*.

Information about any issues relating to the use of this evaluation edition software with this training kit is posted to the Support section of the Microsoft Press Technical Support website (*http://www.microsoft.com/learning/support/books*). For information about ordering the full version of any Microsoft software, please call Microsoft Sales at (800) 426-9400 or visit *http://www.microsoft.com*.

Part 1
Learn at Your Own Pace

1 Introduction to Desktop Support

Exam Objectives in this Chapter:

- This first chapter serves as an overview to the desktop support role and environment and does not specifically cover any exam objective.

Why This Chapter Matters

The goal of this chapter is to introduce you to desktop support and common network configurations and to teach you how best to support the end user in these varied settings. The chapter begins with an introduction to supporting users and then discusses corporate environments, the help and support tier structure, and common job titles and duties. A discussion of workgroups, domains, and reasons for multiple domains is also included. Noncorporate environments are introduced, including Internet service providers (ISPs), call centers, and large and small repair shops.

Lessons in this Chapter:

Before You Begin

The purpose of this course is to teach you to support end users who run Windows XP Professional in a corporate environment or Windows XP Home Edition in a home or small business environment, and to prepare you for the 70-272 certification examination. This course assumes that you have approximately six months of hands-on experience and the following prerequisite knowledge:

- Basic experience using a Microsoft Windows operating system such as Windows XP

- Basic understanding of Microsoft Office applications and Windows accessories, including Microsoft Internet Explorer

- Basic understanding of core operating system technologies, including installation and configuration

- Basic understanding of hardware components and their functions

- Basic understanding of the major desktop components and interfaces and their functions

- Basic understanding of Transmission Control Protocol/Internet Protocol (TCP/IP) settings

- How to use command-line utilities to manage the operating system

- Basic understanding of technologies that are available for establishing Internet connectivity

Lesson 1: Introduction to Supporting Users

The job of desktop support technician (DST) involves much more than answering the phone and resolving a problem. It also involves understanding, communicating with, and pleasing the end user. You must be able to listen to a customer, gather information from that customer, diagnose and resolve or escalate the problem, and properly document the resolution of the problem in the manner dictated by company policy. The end user must also be satisfied with the solution and believe he or she was treated fairly and with respect.

After this lesson, you will be able to

- Identify the types of end users that you will encounter.
- Explain how previous interactions with desktop support could have gone.
- Discuss traits of a good DST.
- Identify what end users expect from you.

Estimated lesson time: 15 minutes

The End User's Level of Expertise

There are many types of end users. Each user has a different level of expertise, and each one has expertise in varying degrees. Some end users have no computer experience at all and barely understand basic computer terms; some have targeted experience; still others have many years of experience. Table 1-1 details the different types of users you might encounter.

Table 1-1 End Users Have Varying Skill Levels

Skill Level	Description
Highly experienced	These users are extremely experienced and most likely know more than you do concerning the problem at hand. Their problems generally need to be escalated quickly.
Generally experienced	These users can use e-mail and the Internet, download and install programs, follow wizards, install and configure programs, set up simple networks, and do minor troubleshooting. Tier 1 or tier 2 support personnel can generally assist these users.

Table 1-1   End Users Have Varying Skill Levels

Skill Level	Description
Targeted experience	These users have experience in one or two applications that they use daily to do their jobs. Other than this experience, they have almost no computing skills. Depending on the application in question, Tier 1 or tier 2 support personnel can generally assist these users.
No experience	These users are completely new to computing and have little or no experience with e-mail, the Internet, or installing or using applications. Tier 1 personnel should be able to handle most of these calls.

After you've gained some experience as a DST, you'll be able to determine how experienced the user is after speaking with him or her for only a few minutes. In the interim, you'll learn how to work with and assist the different types of end users by communicating with them through written scripts and by following specific (and proven) troubleshooting guidelines.

> **Tip**   Keep in mind at all times that you will be assisting all levels of users; never assume that the user knows less than you.

Real World   Leveraging the Expert User

As you work in the desktop support world, you will run into many users who have expertise that you can make use of. Whether the users have more general computing experience than you, are hardware hobbyists, or are simply gurus in particular applications, it is in your best interest to recognize their expertise and learn from it.

In the corporate world especially (which you'll learn more about in Lesson 2), expert users are worth their weight in gold. You will not have time to become an expert in every application that is running within a company, so knowing whom to go to with your questions can help keep things running smoothly. You are also likely to find a user or two in each department who can help field questions when you are not available or whom you can ask to sit down at a user's desk if that user is having trouble explaining the problem to you.

In the noncorporate world, expert users offer a good source for your own continuing education. Listen to what they have to say, and learn from techniques they use when troubleshooting their own problems.

Previous Experiences with Technical Support

Chances are that the end user you are speaking with on the phone or visiting at his or her desk has dealt with a DST before. If that experience wasn't satisfactory, you might have to deal with an angry, dissatisfied, or frustrated client. You might also be the second or third DST trying to solve the problem, or the problem might be a recurring one. If this is the case, concentrate on verifying the problem, be polite and respectful, and use whatever resources it takes to solve the problem quickly and effectively.

Traits of a Good Desktop Support Technician

Companies and clients want to hire and keep the best DSTs that they can find, and they look for several specific traits and qualities. It doesn't matter whether you work in a corporate environment or offer in-home computer-repair services; the traits and skills are the same. To be the best DST you can be, work to demonstrate as many of these qualities as possible.

- **Excellent customer service skills**   Successful DSTs have the ability and emotional intelligence to teach highly technical content to users with any level of experience. They can speak to any user about any problem and define that problem in terms the user can understand (without making the user feel inadequate or dumb). They have skills that any customer service employee would have: they are polite, are concerned for the customer, and have a sincere desire to service the customer's needs. Beyond emotional intelligence, they also have social intelligence. This is the ability to handle their own or others' anxieties, anger, and sadness; be self-motivated; and have empathy for others.

- **Talent for communicating**   Good DSTs can communicate with end users of any level of experience, any personality, and any level of the corporate ladder. They can communicate technical information to nontechnical users and can acquire technical information from those who cannot explain the problem clearly. Good DSTs also take the time to explain in simple terms why the problem occurred, how it can be avoided in the future, and how and where to get help when no DST is available. Good DSTs document the problems, their communications with users, and the solutions they try so that they can communicate even better with users the next time around.

- **Ability to multitask and stay calm under pressure**   DSTs must deal with ongoing problems, multiple open troubleshooting tickets, deadlines for meeting **service level agreements (SLAs)**, accountability to bosses and end users, and ambiguous problems. Throughout these, DSTs must be able to work effectively and coolly under pressure. DSTs must also respond calmly when an end user becomes frustrated or angry and must maintain a professional demeanor at all times.

- **Technical aptitude**   DSTs have a natural aptitude for computers, hardware, and software, and for configuring each. They enjoy working with the technologies, have workstations at home where they troubleshoot problems in their spare time, welcome new technologies, and show a talent for seeing the big picture in terms of networks, components, shared files and folders, and problems. Having the ability to see things holistically is the first step to becoming an expert in your field.

- **Capacity to solve problems**   Talented DSTs have the capacity to solve problems quickly. They are good at solving logic problems, uncovering hidden clues, chasing leads, and discovering and attempting solutions without exacerbating the problem further. Communication and linear and logical troubleshooting are the top skills employers look for. The technical aspect can be taught much more easily than these skills because these have more to do with overall intelligence, personality, and social abilities than technical skills do. You must strive to develop critical thinking and problem-solving skills and learn to "read the signs" when dealing with a problem. The better you are at seeing the signs and the big picture, the better you'll be as a DST. The capacity to solve problems can be improved through training, experience, trial and error, observation, and working with higher-level DSTs.

Lesson Review

The following questions are intended to reinforce key information presented in this lesson. If you are unable to answer a question, review the lesson materials and try the question again. You can find answers to the questions in the "Questions and Answers" section at the end of this chapter.

1. Give yourself five minutes to list as many traits as you can that relate to the three categories listed here.

   ❏ Communication skills

   ❏ Aptitude skills

   ❏ Personal skills

   _____

   _____

   _____

   _____

   _____

2. You are working as a tier 1 support technician. You are speaking to a user whom you quickly assess as being highly experienced. The user starts the conversation by telling you what she has already tried and what she suspects is the cause of her problem. What is the likely outcome of this support call?

_____

_____

_____

3. You are speaking with a user who has been on hold for nearly 20 minutes. The first thing the customer tells you is that he has already spoken with two other DSTs that day and that the "fixes" they recommended have made things even worse for him. How should you handle this?

_____

_____

_____

_____

_____

_____

Lesson Summary

- As a DST, you will encounter users of all skill levels. Never assume that you know more than the user to whom you are talking.

- DSTs must have technical knowledge in many areas, including the operating system; components, such as Microsoft Outlook Express and Internet Explorer; and applications, including Microsoft Outlook, Excel, Access, and others.

- DSTs should be good at getting information from people who might not be able to explain the problem clearly and should be good at explaining technical information to nontechnical users.

Lesson 2: Overview of Corporate Environments

There are several types of environments in which you might be employed. Understanding these environments and your place in them is crucial to your success. This section provides a brief overview of the corporate environment, including common network setups, tier structure, job titles, and job requirements.

After this lesson, you will be able to

- Explain the types of networks that you might encounter.
- Define the tier structure and explain the responsibilities of each tier.
- Identify common support job titles and the responsibilities of those jobs.

Estimated lesson time: 25 minutes

Types of Networks

From a user's perspective, there are three basic types of logical networks: workgroups, domains, and multiple domains. In each of these environments, users are able to share common resources such as files, folders, and printers; and there are security measures available that keep users' personal data, network resources, and company data secure and protected from outside forces.

Exam Tip   Different types of networks involve different capabilities, security measures, and policies. Identifying the scope of a problem (and therefore correctly providing an answer) hinges on correctly identifying the type of network involved. Deciding on the scope should be your first step on the exam and in the real world.

Workgroups

Workgroups are logical groupings of networked computers that share resources; they are often referred to as peer-to-peer networks. Of the three network types, the workgroup is the easiest to set up and maintain but the least secure. Each computer maintains its own local security database, which contains the valid user accounts for logging on to and using that computer. The user accounts secure data on the computer and protect the computer from unwanted access. Because no single computer provides centralized security of user accounts for all of the computers on the network, the network is considered decentralized. Figure 1-1 shows an example of a workgroup.

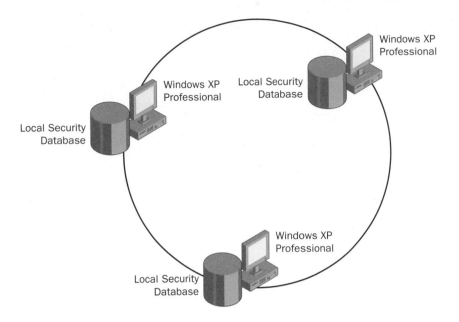

Figure 1-1   A workgroup is often referred to as a peer-to-peer network.

> **Note**   Workgroups are typically configured for home networks, small home offices, and small businesses where the computers are in close proximity to one another and can be connected using a hub, switch, or router. Because they are not the most secure option for a network, they are not often used in larger corporations.

Domains

Domains are logical groupings of networked computers that share a common database of users and centrally managed security on a single server (or group of servers) called a domain controller. A single domain must have one or more domain controllers, and these computers provide **Active Directory** services such as providing access to resources, security, and a single point of administration. Domains are logical groupings, so they are independent of the actual physical structure of the network. Domains can span a building, city, state, country, or even the globe, or they can be configured for a small office. The computers can be connected by dial-up, Ethernet, Integrated Services Digital Network (ISDN) lines, satellite, or even wireless connections. Figure 1-2 shows an example of a domain with two domain controllers.

Note Domains are typically configured for networks in larger companies and corporations because they are the most secure option for a network, offer centralized security and management, and are extensible. Smaller companies generally opt against domains because they have more overhead, are more expensive, and require more attention than workgroups do.

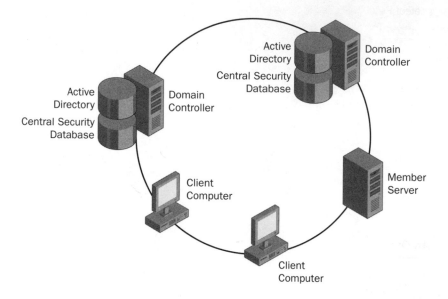

Figure 1-2 Domains share a common database and are centrally managed.

Note Workgroups, domains, and multiple domains describe the logical grouping of computers. Don't confuse this logical grouping with the physical layout of the network. A small network of three computers connected by a single hub can be logically grouped into a domain, just as a larger network consisting of thousands of computers across multiple subnets can also be grouped into a domain. The reason for the distinction between logical and physical structures is one of abstraction. The physical layout has to do with where computers are located and how they are connected to the network. The logical layout has to do with the function of the computer, how it is used, and how it is managed. By separating the two, the administration of computers does not have to be affected by the network infrastructure.

Multiple Domains

Networks can also be arranged into multiple domains. These multiple domains are still managed as a single, cohesive, yet decentralized unit. Multiple administrators manage the network, and the domains represent specific parts of a larger organization. Multiple domains are generally created when the network (and corporation) spans multiple countries or when two established companies merge. In a multiple domain configuration, there must be at least one domain controller in each domain.

> **See Also** To learn more about domains and Active Directory, visit *http://www.microsoft.com /technet*, select Products & Technologies, and select Windows Server 2003 or Active Directory.

Tier Structure

Corporations define technical support roles in tiers, and generally there are four, as detailed in Table 1-2. Each of these four tiers can also have its own tier structure. The tier position that we're concerned with is tier 1, which is italicized in the table. The employees in the corporate tier 1 group are also categorized in three additional, internal, tiers. The internal tier 1 employees usually provide front-line support, and internal tiers 2, 3, and 4 accept escalations. These roles are defined with more detail in the section "Telephone Call Centers" later in this chapter. Your position in the corporation will be in the tier 1, help desk, position.

Table 1-2 An Overview of the Corporate Tier Structure

Tier	Description
Tier 4, architect	Strategic: Analyzes and designs enterprises. Makes budget and purchasing decisions.
Tier 3, engineer	Tactical: Analyzes and designs within a single technology and implements the technology. Handles complex troubleshooting, including escalations from administrators.
Tier 2, administrator	Operational: Provides day-to-day server and software troubleshooting. Performs operating system (OS) management and support.
Tier 1, help desk	*Support: Supports day-to-day client OSs, applications, and hardware troubleshooting. Follows prescriptive guidelines and provides end user phone support.*

Corporate tier structures allow for growth by clearly defining technical support roles and requirements for moving up the tier ladder. The Microsoft Certified Desktop Support Technician (MCDST) certification prepares candidates for jobs in the tier 1 environment and provides a good foundation for moving up in the corporation.

Job Titles and Requirements

As a tier 1 entry-level technical support employee, your job is to provide direct end-user support. At a high level, you should be prepared to perform the following tasks:

- Perform general troubleshooting of the operating system and installed applications

- Provide customer service, including listening to the customer, defining and solving the problem, and educating the user on how to avoid the problem in the future

- Install, configure, and upgrade software, including applications and operating systems

- Monitor and maintain systems

- Document calls and close them or escalate them as required by company policy and time limits set by SLAs

Note   A service level agreement (SLA) defines the parameters of service provided by a company to a user. SLAs typically cover the services to be delivered, fees and expenses, customer responsibilities, documentation requirements, and support policies.

More specifically, you will be consulted to troubleshoot and provide information about a variety of products, including operating systems; applications such as Microsoft Outlook, Microsoft Access, and Microsoft Excel; and operating system components such as Internet Explorer and Outlook Express. You will also be called on to resolve connectivity issues, troubleshoot dual-boot or multiuser computers, and install and configure handheld devices. You will be expected to resolve or escalate 80 percent of the incident requests you receive from end users, employ proper procedures to document the incident, and operate within the environment's SLAs. SLAs might require that a call be resolved in a particular amount of time or within a specified budget.

There are various job titles and job roles for DSTs; common tier 1 entry-level job titles are listed next. When creating a resumé, looking for employment, or interviewing, make sure you are familiar with these titles. Each of these job titles is a tier 1 entry-level job, and all are quite similar.

- Call center support representative
- Customer service representative
- Help desk specialist (or technician)
- Product support specialist
- PC support specialist

Tip   To supplement your DST training, join a relevant newsgroup. With a newsgroup, you can exchange ideas, ask for help, and get answers to common questions quickly. For more information, visit *http://www.microsoft.com/windowsxp/expertzone/newsgroups/default.asp*.

Practice: Identifying Tasks in a Corporate Environment

In this practice, you will explore some of the tasks that are associated with the various tiers. If you are unable to answer a question, review the lesson materials and try the question again. You can find answers to the questions in the "Questions and Answers" section at the end of this chapter.

Scenario

You are a technical support administrator at Proseware, Inc., which supports end users of video games. Proseware also runs online servers for its multiplayer games. You have been asked to divide support into three categories: help desk, administrator, and engineer. You have been told that the help desk will handle questions client-side concerning configuration issues within the game. Administrators will handle configuration problems that the help desk fails to solve and will handle all operating system and hardware issues. The engineer group will handle any technical problems that occur on the server.

Group the following list of tasks according to which support tier you think would handle them. Tiers include: Tier 1-Help Desk; Tier 2-Administrator; and Tier 3-Engineer.

- Adjust display settings
- Troubleshoot video driver problems
- Troubleshoot registration problems that occur on the server
- Adjust audio settings
- Troubleshoot joystick problems
- Configure the game to play on a home network
- Troubleshoot networking issues preventing a customer's computer from connecting to the server
- Register the product online

■ Deal with server crashes resulting from too many requests for service

_____

_____

_____

_____

_____

_____

_____

Lesson Review

The following questions are intended to reinforce key information presented in this lesson. If you are unable to answer a question, review the lesson materials and try the question again. You can find answers to the questions in the "Questions and Answers" section at the end of this chapter.

1. Briefly, what types of businesses, corporations, or companies would choose to configure a workgroup? A domain? A multiple domain? Why?

_____

_____

_____

2. Which of the following is not a job function of a tier 1 corporate desktop support technician? (Check all that apply.)

   A. Perform general troubleshooting of the operating system

   B. Perform general troubleshooting of operating system components, such as Internet Explorer and Outlook Express

   C. Troubleshoot network problems that do not directly affect the end user

   D. Install, configure, and upgrade software, including applications and operating systems

   E. Set group or local security policies for end users, including which security settings a user should have, and determine what he or she can or cannot access on the network

3. For each of the following descriptions, decide whether each refers to a work-group, a domain, or multiple domain network configurations. If the description applies to more than one, list all that apply.

    A. This network configuration is a logical grouping of computers created for the purpose of sharing resources such as files and printers.

    _____

    _____

    B. This network configuration does not use Active Directory services.

    _____

    _____

    C. This network configuration can include multiple domain controllers.

    _____

    _____

    D. This network configuration provides a single point of administration for security.

    _____

    _____

    E. This network configuration is easy to design and implement and is best configured for users in close proximity to one another.

    _____

    _____

Lesson Summary

- DSTs must be prepared to work in various environments, including workgroups, domains, and multiple domains.

- A DST's place in the corporate, ISP, or company hierarchy is generally the tier 1 position and is considered an entry-level position.

- The MCDST certification opens a doorway into tier 1 jobs, identifies the employee as qualified to hold the desired job, and identifies the business owner as qualified to determine and resolve home user problems.

Lesson 3: Overview of Noncorporate Environments

Not all desktop support technicians acquire or hold jobs in a large corporate environment; many obtain employment through telephone call centers, repair shops, private businesses, and ISPs.

After this lesson, you will be able to

- Identify common types of noncorporate support jobs.
- Describe the job activities found in noncorporate support jobs.

Estimated lesson time: 10 minutes

Telephone Call Centers

Telephone call centers accept calls from end users and resolve problems over the telephone. These calls can be hardware or software related, depending on the company and its clients. A DST's place in thsese environments is defined using a tier system similar to that in a corporate environment. Table 1-3 shows a general tier structure for a telephone call center. An entry-level DST falls in either of the first two tiers (italicized in the table), depending on experience.

Table 1-3   Overview of the Telephone Call Center Tier Structure

Experience	Scope of Responsibilities
Tier 4: 3+ years of experience	Receives calls that are escalated from tier 3 personnel and tries to resolve them. This involves complex troubleshooting, and employees in this tier are hardware and software engineers and architects.
Tier 3: 1 to 2 years of experience	Receives calls that are escalated from tier 2 personnel and tries to resolve them. This involves a combination of experience, directed training in specific hardware and software, and application of previous knowledge. These employees might have other certifications.
Tier 2: 6 months to 1 year of experience	*Receives calls that are escalated from tier 1 personnel and tries to resolve them. Like tier 1 employees, the employee works by using a set of predetermined questions and solutions. Supports OS, application, and hardware troubleshooting.*

Table 1-3 Overview of the Telephone Call Center Tier Structure

Experience	Scope of Responsibilities
Tier 1: Less than 6 months of experience	*Answers the phone and works using a script. The employee instructs the user to reboot the computer, disconnect and reconnect, stop and restart an application, and perform other common troubleshooting tasks. Determines the appropriate time to escalate calls to tier 2 personnel.*

Repair Shops and Private Businesses

DSTs also find their niche as members of small repair shops, large repair shop chains, computer sales chains, computer manufacturers, or hardware testing labs. They can also start their own computer-repair business.

If you intend to work as a DST in any of these settings, you should also be either A+ or Network+ certified. Unlike a desktop technician, an employee at a repair shop or one who owns his or her own business has much more hands-on computer work than those who answer phones. These technicians replace hardware, add memory, repair printers, and perform similar tasks, in addition to the tasks required of a desktop technician.

Internet Service Providers

ISPs are companies that provide Internet access to subscribers for a monthly fee. Subscribers can be individuals or entire corporations. Some ISPs do more than offer Internet access, though: they design Web pages, consult with businesses, provide feedback concerning Web page traffic, and send out virus warnings. Some also set up, secure, and maintain e-commerce websites for clients.

If you choose to work for an ISP, you will most likely answer the phones and perform general help desk duties as previously defined. The most common tasks required of an ISP desktop technician include the following:

- Set up new accounts using Outlook or Outlook Express, Netscape Mail, Apple OSX Mail, Eudora, and other e-mail clients
- Configure settings to filter spam by creating rules and blocking senders
- Troubleshoot Internet and e-mail access
- Troubleshoot servers and physical connections
- Resolve problems with various connection types, including dial-up modems, digital subscriber line (DSL), cable, and wireless connections
- Resolve and escalate calls when necessary

ISP desktop technicians must be familiar with Internet technologies, **Domain Name System** (DNS) name resolution, connection types, available modems, and other common ISP tools. ISPs, like other technicians' employers, generally work using a tier system, and moving up the tier is dependent on your experience, education, and training.

Lesson Review

The following questions are intended to reinforce key information presented in this lesson. If you are unable to answer a question, review the lesson materials and try the question again. You can find answers to the questions in the "Questions and Answers" section at the end of this chapter.

1. You have just gotten a job at an ISP and have been assigned a tier 1 position. Which of the following can you expect in your first week at work? (Check all that apply.)

   A. To walk users through re-creating their e-mail accounts or reconfiguring their Internet security settings

   B. To configure local security policies

   C. To answer phones and instruct users to reboot their computer, close and restart applications, and disconnect from and reconnect to the ISP

   D. To read from a script of questions and make decisions based on their answers

   E. To help users reinstall their e-mail clients

2. Taking into account what you've learned about workgroups and domains, network topologies, corporate and noncorporate tier structures, call center environments, hands-on repair shops, and ISPs, describe which environment you would most like to work in. Cite five reasons for your decision.

   _____

   _____

   _____

   _____

   _____

Lesson Summary

- Noncorporate environments in which a DST might work include telephone call centers, repair shops, private businesses, and ISPs.

- Each of the noncorporate environments require different skills, but in each instance, you must be friendly, helpful, capable, and competent.

- If you work for a telephone call center or an ISP, you will likely work in a tier structure much like the structures found in corporate environments.

Case Scenario Exercises

In the following scenarios, you must use what you have learned throughout the lessons in this chapter to answer questions based on a real-world scenario. Read each scenario and answer the questions. If you have trouble, review the chapter and try again. You can find answers in the "Questions and Answers" section at the end of this chapter.

Scenario 1.1

John earned his MCDST and is in the process of obtaining an entry-level job in information technology. He enjoys working with people, but he also enjoys the hands-on aspect of the technology. He has several computers at home, and he has connected them and configured a small domain just for the fun of it. He likes working inside the computer too, adding memory, replacing cards, and so on, and he's certain that someday he wants to own his own computer-repair or network consulting business. He wants to make sure he gets the best work experience possible.

- What type of entry-level job do you think is best for John while he works to meet his goals? Why?

  _____

  _____

  _____

Scenario 1.2

You recently earned your A+ certification and are currently working in a small, family-owned repair shop. You work in the repair section of the shop and do a lot of hands-on computer work, but you don't have much interaction with the public. Although you are extremely talented at repairing hardware, adding memory, repairing printers, and performing similar tasks, and you have exceptionally good problem-solving skills, you know you lack some of the delicate personal skills required of a successful DST. Your boss has even mentioned that you could be a little more personable.

Which of the following offer the best solutions to this problem? (Select two.)

A. Consider moonlighting two or three nights a week as a telephone call support technician. There you'll learn some of the basic personal skills required of a good DST.

B. Quit the repair shop, and go to work immediately for an ISP. You can learn to create websites, you'll learn about e-commerce, and if you're lucky, you'll only have to deal with people face-to-face occasionally.

C. Take a course on interpersonal skills at your local community college. There you'll learn basic communication skills, such as how to listen and how to converse effectively with all types of people.

D. Consider a different line of work. Communication skills, ability, talent, and personal skills come naturally to good DSTs and can't be taught.

Chapter Summary

■ As a DST, you will encounter users of all skill levels. Never assume that you know more than the user to whom you are talking.

■ DSTs must have technical knowledge in many areas, including the operating system; components, such as Microsoft Outlook Express and Internet Explorer; and applications, including Microsoft Outlook, Excel, Access, and others.

■ DSTs must be good at gathering information from people who might not be able to explain the problem clearly and must be good at explaining technical information to nontechnical users.

■ DSTs must be prepared to work in various environments, including workgroups, domains, and multiple domains.

■ A DST's place in the corporate, ISP, or company hierarchy is generally the tier 1 position and is considered an entry-level position.

■ The MCDST certification opens a doorway into tier 1 jobs, identifies the employee as qualified to hold the desired job, and identifies the business owner as qualified to determine and resolve home end-user problems.

■ Noncorporate environments in which a DST might work include telephone call centers, repair shops, private businesses, and ISPs.

■ Each of the noncorporate environments requires different skills, but in each instance, you must be friendly, helpful, capable, and competent.

■ If you work for a telephone call center or an ISP, you will likely work in a tier structure much like the structures found in corporate environments.

Exam Highlights

Before taking the exam, review the key topics and terms that are presented in this chapter. You need to know this information.

Key Points

- Learn to recognize quickly the skill level of the user you are helping. This helps you get the right information from the user and helps you create solutions that the user is comfortable implementing.

- Always identify the scope of a problem. Is it isolated to a single application? A single computer? Is it a network problem? What type of network is involved—peer-to-peer or domain?

Key Terms

Active Directory   A directory service that contains information about a network's users, workstations, servers, printers, and other resources. The Active Directory (found on a domain controller) determines who can access what and to what degree. Active Directory is essential to maintaining, organizing, and securing the resources on a larger network; it allows network administrators to centrally manage resources; and it is extensible, meaning that it can be configured to grow and be personalized for any company.

service level agreement (SLA)   An agreement between parties (such as a call center and the company that hires it) that defines how long a call should take, how much time should be spent on each incident, and what reports and documents must be maintained. The SLA also defines penalties for not meeting those requirements.

Questions and Answers

Lesson 1 Review

Page 1-8 1. Give yourself five minutes to list as many traits as you can that relate to the three categories listed here.

   ❑ Communication skills

   ❑ Aptitude skills

   ❑ Personal skills

   Communication skills Good DSTs communicate with users who have varying experience and job titles; explain technical problems to nontechnical users; obtain technical information from nontechnical users; explain in simple terms how the problem occurred, how to avoid it, and how the user can repair it on his or her own; and leave the user happy and satisfied, with the problem solved.

   Aptitude skills Good DSTs enjoy working with computers and new technologies and tinkering with computers in their spare time, and they see the big picture when diagnosing a problem. They have considerable capacity to solve problems quickly and are good at logic problems, puzzles, and finding solutions to difficult queries.

   Personal skills Good DSTs react calmly under pressure, meet deadlines, document problems and solutions, multitask, and work with end users who might become frustrated or who have had prior unresolved problems.

2. You are working as a tier 1 support technician. You are speaking to a user whom you quickly assess as being highly experienced. The user starts the conversation by telling you what she has already tried and what she suspects is the cause of her problem. What is the likely outcome of this support call?

   If you think the user is right in her assessment of the problem, it is likely that you will escalate her call quickly unless it is a simple service that you can provide.

3. You are speaking with a user who has been on hold for nearly 20 minutes. The first thing the customer tells you is that he has already spoken with two other DSTs that day and that the "fixes" they recommended have made things even worse for him. How should you handle this?

   Of course, your first goal is to be polite and respectful. It is likely that the user will be confrontational about your suggestions and maybe even about your qualifications. Stay calm. You can often put a person at ease with as simple a statement as "I'm sorry you are still having problems. Let's see what we can do about them." Give the user a chance to tell the story of what has happened and what the other DSTs have recommended. You'll likely pick up valuable clues along the way, and it will give the user a chance to be heard and calm down.

Lesson 2 Practice Scenario

Page
1-15
You are a technical support administrator at Proseware, Inc., which supports end users of video games. Proseware also runs online servers for its multiplayer games. You have been asked to divide support into three categories: help desk, administrator, and engineer. You have been told that the help desk will handle questions client-side concerning configuration issues within the game. Administrators will handle configuration problems that the help desk fails to solve and will handle all operating system and hardware issues. The engineer group will handle any technical problems that occur on the server.

Group the following list of tasks according to which support tier you think would handle them. Tiers include: Tier 1-Help Desk; Tier 2-Administrator; and Tier 3-Engineer.

- Adjust display settings
- Troubleshoot video driver problems
- Troubleshoot registration problems that occur on the server
- Adjust audio settings
- Troubleshoot joystick problems
- Configure the game to play on a home network
- Troubleshoot networking issues preventing a customer's computer from connecting to the server
- Register the product online
- Deal with server crashes resulting from too many requests for service

Answers will vary widely, but following are some of the types of activities that each level will handle.

Help desk, tier 1: Adjust display settings; adjust audio settings; register the product online; configure the game to play on a home network

Administrator, tier 2: Troubleshoot networking issues preventing a customer's computer from connecting to the server; troubleshoot video driver problems; troubleshoot joystick problems

Engineer, tier 3: Deal with server crashes resulting from too many requests for service; troubleshoot registration problems that occur on the server

Lesson 2 Review

Page
1-16
1. Briefly, what types of businesses, corporations, or companies would choose to configure a workgroup? A domain? A multiple domain? Why?

Small businesses and home users generally choose workgroups because they are easy to set up and maintain while still offering the security they need. Medium-size companies and larger corporations choose domains because of their single point of administration for security and their Active Directory features. Domains are much more secure than workgroups, and security is extremely important in these settings. Large multinational corporations or corporations that have merged use multiple domains so that each country or merged business can control its own networks.

2. Which of the following is not a job function of a tier 1 corporate desktop support technician? (Check all that apply.)

   A. Perform general troubleshooting of the operating system

   B. Perform general troubleshooting of operating system components, such as Internet Explorer and Outlook Express

   C. Troubleshoot network problems that do not directly affect the end user

   D. Install, configure, and upgrade software, including applications and operating systems

   E. Set group or local security policies for end users, including which security settings a user should have, and determine what he or she can or cannot access on the network

   A, B, and D correctly identify the duties of a tier 1 DST. C is incorrect because desktop support technicians troubleshoot only problems that directly affect end users. They are not responsible for the company's network. E is incorrect because DSTs do not set security policies. That work is done by network administrators in tier 2 or 3.

3. For each of the following descriptions, decide whether each refers to a workgroup, a domain, or multiple domain network configurations. If the description applies to more than one, list all that apply.

   A. This network configuration is a logical grouping of computers created for the purpose of sharing resources such as files and printers.

   Workgroups, domains, and multiple domains. All networks are created for the purpose of sharing resources; it does not matter what logical grouping they use.

   B. This network configuration does not use Active Directory services.

   Workgroup. Workgroups do not use a single point of administration database (domain controller) and therefore do not use Active Directory.

   C. This network configuration can include multiple domain controllers.

   Domains and multiple domains. Domain controllers are used in all types of domain configurations.

   D. This network configuration provides a single point of administration for security.

   Domains and multiple domains. There is not a single point of administration for security in workgroups, but there is in domains.

E. This network configuration is easy to design and implement and is best configured for users in close proximity to one another.

Workgroup. Workgroups are best used for small groups of computers that are in close proximity to one another. It is the easiest type of logical network to configure.

Lesson 3 Review

Page
1-20
1. You have just gotten a job at an ISP and have been assigned a tier 1 position. Which of the following can you expect in your first week at work? (Check all that apply.)

   A. To walk users through re-creating their e-mail accounts or reconfiguring their Internet security settings

   B. To configure local security policies

   C. To answer phones and instruct users to reboot their computer, close and restart applications, and disconnect from and reconnect to the ISP

   D. To read from a script of questions and make decisions based on their answers

   E. To help users reinstall their e-mail clients

   C and D are correct. A desktop technician's first week will require that he or she be placed in the lowest level of the larger tier 1 group. The job duties and responsibilities at this level are minimal; C and D define these clearly. A, B, and E are more complex tasks that are performed by tier 2 or 3 technicians.

2. Taking into account what you've learned about workgroups and domains, network topologies, corporate and noncorporate tier structures, call center environments, hands-on repair shops, and ISPs, describe which environment you would most like to work in. Cite five reasons for your decision.

   Sample answer: I want to work in a corporate environment because I want to learn more about domains, domain controllers, and Active Directory; I want to learn about security, scalability, and databases; I see more room for advancement here than in any other option; I want to have health insurance and a pension plan; I am sure I do not want to work in a call center.

Case Scenario 1.1

Page
1-21
■ What type of entry-level job do you think is best for John while he works to meet his goals? Why?

Although answers will vary, a corporate job might be the best thing for John. There he can gain some hands-on experience with clients at their desks, but he'll also gain experience doing phone work. He'll work with networks that are domains, and he'll have the opportunity to enhance his hands-on skills by checking physical connections and cards and repairing general computer problems. John will also learn how to communicate with many types of people with many levels of experience, thus gaining the personal traits required of a good DST.

Case Scenario 1.2

Page
1-21

Which of the following offer the best solutions to this problem? (Select two.)

A. Consider moonlighting two or three nights a week as a telephone call support technician. There you'll learn some of the basic personal skills required of a good DST.

B. Quit the repair shop, and go to work immediately for an ISP. You can learn to create websites, you'll learn about e-commerce, and if you're lucky, you'll only have to deal with people face-to-face occasionally.

C. Take a course on interpersonal skills at your local community college. There you'll learn basic communication skills, such as how to listen and how to converse effectively with all types of people.

D. Consider a different line of work. Communication skills, ability, talent, and personal skills come naturally to good DSTs and can't be taught.

A and C are the best answers to this question. A is correct because you will learn how to deal with people over the phone, you'll learn some basic communication skills, and you'll learn how to be polite and empathetic with a customer. At three days a week, the experience won't be too stressful. C is correct because interpersonal skills can be learned, and taking a class can help you improve in this area. B and D are incorrect. Quitting and considering a different line of work are drastic ways to deal with this situation. Communication skills, ability, talent, and personal skills don't always come naturally; with practice, experience, mental fortitude, and instruction, they can be learned.

2 Resolving a Service Call

Exam Objectives in this Chapter:

- This chapter provides an introduction to resolving service calls and does not specifically address any exam objective.

Why This Chapter Matters

The purpose of this chapter is to teach you the logical processes involved in resolving a service call. Resolving a call involves gathering information, determining a solution or course of action, attempting and finding solutions or escalating the call, and informing the end user of your findings.

In the first section, you learn what questions to ask and what details to note, such as whether the user has made any recent changes to the operating system or applications. Following that, you learn what steps are involved in determining a solution—starting with locating information, then listing and trying possible solutions, and finally either solving the problem or escalating it to a higher level of expertise. With the problem solved (or out of your hands), you then need to document the call and communicate with the end user about the problem and its solutions.

Understanding these concepts is fundamental to becoming a good desktop support technician (DST), and using problem-solving and personal skills such as these is required on a daily basis.

Lessons in this Chapter:

Before You Begin

This chapter discusses the techniques that are involved with resolving service calls. Before you begin, ensure that you are familiar with the ideas described in Chapter 1, "Introduction to Desktop Support."

Lesson 1: Knowing What to Ask

The most important part of troubleshooting is asking pertinent questions and listening to and making notes of the answers. The end user has many of the answers you need, but you must get the end user to share this information with you. You must listen, communicate, and ask the appropriate questions, all while making the end user feel helpful (and not the one to blame for the problem).

After this lesson, you will be able to

- Describe the questions that you should ask to help determine the problem.
- Explain what the answers to those questions can tell you.

Estimated lesson time: 10 minutes

Asking Who, When, What, Why, and How

A reporter or policeman asks questions to obtain the required information to perform his or her job, and you will ask the same questions in your role as a DST. The information that you acquire helps you to determine why the problem occurred, and with that knowledge you can often resolve the problem on your own. The following sections offer some common questions you should ask and what insights they yield.

Who?

- Who was using the computer when the problem first occurred?
- Who else has been using the computer, and have they experienced similar problems?
- Who has worked on this problem previously, if it has happened before?
- Who has experienced the same problem on another computer (that you know of)?

> **Note**   The answers to the "Who" questions tell you who has firsthand knowledge of the problem and if other users who access the same computer (under a different account) also encounter the problem. If multiple users have access but only one user encounters the problem, you have already narrowed the issue. You will also learn from these questions who has worked on the problem before, and whether other users on the network are having the same problem on their computers. If the latter is true, the problem could be a networkwide problem, such as a **security policy** issue, virus, or other glitch in the entire system.

When?

- When did this problem occur the first time, and has it occurred since?
- When was the last time you downloaded or installed an application?
- When was the last time you installed new hardware?
- When did you last clean up the computer with Disk Cleanup or Disk Defragmenter, delete **temporary files** or **cookies**, or perform similar deletions of data?
- When was the last time you uninstalled any applications?

> **Note**   The answers to the "When" questions tell you how long the user has experienced this problem, if the problem occurred after the user installed new hardware or a new application, and if the user routinely maintains the computer. If the problem occurred after installing or uninstalling hardware or software, you have a good lead. Asking specific questions about maintenance can also be helpful in determining whether the user has recently cleaned out program or system folders or deleted any necessary files.

What?

- What are your thoughts as to what caused the problem?
- What have you tried to troubleshoot the problem yourself?
- What do you think can be done to solve the problem?

> **Note**   The answers to the "What" questions tell you what the user believes happened and give you an opportunity to involve the user in the solution. Asking the user what he or she thinks can be done to solve the problem could also yield a very simple solution. If the user recently reconfigured settings for a program or uninstalled a necessary file or program, you know where to begin. If the user has tried to troubleshoot the problem already, you will need to know what changes he or she has made. Finally, if the user thinks reconfiguring the e-mail account will solve the problem, it's likely because he or she was doing something to it earlier but does not want to admit it.

Why and How?

- Why do you think the problem occurred?
- How do you think the problem occurred?

Note   The answers to the "Why" and "How" questions can often summon a solution quickly. If the user says, "The problem occurred because I spilled coffee on the keyboard" or "The problem occurred because I opened an attachment in an e-mail," you know exactly where to start. Keep in mind, though, that these answers will not always be useful and might sometimes even be deceitful. A user might have opened an attachment, for example, but might deny having done so. Remember, you are the expert.

As you work through these questions with an end user, document the answers carefully, listen to everything the user has to say, be polite and professional, and make notes of possible solutions as you think of them. If necessary, leave the situation for a few minutes to digest the information, and check company documentation, online help and support, or other resources for answers.

Real World   Your Changing Role

When you begin working at a telephone call center, company, home business, or Internet service provider (ISP) as a tier-1 DST, you should expect to ask your end users specific questions that are already written out for you in the form of a script. However, as you move up the ladder and work through the natural progression of gaining expertise and experience, you will move from following a script to building your own repertoire of queries. As you internalize your knowledge, you will start to learn and understand how to resolve problems on your own. Keeping in mind that you will probably start your first tier-1 position reading questions already written for you, in this chapter you will learn what types of questions to ask when you are required to work through the resolution process on your own.

Reproducing the Problem

If you or the end user can reproduce the problem, you will have quite a bit of additional information to work with. Problems that cannot be reproduced, such as applications that shut down for no apparent reason, are much more difficult to diagnose than those that can, such as being unable to send or receive e-mail. If the end user can reproduce the problem, make a note of which applications were open and which components were being used, and troubleshoot those applications and their configurations.

Caution   Don't try to reproduce any problem that has previously caused loss of data or is a known network problem, such as a virus or worm. Doing so can cause additional problems and further damage.

Lesson Review

The following questions are intended to reinforce key information presented in this lesson. If you are unable to answer a question, review the lesson materials and try the question again. You can find answers to the questions in the "Questions and Answers" section at the end of this chapter.

1. Questions asked of clients often trigger quick solutions to basic problems. Match the question on the right to the solution it triggered on the left.

1. Who is affected by this problem?	A. The user states that he recently deleted all temporary files and cookies from his computer, explaining why he is no longer able to automatically sign in to websites he visits.
2. When was the first time you noticed the problem? Was it after a new installation of software or hardware?	B. John cannot send or receive messages using Microsoft Outlook. It is determined that the problem is related only to his configuration of Outlook because other users who log on to the same computer under a different account can use Outlook to send and receive e-mail without any problem.
3. Has the user recently deleted any files or performed any maintenance?	C. The keyboard keys are sticky because soda was spilled on the keyboard.
4. How did this problem occur?	D. The user states that the first time the computer acted strangely was after he installed a new screen saver.

2. You work for an ISP and receive a call from a client stating that he has not been able to retrieve his e-mail all morning. You check the network servers, and everything is working on your end. Which of the following questions could you ask the user that would most likely yield results in this situation? (Pick three.)

   A. When was the last time you installed new hardware?

   B. How long have you been a subscriber with us?

   C. Have you recently installed or switched over to a new e-mail client?

   D. Have you opened any suspicious attachments?

   E. When did you last clean up the computer with Disk Cleanup?

Lesson Summary

- To resolve a service call, you must gather information, determine a solution, find and attempt solutions or escalate the call, test any solutions that you implement, and inform the end user of your findings.

- To solve a problem, first get answers to the questions who, what, where, why, and how. The answers often point to a solution quickly.

Lesson 2: Determining a Solution

After you have asked the proper questions and made note of the answers, you will need to formulate a plan of action for resolving the call. This lesson covers general troubleshooting procedures, how to document solutions, and places you can go for help.

After this lesson, you will be able to

- Explain general troubleshooting procedures.
- Describe places you can go for help in locating answers.
- Explain how to attempt solutions without making the problem worse.

Estimated lesson time: 40 minutes

Understanding General Troubleshooting Procedures

If you work for an ISP or telephone call center, your plan of action might involve only reading a set of directions from a script and escalating the call up a tier, but it is still a course of action. If you have already determined a solution and solved the problem, you need only to document your solution.

If you own your own business, though, or are otherwise on your own when fielding a service call, solving the problem might involve more groundwork. When physically assisting a user either in his or her home or at his or her desk, it isn't quite so easy to turn the call over to someone else. If you own your own business, conferring with someone else can cost you time and money, as well as clients; if you have walked across the corporate campus to field a call, calling in someone else produces the same results. In either instance, when given more responsibility for servicing calls, you will need to have a plan of action for uncovering, documenting, and resolving the call without another technician. In this section, you will learn the steps involved in resolving a service call on your own, as opposed to calling in another technician or escalating the call. In general, a specific procedure should be followed, and a common technique is listed here.

To locate answers and to determine a solution after speaking with the end user, perform these general steps in order (each of which will be detailed in later sections):

1. Locate a solution by searching the computer's help and support files. If you find a solution, attempt to solve the problem and document the solution. If the solution does not work, document that as well, and undo any changes made to the computer.

2. Locate a solution by searching the company's help and support files. If you find a solution, attempt to solve the problem and document the solution. If the solution does not work, document that as well, and undo any changes made to the computer.

3. Search manufacturers' websites. If you find a solution, attempt to solve the problem and document the solution. If the solution does not work, document that as well, and undo any changes made to the computer.

4. Search technical sites. If you find a solution, attempt to solve the problem and document the solution. If the solution does not work, document that as well, and undo any changes made to the computer.

5. Search newsgroups. If you find a solution, attempt to solve the problem and document the solution. If the solution does not work, document that as well, and undo any changes made to the computer.

6. If you do not find a solution, document the information and attempted solutions, and undo any changes made to the computer during the troubleshooting process.

7. Escalate the call.

8. When the problem is solved, document the solution.

The troubleshooting process discussed in this section is further detailed in the flowchart shown in Figure 2-1.

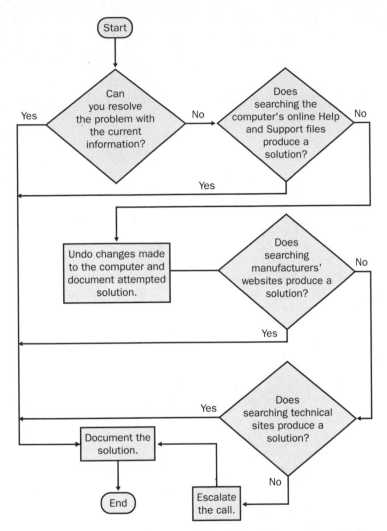

Figure 2-1   Troubleshooting a problem is best done systematically.

Locating the Answers

There are several places to look for help in troubleshooting a computer problem, and if you have good research skills, you will most likely be able to locate a solution without escalating the call. Because escalations require more manpower, more downtime, and more expense for both you and the end user, you should do all you can to resolve calls without having to ask someone else to help. As for finding a solution, chances are good that this isn't the first time an end user has encountered this problem, and the answer will probably be easy to find either in company documents or on the Internet.

Note   The ability to research and find answers isn't an innate ability; a good researcher simply has to know where to look for answers.

Online Help and Support

Online help and support should be the first place you look for information about common operating system problems. Windows Help and Support Center offers information ranging from performing basic tasks, such as logging on and logging off, to complex ones, such as working remotely. It also offers tools to help you access advanced system information, check network diagnostics, and run software and hardware troubleshooting wizards. Figure 2-2 shows the default Help And Support Center for Microsoft Windows XP Professional. It's easy to use; simply browse the categories or type in a few keywords.

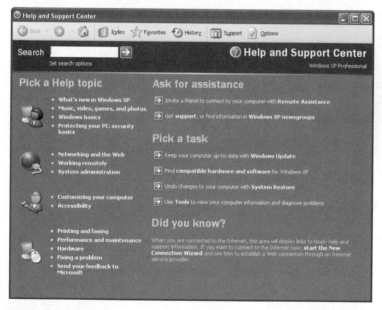

Figure 2-2   The Windows XP Professional default Help And Support Center page offers an abundance of information.

Company Documentation

As time passes, more and more businesses customize the files in the Help And Support Center so that the files offer resources to end users that are specific to their department, job role, company, or domain. This localized help information is useful not only to the end user but to DSTs who don't work for the company and are instead hired as vendors or contract employees. Computer manufacturers already personalize help files for home users and include help files directly related to the user's specific computer configuration. The Microsoft Office System has online resources available directly from the application, too, and these are updated often so that the information is always current.

Exam Tip   Always find out the manufacturer and model of a computer first. Some manufacturers change default Windows settings, include modified help files, and install custom diagnostics software. Often you can take advantage of these inclusions. At a minimum, you should be aware of their presence when proposing solutions.

Targeted help such as this allows users to locate answers to their own problems easily, and it allows you to access information quickly as well. Figure 2-3 shows an example of a customized Help And Support Center interface, created by Sony Corporation for the home user. Notice that there are additional Help topics, including VAIO User Guide, VAIO Multimedia, and VAIO Support Agent Help. These topics are specific to the machine, and they can be quite helpful in troubleshooting computer problems.

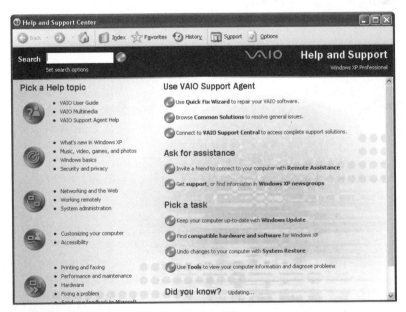

Figure 2-3   Help And Support Center pages can be customized.

Depending on your work environment, this type of customized documentation might be available. At the very least, almost every company will offer some access to a database that contains answers to commonly asked questions. If you cannot find the answer to your troubleshooting query using the default Windows Help And Support files, try these.

Manufacturers' Websites

Many times a problem occurs because a piece of hardware has failed, a **device driver** is corrupt, new software is incompatible with Windows XP or other installed software, or a computer's **basic input/output system (BIOS)** needs updating. You can research these problems and others through a manufacturer's website. This is an especially appropriate tool when troubleshooting a home user's computer or a computer that has recently been upgraded from one operating system to another. If you have yet to find the problem, and a troubleshooting wizard has listed hardware, software, or BIOS problems as the culprit, visit the manufacturer's website for help and updates.

> **Tip** Home users are more likely to install new drivers, applications, and third-party utilities than office users mainly because companies place more limitations on office users. Office users are often not allowed to install devices and applications because of network policies. When troubleshooting a home user's computer, make sure you know what has been installed recently; a new hardware device might be causing the problem. When trouble-shooting for an office user, make sure that the user is (or you are) allowed to implement the proposed solutions.

The Microsoft Knowledge Base

The Microsoft Knowledge Base (available at *http://support.microsoft.com/default.aspx*) offers answers to known issues and can be of significant help when you are trying to solve seemingly irresolvable issues. Figure 2-4 shows the Microsoft Help And Support page where the Knowledge Base and other resources can be accessed. Notice that you can also access announcements, link to visitors' top links, acquire downloads and updates, get product support, and locate other support centers (for Microsoft Office Outlook 2003, Windows 2000, and so on).

The Knowledge Base contains support articles that are identified by an ID number, and you can search for information using that number or using keywords. These articles address known issues with the operating system, third-party software, and hardware, and they provide workarounds and solutions. The Knowledge Base also offers how-to articles, such as KB 291252, "How to Publish Pictures to the Internet in Windows XP," and KB 813938, "How to Set Up a Small Network with Windows Home Edition," the first part of a series of articles on the subject.

Figure 2-4   The Microsoft Knowledge Base offers solutions to known issues.

Search the Knowledge Base after you have tried the foregoing options and when you need to know the following:

- Why a specific piece of hardware such as a camera, scanner, printer, or other device does not work as expected and the problem can be reproduced easily

- Why a specific third-party application will not install, will not start, will not work as expected, or produces error messages

- How to resolve operating system errors, including boot errors, problems during installation, **access violation errors**, and standby problems, and how to resolve other known issues

- How to create boot disks, view system requirements, configure file associations, or perform other common tasks

- How to resolve errors that occur when using operating system components such as accessing System Properties, using Whiteboard, or using System Restore

- What a Stop Error message means and how to resolve it

- How to resolve errors that occur after installing updates

> **Note**   Search the Knowledge Base for the specific error message if a text message exists. This is an especially helpful resource when the error is caused by third-party software or hardware. Information about third-party tools is not available in the Windows XP help files.

TechNet

TechNet (*http://www.microsoft.com/technet/default.mspx/*) offers comprehensive help with applications, operating systems, and components such as Active Directory, Microsoft Internet Explorer, Windows XP Professional, and Office applications, including how to plan, deploy, maintain, and support them. You can also access information on security, get downloads, read how-to articles, read columns, and access troubleshooting and support pages. Because your job will focus on troubleshooting and resolving end user requests, you will likely spend most of your time accessing the troubleshooting pages. A sample TechNet page is shown in Figure 2-5.

Figure 2-5   A sample Microsoft TechNet troubleshooting page.

Much of the information available from TechNet, including the Knowledge Base, is also available through the Microsoft Help And Support page, but TechNet is more geared to IT professionals. You will find that the articles from TechNet are often more technical and sometimes more slanted toward large organizations and networks. Both TechNet and the Microsoft Help And Support page are useful sites, and you will develop a feel for which is the most useful in different situations.

Search the TechNet support pages after you have tried the Microsoft Help And Support page and when you need to do any of the following:

- Locate product documentation

- View the latest security bulletins

- Get information about service packs, Windows updates, and drivers

- Visit the "Bug Center"

- Get help with **dynamic-link library (DLL)** errors

- Subscribe to TechNet

- Locate highly technical information about technologies

> **Note**   TechNet offers two types of annual subscriptions for a single user or a single server, TechNet Standard and TechNet Plus. Prices for subscriptions range from around $350 to $1,000 (U.S.). A one-year subscription delivers up-to-date technical information every month, including the complete Knowledge Base and the latest resource kits, service packs, drivers and patches, deployment guides, white papers, evaluation guides, and much more, all on a set of CDs or DVDs that can be accessed anywhere, anytime, even when you cannot get online. Installing service packs from a disc is much faster than downloading them, offering another reason for considering the subscription. Finally, TechNet Plus offers beta and evaluation software, allowing you to gain experience with software before it is released to the public.

Newsgroups

Newsgroups are a valuable resource for locating answers to problems that you are unable to resolve using any other method. Members of newsgroups are your peers in IT, computer enthusiasts, beginners, and advanced business or home users, and they have various abilities. Some are looking for answers, and some frequent the newsgroups to provide answers to issues they've resolved and to share their expertise. You can join a newsgroup that addresses the application or operating system you need help with, immediately post your question, and almost as quickly receive an answer. Sometimes answers even come from Microsoft experts, such as Microsoft Most Valuable Professionals (MVPs). Microsoft chooses Microsoft MVPs based on their practical expertise in Microsoft technologies, and these MVPs are deemed experts in their fields.

You can access newsgroups in a variety of ways, including:

■ Configuring a newsreader program to access the msnews.microsoft.com news server. This is the best approach because you can access all the newsgroups, making it easier to stay current.

■ Accessing a full list of available newsgroups through the Web. This approach is good if you don't have newsreader software. You can access Microsoft newsgroups on the Web by visiting *http://communities2.microsoft.com/communities/ newsgroups/en-us/default.aspx*.

■ Accessing the Microsoft Help And Support page, the Windows XP Expert Zone, or the TechNet website. Visit those sites and click the Newsgroups link. Some people favor this method because the newsgroups are more clearly identified and are a bit more accessible. However, the newsgroups presented on these sites are just a subset of what is available.

You will find newsgroups for a variety of applications, operating systems, components, and levels of end user. Table 2-1 lists some of the available newsgroup categories, although each category can have multiple newsgroups (such as different newsgroups on Windows XP for subjects such as hardware, customizing, and networking).

Table 2-1   Selecting the Right Newsgroup

For Help With	Join These Knowledge Base Newsgroups
Operating systems	microsoft.public.windowsxp microsoft.public.windowsme microsoft.public.windows.server
Internet Explorer	microsoft.public.windows.inetexplorer
Office applications	microsoft.public.access microsoft.public.excel microsoft.public.frontpage microsoft.public.office microsoft.public.outlook microsoft.public.powerpoint microsoft.public.publisher microsoft.public.word
Connectivity and networking	microsoft.public.windowsxp.network_web microsoft.public.windows.networking microsoft.public.certification.networking
Security	microsoft.public.security microsoft.public.security.virus microsoft.public.windowsxp.security_admin

Table 2-1   Selecting the Right Newsgroup

For Help With	Join These Knowledge Base Newsgroups
Handheld devices	microsoft.public.windows.tabletpc microsoft.public.pocketpc microsoft.public.windowsce

Working Through Possible Solutions

Working through a solution once you have found one requires a little more savvy than simply performing a few mouse clicks and keystrokes and walking away or hanging up the phone. You will have to perform some prerepair and postrepair tasks such as ordering the solutions (if there are more than one), backing up the user's data, and attempting the solutions and documenting the results. If a solution doesn't work, you will have to undo it, try another, and possibly escalate the problem as required by the company.

Attempting Solutions

Most of the time after researching the problem, you will find a single solution to it, and working through that solution will resolve the problem. Solutions you will uncover in a tier-1 position generally involve running a command at the Run line, reconfiguring an e-mail account, installing a patch, re-creating a network connection, reseating a card on the motherboard, or even simply rebooting the computer or removing a floppy disk from the A drive. However, no matter how simple the solution seems, you should always prepare for the worst. Before attempting any solution (besides removing a floppy disk or rebooting), perform as many of the following tasks as you can within your time frame, job scope, and corporate limitations:

- Locate and make a note of previous settings so that you can revert to those if your solution fails or causes additional problems.
- Order the solutions by listing solutions obtained from reputable sources first. (List Help and Support Center, Knowledge Base, TechNet, the manufacturer's website, and so on first, and save solutions found through newsgroups or third-party sites for last.)
- Back up the end user's data to a network resource, CD-R(W), or external hard disk.
- Create a system restore point.
- Perform any additional tasks required by your company.
- Completely document all attempted solutions and their results.

The higher you move up the tier ladder, the more of these you will need to perform or be able to perform. If you provide phone support and work from a script, you might not be able to do any of these, but if you own your own business and visit the user on site, or if you go to a user's desk to solve the problem, you will likely have more leeway (and responsibility) and can do more.

> **Caution**   Protect the end user's data at all costs. If that means postponing an attempt at a risky or undocumented solution until another technician can back up the data or until you can bring in a CD-R(W) drive to back up a home user's data, you must wait.

While working to repair the problem, if you attempt a solution and it doesn't work, you must undo any changed settings, configurations, uninstalled programs, or other specific alterations to a computer before you attempt another solution. This is especially critical if you need to escalate the call; the next technician must see the computer in its previous state. In addition, fully test the solution that you believe resolves the problem. For instance, verify that e-mail can be sent and received after you have changed e-mail account settings, or make sure the user can access a website after you have changed Internet Explorer's privacy settings. Attempt solutions that are within your realm of responsibility, too; don't do a repair installation if that's not on your list of repair options.

Documenting the Problem and Attempted Solutions

Documenting the problem, attempted solutions, and solutions that work are a major part of a DST's job. Although companies, call centers, ISPs, repair shops, and small business owners each have their own way of documenting, documentation tasks usually involve creating (or accessing) a file for a specific client, subscriber, end user, or company computer and updating that file each time there is a service call regarding it. The documentation might be handwritten on a documentation worksheet and then transferred to a computer file later (as in home or desktop tech support), or it might be immediately entered into a computer (as in a call center or in ISP tech support).

Depending on the job you hold and your position in the tier structure, you might be required only to fill in a few fields of a documentation worksheet. However, if you own your own company and keep your own records, you will want to keep much more. Listed next are a few items you should almost always document, no matter what type of job or position you hold:

- The date and time the service call was initiated
- The name, address, phone number, logon information, and any other pertinent data that identifies the end user

- The computer ID, the operating system version, connection type, and installed applications as appropriate

- The problem in definite terms, with as much detail as time allows

- The attempted solutions and the results

- The solution or escalation information

- How long it took to resolve the issue

- Whether the issue has yet to be resolved

Keeping customer and service call documentation (with even minimal information) is crucial to being a good DST, running a successful business, acquiring experience, or advancing in your field. Keeping a separate log of problems and solutions that you have dealt with can also become quite a reference tool; you can refer to your own personal documentation when the problem arises again with another client. In the next section, you will learn to create a personal knowledge base.

Creating a Personal Knowledge Base

There are several options for collecting and maintaining the data you will compile while performing your job as a DST. Microsoft Office Excel and Microsoft Office Access make good databases and organizational tools, and third-party software such as ACT! or Crystal Reports might also be appropriate, depending on how much data you want to keep. Keeping your own personal knowledge base of problems you have encountered and their solutions will make it easier for you to access the answers to those problems the next time they arise.

When creating a personal knowledge base of problems and their solutions, document the following:

- The problem in detail, using keywords so that a search for the problem or one similar to it will produce results

- The cause of the problem, using keywords so that a search for the problem or one similar to it will produce results

- The resource that offered a solution to the problem, including a Uniform Resource Locator (URL)

- The solution

- Problems, if any, that resulted from the solution

- How many times the problem has been encountered and solved

Practice: Determining a Solution

In the following practices, you will practice finding information to help solve specific real-world problems. Following each practice, you will find review questions. If you are unable to answer a question, review the lesson materials and try the question again. You can find answers to the questions in the "Questions and Answers" section at the end of this chapter.

Scenario 1: Finding Solutions in the Knowledge Base

You are a technical support agent for Litware, Inc. A client is having trouble sending e-mail with Microsoft Office Outlook 2000. You cannot find help on the issue by using the Help in Outlook, so you decide to see whether there are any solutions in the Microsoft Knowledge Base.

> **Note** Many of these steps are dependent on the Microsoft website. It is possible that the site will have changed since the writing of this scenario. However, the point of the exercise is to navigate to a particular Knowledge Base article, which is possible even if these steps do not match exactly.

Background

A client sends you the following e-mail using an Internet e-mail account:

I am unable to send messages from Microsoft Outlook 2000. My e-mails come back with the following message:

```
Your message did not reach some or all of the intended recipients.
Subject: Test
Sent: 7/21/2005 11:25 AM
The following recipient(s) could not be reached:
John Doe on 7/21/2005 11:25 AM
A syntax error was detected in the content of the message
The MTS-ID of the original message is: c=US;a= ;1=Server-020127192459Z-145206
MSEXCH:MSExchangeMTA:Site:Server
```

Exercise

1. On the Start menu, choose Internet Explorer.

2. In the Internet Explorer window, in the Address box, type **http://www.microsoft.com** and press ENTER.

3. On the Microsoft home page, in the Resources section, select Support and then select Knowledge Base.

4. On the Search The Knowledge Base page, in the Select A Microsoft Product drop-down list, select Outlook 2000.

5. In the Search For box, type **Your message did not reach some or all of the intended recipients**.

6. In the Using drop-down list, select The Exact Phrase Entered, and then click Go.

7. Click the Back button.

8. In the Search For box, type **A syntax error was detected in the content of the message**. Click Go.

9. On the Support And Troubleshooting page, under Search Results, select OL2000: You Receive A Non-Delivery Report When Outlook 2000 Improperly Formats MDBEF Encoding.

Questions

1. How many articles were found using these search criteria?

_____

_____

2. According to this article, what could be the solution to your client's e-mail problem?

_____

_____

Scenario 2: Finding Solutions at Microsoft TechNet

Litware, Inc., would like to save on transportation costs by using Remote Assistance, rather than always driving to remote client sites. Your boss asks you to see whether his favorite Microsoft column, Professor Windows, has an article about Remote Assistance.

> **Note**   Many of these steps are dependent on the Microsoft websites. It is possible that the sites will have changed since the writing of this exercise. However, the point of the exercise is to navigate to a particular TechNet article, which is possible even if these steps do not match the required steps exactly.

Exercise

1. Log on to Windows XP.

2. On the Start menu, choose Internet Explorer.

3. In the Internet Explorer window, in the Address box, type **http://technet. microsoft.com/default.aspx**.

4. On the Microsoft TechNet page, under the Search For text box, click Advanced Search.

5. On the Search Microsoft.com page, under Microsoft.com Advanced Search, in the All Of These Words box, type **Remote Assistance Professor Windows**.

6. In the Choose A Microsoft.com Site drop-down list, select TechNet. Click Go.

7. On the Search Results From TechNet page, select Windows XP Remote Assistance: Professor Windows, October 2002.

Questions

1. According to the article, what are three ways to use Remote Assistance?

   _____

   _____

2. In Remote Desktop, how many users can be active at a given time? In Remote Assistance?

   _____

   _____

Lesson Review

The following questions are intended to reinforce key information presented in this lesson. If you are unable to answer a question, review the lesson materials and try the question again. You can find answers to the questions in the "Questions and Answers" section at the end of this chapter.

1. Decide where to look first for answers to the scenarios listed here. Match each question on the left to the appropriate choice on the right.

1. After a recent upgrade to Windows XP Professional, a user's scanner no longer functions as it should. You remember that it was listed as incompatible during the upgrade and believe it might be a driver issue. Where will you likely find the new driver?	A. Newsgroup
2. A user cannot access a network application. The application was designed specifically for the company and is not a Microsoft product or any other common third-party application. Where will you likely find information about this application?	B. TechNet

3. You have searched the Knowledge Base and TechNet for the solution to a problem but haven't had any luck. Where should you look now?

C. Knowledge Base

4. You need to search through the latest security bulletins to find out whether the problem you are having is related to a known security problem. Which online resource offers access to these bulletins?

D. Manufacturer website

5. You need to find out why a home user's camera doesn't work with the Windows Picture and Fax Viewer. Specifically, the Rotate tool causes the computer to freeze up each time it is used. Where should you look first?

E. Company documentation

6. You want to access the Hardware Troubleshooter to resolve a problem with a user's sound card. Where can this troubleshooter be found?

F. Help and Support Center

2. Create three simple questions you could ask an end user who is having a problem accessing data on the network server, which would, in turn, provide answers to common connectivity problems. Explain what each solution might uncover. For instance, a yes answer to the question, "Has the computer been moved or bumped recently?" could indicate that a network card is loose inside the computer.

_____

_____

Lesson Summary

- To find a solution, search these resources in the following order: online Help And Support files, company documentation, manufacturers' websites, technical sites, and newsgroups. Apply possible answers in the same order.

- Before attempting any solution, back up the user's data, create a system restore point, and document previous settings and configurations if it is within your job role.

- Always document the service call fully, including the user's name, the computer ID, the problem, the attempted solution, the result, and how long it took to resolve the call.

Lesson 3: Informing and Teaching the End User

The final part of the service call resolution process is to inform the end user what the problem was and how it was resolved. You can then teach the end user how to avoid the problem in the future and how to locate help from the Help and Support Center, company documentation, or other available resources. Finally you can spend a few minutes teaching the user some basic maintenance tasks such as using Disk Defragmenter or Disk Cleanup, as well as some other easy-to-use tools.

After this lesson, you will be able to

- Explain a user's problem and its solution to the user.
- Help a user solve problems using tools built into Windows XP.
- Teach common maintenance tasks to a user.

Estimated lesson time: 15 minutes

Explaining the Problem and Solution to the End User

If a user understands what the problem was and how it was solved, that user can likely prevent the problem in the future or solve the problem if it occurs again. This not only reduces overall costs for the company but also frees you to spend more time working on other tasks. In addition to saving both you and the company time and money by reducing service calls, informing users of the problem and solution is empowering to them, too. Consider this:

- Although it might require some downtime on their end, having end users solve the problem themselves is probably less aggravating to them than reporting the problem and waiting for a technician to call or show up.

- Many users will appreciate knowing how to prevent or solve problems in the future, particularly home or home office users. Most want to know how to prevent and solve problems on their own.

- When users can solve their own problems, it's generally cheaper and minimizes downtime for small business owners and freelance vendors.

Real World   Understanding Your End User

If you get the impression that the end user has absolutely no interest in the information you want to provide, make it brief. Although your main objective is to repair the problem without loss of data, a secondary objective is to avoid annoying the end user. It is not too difficult to gauge a user's level of interest while talking during the problem resolution. Pay attention to how much information the user was able to provide and the questions asked during the process.

Never begrudge a user the time it takes to explain a problem and solution. If explaining the technology behind the fix is too complicated or time-consuming, point the user to some places that provide information. Remember that support costs the user time and costs your company time and money. Also, if the end user is interested and you own your own business, spending a little extra time educating the user will help to improve your relationship and increase the likelihood that he or she will call on you again.

Consider the problems, solutions, and end results of interacting positively and proactively with the end user about problems and their solutions, as detailed in Table 2-2.

Table 2-2   Teach and Inform the End User

Problem and Solution	Solution as Detailed to the End User	Result of Informing and Teaching the End User
The user reports that the computer will not boot. The user has a floppy disk in the drive and needs to remove it.	You inform the user that, when the computer boots, it looks to the floppy disk first for system files. Because there are no system files on the disk, the computer cannot boot.	The next time the user encounters this problem, the user removes the disk and boots the computer without help from technical support.
The user reports that she cannot access network resources. You find that the user is not logged on to the domain.	You inform the user that logging on to the domain is what allows her to access shared resources and that it is a security feature of a domain.	The user understands the idea of being authenticated on the domain and remembers to log on to access network resources.
The user reports that he cannot use System Restore. You determine that it has been disabled.	You inform the user that System Restore must have at least 200 MB of hard disk space to function, and it must be enabled.	The user keeps System Restore enabled.

Table 2-2   Teach and Inform the End User

Problem and Solution	Solution as Detailed to the End User	Result of Informing and Teaching the End User
The user complains that every time she clicks the Outlook Express icon, Outlook opens instead. You determine that Outlook is configured as the default e-mail client and make the appropriate changes.	You inform the end user that she can set defaults for the e-mail client, Web browser, newsgroup reader, calendar, and more on the Programs tab of the Internet Options dialog box.	The end user no longer needs help setting default Internet programs, and she also learns about available Internet options.

Each time you teach end users a new task, they become more confident in their abilities and are more adept at solving their own problems rather than calling for technical support. Although this is good in reducing overall costs and use of resources, it can work against you as well. The old saying, "A little knowledge is a dangerous thing" certainly holds true in this case. While teaching end users new skills, also make sure to let them know (gently) that they can cause problems, too.

> **Tip**   If you can clearly see that the end user you are working with does not have enough experience to deal with the technical information you want to offer, you might be better off not telling the user of the solution. As a DST, you need to have a sense of the end user's prior knowledge to know how much to explain or share. If there is a danger that the new information will result in a misunderstanding or a naive understanding—both of which could get the user into serious trouble in the future—you're probably better off keeping the explanation to a minimum, with a caveat that the end user probably should not "try this at home."

If a user understands what the problem was and how it was solved, that user can likely avoid the problem in the future. When an end user can avoid a problem completely, productivity increases and the overall cost to support that user decreases. It is a waste of resources to simply correct a problem and go back in a week to correct it again. It is much more productive to explain to the user how to keep the problem from happening in the first place. As shown earlier in Table 2-2, end users can often avoid problems if they understand their causes.

Helping the User Solve Problems with Online Help and Support

You can teach end users (in small steps) how to find information and solve problems on their own. There is much information available in the Help and Support Center on a user's own computer, and the information is easy to locate, access, and use. There are also how-to files, as well as lengthy articles on how to perform tasks that range from setting up a home network to working remotely. The troubleshooting wizards are especially helpful, and they provide a great way to get to know the troubleshooting process.

When possible, encourage end users to access the help files and browse through them when they encounter a problem. Most users want to know how to solve problems on their own without waiting for a technician. Small home office users especially appreciate being able to solve their own problems, particularly when a problem occurs late at night or on the weekend, when technicians and technical support aren't available.

Using a Troubleshooting Wizard

You can use the troubleshooting wizards to practice and enhance your troubleshooting skills and to look for answers to common problems. The troubleshooters work through the problem-solving process as you should, suggesting obvious solutions first and then moving on to more complex ones.

Consider the following scenario. A home user is having a problem with Internet connection sharing. Although the user can surf the Internet on her computer, a computer recently connected as a client computer is unable to connect to the Internet through this shared connection. The client computer is the only other computer on the network and connects to the host through a hub. The user states that she only recently acquired the hub and connected the computers to it. She wants you to resolve this problem.

Although this sounds like a potentially difficult situation, this problem can easily be solved using the Internet Connection Sharing Troubleshooter in the Help and Support Center. To locate this troubleshooter (or any other) and resolve this particular problem, follow these steps:

1. Click Start, and then click Help And Support.

2. Select Fixing A Problem under Pick A Help Topic.

3. In the left pane under Fixing A Problem, select Troubleshooting Problems.

4. In the right pane, click List Of Troubleshooters.

5. Select the Internet Connection Sharing link to start the Internet Connection Sharing Troubleshooter.

6. On the What Problem Are You Having? page, select I Cannot Browse The Internet From An Internet Connection Sharing Client Computer, and then click Next.

7. On the Can You Browse The Internet From The Host Computer? page, click Yes, I Can Browse The Internet From The Host Computer, and then click Next.

8. On the Can You Browse The Internet From Another Client Computer? page, select No, I Can't Browse From Any Client Computers On The Home Or Small Office Network, and then click Next.

9. As prompted by the wizard, ask the user whether she has run the Network Setup Wizard. If she has not, run the Network Setup Wizard as defined in the troubleshooting guide. This is the likely cause of the problem because the user stated that the client computer was recently connected to the host through a hub, but she made no mention that a network was officially configured. This should solve the problem. (If this does not solve the problem, continue working through the wizard until the problem has been determined and solved.)

The home user could have accessed this troubleshooter and the problem could have been solved without your assistance if the user had had the proper knowledge of the available tools. However, with the problem solved and the information now at hand, the user can solve the same problem on her own the next time it occurs.

> **Note** Although you want to inform end users of places to obtain information, you don't want them finding a solution on TechNet that requires them to access the registry, change BIOS settings, or perform other potentially dangerous actions. Ensure that end users understand the potential risk of working outside their area of expertise, and verify that they are working only with the Help And Support Center and company-approved documents.

Teaching Common Maintenance Tasks

The end user can be taught how to maintain the computer if company policy allows it. If it is in your job description, if you are visiting an employee's desktop, or if you support home users, take a few minutes to make sure the client understands the basic maintenance options. Routine maintenance can be quite useful in keeping a computer running properly; it can actually prevent problems, and it can even enhance performance.

Using Disk Cleanup

Disk Cleanup is a safe and simple maintenance tool that users can employ to keep their computers running smoothly. Disk Cleanup searches the drives on the computer and then shows the user temporary files, **Internet cache files**, and unnecessary program files that the user can safely delete. Deleting these files frees space on the hard disk, which helps the computer run faster and more efficiently. Removing temporary files also helps performance, because these files can build up on the computer, occupy lots of space, and hinder performance.

To use Disk Cleanup or instruct a user to do so, follow these steps:

1. Click Start, point to All Programs, point to Accessories, point to System Tools, and then click Disk Cleanup. Disk Cleanup often takes a few minutes to open because

it first calculates how much space you will be able to free up on the computer's disk drive.

2. If the computer has multiple partitions, in the Select Drive dialog box, select the drive to clean up from the drop-down list. If this is the first time the drive is being cleaned and more than one drive or partition exists, choose the **system partition** first. Click OK.

3. In the Disk Cleanup dialog box, review the files to be deleted. Click to choose a file type to delete, and select the Recycle Bin check box to empty it also. Figure 2-6 shows an example. Click OK when finished.

4. Click Yes to verify that you want to perform these actions.

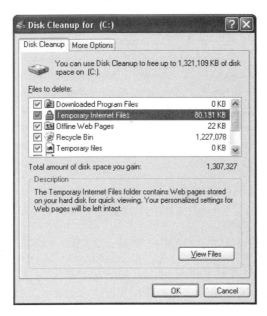

Figure 2-6   Teach end users to use Disk Cleanup weekly.

Using Disk Defragmenter

Disk Defragmenter is another tool that can be used to keep the user's computer running smoothly. The hard disk becomes fragmented as users delete files, move files, delete and install programs and applications, and empty the Recycle Bin. The files on the hard disk aren't stored contiguously as they once were, and this causes the computer to work harder than necessary to locate the file fragments, put them together, and bring up the data.

Persuade the end users you service to run Disk Defragmenter once a month. They'll see better computer performance, have fewer problems in the long term, and learn that maintaining the computer benefits them greatly. To use Disk Defragmenter, follow these steps:

1. Close all open programs.

2. Turn off screen savers and antivirus software, and disconnect from the Internet.

3. Click Start, point to All Programs, point to Accessories, point to System Tools, and click Disk Defragmenter.

4. Highlight a drive to defragment, and either click Analyze to see whether the disk needs defragmenting or click Defragment to begin the process immediately.

Although you might already be familiar with these maintenance tasks, your end users might not be. Share this knowledge with them, and you will likely see them a little less often.

Note   Disk Defragmenter does not provide a built-in way to schedule automatic defragmentation of a drive. This is a major selling point of many third-party defragmentation programs. However, with a small Microsoft Visual Basic Scripting Engine script and the Windows Task Scheduler, you can set up an automated defragmentation schedule quickly and easily. The script and instructions for its use are included in the Tools folder on the CD that is included with this book.

Practice: Exploring the Windows Troubleshooters

In the following exercise, you will explore the troubleshooters included with Windows XP. Following the exercise, you will be asked several questions. If you are unable to answer a question, review the lesson materials and try the question again. You can find answers to the questions in the "Questions and Answers" section at the end of this chapter.

Exercise

1. Click Start, and then click Help And Support.

2. Click the Fixing A Problem link under Pick A Help Topic.

3. Click the Troubleshooting Problems link.

4. Scroll to the section named "Overviews, Articles, and Tutorials," and click the List Of Troubleshooters link.

5. Examine the list of troubleshooters available. You can start any of the troubleshooters by clicking its name. Choose any of the troubleshooters (Display is a good one to start with), and let Windows walk you through its troubleshooting process. Consider stepping through the questions asked in all of the troubleshoot-

ers. It will help you understand what they can solve (and what they cannot), as well as provide valuable insight into the specific settings themselves.

Questions

1. A user complains to you that he is having trouble connecting to the Internet. After asking a few questions, you determine that he is connected to the Internet using a cable modem, that he hooked it up himself, and that it never worked successfully. Which troubleshooters would you suggest the user run?

   _____

   _____

2. You are helping a user who has a small home network. The family's main computer has a laser printer attached to it. The user wants her son to be able to print to the printer from the computer in his bedroom. The network appears to be working since the son can access the shared Internet connection and see the main computer in My Network Places. Which troubleshooters might help?

   _____

   _____

Lesson Review

The following questions are intended to reinforce key information presented in this lesson. If you are unable to answer a question, review the lesson materials and try the question again. You can find answers to the questions in the "Questions and Answers" section at the end of this chapter.

1. Which of the following are tasks you would encourage an average home-based end user to do on his or her own to maintain and support his or her own computer? (Choose all that apply.)

   A. Use Disk Defragmenter monthly.

   B. Access TechNet when in need of technical support, and follow the directions to solve problems on his or her own.

   C. Use Disk Cleanup weekly.

   D. Access the Help and Support Center for how-to articles and to perform specific tasks.

   E. Use Scheduled Tasks to schedule Disk Cleanup to run regularly.

   F. Enable System Restore, and keep it enabled.

2. A user complains to you that he has been getting an error message when trying to download a file saying there is not enough room on his hard drive. Which utility would you suggest the user run?

_____

_____

Lesson Summary

- To lower costs, create informed end users, and reduce how often you have to speak with the same end users, inform them briefly of the problem, the solution, and how to avoid the problem in the future.

- To reduce the likelihood that a computer will develop future problems, inform the user about how to perform routine maintenance tasks such as using Disk Defragmenter and Disk Cleanup.

Case Scenario Exercises

In the following scenarios, you must use what you have learned throughout the lessons in this chapter to answer questions based on a real-world scenario. Read each scenario, and answer the questions. If you have trouble, review the chapter and try again. You can find answers in the "Questions and Answers" section at the end of this chapter.

Scenario 2.1

An end user who runs Windows XP Professional has called technical support regarding his e-mail account. He is certain that he was able to open attachments last week, but an attachment just came arrived today and he cannot open it. The user says the paper clip in Outlook Express is unavailable. The technician asks the user if he has made any changes to Outlook Express, and he says no. He is firm in his answer. The following five steps describe how the technician solved the problem. Put them in the correct order.

1. Inform the user to open Outlook Express, click Tools, click Options, and, on the Security tab, make the appropriate changes.

2. Ask the user what operating system he uses, if any new software or hardware has been installed, if he has switched e-mail clients recently, and other pertinent questions. The user informs you he recently installed a new printer, he uninstalled a screen saver, and he installed Service Pack 1 last weekend.

3. Take a few minutes to inform the user about the maintenance features of Outlook Express, including using Clean Up Now.

4. Look for help in various places, and locate the answer in the Knowledge Base. The technician discovers that installing Service Pack 1 resets the security setting associated with opening attachments in Outlook Express.

5. Verify that the user can now open attachments, and document the results.

Scenario 2.2

An end user calls to report a problem with a locally attached printer. The user is in an office on the other side of the corporate complex, you're busy, and no other technician is available. You find out after asking a few questions that the printer actually works fine, but it just prints slowly. You will not be able to visit the user's desk in person until tomorrow, and you have learned from the user that she has quite a bit of experience with computers.

1. Which of the following solutions (they are all valid) is best under these circumstances?

   A. Tell the user to join a printer newsgroup and ask other users for advice.

   B. Tell the user to open Help And Support, locate the printer troubleshooter, and work through the options. There is an option to allow Windows to investigate the problem, and this might produce a solution.

   C. Tell the user to visit http://www.windrivers.com and download a new driver for the printer.

   D. Tell the user to uninstall and reinstall the printer.

Chapter Summary

- To resolve a service call, you must gather information, determine a solution, find and attempt solutions or escalate the call, test any solutions that you implement, and inform the end user of your findings.

- To solve a problem, first get answers to the questions who, what, where, why, and how. The answers often point to a solution quickly.

- To find a solution, search these resources in the following order: online Help And Support files, company documentation, manufacturers' websites, technical sites, and newsgroups. Apply possible answers in the same order.

- Before attempting any solution, back up the user's data, create a system restore point, and document previous settings and configurations if it is within your job role.

- Always document the service call fully, including the user's name, the computer ID, the problem, the attempted solution, the result, and how long it took to resolve the call.

- To lower costs, create informed end users, and reduce how often you have to speak with the same end users, inform them briefly of the problem, the solution, and how to avoid the problem in the future.

- To reduce the likelihood that a computer will develop future problems, inform the user about how to perform routine maintenance tasks such as using Disk Defragmenter and Disk Cleanup.

Exam Highlights

Before taking the exam, review the key topics and terms that are presented in this chapter. You need to know this information.

Key Points

- Always find out the manufacturer and model of a computer first. Some manufacturers change default Windows settings, include modified help files, and install custom diagnostics software.

- Always try one possible solution at a time. If the solution does not work, undo the solution before moving on to the next. This takes extra time but helps ensure the stability of the user's system and gives you a better idea of what worked and what did not.

Key Terms

basic input/output system (BIOS)   A computer's BIOS program determines in what order the computer searches for system files on boot up, manages communication between the operating system and the attached devices on boot up, and is an integral part of the computer.

device driver   Software that is used to allow a computer and a piece of hardware to communicate. Device drivers that are incompatible, corrupt, outdated, or of the wrong version for the hardware can cause errors that are difficult to diagnose.

Internet cache files   A temporary copy of the text and graphics for all the Web pages that a user has visited. These temporary files are stored in random access memory (RAM) and on your hard disk and can be accessed more quickly than retrieving the files fresh from the Internet every time you visit the page. Internet cache files make browsing the Internet faster because pages you visit often can be loaded more quickly than they can if no cache files exist.

Questions and Answers

Lesson 1 Review

Page 2-5   **1.** Questions asked of clients often trigger quick solutions to basic problems. Match the question on the right to the solution it triggered on the left.

1. Who is affected by this problem?	A. The user states that he recently deleted all temporary files and cookies from his computer, explaining why he is no longer able to automatically sign in to websites he visits.
2. When was the first time you noticed the problem? Was it after a new installation of software or hardware?	B. John cannot send or receive messages using Microsoft Outlook. It is determined that the problem is related only to his configuration of Outlook because other users who log on to the same computer under a different account can use Outlook to send and receive e-mail without any problem.
3. Has the user recently deleted any files or performed any maintenance?	C. The keyboard keys are sticky because coffee was spilled on the keyboard.
4. How did this problem occur?	D. The user states that the first time the computer acted strangely was after he installed a new screen saver.

Answer 1-B is correct. Because only one person is affected by this problem, the "who" question produces a solution to the problem. John's configuration of Outlook must need attention. Answer 2-D is correct because asking "when" produces the information needed to solve the problem. The problem occurred after the user installed a screen saver. Answer 3-A is correct because asking what has been deleted recently produces the cause of the problem. The user recently deleted cookies and temporary files. Answer 4-C is correct because the question "how" produces the simple answer to why the keys are sticky.

2. You work for an ISP and receive a call from a client stating that he has not been able to retrieve his e-mail all morning. You check the network servers, and everything is working on your end. Which of the following questions could you ask the user that would most likely yield results in this situation? (Pick three.)

   A. When was the last time you installed new hardware?

   B. How long have you been a subscriber with us?

   C. Have you recently installed or switched over to a new e-mail client?

   D. Have you opened any suspicious attachments?

   E. When did you last clean up the computer with Disk Cleanup?

Answers B, C, and D are correct. Answer B is correct because a new subscriber will likely have problems with the configuration of the new e-mail account or will have made typographical errors. Answer C is correct because switching to a new e-mail client can cause compatibility issues. Answer D is correct because opening a suspicious attachment might have unleashed a virus. Answer A is incorrect because it is unlikely that a new hardware installation would create a sudden problem retrieving e-mail. Answer E is incorrect because using Disk Cleanup will not affect a user's ability to retrieve e-mail.

Lesson 2 Practice: Scenario 1

Page 2-20   **1.** How many articles were found using these search criteria?

At least six.

2. According to this article, what could be the solution to your client's e-mail problem?

Installing the Outlook 2000 Post-Service Pack Hotfix Roll-Up Package from June 7, 2003.

Lesson 2 Practice: Scenario 2

Page 2-21   **1.** According to the article, what are three ways to use Remote Assistance?

You can use Remote Assistance via instant messaging, e-mail, or a file.

2. In Remote Desktop, how many users can be active at a given time? In Remote Assistance?

In Remote Desktop, only one user is active at a given time. In Remote Assistance, both the person requesting assistance and the person providing the assistance can be active.

Lesson 2 Review

Page 2-22   **1.** Decide where to look first for answers to the scenarios listed here. Match each question on the left to the appropriate choice on the right.

1. After a recent upgrade to Windows XP Professional, a user's scanner no longer functions as it should. You remember that it was listed as incompatible during the upgrade and believe it might be a driver issue. Where will you likely find the new driver?	A. Newsgroup
2. A user cannot access a network application. The application was designed specifically for the company and is not a Microsoft product or any other common third-party application. Where will you likely find information about this application?	B. TechNet
3. You have searched the Knowledge Base and TechNet for the solution to a problem but haven't had any luck. Where should you look now?	C. Knowledge Base
4. You need to search through the latest security bulletins to find out whether the problem you are having is related to a known security problem. Which online resource offers access to these bulletins?	D. Manufacturer website

5. You need to find out why a home user's camera doesn't work with the Windows Picture and Fax Viewer. Specifically, the Rotate tool causes the computer to freeze up each time it is used. Where should you look first?

E. Company documentation

6. You want to access the Hardware Troubleshooter to resolve a problem with a user's sound card. Where can this troubleshooter be found?

F. Help and Support Center

Answer 1-D is correct. Manufacturers often offer new drivers when new operating systems become available. Answer 2-E is correct. Because the application is a company product, the company documentation offers the best place to search for answers. Answer 3-A is correct. After searching the Knowledge Base and TechNet, newsgroups are a good place to look. Answer 4-B is correct. TechNet offers these resources. Answer 5-C is correct. The Knowledge Base offers information on known issues between the operating system and third-party hardware and software. Answer 6-F is correct. The Hardware Troubleshooter is available from Help and Support.

2. Create three simple questions you could ask an end user who is having a problem accessing data on the network server, which would, in turn, provide answers to common connectivity problems. Explain what each solution might uncover. For instance, a yes answer to the question, "Has the computer been moved or bumped recently?" could indicate that a network card is loose inside the computer.

Answers to this question may vary, but following are three typical questions you could ask.

Have you or anyone else who uses the computer changed any settings recently? Changes to computer settings such as the computer name can render a computer unable to connect.

Is the network cable plugged in to both the computer and the outlet or hub?

Did you log on properly when the computer booted up? Failing to log on to the domain will cause access to network resources to be denied.

Lesson 3 Practice

Page 2-30   1. A user complains to you that he is having trouble connecting to the Internet. After asking a few questions, you determine that he is connected to the Internet using a cable modem, that he hooked it up himself, and that it never worked successfully. Which troubleshooters would you suggest the user run?

The following troubleshooters could be helpful: Home Networking, Hardware, Drives and Network Adapters, and Internet Connection Sharing.

2. You are helping a user who has a small home network. The family's main computer has a laser printer attached to it. The user wants her son to be able to print to the printer from the computer in his bedroom. The network appears to be working since the son can access the shared Internet connection and see the main computer in My Network Places. Which troubleshooters might help?

The following troubleshooters could be helpful: Hardware, File and Print Sharing, and Printing.

Lesson 3 Review

Page 2-31   **1.** Which of the following are tasks you would encourage an average home-based end user to do on his or her own to maintain and support his or her own computer? (Choose all that apply.)

    A. Use Disk Defragmenter monthly.

    B. Access TechNet when in need of technical support, and follow the directions to solve problems on his or her own.

    C. Use Disk Cleanup weekly.

    D. Access the Help and Support Center for how-to articles and to perform specific tasks.

    E. Use Scheduled Tasks to schedule Disk Cleanup to run regularly.

    F. Enable System Restore, and keep it enabled.

Answers A, C, D, E, and F are correct because these are simple and generally fail-safe ways users can maintain their computers. Answer A is correct because running Disk Defragmenter monthly will keep the computer running smoothly and keep the hard disks organized. Answer C is correct because Disk Cleanup will delete temporary files before they become large enough to create a problem for the user. Answer D is correct because the Help and Support Center offers wizards to help in solving problems. Answer E is correct because Scheduled Tasks offers a nice way to run cleanup tasks. Answer F is correct because System Restore is a good utility to use when the computer encounters a serious problem. Answer B is incorrect because TechNet is written with the IT professional in mind. Home users are much better off using the Help and Support site.

2. A user complains to you that he has been getting an error message when trying to download a file saying there is not enough room on his hard drive. Which utility would you suggest the user run?

Disk Cleanup could help the user recover considerable disk space and would be a good place to start. If Disk Cleanup does not recover enough space to allow the user to work comfortably, you can then move on to other solutions (such as removing unnecessary programs).

Case Scenario Exercises: Scenario 2.1

Page 2-32 An end user who runs Windows XP Professional has called technical support regarding his e-mail account. He is certain that he was able to open attachments last week, but one just came in today and he cannot open it. The user says the paper clip in Outlook Express is unavailable. The technician asks the user if he has made any changes to Outlook Express, and he says no. He is firm in his answer. The following five steps describe how the technician solved the problem. Put them in the correct order.

1. Inform the user to open Outlook Express, click Tools, click Options, and on the Security tab, make the appropriate changes.

2. Ask the user what operating system he uses, if any new software or hardware has been installed, if he has switched e-mail clients recently, and other pertinent questions. The user informs you he recently installed a new printer, he uninstalled a screen saver, and he installed Service Pack 1 last weekend.

3. Take a few minutes to inform the user about the maintenance features of Outlook Express, including using Clean Up Now.

4. Look for help in various places, and locate the answer in the Knowledge Base. The technician discovers that installing Service Pack 1 resets the security setting associated with opening attachments in Outlook Express.

5. Verify that the user can now open attachments, and document the results.

> The correct order is 2, 4, 1, 5, and 3. Troubleshooting involves being able to do steps in the correct order to produce the desired solution. Step 2 involves collecting information, step 4 involves locating a solution, step 1 involves working through the solution, step 5 involves verifying the solution, and step 3 involves teaching the end user.

Case Scenario Exercises: Scenario 2.2

Page 2-33 An end user calls to report a problem with a locally attached printer. The user is in an office on the other side of the corporate complex, you're busy, and no other technician is available. You find out after asking a few questions that the printer actually works fine, but it just prints slowly. You will not be able to visit the user's desk in person until tomorrow, and you have learned from the user that she has quite a bit of experience with computers.

1. Which of the following solutions (they are all valid) is best under these circumstances?

    A. Tell the user to join a printer newsgroup and ask other users for advice.

    B. Tell the user to open Help And Support, locate the printer troubleshooter, and work through the options. There is an option to allow Windows to investigate the problem, and this might produce a solution.

    C. Tell the user to visit *http://www.windrivers.com* and download a new driver for the printer.

    D. Tell the user to uninstall and reinstall the printer.

    > Answer B is correct. The Help And Support files offer many valuable troubleshooters that both DSTs and end users can employ. Answers A, C, and D are not the best choices under these circumstances because they will not produce a dependable, acceptable, and valid solution quickly.

3 Troubleshooting the Operating System

Exam Objectives in this Chapter:

- Configure the operating system to support applications
- Answer end-user questions that are related to configuring the operating system to support an application
- Resolve issues related to operating system features
- Resolve issues related to customizing the operating system to support applications

Why This Chapter Matters

This chapter teaches you how to resolve many of the most common end-user requests that involve basic operating system components as they relate to running applications. The components covered in this chapter include the taskbar, Start menu, regional settings, folder settings, and file association settings.

The chapter begins with the taskbar and Start menu and introduces the most common issues that you will see as a tier 1 desktop support technician (DST). Issues involving the taskbar usually revolve around missing icons, a locked or missing taskbar, or the automatic grouping of items. Common issues with the Start menu involve how to personalize it by adding or removing items, reordering items, or performing similar customizations.

You will also learn how to configure and troubleshoot various regional settings such as currency, date, and time; to configure input languages; and resolve language-related keyboard problems. Finally you will learn about folder settings and file associations and the most common end-user requests that are associated with these components. Common file and folder requests include changing how a folder opens and what is shown, viewing hidden or system files, and changing the way a particular program or file opens.

Lessons in this Chapter:

Before You Begin

Before you begin this chapter, you should have basic familiarity with the Windows XP interface. You should also have access to a computer running Windows XP on which you can experiment with changing various settings.

Lesson 1: Resolving Taskbar and Start Menu Issues

The taskbar and the Start menu are the two main liaisons between the end user and his or her computer. The taskbar defines for the user the files and programs that are currently open and running and the programs that are running in the background. The taskbar also allows the user to switch easily between open files and applications, group items, and open the most often used programs quickly. The Start menu provides access to the other available programs, network places, connections, help and support files, recent documents, and more.

After this lesson, you will be able to

- Identify the types of questions that relate to the Start menu and taskbar.
- Troubleshoot and customize the notification area.
- Troubleshoot and customize the taskbar.
- Troubleshoot and customize the Start menu.

Estimated lesson time: 50 minutes

Common Start Menu and Taskbar Requests

Because of the amount of time the end user spends using these two components, you may come across several configuration (or troubleshooting) requests, including the following:

- The taskbar is always disappearing, and I'd like that to stop. I also want to be able to move the taskbar to another area of the screen.

- John, my colleague down the hall, has an icon next to his Start menu that he uses to open our accounting program. I do not have any icons there. How do I create one of those so that I do not always have to locate the program on the Start menu or place a shortcut on the desktop?

- I do not have enough room on my taskbar to show all of my open programs, and I have to scroll to see the additional programs. Is there some way of grouping the programs together?

- Can I remove or hide the icons for my antivirus software, my pop-up stopper program, and other programs that run in the background? If I remove them, do they stop running?

- There are a lot of icons in the notification area that I do not think I need. How can I get rid of those for good? I do not think they should be running in the background, and I do not even know what some of them are.

- There are lots of programs in my Start menu that I do not need, and some I need that are not there. Can you fix that for me?

- I want to be able to open My Network Places, open Control Panel, and access System Administrative Tools from the Start menu, but I do not want my recent documents to be listed. I also do not want to see the My Music or My Pictures folder or any other folders that are not work related.

To answer these questions, you must understand the options that are available and how to access and configure them. By the time you reach the end of this lesson you will be able to resolve all of these issues and more.

> **Note**   These questions and their answers constitute Review Question 1.

Troubleshooting the Notification Area

The notification area shows the time, volume control, and icons for programs that start and run automatically. These program icons can be for antivirus programs, music programs, CD-burning programs, or third-party programs that have been downloaded or purchased. If an item is in the notification area, its program is running in the background, making it quickly available when needed. The notification area also shows icons for network connections, and it can show whether the connections are enabled or disabled.

In this section, you will learn to configure and troubleshoot the notification area. Troubleshooting can also include cleaning up the area by removing unnecessary programs. After completing this section, you will be able to do the following:

- Add items to the notification area if the program supports it

- Hide inactive icons so that the notification area does not take up too much room on the taskbar

- Remove icons and close running programs temporarily

- Remove icons and close running programs permanently

Adding Items to the Notification Area

You can add an icon to the notification area only if the program supports that feature in its preferences or configuration options, and many times icons are added by default when a new program is installed. (There is no support for dragging and dropping a program in the notification area.) You can also add icons for network connections, including **Ethernet** connections to **local area networks (LANs)**, wireless connections through **wireless access points**, and dial-up connections to the Internet.

If a user requests that you add an icon to the notification area for an application such as an antivirus program, open the program and browse through the available options and preferences. If an option to show or remove the program in the notification area is available, it should look similar to what is shown in Figure 3-1.

Figure 3-1   Microsoft OneNote offers the option to remove the icon from the tray.

> **Note**   When you remove an item from the notification area, it does not necessarily disable the program; it may only remove the icon. Check the instructions for an application to make sure.

If a user requests that you add an icon to the notification area for any network or Internet connection on a computer running Microsoft Windows XP, follow these steps:

1. Click Start, click Connect To, and then click Show All Connections. If the Connect To option is not available on the Start Menu, in Control Panel, open Network Connections.

2. Right-click the connection that you want to show in the notification area, and then click Properties

3. On the General tab of the connection's Properties dialog box, select the Show Icon In Notification Area When Connected check box, and then click OK.

Figure 3-2 shows a notification area that has three active network connections. One is a wireless connection, one is a dial-up Internet connection, and one is a connection to a LAN. It also shows antivirus software and a third-party pop-up stopper application.

Figure 3-2   The notification area shows active programs and connections.

Hiding Inactive Icons

If the computer has several programs that start automatically when Microsoft Windows loads and there are multiple icons in the notification area as shown in Figure 3-2, the end user might complain that the notification area is taking up too much space on the taskbar. If this happens, enable Hide Inactive Icons, and the icons for programs that are not active but are still running in the background will be hidden. To hide inactive icons, follow these steps:

1. Right-click an empty area of the taskbar, and choose Properties.

2. On the taskbar tab, select the Hide inactive icons check box. Click OK.

The inactive icons are hidden behind the arrow. Figure 3-3 shows a notification area configured with hidden icons. Compare this with Figure 3-2; both show the same notification area.

Figure 3-3   Hidden icons in the notification area are accessed by clicking the arrow.

Exam Tip   Keep in mind that items in the notification area can be hidden behind the arrow. You (or the user) might not see them, but that does not mean they are not there. Check there before you access the program's preferences or restart the program.

Removing Icons and Temporarily Closing Programs That Are Running

To close a program and remove an item from the notification area temporarily so that you can free up resources, disable the program, or briefly unclutter the notification area, right-click the icon and look at the choices. Figure 3-4 shows the choices for MSN Messenger 6.1, a program that a home user might have installed.

Figure 3-4   Click Exit to close this program and remove the icon from the notification area.

The choices for removing the icon and editing the program differ depending on the application or connection. Common options include the following:

- Exit
- Disable
- Close
- End
- Preferences (locate the Exit command in the dialog box)

Removing icons from the notification area in this manner is not permanent; it only removes an icon until the program is started again or you reboot the computer. Removing items permanently requires a little more work.

Removing Icons and Permanently Closing Programs That Are Running

A cluttered notification area is a good indicator that too many programs are starting when you start Windows. Having too many programs running can be the cause of many common problems, including a slower than necessary startup process, an unstable system, or a computer that generally displays slow response times when accessing applications or performing calculations. When a user complains that the system exhibits these systems, check the notification area first.

Even if the computer seems to be running smoothly, you should remove items from a computer's notification area if the applications are never used. There is no reason to allow unused programs to start each time Windows does; this only drains necessary system resources.

If you decide to remove programs from the notification area permanently, follow these steps:

1. Click Start, and then click Run.

2. In the Run dialog box, type **msconfig.exe** and click OK.

3. In the System Configuration Utility dialog box, click the Startup tab.

4. Scroll through the list, as shown in Figure 3-5, and clear the check box of any third-party item you do not want to start automatically when Windows does.

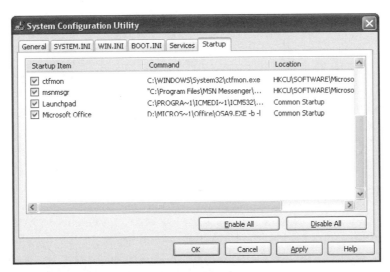

Figure 3-5   The System Configuration Utility dialog box offers lots of information.

5. Restart the computer, and when prompted by the System Configuration Utility, verify that you understand that changes have been made.

Real World   Users May Not Know What to Call Things

Part of your job as a DST is learning to listen to users. Remember that users are not trained and often do not know the proper terminology to use. For example, you may know what the notification area is, but it is not a name that is posted anywhere obvious or that just suggests itself. If a user is trying to explain something to you, feel free to let the user know the proper terminology, but try not to make it sound like something he or she should have known.

If you are explaining something to a user, use the proper terminology so that the user has the chance to hear it, but be prepared to help him or her navigate the first couple of times. Users are often embarrassed to speak up and tell you they do not know what something is. Use landmarks that everyone understands to help guide the way. For example, you might tell a user, "Look in the notification area; it's on the bottom right where the clock and all the other icons are."

Locking and Unlocking the Taskbar

By default, the taskbar's position on the desktop is locked, which means that it cannot be moved to any other location and cannot be resized, and that toolbars that are displayed on the taskbar cannot be moved or resized. If a user wants to unlock the taskbar, the procedure is easy: right-click an empty area of the taskbar, and from the resulting list, deselect Lock The Taskbar. Remember to lock it back when you get things the way the user wants them. When locked, the taskbar is protected from accidental changes and you gain a little extra room because the toolbar handles are not displayed.

Note   If a toolbar is enabled and the taskbar is locked, there will be no handle (the rows of dotted lines) in front of the toolbar area. If a toolbar is enabled and the taskbar is unlocked, the handle is visible, as shown in the figures in this chapter. You can reposition a toolbar or even move it off the taskbar entirely by dragging the handle when the taskbar is unlocked.

Grouping Similar Items and Enabling Quick Launch

Two additional ways to enhance the taskbar are enabling Group Similar Taskbar Buttons and enabling the Quick Launch toolbar, which are available options in the Taskbar And Start Menu Properties dialog box. Grouping similar open items saves room on the taskbar by grouping similar entries together; enabling Quick Launch lets you permanently add icons to the Quick Launch area of the taskbar for any program a user accesses often.

Enabling Group Similar Taskbar Buttons

As a DST, you will work with users of all levels. Some users will just be learning how to use e-mail, some will work with a single program and one or two files most of the day, and others will work with multiple programs and have multiple open files. Users who multitask among multiple programs and have several open files will likely have a crowded taskbar and might ask you about their options for organizing the files and programs shown on the taskbar.

Figure 3-6 shows a crowded taskbar, and Figure 3-7 shows the same taskbar with the grouping option enabled. Both taskbars include three open Windows Explorer folders, three open Microsoft Excel worksheets, two open graphics in Microsoft Paint, and three open Microsoft Word documents. In Figure 3-6, you cannot see some of these open files without using the arrow on the taskbar.

Figure 3-6   A crowded taskbar is disorganized and hard to use.

Figure 3-7   Grouping similar taskbar buttons makes programs and documents easier to find.

If the user wants you to configure his or her computer to use these grouping options, open the Taskbar And Start Menu Properties dialog box as detailed earlier. On the Taskbar tab, select the Group Similar Taskbar Buttons check box and click OK.

Enabling Quick Launch

Quick Launch is the area of the taskbar directly to the right of the Start menu that contains icons for your most-used programs. If you enable Quick Launch right after installing Windows XP, you will have three icons: E-Mail, Launch Internet Explorer Browser, and Show Desktop, as shown in Figure 3-8. Clicking the respective icons opens these programs. You can also customize the Quick Launch area to include whichever programs you access most often, and you can even resize it if the taskbar is unlocked. (Figure 3-9 shows a customized Quick Launch area.) Some programs also add icons to the Quick Launch area automatically during the program's installation, so what you see when you first enable Quick Launch will vary.

Figure 3-8   Quick Launch is shown here with the taskbar unlocked.

If a user contacts you and wants to use Quick Launch or asks you to add or remove program icons from it, follow these steps:

1. Right-click an empty area of the taskbar, and choose Properties.

2. In the Taskbar And Start Menu dialog box, click the Taskbar tab.

3. Select the Show Quick Launch check box, and then click OK.

4. To remove any item from the Quick Launch area, right-click the icon and select Delete. Click Yes in the Confirm File Delete dialog box. (You will not be deleting the program, only removing the icon from the Quick Launch area.)

5. To add any item to the Quick Launch area, locate the program in Windows Explorer, the Start menu, or the All Programs list; right-click it; drag the program to the Quick Launch area; and then choose Create Shortcuts Here. If this option is not available, choose Copy Here. A new icon will be added to the Quick Launch area.

> **Tip**   An even quicker way to get things onto your Quick Launch toolbar is to drag them there. Use your right mouse button to drag any shortcut from the Start menu (or desktop or any folder) to the Quick Launch area. When you let go of the mouse button, a menu pops up asking whether you want to copy or move the shortcut. Choose Copy to add the item to Quick Launch and also leave a copy in its original location. You might move items to the Quick Launch bar if, for example, you are cleaning shortcuts off of a cluttered desktop.

Figure 3-9 shows a personalized Quick Launch area with icons (from left to right) for Microsoft Outlook Express, Microsoft Internet Explorer, Microsoft Photo Editor, MSN Messenger 6.1, Help and Support, Backup, and Control Panel. Depending on the user's needs and preferences, you might be called on to create a Quick Launch area like this one.

Figure 3-9   A personalized and resized Quick Launch area is shown here with the taskbar unlocked.

Troubleshooting a Locked, Hidden, or Missing Taskbar

If an end user contacts you about a locked, hidden, or missing taskbar, carrying out the repair is most likely a simple procedure; this taskbar issue is also a surprisingly common complaint. Most of the time, the Start Menu And Taskbar Properties dialog box simply has the Lock The Taskbar, Auto-Hide The Taskbar, or Keep The Taskbar On Top Of Other Windows check box selected. Clearing the check box solves the problem immediately.

- **Lock The Taskbar**   When this check box is selected, the user cannot move or resize the taskbar by dragging. The user might complain that the taskbar is "locked."

- **Auto-Hide The Taskbar**   When this check box is selected, the taskbar is hidden until the user moves his or her mouse over the area where the taskbar should be. The user might complain that the taskbar is "missing" or "malfunctioning."

- **Keep The Taskbar On Top Of Other Windows**   When this check box is selected, the taskbar stays on top of all other running applications. The user might complain that the taskbar is "always in the way."

The user might also complain that the taskbar is too large or in the wrong area of the desktop. When this happens, inform the user that he or she can drag the top of the taskbar (when the mouse pointer becomes a two-headed arrow) to resize it. Moving the taskbar to another area of the screen is achieved by dragging it there.

Advanced Troubleshooting

If you cannot solve a taskbar problem by using the preceding techniques, the problem is more advanced. Table 3-1 lists some known issues with the taskbar and the Knowledge Base article number and brief solution.

Table 3-1 Advanced Taskbar Problems and Solutions

Problem	Knowledge Base Article Number and Brief Solution
The taskbar is missing when you log on to Windows.	KB 318027. This behavior can occur if the Windows settings for a particular user account are corrupted. The solution involves checking for bad drivers, followed by creating a new user account, followed by performing an in-place repair of the operating system.
The taskbar stops responding intermittently.	KB 314228. This is caused if the Language Bar is minimized and a Windows-based program is busy. Installing the latest service pack solves this problem.
After moving the taskbar from the bottom of the screen to the right side, the background picture is not displayed correctly.	KB 303137. Microsoft has confirmed that this is a problem. To solve this problem, click once on an empty area of the desktop and then press F5 to refresh the background.

Table 3-1   Advanced Taskbar Problems and Solutions

Problem	Knowledge Base Article Number and Brief Solution
A part of the ToolTips or a message from the status area remains behind or partially displayed on the status area of the taskbar after it should be gone.	KB 307499. To resolve this behavior, right-click another location that does not contain the leftover message, click the displayed message, move the mouse pointer over the icon, or resize the taskbar.

If the end user's problem is among these, search the Knowledge Base for additional articles and solutions.

See Also   Refer to Chapter 2, "Resolving a Service Call," for more troubleshooting techniques, including the order in which available information should be sought and which techniques you should attempt.

Configuring Taskbar Toolbars

Adding any taskbar toolbar adds a link on the taskbar that can be used to quickly access the chosen component. For instance, adding the Desktop toolbar allows you to easily access items on the desktop by clicking the link to them on the taskbar. Adding the Links toolbar allows a user to access Internet sites stored in their Links folder (in Internet Explorer Favorites) from the taskbar.

You can add toolbars to the taskbar by right-clicking the taskbar, pointing to Toolbars, and making the appropriate selection from the choices available. Some choices you can add include the following:

- Address
- Windows Media Player
- Links
- Language Bar
- Desktop
- Quick Launch
- New Toolbar

If users need access to any of these items often, inform them of the ability to add them.

Troubleshooting the Start Menu

Usually service calls regarding the Start menu involve what is or is not on it. A CEO might want My Network Connections, My Recent Documents, Internet, E-Mail, and the company's accounting program. The lead artist in the graphics department might want My Pictures, Printers and Faxes, My Music, and his or her favorite art program. When you are queried to personalize the Start menu, the combinations of ways in which the service call comes in are numerous. Figure 3-10 shows an example of a personalized Start menu.

Figure 3-10   A customized Start menu offers personalized access to programs.

Two types of Start menus are available in Windows XP, the Start menu and the Classic Start menu. In this section, you learn about the Start menu and how to resolve the most basic troubleshooting calls. The tasks include adding or removing programs or Start menu items, permanently pinning items to the Start menu, and reordering the All Programs list. The Classic Start menu is discussed briefly in the next section.

Adding or Removing Items in the All Programs List

Adding and removing items in the All Programs list on the Start menu are common requests from end users. You can add a program in many ways, but you will learn the easiest way here. Removing a program is the simpler of the two tasks.

To add an item to the All Programs list, follow these steps:

1. Right-click the Start menu, and choose Open All Users.
2. Click File, point to New, and click Shortcut.

3. In the Create Shortcut dialog box, click Browse.

4. Locate the local or network program, file, folder, computer, or Internet address to create a shortcut for, and click OK.

5. Click Next. On the Select A Title For The Program page, type a name for the shortcut and click Finish.

6. Close the Documents And Settings\All Users\Start Menu window.

To see the new addition, click Start, point to All Programs, and look toward the top of the All Programs list. You can now move that item by dragging it to any other area of the All Programs list, the Frequently Used Programs area of the Start menu, or the pinned items list. You can also add a shortcut for an item to the Start menu by dragging the item's icon to a position on the Start menu.

To remove an item from the All Programs list, simply right-click it and choose Delete. Click Yes when prompted to verify this action.

> **Note** You can reorder items on the All Programs list by dragging and dropping, or you can order them alphabetically by right-clicking any entry and choosing Sort By Name.

Adding or Removing Items on the Start Menu

End users often initiate a service call because a colleague one cubicle over has something on the Start menu that they do not, or there are items on the Start menu that they simply do not need. They might call to say that sometimes the program they want is in the frequently used area of the Start menu and sometimes it isn't, and they would like it to always be available. Start menu items can include just about anything, such as frequently accessed programs, pinned items, and operating system components such as Control Panel, My Network Places, Help and Support, Search, Run, and similar items.

Items are added to the frequently used programs area as they are opened, and they are moved up or down the list automatically depending on how often they are used. When a computer is new and there are no items in this list, a program is added to it by opening it once. As programs continue to be opened and used, the list automatically displays the programs by how frequently they are used. If specific items on the list are not needed, they can be removed by right-clicking and choosing Remove From This List. In addition, all items can be removed and the frequently used programs can be disabled, cleared, or reconfigured from the Customize Start Menu dialog box by following these steps:

1. Right-click the Start button, and choose Properties.

2. In the Taskbar And Start Menu Properties dialog box, verify that Start Menu is selected, and click Customize.

3. In the Customize Start Menu dialog box, in the Programs section, click Clear List to clear all items from the frequently used programs area of the Start menu.

4. To increase or decrease the number of programs shown, change the value for Number Of Programs On Start Menu by using the arrows. Zero disables the Start menu. Figure 3-11 shows an example of the Start Menu dialog box. Click OK and click OK again to apply the changes.

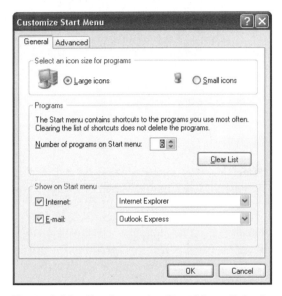

Figure 3-11   The Customize Start Menu dialog box offers many ways to personalize the Start menu.

You can pin or unpin an item on the Start menu by right-clicking the item in the Start menu or All Programs list and choosing Pin To Start Menu. Pinning an item to the Start menu places it in the upper left corner of the Start menu with other pinned items such as Internet and e-mail, allowing for easier access. This option is also available for items in the frequently used items area.

Finally, if a user asks you to add or remove an operating system component, such as Favorites, Control Panel, Run, My Documents, or My Pictures to or from the Start menu or to configure how it is displayed, follow these steps:

1. Right-click Start, and choose Properties.

2. In the Taskbar And Start Menu Properties dialog box, verify that Start Menu is selected, and click Customize.

3. In the Customize Start Menu dialog box, click the Advanced tab.

4. In the Start Menu Items window, scroll through the options. Selecting an item will show it on the Start menu. Other choices for an item include the following:

- ❑ **Display As A Link**   The item will be displayed on the Start menu.

- ❑ **Display As A Menu**   The item will be displayed, and a menu will be available that contains the objects in that folder.

- ❑ **Don't Display This Item**   The item will not be displayed.

5. In the Recent Documents area, click Clear List to clear the list of recently opened documents, or clear List My Most Recently Opened Documents to prevent items from being shown. Click OK twice to apply the changes and exit.

Note   Remember, if the troubleshooting call goes beyond these basic configuration issues, visit the Knowledge Base for help.

Troubleshooting the Classic Start Menu

The Classic Start menu is another option for end users. If, after an upgrade, end users complain that the Start menu is too complicated or that they want it to look more like their old Microsoft Windows 98 or Windows 2000 computer did, this is the menu you pick. Troubleshooting the Classic Start menu is similar to troubleshooting the Start menu as detailed earlier except for the minor differences in the Customize dialog box. Figure 3-12 shows the Customize Classic Start Menu dialog box.

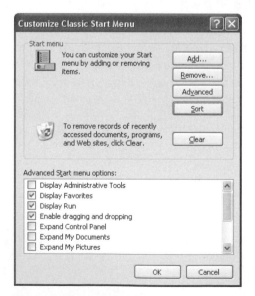

Figure 3-12   Customizing the Classic Start menu is also achieved through a dialog box.

In the Customize Classic Start Menu dialog box, you can do the following:

- Click Add to add any item to the Start menu.

- Click Remove to remove any item from the Start menu.

- Click Advanced to start Windows Explorer to add or remove items from the Start menu.

- Click Clear to remove records of recently accessed documents, programs, and websites.

- Click any item in the Advanced Start Menu Options list to show that item.

Practice: Resolve Taskbar and Start Menu Issues

In this practice, you will configure an icon so that it is always hidden in the notification area, configure an application to start with Windows and then disable the automatic starting by using the msconfig command, add a shortcut to the Quick Launch toolbar, and then add the Network Connections folder to the Start menu.

Exercise 1: Configure the Notification Area

1. Log on to Windows XP.
2. Right-click the taskbar, and select Task Manager.
3. Minimize the Task Manager window.
4. Observe the CPU Usage icon in the notification area.
5. Right-click any empty spot on the taskbar or in the notification area, and select Properties.
6. In the Taskbar And Start Menu Properties dialog box, in the Notification Area section, click Customize.
7. In the Customize Notifications dialog box, select Current Items, and click Hide When Inactive to the right of CPU Usage, in the Behavior column.
8. From the Behavior drop-down list, select Always Hide, and click OK.
9. In the Taskbar And Start Menu Properties dialog box, click OK.
10. Notice that the Task Manager icon is no longer visible in the notification area.
11. To reset the default settings for the notification area, right-click any empty spot on the taskbar or in the notification area and select Properties.
12. In the Taskbar And Start Menu Properties dialog box, in the Notification section, click Customize.

13. In the Customize Notifications dialog box, click Restore Defaults, and click OK.

14. In the Taskbar And Start Menu Properties dialog box, click OK.

Exercise 2: Configure Startup Applications

1. Log on to Windows XP by using an account with Administrator permissions.

2. On the Start menu, choose All Programs, right-click the Startup folder, and choose Open All Users.

3. In the Startup folder, choose New on the File menu, and then choose Shortcut.

4. In the Create Shortcut dialog box, type calc.exe and click Next.

5. In the Select A Title For The Program dialog box, type Calculator and click Finish.

6. Log off Windows, and log back on. The calculator should run as soon as you log on because a shortcut for it is now in the Startup folder.

Exercise 3: Add a Shortcut to the Quick Launch Toolbar

1. Log on to Windows XP.

2. Right-click any open area on the taskbar, and choose Properties.

3. In the Taskbar And Start Menu Properties dialog box, in the Taskbar Appearance section, select the Show Quick Launch check box and click OK.

4. On the Start menu, point to All Programs, right-click the Accessories folder, and choose Open All Users.

5. Drag the Calculator icon from the Accessories window to a position on the Quick Launch toolbar.

6. Click the Calculator icon on the Quick Launch toolbar to open the Calculator. Close the Calculator when you are done.

7. To delete the Calculator icon from the Quick Launch toolbar, right-click the icon and choose Delete.

Exercise 4: Add the Network Connections Folder to the Start Menu

1. Right-click the Start menu, and choose Properties.

2. In the Taskbar And Start Menu Properties dialog box, on the Start Menu tab, click Customize.

3. In the Customize Start Menu dialog box, on the Advanced tab, in the Start Menu Items list, locate Network Connections and select Link To Network Connections Folder.

4. Click OK.

5. In the Taskbar And Start Menu Properties dialog box, click OK.

6. Verify that the item was successfully added to the Start menu.

Lesson Review

The following questions are intended to reinforce key information presented in this lesson. If you are unable to answer a question, review the lesson materials and try the question again. You can find answers to the questions in the "Questions and Answers" section at the end of this chapter.

1. Match the end-user request on the left with the solution on the right.

1. The Taskbar is always disappearing, and I'd like that to stop. I also want to be able to move the taskbar to another area of the screen.	A. Open the Taskbar And Start Menu Properties dialog box. On the Taskbar tab, select the Show Quick Launch check box. Then, on the Start menu, locate the program to display in the Quick Launch area, right-click it, and drag and drop it there. Select Copy Here.
2. John, my colleague down the hall, has an icon next to his Start menu that he uses to open our accounting program. I do not have any icons there. How do I create one of those so I do not always have to locate the program in the Start menu or place a shortcut on the desktop?	B. Open the Taskbar And Start Menu Properties dialog box. On the Taskbar tab, select the Group Similar Taskbar Buttons check box.
3. I do not have enough room on my taskbar to show all of my open programs, and I have to scroll to see the additional programs. Is there some way of grouping the programs?	C. Open the Taskbar And Start Menu Properties dialog box. On the Taskbar tab, clear the Auto-Hide The Taskbar check box. Then verify that the Lock The Taskbar check box is cleared. Instruct the user to move the taskbar by dragging.
4. Can I remove or hide the icons for my antivirus software, my pop-up stopper program, and other programs that run in the background? If I remove them, do they stop running?	D. Notification area icons can be removed by setting preferences in the program's configuration choices. If you right-click an item in the notification area and its shortcut menu lets you choose Exit or Close, the program will stop running when you choose the appropriate option.
5. In my notification area, there are a lot of icons that I do not think I need. How can I get rid of those for good? I do not think they should be running in the background, and I do not even know what some of them are.	E. Open the Taskbar And Start Menu Properties dialog box. On the Start Menu tab, click Customize. In the Customize Start Menu (or Customize Classic Start Menu) dialog box, make the appropriate changes.

6. On my Start menu are lots of programs that I do not need and some that I need but are not there. Can you fix that for me?

7. I want to be able to open My Network Places, open Control Panel, and access System Administrative Tools from the Start Menu, but I do not want my recent documents to be listed. I also do not want to see My Music, My Pictures, or any of that other stuff that is not work-related.

F. Click Start, and click Run. At the Run line, type **msconfig.exe** and click OK. On the Startup tab, clear the check boxes for the items that you do not want to start when the computer boots.

G. Open the Taskbar And Start Menu Properties dialog box. On the Start Menu tab, select Classic Start Menu and click Customize. Use the Add and Remove buttons to customize the menu. Apply the changes. If desired, select Start Menu to return to the default Start Menu look.

2. You want to have as few items as possible on the taskbar. Which of the following items can you easily remove from the taskbar?

   A. The Start button

   B. The system clock

   C. The notification area

   D. Quick Launch items

   E. Inactive icons in the notification area

Lesson Summary

■ To resolve problems involving the taskbar, use the Taskbar And Start Menu Properties dialog box. On the Taskbar tab, you can lock or hide the taskbar, group similar items, show Quick Launch, hide inactive icons, and keep the taskbar on top of other windows.

■ To resolve problems involving the Start menu, use the Taskbar And Start Menu Properties dialog box. On the Start menu tab, click Customize to define what should and should not appear on the taskbar, clear the taskbar of recently used programs or documents, and more.

Lesson 2: Customizing Regional and Language Settings

Regional and language options, available from Control Panel, define the standards and formats the computer uses to perform calculations; provide information such as date and time; and display the correct format for currency, numbers, dates, and other units. These settings also define a user's location, which enables help services to provide local information such as news and weather. Language options define the input languages (one computer can accept input in many different languages); therefore, the computer must be configured with the proper settings.

After this lesson, you will be able to

- Configure the correct currency, date, and time for a user.
- Configure input languages.
- Troubleshoot language-related problems.

Estimated lesson time: 20 minutes

Regional and Language Settings

Almost all regional and language configuration and troubleshooting tasks are performed in Control Panel by clicking Date, Time, Language, And Regional Options and then clicking Regional And Language Options. Figure 3-13 shows the Regional And Language Options dialog box.

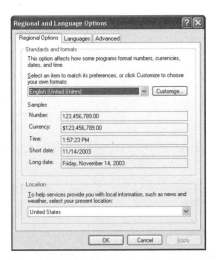

Figure 3-13   The Regional And Language Options dialog box offers a place to select available languages and customize formatting.

As a DST, you could be asked to help users configure and troubleshoot these settings. In many instances, users need to add a region or an input language because they travel, work, or live in two different countries or regions; an input language needs to be added because users who share a computer speak different languages; or a currency, time, and date need to be changed temporarily on a user's laptop while he or she is on a business trip. You learn how to perform these tasks in the next few sections.

Configuring Correct Currency, Time, and Date

When a user requests a change to the currency, time, or date standards and formats on a computer, you make those changes in the Regional And Language Options dialog box on the Regional Options tab, shown earlier in Figure 3-13. Changing the standard and format is as simple as clicking the drop-down list in the Standards And Formats area and selecting a new option. In Figure 3-14, English (United States) is no longer selected; French (France) is. Notice that the date is written in French, that the currency has changed, and that the date, January 12, 2004, is written 12/01/2004, which is different from the English version, which is 1/12/2004.

Figure 3-14 Changing standard and format options changes the currency, date, language, and more.

To make changes and to access the other regional and language options, follow these steps:

1. Open Control Panel. In Category view, click Date, Time, Language, And Regional Options, and then click Regional And Language Options. (In Classic view, double-click on Regional And Language Options.)

2. Click the Regional Options tab.

3. In the Standards And Formats section, click the drop-down list to view the additional choices. Select one of these choices.

4. In the Location section, choose a country or region from the list to change the default location.

5. To further customize the settings, click Customize.

6. When finished, click OK in each open dialog box to exit.

Customizing Regional Options

If a user requests a specific change to the default settings, such as changing the currency symbol, the time or date format, or the system of measurement, but wants to keep other default settings intact, click Customize, as shown in Figure 3-13, and make the appropriate changes. Each option has a drop-down list, and selecting a different option requires only selecting it from the list.

Configuring Input Languages

The input language configured for the computer tells Windows how to react when text is entered using the keyboard. A user might want you to add a language if he or she works or travels between two or more countries that use different languages and he or she needs to work in those languages or perform calculations with the currencies in those countries. With multiple languages configured, the user can toggle between them as needed. In addition, users might want to change language settings even if they do not travel but do work with an international group or conduct business with other countries.

To add (or remove) an input language, follow these steps:

1. From Control Panel, open Regional And Language Options.

2. Click the Languages tab, and in the Text Services And Input Languages section, click Details.

3. In the Text Services And Input Languages dialog box, click Add to add a language.

4. In the Add Input Language dialog box, select the language you want to add. To choose a specific keyboard layout, select the Keyboard Layout/IME check box and choose the appropriate layout. To add a keyboard layout or **input method editor (IME)**, you need to have installed it on your computer first. Click OK.

5. Back in the Text Services And Input Languages dialog box, select which language should be the default language from the Default Input Language drop-down list, and click OK.

Figure 3-15 shows two available languages, English (United States)—US and Italian (Italy)—Italian. The user can now switch between these languages easily by using the Language Bar (located on the taskbar).

Figure 3-15 Two languages are now available for the user.

Troubleshooting Language-Related Problems

When users have multiple languages configured, language-related problems are bound to occur. One of the more common issues occurs when a user with multiple languages configured accidentally changes the default language in use by unintentionally hitting the key combination that switches between them. By default, pressing left ALT+SHIFT switches between languages. Users who accidentally hit that combination might suddenly find themselves with a keyboard that does not act as it is supposed to, and they will not have any explanation for why it happened. You will have to use the Language Bar to switch back to the default language, and you might want to disable this feature while you are at the computer.

> **Exam Tip** Consider regional settings as a possibility when keyboard errors are reported or when users report that symbols do not look correct.

Here are some other common language-related problems to look for:

- If a user complains that while using the On-Screen Keyboard accessibility tool, most keys on the screen do not blink when he or she presses a key on the physical keyboard, inform the user that this behavior is intended and correct. (See KB 294519.)

- If after installing a new IME as the default keyboard layout, the user complains that the previous keyboard layout is still being used, install the latest service pack to resolve the problem. (See KB 318388.)

- If a user complains that after choosing a new language he or she is unable to view the menus and dialog boxes in that language, inform the user that the Windows Multilingual User Interface Pack must be purchased and installed for these items to be changed. (See Microsoft Help and Support Center.)

Less common and more complex problems are addressed in the Knowledge Base. Remember to search there for answers if the problem cannot be resolved through general reconfiguration and common troubleshooting techniques.

Practice: Configure Language Options

In this practice, you will assign a different input language and disable the ALT+SHIFT language toggle keyboard shortcut.

Exercise 1: Assign Russian as the Input Language

1. Log on to Windows XP.

2. On the Start menu, choose Control Panel.

3. Click Date, Time, Language, And Regional Options. (Note that if Control Panel is configured to show the Category view, you must click Switch To Classic View before performing this step.)

4. Click Regional And Language Options.

5. In the Regional And Language Options dialog box, on the Languages tab, in the Text Services And Input Languages section, click Details.

6. In the Text Services And Input Languages dialog box, in the Installed Services section, click Add.

7. In the Add Input Language dialog box, in the Input Language drop-down list, select Russian. Click OK.

8. In the Text Services And Input Languages dialog box, click OK.

9. In the Regional And Language Options dialog box, click OK.

10. On the Start menu, choose All Programs, Accessories, and then choose Notepad.

11. In the Untitled–Notepad window, type some random letters. Press the left ALT+SHIFT keys, and type some more random characters. Notice that the input language is toggled.

12. Close Notepad.

Exercise 2: Disable the ALT+SHIFT Language Toggle Option

1. On the Start menu, choose Control Panel. In Control Panel, click Date, Time, Language, And Regional Options. (Note that if Control Panel is configured to show the Category view, you must click Switch To Classic View before performing this step.)

2. Click Regional and Language Options.

3. In the Regional And Language Options dialog box, on the Languages tab, in the Text Services And Input Languages section, click Details.

4. In the Text Services And Input Languages dialog box, in the Preferences section, click Key Settings.

5. In the Advanced Key Settings dialog box, click Change Key Sequence.

6. In the Change Key Sequence dialog box, clear the Switch Input Languages check box, and click OK.

7. In the Advanced Key Settings dialog box, click OK.

8. In the Text Services And Input Languages dialog box, click OK.

9. In the Regional And Language Options dialog box, click OK.

Lesson Review

The following questions are intended to reinforce key information presented in this lesson. If you are unable to answer a question, review the lesson materials and try the question again. You can find answers to the questions in the "Questions and Answers" section at the end of this chapter.

1. You are an architect who creates blueprints for clients all over the world, so you use the metric system instead of the U.S. system of measurement. Your company handles all other communications, including billing. Your regional settings are configured to use the English (United States) standard. Which of the following is the best option for changing the default system of measurement on your computer from U.S. to metric?

   A. Change the default regional options for standards and formats to English (Canada). Canada is the nearest country that uses the metric system.

   B. Change the default regional options for standards and formats to English (United Kingdom). The United Kingdom uses the metric system, and many of your clients live there.

    C. Keep the English (United States) setting, but customize the measurement system to use the metric system. Do not make any other changes.

    D. Install a metric keyboard.

2. A user has multiple languages configured on her laptop and needs access to the Language Bar quite often. However, she does not want the Language Bar to be open continuously, taking up space on the taskbar. What can you tell the user to do? Select the best answer.

    A. In Regional And Language Options, remove and reinstall the languages each time she needs them.

    B. In the Text Services And Input Languages dialog box, select the Turn Off Advanced Text Services check box.

    C. Add the Language Bar to the taskbar only when it is needed by right-clicking the taskbar, pointing to Toolbars, and choosing Language Bar.

    D. None of the above. When multiple languages are configured, the Language Bar is always on the taskbar.

Lesson Summary

- To allow a user to work in different languages on one computer, make changes in the Regional And Language Options dialog box. There you can select and configure options for currency, time, and dates and select input languages.

- In troubleshooting language-related problems, the most common problem is that a user has unknowingly switched to another language and is having problems with keyboard function.

Lesson 3: Customizing Folder Options

Folder options specify how folders function and the content that is displayed.

After this lesson, you will be able to

- Configure folder options.
- Troubleshoot Folder view settings.
- Identify the best practices for setting folder options.

Estimated lesson time: 15 minutes

Configuring Folder Options

You can use Folder options to resolve many types of service calls and requests from end users. You can access folder settings from Control Panel or from the Tools menu in Windows Explorer. Listed next are brief descriptions of the four available tabs in the Folder Options dialog box and some common tasks that you can perform by using them:

- **General tab**   Use the options on this tab to change how folders look and how they open. Windows can be configured to use Windows classic folders for a pre–Windows XP look and feel, and opening a folder inside another folder can be configured to appear in different ways. Folders can be configured so that the new folder opens either in the same window or in a different one. Folders can also be configured to open with a single or double click.

- **View tab**   Use the options on this tab to apply folder views systemwide (Details, Tiles, Icons, and so on) or to reset the folder views to their default. Configure advanced settings to remember (or not remember) each folder's view settings, to show (or not show) pop-up descriptions of folder and desktop items, to use (or not use) Simple File Sharing, to automatically search for network folders and printers, and more.

- **File Types tab**   Use the options on this tab to view, add, or reconfigure which types of files open with which particular program. When an end user requests that a specific file open with a specific program, make that change here. (File types are covered in Lesson 4.)

- **Offline files**   If **Fast User Switching** is not enabled, offline files can be enabled here. When offline files are enabled, a user can work on network files even if he or she is not connected to the network. (Offline files are a tested objective on the 70-271 exam.)

> **Note**   Open the Folder Options dialog box by opening Control Panel, clicking Appearance And Themes, and opening Folder Options.

Troubleshooting Folder View Settings

When a user requests help regarding how folders are viewed, how windows open, and what can and cannot be seen inside a folder, check the configured folder options first. There you can discover the cause of many common problems and resolve them easily.

Before starting any troubleshooting in the Folder Options dialog box, ask the user if he or she has made any changes there already. If a user tells you he or she has made changes to the folder options but cannot remember what the changes were, use the Restore Defaults button on the General tab and the View tab to restore the defaults. Many times this solves the problem. Table 3-2 shows some other common problems and their resolutions, all of which are available in the Folder Options dialog box.

Table 3-2   Common Folder View Issues and Their Solutions

Common Problem	Solution
A user reports that each time he opens a folder or clicks an icon in Control Panel, it opens a separate window. Sometimes he has 15 open windows on his desktop, and he finds it quite annoying. He wants you to change this behavior.	In the Folder Options dialog box, on the General tab, in the Browse Folders area, select Open Each Folder In The Same Window.
A user reports that she needs to view encrypted and compressed folders in a different color when using Windows Explorer to locate them. She wants to know how to do this.	In the Folder Options dialog box, on the View tab, select the Show Encrypted Or Compressed NTFS Files In Color check box.
A user reports that his co-workers often see new folders and printers in My Network Places, but he never does. He has to search for and add them manually. He wants you to resolve this problem.	In the Folder Options dialog box, on the View tab, select the Automatically Search For Network Folders And Printers check box.
Your CEO fancies himself a power user and wants to be able to view and access protected system files and hidden files and folders. How do you allow this?	In the Folder Options dialog box, on the View tab, select the Show Hidden Files And Folders check box and clear the Hide Protected Operating System Files (Recommended) check box.
A user who has recently upgraded from Windows 98 to Windows XP does not like the "Web" look associated with the folders and the interface. What can you do in the Folder Options dialog box to make the user more comfortable?	In the Folder Options dialog box, on the General tab, click Use Windows Classic Folders.

Note   If you change the Tasks setting in the Folder Options dialog box (on the General tab) to Use Windows Classic Folders instead of Show Common Tasks In Folders, you will not have the option in Control Panel to switch to Category view. Users might miss this feature and have a difficult time connecting the missing options with selecting this setting.

Exam Tip   Go over all the folder options available before the exam, but particularly try to remember those listed in Table 3-2.

Adopting Best Practices

Because changing default folder behavior is so simple (just select or clear any check box in the Folder Options dialog box), you might think that changes performed here are harmless. This is not true. Here are some reasons to leave the default options configured:

■ Although you can easily allow users to view hidden files and folders or access system files, you should avoid it at all costs. Changes made to these files, especially system files, can make the computer inoperable. If the changes are severe enough, you might have to perform a repair installation.

■ Although you might be tempted to disable Simple File Sharing to give a user more options for configuring security on his or her small workgroup or home network, it is not always necessary and might confuse the end user. In addition, the user might try to configure complicated options and create unnecessary file sharing problems.

■ Although you might think that switching a user to use Windows classic folders just because he or she is initially uncomfortable with the interface is helpful, in the long run it might be better for that user to learn to work with the new technology. Technologies will change, and it is generally beneficial to keep up.

Practice: Configure Folder Options

In this practice, you will configure four folder options. First you will set each new folder opened to have its own window. Second you will set folders to behave more like Web pages so that the user needs to click only once to open an item rather than double-click. Third you will make file extensions visible. Finally you will make hidden folders visible.

1. Log on to Windows XP.

2. On the Start Menu, choose Control Panel.

3. Click Appearance and Themes. (Note that if Control Panel is configured to show the Category view, you must click Switch To Classic View before performing this step.)

4. Click Folder Options.

5. In the Folder Options dialog box, on the General tab, in the Tasks section, select Use Windows Classic Folders.

6. In the Browse Folders section, select Open Each Folder In The Same Window.

7. In the Click Items As Follows section, select Single-Click To Open An Item (Point To Select).

8. On the View tab, in the Advanced Settings list, under Files And Folders, clear the Hide Extensions For Known File Types check box.

9. In the Advanced Settings list, under Hidden Files And Folders, select Show Hidden Files And Folders. Click OK.

10. In Control Panel, select Folder Options, and on the General tab, click Restore Defaults. On the View tab, click Restore Defaults. Click OK.

Lesson Review

The following questions are intended to reinforce key information presented in this lesson. If you are unable to answer a question, review the lesson materials and try the question again. You can find answers to the questions in the "Questions and Answers" section at the end of this chapter.

1. After configuring folder options, you notice you can no longer switch to Category view in Control Panel. What must you do to resolve this problem?

   A. Clear the Use Windows Classic Folders check box in the Folder Options dialog box.

   B. Select the Use Windows Classic Folders in the Folder Options dialog box.

   C. In Control Panel, click View, select Choose Details, and select the Show Tasks check box.

   D. In Control Panel, click the View tab, select Choose Details, and clear the Hide Task Options check box.

2. There are many ways to access the Folder Options dialog box. Which of the following are valid examples?

   A. In Windows Explorer, click Tools, and click Folder Options.

   B. In the My Documents folder, click Tools, and click Folder Options.

   C. In Control Panel, open Folder Options.

   D. In My Computer, click Tools, and click Folder Options.

   E. From the All Programs list, under Accessories, click Folder Options.

Lesson Summary

- To configure how folders open, how they look, and what they contain, use the Folder Options dialog box. There you can choose to show hidden files and folders, open folders with a single click, configure how encrypted and compressed files look, and more.

- Often simply restoring folder options to their default settings is enough to fix a user's problem, but you should still examine a user's configuration and try to understand the problem. The user might also want some options reconfigured.

Lesson 4: Troubleshooting Issues with File Associations

File extensions define the file type. A file with the extension .doc is a document; a file with the extension .mp3 is an MP3 music file. The file extension tells Windows what type of file it is opening and what program should be used to open it. As a DST, you will be called on to troubleshoot file associations. Specifically, you will be asked to add and troubleshoot file types that are not recognized by the operating system and to configure a specific file type to always open with a specific program.

After this lesson, you will be able to

- Identify common file types.
- Change the way a file type opens.
- Troubleshoot file associations.

Estimated lesson time: 20 minutes

Understanding Common File Types

Table 3-3 shows some common file types and the programs they will most likely be configured to open with automatically. In the far right column, additional programs are listed that can be used to open the same file. Users might ask you to change which program is used to open a specific file type because they prefer one program to another or because company policy requires them to use a specific program.

Table 3-3   Common File Types and the Programs Used to Open Them

File Extension	Common Default Programs	Alternative Programs
.avi	Windows Media Player	Third-party media tools
.bmp	Paint	Microsoft Photo Editor, third-party graphics programs, Internet Explorer
.doc	Word	WordPad, Notepad, or third-party word processing programs
.gif, .jpg, .jpeg, .tiff	Paint, Windows Picture and Fax Viewer	Third-party graphics programs, Internet Explorer
.htm, .html	Internet Explorer, Notepad	WordPad, Microsoft FrontPage, third-party Web browsers
.mp3, .wav	Windows Media Player	Third-party media tools
.txt	Notepad	WordPad, Internet Explorer, Word
.xls	Excel	Third-party database applications

This is by no means a complete list; these are only a few of the hundreds of available file types. However, it does make clear that different files can be opened using various programs. Although the CEO's secretary might be happy with .jpg files opening in Windows Picture and Fax Viewer, chances are good that a member of the graphics department will need that file to open in a more advanced graphics program.

> ### Real World   When Not to Change File Extensions
>
> Some programs will not function properly when you change certain file extensions. A good example of this is programs that install an alternative Web browser that is used to access their database through a browser interface. While such programs should be written to allow any browser to be used, they often are not. Even if the user wants to use Internet Explorer as the default Web browser, in such an instance the user will not be able to.
>
> If you come across such a program (and you should always check to see what is installed on a user's system), explain to the user that you will not be able to change the file extension. Instead, teach the user to open the program he or she wants to use (such as a Web browser) and then either use the program's interface to open the file or use the Open With command.

Changing the Default Way That a File Type Opens

If a user requests that a specific type of file open with a specific program every time that file type is encountered, you will want to change the details for that particular file extension to create a permanent default for that file type. For instance, if a user requests that all .gif files always open with Windows Picture and Fax Viewer, you can set this by following these steps:

1. Open Control Panel, and open Folder Options.

2. Click the File Types tab, scroll down, and select GIF.

3. In the Details For 'GIF' Extension area, next to Opens With: *<program name>*, click Change.

4. In the Open With dialog box, shown in Figure 3-16, click Windows Picture And Fax Viewer and click OK. Click Close in the Folder Options dialog box.

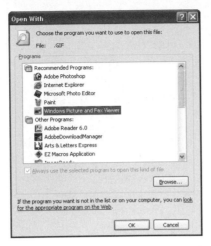

Figure 3-16 The Open With dialog box offers personalization options for the user.

From here on, or until this new default behavior is changed manually, all .gif files will open using Windows Picture and Fax Viewer. You can use this same procedure to change any file type and the program it opens with.

Changing the Way That a File Type Opens One Time

If a user wants the file to open with a different program only one time, it is as simple as right-clicking. Perhaps a user who has never edited a picture has one she wants to brighten using the tools in Photo Editor, but all of her graphics files open in the Windows Picture and Fax Viewer by default. You can instruct the user to open the picture in another program easily, following these steps:

1. Browse to the file using Windows Explorer or My Computer, or by opening My Documents, My Pictures, or another folder that contains the file.

2. Right-click the file to open, point to Open With, and select the program from the list. The file will open in the designated program.

Note The Open With dialog box includes the Always Use The Selected Program To Open This Kind Of File check box. If this check box is selected, the program will always open with this type of file. Do not select this check box if you do not want to make this the default program.

Problems occur when there are no choices in the Open With list. This happens because Windows does not recognize the file and does not know which program to use to open it. This problem is covered in the next section.

Troubleshooting File Associations

There are two common file association problems that end users encounter. Either they right-click the file, point to Open With, and see no available choices, or they attempt to open the file and fail because the file type is not recognized. (These unknown files and their file types are almost exclusively created using third-party applications or a company's specially designed applications.)

If, after right-clicking a file, the Open With dialog box provides no choices, you need to inform the user to select Choose Program (available from the Open With list choices) to tell Windows what program to use to open the file. If there are no recommended programs, the user needs to browse to the program that opens the file. After selecting the appropriate program, the user can open the file. If the program is unavailable, you will need to install a program that can be used and is compatible with that particular file type.

When Open With is unavailable and the user selects Open, or if a user attempts to open a file with an unknown file extension, the user receives the message shown in Figure 3-17. This message appears when a user tries to open a file and the associated program is not installed or available, or when the file type is not registered and recognized by the operating system. In this dialog box, you can either use a Web service to locate the program the file opens with or manually select the program from the list. To manually select a program, choose Select The Program From A List, locate the program, and click OK.

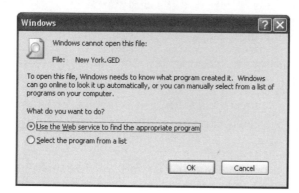

Figure 3-17   The result when a file type is not recognized by Windows.

Adding a New File Extension

If you have encountered a file type that Windows is not familiar with, you will need to add that file extension in the Folder Options dialog box on the File Types tab. Then Windows will know that the file type is valid and will know which program to associate it with.

To add a file type, follow these steps:

1. Open Control Panel, and open Folder Options.

2. On the File Types tab, click New.

3. In the Create New Extension dialog box, type the file extension in the File Extension field. Click OK.

4. Locate the new file type at the top of the Registered File Types list, as shown in Figure 3-18. Notice that the new file type does not have a program associated with it. In the Opens With area, click Change to choose the program with which to open files of that type.

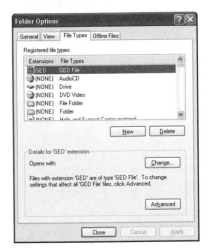

Figure 3-18   Adding a file type is achieved through the Folder Options dialog box.

5. In the Windows dialog box, choose Select The Program From A List and click OK.

6. In the Open With dialog box, select the program. (An installed program must be able to open the file.) Click OK. In the Folder Options dialog box, click Close.

Note   You can also modify file types by clicking Advanced on the File Types tab. Actions such as Open, Play, and Print can be set as the default action when a file is selected and opened.

Practice: Configure File Associations

In this practice, you will configure text files to open in WordPad by default instead of in Notepad.

1. Log on to Windows XP.

2. On the Start menu, choose Control Panel.

3. Click Appearance and Themes. (Note that if Control Panel is configured to show the Category view, you must click Switch To Classic View before performing this step.)

4. Click Folder Options.

5. In the Folder Options dialog box, on the File Types tab, in the Registered File Types list, in the Extensions column, select TXT. In the Details For 'TXT' Extension section, click Change.

6. In the Open With dialog box, under Recommended Programs, select WordPad. Click OK.

7. Close the Folder Options dialog box, and then close Control Panel.

8. Right-click any open space on the desktop, point to New, and then select Text Document.

9. Double-click the new text document to see that it opens in WordPad instead of Notepad.

10. On the Start menu, choose Control Panel. Click Appearance and Themes and then click Folder Options.

11. In the Folder Options dialog box, on the File Types tab, in the Registered File Types list, in the Extensions column, select TXT.

12. In the Details For 'TXT' Extension section, select Restore.

13. In the Folder Options dialog box, click Close.

Lesson Review

The following questions are intended to reinforce key information presented in this lesson. If you are unable to answer a question, review the lesson materials and try the question again. You can find answers to the questions in the "Questions and Answers" section at the end of this chapter.

1. In the following table, match the user request on the left with the part of the operating system that is used to resolve that request on the right.

1. A user wants to open folders using a single click, not a double click.	A. Taskbar And Start Menu Properties dialog box, Taskbar tab.
2. A user wants open programs to be grouped on the taskbar.	B. Configure the folder options from the View menu of any open folder. Open the Folder Options dialog box, and on the View tab, click Apply To All Folders.
3. A user wants all of her folders to open and display folder items as icons, not the current setting of tiles.	C. Folder Options dialog box, File Types tab, Registered File Types window, Change.

4. A user wants his JPEG files to always open in Paint.	D. Folder Options dialog box, General tab.
5. A user complains that there is no Security tab when she shares a file.	E. Folder Options dialog box, View tab, Advanced Settings.
6. A user complains that the pop-up descriptions for folder and desktop items no longer appear when he hovers over the item with the mouse.	F. Folder Options dialog box, View tab, disable Simple File Sharing.

2. Which of the following allows you to open a file with an unknown file type? (Each choice offers a complete solution. Choose two.)

    A. Install the application used to create the file, and then open the file in that program.

    B. Register the file type in the Folder Options dialog box, and associate it with a program already installed on the computer that has the capability to open the file.

    C. Use the Web to determine which programs can be used to open the file.

    D. Register the file type, and let Windows choose a program to open the file with.

Lesson Summary

- File extensions define the application Windows uses to open a file. Often more than one installed application could be used to open a file type.

- To open a file with an application other than the one defined for its file type, use the Open With dialog box by right-clicking on a file and choosing Open With.

- To define which program should be used to open a specific file type, to add new file types, and to edit what happens when a particular program opens a file, use the Folder Options dialog box by clicking the File Types tab.

Lesson 5: Using the Windows XP Troubleshooting Tools

A number of troubleshooting tools ship with Windows XP that can be extremely helpful in resolving many of the problems you will encounter while performing your job as a DST.

After this lesson, you will be able to

- Use various Windows XP troubleshooting tools.
- Explain to a user when to use each troubleshooting tool.

Estimated lesson time: 15 minutes

Commonly Used Troubleshooting Tools

Troubleshooting tools generally prove useful when the user receives error messages during Windows startup, while opening or saving files, when starting applications, or when accessing hardware.

In this section, you will learn about five of these tools:

- **Msconfig** A command-line tool (one that you can run from the Command Prompt or using the Run dialog on the Start menu) that opens the System Configuration Utility, which you can use to troubleshoot and resolve startup errors and resolve unwanted prompts by third-party applications

- **Msinfo32** A command-line tool that opens the System Information window, which provides detailed information about the computer system configuration

- **Chkdsk** A command-line tool that creates a status report of the integrity of the hard disk and corrects errors on the disk

- **Disk Defragmenter** A program included with Windows XP that analyzes hard disks and locates and consolidates fragmented files and folders

- **SFC /Scannow** A command-line tool that scans and verifies all protected system files on the computer and replaces any missing files

The next five sections introduce these tools; for more information, see the related Windows XP Help files.

Using Msconfig

Use Msconfig when troubleshooting errors that occur during the startup process, to rid the computer of third-party software prompts after startup, to discover and resolve problems with running services, or to resolve errors regarding the boot paths configured on multiboot computers.

To use Msconfig to open and use the System Configuration Utility, follow these steps:

1. From the Start menu, select Run.

2. In the Run dialog box, type **msconfig** and click OK.

3. From the System Configuration Utility dialog box, browse through the available tabs and make changes as appropriate:

   a. **General** Use these options to tell Windows XP how to start the computer. There are three choices: Normal Startup, which loads all device drivers and services; Diagnostic Startup, which loads only basic devices and services; and Selective Startup, which loads only the items manually configured from the other tabs. System Restore can also be launched from this tab. Experiment with these choices to resolve startup problems.

   b. **SYSTEM.INI** Use these options to tell Windows XP which items configured in the System.ini file to load when starting. You will need to have quite a bit of experience with the startup files, drivers, and other items to use these tools effectively.

   c. **WIN.INI** Use these options to tell Windows XP which items configured in the Win.ini file to load when starting. You will need to have quite a bit of experience with the startup files, drivers, and other items to use these tools effectively.

   d. **BOOT.INI** Use these options to configure dual-boot computers, check boot paths, set a boot path as a default, configure how long to wait before booting to the default, and more.

   e. **Services** Use these options to select or deselect which services on the Windows XP computer will load during startup. Deselecting services can help you pinpoint the exact service that is causing problems on the machine.

   f. **Startup** Use these options to select or deselect which startup items are loaded during the startup process. Deselecting third-party startup items will rid the computer of that software's prompts to register, upgrade, update, or purchase and will stop the item from loading on startup. Use this option to rid the notification area of unnecessary running programs.

   Click OK, and then restart the computer. During startup, you will be prompted that the startup configuration has changed.

Caution   Be careful when modifying the startup files; you might make it impossible to start Windows. Many of these options should be reserved for experienced and advanced technicians. When in doubt, consult a more experienced technician or the Windows XP or KB help files.

Using Msinfo32

Use Msinfo32 when you need to obtain information about the local or remote computer's hardware configuration, computer components, installed software, or drivers (signed or unsigned); or when you need to get information about the BIOS version; verify that memory is installed and available; check product activation status; determine hardware conflicts; and more.

To use Msinfo32 to open the System Information window and to browse through the available data, follow these steps:

1. From the Start menu, select Run.

2. In the Run dialog box, type **msinfo32** and click OK.

3. From the left pane, expand each of the trees to view the available data, as shown here and as illustrated in Figure 3-19.

    a. **Hardware Resources**   View and determine conflicts between hardware devices and see interrupt requests (IRQs), memory, and more.

    b. **Components**   View information about multimedia hardware, sound and display devices, modems, storage, printing devices, and more.

    c. **Software Environment**   View information about system drivers, print jobs, network connections, running tasks, services, and more.

    d. **Internet Settings**   View information about Internet settings, including the browser version and type, content and cache settings, and more.

    e. **Applications**   View installed applications and information logged during use of the applications. Figure 3-19 shows an example of the Microsoft Office 2003 Environment tree and a description of the last Web connection error encountered by the application.

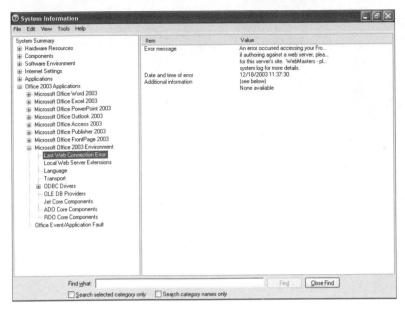

Figure 3-19   The System Information utility offers an incredible wealth of information.

4. Close the System Information window when finished.

Using Chkdsk

Use Chkdsk (Check Disk) to view the file system type (NTFS or FAT) and to verify the integrity of the disks installed on the computer. By adding the appropriate parameter (/F), you can also fix errors on the disk.

To use Chkdsk to check the integrity of the hard disk and automatically fix any errors it finds, follow these steps:

1. From the Start menu, point to All Programs, point to Accessories, and select Command Prompt.

2. To see all of the Chkdsk parameters, at the command prompt, type **chkdsk /?**. The Help report is shown in Figure 3-20. (If you do not have any experience at the command line, review these options carefully. Do some independent study to become familiar with command-line tools.)

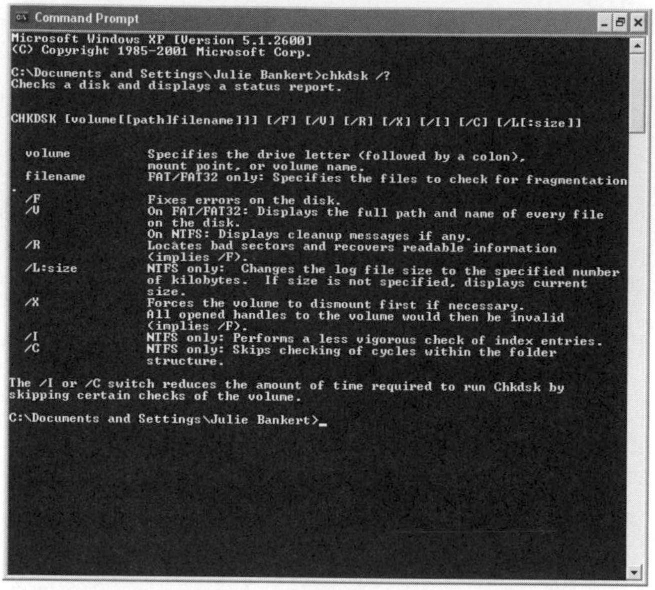

Figure 3-20 Chkdsk offers several parameters.

3. At the command prompt, type **chkdsk /F** to run Check Disk and automatically correct disk errors.

Using Disk Defragmenter

Disk Defragmenter looks for and consolidates fragmented files, those that are saved in various areas of the hard drive rather than in one place. Opening defragmented files takes less time than opening fragmented ones because the information is stored together on the disk rather than haphazardly. Use Disk Defragmenter when the user complains that the computer seems slower than usual, when the user has not used Disk Defragmenter in the past or does not use it on a regular basis, and when no distinct problems can be found for the slowdown.

To use Disk Defragmenter, follow these steps:

1. From the Start menu, point to All Programs, point to Accessories, point to System Tools, and select Disk Defragmenter.

2. To analyze the disk to see whether it needs defragmenting, select the disk from the top pane, and select Analyze from the bottom.

3. If the computer's hard disk needs to be defragmented, you will be prompted, as shown in Figure 3-21. Click Close.

4. Back up the user's files.

5. Disconnect from the Internet, turn off all antivirus software, turn off all screen savers, and close all running programs (except Disk Defragmenter).

6. To defragment the volume, select Defragment. Close all dialog boxes and windows when the process is complete.

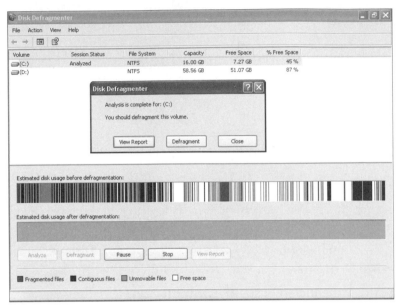

Figure 3-21   After analyzing the disk, Disk Defragmenter prompts to defragment the disk.

Note   Disk Defragmenter might take quite some time to complete, depending on the disk size and the level of fragmentation. Consider running this application at the end of the day or at night, and do not disturb the computer while it is running.

Using SFC /Scannow

System File Checker (SFC) is a command-line utility that allows a technician or user to determine whether any protected system files are missing. Missing system files can cause problems with the boot process or problems when operating system components are opened.

To use the SFC /Scannow utility to determine whether there are any missing files and to replace them, follow these steps:

1. From the Start menu, point to All Programs, point to Accessories, and select Command Prompt.

2. Type **SFC /scannow** (note the space after SFC) and press ENTER or RETURN.

3. If prompted, insert the Windows XP CD-ROM.

4. Wait while Windows verifies that all protected files are intact and in their original versions.

There are many other command-line tools to choose from. To locate information about these tools, open the Windows Help and Support Center and search for *command-line tools*.

Practice: Explore Windows Troubleshooting Tools

In this practice, you will use msconfig to disable the Calculator from starting with Windows, as you configured at the end of Lesson 1. You will also use Disk Defragmenter to defragment your hard drive.

Exercise 1: Use Msconfig to Disable a Startup Application

1. Log on to Windows XP.

2. On the Start menu, choose Run. In the Run dialog box, in the Open text box, type **msconfig** and press ENTER.

3. In the System Configuration Utility, select the Startup tab. In the Startup Item column, clear the Calculator check box and click OK.

4. In the System Configuration dialog box, click Restart.

5. When Windows starts up, log on. Note that the Calculator does not launch this time.

6. In the System Configuration Utility dialog box that appears, select the Don't Show This Message Or Launch The System Configuration Utility When Windows Starts check box. Click OK.

Exercise 2: Use Msinfo32 to Find Information About Your Display Adapter

1. Log on to Windows XP.

2. On the Start menu, choose Run. In the Run dialog box, in the Open text box, type **msinfo32** and press ENTER.

3. In the System Information window, under System Summary, double-click Components to expand that node.

4. Click the Display component.

5. The information on the right shows the manufacturer, model, and settings for your display adapter.

Lesson Review

The following questions are intended to reinforce key information presented in this lesson. If you are unable to answer a question, review the lesson materials and try the question again. You can find answers to the questions in the "Questions and Answers" section at the end of this chapter.

1. Which of the following troubleshooting tools that are included with Windows XP should you use to repair problems that are related to missing protected system files?

   A. Msconfig

   B. Msinfo32

   C. Chkdsk

   D. Disk Defragmenter

   E. SFC /Scannow

2. In the following table, match the troubleshooting tool on the left with the task that the tool is used for on the right.

1. Msconfig	A. A command-line tool that creates a status report of the integrity of the hard disk and corrects errors on the disk
2. Msinfo32	B. A command-line tool that scans and verifies all protected system files on the computer and replaces any missing files
3. Chkdsk	C. A command-line tool that opens the System Configuration Utility, which can be used to troubleshoot and resolve startup errors and get rid of unwanted prompts by third-party applications
4. Disk Defragmenter	D. A command-line tool that opens the System Information window, which provides detailed information about the computer system configuration
5. SFC /Scannow	E. A program included with Windows XP that analyzes hard disks and locates and consolidates fragmented files and folders

Lesson Summary

- Use Msconfig to troubleshoot errors that occur during the boot process, to rid the computer of third-party software prompts after startup, to discover and resolve problems with running services, or to resolve errors regarding the boot paths configured on multiboot computers.

- Use Msinfo32 when you need to obtain information about the local or remote computer's hardware configuration, computer components, installed software, or drivers (signed or unsigned); or when you need to get information about the BIOS version.

- Use Chkdsk (Check Disk) to view the file system type (NTFS or FAT) and to verify the integrity of the disks installed on the computer.

- Use Disk Defragmenter to consolidate fragmented files, those that are saved in various areas of the hard drive rather than in one place.

- Use SFC /Scannow to determine whether any protected system files are missing.

Case Scenario Exercises

In the following scenarios, you must use what you have learned throughout the lessons in this chapter to answer questions based on a real-world scenario. Read each scenario, and answer the questions. If you have trouble, review the chapter and try again. You can find answers in the "Questions and Answers" section at the end of this chapter.

Scenario 3.1

Jessica calls the technical support line to report that she can no longer locate her messaging program. When you ask her to explain the problem in more detail, you discover that she believed the icon was taking up too much space "in the area of the taskbar where the clock is," so she removed it by right-clicking and choosing Exit. Now she cannot find it and is afraid she has deleted it from her system. What is the problem, and how can it be resolved?

A. Jessica completely removed the program from her system when she removed it from the notification area. Reinstall the component from the operating system's CD-ROM.

B. Jessica has exited the program but not uninstalled it. Because it is an application configured to start when Windows boots, you inform her that the only way to start the program again is to reboot the computer.

C. Jessica must log on to the network domain so that the missing program files can be downloaded.

D. Jessica removed the program icon and closed the program only temporarily. The icon can be added back to the notification area by rebooting the computer or by starting the program from the All Programs menu.

Scenario 3.2

After an upgrade from Microsoft Windows 2000 Professional to Windows XP Professional, a user reports that "the Start menu is too confusing and everything looks weird," and he wants you to remove Windows XP and put Windows 2000 back on his computer. Knowing that you cannot do that because the company is upgrading all of its machines, which of the following can you do to make this user more comfortable with the new operating system?

   A. Change the Start menu type to the Classic Start menu.

   B. Disable Hide Inactive Icons.

   C. Use the Windows Classic theme.

   D. Do not show the Favorites, My Music, or My Pictures folders on the Start menu.

   E. In the Folder Options dialog box, select Use Windows Classic Folders.

   F. Use Classic View in Control Panel.

Troubleshooting Lab

In this lab, you will perform two common activities for DSTs who are troubleshooting issues with hard drives. The issues range from intermittent application errors to slow performance. You will first run Check Disk on your hard drive to verify the integrity of the disks and then run Disk Defragmenter.

Exercise 1: Run Check Disk and Fix Errors

   1. Log on to Windows XP.

   2. From the Start menu, point to All Programs, point to Accessories, and select Command Prompt.

   3. At the command prompt, type **chkdsk /F**.

   4. Windows returns a message telling you that it cannot fix errors on the system drive while it is in use and asking whether you want to schedule a scan for the next time you start Windows. Press the Y key, and then press ENTER.

   5. Close the Command Prompt window.

   6. On the Start menu, select Turn Off Computer, and then select Restart.

   7. Watch while Windows restarts. Before you get to the logon screen, Windows notifies you that a Chkdsk scan has been scheduled and gives you the opportunity to cancel it by pressing any key. Let the scan run, and watch its progress. When it is done, the logon screen is displayed.

Exercise 2: Defragment a Disk

1. Log on to Windows XP.

2. From the Start menu, point to All Programs, point to Accessories, point to System Tools, and select Disk Defragmenter.

3. Disconnect from the Internet, turn off all antivirus software, turn off all screen savers, and close all running programs (except Disk Defragmenter).

4. Select a disk, and then click Defragment.

5. Close all dialog boxes and windows when the process is complete.

Chapter Summary

■ To resolve problems involving the taskbar, use the Taskbar And Start Menu Properties dialog box. On the Taskbar tab, you can lock or hide the taskbar, group similar items, show Quick Launch, hide inactive icons, and keep the taskbar on top of other windows.

■ To resolve problems involving the Start menu, use the Taskbar And Start Menu Properties dialog box. On the Start menu tab, click Customize to define what should and should not appear on the taskbar, clear the taskbar of recently used programs or documents, and more.

■ To allow a user to work in different languages on one computer, make changes in the Regional And Language Options dialog box. There you can select and configure options for currency, time, and dates and select input languages.

■ When troubleshooting language-related problems, the most common problem is that a user has unknowingly switched to another language and is having problems with keyboard function.

■ To configure how folders open, how they look, and what they contain, use the Folder Options dialog box. There you can choose to show hidden files and folders, open folders with a single click, configure how encrypted and compressed files look, and more.

■ Often simply restoring folder options to their default settings is enough to fix a user's problem, but you should still examine a user's configuration and try to understand the problem. The user might also want some options reconfigured.

■ File extensions define the application Windows uses to open a file. Often more than one installed application can be used to open a file type.

■ To open a file with an application other than the one defined for its file type, use the Open With dialog box by right-clicking on a file and choosing Open With.

■ To define which program should be used to open a specific file type, to add new file types, and to edit what happens when a particular program opens a file, use the Folder Options dialog box by clicking the File Types tab.

■ Use Msconfig to troubleshoot errors that occur during the boot process, to rid the computer of third-party software prompts after startup, to discover and resolve problems with running services, or to resolve errors regarding the boot paths configured on multiboot computers.

■ Use Msinfo32 when you need to obtain information about the local or remote computer's hardware configuration, computer components, installed software, or drivers (signed or unsigned); or when you need to get information about the BIOS version.

■ Use Chkdsk (Check Disk) to view the file system type (NTFS or FAT) and to verify the integrity of the disks installed on the computer.

■ Use Disk Defragmenter to consolidate fragmented files, those that are saved in various areas of the hard drive rather than in one place.

■ Use SFC /Scannow to determine whether any protected system files are missing.

Exam Highlights

Before taking the exam, review the key topics and terms that are presented in this chapter. You need to know this information.

Key Points

■ Icons in the notification area might be hidden. Check behind the arrow before you access the program's preferences or restart a program.

■ Consider regional settings as a possibility when keyboard errors are reported or when users report that symbols do not look right.

■ Study the common requests users make that involve folder options. In particular, remember that you can make encrypted and compressed information visible by color in Windows and that many files are hidden by default.

Key Terms

Fast User Switching   A feature of Windows XP Home and Professional, available for users who are not members of domains, which makes it possible for users to switch quickly between user accounts without having to actually log off and on or reboot the computer. Running programs do not need to be closed before switching users.

LAN   See local area network

local area network (LAN)   A group of computers in a small geographic area such as a home, an office, or a floor of an office building. LANs can be workgroups or domains, can connect wirelessly or using Ethernet and a hub, or can connect by more complex connections such as fiber-optic lines.

Questions and Answers

Lesson 1 Review

Page
3-19

1. Match the end-user request on the left with the solution on the right.

1. The Taskbar is always disappearing, and I'd like that to stop. I also want to be able to move the taskbar to another area of the screen.	A. Open the Taskbar And Start Menu Properties dialog box. On the Taskbar tab, select the Show Quick Launch check box. Then, on the Start menu, locate the program to display in the Quick Launch area, right-click it, and drag and drop it there. Select Copy Here.
2. John, my colleague down the hall, has an icon next to his Start menu that he uses to open our accounting program. I do not have any icons there. How do I create one of those so I do not always have to locate the program in the Start menu or place a shortcut on the desktop?	B. Open the Taskbar And Start Menu Properties dialog box. On the Taskbar tab, select the Group Similar Taskbar Buttons check box.
3. I do not have enough room on my taskbar to show all of my open programs, and I have to scroll to see the additional programs. Is there some way of grouping the programs?	C. Open the Taskbar And Start Menu Properties dialog box. On the Taskbar tab, clear the Auto-Hide The Taskbar check box. Then verify that the Lock The Taskbar check box is cleared. Instruct the user to move the taskbar by dragging.
4. Can I remove or hide the icons for my antivirus software, my pop-up stopper program, and other programs that run in the background? If I remove them, do they stop running?	D. Notification area icons can be removed by setting preferences in the program's configuration choices. If you right-click an item in the notification area and its shortcut menu lets you choose Exit or Close, the program will stop running when you choose the appropriate option.
5. In my notification area, there are a lot of icons that I do not think I need. How can I get rid of those for good? I do not think they should be running in the background, and I do not even know what some of them are.	E. Open the Taskbar And Start Menu Properties dialog box. On the Start Menu tab, click Customize. In the Customize Start Menu (or Customize Classic Start Menu) dialog box, make the appropriate changes.

6. On my Start menu are lots of programs that I do not need and some that I need but are not there. Can you fix that for me?

F. Click Start, and click Run. At the Run line, type **msconfig.exe** and click OK. On the Startup tab, clear the check boxes for the items that you do not want to start when the computer boots.

7. I want to be able to open My Network Places, open Control Panel, and access System Administrative Tools from the Start Menu, but I do not want my recent documents to be listed. I also do not want to see My Music, My Pictures, or any of that other stuff that is not work-related.

G. Open the Taskbar And Start Menu Properties dialog box. On the Start Menu tab, select Classic Start Menu and click Customize. Use the Add and Remove buttons to customize the menu. Apply the changes. If desired, select Start Menu to return to the default Start Menu look.

1-C. 2-A. 3-B. 4-D. 5-F. 6-G. 7-E.

2. You want to have as few items as possible on the taskbar. Which of the following items can you easily remove from the taskbar?

   A. The Start button

   B. The system clock

   C. The notification area

   D. Quick Launch items

   E. Inactive icons in the notification area

B, D, and E are the correct answers. All of these can be easily removed using the Taskbar And Start Menu Properties dialog box. A is not correct because the Start button cannot be removed, and C is incorrect because even though you can remove everything from the notification area, the tray itself is still visible on the taskbar.

Lesson 2 Review

Page 3-26

1. You are an architect who creates blueprints for clients all over the world, so you use the metric system instead of the U.S. system of measurement. Your company handles all other communications, including billing. Your regional settings are configured to use the English (United States) standard. Which of the following is the best option for changing the default system of measurement on your computer from U.S. to metric?

   A. Change the default regional options for standards and formats to English (Canada). Canada is the nearest country that uses the metric system.

   B. Change the default regional options for standards and formats to English (United Kingdom). The United Kingdom uses the metric system, and many of your clients live there.

C. Keep the English (United States) setting, but customize the measurement system to use the metric system. Do not make any other changes.

D. Install a metric keyboard.

C is the correct answer because changing the measurement system is a customization option. No other changes are necessary. A and B are incorrect because changing the default standards and formats also changes currency, time, date, and similar settings. D is incorrect because there is no metric keyboard.

2. A user has multiple languages configured on her laptop and needs access to the Language Bar quite often. However, she does not want the Language Bar to be open continuously, taking up space on the taskbar. What can you tell the user to do? Select the best answer.

A. In Regional And Language Options, remove and reinstall the languages each time she needs them.

B. In the Text Services And Input Languages dialog box, select the Turn Off Advanced Text Services check box.

C. Add the Language Bar to the taskbar only when it is needed by right-clicking the taskbar, pointing to Toolbars, and choosing Language Bar.

D. None of the above. When multiple languages are configured, the Language Bar is always on the taskbar.

C is the correct answer. The Language Bar, like other toolbars, can be added and removed from the taskbar as needed. A is too drastic, and although the solution would work, this is not the best answer. B does not have anything to do with the taskbar, and D is incorrect because C is the answer.

Lesson 3 Review

1. After configuring folder options, you notice you can no longer switch to Category view in Control Panel. What must you do to resolve this problem?

A. Clear the Use Windows Classic Folders check box in the Folder Options dialog box.

B. Select the Use Windows Classic Folders in the Folder Options dialog box.

C. In Control Panel, click View, select Choose Details, and select the Show Tasks check box.

D. In Control Panel, click the View tab, select Choose Details, and clear the Hide Task Options check box.

A is the correct answer. Category view is unavailable in Control Panel if Windows Classic view is selected. B is incorrect for this reason, and C and D are not valid options on the View menu in Control Panel.

2. There are many ways to access the Folder Options dialog box. Which of the following are valid examples?

   A. In Windows Explorer, click Tools, and click Folder Options.

   B. In the My Documents folder, click Tools, and click Folder Options.

   C. In Control Panel, open Folder Options.

   D. In My Computer, click Tools, and click Folder Options.

   E. From the All Programs list, under Accessories, click Folder Options.

   A, B, C, and D all offer ways to open folder options. E does not.

Lesson 4 Review

Page
3-38

1. In the following table, match the user request on the left with the part of the operating system that is used to resolve that request on the right.

1. A user wants to open folders using a single click, not a double click.	A. Taskbar And Start Menu Properties dialog box, Taskbar tab.
2. A user wants open programs to be grouped on the taskbar.	B. Configure the folder options from the View menu of any open folder. Open the Folder Options dialog box, and on the View tab, click Apply To All Folders.
3. A user wants all of her folders to open and display folder items as icons, not the current setting of tiles.	C. Folder Options dialog box, File Types tab, Registered File Types window, Change.
4. A user wants his JPEG files to always open in Paint.	D. Folder Options dialog box, General tab.
5. A user complains that there is no Security tab when she shares a file.	E. Folder Options dialog box, View tab, Advanced Settings.
6. A user complains that the pop-up descriptions for folder and desktop items no longer appear when he hovers over the item with the mouse.	F. Folder Options dialog box, View tab, disable Simple File Sharing.

1-D. 2-A. 3-B. 4-C. 5-F. 6-E.

2. Which of the following allows you to open a file with an unknown file type? (Each choice offers a complete solution. Choose two.)

   A. Install the application used to create the file, and then open the file in that program.

   B. Register the file type in the Folder Options dialog box, and associate it with a program already installed on the computer that has the capability to open the file.

C. Use the Web to determine which programs can be used to open the file.

D. Register the file type, and let Windows choose a program to open the file with.

A and B are the correct answers. A is correct because installing the application used to create the file will allow a user to open that file. B is correct because the file type is registered and a program is available to open the file. C is incorrect because a compatible program must be installed or available, and simply knowing what programs can be used to open the file is not enough. D is incorrect because Windows cannot automatically select a program. That is done manually.

Lesson 5 Review

Page 3-47

1. Which of the following troubleshooting tools that are included with Windows XP should you use to repair problems that are related to missing protected system files?

A. Msconfig

B. Msinfo32

C. Chkdsk

D. Disk Defragmenter

E. SFC /Scannow

E is the correct answer. System File Checker scans the protected system files and copies missing files from the Windows XP CD. None of the other options scan, check, or replace missing system files.

2. In the following table, match the troubleshooting tool on the left with the task that the tool is used for on the right.

1. Msconfig	A. A command-line tool that creates a status report of the integrity of the hard disk and corrects errors on the disk
2. Msinfo32	B. A command-line tool that scans and verifies all protected system files on the computer and replaces any missing files
3. Chkdsk	C. A command-line tool that opens the System Configuration Utility, which can be used to troubleshoot and resolve startup errors and get rid of unwanted prompts by third-party applications
4. Disk Defragmenter	D. A command-line tool that opens the System Information window, which provides detailed information about the computer system configuration
5. SFC /Scannow	E. A program included with Windows XP that analyzes hard disks and locates and consolidates fragmented files and folders

1-C. 2-D. 3-A. 4-E. 5-B.

Case Scenario Exercises: Scenario 3.1

Page
3-48
Jessica calls the technical support line to report that she can no longer locate her messaging program. When you ask her to explain the problem in more detail, you discover that she believed the icon was taking up too much space "in the area of the taskbar where the clock is," so she removed it by right-clicking and choosing Exit. Now she cannot find it and is afraid she has deleted it from her system. What is the problem, and how can it be resolved?

A. Jessica completely removed the program from her system when she removed it from the notification area. Reinstall the component from the operating system's CD-ROM.

B. Jessica has exited the program but not uninstalled it. Because it is an application configured to start when Windows boots, you inform her that the only way to start the program again is to reboot the computer.

C. Jessica must log on to the network domain so that the missing program files can be downloaded.

D. Jessica removed the program icon and closed the program only temporarily. The icon can be added back to the notification area by rebooting the computer or by starting the program from the All Programs menu.

The answer is D. Exiting a program from the notification area only closes the program temporarily. The icon can be added again simply by starting the program or by rebooting. B is only partially valid. Rebooting the computer will add the messaging icon back to the tray, but it is not the only way to add it back. A and C are not valid because the program was never uninstalled and there are no missing files.

Case Scenario Exercises: Scenario 3.2

Page
3-49

After an upgrade from Microsoft Windows 2000 Professional to Windows XP Professional, a user reports that "the Start menu is too confusing and everything looks weird," and he wants you to remove Windows XP and put Windows 2000 back on his computer. Knowing that you cannot do that because the company is upgrading all of its machines, which of the following can you do to make this user more comfortable with the new operating system?

A. Change the Start menu type to the Classic Start menu.

B. Disable Hide Inactive Icons.

C. Use the Windows Classic theme.

D. Do not show the Favorites, My Music, or My Pictures folders on the Start menu.

E. In the Folder Options dialog box, select Use Windows Classic Folders.

F. Use Classic View in Control Panel.

All of the answers are excellent ways to help the end user feel more comfortable in his new environment and are thus all correct.

4 Microsoft Outlook and Outlook Express

Exam Objectives in this Chapter:

- Configure and troubleshoot Microsoft Office applications
    - ❑ Configure and troubleshoot e-mail account settings
- Configure and troubleshoot Microsoft Office Outlook Express
    - ❑ Answer end-user questions related to configuring Outlook Express
    - ❑ Configure and troubleshoot newsreader account settings
    - ❑ Configure and troubleshoot e-mail account settings
- Resolve issues related to Outlook Express features
- Resolve issues related to customizing an Office application
    - ❑ Manage Microsoft Outlook data, including configuring, importing and exporting data, and repairing corrupted data
- Resolve issues related to customizing Outlook Express

Why This Chapter Matters

The purpose of this chapter is to teach you to support end users who run Microsoft Windows 2000 Professional, Windows XP Home Edition, or Windows XP Professional and who use Microsoft Office Outlook or Outlook Express as their e-mail client. In this chapter, you will learn to create, configure, and troubleshoot e-mail accounts and newsgroups, keep Outlook and Outlook Express running smoothly by maintaining the stored data, and resolve common end-user requests, such as:

- Importing address books and messages from other computers or exporting address books and messages to laptops and other portable devices.
- Setting up a newsgroup.
- Configuring a home account so that e-mail can be retrieved from the network server.
- Leaving a copy of e-mails on the network server.
- Resolving problems related to user name, display name, or e-mail account settings.

> **Note**   MSCDT Exam 70-272 covers both Outlook and Outlook Express, but most of the focus in this chapter is on Outlook. Because Outlook Express is a limited version of Outlook, the procedures involved in using it are similar to the procedures for using Outlook, with minor changes. Of course, the full version of Outlook is much more comprehensive and offers many more features. Be sure you are familiar with both versions and that you can perform the tasks outlined in this chapter in either application.

Lessons in this Chapter:

Before You Begin

Before you begin this chapter, you should have basic familiarity with the Windows XP interface. You should also have a working knowledge of e-mail software. Finally, you should have access to a computer running Windows XP and Microsoft Office Outlook on which you can experiment with changing various settings.

Lesson 1: Configuring E-Mail Accounts

As a desktop support technician (DST), you must be able to configure e-mail accounts by using Outlook and Outlook Express. Creating accounts also includes testing, troubleshooting, and importing or exporting existing address books and messages.

After this lesson, you will be able to

- Identify common e-mail protocols.
- Create e-mail accounts in Outlook 2003 and Outlook Express.
- Work with address books and messages.

Estimated lesson time: 45 minutes

Understanding E-Mail Protocols

Post Office Protocol 3 (POP3) and Simple Mail Transfer Protocol (SMTP) are **protocols** for moving e-mail across the Internet. SMTP is used to send e-mail from one server to another or from a client computer to a mail server. POP3, and another protocol called Internet Message Access Protocol (IMAP), are used to retrieve e-mail from those servers.

When supporting users, you are primarily going to be concerned with the receiving protocols, POP3 and IMAP. Of these two, POP3 is by far the most commonly used. With a POP3 e-mail account, messages are received and held on a mail server (either on a local network or at an Internet service provider [ISP]). The user's client software accesses the server and downloads those messages at the user's convenience. The client software deletes the messages from the server after they are downloaded. IMAP, an extension of POP3, is similar except that instead of the messages being downloaded from the server, they are stored on the server and the user works with them there.

Creating Accounts

Creating accounts using either Microsoft Outlook 2003 or Outlook Express is achieved by using a wizard. You can set up several types of e-mail accounts in Outlook 2003, including an e-mail account for Microsoft Exchange Server, POP3, IMAP, **Hypertext Transfer Protocol (HTTP)**, and additional e-mail account types, including those that access third-party mail servers. As a DST in a tier-1 or tier-2 position, you will be called on to set up only POP3, IMAP, and HTTP accounts. Domain administrators will set up accounts to Exchange servers and third-party servers.

> **Note** In this section, you will learn to create new e-mail accounts in Microsoft Office Outlook 2003; Outlook Express is briefly discussed at the end of this section.

In the following example, you will learn to add a POP3 account, and the procedures for adding an IMAP or HTTP account are quite similar. To add a POP3 e-mail account for an Outlook 2003 client, follow these steps:

1. Open Outlook 2003.

2. Click Tools, and click E-Mail Accounts to open the E-Mail Accounts Wizard.

3. On the E-Mail Accounts page, choose Add A New E-Mail Account, and click Next.

4. On the Server Type page, click POP3, and click Next.

5. On the Internet E-Mail Settings (POP3) page, shown in Figure 4-1, type the required information.

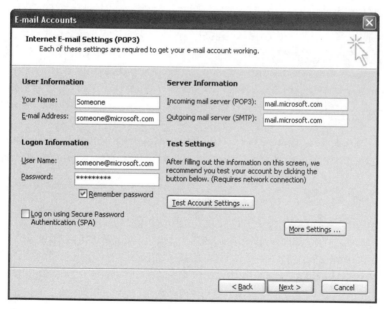

Figure 4-1 Internet e-mail settings.

❏ **Your Name**   The user's name as it should appear in the From: line of e-mail messages that are sent from the user.

❏ **E-Mail Address**   The user's full e-mail address, including the suffix (that is, user@domainname.com).

❏ **User Name**   The user name that is required to authenticate to the mail server. This can be a name or the e-mail address. If you are setting up an account for a user with an ISP, the ISP should have provided the information to the user.

❏ **Password**   The password that is required to authenticate to the mail server.

❏ **Incoming Mail Server (POP3)**   The name of the incoming mail server. The names of incoming and outgoing servers should also have been provided by the user's ISP (if you are setting up an ISP account). If the user cannot find this information, it is often available on the ISP's website.

❏ **Outgoing Mail Server (SMTP)**   The name of the outgoing mail server.

❏ **Log On Using Secure Password Authentication (SPA)**   Select this check box if the server requires it. (Most do not.)

6. Click Test Account Settings. If an error occurs, as shown in Figure 4-2, double-check the information entered in step 5. If problems persist, contact your network administrator for the correct settings, and if an administrator is not available, refer to Lesson 4, "Troubleshooting Outlook," in this chapter.

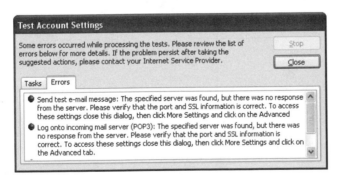

Figure 4-2   Test account settings.

7. If you know you need to configure advanced options such as additional user information, additional SMTP settings, or connection options or to configure the account to leave a copy of messages on the server, click More Settings. For a home user, the defaults are generally fine, and for many corporate users, the same is true. Click Next, and then click Finish to close the wizard. If advanced options are necessary or the e-mail account does not work properly, you will need to config-ure advanced options, which are detailed in the following section.

Configuring Advanced E-Mail Account Settings

If you need to configure advanced settings, either while you are creating an e-mail account or after it has been created, you can do so from the Internet E-Mail Settings dialog box, shown in Figure 4-3. This dialog box can be accessed by clicking More Set-tings while creating the account on the Internet E-Mail Settings page (shown earlier in Figure 4-1) or by editing an existing account.

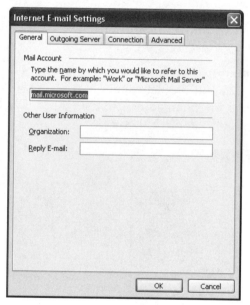

Figure 4-3   The Internet E-Mail Settings dialog box.

There are several additional settings, detailed in Table 4-1.

Table 4-1   Internet E-Mail Settings

Tab	Setting and Description
General	■ **Mail Account** The name of the account as the user would like to refer to it. This can be any name. ■ **Organization** The name of the user's organization. This is optional. ■ **Reply E-Mail** The e-mail address that should be used to accept replies to messages sent to this address. If no address is configured, all replies are sent to the configured e-mail address.
Outgoing Server	■ **My Outgoing Server (SMTP) Requires Authentication** Select this check box to specify that the SMTP server requires a user name and password. When this is selected, other options become available: Use The Same Settings As My Incoming Mail Server, Log On Using (User Name, Password), and Log On Using Secure Password Authentication (SPA). ■ **Log On To Incoming Mail Server Before Sending E-Mail** Many mail providers require that you log on to an incoming server before you are allowed to use their outgoing server. This ensures that you have a valid account there and prevents people without accounts from using the outgoing server to send messages anonymously (a favorite tactic of spammers). Normally, a user will not need this option selected since he or she is already logging on to the account when checking e-mail. You might need to configure this option if the user receives mail from a different server than the ISP or network provider to which the user is connected.
Connection	■ **Connect Using My Local Area Network (LAN)** Select this option to connect to the mail server using the LAN. This is appropriate when the user is connected to the Internet through a dedicated connection, such as on a company network or using a cable or DSL connection. ■ **Connect Via Modem When Outlook Is Offline** Select this option when a user connects over his or her LAN but needs to connect with a modem if working away from the network. ■ **Connect Using My Phone Line** Select this option when a user always connects to the mail server using his or her own phone line. ■ **Connect Using Internet Explorer's Or A 3rd Party Dialer** Select this option to use the same settings configured for Internet Explorer or when a third-party connection is used. ■ **Modem** Select a dial-up connection from the drop-down list. ■ **Properties** Click the Properties button to access advanced modem properties. ■ **Add** Click the Add button to add another networking connection.

Table 4-1   Internet E-Mail Settings

Tab	Setting and Description
Advanced	■ **Incoming Server (POP3)** Type the port number of the POP3 server. Generally, it is 110. ■ **This Server Requires An Encrypted Connection (SSL)** Select this check box if the server requires an encrypted connection. ■ **Outgoing Server (SMTP)** Type the port number of the SMTP server. Generally, it is 25. ■ **Server Timeouts** Specifies how long to wait for a response from the mail server before giving up. Slower connections require more time to respond; faster connections require less. ■ **Leave A Copy Of Messages On The Server** Select this check box if messages are to be left on the server even after users have deleted them from their hard drives. This is useful if a user needs to check messages from two different locations. Set the primary location so that messages are removed from the server when the user checks mail from that location. Set the secondary location so that it does not delete messages. The user can check for new messages from the secondary location but will still receive the messages at the primary location. ■ **Remove From Server After ___ Days** If the e-mail account is configured to leave messages on the server, this tells Outlook how long to leave them there before deleting them. ■ **Remove From Server When Deleted From Deleted Items** If the e-mail account is configured to leave messages on the server, this setting deletes those e-mails when they are deleted from the user's Deleted Items folder.

If you need to set any of these additional options and did not do so when you created the account, you can do so by modifying an existing account. To configure the additional settings for an existing account, follow these steps:

1. Open Outlook 2003, click Tools, and click E-Mail Accounts.

2. On the E-Mail Accounts page, click View Or Change Existing E-Mail Accounts, and click Next.

3. On the E-Mail Accounts page, select the account to change, and click Change.

4. On the Internet E-Mail Settings (POP3) page, click More Settings.

5. In the Internet E-Mail Settings dialog box, click any tab and enter or configure the required information. Click OK when finished to close the Internet E-Mail Settings dialog box.

6. Click Finish on the E-Mail Accounts page.

With the e-mail account configured, send a test e-mail from the new account and to the new account to verify that e-mail can be both sent and received. If there are problems, refer to Lesson 4, "Troubleshooting Outlook," in this chapter.

Connecting to an Exchange Server Account

If you are working in a corporate environment, it is likely that the company will use an internal mail server such as Microsoft Exchange Server to provide e-mail services within the company. After an Exchange administrator has configured a mailbox for a user on an Exchange server, connecting Outlook 2003 to that mailbox is not difficult.

> **Note**   If a company is using Exchange Server as its e-mail server, the chances are high that they have settled on Outlook as the default mail client for use in the company. Used together, Outlook and Exchange offer a lot of advanced functionality. However, it is possible that some users, especially those connecting remotely, will use Outlook Express or a third-party e-mail client to connect. Fortunately, Exchange Server supports POP3 connections, so you can connect a mail client to it the same way you would to a POP3 server. This section details the connection of Outlook 2003 to an Exchange Server using the Message Application Programming Interface (MAPI) protocol, the likely choice for connections inside a company network.

To connect to an Exchange server mailbox using Outlook 2003, you have two options. If you have not run Outlook 2003 since you installed it, you can start up Outlook and set up the Exchange Server account during the startup wizard that runs the first time you start Outlook. If you have already set up accounts in Outlook and need to add an Exchange Server account, you will need to do it using the Mail tool in the Windows Control Panel. You cannot add an Exchange account while Outlook is running. This section shows you how to set up an Exchange account using the Control Panel method; if you are using the Outlook Startup Wizard instead, you will find the process nearly identical.

To add an Exchange Server mailbox to an existing Outlook profile, use the following steps:

1. On the Start menu, select Control Panel.

2. In Control Panel, click User Accounts.

3. In the User Accounts window, click Mail.

4. In the Mail Setup – Outlook window, click E-Mail Accounts.

5. Select the Add A New E-Mail Account option, and click Next.

6. On the Server Type page, select the Microsoft Exchange Server option, and click Next.

7. On the Server Type page, select Microsoft Exchange Server, and click Next.

8. On the Exchange Server Settings page, type the name or IP address of the Microsoft Exchange Server, and type the user name. Both of these should have been provided to the user by the Exchange administrator.

9. Click Check Name to have the E-Mail Accounts Wizard verify that the mailbox you typed exists on the Exchange server. If the verification is successful, you see the server and user name appear in underlined text in the fields (as shown in Figure 4-4). Click Next.

10. On the Congratulations page, click Finish.

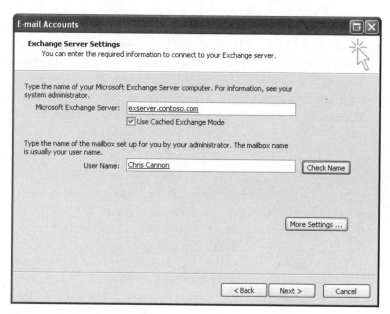

Figure 4-4   Connecting to an Exchange Server mailbox.

Working with Address Books and Messages

When Outlook 2003 is run for the first time after being installed on a user's computer, Outlook offers to import mail, addresses, and mail account settings from an existing e-mail application that is already installed on the computer. For many users, this is Outlook Express, but it can also be Eudora Light or Eudora Pro. In addition, data from previously saved files, such as Microsoft Office Excel or Microsoft Office Access files, can be imported. You can even import messages from previous Outlook data files.

Users might also need to export address books and messages for the purpose of backing them up or moving them to another location. Importing and exporting tasks are performed by using the Import And Export Wizard, available on the Outlook File menu.

Importing Address Books and Messages

Address books and e-mail messages can be imported in many ways, and in this section we cover two of them. You will learn to import mail messages and address books from Outlook Express and Eudora (Pro and Light), and you will learn to import mail and messages from an Excel file. Although there are other options, including importing the data from a previously exported text or comma-separated values (CSV) file, an Access file, a personal folder file, or an application such as Lotus Organizer or ACT!, the procedures are basically the same as the two you will see here.

To import Internet e-mail and addresses from Outlook Express, Eudora Light, or Eudora Pro, follow these steps:

1. Open Outlook. On the File menu, click Import And Export.

2. On the first page of the Import And Export Wizard, click Import Internet Mail And Addresses, and click Next.

3. On the Outlook Import Tool page, select the Internet Mail application to import from. Figure 4-5 shows this page with Outlook Express selected.

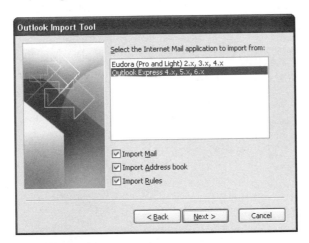

Figure 4-5   The Outlook Import Tool.

4. Select the items to import. Choose any combination of Import Mail, Import Address Book, and Import Rules. Click Next.

5. If you are importing only e-mail messages or rules, click Finish. If you are also importing an address book, click Next.

6. If importing addresses, on the Import Addresses page, choose one of the following options and then click Finish:

  ❏ **Replace Duplicates With Items Imported** Existing data will be overwritten with the data imported.

  ❏ **Allow Duplicates To Be Created** Existing data will not be overwritten, and duplicates will be added.

  ❏ **Do Not Import Duplicate Items** Existing data will be kept, and duplicate information will not be copied.

7. To save a report of the Import Summary, click Save In Inbox on the Import Summary page.

To import data from another program or file, follow these steps:

1. Open Outlook. On the File menu, click Import And Export.

2. In the Import And Export Wizard, select Import From Another Program Or File, and click Next.

3. On the Import A File page, select Microsoft Excel. (To import from another program, select another option.) Click Next.

4. Click Browse to locate the file. Select the appropriate option for dealing with duplicate entries. Click Next.

5. On the Import A File page, choose the appropriate folder from the Select Destination Folder list. Figure 4-6 shows an example. Click Next.

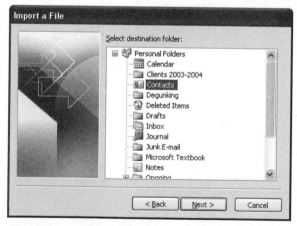

Figure 4-6   Importing a file to the Contacts folder.

6. To map custom fields or to change the folder selected, click Map Custom Fields or Change Destination. When mapping custom fields, drag and drop the field on the left (configured fields) to the field on the right (address book fields). When finished, click Next. Click Finish.

Exporting Address Books and Messages

For the purpose of backing up an address book or a message, or to store the information on a hard drive for the purpose of exporting to another computer later, use the Import And Export Wizard as detailed in the preceding sections. When prompted, select Export To A File (instead of selecting any importing choice). You will be prompted to save the file as one of the following:

■ **Comma-Separated Values (DOS)**   Choose this if you need to export the data so that it can later be imported into a third-party e-mail client.

■ **Comma Separated Values (Windows)**   Choose this if you need to export a file for use in Microsoft Office Word, Microsoft Office PowerPoint, or third-party applications.

■ **Microsoft Access**   Choose this to save the data in a Microsoft Access file.

■ **Microsoft Excel**   Choose this to save the data in a Microsoft Excel file.

■ **Personal Folder File (.pst)**   Choose this if you need to organize and back up your Outlook data. These data files can be read only by Outlook. Only the content is preserved; permissions, rules, forms, views, and descriptions are not preserved.

■ **Tab-Separated Values (DOS)**   Choose this if you need to export the data so that it can later be imported into a third-party e-mail client.

■ **Tab-Separated Values (Windows)**   Choose this if you need to export a file for use in Word, PowerPoint, or third-party applications.

After making the appropriate choice, click Next, and continue through the wizard as detailed in earlier sections.

> **Exam Tip**   For the exam, be sure you know the programs and formats from which Outlook and Outlook Express can import and those to which they can export.

Real World   Backing Up Outlook

Outlook 2003 stores all items (messages, calendar entries, contacts, notes, and so on) in a single database file known as a personal storage file. By default, this file is named Outlook.pst, and you can find it in C:\Documents and Settings\user-name\Local Settings\Application Data\Microsoft\Outlook. This folder is also the default storage location for archived information, which is stored by default in a separate personal storage file named Archive.pst.

If one of the accounts you use in Outlook 2003 is an Exchange Server mailbox, you should note that all messages associated with that account are actually stored on the Exchange server and not as part of the local .pst file. If you are using Outlook 2003 in cached mode, messages on the Exchange server are copied to a temporary file (called an offline folder, or .ost, file) on the local computer so that the user can work while disconnected from the Exchange server.

Outlook 2003 stores other program information in C:\Documents and Settings\username\Application Data\Microsoft\Outlook. (Notice that the only difference in this path is that the Local Settings folder is not involved.) In this folder, you will find the following files:

- Outcmd.dat stores Outlook menu customizations.
- Outitems.log identifies Outlook items to be placed automatically in the journal.
- Outlook.NK2 lists nicknames used for AutoComplete.
- Outlook.srs stores Outlook Send/Receive group settings.
- Outlook.xml stores navigation bar customizations.
- OutlPrnt stores customized print settings.

If you plan to troubleshoot Outlook 2003, you can save yourself a lot of headaches and embarrassment by making a backup copy of these two Outlook folders somewhere else on the user's computer.

Using Outlook Express

The goal of this section is to introduce you to Outlook Express and to detail the most common tasks you will be asked to perform. Although using Outlook Express is similar to using Outlook, the processes are not exactly the same for both. As a DST, you must support both Outlook (commonly used in corporations, companies, and small businesses) and Outlook Express (commonly used by home users and small home-based businesses). In this section, you will learn the most basic Outlook Express tasks, such as creating a POP3 or IMAP account for a home user, testing and troubleshooting that account, and importing an existing address book and messages.

> **Note**   Teach your end users to export their address book to a floppy disk. The floppy disk makes an excellent backup.

Creating a POP3 or IMAP Account

To create a POP3 account using Outlook Express for a small business owner or home user, follow these steps:

1. Open Outlook Express.

2. Click Tools, and then click Accounts.

3. Click the Mail tab. Click Add, and then click Mail.

4. Using the Internet Connection Wizard, on the Your Name page, type the name of the user as he or she wants it to appear to others. Because this is a display name only, any name is fine. Click Next.

5. On the Internet E-Mail Address page, type the e-mail address. Click Next.

6. On the E-Mail Server Names page, in the My Incoming Mail Server Is A ___ Server drop-down list, choose POP3, IMAP, or HTTP. In the Incoming Mail (POP3, IMAP, Or HTTP) Server box, type the name of the incoming mail server. In the Outgoing Mail (SMTP) Server box, type the name of the outgoing mail server. Figure 4-7 shows an example. Click Next.

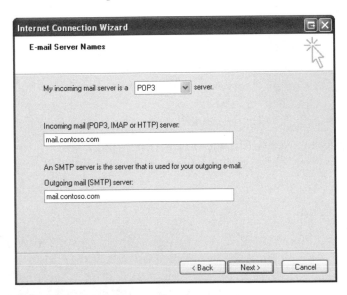

Figure 4-7   Configure e-mail server names.

7. On the Internet Mail Logon page, type the account name and password. If the home user requests it, select the Remember Password check box. Click Next.

8. Click Finish when prompted, and click Close in the Internet Accounts dialog box.

Testing and Troubleshooting

You will want to verify that the account works as it should. To test and troubleshoot the new account, follow these steps:

1. Open Outlook Express, and click Create Mail.

2. In the To: box, type the address of the e-mail account you just created. This is the user's account. In the Subject box, type **Test**, and then click Send.

3. After the e-mail has been sent, click Send/Recv. Verify that the e-mail was sent and received. If an error occurs or if the display name is incorrect, troubleshoot the account using the steps listed next.

If an error was received while you were testing the account, specifically a failure notice issued by the ISP that the e-mail could not be sent, that an error occurred when trying to receive the e-mail, or that the display name is incorrect, follow these steps:

1. Click Tools, and click Accounts.

2. Click the Mail tab, and select the account that was just configured and is not working.

3. Click Properties.

4. On the General tab, verify the user information, including name and e-mail address. Make the appropriate corrections.

5. On the Servers tab, verify the server information, including incoming server name, incoming and outgoing mail servers, account name, password, and authentication settings. If in doubt, contact the ISP to double-check the settings. Make the appropriate corrections. Click OK, and then click Close. Send another test e-mail.

6. If the e-mail still fails, verify that the user is connected to the Internet, verify with the ISP that the e-mail address used is the correct one, and verify the names of the mail servers.

Importing and Exporting

With the account working properly, you can now import a user's address book and existing messages. There are multiple ways to import an address book, as you learned earlier. However, when configuring a new account for a home user, the easiest way to import an address book is to have previously exported it as a CSV text file. Working with an address book using this technique works in almost any situation, including moving address books between computers (such as from a home PC to a laptop or from an old computer to a new one) and moving an existing address book from an old e-mail account configuration to a new one on the same or on different computers. It also provides an excellent way to back up the address book, and teaching the end user to do this is a good idea.

In this example, you will learn how to first export an existing address book as a CSV text file and then how to import it into the new account. To export the address book, follow these steps:

1. Open Outlook Express on the old computer, laptop, or existing computer; click File; point to Export; and click Address Book.

2. In the Address Book Export Tool, select Text File (Comma Separated Values) and click Export.

3. In the CSV Export dialog box, click Browse and choose a location in which to save the file. Name the file, and then click Save in the Save As dialog box. Click Next.

4. In the second CSV Export dialog box, select the fields to export. Be sure you select First Name, Last Name, and E-Mail Address. Click Finish.

5. Click OK when prompted that the export process is complete, and then click Close to close the Address Book Export Tool.

To import the address book, follow these steps:

1. Click File, point to Import, and select Other Address Book.

2. In the Address Book Import Tool dialog box, shown in Figure 4-8, select Text File (Comma Separated Values). Click Import.

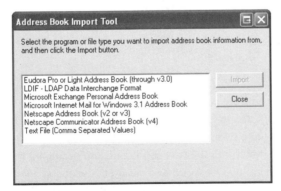

Figure 4-8   Import an address book.

3. In the CSV Import dialog box, click Browse. Locate the exported address book, and click Open. Click Next in the CSV Import dialog box.

4. In the second CSV Import dialog box, select the fields to import and click Finish. Be sure you select First Name, Last Name, and E-Mail Address.

5. Click OK when prompted that the import process is complete, and then click Close to close the Address Book Import Tool.

Finally, importing existing messages is achieved as follows:

1. Open Outlook Express, click File, point to Import, and select Messages.

2. In the Select Program dialog box, select Microsoft Outlook Express 6. Click Next.

> **Note**   The program from which you choose to import governs what you see from this point on. This procedure details the steps for importing from an Outlook Express 6 message store.

3. In the Import dialog box, select the appropriate identity and click Next.

4. In the Location Of Messages dialog box, accept the defaults (unless the mail folder has been moved), and click Next. If the mail folder has been moved, you will need to use the Browse button to locate it before clicking Next.

5. In the Select Folders dialog box, select All Folders or Selected Folders. If Selected Folders is chosen, select the folders to import. To select more than one folder, hold down the CTRL key. Click Next.

6. Click Finish after the messages are imported successfully.

> **Note**   As with Outlook, there are various ways to import and export data. Make sure you are familiar with the additional techniques.

Practice: Set Up and Configure E-Mail Accounts

In this practice, you will configure Outlook 2003 as a POP3 client and as an IMAP client. You will also back up Outlook data.

> **Note**   You will need to have a computer running Windows XP with Office 2003 installed to complete these practices. To work through Exercise 1, it must be the first time that you have started Outlook following installation. When setting up an e-mail account, it is helpful if you have an actual mail server (such as at your ISP) to use to configure accounts. If you do not, you can still enter the information in Outlook 2003 and set up the account; you just will not be able to test the setup.

Exercise 1: Configure Outlook 2003 as a POP3 Client by Using the Outlook 2003 Startup Wizard

1. Log on to Windows XP.

2. On the Start menu, choose E-Mail. If Outlook 2003 is not configured as your default e-mail software, on the Start menu, point to All Programs and then to Microsoft Office, and select Microsoft Office Outlook 2003.

3. In the Outlook 2003 Startup Wizard, click Next.

4. On the Account Configuration page, verify that Yes is selected, and click Next.

5. In the E-Mail Accounts Wizard, on the Server Type page, select POP3, and click Next.

6. On the Internet E-Mail Settings (POP3) page, under User Information, in the Your Name text box, type your name. In the E-Mail Address text box, type your e-mail address. If you are setting up a nonworking account, you can enter anything here.

7. Under Logon Information, in the Password text box, type your password. Again, it does not matter what you enter if you are setting up a nonworking account.

8. Under Server Information, in the Incoming Mail Server (POP3) text box, and in the Outgoing Mail Server (SMTP) text box, type the name of your server (or just make up a name for a nonworking account). Click Next.

9. On the Congratulations page, click Finish.

10. In the Microsoft Office 2003 Activation Wizard, verify that I Want To Activate The Software Over The Internet is selected, and click Next.

11. In the Microsoft Office 2003 Activation Wizard, click Close.

Exercise 2: Configure Outlook 2003 as an IMAP Client by Using the Mail Control Panel

1. Log on to Windows XP.

2. On the Start menu, choose Control Panel.

3. In Control Panel, click User Accounts.

4. In the User Accounts window, click Mail.

5. In the Mail Setup – Outlook dialog box, click Show Profiles.

6. In the Mail dialog box, click Add.

7. In the New Profile dialog box, in the Profile Name text box, type **IMAP** and click OK.

8. In the E-Mail Accounts Wizard, in the E-Mail section, verify that Add A New E-Mail Account is selected and click Next.

9. On the Server Type page, select IMAP and click Next.

10. On the Internet E-Mail Settings (IMAP) page, under User Information, in the Your Name text box, type your name. In the E-Mail Address text box, type your e-mail address.

11. Under Logon Information, in the Password text box, type your password.

12. Under Server Information, in the Incoming Mail Server (IMAP) text box, and in the Outgoing Mail Server (SMTP) text box, type the names of your servers. Click Next.

13. On the Congratulations page, click Finish.

14. In the Mail dialog box, select Prompt For A Profile To Be Used. Click OK.

15. Start Outlook 2003.

16. In the Choose Profile dialog box, in the Profile Name drop-down list, select IMAP and click OK. You should now be able to test your new IMAP account.

Exercise 3: Create a Connection to an Exchange Server

To complete this practice, you will need the application named MiniDir, which is found in the Tools folder on the CD included with this book. This application simulates an Exchange server for the purposes of creating an account within Outlook. Please note that the MiniDir application does not allow you to send or receive messages. Its only purpose is to simulate the experience of setting up an Outlook account.

1. Log on to Windows XP.

2. On the Start menu, point to All Programs and then to Accessories, and select Windows Explorer.

3. In the Folders pane of Windows Explorer, expand the My Computer node, and then select Local Disk (C:).

4. On the File menu, point to New, and then select Folder.

5. The new folder is created in the right-hand pane and selected automatically. Type **MiniDir** to change the name of the folder.

6. Insert the CD that was included with this book. If a splash screen opens automatically, close it.

7. In the Folders pane of Windows Explorer, navigate to your CD drive and select the Tools folder on the CD.

8. Select the MiniDir application (it is a single file), and then, on the Edit menu, select Copy.

9. In the Folders pane of Windows Explorer, navigate to the new MiniDir folder that you created on the C drive. On the Edit menu, select Paste. You should now see a copy of the MiniDir application in the MiniDir folder you created.

10. Close the Windows Explorer window.

11. On the Start menu, point to All Programs and then to Accessories, and select Command Prompt.

12. In the Command Prompt window, type **cd c:\minidir** and press ENTER.

13. Type **minidir.exe** and press ENTER. At this point, the MiniDir application is running, although you see no visual indication of it other than the phrase "Hit RETURN to terminate MiniDir" in the Command Prompt window. Minimize the Command Prompt window, and leave MiniDir running for the remainder of this exercise.

14. On the Start menu, select Control Panel.

15. In Control Panel, click User Accounts.

16. In the User Accounts window, click Mail.

17. In the Mail Setup – Outlook window, click E-Mail Accounts.

18. Select the Add A New E-Mail Account option, and click Next.

19. On the Server Type page, select the Microsoft Exchange Server option, and click Next.

20. On the Start menu, point to All Programs and then to Accessories, and select Command Prompt to open a second Command Prompt window. In this window, type **ipconfig** and note the IP address listed for your local area connection.

21. On the Exchange Server Settings page of the E-Mail Accounts Wizard, in the Microsoft Exchange Server field, type the IP address you identified in the preceding step.

22. In the User Name field, type **Test User**.

23. Click Check Name. You should see both the Exchange Server address and the user name become underlined. Click Next.

24. On the Congratulations page, click Finish, and you are returned to the Mail Setup – Outlook dialog box. Click E-Mail Accounts.

25. On the E-Mail Accounts page, select the View Or Change Existing E-Mail Accounts option and click Next.

26. In the list of accounts, select the new Microsoft Exchange Server account you just created and click Remove. Click Yes to confirm the removal. Click Finish.

27. Click Close to exit the Mail Setup – Outlook dialog box.

28. Locate the Command Prompt window that you used to determine your IP address. Type **Exit** and press ENTER to close the window.

29. Locate the Command Prompt window that you used to run the MiniDir application. Press ENTER to end the MiniDir application. Type **Exit** and press ENTER to close the window.

Exercise 4: Back Up Outlook Data

1. Log on to Windows XP.

2. On the Start menu, choose E-Mail. If Outlook 2003 is not configured as your default e-mail software, on the Start menu, point to All Programs, then to Microsoft Office, and select Microsoft Office Outlook 2003.

3. On the File menu, choose Import And Export.

4. In the Import And Export Wizard, in the Choose An Action To Perform list, select Export To A File. Click Next.

5. On the Export To A File page, in the Create A File Of Type list, select Personal Folder File (.pst) and click Next.

6. On the Export Personal Folders page, in the Select A Folder To Export From list, click Personal Folders (the outermost folder), select the Include Subfolders check box, and then click Next.

7. On the Export Personal Folders page, click Browse.

8. In the Open Personal Folders dialog box, click the Desktop icon on the left, and click OK.

9. On the Export Personal Folders page, click Finish.

10. In the Create Microsoft Personal Folders dialog box, click OK.

Lesson Review

The following questions are intended to reinforce key information presented in this lesson. If you are unable to answer a question, review the lesson materials and try the question again. You can find answers to the questions in the "Questions and Answers" section at the end of this chapter.

1. A user has a POP3 e-mail account from an ISP, and he reports that he cannot send e-mail. He can receive e-mail. Which of the following is most likely the problem?

    A. The Mail Account name in the Internet E-Mail Settings dialog box (accessed by clicking More Settings in the E-Mail Accounts dialog box) has a typographical error.

    B. The SMTP server name is incorrectly configured in the user's e-mail settings.

    C. The ISP's POP3 mail server is down.

    D. The user has not typed in the correct password.

2. A client who has been using Outlook Express has recently installed Microsoft Office 2003. He reports that when he opened Outlook for the first time, he tried to create an e-mail account, but as the procedure progressed, he got confused and clicked Cancel in the remaining dialog boxes instead of working through them. He now reports that he can send and receive e-mail, but he cannot access his address book and he cannot locate his old mail messages. What should you tell the user to do?

    A. Uninstall and reinstall Outlook 2003. After the application has been reinstalled, tell him to call back, and you will walk him through the procedure.

    B. Delete the existing account using the E-Mail Accounts Wizard. Re-create the account using the same wizard, and follow the prompts for importing the address book and mail messages.

    C. Click Tools, and click Address Book. In the Address Book window, click File, and click Import And Export. Import the address book used for Outlook Express.

    D. Open Outlook, and on the File menu, click Import And Export. Work through the Import And Export Wizard to import both mail messages and the address book.

3. There are several ways to export address books and e-mail messages. Match the user's requirements on the left with the best export option on the right.

1. The address book will be stored in a Word document.	A. Personal folder files
2. The address book will be stored as a database file.	B. Microsoft Excel
3. Messages will be stored as a backup of Outlook data and will not be used by any other program.	C. CSV (Windows)
4. The address book will be stored as an .xls file.	D. Microsoft Access

Lesson Summary

- POP3 and IMAP are protocols used by clients to receive e-mail from servers. SMTP is a protocol used by clients and servers to send e-mail.

- To create, test, and troubleshoot e-mail accounts in Outlook and Outlook Express, use the Internet Accounts dialog box. From there you can add accounts, view properties, and make changes to existing accounts.

- Importing and exporting messages and address books provides a good method for backing up and restoring Outlook and Outlook Express, and a method for migrating from other e-mail software.

Lesson 2: Configuring Newsreader Settings

Newsgroups are collections of messages that are stored on news servers. These news servers are maintained by third-party entities such as Microsoft, for the purpose of assisting others in finding information and answers to questions quickly. Messages posted to the newsgroups can generally be read by anyone, and anyone can post to them. In this section, you will learn how to add the News entry to the Go menu, how to start the Outlook Express newsreader, how to use Outlook News as the default news client, how to join a newsgroup, and how to troubleshoot newsgroup accounts.

After this lesson, you will be able to

- Configure Outlook as a newsreader.
- Add newsgroups to a newsreader.
- Resolve common service calls involving newsreaders.

Estimated lesson time: 20 minutes

Setting Up Outlook News as the Default News Client

The first time you or an end user sets up Outlook to join a newsgroup, you must add the News command to the Go menu by following these steps:

1. Open Outlook, right-click an empty area of the Standard toolbar, and select Customize.

2. Click the Commands tab, and in the Categories list, select Go.

3. In the Commands list, select News, and drag it to the Go menu. When the menu list appears, point to where you want News to appear in the list and release the mouse button. Figure 4-9 shows the new Go menu choices. Click Close in the Customize dialog box.

Figure 4-9   The new Go menu.

4. To set up a newsgroup, click Go, and then click News.

> **Note**   If the News option is not available in the Customize dialog box, from Control Panel, Internet Options, and the Programs tab, choose Outlook Express to be the default newsreader.

Adding a Newsgroup

If an end user has Outlook Express installed, Outlook Express is most likely already configured as the default newsreader. To configure Outlook News to be the new default newsreader, follow these steps:

1. Open Outlook, click Go, and choose News.

2. Wait while the Outlook Newsreader opens, and click Yes to verify that Outlook should now be the default program used. If the user has currently joined newsgroups using Outlook Express, those newsgroups will be available once this is done.

If the user has not joined any newsgroups previously, you will be asked to help the user set up a newsgroup account. The procedure to join a newsgroup is the same in either Outlook or Outlook Express:

1. Click Tools, click Accounts, and in the Internet Accounts dialog box, click the News tab.

2. Click Add, and click News.

3. On the Internet Connection Wizard page, type the display name and click Next.

4. On the Internet News E-Mail Address page, type the e-mail address to be associated with this account, and click Next. (Consider masking the e-mail account name to protect the user from unsolicited junk e-mail.)

5. On the Internet News Server Name page, type the name of the News (NNTP) Server. This name must be obtained from the newsgroup host. The Microsoft news server name is msnews.microsoft.com. If the news server requires the user to log on, select the My News Server Requires Me To Log On check box. If this check box is selected, click Next and type in the user name and password.

6. Click Finish to close the wizard, and click Close in the Internet Accounts dialog box.

7. When prompted by Outlook to download newsgroups from the accounts just added, click Yes.

8. In the Newsgroup Subscriptions dialog box, locate the newsgroups to add and click Subscribe. Click OK to close the dialog box.

9. In the left pane, select an added newsgroup to connect.

Common Newsgroup Service Calls

Common service calls associated with newsgroups include blocking messages from a particular sender, blocking unwanted messages, and resolving problems with sending or receiving **posts**. Users might also need to cancel a subscription to a newsgroup or view newsgroups without subscribing at all.

Blocking Senders and Unwanted Messages

Users might decide that some posts or newsgroup participants are not desirable or useful and might ask you to block those senders or messages. Blocked messages go directly to the Delete folder and are not displayed. To block messages from a sender or a domain, follow these steps:

1. Open the newsreader, and from the list of messages in a newsgroup, open a message from the sender to block.

2. Click Message, and click Block Sender. Click OK to block all messages from that sender.

Resolving Send and Receive Errors

Send and receive errors can be caused in a variety of ways, including misspelled news server names, server **time-outs**, problems with passwords, and problems with ISP settings. Listed here are some common problems and solutions:

- **Time-out errors**   Newsgroup servers will time out and give an error message if it takes longer than allotted to download newsgroup messages. To solve this problem, click Tools, click Accounts, select the news server to change, and click Properties. On the Advanced tab, in the Server Timeouts area, move the slider to the right. Click OK, and click Close.

- **Can connect to ISP but cannot access newsgroups**   Failure to access a newsgroup when Internet connectivity is working is generally caused by incorrect advanced options settings. Click Tools, click Accounts, select the news server, and click Properties. On the Server, Connection, and Advanced tabs, check the settings and verify that they are correct. Keep an eye out for typographical errors. Make the appropriate changes, click OK, and click Close.

- **Cannot connect to news server**   The inability to connect to a news server is often related to the settings configured for the news server, including the user name, password, or news server name. Click Tools, click Accounts, click the news server name, and click Properties. Check the following:

    - On the Server tab, verify the New Account name and user information.

    - On the Advanced tab, verify that the server name is spelled correctly. If the server requires the end user to log on, verify the account name and password.

❑ On the Advanced tab, verify the News (NNTP) port number (this is generally 119), clear the This Server Requires A Secure Connection (SSL) check box if a secure connection is not necessary, and select or clear the Ignore News Sending Format And Post Using check box as desired.

Other common problems with newsgroups can be resolved using newsgroups, the Microsoft Knowledge Base, and similar resources.

Viewing Newsgroups Without Subscribing

A user can view newsgroup content in any of several ways without subscribing, including visiting the newsgroup's website, but the easiest way is through the Help options in Outlook. In the following example, you use the Help options available in Outlook to access the Outlook New Users newsgroup:

1. Open Microsoft Outlook, and in the upper right corner where it shows Type A Question For Help, type **newsgroups** and press ENTER. (You must be online.)

2. Scroll down the Search Results pane, and choose Get Answers From Other Users, as shown in Figure 4-10.

Figure 4-10   Visit a newsgroup without joining.

3. The Discussions In Outlook New Users newsgroup Web page opens. There you can browse messages, search for topics, read posts, post replies, and locate other newsgroups.

> **Note**   Newsgroups can be an effective way to help end users become more autonomous and find solutions to their own problems. If you have time during a service call, point users to this feature.

Unsubscribing to a Newsgroup

To unsubscribe to a newsgroup, open the newsreader and locate the newsgroup to unsubscribe from. Right-click the newsgroup, and choose Unsubscribe.

Practice: Configure Newsreader Settings

In this practice, you will configure a newsgroup in Outlook Express.

1. Log on to Windows XP.

2. On the Start menu, choose All Programs, and then choose Outlook Express. When asked whether you want to make Outlook Express your default mail client, click No.

> **Note**   If this is the first time you have run Outlook Express, you will be prompted to create a new e-mail address. If this happens, click Cancel to cancel the wizard, and then click Yes when it asks whether you are sure you want to cancel. You will then be shown the Outlook Express window.

3. From the Tools menu, select Accounts. In the Internet Accounts dialog box, click Add and select News.

4. In the Internet Connection Wizard, on the Your Name page, in the Display Name text box, type your name and then click Next.

5. On the Internet News E-Mail Address page, in the E-Mail Address text box, type your e-mail address. Click Next.

6. On the Internet News Server Name page, in the News (NNTP) Server text box, type **msnews.microsoft.com**, and click Next.

7. On the Congratulations page, click Finish.

8. In the Internet Accounts dialog box, click Close. In the Outlook Express message box, click Yes. After a few seconds of downloading newsgroups, you are shown the Newsgroup Subscriptions dialog box.

9. In the Newsgroup Subscriptions dialog box, on the All tab, scroll through the list of newsgroups and find the ones that interest you. When you find one, subscribe to it by selecting the newsgroup and then clicking Subscribe.

10. When you are finished subscribing to newsgroups, click OK.

11. In Outlook Express, in the Folders pane, find the server you just set up and select one of the newsgroups on it. Outlook Express downloads messages for that newsgroup and displays them in the right-hand pane.

Lesson Review

The following questions are intended to reinforce key information presented in this lesson. If you are unable to answer a question, review the lesson materials and try the question again. You can find answers to the questions in the "Questions and Answers" section at the end of this chapter.

1. Configuring a newsgroup in Outlook 2003 involves several steps, each of which is listed next. Place the steps in the correct order.

   A. Open the newsreader from the Go menu.

   B. Type the name of the news (NNTP) server.

   C. Subscribe to the downloaded newsgroups.

   D. Use the Customize dialog box to drag the News command to the Go menu on the Menu bar.

   E. Create a news account by clicking Tools, clicking Accounts, and on the News tab, clicking Add.

2. A user has asked you whether there is any way to prevent a particular person's posts from showing up in the newsreader since that person posts hundreds of advertisements each week. What can you tell the user?

   _____

   _____

Lesson Summary

■ To join a newsgroup and set Outlook as the default newsgroup reader, drag the News command to the Go menu, and use the News option to add or remove newsgroup accounts.

■ Common service calls associated with newsgroups include blocking messages from a particular sender, blocking unwanted messages, and resolving problems with sending or receiving posts.

Lesson 3: Maintaining Outlook

Maintaining Outlook is similar to maintaining Outlook Express; a user can empty the Deleted Items folder when he or she exits the program, use AutoArchive to manage the mailbox size by deleting old items or moving them to an archive file, and use Mailbox Cleanup to manage the size of the mailbox or delete files that are a certain age or size. Users might also want to configure junk e-mail settings. You will be called on to perform these tasks, but to reduce service calls to clients, make sure you teach your end users to use these tools regularly.

After this lesson, you will be able to

- Configure Outlook to empty deleted items on exit.
- Configure AutoArchive in Outlook.
- Perform mailbox cleanup tasks in Outlook.
- Configure Outlook's Junk E-mail feature.
- Block HTML content in Outlook.

Estimated lesson time: 25 minutes

Emptying the Deleted Items Folder on Exit

One way to keep Outlook maintained is to empty the items in the Deleted Items folder each time Outlook is closed. Emptying the Deleted Items folder when exiting keeps that folder clean, and this step might be necessary to keep a user's mailbox within specific file size limits, especially if the user's mailbox is stored on a network server.

Note   The rest of this chapter focuses on Outlook, but tasks done in Outlook Express are performed similarly, as demonstrated in earlier sections.

Deleting files on exit is an option in the Options dialog box, set as follows:

1. In Outlook, click Tools, and click Options.
2. In the Options dialog box, click the Other tab.
3. Select the Empty The Deleted Items Folder Upon Exiting check box.
4. Click OK to close the Options dialog box.

> **Note**   Do not select the Empty The Deleted Items Folder Upon Exiting check box unless you absolutely have to. Users will find that they access this folder often to review deleted messages.

AutoArchive

AutoArchive can be used to keep a mailbox manageable by archiving old items to a separate personal storage file and by deleting content that meets specific criteria for age. AutoArchive is on by default and runs in the background, clearing items that meet set expiration conditions. These expiration options apply to both e-mail and meeting items with content that is no longer valid after a certain date.

AutoArchive can be configured in a number of ways and can be set to perform (or not perform) the following tasks:

- Run automatically after a specific number of days.

- Prompt the user before it runs.

- Archive or delete old items after a specific number of months, weeks, or days.

- Delete expired items in e-mail folders.

- Show archive folders in the folder list.

- Move items to a specific place.

- Permanently delete old items.

- Set a **retention policy** if it is applied by a network administrator.

Because users often forget to manage and maintain their e-mails, AutoArchive should be configured to run using its defaults unless the user or corporate policy prevents it. AutoArchive can be accessed from the Options dialog box as follows:

1. Click Tools, click Options, and click the Other tab.

2. Click AutoArchive.

3. Make changes by selecting or clearing check boxes and using the arrows to set numeric configurations.

Mailbox Cleanup

When possible, inform users of Outlook's Mailbox Cleanup feature, which lets users easily manage the size of their mailboxes and improve the overall performance of Outlook. From the Mailbox Cleanup dialog box, users can do the following:

■ View the total size of the mailbox and the individual folders in it, including the Deleted Items folder.

■ Sort, delete, and archive items by date or size.

■ Find and delete unread e-mail (junk e-mail or spam), e-mail from a particular sender, e-mail that has an attachment, items in the Deleted Items folder, items sent to a particular person, and more.

■ View and delete items in the **Conflicts folder**.

To open and use the Mailbox Cleanup utility (as shown in Figure 4-11), follow these steps:

1. Click Tools, and click Mailbox Cleanup.

❑ To view the mailbox size, click View Mailbox Size. Click Close to return to the Mailbox Cleanup dialog box.

❑ To use AutoArchive, configure the settings for date and size using the arrows next to the Find Items Older Than and Find Items Larger Than areas, and click AutoArchive.

❑ To view the size of the Deleted Items folder, click View Deleted Items Size. Click Close to return to the Mailbox Cleanup dialog box.

❑ To empty the Deleted Items folder, click Empty. Click Yes to verify your choice.

2. To perform an advanced search for files, in the Mailbox Cleanup dialog box, set the criteria using the arrows next to the Find Items Older Than and Find Items Larger Than areas, and then click Find. The Advanced Find dialog box opens with three tabs: Messages, More Choices, and Advanced. You use these tabs to configure advanced search options, and you use the Edit menu to select and delete the items if desired.

Figure 4-11   The Mailbox Cleanup dialog box.

Each tab in the Advanced Find window offers multiple options for sorting the files that matched the original criteria in step 3 in the preceding example. For instance, to locate all unread e-mail and delete it (this is almost always junk e-mail), click the More Choices tab, select the Only Items That Are check box, and choose Unread from the drop-down list. Every item stored that has not been read that matches the criteria for age and size set earlier will appear. To delete these files, click Edit, then click Select All, and then press DELETE on the keyboard.

E-mail can also be sorted by who sent it, who it was sent to, whether or not it contains an attachment or is flagged, and whether it meets specific size requirements. E-mail can also be sorted based on the words that appear in the subject line or body. This is an excellent tool for getting rid of unwanted e-mail stored on the computer, e-mail regarding a specific project that has been completed, or e-mail from a group or specific person.

Exam Tip   Learn the options that are available to you in the Outlook Mailbox Cleanup feature. This is valuable information on the exam and in the real world.

Junk E-Mail Options

Outlook has a built-in Junk E-Mail feature that is available on the Actions menu. The Junk E-Mail Options dialog box is shown in Figure 4-12. Junk e-mail options can be set to move messages that appear to be unwanted to a special junk e-mail folder. As you can see in Figure 4-12, the Junk E-Mail Options dialog box has the following four tabs:

- **Options**   Use the options on this tab to configure the level of junk e-mail protection. The level can be configured for no protection or for low or high protection, or so that the recipient receives e-mail only from specified contacts. These settings can also be configured so that suspected junk e-mail is automatically deleted and bypasses the Junk E-Mail folder.

- **Safe Senders**   Use the options on this tab to configure a safe senders list. E-mail from addresses or domain names on this list will never be treated as junk e-mail. Also available is the Always Trust E-Mail From My Contacts check box.

- **Safe Recipients**   Use the options on this tab to configure a safe recipients list. E-mail sent to addresses or domain names on this list will never be treated as junk e-mail.

- **Blocked Senders**   Use the options on this tab to configure a blocked senders list. E-mail from addresses or domain names on this list will always be treated as junk e-mail.

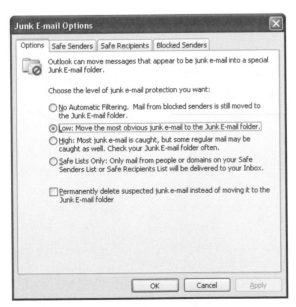

Figure 4-12   The Junk E-Mail Options dialog box.

As a DST, you will be asked to address issues involving junk e-mail. For clients who use Outlook, your first suggestion should be to configure junk e-mail options. (For Outlook Express users, configure rules and block senders.) Be sure you tell users to check their Junk E-Mail folder occasionally, though, because sometimes valid e-mail gets sent there.

To use and configure Outlook's default Junk E-Mail Options, follow these steps:

1. Click Actions, point to Junk E-Mail, and click Junk E-Mail Options.

2. On the Junk E-Mail Options tab, shown in Figure 4-12, choose the desired level of junk e-mail protection.

3. On the Safe Senders, Safe Recipients, and Blocked Senders tabs, click Add to add a particular sender or domain. Click OK.

> **Caution**   If junk e-mail levels are set to High, most junk e-mail will be caught, but some valid mail might be caught as well. Be careful when choosing this setting, and make sure that important contacts are configured as safe senders.

Users can also easily add senders to the safe senders or blocked lists as e-mail arrives. With the e-mail selected in Outlook, click Actions, point to Junk E-Mail, and click any of the following:

- Add Sender To Blocked Senders List

- Add Sender To Safe Senders List

- Add Sender's Domain (@example.com) To Safe Senders List

- Add Recipient To Safe Recipients List

- Mark As Not Junk (available only when the user is accessing e-mail from the Junk E-Mail folder)

These settings allow users to add blocked senders, safe senders, and safe recipients easily. Teach end users how to do this when possible.

Blocking HTML Content in Outlook

In addition to displaying messages in a plain text format, Outlook can also display messages using the same HTML format used for creating Web pages. Although using HTML format offers the advantages of using rich-text formatting options and including graphics and other types of content in a message, a potential downside of HTML messages is that they often include content that must be downloaded from an external server. This is particularly true of newsletters, form letters, and many types of junk e-mail messages.

In fact, HTML content is frequently used by senders of junk e-mail to include references to images that reside on their Web servers (sometimes messages that are only a single pixel in size). When the user opens such a message, many e-mail programs automatically download and display the images, verifying to the sender that you have an active e-mail address. By default, Outlook 2003 blocks external content from being automatically downloaded and displayed in HTML-formatted messages. To display such content, a user must right-click the message and specify that Outlook download and display the content.

> **Note**   With Windows XP Service Pack 2 installed, Outlook Express also has the ability not to automatically download external content. You can even configure Outlook Express to only display messages in plain text format. As a result, potentially unsafe attachments that are sent through e-mail and instant messages are isolated so that they cannot affect other parts of the system.

Practice: Configure Outlook Maintenance Settings

In this practice, you will configure Outlook 2003 so that the Deleted Items folder is emptied automatically on exit, set AutoArchive options, and compact Outlook data.

Exercise 1: Empty the Deleted Items Folder upon Exiting Outlook 2003

1. Log on to Windows XP.
2. On the Start menu, choose E-Mail. If Outlook 2003 is not configured as your default e-mail software, on the Start menu, point to All Programs and then to Microsoft Office, and select Microsoft Office Outlook 2003.
3. On the Tools menu, choose Options.
4. In the Options dialog box, on the Other tab, select the Empty The Deleted Items Folder Upon Exiting check box.

Exercise 2: Set AutoArchive Options

1. Log on to Windows XP.
2. On the Start menu, choose E-Mail. If Outlook 2003 is not configured as your default e-mail software, on the Start menu, point to All Programs and then to Microsoft Office, and select Microsoft Office Outlook 2003.
3. On the Tools menu, choose Options.
4. In the Options dialog box, on the Other tab, click AutoArchive.
5. In the AutoArchive dialog box, select the Run AutoArchive Every check box.

6. Clear the Prompt Before AutoArchive Runs check box. In the Default Folder Settings For Archiving section, in the Clean Out Items Older Than selection box, select the number of months you want to be the maximum age for items to stay in Outlook before being archived.

7. Click Apply These Settings To All Folders Now, and then click OK.

Exercise 3: Compact Outlook Data

1. Log on to Windows XP.

2. On the Start menu, choose E-Mail. If Outlook 2003 is not configured as your default e-mail software, on the Start menu, point to All Programs and then to Microsoft Office, and select Microsoft Office Outlook 2003.

3. On the Tools menu, choose Options.

4. In the Options dialog box, on the Mail Setup tab, click Data Files.

5. In the Outlook Data Files dialog box, click Settings.

6. In the Personal Folders dialog box, click Compact Now. Compacting time will vary with the size of the .pst file.

Note   Sometimes compacting .pst files can repair faults in the files.

7. In the Personal Folders dialog box, click OK.

8. In the Outlook Data Files dialog box, click Close.

9. In the Options dialog box, click OK.

Lesson Review

The following questions are intended to reinforce key information presented in this lesson. If you are unable to answer a question, review the lesson materials and try the question again. You can find answers to the questions in the "Questions and Answers" section at the end of this chapter.

1. A user reports that he received an error message from the company's e-mail server. The message stated that he has met his quota for space on the server and needs to delete some of the e-mail he has stored there. He informs you that he has deleted some unnecessary folders from Outlook, reduced the items in his Sent Items folder, and emptied the Deleted Items folder. He wants help configuring the computer so that he does not receive these messages in the future. Which of the following applications or utilities is the best choice for configuring his computer?

   A. AutoArchive

   B. Mailbox Cleanup

C. Junk E-Mail

D. Macros

2. A user reports that he set up AutoArchive in Outlook 2003 to permanently delete items that are two weeks old, no matter which folder they are in. However, the items are not being deleted after 14 days, but instead are being deleted every 21 days. What is the likely cause of this?

   A. A retention policy has been set by network administrators.

   B. The deleted items have been moved to the Junk E-Mail folder.

   C. The settings configured in Mailbox Cleanup conflict with the settings configured in AutoArchive. Mailbox Cleanup has priority when conflicts arise.

   D. AutoArchive has been disabled because there is less than 200 MB of free space on the computer hard disk.

Lesson Summary

- Configuring Outlook to empty deleted items when exiting is one way to keep the size of your Outlook file down. Be careful with this setting, though, as many users need to refer to deleted items occasionally.

- AutoArchive automatically moves items of a certain age to a separate personal storage file, helping keep the size of the Outlook data file down and keeping old messages out of a user's way.

- The Mailbox Cleanup feature in Outlook lets users find, sort, delete, and archive messages according to a number of criteria, such as item age, sender, folder, and so on.

- Outlook 2003 features robust Junk E-Mail features that move unwanted messages to a separate folder and keep them out of the way.

- By default, Outlook 2003 (and Outlook Express when Windows XP Service Pack 2 is installed) does not download external HTML content.

Lesson 4: Troubleshooting Outlook

Most problems that occur with Outlook have to do with incorrect user names, passwords, and e-mail addresses, and these issues result in problems with sending and receiving e-mail. Other problems occur when end users make their own changes to the application, which can cause problems with the interface or the ability to connect to the ISP or e-mail server. In this section, you learn how to resolve common problems such as these.

After this lesson, you will be able to

- Resolve problems resulting from an incorrect name or e-mail address.
- Resolve common interface problems.

Estimated lesson time: 10 minutes

Resolving an Incorrect Name or E-Mail Address

If any typographical errors were made during the creation of the user's e-mail account, if the user changed departments and needs his or her e-mail name or address altered, if the user wants replies to go to a different e-mail address than the one configured, or if the user has independently made changes to his or her e-mail settings, he or she might encounter problems in sending or receiving e-mail, or he or she might report that the name or organization is not correct on e-mails sent to others. Users who change positions, get promoted, earn degrees or certifications, or get married might want a new title (or name) in their e-mail as well. If a user reports errors or needs changes along these lines, make the changes from the E-Mail Accounts Wizard as follows:

1. Open Outlook, click Tools, and click E-Mail Accounts.

2. In the E-Mail Accounts Wizard, under E-Mail, click View Or Change Existing E-Mail Accounts. Click Next.

3. In the E-Mail Accounts dialog box, select the e-mail account to configure. Click Change.

4. Verify the values for User Information, Server Information, and Logon Information, and make changes as needed. Click Test Settings to verify that the information is correct.

5. Click More Settings, and in the Internet E-Mail Settings dialog box, view the tabs and make changes as needed. Click OK when finished. Click Next and Finish to close the E-Mail Accounts Wizard.

Almost all problems relating to typographical errors or changing a user's name or e-mail address can be resolved by using this utility.

Common Interface Problems

The Outlook interface can be changed to reflect the needs and preferences of any user. For the most part, changes made to the interface are achieved by using the View menu options, using the Go menu options, and by customizing the toolbars using the Customize dialog box. Although interface changes are generally easy to configure, when new users make changes on their own they sometimes encounter problems later in locating items they need. Table 4-2 details some items that a user might report as missing and the procedure for getting those particular components back. Figure 4-13 shows Outlook 2003 and the available panes and toolbars.

Table 4-2   Missing Interface Components

End-User Issue	Procedure for Resolution
Navigation pane is missing.	Click View, and check Navigation Pane.
Reading Pane is missing or in the wrong area of the interface.	Click View, point to Reading Pane, and click Right or Bottom.
E-mails are arranged in the wrong order.	Click View; point to Arrange By; and choose Date, Conversation, From, To, Folder, Size, Subject, Type, Flag, Attachments, E-Mail Account, Importance, Categories, or Custom.
Cannot preview e-mail messages in Inbox.	Click View, and click AutoPreview.
Missing Task pane, Standard toolbar, Advanced toolbar, or Web toolbar.	Right-click the Menu bar, and select the missing item.
Missing Status Bar.	Click View, and check Status Bar.
Cannot view items in the Navigation pane, or the Navigation pane has changed.	Click Go, and click the item to display in the Navigation pane.
Needed commands are missing from the toolbars and menus.	Right-click an empty area of the Menu bar, click Customize, and from the Commands tab, choose the items to add. Drag the item to the correct area of the toolbar or menu. Click the Options tab to reset menus and toolbars and perform other customizations.
Items in the Navigation pane are not needed.	Click Tools, click Options, and click the Other tab. Click Navigation Pane Options, and in the Navigation Pane Options dialog box, clear unwanted items.

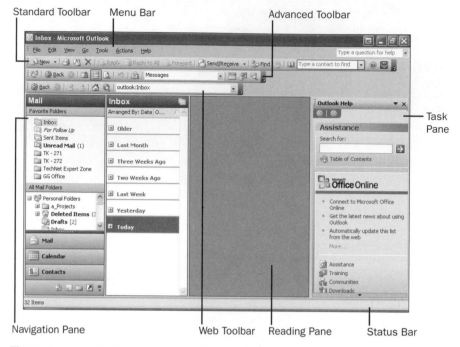

Figure 4-13   Default panes and toolbars in Outlook.

Many other settings are available for end users, all of which can be configured through the available menus and dialog boxes. Familiarize yourself with all aspects of both Outlook and Outlook Express.

Practice: Test Outlook 2003 Account Settings

In this practice, you will test account settings in Outlook 2003.

1. Log on to Windows XP.

2. Open Outlook, select the Tools menu, and select E-Mail Accounts.

3. In the E-Mail Accounts Wizard, under E-Mail, click View Or Change Existing E-Mail Accounts. Click Next.

4. In the E-Mail Accounts dialog box, select the e-mail account to configure. Click Change.

5. Verify the values for User Information, Server Information, and Logon Information, and make changes as needed.

6. Click Test Settings to verify that the information is correct.

7. Click More Settings, and in the Internet E-Mail Settings dialog box, view the tabs and make changes as needed. Click OK when finished. Click Next and Finish to close the E-Mail Accounts Wizard.

Lesson Review

The following questions are intended to reinforce key information presented in this lesson. If you are unable to answer a question, review the lesson materials and try the question again. You can find answers to the questions in the "Questions and Answers" section at the end of this chapter.

1. A user has recently set up an e-mail account in Outlook and is having trouble accessing his e-mail server. When he tries to send and receive in Outlook, he gets a dialog box that asks for his user name and password. No matter what he types in the box, it does not work. Why might Outlook be showing the user this dialog box? What can you do to help the user?

   _____

   _____

2. Match the interface problem on the left with the solution on the right.

1. Navigation pane is missing.	A. Click Go, and click the item to display in the Navigation pane.
2. Reading Pane is missing or in the wrong area of the interface.	B. Click View, and check Navigation Pane.
3. E-mails are arranged in the wrong order.	C. Right-click the Menu bar, and select the missing item.
4. Missing Task pane, Standard toolbar, Advanced toolbar, or Web toolbar.	D. Click Tools, click Options, and click the Other tab. Click Navigation Pane Options, and in the Navigation Pane Options dialog box, clear unwanted items.
5. Cannot view items in the Navigation pane, or the Navigation pane has changed.	E. Click View; point to Arrange By; and choose Date, Conversation, From, To, Folder, Size, Subject, Type, Flag, Attachments, E-Mail Account, Importance, Categories, or Custom.
6. Items in the Navigation pane are not needed.	F. Click View, point to Reading Pane, and click Right or Bottom.

Lesson Summary

- Errors made while entering user names and passwords lead to errors retrieving messages. To resolve such problems, always double-check server names, user names, and passwords against what has been entered. Use Outlook's automatic testing features to make sure account information is entered correctly.

- The Outlook interface can be changed to reflect the needs and preferences of any user. For the most part, changes made to the interface are achieved by using the View menu options, by using the Go menu options, and by customizing the toolbars by using the Customize dialog box.

Lesson 5: Resolving Common User Requests in Outlook

End users will eventually need help configuring other Outlook features in addition to setting up e-mail accounts, adding newsgroups, or troubleshooting connectivity.

After this lesson, you will be able to

- Configure Outlook to leave a copy of e-mail on a server.
- Configure common composition options.
- Set up an Internet Accounts file.

Estimated lesson time: 15 minutes

Leaving a Copy of E-Mail on the Server

When users travel, they have an account on their laptop so that they can access e-mail while on the road. Creating this account is similar to creating any e-mail account except that the users need to be able to dial in to (or otherwise connect to) the e-mail server at their workplace. Sometimes a user dials directly in to a company server; other times a user accesses the server through his or her ISP. (You will learn to create accounts such as these in Chapter 8, "Common Connectivity Problems.")

After the account is set up, you will need to configure Outlook to leave e-mail on the network server until the user returns to work to retrieve it and delete it permanently. If this is not set up properly, the user will have some e-mail messages on the laptop, some on the home computer, and some on the office computer. Keeping track of e-mail using this type of system is inefficient.

To configure a user's laptop so that Outlook will leave messages on the network server or ISP server until the user deletes them manually from his or her office computer, follow these steps:

1. Click Tools, click Options, and click the Mail Setup tab.

2. Click E-Mail Accounts, and on the E-Mail Accounts page, click View Or Change Existing E-Mail Accounts, and click Next.

3. On the E-Mail Accounts page, select the e-mail account to configure, and click Change.

4. On the Internet E-Mail Settings page, click More Settings.

5. In the Internet E-Mail Settings dialog box, click the Advanced tab, shown in Figure 4-14.

6. Select the Leave A Copy Of Messages On The Server check box, and if applicable select the Remove From Server After ___ Days or the Remove From Server When Deleted From Deleted Items check box.

7. Click OK, click Next, and click Finish.

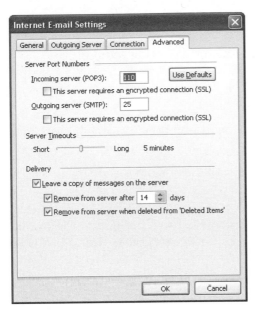

Figure 4-14   Leave a copy of messages on the server.

Depending on the choices made here, messages will remain on the server for a specified number of days or until they are manually deleted. This gives the user a method for keeping the e-mail account synchronized when multiple computers are used.

> **Exam Tip**   You will notice that particular attention has been paid in this chapter to configuring mail client software to leave a copy of messages on servers for users who check mail from more than one location. Remember how to configure this option in Outlook and Outlook Express.

Configuring Composition Options

Because most users use Outlook to send and receive e-mail on a daily basis, composition options will certainly be important to them. Several options are available, including formatting, spelling and grammatical editing, and creating signatures. End users might ask you to assist them in configuring these options.

All of the composition options that a user needs are located in the Options dialog box. (Click Tools, and then click Options.) On the Mail Format tab, a user can configure the following settings:

■ Compose messages in Hypertext Markup Language (HTML), rich text, or plain text.

■ Choose an editor (for example, Microsoft Office Word 2003).

- Choose stationery and fonts for new messages, when replying and forwarding, and when sending e-mail using plain text.

- Create signatures.

On the Spelling tab, the user can configure the following settings:

- Suggest replacements for misspelled words.

- Check spelling before sending an e-mail.

- Ignore words in uppercase, words with numbers, or original text in a reply or forward.

- Configure AutoCorrect options, and edit the custom dictionary.

- Choose an international dictionary.

Making these configuration changes is achieved by configuring the available drop-down lists, selecting or clearing options, or accessing other dialog boxes by clicking buttons.

The .iaf File

Outlook Express can be used to create an .iaf, or Internet Accounts file, to back up and store information about the mail folders and mail and news account settings for a single Outlook Express identity. Backing up this information makes it easy to restore, if necessary, following a computer crash or in the event a new computer is obtained or purchased. These .iaf files will not store subscribed newsgroup information, message rules, or blocked senders, and they will not retain information about custom toolbars either, but they offer a quick and easy way to back up and restore settings.

To export the settings to an .iaf file using Outlook Express, follow these steps:

1. In Outlook Express, click Tools, and click Accounts.

2. In the Internet Accounts dialog box, select an account and click Export.

3. In the Export Internet Account dialog box, browse to a location to save the file or accept the defaults. Name the file, and click Save.

4. In the Internet Accounts dialog box, click Close.

As necessary, use the same procedure (clicking Import instead of Export) to restore the file to the e-mail account.

Practice: Resolve Common Outlook User Requests

In this practice, you will disable the Send Immediately When Connected option in Outlook 2003, configure an e-mail account to leave a copy of messages on the server after downloading messages, enable automatic download of images in e-mail, and turn on the Outlook 2003 Junk E-Mail feature.

Exercise 1: Disable Send Immediately When Connected

1. Log on to Windows XP.

2. Open Outlook 2003.

3. On the Tools menu, choose Options.

4. In the Options dialog box, on the Mail Setup tab, clear the Send Immediately When Connected check box.

5. Click OK to return to Outlook.

Exercise 2: Enable Leave Messages On Server

1. Log on to Windows XP.

2. Open Outlook 2003.

3. On the Tools menu, choose Options.

4. On the Mail Setup tab, click E-Mail Accounts.

5. In the E-Mail Accounts Wizard, verify that View Or Change Existing E-Mail Accounts is selected, and then click Next.

6. On the E-Mail Accounts page, choose an account and click Change.

7. On the Internet E-Mail Settings (POP3) page, click More Settings.

8. In the Internet E-Mail Settings dialog box, on the Advanced tab, select the Leave A Copy Of Messages On The Server check box. Click OK.

9. In the E-Mail Accounts Wizard, on the Internet E-Mail Settings (POP3) page, click Next.

10. On the E-Mail Accounts page, click Finish.

Exercise 3: Enable Automatic Download of Images in E-Mails

1. Log on to Windows XP.

2. Open Outlook 2003.

3. On the Tools menu, choose Options.

4. On the Security tab, click Change Automatic Download Settings.

5. In the Automatic Picture Download Settings dialog box, clear the Don't Download Pictures Or Other Content Automatically In HTML E-Mail check box. Click OK.

6. In the Options dialog box, click OK.

Caution   Blocking pictures in e-mail messages can help protect privacy. Pictures often require Outlook to download content from an Internet server. The communication involved in downloading the content can verify your e-mail address and possibly make you the target of more junk e-mail. Be sure you explain this to clients before modifying this setting.

Exercise 4: Limit Junk E-Mail

1. Log on to Windows XP.

2. Open Outlook 2003.

3. On the Actions menu, choose Junk E-Mail, and then choose Junk E-Mail Options.

4. In the Junk E-Mail Options dialog box, select High: Most Junk E-Mail Is Caught, But Some Regular Mail May Be Caught As Well. Check Your Junk E-Mail Folder Often. Click OK.

Lesson Review

The following questions are intended to reinforce key information presented in this lesson. If you are unable to answer a question, review the lesson materials and try the question again. You can find answers to the questions in the "Questions and Answers" section at the end of this chapter.

1. A user reports that he configured specific fonts to use when composing a new message, when replying and forwarding messages, and when using stationery. However, each time he composes a message or replies or forwards one, the same

font is always used. It is the 12-point Courier New font that he configured for composing and reading plain text. When he closes the Fonts dialog box, he selects the Always Use My Fonts check box, but he still can only compose e-mail using 12-point Courier New. What is the cause of the problem?

   A. The fonts chosen for new mail, for replying, and for forwarding are not installed on the computer or are corrupt. Reinstall the fonts.

   B. The display settings on the computer are set to 800 x 600 pixels. Reconfigure the display settings to 1024 x 768.

   C. The mail format settings are configured to compose messages in plain text. Configure them to use HTML or rich text.

   D. The advanced settings for Internet Format (on the Mail Format tab of the Options dialog box) are set to encode attachments in UUENCODE format when a plain text message is sent.

2. A user wants to be able to check her e-mail from her home computer and from her notebook computer when she travels. She has a POP3 account with her ISP. How can you help her?

_____

_____

Lesson Summary

■ When users need to check e-mail from more than one computer, you can configure an e-mail account on a second computer to leave a copy of messages on a server after e-mail is checked.

■ End users often ask for help configuring composition options. Several options are available, including formatting, spelling and grammatical editing, and creating signatures.

■ Outlook Express can be used to create an .iaf, or Internet Accounts file, to back up and store information about the mail folders and mail and news account settings for a single Outlook Express identity.

Case Scenario Exercises

In the following scenarios, you must use what you have learned throughout the lessons in this chapter to answer questions based on a real-world scenario. Read each scenario, and answer the questions. If you have trouble, review the chapter and try again. You can find answers in the "Questions and Answers" section at the end of this chapter.

Scenario 4.1

A home user has purchased a new computer and plans to get rid of the old one. She has backed up her My Documents, My Pictures, and My Videos folders to three CDs. The only other thing the user wants to transfer to the new computer is her address book. She does not want to transfer her messages, e-mail account settings, or news account settings. What is the fastest way to move this data to the new computer? She uses Outlook Express.

  A. From the old computer, use Outlook Express to export the address book to a floppy disk, and then use that disk to import the address book into the new computer. Use the CDs already burned to transfer the folder data.

  B. Connect the two computers by using a null-modem cable, and use the Files And Settings Transfer Wizard to transfer the data.

  C. Connect the two computers by using a hub and Ethernet cables, and then drag and drop the folders between computers. At the new computer, import the address book by using the Import command.

  D. At the new computer, use Outlook Express to import the address book from the old computer. Use a null-modem cable to connect. Use the CDs already burned to transfer the folder data.

Scenario 4.2

A small business user in a graphics company reports that he recently set his junk e-mail option to High because he has been getting an incredible amount of spam lately. After asking a few questions, you discover that he joined three newsgroups last month and created his own company website, where he posted his e-mail address. He reports that although most junk e-mail is caught, he is getting complaints from his clients that he is not responding to their e-mails in a timely fashion. He wants to block the junk e-mail, but he also wants to receive the large attachments and pictures that Outlook thinks are junk e-mail. What should you advise this user to do? Although more than one answer is viable, choose the single best answer.

A. Unsubscribe from the newsgroups. As long as he is subscribed to them, he will continue to get junk e-mail. Remove his e-mail address from his website, and replace it with his phone number.

B. Add each client to the safe senders list in the Junk E-Mail Options dialog box.

C. Open the Junk E-Mail folder, and for each item, click Actions, point to Junk E-Mail, and select Add Sender To Blocked Senders List.

D. Open the Junk E-Mail folder, and for each item that is a valid e-mail, click Actions, point to Junk E-Mail, and select Add Sender To Safe Senders List.

Troubleshooting Lab

A newly created division of Consolidated Messenger requires e-mail access. This new department will be using Microsoft Office Outlook 2003 as its e-mail client. Furthermore, the users will be asked to configure Outlook 2003 themselves, according to your instructions. You need to create detailed instructions on how to configure Outlook 2003 as a POP3 client. You also need to include instructions on testing the account after it is created.

Using WordPad or Microsoft Word, create a set of instructions for new users of Outlook 2003 on setting up a POP3 e-mail account. You may assume that this is the first time these users have started Outlook 2003, so they will be using the Outlook 2003 Startup Wizard to create the account. Once the account setup is finished, instruct users how to test their account settings. Use the following parameters when creating your instructions:

■ POP3 server name: pop3.consolidatedmessenger.com.

■ SMTP server name: smtp.consolidatedmessenger.com.

■ User name: These are the same user names used to log on to the company network.

■ Password: E-mail passwords have been distributed to users.

■ E-mail address: *username@consolidatedmessenger.com*.

Chapter Summary

- POP3 and IMAP are protocols used by clients to receive e-mail from servers. SMTP is a protocol used by clients and servers to send e-mail.

- To create, test, and troubleshoot e-mail accounts in Outlook and Outlook Express, use the Internet Accounts dialog box. From there, you can add accounts, view properties, and make changes to existing accounts.

- Importing and exporting messages and address books provides a good method for backing up and restoring Outlook and Outlook Express, as well as a method for migrating from other e-mail software.

- To join a newsgroup and set Outlook as the default newsgroup reader, drag the News command to the Go menu, and use the News option to add or remove newsgroup accounts.

- Common service calls associated with newsgroups include blocking messages from a particular sender, blocking unwanted messages, and resolving problems with sending or receiving posts.

- Configuring Outlook to empty deleted items when exiting is one way to keep the size of your Outlook file down. Be careful with this setting, though, because many users need to refer to deleted items occasionally.

- AutoArchive automatically moves items of a certain age to a separate personal storage file, helping keep the size of the Outlook data file down and keeping old messages out of a user's way.

- The Mailbox Cleanup feature in Outlook lets users find, sort, delete, and archive messages according to a number of criteria, such as item age, sender, folder, and so on.

- Outlook 2003 features robust Junk E-Mail features that move unwanted messages to a separate folder and keep them out of the way.

- Errors made while entering user names and passwords lead to errors retrieving messages. To resolve such problems, always double-check server names, user names, and passwords against what has been entered. Use Outlook's automatic testing features to make sure account information is entered correctly.

- The Outlook interface can be changed to reflect the needs and preferences of any user. For the most part, changes made to the interface are achieved by using the View menu options, by using the Go menu options, and by customizing the toolbars by using the Customize dialog box.

- To resolve common end-user requests, learn techniques such as leaving a copy of the e-mail on a network server, exporting .iaf files, and setting composition options for spelling, grammar, and signatures.

Exam Highlights

Before taking the exam, review the key topics and terms that are presented in this chapter. You need to know this information.

Key Points

■ Outlook and Outlook Express can import messages and address book information from other installations of Outlook, Outlook Express, and Eudora. They can also import from text of comma-separated value files. Both programs can export to these formats, as well as to Microsoft Access and Microsoft Excel formats.

■ The Outlook Mailbox Cleanup feature lets users find, sort, delete, and archive messages according to a number of criteria, such as item age, sender, folder, and so on.

■ Remember how to configure mail client software to leave a copy of messages on servers for users who check mail from more than one location in both Outlook and Outlook Express.

Key Terms

HTTP e-mail account   An e-mail account that connects to an HTTP e-mail server, such as Hotmail. HTTP accounts can be added to Outlook 2003 or to Outlook Express and can download e-mail and synchronize mailbox folders.

protocol   A set of agreed-on rules for communicating among computers. Protocols are industry standards, and both the sending and receiving computer must agree on the protocols used for communication to take place.

time-out   An error caused by an e-mail or news post that takes longer than the allotted time to download. Time-out errors can be eliminated by increasing how much time Outlook is allotted to download messages from a mail server.

Questions and Answers

Lesson 1 Review

Page 4-22   **1.** A user has a POP3 e-mail account from an ISP, and he reports that he cannot send e-mail. He can receive e-mail. Which of the following is most likely the problem?

   A. The Mail Account name in the Internet E-Mail Settings dialog box (accessed by clicking More Settings in the E-Mail Accounts dialog box) has a typographical error.

   B. The SMTP server name is incorrectly configured in the user's e-mail settings.

   C. The ISP's POP3 mail server is down.

   D. The user has not typed in the correct password.

The correct answer is B. The SMTP mail server is responsible for sending e-mail. Answer A is incorrect because the name used in the Internet E-Mail Settings dialog box is a friendly name. A typographical error would not cause a connectivity problem. Answer C is incorrect because a POP3 server is used by a client to receive e-mail. Answer D is incorrect because ISPs use the same password to send and receive e-mail.

2. A client who has been using Outlook Express has recently installed Microsoft Office 2003. He reports that when he opened Outlook for the first time, he tried to create an e-mail account, but as the procedure progressed, he got confused and clicked Cancel in the remaining dialog boxes instead of working through them. He now reports that he can send and receive e-mail, but he cannot access his address book and he cannot locate his old mail messages. What should you tell the user to do?

   A. Uninstall and reinstall Outlook 2003. After the application has been reinstalled, tell him to call back, and you will walk him through the procedure.

   B. Delete the existing account using the E-Mail Accounts Wizard. Re-create the account using the same wizard, and follow the prompts for importing the address book and mail messages.

   C. Click Tools, and click Address Book. In the Address Book window, click File, and click Import And Export. Import the address book used for Outlook Express.

D. Open Outlook, and on the File menu, click Import And Export. Work through the Import And Export Wizard to import both mail messages and the address book.

The correct answer is D. The Import And Export Wizard can be used to import both mail messages and an address book. Answer A is incorrect because uninstalling and reinstalling is too drastic of an approach. Answer B is incorrect because there are no prompts in the E-Mail Accounts Wizard for importing mail messages and an address book. Answer C is incorrect because it is not a valid option.

3. There are several ways to export address books and e-mail messages. Match the user's requirements on the left with the best export option on the right.

1. The address book will be stored in a Word document.	A. Personal folder files
2. The address book will be stored as a database file.	B. Microsoft Excel
3. Messages will be stored as a backup of Outlook data and will not be used by any other program.	C. CSV (Windows)
4. The address book will be stored as an .xls file.	D. Microsoft Access

1-C. CSV (Windows) stores data so that it can be used by Word, PowerPoint, and third-party programs. 2-D. Microsoft Access is a database application. 3-A. Personal folder files are used only by Outlook for organizing and backing up Outlook data. 4-B. Microsoft Excel stores files with the .xls extension.

Lesson 2 Review

Page 4-30 **1.** Configuring a newsgroup in Outlook 2003 involves several steps, each of which is listed next. Place the steps in the correct order.

A. Open the newsreader from the Go menu.

B. Type the name of the news (NNTP) server.

C. Subscribe to the downloaded newsgroups.

D. Use the Customize dialog box to drag the News command to the Go menu on the Menu bar.

E. Create a news account by clicking Tools, clicking Accounts, and on the News tab, clicking Add.

The correct order is D, A, E, B, C.

2. A user has asked you whether there is any way to prevent a particular person's posts from showing up in the newsreader since that person posts hundreds of advertisements each week. What can you tell the user?

The Outlook newsreader and Outlook Express both feature a way to block particular senders. Once you do this, posts from that sender do not show up in the newsreader window.

Lesson 3 Review

Page 4-38   **1.** A user reports that he received an error message from the company's e-mail server. The message stated that he has met his quota for space on the server and needs to delete some of the e-mail he has stored there. He informs you that he has deleted some unnecessary folders from Outlook, reduced the items in his Sent Items folder, and emptied the Deleted Items folder. He wants help configuring the computer so that he does not receive these messages in the future. Which of the following applications or utilities is the best choice for configuring his computer?

    A. AutoArchive

    B. Mailbox Cleanup

    C. Junk E-Mail

    D. Macros

Answer A is correct because AutoArchive will move old items to an archive file on the computer and automatically delete those items that are a specific number of days old. Answer B is incorrect because Mailbox Cleanup is used to sort and delete files. Although AutoArchive can be started from inside Mailbox Cleanup, most of the options for it are not available. Answer C is incorrect because the Junk E-Mail utility works only with junk e-mail and does not automatically archive any e-mails or delete e-mail automatically. Answer D is incorrect because macros do not have anything to do with maintaining Outlook and folder size.

2. A user reports that he set up AutoArchive in Outlook 2003 to permanently delete items that are two weeks old, no matter which folder they are in. However, the items are not being deleted after 14 days but instead are being deleted every 21 days. What is the likely cause of this?

    A. A retention policy has been set by network administrators.

    B. The deleted items have been moved to the Junk E-Mail folder.

    C. The settings configured in Mailbox Cleanup conflict with the settings configured in AutoArchive. Mailbox Cleanup has priority when conflicts arise.

    D. AutoArchive has been disabled because there is less than 200 MB of free space on the computer hard disk.

Answer A is correct. Retention policies for e-mail archiving and deletion override AutoArchive settings. Answer B is incorrect because deleted items would not be placed in this folder. Answer C is incorrect because using AutoArchive settings in Mailbox Cleanup simply runs the AutoArchive component with its configured settings. Answer D is incorrect because AutoArchive does not become disabled because of disk space issues.

Lesson 4 Review

Page 4-43   **1.** A user has recently set up an e-mail account in Outlook and is having trouble accessing his e-mail server. When he tries to send and receive in Outlook, he gets a dialog box that asks for his user name and password. No matter what he types in the box, it does not work. Why might Outlook be showing the user this dialog box? What can you do to help the user?

Outlook is displaying this dialog box because it is having trouble authenticating the user's credentials with the e-mail server. Many times this happens when there is a networking problem. However, since the account has recently been set up, it is more likely that the user name or password was entered incorrectly during setup. You can test this by going to the E-Mail Accounts dialog box, selecting the account involved, and using the Test Settings feature.

2. Match the interface problem on the left with the solution on the right.

1. Navigation pane is missing.	A. Click Go, and click the item to display in the Navigation pane.
2. Reading Pane is missing or in the wrong area of the interface.	B. Click View, and check Navigation Pane.
3. E-mails are arranged in the wrong order.	C. Right-click the Menu bar, and select the missing item.
4. Missing Task pane, Standard toolbar, Advanced toolbar, or Web toolbar.	D. Click Tools, click Options, and click the Other tab. Click Navigation Pane Options, and in the Navigation Pane Options dialog box, clear unwanted items.
5. Cannot view items in the Navigation pane, or the Navigation pane has changed.	E. Click View; point to Arrange By; and choose Date, Conversation, From, To, Folder, Size, Subject, Type, Flag, Attachments, E-Mail Account, Importance, Categories, or Custom.
6. Items in the Navigation pane are not needed.	F. Click View, point to Reading Pane, and click Right or Bottom.

1-B, 2-F, 3-E, 4-C, 5-A, 6-D

Lesson 5 Review

Page 4-48   **1.** A user reports that he configured specific fonts to use when composing a new message, when replying and forwarding messages, and when using stationery. However, each time he composes a message or replies or forwards one, the same font is always used. It is the 12-point Courier New font that he configured for composing and reading plain text. When he closes the Fonts dialog box, he selects the Always Use My Fonts check box, but he still can only compose e-mail using 12-point Courier New. What is the cause of the problem?

A. The fonts chosen for new mail, for replying, and for forwarding are not installed on the computer or are corrupt. Reinstall the fonts.

B. The display settings on the computer are set to 800 x 600 pixels. Reconfigure the display settings to 1024 x 768.

C. The mail format settings are configured to compose messages in plain text. Configure them to use HTML or rich text.

D. The advanced settings for Internet Format (on the Mail Format tab of the Options dialog box) are set to encode attachments in UUENCODE format when a plain text message is sent.

Answer C is correct. If messages are composed in plain text, the plain text font will be applied. Answer A is incorrect because the font would not be listed if it were not available. Answer B is incorrect because the display settings do not have anything to do with the configured fonts. Answer D is incorrect because it applies only when a plain text message is selected.

2. A user wants to be able to check her e-mail from her home computer and from her notebook computer when she travels. She has a POP3 account with her ISP. How can you help her?

The best way to set her accounts up in this situation would be to configure her account on her home computer normally and then configure the account on the notebook computer to leave a copy of the messages on the server when it checks e-mail. This way, all messages eventually come to the home computer for permanent storage.

Case Scenario Exercises: Scenario 4.1

Page 4-50 A home user has purchased a new computer and plans to get rid of the old one. She has backed up her My Documents, My Pictures, and My Videos folders to three CDs. The only other thing the user wants to transfer to the new computer is her address book. She does not want to transfer her messages, e-mail account settings, or news account settings. What is the fastest way to move this data to the new computer? She uses Outlook Express.

A. From the old computer, use Outlook Express to export the address book to a floppy disk, and then use that disk to import the address book into the new computer. Use the CDs already burned to transfer the folder data.

B. Connect the two computers by using a null-modem cable, and use the Files And Settings Transfer Wizard to transfer the data.

C. Connect the two computers by using a hub and Ethernet cables, and then drag and drop the folders between computers. At the new computer, import the address book by using the Import command.

D. At the new computer, use Outlook Express to import the address book from the old computer. Use a null-modem cable to connect. Use the CDs already burned to transfer the folder data.

Answer A is correct because it is the fastest way to perform the data exchange. Answers B, C, and D are all incorrect because the user is replacing the old computer with the new one and has no intention of keeping the old one. Because of that, networking the computers using either Ethernet or a null-modem cable would take too much time and effort and would not be the best choice.

Case Scenario Exercises: Scenario 4.2

Page 4-50 A small business user in a graphics company reports that he recently set his junk e-mail option to High because he has been getting an incredible amount of spam lately. After asking a few questions, you discover that he joined three newsgroups last month and created his own company website, where he posted his e-mail address. He reports that although most junk e-mail is caught, he is getting complaints from his clients that he is not responding to their e-mails in a timely fashion. He wants to block the junk e-mail, but he also wants to receive the large attachments and pictures that Outlook thinks are junk e-mail. What should you advise this user to do? Although more than one answer is viable, choose the single best answer.

A. Unsubscribe from the newsgroups. As long as he is subscribed to them, he will continue to get junk e-mail. Remove his e-mail address from his website, and replace it with his phone number.

B. Add each client to the safe senders list in the Junk E-Mail Options dialog box.

C. Open the Junk E-Mail folder, and for each item, click Actions, point to Junk E-Mail, and select Add Sender To Blocked Senders List.

D. Open the Junk E-Mail folder, and for each item that is a valid e-mail, click Actions, point to Junk E-Mail, and select Add Sender To Safe Senders List.

Answer B is the best answer. E-mail addresses added to the safe senders list will never be mistaken for junk e-mail. Answer A is incorrect because the user should be able to access newsgroups and have his e-mail address on his website if he desires. Answer C is incorrect because this process would take too long and would be ineffective. Spammers change their addresses regularly. Answer D is incorrect because it would affect the user's e-mail only after the items had been sent to the Junk E-Mail folder.

5 Supporting Microsoft Internet Explorer

Exam Objectives in this Chapter:

- Configure and troubleshoot Microsoft Internet Explorer
- Resolve issues related to Internet Explorer support features
- Resolve issues related to customizing Internet Explorer

Why This Chapter Matters

The purpose of this chapter is to introduce Microsoft Internet Explorer and to explore common end-user requests. As a desktop support technician (DST), you will be asked to resolve a wide range of service calls regarding Internet Explorer, including personalizing the interface, changing the way that Web pages look on the monitor, and showing users how to access History files or search for related websites. You will also be called on to perform troubleshooting tasks. These calls generally have to do with the inability to view Web pages or problems with the speed at which Web pages are loaded, but the requests can also be about performing maintenance tasks, such as deleting temporary files or asking for advice on dealing with cookies.

Before You Begin

Before you begin this chapter, you should have basic familiarity with the Microsoft Windows XP interface. You should also have a working knowledge of Microsoft Internet Explorer and using the Web. Finally, you should have access to a computer running Windows XP and Microsoft Internet Explorer on which you can experiment with changing various settings.

Lesson 1: Personalizing Internet Explorer

As a DST, many of the requests that you will receive will have more to do with making something "look right" than actually performing an advanced troubleshooting task. In addition to making the interface pleasing to the eye, though, you will also be asked to make it more functional.

After this lesson, you will be able to

- Format colors, font styles, and font sizes on Web pages.
- Add language preferences so that websites, if content is available, can be viewed in another language.
- View data, including Web browsing history, related sites, search results, and folders.
- Set a home page.
- Personalize Microsoft Internet Explorer's title bar.

Estimated lesson time: 45 minutes

Configuring Accessibility

Users who have trouble viewing Web pages because of the colors, font size, or font type might ask you to configure Internet Explorer so that Web pages are easier to read and view. You can make these changes by using Internet Explorer menus and the Internet Options dialog box as detailed in the next two sections. However, these changes are not always applied when a user visits a website. For users to use these settings at all websites that they visit, you will need to tell them how to apply the changes by using the accessibility options and configuring Internet Explorer to use these settings to override existing Web page defaults.

In the following three sections, you will learn to change the text size, default colors, and fonts, and how to configure the new settings to override any existing and specific Web settings.

▶ **Changing Text Size**

If an end user asks you to change the default text size on a Web page, follow these steps:

1. Open Internet Explorer, point to View, and point to Text Size.

2. Select from the following choices: Largest, Larger, Medium, Smaller, and Smallest.

▶ **Changing Colors and Fonts**

If an end user asks you to change the default colors and fonts used when she visits Web pages, follow these steps:

1. Open Internet Explorer, and on the Tools menu, select Internet Options.

2. In the Internet Options dialog box, select the General tab, and select Colors.

3. In the Colors dialog box that opens, shown in Figure 5-1, follow these steps:

   a. Under Colors, clear the Use Windows Colors check box, and select the color box next to Text. Select a new color for the text, and click OK.

   b. Under Colors, select the color box next to Background. Select a new color for the background, and click OK.

   c. Under Links, select the color box next to Visited. Select a new color, and click OK.

   d. Under Links, select the color box next to Unvisited. Select a new color, and click OK.

   e. Under Links, select the Use Hover Color check box. Click the color box next to Hover. Select a color, and click OK.

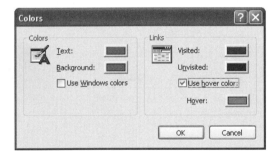

Figure 5-1   The Colors dialog box lets users customize the colors they see when visiting Web pages.

4. Click OK to close the Colors dialog box.

5. In the Internet Options dialog box, select Fonts.

6. In the Fonts dialog box, select a language script (if a change is needed), select a Web page font, and select a plaintext font. Internet Explorer uses Web page fonts to display formatted text on a Web page; it uses plaintext fonts to display unformatted text. Click OK.

7. Click OK to close the Internet Options dialog box.

Overriding Settings That Are Specified by Websites

The settings that are configured in Internet Explorer for text size, colors, and fonts might or might not be applied, depending on the website visited. Web pages that have no colors specified use the colors the user has configured, and the same is true of fonts. However, a Web page that specifies color or font overrides the choices that the user specifies.

▶ **Overriding Color and Font Preferences**

To ensure that the end user's preferences for colors and fonts are always applied, follow these steps:

1. Open Internet Explorer, and on the Tools menu, select Internet Options.

2. In the Internet Options dialog box, select the General tab, and select Accessibility.

3. In the Accessibility dialog box, under Formatting, select the appropriate check boxes:

   a. Ignore Colors Specified On Web Pages

   b. Ignore Font Styles Specified On Web Pages

   c. Ignore Font Sizes Specified On Web Pages

4. Click OK in the Accessibility dialog box, and click OK again in the Internet Options dialog box.

Exam Tip   If a user complains that a Web page does not look the way it should, be sure you check whether a custom appearance is set and whether that custom appearance is configured to override the styles on Web pages.

Toolbar Button Icon Size

While on the phone or at an end user's desk resolving an accessibility option call, ask the user whether she would like to customize the size of the toolbar button icons while you are there. If a user has asked you to make the Web text larger, she might also appreciate having larger toolbar icons, too. If the user has asked you to make Web page text smaller, she might also appreciate smaller toolbar icons.

▶ **Customizing Toolbar Buttons**

If the user wants to customize the toolbar button icons, walk him or her through the following procedure:

1. Open Internet Explorer, and right-click any toolbar button or icon. On the shortcut menu, choose Customize.

2. In the Customize Toolbar dialog box, in the Icon Options drop-down list, choose Large Icons or Small Icons based on the user's preference.

3. In the Text Options drop-down list, choose Show Text Labels, Selective Text On Right, or No Text Labels to finish the customization. Because the changes are applied immediately, the user can decide what she wants before committing by closing the dialog box. Once an appropriate choice has been made, click Close.

Using the Profile Assistant

The Profile Assistant is another option available to Internet Explorer users. The Profile Assistant stores personal information, which can then be sent automatically to a website when that information is requested. The Profile Assistant saves the information in a secure location on the client's computer and prompts the user to send the information if the website supports this technology. The user can accept or deny this service each time she encounters it. This saves time for the user because she does not have to enter the same information each time she visits a new website, and it allows her to determine when and for what sites the Profile Assistant is used. As a DST, you might get requests from users who would like an easier way to enter personal information than by keying it in manually each time.

▶ **Configuring the Profile Assistant**

To configure the Profile Assistant, open Internet Explorer, and follow these steps:

1. From the Tools menu, select Internet Options.

2. On the Content tab, under Personal Information, select My Profile. Note that the first time you open a profile, you are asked to create an entry in your address book (or choose an existing entry) to represent the profile.

3. In the Properties dialog box for the user, configure as much information as desired by accessing the following tabs: Name, Home, Business, Personal, Other, **NetMeeting**, and Digital IDs. (Digital IDs will be detailed later in this chapter.)

4. Click OK to close the Properties dialog box when you have finished; click OK in the Internet Options dialog box to close it.

Configuring Languages

Internet Explorer can display Web pages in many different languages, and if users' Web surfing takes them to sites that are written in another language, Internet Explorer can update the computer with the character sets needed to view those sites. If you have multilingual end users and clients, you might be asked to configure Internet Explorer to work with these languages.

▶ **Changing Language Settings**

To specify another language for Web page content, follow these steps:

1. Open Internet Explorer, and from the Tools menu, select Internet Options.

2. On the General tab, select Languages.

3. In the Language Preference dialog box, select Add.

4. In the Add Language dialog box, select the language to add, as shown in Figure 5-2, and click OK.

Figure 5-2 Users can add almost any language to Internet Explorer.

5. Arrange the languages in order of priority by selecting them and using the Move Up or Move Down button. If a website offers multiple languages, content will appear in the language that has the highest priority. Click OK in the Language Preference dialog box.

6. Click OK to close the Internet Options dialog box.

> **Note** Most Web pages contain information that tells Internet Explorer which language and character set to use. However, not all pages contain that information. When this is the case, Internet Explorer can usually determine the character set to use if Auto-Select is turned on. In Internet Explorer, click View, point to Encoding, and make sure Auto-Select is selected. If it isn't, select it. Notice that you can also select a specific encoding from the list.

Resolving Common Interface Requests

End users often have requests that deal with locating information while using Internet Explorer and customizing Internet Explorer's interface. Users might need to locate a website that they visited last week; they might be searching for information that is related to information they have previously found; they might need to be able to view search options, their Favorites, the Media bar, History, or their hard disk folders while they browse the Internet; or, they might ask you to configure a home page or troubleshoot when they cannot set one themselves. You will learn how to resolve all of these requests in this section.

Viewing History

Users sometimes call to ask how they can access a site that they have previously visited. Users might add that they have forgotten the site name and **Uniform Resource Locator (URL)** but require the information they found earlier on the site. You will be required to help them locate the site again.

The History files can help you locate previously viewed websites that have been visited over the last three weeks, and the sites can be viewed in various ways:

- By date
- By site
- By most visited
- By order visited today

▶ **Locating a Previously Visited Site**

To assist a user in locating a previously viewed site, follow these steps:

1. Open History by either choosing the History button on the Standard toolbar or accessing it from the View menu. From the View menu, point to Explorer Bar, and select History.

2. On the Explorer bar, select View to see the History categories. Sort the files by choosing By Date, By Site, By Most Visited, or By Order Visited Today. Figure 5-3 shows the categories on the Explorer bar viewed by date.

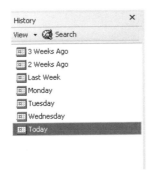

Figure 5-3   The Explorer bar with History sorted by date offers customized searching.

3. Select any category to expand it, and choose any site in the list to return to the site.

> **Note**   Viewing the History sites by name organizes the site alphabetically. This can be useful if the user remembers a company name. Often a company's name is the same as its website name.

Viewing Related Sites

The Related button is an available Standard toolbar button that can be an extremely helpful tool for users who need to access related information quickly. Clicking the Related icon opens the Explorer bar and offers a list of other Internet sites that contain information that is similar to what the user is currently viewing. Figure 5-4 shows an example. In this figure, the user is viewing the Windows XP Expert Zone, and the related information on the Explorer bar shows websites that offer similar information.

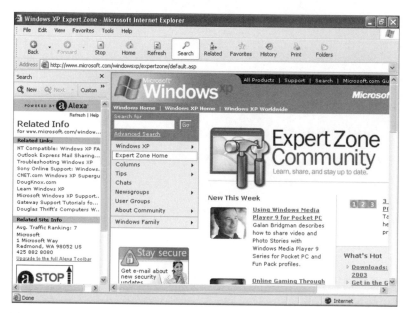

Figure 5-4   Locate related information using the Related button.

By default, Internet Explorer does not include the Related button on the toolbar, so the first step is to put it there. The following procedure also works for adding or removing other icons.

▶ **Using the Related Button**

To assist a user in using the Related button, follow these steps:

1. Open Internet Explorer, and right-click any Standard toolbar button. Select Customize.

2. In the Customize Toolbar dialog box, in the left pane under Available Toolbar Buttons, locate Related.

3. Select Related, and then select Add, and the Related button appears in the right pane under Current Toolbar Buttons.

4. Use the Move Up or Move Down button to place the new button anywhere on the toolbar. Click Close when finished.

Now, any time users need to locate information that is similar to what they are viewing, they need only to click the Related button. The Explorer bar will open automatically.

Viewing and Customizing the Explorer Bar

The Explorer bar was introduced briefly in the preceding section, but there are other Explorer bar options. To access these options, from the View menu, point to Explorer Bar, and select from the following:

- **Search**   The Search Explorer bar can help an end user find a Web page, a person's address, a business, or a map; or look up a word, find a picture, or look through previous searches. You can also use the Search Explorer bar to search websites by keywords, as with any other **search engine**. MSN Search performs these searches.

- **Favorites**   The Favorites Explorer bar shows all of the end user's favorites in the Explorer bar. This allows the user easy access to all of his or her favorite websites.

- **Media**   The Media Explorer bar opens WindowsMedia.com, where music videos, movie previews, radio stations, and news can be accessed quickly.

- **History**   The History Explorer bar leaves the History folders open and available at all times. Using the History bar, a user can access previously viewed websites easily.

- **Folders**   The Folders Explorer bar shows the folders on the user's hard disk. This makes accessing those folders as easy as clicking them. When a user opens a folder, the folder's contents appear in the right pane of Internet Explorer. Using the Back button returns the user to the previously viewed folder or Web page.

> **Note**   Users can close the Explorer bar by clicking the X in the upper right corner of the bar or by clearing it on the View, Explorer Bar menu.

Finally, although it is not technically an Explorer bar, selecting Tip Of The Day from the Explorer Bar menu opens a third pane at the bottom of the Web page; Internet Explorer will display tips in this pane. This might be a good choice for a new user, and you can suggest it when troubleshooting his or her Internet Explorer configuration either on the phone or at the user's desk.

Setting a Corporate Home Page

Another common request of end users is to configure a home page that opens each time the user opens Internet Explorer. This home page can be the company's website home page, a search engine, or a small business owner's own website, among others.

▶ **Configuring a Home Page**

To configure a home page, follow these steps:

1. Use Internet Explorer to browse to the website to set as the home page.

2. From the Tools menu, select Internet Options.

3. In the Internet Options dialog box, select the General tab.

4. In the Home Page area, type an address or select Use Current to make the current page the home page.

Note   If a user complains that he cannot change his home page, chances are that it is against company policy. The home page is probably set, and rules are in place for changing it in the company's **Group Policy**.

Personalizing the Title Bar

If a home user or a computer administrator wants to customize the Title bar of Internet Explorer with a browser title or custom logo, or if he or she wants to make customizations to the Standard toolbar, such as changing the toolbar background or adding buttons, you will need to know how to create and modify Group Policy settings. Administrators of a single computer or administrators in a workgroup can configure Group Policy. Group Policy settings configured on a single computer running Microsoft Windows XP Professional affect everyone who logs on to that computer. (In a domain, network administrators configure Group Policy, and these changes affect everyone who logs on to the domain.)

▶ **Creating a Customized Toolbar**

To use Group Policy to change how the Internet Explorer interface looks by creating a customized title bar, or to further customize it for a small business owner or home user, follow these steps:

1. From the Start menu, select Run.

2. In the Run dialog box, type **gpedit.msc**. The gpedit.msc command opens the Group Policy console. Click OK.

3. In the Group Policy console, expand User Configuration (if necessary), expand Windows Settings, and expand Internet Explorer Maintenance. The left pane of the Group Policy console is shown in Figure 5-5.

Figure 5-5 The Group Policy console's left pane offers various customizable options.

4. In the left pane, select Browser User Interface, and in the right pane, double-click Browser Title.

5. In the Browser Title dialog box, select the Customize Title Bars check box, and then type in the user's name, company name, or other customization. The new Internet Explorer Title bar will read "Microsoft Internet Explorer Provided By" followed by what you type. Click OK.

6. In the right pane of the Group Policy console, double-click Custom Logo.

7. In the Custom Logo dialog box, select the Customize The Static Logo Bitmaps or Customize The Animated Bitmaps check box. (You can configure either or both.) Click Browse to locate the image. In the Browse dialog box, locate the image and click Open. Click OK in the Custom Logo box to apply it.

8. Open Internet Explorer, and view the changes. If satisfied, close the Group Policy console.

You can make many other changes to Internet Explorer by using the Group Policy console. You might have noticed that the Browser User Interface node also includes an option called Browser Toolbar Customizations, which allows the user to customize and even add toolbar buttons. In addition, you can make the following customizations under Internet Explorer Maintenance to customize URLs (refer to Figure 5-5):

■ In the left pane, select URLs, and in the right pane, choose Important URLs. Here you can customize the home page URL, the Search bar URL, and the online support page URL. The online support page is created by the company and then made available to users.

- In the left pane, click URLs, and in the right pane, choose Favorites And Links. Here, you can customize the Favorites folder and the Links bar by adding links to sites related to the company or the service the company offers. For instance, you can add Favorites folders for Help And Support or Corporate Online Help pages.

> **Note** For information about how to configure Automatic Updates by using Group Policy, refer to Microsoft Knowledge Base article 328010. This KB article also contains a white paper on software update services.

Configuring Content Advisor

Another customizable option a user might ask about is Content Advisor. Content Advisor allows a user to control the Internet content that can be viewed on a single computer. The Content Advisor dialog box, shown in Figure 5-6, allows an administrator to configure which websites and content can and cannot be viewed based on the user's preferences and the guidelines of the Internet Content Rating Association (ICRA). ICRA's goal is to protect children from potentially harmful content while still preserving free speech on the Internet. Rating categories include Language, Nudity, Sex, and Violence. Content Advisor also allows the user to specify customized and approved or disallowed sites.

Figure 5-6 Content Advisor can be used to limit the Web content that can be viewed.

▶ **Configuring and Using Content Advisor**

Content Advisor is accessed and configured by using Internet Explorer's Internet Options dialog box:

1. Open Internet Explorer, select Internet Options, and from the Internet Options dialog box, select the Content tab.

2. From the Content Advisor section, select Enable or Settings.

3. From the Ratings tab, select a category. Move the slider to the left for more restrictive settings; move the slider to the right for less restrictive settings. As you move the slider, read the descriptions of the rating levels in the Descriptions area. Repeat this step for all four categories: Language, Nudity, Sex, and Violence.

4. To add a site to the Approved Sites list or to disallow access to any website, select the Approved Sites tab and enter the name of the website in the Allow This website area. Choose Always to make the page always viewable, or Never to make sure it cannot be viewed.

5. From the General tab under User Options, if desired, select Users Can See Sites That Have No Rating or Supervisor Can Type A Password To Allow Users To View Restricted Content, or both. If desired, select Create Password or Change Password and configure an administrator password. Click OK to close this dialog box.

6. To configure advanced settings such as using a specific ratings bureau or importing or installing rules, select the Advanced tab and make the appropriate changes. Click OK to close Content Advisor.

7. Click OK to close the Internet Options dialog box.

Practice: Personalize Internet Explorer

In this practice, you will set a home page, configure accessibility options, choose languages for Internet Explorer, view History, configure Internet Explorer to start with a blank home page, and configure a favorite site for offline use.

Exercise 1: Setting a Home Page

1. Log on to Windows XP.

2. On the Start menu, select Internet Explorer.

3. On the Standard toolbar, click the Stop button (a red X).

4. In Internet Explorer, on the Tools menu, select Internet Options.

5. In the Internet Options dialog box, on the General tab, in the Home Page section, in the Address text box, type **http://support.microsoft.com** and click OK.

Exercise 2: Configuring Accessibility

1. Log on to Windows XP.

2. On the Start menu, select Internet Explorer.

3. In Internet Explorer, in the Address text box, type **http://www.microsoft.com**.

4. On the View menu, select Text Size and then select Largest.

5. In Internet Explorer, on the Tools menu, select Internet Options.

6. In the Internet Options dialog box, click Accessibility. In the Accessibility dialog box, in the Formatting section, select the Ignore Font Sizes Specified On Web Pages check box, and click OK.

7. Click Colors.

8. In the Colors dialog box, click the Unvisited color swatch.

9. In the Color selector box, in the Basic Colors section, select a bright color swatch without blue in it, such as hot pink. Click OK.

10. In the Colors dialog box, click OK.

11. In the Internet Options dialog box, on the General tab, click Accessibility.

12. In the Accessibility dialog box, in the Formatting section, select the Ignore Colors Specified On Web Pages check box. Click OK.

13. In the Internet Options dialog box, click OK.

Exercise 3: Choosing Languages

1. Log on to Windows XP.

2. On the Start menu, select Internet Explorer.

3. In Internet Explorer, on the Tools menu, select Internet Options.

4. In the Internet Options dialog box, click Languages.

5. In the Languages Preference dialog box, click Add.

6. In the Add Language dialog box, select a language, and click OK.

7. In the Language Preference dialog box, click Cancel. (If you wanted to change the language preference, you would click OK.)

8. In the Internet Options dialog box, click OK.

Exercise 4: Viewing History

1. Log on to Windows XP.

2. On the Start menu, select Internet Explorer.

3. In Internet Explorer, to create a browsing history, browse to about 10 separate pages within the support.microsoft.com Web space.

4. On the Standard toolbar, click the History button (a clock with an arrow curving counterclockwise).

5. On the History toolbar, in the View drop-down list, select By Order Visited Today.

Exercise 5: Starting Internet Explorer with a Blank Home Page

1. Log on to Windows XP.

2. On the Start menu, select Run. In the Run dialog box, in the Open text box, type **iexplore - nohome** and press ENTER.

3. In Internet Explorer, on the Tools menu, select Internet Options.

4. In Internet Explorer, on the Standard toolbar, click the Home button.

5. On the Tools menu, select Internet Options.

6. In the Internet Options dialog box, on the General tab, in the Home Page section, click Use Blank. Click OK.

Lesson Review

The following questions are intended to reinforce key information presented in this lesson. If you are unable to answer a question, review the lesson materials and try the question again. You can find answers to the questions in the "Questions and Answers" section at the end of this chapter.

1. A user reports that he has changed his text size to Largest, but when he visits sites, sometimes the text on the sites is large and sometimes it is not. He reports this happens occasionally with colors and font styles, too. What does the user need to do to make sure these settings are always used, no matter what website he visits?

   A. Use the Internet Options dialog box in Internet Explorer, and from the General tab, select Accessibility, and make the appropriate changes in the Accessibility dialog box.

   B. Open Control Panel, open Accessibility Options, and on the Display tab, select the Override Web Settings check box.

   C. Use the Internet Options dialog box in Internet Explorer, select the General tab, choose Advanced, and in the Accessibility choices, select the Override Web Settings check box.

   D. Use the Internet Options dialog box in Internet Explorer, select the General tab, choose Accessibility, and in the Accessibility dialog box, select the Format Documents Using My Style Sheet check box.

2. A small business owner wants to personalize the Internet Explorer title bar on the computer that visitors access when they come into her store. She also wants to configure a default home page that users cannot change. Which of the following commands is used on the Run line to open the appropriate application for configuring these computerwide settings?

   A. msconfig.exe

   B. sigverif.exe

   C. cmd.exe

   D. gpedit.msc

3. A home user wants you to configure his Windows XP computer so that his 12-year-old son cannot access websites that contain offensive language, nudity, sexual references, or violence that involves fighting or killing. He would like to be able to override those settings, if ever necessary, by using an administrator password. The user wants to spend the least amount of money possible. What should you tell the user to do?

   A. Tell the user to purchase and install inexpensive third-party parental control software. Teach the user how to configure it.

   B. Configure Content Advisor, included with Windows XP.

   C. Create a separate account for the son, and purchase and install parental control software. Apply the software only to the son's account.

   D. Configure digital certificates, included with Windows XP, and accept digital certificates only from reputable sites.

   E. Configure the Profile Assistant to limit what sites the son has access to.

Lesson Summary

■ To personalize Internet Explorer, users can change the text size, colors, fonts, and font styles shown on Web pages, and they can customize the toolbars.

■ To configure languages so that websites can be viewed in a user's native language, change the language option in the Internet Options dialog box of Internet Explorer.

■ To secure and personalize a Web user's experience, Content Advisor, Digital Certificates, and the Profile Assistant can be configured.

Lesson 2: Maintaining Internet Explorer

Maintaining Internet Explorer is an important task, but many end users either do not take the time to maintain it or do not know what should be done or how often. As a DST, you will be called on to help end users resolve problems that stem from this lack of maintenance.

After this lesson, you will be able to

- Identify problems resulting from temporary file storage.
- Remove temporary files manually by using Internet Explorer or Disk Cleanup.
- Explain the use of cookies.
- Configure cookie use and privacy settings in Internet Explorer.

Estimated lesson time: 30 minutes

Controlling Temporary Files

Temporary Internet files are automatically saved to hard disk to speed up the display of frequently visited Web pages. Internet Explorer saves the files in the Temporary Internet Files folder, which can contain **cookies**, graphics, Web pages, and **JavaScript** files, among other things. Because Internet Explorer can open files saved to the computer faster than it can obtain and open files from the Internet, maintaining the files in this folder is quite important to successful, fast Web browsing.

However, problems occur when the Temporary Internet Pages **cache** is full. Resolving these problems is as simple as deleting the files in the Temporary Internet Files folder. Unfortunately, recognizing problems caused by a full Temporary Internet Files folder can be difficult. Here are some common warning signs of a full Temporary Internet Files folder:

- An end user reports he cannot use the Save Picture As command to save a graphics file to his hard disk as a .jpeg or .gif, but the file can be saved as a .bmp file. The file name might also appear as Untitled.
- An end user reports problems viewing History files by date, or no data appears.
- An end user reports that when he selects Source on the View menu to view the source for a Web page, the source code does not appear as expected.
- An end user reports that when he visits the Windows Update Product Catalog website, he receives the message Cannot Display Page. (This happens because the user has an earlier version of the site control in his or her browser cache and the cache is full.)
- An end user reports that he gets unrecoverable errors (faults) when using Internet Explorer.

Although these problems can occur for other reasons, deleting the files in the Temporary Internet Files folder often solves the problem. In the next few sections, you learn several ways to manage and delete temporary Internet files.

Using Disk Cleanup

Disk Cleanup is a maintenance tool that is included with Windows XP. You can use Disk Cleanup to resolve problems, but you can also teach your end users to use it to maintain their computers on their own. Disk Cleanup deletes files in the **Downloaded Program Files** folder, the Temporary Internet Files folder, the **Temporary Files** folder, the Recycle Bin, and more. Deleting these files regularly helps keep the computer running smoothly.

▶ **Deleting Files With Disk Cleanup**

To use Disk Cleanup, follow these steps:

1. From the Start menu, point to All Programs, point to Accessories, point to System Tools, and select Disk Cleanup.

2. In the Select Drive dialog box, select the drive to clean up from the Drives drop-down list, and click OK.

3. In the Disk Cleanup dialog box, shown in Figure 5-7, select the folders and the items to clean up. You can read a description of what is in each folder by clicking it once.

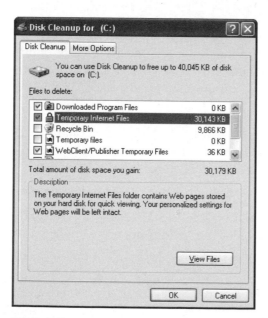

Figure 5-7   Disk Cleanup can be used to delete unnecessary files.

4. To view any of the files, click View Files.

5. Click OK to start the cleaning process. Click Yes to verify that you want to perform these actions.

> **Note**   Urge your end users to use Disk Cleanup at least once a month.

Real World   **Reclaiming Wasted Space**

Disk Cleanup can help free up disk space by deleting common temporary files found in various locations across your hard drive. However, the space reclaimed using Disk Cleanup is usually not very much by today's standards. A crowded disk can slow the responsiveness of Windows and running applications, including Internet Explorer. Here are some other ways you can help users free up disk space:

- Remove unused applications. Use Add Or Remove Programs in Control Panel to see all the applications installed on the system. Scan for any applications that users do not need anymore. (Always check with the user before removing applications, of course.) There may even be applications the user does not know about.

- Archive old or large documents. If the user has a CD or DVD writer, consider archiving older documents to disk to free up disk space. If there are especially large documents (such as videos), consider moving those to disk as well.

- Teach users to use the tools described in Chapter 3 to perform routine maintenance on their hard disks. These tools include Check Disk and Defragmenter.

- Use Disk Compression to compress documents so that they take up less space.

Manually Deleting Files

There is another way to delete temporary Internet files besides using Disk Cleanup: you can manually delete the files yourself from the Temporary Internet Files folder. This folder is located in the %SystemDrive%\Documents And Settings*username*\Local Settings\Temporary Internet Files folder. You will have to have Show Hidden Files And Folders selected on the View tab of the Folder Options dialog box if you want to browse to this folder.

A quick way to delete all temporary Internet files is to choose Internet Options from the Tools menu of Internet Explorer and then select Delete Files on the General tab of the Internet Options dialog box. If you do not want to delete all of the files in the folder, you can access the folder from within Internet Explorer (and you do not have to have the option to view hidden files turned on).

▶ **Deleting Files Manually**

To access the Temporary Internet Files folder and to manually delete the files in it, follow these steps:

1. Open Internet Explorer, and from the Tools menu, select Internet Options.

2. In the Internet Options dialog box, on the General tab in the Temporary Internet Files area, select Settings.

3. In the Settings dialog box, shown in Figure 5-8, select View Files.

4. Select the file that you want to delete (or press CTRL+A to select all files), and choose Delete from the File menu. You can also press the DEL key on the keyboard.

5. Click Yes to verify that you want to delete these files. Close the Temporary Internet Files window.

6. Click OK to close the Settings dialog box, and click OK again to close the Internet Options dialog box.

Figure 5-8   The Settings dialog box allows a user to work with temporary Internet files manually.

Note   You can also view ActiveX and Java controls that have been downloaded and installed on the computer by clicking View Objects in the Settings dialog box. These files can also be deleted.

Deleting Files on Exit

If you have a user who has recurring problems with a full Temporary Internet Files folder, if a user does not want to have temporary Internet files saved to his or her computer, or if company policy requires that no temporary files be saved to any users' hard disks, you can configure temporary Internet files to be deleted each time the user closes Internet Explorer.

▶ **Deleting Files When Exiting**

To configure Internet Explorer to delete the files in the Temporary Internet Files folder each time the user closes Internet Explorer, follow these steps:

1. Open Internet Explorer, and from the Tools menu, select Internet Options.

2. On the Advanced tab, scroll down to the Security section.

3. Select the Empty Temporary Internet Files Folder When Browser Is Closed check box. Click OK.

Each time the user closes Internet Explorer, the temporary files will be automatically deleted.

Exam Tip   Make sure you understand how to delete temporary Internet files by using Disk Cleanup and from within Internet Explorer. Experiment with the various settings that govern temporary files to make sure you understand their use.

Configuring Temporary Internet File Settings

As shown in Figure 5-8, you can configure any of several settings for temporary Internet files, including how often Internet Explorer checks a Web page for newer versions, how much disk space should be set aside to hold temporary files, and where the Temporary Internet Files folder is stored. It is important to understand what each of these settings offers because end users will often have specific needs that will require you to make changes to these default settings.

There are four settings for how often Internet Explorer should look for newer versions of stored pages, and these options are detailed in Table 5-1. Reasons for changing the settings are also outlined.

Table 5-1   How Often Should Internet Explorer Check for Newer Versions of Web Pages?

Setting	When It Should Be Selected	What the End Result Will Be
Every Visit To The Page	Choose this option when you always need a newer version of the page, such as a stock page, weather alert page, or news page.	Selecting this option slows down browsing for pages already viewed because a new page must be retrieved from the Internet each time the page is visited. Retrieving pages from the Internet takes much longer than retrieving them from the Temporary Internet Files folder on the hard disk.
Every Time You Start Internet Explorer	Choose this option when you need to see the latest version of the page when you first open Internet Explorer each day (or each session). This might be necessary for corporate users who have to check for daily changes to the company's website.	Selecting this option increases browsing speed throughout a session but is slower than the following two options.
Automatically	Choose this default option when you want Internet Explorer to look for newer versions of pages automatically. This is generally the best option for home users and most company personnel.	Selecting this option configures Internet Explorer to check for new versions of pages viewed in a previous session. Internet Explorer determines over time how often you view the page and makes allowances for how often the site should be checked for new content.
Never	Choose this option if you do not want Internet Explorer ever to check for newer versions of previously viewed pages. This setting is appropriate for users who access sites that rarely change or if users are charged for bandwidth. Instruct users to click the Refresh button to check for changes at any time.	Selecting this option speeds up browsing because all previously viewed pages are cached, and the information for those pages is retrieved from the hard disk each time the site is accessed.

In the Settings dialog box, you can also configure how much hard disk space is allotted to the Temporary Internet Files folder. Because temporary Internet files make surfing previously viewed pages faster, you should configure an ample amount of space. If a user complains that browsing is slower than she thinks it should be or slower than it used to be, or if you have already seen the warning signs or dealt with a full Temporary Internet Files folder, consider allotting more space for the folder. If the end user is low on disk space, you should reduce the amount of space that is reserved for temporary Internet files.

Finally, if it is necessary for backup, or if you want to store the Temporary Files folder on another drive or partition, you can move the folder by selecting Move Folder. In the Browse For Folder dialog box, browse to the new folder and click OK.

Configuring Cookie Use in Internet Explorer

Cookies are small text files that are placed on a computer by some websites that the user visits. The website reads these text files the next time the user visits the site, letting the site keep track of a user's preferences. This way, the Web browsing experience is personalized because sites remember details such as a logon name, which operating system is used, which version of Microsoft Windows Media Player is running, and what a user prefers to view while visiting. A website might also know what has been previously purchased, and it can guess what a user will want to see on the next visit.

> **Note**   Cookies can also store personally identifiable information such as a name, an e-mail address, a telephone number, or even a person's marital status. However, websites gain this information only by asking for it outright. Make sure your end users know that cookies cannot obtain any personally identifiable information from them unless they specifically provide it.

Although most cookies are legitimate, some are not. Unsatisfactory cookies are those that are used to provide personally identifiable information for a secondary purpose, such as selling your e-mail address to third-party vendors or sharing your name and address with other companies. Because there are unsatisfactory cookies, it is important to understand the different types of cookies, how to delete cookies, and how to change privacy settings to prevent various types of cookies from being saved to the computer. Your company might require changes to be made to the default settings for cookies, too, so you need to know how to make changes if asked.

Types of Cookies

There are several types of cookies:

- **Persistent**   These cookies remain on a computer even when Internet Explorer is closed, the user has disconnected from the Internet, or the computer has been turned off. Persistent cookies store information such as logon name, password, e-mail address, color schemes, purchasing history, and other preferences, so that when you revisit a site, this information is available and can be applied.

- **Temporary**   These cookies are stored on a computer only during a single browsing session and are deleted when Internet Explorer is closed. Websites use temporary cookies to determine the client browser, language, and screen resolution that the user is using. This allows a user to move back and forth among the Web pages at the site without losing previously entered information. If you disable temporary cookies, a user will not be able to access a site that requires them.

- **First-party**   These cookies are sent to a computer from the website being viewed. They might be persistent or temporary and are generally harmless.

- **Third-party**   These cookies are sent to a computer from a website that is not currently being viewed. They generally come from advertisers on the website that is being viewed, and these cookies track Web page use for advertising and marketing purposes. Third-party cookies might be persistent or temporary, and most are blocked by default by using the Medium privacy setting.

- **Session**   A session cookie is a temporary cookie that is deleted from a computer when Internet Explorer is closed.

Internet Explorer offers companies and end users several options for working with cookies, and the cookies stored on a computer can be deleted easily. Users have complete control over which types of cookies are stored, and users can even be prompted before a cookie is placed on the computer.

▶   **Deleting Cookies**

Because cookies can store user names, passwords, and other personally identifiable information, deleting cookies is necessary when a computer is transferred to another user at a company or sold. For security reasons, you might also be asked to delete cookies occasionally.

To delete the cookies on any computer running Windows XP, follow these steps:

1. Open Internet Explorer, and from the Tools menu, select Internet Options.

2. On the General tab, select Delete Cookies.

3. In the Delete Cookies dialog box, click OK to verify that you want to delete the cookies in the Temporary Internet Files folder. Click OK to close the Internet Options dialog box.

> **Note**   When you delete cookies from a computer, no user names, member names, passwords, ID numbers, or similar information is retained. When a user revisits a site that requires this information, he will have to reenter this information.

Configuring Privacy Settings

The privacy settings of Internet Explorer allow users and companies to personalize what types of cookies can be saved to the computer and under what circumstances. You can configure Internet Explorer to prompt a user every time a cookie is to be placed on the computer, to handle cookies differently for different websites, to allow some cookies and block others, or to block all cookies. These settings apply to websites in the Internet zone only; Local Intranet, Trusted Sites, and Restricted Sites zones all have their own configuration.

▶ **Changing Default Privacy Settings**

When asked by an end user or a manager or required by company policy to change the default privacy settings for cookie handling, follow these steps:

1. Open Internet Explorer, and from the Tools menu, select Internet Options.

2. Select the Privacy tab. If the Default button is unavailable, no advanced cookie-handling settings have been configured. If the Default button is available, advanced settings have already been configured. To view the default settings, click Default if it is available. Figure 5-9 shows the default settings.

Figure 5-9   Default privacy settings can be changed from the Privacy tab of the Internet Options dialog box.

3. Move the slider to select one of the following (from least secure to most secure):

   ❑ **Accept All Cookies**   All cookies are saved, and websites can read the cookies they created.

   ❑ **Low**   Only third-party cookies that do not have a compact privacy policy or that use personally identifiable information without a user's implicit consent are restricted.

   ❑ **Medium**   The same as the low setting, but also restricts first-party cookies that use personally identifiable information without a user's implicit consent.

   ❑ **Medium-High**   The same as the medium setting but also restricts third-party cookies that collect personally identifiable information without a user's explicit consent.

❏ **High**   Blocks all cookies that do not have a compact privacy policy and all cookies that use personally identifiable information without a user's explicit consent.

❏ **Block All Cookies**   Blocks all cookies, and existing cookies on the computer cannot be read by the websites that created them.

Exam Tip   Memorize the different types of cookies, and understand their use. Also memorize which types of cookies are blocked at each privacy setting. Privacy settings are important on the exam and in the real world.

4. Click OK to close the Internet Options dialog box and apply the changes, or select Advanced on the Privacy tab to override any particular privacy setting's defaults. If Advanced is selected, continue to step 5.

5. In the Advanced Privacy Settings dialog box, select the Override Automatic Cookie Handling check box. From the First-Party Cookies choices, select Accept, Block, or Prompt as desired; and from the Third-Party Cookies area, select Accept, Block, or Prompt as desired. To always allow session cookies, select the Always Allow Session Cookies check box. (See Figure 5-10.) Click OK, and click OK again in the Internet Options dialog box to apply the changes.

Figure 5-10   The Advanced Privacy Settings dialog box can be used to tweak privacy settings.

Some websites require cookies, so blocking all cookies can cause a user to have problems viewing a site; the site might fail to function properly. In addition, changing cookie settings can also affect how cookies already stored on the computer act when they are needed. Be alert when making changes to the default; you can create more problems than you are solving, if not careful.

Practice: Maintain Internet Explorer

In this practice, you will delete temporary Internet files manually, configure Internet Explorer to delete temporary Internet files automatically, delete cookies, and change the cached pages update setting.

Exercise 1: Delete Temporary Internet Files Manually

1. Log on to Windows XP using an account with Administrator privileges.
2. On the Start menu, select Internet Explorer.
3. In Internet Explorer, on the Tools menu, select Internet Options.
4. In the Internet Options dialog box, on the General tab, in the Temporary Internet Files section, click Settings.
5. In the Settings dialog box, click View Files.
6. In the Temporary Internet Files folder, on the Edit menu, select Select All. Press the DELETE key.
7. In the Warning message box, click Yes. Close the Temporary Internet Files folder. In the Settings dialog box, click OK.

Exercise 2: Configure Internet Explorer to Delete Temporary Internet Files Automatically on Exit

1. Log on to Windows XP.
2. Start Internet Explorer.
3. On the Tools menu, select Internet Options.
4. In the Internet Options dialog box, on the Advanced tab, in the Settings list, in the Security section, select the Empty Temporary Internet Files Folder When Browser Is Closed check box.

Exercise 3: Delete Cookies

1. Log on to Windows XP.
2. Start Internet Explorer.
3. On the Tools menu, select Internet Options.
4. In the Internet Options dialog box, on the General tab, in the Temporary Internet Files section, click Delete Cookies.
5. In the Delete Cookies message box, click OK.

Exercise 4: Change the Cached Pages Update Settings

1. Log on to Windows XP.

2. Start Internet Explorer.

3. On the Tools menu, select Internet Options.

4. In the Internet Options dialog box, on the General tab, in the Temporary Internet Files section, click Settings.

5. In the Settings dialog box, under Check For Newer Versions Of Stored Pages, select Every Visit To The Page. Click OK. In the Internet Options dialog box, click OK.

Lesson Review

The following questions are intended to reinforce key information presented in this lesson. If you are unable to answer a question, review the lesson materials and try the question again. You can find answers to the questions in the "Questions and Answers" section at the end of this chapter.

1. Which of the following are indications of a full Temporary Internet Files folder? (Choose all that apply.)

    A. When using the Save As command, pictures can be saved only as bitmaps and cannot be saved as .jpeg or .gif files.

    B. No History files appear in the History folder.

    C. Page faults appear.

    D. Access to frequently accessed Web pages is slow.

2. Match the type of cookie on the left with its description on the right.

1. Persistent	A. These cookies are sent to a computer from the website being viewed. They can be persistent or temporary and are generally harmless.
2. Temporary	B. These cookies are sent to a computer from a website not currently being viewed. They generally come from advertisers on the website being viewed for the purpose of tracking Web page use for advertising and marketing purposes. They can be persistent or temporary, and most of these cookies are blocked by default, using the Medium privacy setting.
3. First-party	C. These cookies are stored on a computer during only a single browsing session and are deleted when Internet Explorer is closed. They are used by websites to determine the client browser, the language, and the screen resolution that are used, and they allow a user to move back and forth among the Web pages at the site without losing previously entered information. If these cookies are disabled, a user will not be able to access a site that requires them.

4. Third-party	D. A temporary cookie that is deleted from a computer when Internet Explorer is closed.
5. Session	E. These cookies remain on a computer even when Internet Explorer is closed, the user has disconnected from the Internet, or the computer has been turned off. These cookies store information such as logon name, password, e-mail address, color schemes, purchasing history, and other preferences, so that when a site is revisited, this information is available and can be applied.

3. Company policy requires that all cookies saved to a user's computer must have a compact privacy policy that conforms to Platform for Privacy Preferences (P3P) standards. No cookies shall be saved if they do not conform. Which of the following default privacy settings can be used? (Select all that apply.)

   A. Accept All Cookies

   B. Low

   C. Medium

   D. Medium-High

   E. High

   F. Block All Cookies

Lesson Summary

- Problems occur when the Temporary Internet Pages cache is full. You can delete these files manually or by using the Disk Cleanup tool that comes with Windows XP.

- Cookies are small text files placed on a computer by some websites that the user visits, normally to track user preferences.

- Types of cookies include persistent, temporary, first-party, third-party, and session.

- You can review and delete cookies from within Internet Explorer from the General tab of the Internet Options dialog box.

Lesson 3: Troubleshooting Internet Explorer

DSTs are often called on to troubleshoot problems with Internet Explorer, and these service calls are generally one of three types. They are end-user requests to make Internet Explorer work faster and smarter, look better, have more functionality, or resolve simple interface issues; corporate requests to configure security zones (which usually results in additional security zone service calls); and requests to resolve problems that have to do with the inability to view Web pages properly. This section covers all of these topics.

After this lesson, you will be able to

- Identify and resolve common user requests involving Internet Explorer.
- Configure and troubleshoot Internet Explorer security zones.
- Resolve problems viewing Web pages.

Estimated lesson time: 45 minutes

Resolving Common User Requests

End users will have various requests that involve how Internet Explorer looks and acts, and they will ask you to resolve problems with the interface. You can resolve many of these problems by customizing the Standard toolbar, changing what is selected in the View menu, or personalizing the Advanced settings in the Internet Options dialog box.

Note   This section assumes that Internet Explorer is connected to the Internet properly. Chapter 8, "Common Connectivity Problems," focuses on connectivity problems.

Missing Toolbar, Links Bar, or Status Bar

A common complaint from end users is that an Internet Explorer toolbar is missing or that the toolbar they used to have is not available anymore. The toolbars that can be configured include the Standard toolbar, the Address bar, and the Links bar. Users might also complain that they cannot see the information at the bottom of the screen that shows the security zone they are in, denoting a missing Status bar. You can add and remove these toolbars by using the View menu, and you can customize the placement of the Standard toolbar, Address bar, and Links bar by dragging and dropping.

To show or hide any of the toolbars, follow these steps:

1. Open Internet Explorer, and from the View menu, point to Toolbars.

2. The Toolbars list contains Standard Buttons, Address Bar, Links, Lock The Toolbars, and Customize Selection. Toolbars marked with a check are showing; toolbars without a check are not.

3. To select or clear a toolbar, select it from the list. Figure 5-11 shows an example of all three toolbars. In this example, the Links bar is incorporated into the Address bar.

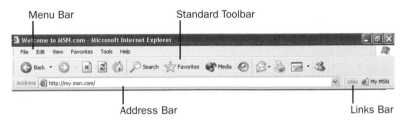

Figure 5-11   The toolbars can be customized to suit any user's needs.

To customize the placement of the Standard toolbar, Address bar, or Links bar, follow these steps:

1. In Internet Explorer, make sure the toolbars are unlocked by going to the View menu, pointing to Toolbars, and ensuring that Lock The Toolbars does not have a check next to it. If it does, choose the command to toggle it off.

2. Position the pointer at the far left of the toolbar you want to move.

3. Click and hold the mouse button; the pointer will change to a four-headed arrow.

4. Drag the toolbar to a new position to combine it with an existing toolbar or to move its position on the screen.

5. Position the pointer on the light dotted lines that separate combined toolbars until the pointer becomes a two-headed arrow. Drag to resize the toolbar.

> **Note**   The Standard toolbar, Address bar, and Link bar must remain at the top of the Internet Explorer window. They cannot be moved to the left, right, or bottom of the screen (as the Taskbar can).

Locked Toolbar

If a user complains that the toolbar is locked and cannot be moved, click View, point to Toolbars, and clear Lock The Toolbars.

Personalizing the Favorites Menu

When users call to report that they cannot access all of their favorites or that they have saved favorites but they are not listed in the Favorites list, it is most likely because the Personalized Favorites Menu option is enabled in the Advanced options of Internet Explorer. Personalized menus keep the Favorites list clean by hiding links that are not used very often. The list shows only those links that are accessed frequently. Tell the users that they can access the less frequently accessed links by clicking the down arrow at the end of the Favorites list.

▶   **Enabling Personalized Favorites Menus**

If the user asks you to change this behavior or if the user wants you to enable personalized favorites, follow these steps:

1. Open Internet Explorer, and from the Tools menu, select Internet Options.

2. From the Advanced tab, scroll down to the Browsing section, and select or clear the Enable Personalized Favorites Menu check box. Click OK.

> **Note**   Applying the change to personalized favorites might require you to close and restart Internet Explorer.

Importing and Exporting Internet Favorites

If you use Internet Explorer on multiple computers, you can easily share favorite items among computers by exporting them on one computer and then importing them on another. Exporting favorites is also a good way to back them up, share them with a friend, or even create a single Web page with links to all your favorites.

▶   **Exporting Internet Favorites**

To export Internet Favorites to an .htm file, follow these steps:

1. On the File menu of Internet Explorer, select Import And Export.

2. On the Welcome page of the Import/Export Wizard, click Next.

3. Select the Export Favorites option, and click Next.

4. You can specify the primary Favorites folder or any particular subfolder for your export. When you select a folder for export, all subfolders in that folder will also be exported. Select the folder you want to export, and click Next.

5. Click Browse, select a location and name for the export file, and click Save. Click Next, and then click Finish.

6. Internet Explorer informs you that the export is successful. Click OK.

The exported file is saved as a Web page. Double-click it to open it in Internet Explorer, and you will see a list of all your favorites, complete with hyperlinks. You can transfer this file to another computer and import it, back it up to a safe place, or even use it as a Web page.

▶ **Importing Internet Favorites**

To import Internet Favorites from an .htm file, follow these steps:

1. On the File menu of Internet Explorer, select Import And Export.

2. On the Welcome page of the Import/Export Wizard, click Next.

3. Select the Import Favorites option, and click Next.

4. Click Browse, locate and select the .htm file you want to import, and then click Save.

5. Click Next, and then select a folder in which the imported favorites will be placed. Click Next, and then click Finish.

6. After Internet Explorer informs you that the import is successful, click OK.

Using AutoComplete

AutoComplete is a feature that helps end users work, browse, and purchase items on the Internet faster than they could normally by automatically listing possible matches for Web addresses, forms, and user names and passwords on forms. Although this can be a good feature for a computer administrator who does not share a computer, for the average home user or the owner of a small home-based business, it is not a good idea under all circumstances.

You should not use AutoComplete when the computer is located in a nonsecure environment, such as a break room, lunchroom, or kiosk, or when two or more people share a computer and a computer account. In addition, when a computer is transferred to a new user or sold to another person, the AutoComplete form and password information should be cleared.

▶ **Enabling or Disabling AutoComplete**

As a DST, you will be asked to enable or disable AutoComplete (depending on the circumstance), enable or disable Internet Explorer's ability to save passwords, and clear the AutoComplete history. To do these, follow these steps:

1. Open Internet Explorer, and from the Tools menu, select Internet Options.

2. On the Content tab, and in the Personal Information area, select AutoComplete.

3. To enable or disable AutoComplete, in the AutoComplete Settings dialog box, select or clear Use AutoComplete for the Web Addresses, Forms, and User Names And Passwords On Forms check boxes.

4. To clear the AutoComplete history for forms, select Clear Forms.

5. To clear the AutoComplete history for passwords, select Clear Passwords.

6. To remove the ability of Internet Explorer to save any passwords in the future, clear the Prompt Me To Save Passwords check box.

7. Click OK to close the AutoComplete Settings dialog box, and click OK to close the Internet Options dialog box.

Exam Tip   Do not confuse AutoComplete with Inline AutoComplete. Inline AutoComplete completes entries in the Address bar of Internet Explorer as you type, based on entries you have used before, and offers a list of choices under the Address bar or other links that start the same way. AutoComplete offers choices under the Address window as well, but does not complete the entry in the Address bar as you type.

Using Inline AutoComplete

Inline AutoComplete completes entries in the Address bar as you type, based on entries you have used before, and offers a list of choices under the Address bar for other links that start the same way.

► **Enabling Inline AutoComplete**

You can enable Inline AutoComplete, using the Advanced options of Internet Explorer, by following these steps:

1. Open Internet Explorer, and from the Tools menu, select Internet Options.

2. From the Advanced tab, scroll down to the end of the Browsing section.

3. Select the Use Inline AutoComplete check box. Click OK.

Using Default Search Actions

Users can perform searches in a number of ways, including using the Search Explorer bar, using a Web browser or search engine, or typing their requests in the Address bar. If a user's choice is to search for information using the Address bar, the results of that search can be shown in several ways. In addition, searching from the Address bar can be disabled. Here are the Advanced choices for searching from the Address bar:

- Display results, and go to the most likely site.

- Do not search from the Address bar.

- Just display the results in the main window.

- Just go to the most likely site.

▶ **Changing Default Actions**

The default is to go to the most likely site, but you can change that default, as follows:

1. Open Internet Explorer, and from the Tools menu, select Internet Options.

2. Click the Advanced tab, and scroll down to Search From The Address Bar.

3. In the When Searching list, select the appropriate choice. Click OK.

Changing the HTML Editor

Some end users' jobs require them to view the source code on a Web page, and they need a Hypertext Markup Language (HTML) editor program to use with Internet Explorer to view and edit that source code. By default, Internet Explorer uses Notepad. However, if a user wants to use Microsoft FrontPage or another HTML editor, you need to change this default.

▶ **Changing the Default Editor**

To change the default HTML editor in Internet Explorer, follow these steps:

1. Open Internet Explorer, and from the Tools menu, select Internet Options.

2. Select the Programs tab.

3. In the HTML Editor drop-down list, choose the appropriate program. Click OK.

Script Errors

Users might report that script error notifications appear on their monitors while surfing websites, and they might also complain that they are continually asked whether they want to debug those errors. You might also have users with the opposite problem; a developer or technician might need to see these errors when testing a new website. Whatever the case, script options exist in the Advanced options of Internet Explorer, and they can be easily enabled or disabled.

▶ **Enabling and Disabling Script Debugging**

To enable or disable script debugging, or if a user should be notified of all script errors, follow these steps:

1. Open Internet Explorer, and from the Tools menu, select Internet Options.

2. From the Advanced tab, in the Browsing section, select or clear the following check boxes and then click OK: Disable Script Debugging and Display A Notification About Every Script Error.

3. Click OK to close the Internet Options dialog box.

Download Complete Notification

By default, Internet Explorer notifies users when a download is complete by leaving the download dialog box open and sometimes playing a sound. It is possible, though, that a user has turned the notification off (there is a check box on the download dialog box that makes this an easy thing to do) and now would like to turn the feature back on.

▶ **Enabling Download Notification**

To enable download-complete notification, follow these steps:

1. Open Internet Explorer, and from the Tools menu, select Internet Options.

2. From the Advanced tab, and in the Browsing section, select the Notify When Downloads Complete check box.

3. Click OK to close the Internet Options dialog box.

As you learned in this section, you can resolve many problems by using the View menu or the Internet Options dialog box. The Content tab, Programs tab, and Advanced tab of the Internet Options dialog box allow you to change the program defaults and personalize Internet Explorer. The View menu enables personalization of the toolbars. Many user requests can be handled by making changes here.

Troubleshooting Security Zones

There are four security zones in Internet Explorer: Internet, Local Intranet, Trusted Sites, and Restricted Sites. The Internet zone contains all websites. Local Intranet, Trusted Sites, and Restricted Sites zones do not include any sites by default and thus must have websites manually placed in them. Each of the four zones has default security settings (Low, Medium-Low, Medium, and High) that determine the type of content that can be downloaded and run (such as **ActiveX controls**) and what users are able to do (such as install desktop items). For any zone, you can change the security level and modify the security defaults.

You will be asked to resolve problems that have to do with zone configurations; these will mainly be issues regarding the inability to view or access something or to comply with company security directives. To resolve these types of calls, you will need an understanding of the default settings for each zone. Table 5-2 details the four zones and their default settings for ActiveX controls and installation of desktop items. There are other settings for each zone, but these are the items you will commonly need to modify. (Default settings can be changed.)

Exam Tip   Make sure you understand and are familiar with all of the security zone settings.

Table 5-2 Security Zones and Default Settings

Security Zone	Default Security Levels
High (default for the Restricted Sites zone)	**Disable** Download unsigned ActiveX controls; initialize and script ActiveX controls not marked as safe. **Disable** Run ActiveX controls and plug-ins; script ActiveX controls marked safe for scripting. **Disable** Download signed ActiveX controls; install desktop items.
Medium (default for the Internet zone)	**Disable** Download unsigned ActiveX controls; initialize and script ActiveX controls not marked as safe. **Enable** Run ActiveX controls and plug-ins; script ActiveX controls marked safe for scripting. **Prompt** Download signed ActiveX controls; install desktop items.
Medium-Low (default for the Local Intranet zone)	**Disable** Download unsigned ActiveX controls; initialize and script ActiveX controls not marked as safe. **Enable** Run ActiveX controls and plug-ins; script ActiveX controls marked safe for scripting. **Prompt** Download signed ActiveX controls; install desktop items.
Low (default for the Trusted Sites zone)	**Prompt** Download unsigned ActiveX controls; initialize and script ActiveX controls not marked as safe. **Enable** Run ActiveX controls and plug-ins; script ActiveX controls marked safe for scripting. **Enable** Download signed ActiveX controls; install desktop items.

Note File and font downloads are enabled by default on all Internet security zones.

Service calls involving security zones can have to do with an end user's need to have more (or less) access to Web content than she currently has or to place a website in a specific zone and use that zone's default security settings. You might also receive calls to configure users' computers to comply with a company security policy requirement to enable or disable a specific security setting. In this section, you will learn to do all of these things.

▶ **Changing Internet Zone Defaults**

To make changes to the Internet zone's default settings (this same technique works to change any zone's default settings), follow these steps:

1. Open Internet Explorer, and from the Tools menu, select Internet Options.

2. From the Security tab, select the Internet zone if it is not selected already.

3. Click Default Level, and move the security slider that appears up or down to change the default security setting for the zone. It is best to leave the Internet zone at either Medium (the default) or High. Lower settings will reduce security; higher settings will reduce functionality.

4. Select Custom Level.

5. In the Security Settings dialog box, scroll down the list to select the item to change. Make the appropriate change by selecting the desired option. Click OK to close the Security Settings dialog box, and click OK to close the Internet Options dialog box.

▶ **Adding a Website to the Trusted Sites Zone**

To add a website to the Trusted Sites zone (this same technique works to add a site to the Restricted Sites zone), follow these steps:

1. Open Internet Explorer, and from the Tools menu, select Internet Options.

2. Select the Security tab.

3. Select Trusted Sites, and choose Sites.

4. In the Add This Web Site To The Zone box, type the address to add. If adding a trusted site, you must begin the website URL with *https://*, which denotes a secure site. Click Add.

5. Click OK to close the Trusted Sites dialog box, and click OK again to close the Internet Options dialog box.

▶ **Adding a Website to the Local Intranet Zone**

To add a website to the Local Intranet zone, follow these steps:

1. Open Internet Explorer, and from the Tools menu, select Internet Options.

2. Select the Security tab.

3. Select Local Intranet, and then choose Sites.

4. In the Local Intranet dialog box, select the websites that should be included in the Local Intranet zone. Figure 5-12 shows the choices.

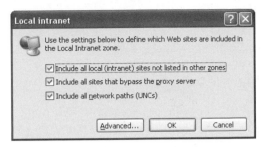

Figure 5-12   Local Intranet zone settings can be set to configure local sites.

5. In the Local Intranet dialog box, choose Advanced.

6. In the Add This Web Site To The Zone box, type any other websites to add. Click Add to add each.

7. Click OK in the Local Intranet dialog box, click OK again in the first Local Intranet dialog box, and click OK to close the Internet Options dialog box.

Common Service Calls

As a DST, you will need to know when to change which security setting, and you will often be asked to make the change without giving the user a security setting that is too lenient or one that is against company policy. This takes familiarity with the process (shown earlier) and an understanding of the security setting options. To help you become more familiar with common requests, Table 5-3 shows some examples of service calls and their resolutions.

Table 5-3   Common Security Service Calls and Resolutions

Service Call Scenario	Resolution
A Web designer calls to report that he needs to be able to download signed ActiveX controls for the purpose of testing a website he is creating. However, each time a signed ActiveX control is downloaded, he gets a prompt. He wants this behavior to stop.	Personalize his default security settings, and change the setting for Download Signed ActiveX Controls from Prompt to Enable.
A user reports that when she connects to a site on her local intranet, she cannot download unsigned ActiveX controls. She needs to be able to do this to perform work-related tasks. You need to change this so that she can download unsigned ActiveX controls without changing the security zone.	Personalize her default security settings, and change the setting for Download Unsigned ActiveX Controls from Disable to Enable or Prompt.
Your boss tells you that he does not want his workers to be able to install desktop items for anything they have downloaded from the Internet. He asks you not to change any other behavior on their computers.	Personalize the default security settings on each computer, and change the setting for Install Desktop Items from Prompt to Disable.

As you become more familiar with the terms and security settings options, you will be able to quickly identify problems and their solutions. In many instances, you can resolve problems by making simple changes to the default security settings.

Resolving Problems with Viewing Web Pages

There are several reasons why users will not be able to view Web pages properly, and many times it is because they have made changes to the defaults on their own. Problems can also occur because of default security settings: a site is in the Restricted Sites zone or the site requires cookies to be placed on the computer and cookies are not allowed. Users might report specific errors as well: they get internal page faults, or they cannot hear sounds, see videos, or view pictures. These are common problems, and solutions to them are detailed in this section.

Screen Resolution

If a user reports problems with viewing a single Web page, but other pages look fine, check to see whether there is a note at the bottom of the page that says, "This page is best viewed using 800 by 600 screen resolution" or something similar. If it is a corporate website or one that the user relies on heavily, he might need to reconfigure his display settings permanently. Display settings are changed in Control Panel.

Cookie Handling

Many websites require cookies to be enabled on a user's computer if the user wants to visit and browse the site. A user will be unable to view Web pages that have this requirement if the user's privacy settings are configured to block all cookies, if the privacy settings are set to High, or if the company has a strict cookie policy that blocks first-party cookies or does not allow session cookies. When Internet Explorer blocks content, it notifies the user through the Information Bar.

Allowing a user access to sites requires that the default privacy settings be changed. Changing privacy settings was detailed in the section "Configuring Privacy Settings," earlier in this chapter.

The Information Bar

The Internet Explorer Information Bar installed as part of Windows XP Service Pack 2 replaces many of the common dialog boxes that prompt users for information and provides a common area for displaying information. Notifications such as blocked ActiveX installs, blocked pop-up windows, and downloads all appear in the Information Bar, which appears below the toolbars and above the main browsing window, as shown in Figure 5-13. Either clicking or right-clicking the Information Bar brings up a menu that relates to the notification that is presented.

Figure 5-13   The Internet Explorer Information Bar provides a common notification area.

Note   Microsoft does not use pop-up ads or windows on the Microsoft.com site. The Internet Explorer window in Figure 5-13 was created to show the functionality of the new Information Bar and Pop-Up Blocker features in Windows XP Service Pack 2.

Pop-Up Blocker

Internet Explorer also provides a pop-up blocker for blocking pop-up windows that some sites use for advertising purposes. When a site tries to open a pop-up window, Internet Explorer blocks the window from opening and displays a notification in the Information Bar. Clicking the Information Bar allows you to show the blocked pop-up, allow all pop-ups on the current site, and configure other settings.

You can enable or disable the Pop-Up Blocker by using the Privacy tab in the Internet Options dialog box. Just select or clear the Block Pop-Ups check box. Click Settings to open the Pop-Up Blocker Settings dialog box, as shown in Figure 5-14. The Allowed Sites list shows all the sites that you have allowed to display pop-up windows, whether by adding those sites on this dialog box or by adding them using the Information Bar. Type the name of a site and click Add to add a new site to the list of allowed sites.

Figure 5-14   Add sites that are allowed to display pop-up windows and configure what happens when a pop-up window is blocked.

In the Notifications and Filters sections, you can perform the following actions:

- Have Internet Explorer play a sound when a pop-up window is blocked.

- Configure whether Internet Explorer shows the Information Bar when a pop-up window is blocked.

- Set the filter level for blocking pop-up windows. The default setting is Medium, which blocks most pop-up windows and works well for most people. If a user complains of still getting too many pop-up windows, you can set the level to High. However, the High setting blocks all external windows from opening—including those that the user might want. Teach the user how to hold down the CTRL key while clicking a link to allow a pop-up window to open. The Low setting allows pop-up windows from most secure sites to open. Teach users to experiment with settings until they find ones that works best for them.

Sounds, Videos, and Pictures

Some of the Advanced options of Internet Explorer restrict what can and cannot be seen on a Web page. These settings are often configured to speed up access to a page by not playing videos or showing pictures when the site is loaded, and sound can be disabled as well. If a user reports problems that are associated with sound, video, or pictures, check the Advanced options first by following these steps:

1. Open Internet Explorer, and from the Tools menu, select Internet Options.

2. Click the Advanced tab, and scroll down to the Multimedia section.

3. Verify that the appropriate items are selected:

❑ Play Animations In Web Pages

❑ Play Sounds In Web Pages

❑ Play Videos In Web Pages

❑ Show Pictures

4. On the Advanced tab, verify that the Show Image Download Placeholders check box is cleared. Click OK.

Invalid Page Faults

A **page fault** is a normal process that occurs when a program requests data that is not currently loaded into the computer's real memory. When this occurs, Windows attempts to retrieve the data from the virtual memory stored on hard disk. If the data cannot be mapped to virtual memory, the result is an invalid page fault—and often a crashed application. Invalid page faults are often difficult to diagnose. Connectivity settings; a full Temporary Internet Files folder; and third-party Internet software, including firewalls, file-sharing software, Internet optimizers, and on-screen animation programs, can cause page faults. Network protocols, cookies, corrupted Favorites, services, and Internet software installations can also cause invalid page faults. Invalid page faults can be represented by several different types of errors, including:

■ An actual invalid page fault error.

■ Iexplore.exe has generated errors and must be shut down.

■ Page could not be displayed.

■ Could not open the search page.

■ An access violation occurred in MSHTML.DLL.

If specifics about the error are provided in the error message (as in the last item in the preceding list), visit the Microsoft Knowledge Base (*http://support.microsoft.com/default.aspx*) and type in the exact error. Downloading and installing a hotfix might solve this particular error. These are the easiest of all page faults to find solutions for. If no specifics are given, you will have to resolve the errors using trial-and-error troubleshooting techniques.

Note   Before you do too much troubleshooting, verify that the user has the most recent version of Internet Explorer and the latest service packs for both the operating system and Internet Explorer. To check the version number and which service packs are installed, open Internet Explorer, and from the Help menu, select About Internet Explorer.

If you are at the user's desk when the error occurs, use the Internet Explorer Reporting tool to report the error, and then view the error details. If the error report gives any indication of the cause of the error, disable the program or service associated with it. If that does not work and the user has the most up-to-date service packs installed, continue troubleshooting in the following order:

1. Verify that the proxy settings for the local area network (LAN), if they exist, are correctly configured. You can locate these settings by clicking LAN Settings on the Connections tab of the Internet Options dialog box.

2. Disable third-party browser extensions, such as Bonzai Buddy, Comet Cursor, and other third-party downloaded components. Applications such as these can often be disabled from the system tray or from the application itself, and uninstalling the component from Control Panel is the best option if one of these programs caused the page fault.

3. Delete all temporary Internet files and ActiveX controls. You can do this on the General tab of the Internet Options dialog box.

4. Delete cookies. You can do this on the General tab of the Internet Options dialog box.

5. Troubleshoot the Favorites folder. It is possible that corruption in the Favorites folder or some of the files it holds is to blame. Try moving the contents of the user's Favorites folder to a temporary folder. If that solves the problem, add the shortcuts back to the Favorites folder a few at a time. If the problem recurs, it is usually easy to find the culprit.

6. Verify that the system has enough RAM and that the RAM is performing properly.

If these techniques do not solve the problem, consult the Microsoft Knowledge Base, TechNet, and newsgroups as detailed in Chapter 2, "Resolving a Service Call."

Practice: Configure Security Zones in Internet Explorer

In this practice, you will configure Internet Explorer security zones.

1. Log on to Windows XP using an account with Administrator privileges.

2. On the Start menu, select Internet Explorer.

3. In the Internet Options dialog box, on the Security tab, in the Security Level For This Zone section, click Default Level.

4. Move the slider to the High position. Click Apply. Click Custom Level.

5. In the Security Settings dialog box, click Cancel.

6. In the Internet Options dialog box, in the Select A Web Content Zone To Specify Its Security Settings section, select Trusted Sites.

7. In the Security Level For This Zone section, click Default Level.

8. In the Trusted Sites section, click Sites.

9. In the Trusted Sites dialog box, in the Add This Web Site To The Zone text box, type **https://www.microsoft.com**. Click Add. Click OK. Click OK again to close the Internet Options dialog box.

10. In Internet Explorer, in the Address text box, type **http://www.google.com** and press ENTER.

11. On the Google Web page, right-click any hyperlink and select Save Target As. In the Security Alert message box, click OK.

12. In the Address text box, type **https://www.microsoft.com** and press ENTER.

13. On the Microsoft Web page, right-click any hyperlink and select Save Target As. In the Save As dialog box, click Cancel.

Lesson Review

The following questions are intended to reinforce key information presented in this lesson. If you are unable to answer a question, review the lesson materials and try the question again. You can find answers to the questions in the "Questions and Answers" section at the end of this chapter.

1. A company has placed a computer in a break room so that users can access it on their lunch and coffee breaks. How should the computer be configured? (Choose all that apply.)

    A. Disable AutoComplete.

    B. Clear forms and clear passwords from the AutoComplete Settings dialog box.

    C. Disable Personalized Favorites.

    D. Set privacy settings to block all cookies.

    E. Configure a custom level for the Internet zone to disable the installation of desktop icons.

2. You need to configure a security setting for the Internet zone for users who access websites from a computer located in the company's lunchroom. Network administrators have configured Group Policy, physically secured the computer, and performed similar tasks, and have asked you to configure a security level for the Internet zone that will apply the following rules by default:

    ❑ **Disable** Download unsigned ActiveX controls; initialize and script ActiveX controls not marked as safe.

❑ **Enable** Run ActiveX controls and plug-ins; script ActiveX controls marked safe for scripting.

❑ **Prompt** Download signed ActiveX controls; install desktop items.

Which security level offers these default settings for the Internet zone?

_____

_____

Lesson Summary

■ Many of the interface requests that you receive can be resolved by customizing the Standard toolbar, changing what is selected in the View menu, or personalizing the Advanced settings in the Internet Options dialog box.

■ There are four security zones: Internet, Local Intranet, Trusted Sites, and Restricted Sites. The Internet zone contains all websites. Local Intranet, Trusted Sites, and Restricted Sites zones do not include any sites by default and thus must have websites manually placed in them.

■ Many factors can cause problems with viewing Web pages, including connectivity issues, security zone configuration, privacy settings, Internet Explorer configuration, and even the graphics settings in Windows XP.

Case Scenario Exercises

Scenario 5.1

All computers in your office have recently been upgraded from Microsoft Windows 98 to Windows XP. A clean installation was performed on each computer, and all service packs were installed. The installation went smoothly. However, the stockbrokers in your office are complaining that they are not getting up-to-date quotes when they visit their favorite, frequently viewed websites. They have been accessing these sites for two years without incident. What is most likely wrong, and how can this problem be resolved?

A. The application the stockbrokers use to get stock quotes is not compatible with Windows XP and needs to be replaced with a newer version.

B. The Temporary Internet Files folder is full and needs to be emptied.

C. The settings for the temporary files need to be changed to check for newer versions of stored pages every time the page is visited.

D. The Temporary Files folder was moved during the upgrade, and Internet Explorer does not know where to store temporary files and therefore is not saving any.

Scenario 5.2

A user reports that each time she accesses a particular website, she is inundated with content that she does not want to see, and she thinks this might have to do with ActiveX, Java applets, or scripts running on the site. The user reports that the site takes a long time to load, too. She wants to visit this site and read only the data; she has no interest in the other items on the site. You need to make this site available without making any changes to the default settings for the Internet zone. What should you do?

A. Add this site to the Local Intranet zone.

B. Add this site to the Trusted Sites zone.

C. Add this site to the Restricted Sites zone.

Troubleshooting Lab

You are working for a company that provides computer support for several small businesses. You get a call from a user who complains that when she tries to send an e-mail message from within Internet Explorer, it creates a new message using Outlook Express. However, she uses Outlook as her e-mail software. She would like you to configure Internet Explorer so that she can create a message using Outlook. After talking with her for a few more minutes, you also find that she would like the following programs to be configured to work within Internet Explorer:

- HTML editor: Notepad

- E-mail client: Hotmail

- Newsgroup reader: Outlook Express

- Internet call: NetMeeting

- Calendar: Microsoft Office Outlook

- Contact list: Address Book

How would you configure these programs within Internet Explorer?

Chapter Summary

- To personalize Internet Explorer, users can change the text size, colors, fonts, and font styles shown on Web pages, and they can customize the toolbars.

- To configure languages so that websites can be viewed in a user's native language, change the language option in the Internet Options dialog box of Internet Explorer.

- To secure and personalize a Web user's experience, Content Advisor, Digital Certificates, and the Profile Assistant can be configured.

- To resolve common end-user requests, you will have to import favorites, configure settings for cookies, set a home page, personalize the title bar, and configure the Explorer bar.

- To maintain Internet Explorer, use Disk Cleanup regularly and configure Temporary Internet File folder settings.

- To troubleshoot Internet Explorer, check security zones, privacy settings, and the Advanced configuration options of Internet Explorer.

Exam Highlights

Before taking the exam, review the key topics and terms that are presented in this chapter. You need to know this information.

Key Points

- If a user complains that a Web page does not look the way it should, be sure you check whether a custom appearance is set and whether that custom appearance is configured to override the styles on Web pages.

- You can remove temporary Internet files cached on a user's hard disk by using the Disk Cleanup tool that comes with Windows XP or by using the Internet Options dialog box in Internet Explorer. Deleting temporary files can fix a number of problems, ranging from slow performance to problems logging in to websites.

- Remember the five kinds of cookies—temporary, persistent, first-party, third-party, and session. Also remember what types of cookies are blocked at the different privacy settings.

Key Terms

cookie   A small text file that a website creates and stores on a computer. Cookies detail what users' preferences are, what users purchased, and any personal information offered by the user.

Group Policy   A policy created by an administrator that affects all users on a computer or all users in a domain and generally set by domain administrators on a domain level. Group Policy is used to specify how a user's desktop looks, what wallpaper is used, and how the Internet Explorer Title bar looks, to name only a few options.

search engine   An application that can search through every page on every website on the Internet for the purpose of offering those pages when a user searches for information. Major search engines include Google and Yahoo!.

temporary files   Cached files. Temporary Internet files allow a user to use the Back and Forward buttons, access History, and use offline files and folders. Retrieving information from the Temporary Internet Files folder is much faster than retrieving information from the Internet.

Uniform Resource Locator (URL)   The URL of a website is its friendly name, for instance, *http://www.microsoft.com*.

URL   *See* Uniform Resource Locator (URL).

Questions and Answers

Lesson 1 Review

Page
5-15

1. A user reports that he has changed his text size to Largest, but when he visits sites, sometimes the text on the sites is large and sometimes it is not. He reports this happens occasionally with colors and font styles, too. What does the user need to do to make sure these settings are always used, no matter what website he visits?

    A. Use the Internet Options dialog box in Internet Explorer, and from the General tab, select Accessibility, and make the appropriate changes in the Accessibility dialog box.

    B. Open Control Panel, open Accessibility Options, and on the Display tab, select the Override Web Settings check box.

    C. Use the Internet Options dialog box in Internet Explorer, select the General tab, choose Advanced, and in the Accessibility choices, select the Override Web Settings check box.

    D. Use the Internet Options dialog box in Internet Explorer, select the General tab, choose Accessibility, and in the Accessibility dialog box, select the Format Documents Using My Style Sheet check box.

    Answer A is correct. Answers B and C are not valid choices (because they do not exist) and are therefore not correct. Answer D is a valid choice but will not override Web settings using the text size, fonts, and colors selected by the user.

2. A small-business owner wants to personalize the Internet Explorer title bar on the computer that visitors access when they come into her store. She also wants to configure a default home page that users cannot change. Which of the following commands is used on the Run line to open the appropriate application for configuring these computerwide settings?

    A. msconfig.exe

    B. sigverif.exe

    C. cmd.exe

    D. gpedit.msc

    Answer D is correct because gpedit.msc opens the Group Policy console, and this console can be used to apply group policies computerwide. Answer A is incorrect because this command opens the System Configuration utility. Answer B is incorrect because sigverif.exe opens the File Signature Verification utility. Answer C is incorrect because cmd.exe opens a command prompt.

3. A home user wants you to configure his computer running Windows XP so that his 12-year-old son cannot access websites that contain offensive language, nudity, sexual references, or violence that involves fighting or killing. He would like to be able to override those settings if ever necessary by using an administrator password. The user wants to spend the least amount of money possible. What should you tell the user to do?

   A. Tell the user to purchase and install inexpensive third-party parental control software. Teach the user how to configure it.

   B. Configure Content Advisor, included with Windows XP.

   C. Create a separate account for the son, and purchase and install parental control software. Apply the software only to the son's account.

   D. Configure digital certificates, included with Windows XP, and accept digital certificates only from reputable sites.

   E. Configure the Profile Assistant to limit what sites the son has access to.

   Answer B is correct. Content Advisor, included with Windows XP, is an inexpensive way to control what sites and content are accessed on the Internet. Answers A and C are incorrect because third-party software generally costs money and is not necessary in this situation. Answer D is incorrect because digital certificates verify identity on the Internet; they are not used to judge or rate content. Answer E is incorrect because the Profile Assistant is used only for identification purposes.

Lesson 2 Review

Page
5-28

1. Which of the following are indications of a full Temporary Internet Files folder? (Choose all that apply.)

   A. When using the Save As command, pictures can be saved only as bitmaps and cannot be saved as .jpeg or .gif files.

   B. No History files appear in the History folder.

   C. Page faults appear.

   D. Access to frequently accessed Web pages is slow.

   Answers A, B, and C are correct. Answer D is incorrect because a full Temporary Internet Files folder would imply that frequently accessed Web pages are cached.

2. Match the type of cookie on the left with its description on the right.

1. Persistent	A. These cookies are sent to a computer from the website being viewed. They can be persistent or temporary and are generally harmless.
2. Temporary	B. These cookies are sent to a computer from a website not currently being viewed. They generally come from advertisers on the website being viewed for the purpose of tracking Web page use for advertising and marketing purposes. They can be persistent or temporary, and most of these cookies are blocked by default using the Medium privacy setting.

3. First-party	C. These cookies are stored on a computer during only a single browsing session and are deleted when Internet Explorer is closed. They are used by websites to determine the client browser, the language, and the screen resolution that are used, and they allow a user to move back and forth among the Web pages at the site without losing previously entered information. If these cookies are disabled, a user will not be able to access a site that requires them.
4. Third-party	D. A temporary cookie that is deleted from a computer when Internet Explorer is closed.
5. Session	E. These cookies remain on a computer even when Internet Explorer is closed, the user has disconnected from the Internet, or the computer has been turned off. These cookies store information such as logon name, password, e-mail address, color schemes, purchasing history, and other preferences, so that when a site is revisited, this information is available and can be applied.

1. E. 2. C. 3. A. 4. B. 5. D.

3. Company policy requires that all cookies saved to a user's computer must have a compact privacy policy that conforms to P3P standards. No cookies shall be saved if they do not conform. Which of the following default privacy settings can be used? (Select all that apply.)

   A. Accept All Cookies

   B. Low

   C. Medium

   D. Medium-High

   E. High

   F. Block All Cookies

   Answer E is correct. The other settings do not require cookies to conform to P3P requirements.

Lesson 3 Review

Page 5-45

1. A company has placed a computer in a break room so that users can access it on their lunch and coffee breaks. How should the computer be configured? Choose all that apply.

   A. Disable AutoComplete.

   B. Clear forms and clear passwords from the AutoComplete Settings dialog box.

   C. Disable Personalized Favorites.

D. Set privacy settings to block all cookies.

E. Configure a custom level for the Internet zone to disable the installation of desktop icons.

Answers A, B, and E are correct. Disabling AutoComplete and clearing AutoComplete settings protect users from others obtaining their user names and passwords. Disabling the installation of desktop icons keeps the desktop clean. Answer C is incorrect because the way in which the Favorites list appears is not a security issue. Answer D is incorrect because blocking all cookies will make many websites nonfunctional.

2. You need to configure a security setting for the Internet zone for users who access websites from a computer located in the company's lunchroom. Network administrators have configured Group Policy, physically secured the computer, and performed similar tasks, and they have asked you to configure a security level for the Internet zone that will apply the following rules by default:

❑ **Disable** Download unsigned ActiveX controls; initialize and script ActiveX controls not marked as safe.

❑ **Enable** Run ActiveX controls and plug-ins; script ActiveX controls marked safe for scripting.

❑ **Prompt** Download signed ActiveX controls; install desktop items.

Which security level offers these default settings for the Internet zone?

The High security level offers the desired settings. On the Security tab of the Internet Options dialog box, select the Internet zone, click Default Levels, and set the slider to High.

Case Scenario Exercises: Scenario 5.1

Page 5-46 All computers in your office have recently been upgraded from Microsoft Windows 98 to Windows XP. A clean installation was performed on each computer, and all service packs were installed. The installation went smoothly. However, the stockbrokers in your office are complaining that they are not getting up-to-date quotes when they visit their favorite, frequently viewed websites. They have been accessing these sites for two years without incident. What is most likely wrong, and how can this problem be resolved?

A. The application the stockbrokers use to get stock quotes is not compatible with Windows XP and needs to be replaced with a newer version.

B. The Temporary Internet Files folder is full and needs to be emptied.

C. The settings for the temporary files need to be changed to check for newer versions of stored pages every time the page is visited.

D. The Temporary Files folder was moved during the upgrade, and Internet Explorer does not know where to store temporary files and therefore is not saving any.

Answer C is correct. By default, temporary files are configured to look for newer versions of pages automatically, which is not as often as the stockbrokers need. Answer A is incorrect because incompatible software would have been reported by Windows XP during the upgrade. The scenario states that the upgrade went smoothly. Answer B is incorrect because, although a full Temporary Internet Files folder could cause problems, it would not cause problems on multiple computers at the same time. Answer D is incorrect because the Temporary Files folder is accessible after a clean installation.

Case Scenario Exercises: Scenario 5.2

Page 5-47 A user reports that each time she accesses a particular website, she is inundated with content that she does not want to see, and she thinks this might have to do with ActiveX, Java applets, or scripts running on the site. The user reports that the site takes a long time to load, too. She wants to visit this site and read only the data; she has no interest in the other items on the site. You need to make this site available without making any changes to the default settings for the Internet zone. What should you do?

A. Add this site to the Local Intranet zone.

B. Add this site to the Trusted Sites zone.

C. Add this site to the Restricted Sites zone.

Answer C is correct. Adding sites to the Restricted Sites zone disables features such as ActiveX controls and Java. Answers A and B are incorrect because these zones do not restrict websites but instead do just the opposite.

Troubleshooting Lab

Page 5-47 You are working for a company that provides computer support for several small businesses. You get a call from a user who complains that when she tries to send an e-mail message from within Internet Explorer, it creates a new message using Outlook Express. However, she uses Outlook as her e-mail software. She would like you to configure Internet Explorer so that she can create a message using Outlook. After talking with her for a few more minutes, you also find that she would like the following programs to be configured to work within Internet Explorer:

- HTML editor: Notepad
- E-mail client: Hotmail
- Newsgroup reader: Outlook Express
- Internet call: NetMeeting

■ Calendar: Microsoft Office Outlook

■ Contact list: Address Book

How would you configure these programs within Internet Explorer?

You should configure these programs on the Programs tab of the Internet Options dialog box, shown in Figure 5-15.

Figure 5-15 Use the Programs tab of the Internet Options dialog box to configure the programs used by Internet Explorer.

6 Installing and Configuring Office Applications

Exam Objectives in this Chapter:

- Configure and troubleshoot Office applications
    - Answer end-user questions related to configuring Office applications
    - Set application compatibility settings
    - Troubleshoot application installation problems
- Resolve issues related to customizing an Office application
    - Answer end-user questions related to customizing Office applications
    - Customize toolbars
    - Configure proofing tools
    - Personalize Office features

Why This Chapter Matters

The goal of this chapter is to teach you how to install and configure Microsoft Office applications for end users in either a corporate or a home environment. Installation includes verifying that the software to be installed is compatible with the computer's operating system and hardware, understanding and verifying license and minimum hardware requirements, and using program compatibility mode when software is not compatible. After installation, you will learn how to configure the applications to meet the user's specific needs. Configuration tasks include setting up proofing tools, using fonts and localized templates, personalizing dictionaries, customizing menus and toolbars, and configuring print options.

Lessons in this Chapter:

Before You Begin

Before you begin this chapter, you should have basic familiarity with the Microsoft Windows XP interface. You should have access to a computer running Windows XP, and you should also have the installation CD for Microsoft Office 2003.

Lesson 1: Preparing for an Office Installation

Although many people (mostly end users) simply put a program's installation CD in the CD-ROM drive and follow the prompts to install it, this is not a prudent way for a professional Desktop Support Technician (DST) to install applications for end users. Part of a DST's job is to verify that the program is compatible with the user's system, that the computer meets the application's minimum requirements, that the company or user has a valid license, and that the program will function as it should in the environment in which it will be used.

After this lesson, you will be able to

- Verify an application's compatibility with a user's system.
- Verify that a user's system meets minimum requirements for an application.
- Use program compatibility options in Windows XP to support older applications.

Estimated lesson time: 30 minutes

Verifying Compatibility

When a user asks you to install an application, your first job is to check the software box, the CD, online support (such as the manufacturer's website), or other documentation to verify that the software is compatible with Microsoft Windows XP. One of the primary reasons that application installations fail is that the application is incompatible with the operating system. In most instances, compatibility information is readily available. Figure 6-1 shows examples of the logos you should look for on box covers and websites, indicating that the application is compatible with Windows XP.

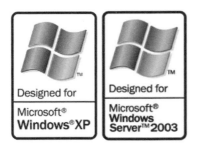

Figure 6-1   Verify compatibility from the software's box or other documentation.

Some applications offer much more information, usually from a page that lists system requirements. These requirements might state that specific hardware must be installed on the computer for components in the application to work (and thus be compatible). For example, although Microsoft Office System can be installed on almost any computer that runs Microsoft Windows 2000 with Service Pack 3 or Windows XP or later, to use certain features, other hardware must be installed for the features to function correctly. For instance, the following components need specific hardware to work:

- **Speech recognition** For speech recognition to work properly with Windows 2000 (with Service Pack 3 or later) or Windows XP, the computer must have a close-talk microphone and an audio output device.

- **Advanced Outlook functionality** For advanced Microsoft Office Outlook 2003 options to work properly, a Microsoft Exchange server is required.

- **Collaboration functionality** For advanced collaboration functionality, Microsoft Windows Server 2003 must be available, and Windows SharePoint must be installed.

- **Internet functionality** For Internet tools and options, such as online support features, updating Office 2003 and Outlook 2003 to work properly, Internet connectivity must be available.

Verifying an application's compatibility is an important part of the installation procedure. If you determine that a program is incompatible, consider your options, including purchasing new hardware, searching for an upgrade to the application, or choosing not to install the program at all.

Meeting Minimum Requirements

Documented minimum requirements list the basic hardware and operating system components necessary for the program to function minimally (usually without additional features such as speech recognition or advanced functionality). Minimum requirements detail which type of processor is needed, how much random access memory (RAM) is required, how much hard disk space must be available, which type of operating system can be used, and which kind of display is needed for the program to open and run.

Recommended requirements are also generally included in the same documentation. Recommended requirements state which hardware is necessary for the application to function effectively and efficiently. These standards are often required to keep the computer running efficiently while performing tasks.

Table 6-1 shows an example of the documented minimum and recommended requirements for Microsoft Office Professional Edition 2003. You can also find this information online at *http://www.microsoft.com/office/editions/prodinfo/sysreq.mspx.*

Table 6-1   Office Professional Edition 2003 Minimum Requirements

Component	Minimum Requirement	Recommended Requirement
Computer and processor	Personal computer with a 233-MHz processor	Personal computer with an Intel Pentium III or equivalent processor; Pentium 4 provides optimal performance
Memory (RAM)	128 MB	More than 128 MB
Hard disk space	400 MB	An additional 290 MB of space for options and installation files cache
Operating system	Windows 2000 (with Service Pack 3 or later), Windows XP, or Windows Server 2003	Windows 2000 (with Service Pack 3 or later), Windows XP, or Windows Server 2003
Display	Super VGA (800 × 600) and 256 colors	Super VGA (800 × 600) or higher

Installing additional options requires more hardware. Using the optional installation of Outlook 2003 with Business Contact Manager requires a PC with a Pentium 450-MHz or faster processor, 260 MB or more of RAM, and 190 MB of additional disk space.

Note   Most of the time, you will want the user's computer to exceed the minimum requirements. Simply meeting minimum requirements will allow the program to run, but exceeding the requirements will help the program run faster and more efficiently. In almost all cases, meeting or exceeding recommended requirements is best.

Real World   Having the Proper Licenses

Installing and running a software program almost always requires a license, an activation code, a validation code, or a product identification number. Generally, you find these numbers on the CD itself, on the CD case, on the box, or, if the application was downloaded from the Internet, in an e-mail. As a DST, particularly if you work in a private shop or visit users' homes, users ask you to install software for them. It is in your best interest and the users' to make sure that the software you are using is properly licensed. If you cannot verify licensing, explain to the user why you are not comfortable installing the software.

In some instances, you must enter the code prior to installation, as with Microsoft Office. Other times you must input a product ID during installation, and activation occurs after you complete the installation, as with Windows XP. Sometimes you enter an unlock code the first time you use the application, which then activates the program. Whatever the case, you need to verify that the end user or the company has a valid license, product ID, or activation code prior to beginning the installation. Figure 6-2 shows an example of a product ID requirement prior to installation.

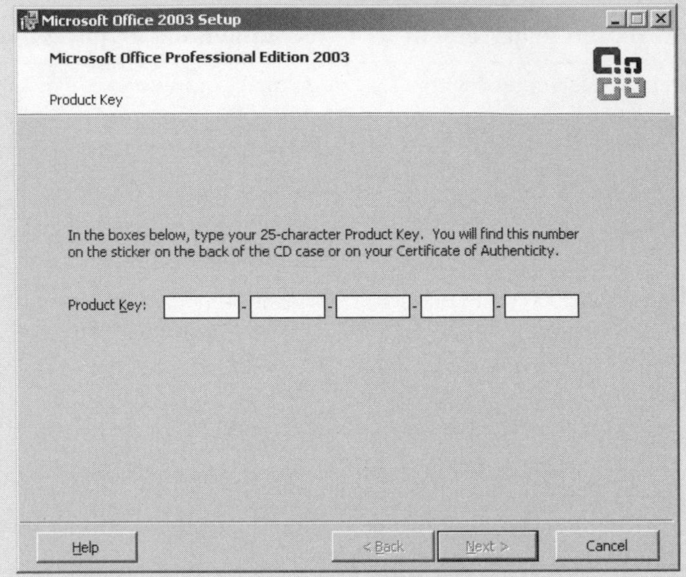

Figure 6-2   A product key must be available to install most software.

Using Program Compatibility Options

Although most programs run properly on Windows XP, some older applications (especially games) that were written for a specific operating system such as Microsoft Windows 95 or Windows 98 do not work as expected (or do not install at all). When this happens, install or run the program using one of the available program compatibility options in Windows XP. Choosing a program compatibility mode for a program allows that program to run in its native environment, which should cause the program to run properly and perform as expected.

When Not to Use Compatibility Modes

Program compatibility modes are not meant for all programs. For example, you should never use a program compatibility mode to force system tools (such as antivirus or CD-burning software) that are written for another operating system to work on Windows XP. System tools such as these run in the Win32 Subsystem kernel mode and can cause serious problems if installed and run incorrectly. System tools include but are not limited to the following:

- Antivirus software
- Firewalls
- CD-burning software

- Backup utilities
- Disk management software
- Disk partitioning software

When in doubt, purchase a newer version or an upgrade to the software, or do not install it.

Program Compatibility Modes

If a program is already installed and is not performing properly, you can change the compatibility mode for it by right-clicking the program's icon and selecting the Compatibility tab in the Properties dialog box. You can choose one of four compatibility modes—Windows 95, Windows 98/Me, Windows NT 4.0 (Service Pack 5), or Windows 2000—by following these steps:

1. Locate the problem application in the All Programs list or by browsing to it using Windows Explorer.

2. Right-click the program name or icon, and choose Properties. In the Properties dialog box, select the Compatibility tab, shown in Figure 6-3.

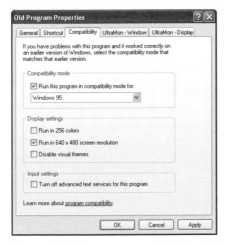

Figure 6-3 Program compatibility settings are located under the Compatibility tab.

3. In the Compatibility Mode area, select the Run This Program In Compatibility Mode For check box and choose an operating system from the drop-down list.

4. In the Display Settings area, select any of these check boxes: Run In 256 Colors, Run In 640 × 480 Screen Resolution, or Disable Visual Themes. If the program has problems handling the higher-quality video of Windows XP, you should try one of these settings. (If, after configuring these settings, you still find that the program does not run properly, try tweaking the settings.)

5. If available in the Input Settings area, select the Turn Off Advanced Text Services For This Program check box. Advanced Text Services can interfere with earlier software, especially games.

6. Click OK, and then start the program and verify that it runs properly.

> **Exam Tip**   Familiarize yourself with the particular settings that are available on the Compatibility tab and with the overall compatibility modes that you can select.

Program Compatibility Wizard

The Program Compatibility Wizard lets you install and test a program in different environments and with various settings to see which mode can best run the application. For instance, if the program was originally designed to work on a computer running Windows 95, installing it using the Windows 95 program compatibility mode will allow the program to run in its native environment, and it will likely run properly.

To use the Program Compatibility Wizard to install an older program, follow these steps:

1. From the Start menu, open Help And Support.

2. In the Search box, type **Program Compatibility Wizard**.

3. In the Search Results box, click Getting Older Programs To Run On Windows XP. In the right-hand pane, in step 1 under the section titled "To Run The Program Compatibility Wizard," click the Program Compatibility Wizard link.

> **Note**   You can also access the Program Compatibility Wizard by clicking Start and then Run, typing **hcp://system/compatctr/compatmode.htm** in the Open text box, and then clicking OK.

4. Click Next to start the wizard.

5. On the How Do You Want To Locate The Program That You Would Like To Run With Compatibility Settings? page, select how you want to locate the program:

   A. I Want To Choose From A List Of Programs. If you choose this option, the Program Compatibility Wizard scans your hard drive, CD-ROM drive (if a CD is inserted), and floppy drive (if a floppy disk is present). The wizard then presents you with a list of setup programs it has found. Choose a program from the list, and click Next. Move to step 6.

   B. I Want To Use The Program In The CD-ROM Drive. If you choose this option, the Program Compatibility Wizard scans your CD-ROM drive. Move to step 6.

    C. I Want To Locate The Program Manually. If you choose this option, the Program Compatibility Wizard lets you type the path or browse for an installation file. After you have indicated the file, click Next. Move to step 6.

  6. On the Select A Compatibility Mode For The Program page, make the appropriate selection (Microsoft Windows 95, Microsoft Windows NT 4.0 [Service Pack 5], Microsoft Windows 98/Windows Me, or Microsoft Windows 2000), or choose not to apply a compatibility mode. Click Next.

  7. On the Select Display Settings For The Program page, select a display setting. Read the program's documentation to verify that you are making the correct selection. (You do not have to make a selection.) Click Next.

  8. Install the program.

  9. On the Did The Program Work Correctly? page, make one of the following selections, and then click Next:

    ❑ Yes, Set This Program To Always Use These Compatibility Settings

    ❑ No, Try Different Compatibility Settings

    ❑ No, I Am Finished Trying Compatibility Settings

  10. On the Program Compatibility Data page, choose Yes or No to send a compatibility data report to Microsoft. Click Next, and then click Finish.

If later the program does not run as expected, right-click the program icon, click the Compatibility tab, and select another compatibility option.

Using System Restore

One of the best, and most underused, safety features of Windows XP is a tool named System Restore. System Restore monitors changes to a system and to some application files and periodically creates restore points. At any time, you can revert a system to one of these restore points. Restore points are created automatically every day. Some applications, such as Office 2003, automatically create restore points prior to installation. Best of all, you can create a restore point manually anytime you want.

When you are troubleshooting a system or installing software for a user, you should make it a habit to create a restore point before you do anything else. You should also create restore points before making any important system changes. It is a small step to take, and the payoff can be enormous.

▶ **Creating a Restore Point**

To create a restore point using System Restore, use the following steps:

  1. On the Start menu, point to All Programs, then to Accessories, and then to System Tools, and select System Restore.

2. Select the Create A Restore Point option, and click Next.

3. Type a description for the restore point (something like "about to install new video driver") and click Create.

4. Click Close to exit System Restore.

▶ **Reverting to a Restore Point**

To have a computer revert to a previous restore point by using System Restore, follow these steps:

1. On the Start menu, point to All Programs, then to Accessories, and then to System Tools, and select System Restore.

2. Select the Restore My Computer To An Earlier Time option, and click Next.

3. Use the calendar to select the day that contains the restore point to which you want to revert. Days in bold text contain restore points. After you have selected the day, select the specific restore point on the list to the right. Click Next.

4. Confirm that you have selected the desired restore point, and click Next. Windows reverts to the saved settings and restarts. Click OK to exit System Restore.

Real World   Allowing Corporate Users to Install Their Own Programs

Many companies have local or group policies in place that prevent users from installing their own programs. In these environments, you can expect service calls from end users who are upset about this policy because they want to install the latest holiday screen saver, greeting card software, or music file sharing download application. Let the users know that these policies are in place for many reasons, but emphasize that letting them install any program they want can be quite dangerous for the company, the computer, and for the users' data. (Many programs such as these are also detrimental to a user's productivity.)

If a user does have the appropriate permissions to install a program, make sure he or she is aware of the preinstallation tasks detailed in this section, that he or she creates a system restore point prior to installation, and that his or her data is backed up.

Practice: Prepare for an Office 2003 Installation

In this practice, you will check system requirements for an installation, create a restore point, and configure program compatibility.

Exercise 1: Check System Requirements

1. Log on to Windows XP.

2. On the Start menu, select Run. In the Run dialog box, in the Open text box, type **msinfo32**, and press ENTER.

3. In the System Information window, note the following information from the System Summary:

   ❑ Operating system

   ❑ Processor

   ❑ Total physical memory

4. Expand the Components node in the left-hand pane, and then select Display. Copy the following information from the right-hand pane:

   ❑ Video card name

   ❑ Adapter RAM

   ❑ Current resolution and bits/pixel settings

5. Close the System Information window.

6. On the Start menu, select My Computer.

7. In the My Computer window, right-click Local Drive (C:), and select Properties.

8. In the Local Disk (C:) Properties dialog box, on the General tab, note the free space on drive C.

Exercise 2: Create a Restore Point

1. Log on to Windows XP.

2. On the Start menu, point to All Programs, then to Accessories, and then to System Tools, and select System Restore.

3. Select the Create A Restore Point option, and click Next.

4. Type a description for the restore point (something like "about to install new video driver"), and click Create.

5. Click Close to exit System Restore.

Lesson Review

The following questions are intended to reinforce key information presented in this lesson. If you are unable to answer a question, review the lesson materials and try the question again. You can find answers to the questions in the "Questions and Answers" section at the end of this chapter.

1. A user wants you to install Office Professional Edition 2003 on his computer. He uses Windows XP Home Edition and has a Pentium III processor, 512 MB of RAM, 40 GB of free hard disk space, and a generic plug-and-play Super VGA monitor capable of 800-x-600 resolution. Which of the following upgrades (if any) will be needed so that the program will run well (thus meeting recommended requirements)? (Choose all that apply.)

   A. Upgrade from Windows XP Home Edition to Windows XP Professional Edition.

   B. Upgrade to a Pentium 4 or equivalent.

   C. Add more RAM.

   D. Partition the hard disk into two 20-GB sections. Office cannot work with large disk drives.

   E. Install Service Packs 1 and 2.

   F. Upgrade to a flat-screen monitor or a monitor with resolution that can be configured at 1024 x 768.

   G. Nothing needs to be upgraded.

2. Which of the following types of software would it be safe to run under Windows XP, using an application compatibility mode?

   A. A game that was written for Windows 95

   B. Backup software that was written for Windows 98

   C. Disk partitioning software that was written for Windows 2000

   D. Antivirus software that was written for Windows 2000

Lesson Summary

■ One of the primary reasons that application installations fail is that the application is incompatible with the operating system. You should always verify compatibility before installing software.

■ You should also make sure that the system on which you are going to install software meets that software's minimum system requirements.

■ If you need to install older programs that were not written for earlier versions of Windows, Windows XP includes an application compatibility feature that allows programs to run in their native environments.

Lesson 2: Installing Office 2003

After you verify that the application is compatible with the operating system and the computer's hardware is set up, that the user has the proper licenses, and that the computer meets the minimum or recommended requirements, installing the program can occur in a number of ways. You can install an application by using an installation CD or shared files on a network server. Some companies automate installation by using Group Policy or other methods, further simplifying the process for users.

After this lesson, you will be able to

- Explain general application installation concepts.
- Identify and resolve common installation problems.
- Identify log files that might be useful in troubleshooting installation problems.

Estimated lesson time: 25 minutes

General Installation Concepts

During the installation of many applications, you will be prompted throughout to answer questions about or agree to the license agreement and to decide what should be installed and where and what to do with temporary files after the installation is complete.

License Agreements

Generally, license agreements document for the user or the company how the software can be used. License agreements include information about but not limited to the following:

- Guidelines for how often and where you can install the software. You can install some applications on only a single personal computer, others on a personal computer and a laptop, and others on multiple computers. Some software can be installed on network servers and requires a license for each user or computer that accesses the software on the network.
- Guidelines for Remote Desktop and Remote Assistance use.
- Guidelines for mandatory product activation (covered in the next section).
- Restrictions on using the application to create or promote inappropriate content or any item that can damage or disable Internet-based services.
- Guidelines for selling, renting, or transferring the application.
- Warranties, applicable laws, severability clauses, and other legal issues.

You should read the license agreement carefully and then agree to it. Understand that agreeing to the license agreement is equivalent to signing a legal contract, though, and it is legally binding. Make sure you read the agreement and truly agree with and are aware of the rules and regulations stated in it. (You will not be able to install the program without accepting the license agreement.)

More About Product Activation

As mentioned in the preceding section, many software manufacturers, including Microsoft, require the user to activate the product online or by phone or fax within a specified number of days from the time the software was installed or first used. If the product is not activated in that specified period, the software will cease to work and will only prompt the user to activate it each time it is opened. As an example, Microsoft Windows XP must be activated within 30 days of its first use. If the user does not or cannot activate the product (perhaps it is a pirated copy), the operating system fails to function after the 30-day grace period. Product activation is part of Microsoft's effort to combat piracy and unauthorized use of its products.

> **Note**   To activate Windows XP by phone in the U.S., call (888) 652-2342. For more information about product activation, read Microsoft's Knowledge Base articles 302806 and 302878.

Product activation prevents users from installing the software on multiple computers and from sharing the software with users who do not want to purchase the software, and it prevents casual copying of the software.

Choosing Components

When you install a suite of Office applications (or other multifaceted application) such as Microsoft Office Professional Edition 2003, you will be prompted to select an installation type and to decide which components to install. The components that you choose can be installed in various ways, depending on the amount of resources on the computer.

Installation types for Office Professional Edition 2003 include Upgrade, Complete Install, Minimal Install, Typical Install, and Custom Install (all of which are common options). Figure 6-4 shows these options, as well as the option to browse to a new location to save the installation files.

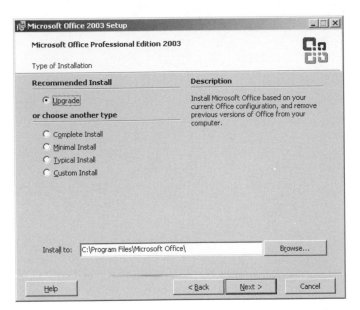

Figure 6-4   There are several installation types to choose from.

Components of Office Professional Edition 2003 include Microsoft Office Word 2003, Excel 2003, PowerPoint 2003, Outlook 2003, Publisher 2003, and Access 2003. When installing Office Professional Edition 2003, choosing Custom Install is almost always the best choice because you control which programs are installed, where they are installed, and which additional components are included with the installation.

When installing using Custom Install, you can choose how to install each component:

- **Run From My Computer**   Copies files and writes registry entries and shortcuts for the selected component or components. This allows the user to run the components locally, without having to insert the CD or access the files from a network drive.

- **Run All From My Computer**   Copies files and writes registry entries and shortcuts for the selected component or components and all of their subfolders. This allows the user to run the components locally, without having to insert the CD or access the files from a network drive.

- **Install On First Use**   Does not copy the files to the user's hard disk until the component is first used. At that time, the component is automatically copied either from the CD or a network location.

- **Not Available**   Does not copy and will never copy the selected component.

Figure 6-5 shows a custom installation with all of the components selected to run from the computer. When performing an installation, you will be prompted to make the appropriate choices.

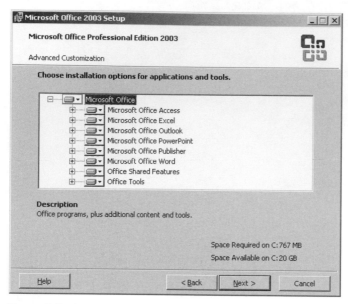

Figure 6-5   In this figure, all components are selected to run from the computer.

Install to File Folder

You might be asked to configure the computer to store the installation files in a location other than the user's hard disk. The files might be stored on a different partition or on a network drive. If company policy requires it or if a user's computer has multiple partitions, click Browse in the installation type stage (shown in Figure 6-4) and select the desired location.

Deleting Temporary, Backup, or Installation Files

Depending on the program that you install, you might be prompted to delete backup files, temporary files, or installation files. Most of the time, temporary files are deleted automatically, but running Disk Cleanup after an installation is not a bad idea if you did not see any temporary files being deleted toward the end of the installation and feel that they have been left on the computer.

Backup files are usually deleted automatically, too, but if you have enough disk space and are prompted to save or delete them, it will not hurt to leave them on the computer. Installation files can be deleted if you are prompted, but for the most part, accepting the defaults offered during the installation process is fine. When you install Microsoft Office, it is recommended that you keep the installation files. Figure 6-6 shows an example of the backup files being automatically deleted.

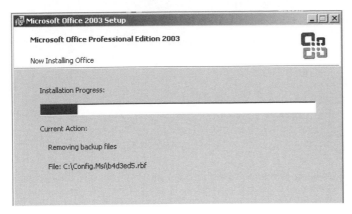

Figure 6-6   Deleting backup files is usually done automatically.

> **Note**   When an end user opens a program or a component for the first time, he or she might be asked to enter specific user information, including e-mail address, name, business, and so on. Make sure you start the program and enter this information before leaving the user's desk or ending the service call.

Getting Required Updates After Installation

After installing Office Professional Edition 2003, you will most likely be prompted to obtain the newest updates from the Microsoft Office Online website. If prompted, follow the directions for obtaining the updates; the updates will be downloaded and installed automatically.

Checking for Updates Manually

An experienced technician will remember to manually check for updates often, and you should instruct users to do so as well. Checking for updates on a schedule, for instance, once a week or once a month, helps keep the computer safe and running properly. To check for Office updates manually:

1. Open any Office application—such as Microsoft Excel, Word, PowerPoint, or Access—and from the Help menu, select Check For Updates. Figure 6-7 shows the option from Excel.

Figure 6-7   Manually check for updates by using the Help menu in any Office application.

2. Internet Explorer will automatically open to *http://office.microsoft.com/officeupdate /default.aspx*. Select Check For Updates.

3. If new updates are available, select or deselect the ones to install, and select Start Installation. Figure 6-8 shows the Office Update website with two updates available.

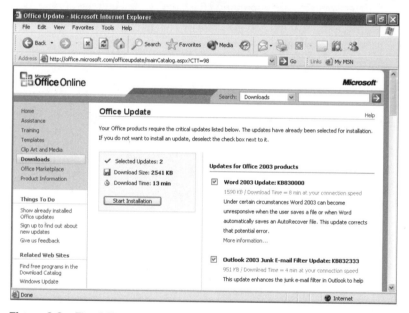

Figure 6-8   The Office Update website shows available updates.

4. When prompted, click Next to confirm installation. Continue following the Office Update Installation Wizard prompts until the updates are installed. Depending on the updates selected, this process might require you to insert the Microsoft Office CD, close running applications, or restart your computer upon completion.

Troubleshooting Common Installation Problems

Problems that occur during installations vary, but most are caused by a lack of hardware resources on the computer, compatibility problems, a bad CD-ROM, corrupt or inaccurate downloaded files, a user's failure to follow installation instructions, or an incorrect product ID or validation code. Table 6-2 lists some of the most common problems, possible causes, and their solutions.

Table 6-2   Common Installation Problems

Installation Problem	Possible Cause	Possible Solution
Disk space or RAM errors.	The computer does not meet the minimum requirements documented for the software.	Install an additional drive or free up enough drive space, or add more physical memory (RAM).
Missing or corrupt files.	The CD might be bad, or downloaded files might be corrupt or missing.	Request a new CD from the manufacturer, or download the files again.
Permission-denied errors.	An administrator might need to install the software, or network policies prevent software installations.	Contact an administrator or log on as one.
Errors including Can't Copy File To Disk, Permission Denied, and Can't Access Hard Disk.	Antivirus software might be preventing the application from installing.	Disable the antivirus software temporarily.
Product ID, validation code, or unlock code does not work.	You might have made typographical errors when entering the code; for example, you might have entered a zero instead of the letter O. In addition, validation codes might be case sensitive. The code might be invalid because the program has already been installed on another computer.	Try entering the code again, substituting zeros for the letter O and vice versa. Make sure you enter the code using the correct case. If the code continues to fail, call the company's tech support line, ask an administrator for assistance, or read the license agreement to see whether there are limitations on installations.
Activation failure.	The activation might fail because the program has already been installed on another computer or because the computer is not connected to the Internet.	Read the license agreement to see whether there are limitations on installations, connect to the Internet if necessary, or activate the product over the phone.

Table 6-2   Common Installation Problems

Installation Problem	Possible Cause	Possible Solution
Installation hangs, gives illegal operation errors, or fails.	These problems can be caused any number of ways, including the failure to close open programs before installing, failure to follow installation instructions, having incompatible hardware, or not having enough memory.	Try reinstalling, and carefully follow the instructions shown. Access the company's website, and search for installation help and support files if necessary. Many programs have known issues with specific hardware and operating systems.

Chances are that someone else has already seen any error message that you see and a solution has been found and documented. Most manufacturers have Web pages that address these specific problems. If an installation problem persists, visit the manufacturer's website and see whether a solution is available.

> **Exam Tip**   In Windows XP, you must have administrative permissions to install most programs. Some programs, such as Office 2003, are good about warning you of this fact before you start the installation; some programs are not. When a program does not warn you, it can sometimes seem as though the installation is successful, and problems do not pop up until later.

Using Log Files

If the installation problems cannot be solved by the techniques that are listed in the preceding section or by researching the Microsoft Knowledge Base, consider viewing the log files that Office creates during installation; you can use these files to troubleshoot installation problems. There are four file types (depending on the installation), and these log files are automatically created in the \Temp folder on the user's hard disk:

- Office Professional Edition 2003 Setup(000x).txt—the Setup.exe log file
- Office Professional Edition 2003 Setup(000x)_Task(000x).txt—the Windows Installer log file
- MSI*.log—Windows Installer log file
- Offcln11.log—a log file created if you have uninstalled Office 2003 previously

You can get more information about these files and how to read them from the Microsoft Knowledge Base article 826511, "How to Use an Office 2003 Setup Log File to Troubleshoot Setup Problems."

Practice: Install Microsoft Office 2003

In this practice, you will install Office 2003. To complete this practice, you will need the Office 2003 Evaluation CD that comes with this book or your own copy of the software.

1. Log on to Windows XP by using an account with administrator privileges.

2. Insert the Microsoft Office Professional Edition 2003 CD into the CD-ROM drive.

3. The Microsoft Office 2003 Setup Wizard should start automatically. If it does not, on the Start menu, select My Computer, and in the My Computer window, open your CD-ROM drive. Double-click Setup.exe to start the wizard.

4. In the Microsoft Office 2003 Setup Wizard, enter your user name, initials, and organization name, and then click Next.

5. Read the licensing agreement, and then select the I Agree To The Terms In The Licensing Agreement option. Click Next.

6. Make sure that the Typical Install option is selected, and click Next.

7. Verify the installation details, and click Install.

8. After the installation is finished, you are informed that the update completed successfully. Ensure that both the Check The Web For Updates And Additional Downloads and the Delete Installation Files check boxes are cleared. Click Finish.

Lesson Review

The following question is intended to reinforce key information presented in this lesson. If you are unable to answer the question, review the lesson materials and try the question again. You can find answers to the question in the "Questions and Answers" section at the end of this chapter.

The following table lists some common installation problems and their causes. To answer this question, match the installation problem on the left with the likely cause on the right.

1. The program installed correctly but fails online activation.	A. The program was probably downloaded from the Internet, and the download was not successful.
2. The error Can't Copy File To Disk prevents installation from starting or completing.	B. The computer does not meet minimum hardware requirements.
3. The installation of the program stops, and an error message appears that states that some of the downloaded files are missing or corrupt.	C. An antivirus program is running.

| 4. Installation stops, hangs, or quits. | D. There might be a typographical error created by the user. |
| 5. The validation code will not validate the software. | E. The program has already been installed on another computer, and licensing restrictions and requirements are preventing the successful installation of the program. |

Lesson Summary

- During a typical application installation, you will need to agree to licensing requirements, select the components to install, select the installation location, and possibly activate the product after installation is finished.

- You should teach users to check for program updates frequently.

- Most installation problems are caused by a lack of hardware resources on the computer, compatibility problems, a bad CD-ROM, corrupt or inaccurate downloaded files, a user's failure to follow installation instructions, or an incorrect product ID or validation code.

Lesson 3: Personalizing Office Features

After you install a program, it needs to be personalized to suit the user who will be working with the program. Personalization comes in many forms, but for the most part, users will want you to help them customize toolbars and menus, change formatting and printing options, and change the default location of saved files.

After this lesson, you will be able to

- Add, remove, and customize toolbars.
- Customize commands on toolbars and menus.
- Locate and configure important program options.

Estimated lesson time: 30 minutes

Adding, Removing, and Customizing Toolbars

Every application has at least one toolbar, and some applications offer many. Both Microsoft Office Excel Professional Edition 2003 and Microsoft Office Word Professional Edition 2003 offer 20 toolbars. Users will not want all of the available toolbars on their screen at the same time, but they might want to add the ones they use often or remove the ones they do not use. In addition, users might want to customize their toolbars by using the available toolbar options (such as showing items on a single row or on two rows, or using large icons).

Common Toolbars

Some toolbars are fairly common and appear in multiple Office applications. To customize an application for a specific user in a specific department, you will need to be aware of the most common options:

- **Standard**   This toolbar contains standard features, including options for opening a new or existing document, saving and printing, and using features such as spell check and cut, copy, and paste. This toolbar should be made available to most users.

- **Formatting**   This toolbar contains features that include font selection and size; formatting options such as bold, italic, and underline; and justification and numbering options. This toolbar should be made available to most users, especially those who create presentations, graphics, or publications.

- **Web**   This toolbar contains options for accessing Favorites, a home page, and previously viewed network documents and websites. This toolbar should be made available to those whose work requires them to access the Internet or network places frequently.

- **Task pane**   This toolbar offers a fast and easy way to obtain information about the Office program or component. This toolbar should be made available to new users and those who need to locate information from the Knowledge Base, newsgroups, or other technical help sites quickly.

- **Drawing**   This toolbar offers options to quickly draw shapes and to insert Word-Art, clip art, pictures, diagrams, or charts. This toolbar should be made available to users who create publications, company memos, or other documents with images or who otherwise need access to the drawing tools.

Figure 6-9 shows these toolbars (and the Menu bar) in Word 2003.

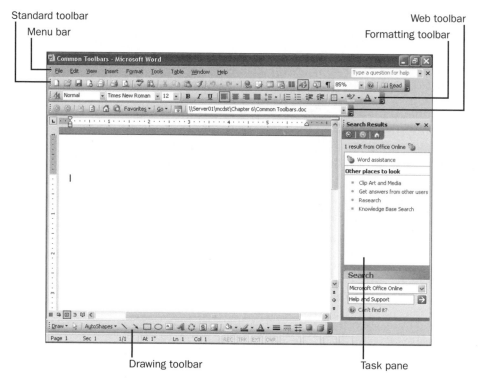

Figure 6-9   Common toolbars are shown here.

Toolbar Customizations

Toolbars can be added, removed, and customized. To add or remove toolbars in any Microsoft Office application, click View, point to Toolbars, and select or clear any toolbar to show or hide it. Figure 6-10 shows an example. (You can also add or delete toolbars by right-clicking on the Menu bar.)

Figure 6-10   Adding toolbars from the View menu by selecting them.

You can also customize what is shown on toolbars, and there are several ways to access the customization options:

- Right-click the Menu bar, click Customize, and select the Options tab.

- From the View menu, point to Toolbars, and select Customize, and select the Options tab.

- From the Tools menu, select Customize, and select the Options tab.

Each of these methods opens the Customize dialog box shown in Figure 6-11. Several options are available:

- **Show Standard And Formatting Toolbars On Two Rows**   Selecting this option places both toolbars on the same row to save space on the user's screen.

- **Always Show Full Menus**   Selecting this option causes menus to always show all of their options and does not show **personalized menus**.

- **Show Full Menus After A Short Delay**   Selecting this option causes menus to show personalized menus and then shows the full menu after a short delay.

- **Reset Menu And Toolbar Usage Data**   Selecting this button restores the default set of commands on the menus and toolbars and undoes any explicit customization.

- **Large Icons**   Selecting this option causes the icons on the toolbars to become larger.

- **List Font Names In Their Font**   Selecting this option causes lists of fonts to be displayed in their font names. This makes selecting a font easier; the font list contains a preview of each font available.

- **Show ScreenTips On Toolbars**   Selecting this option shows ScreenTips on toolbars.

- **Show Shortcut Keys In ScreenTips**   Selecting this option shows shortcut keys in ScreenTips.

- **Menu Animations**   Selecting an option from the drop-down list enables menus to be shown using a specified animation: System Default, Random, Unfold, Slide, or Fade.

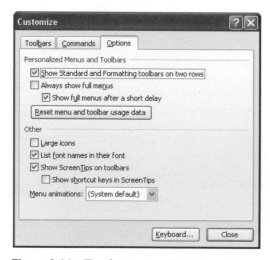

Figure 6-11   The Customize dialog box allows a user to personalize an Office application.

> **Note**   You can move toolbars by dragging them from their leftmost ends. The mouse pointer becomes a four-headed arrow when placed over the correct area for moving the toolbar.

Further Customizing Menus, Toolbars, and Their Commands

Some end users will have specific requests concerning the customization of their toolbars; they might ask you to make several adjustments, including these:

- Adding commands to the Menu bar
- Adding commands to menu lists

- Rearranging the categories on the Menu bar
- Rearranging the commands in the menu lists
- Resetting the menus and toolbars to their defaults

You can make all of these adjustments by using the Customize dialog box.

Sample Service Call

A user in the graphics department of your company uses Microsoft Office PowerPoint 2003 to create company documentation and slides for presentations. He needs to have as much workspace as possible and wants you to make several changes:

- Remove all of the toolbars and the Task pane.
- Add the commands Insert Table and Publish As Web Page to the Menu bar.
- Add the Draw Table command to the Tools menu list.
- Move the Can't Repeat or Repeat command to the top of the Edit menu.
- Move the Slide Show category on the Menu bar to the end of the Menu bar.

Here is how you would make these changes:

1. From the Start menu, point to All Programs, point to Microsoft Office, and select Microsoft Office PowerPoint 2003.

2. To remove the toolbars and the task pane, right-click the Menu bar and clear every item's check box.

3. Right-click the Menu bar, and select Customize.

4. On the Commands tab, in the Categories pane, select Table.

5. In the Commands pane, select Table, and drag it to the Menu bar.

6. In the Categories pane, select Web.

7. In the Commands pane, select Publish As Web Page, and drag it to the Menu bar. The Menu bar now has the available commands added.

8. In the Categories pane, select Table.

9. In the Commands pane, drag the Draw Table command to the Tools menu list. Figure 6-12 shows how this will look. Drop the Draw Table command underneath the Spelling command.

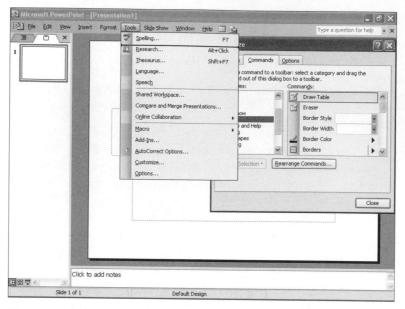

Figure 6-12   Adding a command to a menu list by dragging it.

You can rearrange commands on the Menu bar and in the menu lists by using the Rearrange Commands dialog box. To make these changes, follow these steps:

1. In the Customize dialog box, select Rearrange Commands.

2. In the Rearrange Commands dialog box, under Choose A Menu Or Toolbar To Rearrange, verify that Menu Bar is selected, and from the Menu Bar drop-down list, select Edit.

3. In the Controls area, select Can't Repeat. Click Move Up to move this item to the top of the list.

4. Under Choose A Menu Or Toolbar To Rearrange, click Toolbar. Menu Bar will be selected.

5. In the Controls area, select Slide Show. Click Move Down four times to move this to the end of the Menu Bar list.

6. Note that Reset is available in the Rearrange Commands dialog box. Click Close. Click Close again to exit the Customize dialog box. Figure 6-13 shows the result.

Figure 6-13   A customized Menu bar.

Resetting Toolbars to Their Default State

If users complain that buttons are missing from toolbars (or commands from menus), or that items are rearranged, an easy way to fix the problem is to return toolbars to their default settings.

To reset a toolbar to its default state, use the following steps:

1. On the Tools menu, select Customize.

2. In the Customize dialog box, switch to the Toolbars tab.

3. Select the toolbar you want to reset, and click Reset.

4. If you are using Microsoft Word, a Reset Toolbar dialog box opens. Select the template or document in which you want to reset the toolbar (select Normal.dot to make the changes global), and click OK. Click Close to close the Customize dialog box.

5. If you are using any other Office application, a dialog box opens that asks you to confirm the reset, but you do not choose a document or template. Click OK to confirm, and then click Close to close the Customize dialog box.

Customizing Using the Options Dialog Box

There are literally thousands of ways to customize the various applications in Microsoft Office 2003. Many of these options are available through the Tools menu and the Options choice. The Options dialog box configuration choices and tabs differ depending on the program selected. You should familiarize yourself with the available options in all of the Office applications as well as any third-party applications you see regularly.

Figures 6-14, 6-15, and 6-16 show various Options dialog boxes. Although there is not enough room to cover all of the options for each Office application in this chapter, we cover some of the more common options that are available through the Word 2003 Options dialog box.

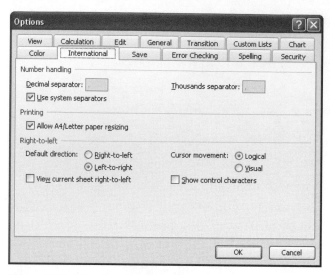

Figure 6-14   The Excel Options dialog box.

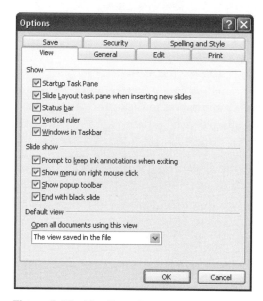

Figure 6-15   The PowerPoint Options dialog box.

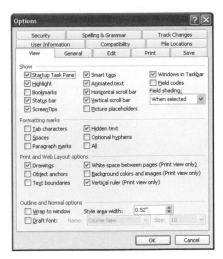

Figure 6-16 The Word Options dialog box.

Note In the remaining sections of this chapter, Word 2003 is used as the default application for detailing the options for configuring Office applications. Other components and programs offer comparable options and are used similarly.

View Options

The options on the View tab of the Word 2003 Options dialog box are shown in Figure 6-16. You can make many customizations with the options on this tab. Common options that users might want you to modify include these:

- **Startup Task Pane** The Startup Task Pane is the pane on the right side that offers links to Microsoft Office Online, search options, and a list of recently viewed documents.

- **Tab Characters, Spaces, Paragraph Marks, Hidden Text, and Optional Hyphens** Formatting marks can be shown for tab characters, spaces, paragraph marks, and more.

- **Drawings** Clearing the Drawings check box hides objects created with the Word drawing tools to speed up the display of documents that contain drawings.

- **Wrap To Windows** Choosing this option wraps text to the document window, making it easier to read on the screen.

Note As with the remaining sections, familiarize yourself with all of the available options. To see what each option does, click the question mark in the upper right corner of the Options dialog box, and then click any option with the mouse.

General Options

You can make many customizations with the options on the General tab. Common options that users might want you to modify include these:

- **Provide Feedback With Animation** and **Provide Feedback With Sound**   Users might want to use sound (by selecting the Provide Feedback With Sound check box) or not view animations (by clearing the Provide Feedback With Animation check box) when using Word 2003.

- **Help For WordPerfect Users**   Selecting this box allows WordPerfect users to view help files.

- **Allow Background Open Of Web Pages**   Users might want to open Hypertext Markup Language (HTML) files and still use Word to complete other tasks.

- **Allow Starting In Reading Layout**   Users might not want documents to automatically open in Reading layout.

Edit Options

You can also make many customizations with the options on the Edit tab. Common options that users might want you to modify include these:

- **Typing Replaces Selection**   When this check box is selected, the selected text is deleted as the user types. When the check box is cleared, Word inserts the text in front of the selected text.

- **Picture Editor**   Microsoft Office Word is the default picture editor, but you can change this option if you have another picture editor installed.

- **Enable Click And Type**   Click And Type allows a user to insert text, graphics, tables, and other items in a blank area of a document by double-clicking. This might not be desirable.

Print Options

You can make many customizations with the options on the Print tab. Common options that users might want you to modify include the following:

- **Draft Output**   This setting prints the document with minimal formatting, which speeds up the print process. Not all printers support this function.

- **Reverse Print Order**   This setting prints pages in reverse order.

- **Include With Document**   The options in this section control the printing of field codes, Extensible Markup Language (**XML**) **tags**, and so on.

- **Default Tray**   Configure a default print tray for printers that support this feature.

Save Options

You can make many customizations with the options on the Save tab. Common options that users might want you to modify include these:

- **Always Create Backup Copy**   Select this check box to create a backup copy of each document.

- **Allow Background Saves**   Documents are automatically saved in the background every 10 minutes. A user might want to disable this to avoid saving changes to a file before he or she is ready.

- **Save Word Files As**   You can save Word files as Word documents, XML documents, single-file Web pages, Web pages, or document templates.

File Locations

You can make many customizations with the options on the File Locations tab. Common options that users might want you to modify include these:

- Changing the location where documents are stored

- Changing the location where clip art is stored

- Changing the location of **AutoRecover files**

Making changes on the File Locations tab requires more than selecting or clearing a check box or making a selection from a drop-down list. To modify the location of saved files, click Modify. In the Modify Location dialog box, browse to the new location and click OK. Note that you can create a new folder in the desired location by selecting the Create New Folder icon in the Modify Location dialog box. A user might want to change the default location of saved files to make backing up documents easier or to make locating AutoRecover files more intuitive.

> **Note**   When a user reports that his or her computer or application shut down unexpectedly and a working file was lost, browse to the location of the AutoRecover files. You will almost always find the last saved version there.

Security Options

You can make many customizations with the options on the Security tab. Common options that users might want you to modify include these:

- Creating a password to open a file and setting advanced **encryption** options

- Creating a password to modify the file

- Configuring the file for read-only

- Removing personal information from the file's properties when the file is saved

These options and others can be used to keep a user's files and information safe, even when others have access to the files.

Practice: Personalize Office Features

In this practice, you will add a toolbar to the Word 2003 interface, create a custom toolbar, and add items to a menu list. This practice requires you to have successfully completed the installation of Office 2003, as detailed in the practice at the end of Lesson 2.

Exercise 1: Add and Use a Toolbar

1. Log on to Windows XP.

2. On the Start menu, point to All Programs, point to Microsoft Office, and select Microsoft Office Word 2003.

> **Note**   If this is the first time you have run Word, you will be prompted to activate Office 2003. You must be connected to the Internet for this to work. Make sure the I Want To Activate The Software Over The Internet option is selected, and click Next. After activation is complete, click Close.

3. On the View menu, point to Toolbars, and then select Web Tools.

Exercise 2: Create a Custom Toolbar

1. Log on to Windows XP.

2. On the Start menu, select All Programs, select Microsoft Office, and then select Microsoft Office Word 2003.

3. In Microsoft Office Word 2003, right-click any toolbar and select Customize.

4. In the Customize dialog box, on the Toolbars tab, click New.

5. In the New Toolbar dialog box, in the Toolbar Name text box, type **Date and Time**. Click OK.

6. In the Customize dialog box, on the Commands tab, in the Categories list, select Insert. In the Commands list, drag the Date and Time commands to the newly created Date And Time toolbar.

7. In the Customize dialog box, click Close.

8. Drag the Date And Time toolbar to the toolbar area at the top of the Microsoft Word window, and dock it there.

Exercise 3: Add Items to a Menu List

1. Log on to Windows XP.

2. On the Start menu, select All Programs, select Microsoft Office, and then select Microsoft Office PowerPoint 2003.

3. Right-click the Menu bar, and select Customize.

4. In the Customize dialog box, on the Commands tab, in the Categories list, select New Menu.

5. In the Commands list, drag New Menu to the end of the Menu bar, just after Help.

6. In the Categories list, select Tools.

7. In the Commands list, drag Macros, Record New Macro, and Visual Basic Editor to the New menu.

8. On the Menu bar, right-click New Menu and select Name: New Menu. Type **Macro** and press ENTER.

9. Click Close to close the Customize dialog box.

10. Close PowerPoint.

Lesson Review

The following questions are intended to reinforce key information presented in this lesson. If you are unable to answer a question, review the lesson materials and try the question again. You can find answers to the questions in the "Questions and Answers" section at the end of this chapter.

1. An employee in the marketing department of your company works in Excel most of the day, but she spends an equal amount of time on the Internet. There she obtains product information and competitor prices from websites to create quotes. She is also new to Excel and often has to access the Help and Support files. You want to help her work faster and smarter. What can you suggest? (Choose all that apply.)

   A. Add the Web toolbar to Excel.

   B. Customize the toolbars, and reset the menu and toolbar usage data.

   C. Add the Task pane to the Excel interface.

   D. Add the Formula Auditing toolbar to Excel.

2. An employee in the graphics department of your company uses Microsoft Office PowerPoint Professional Edition 2003 to create documentation for company meetings with prospective clients. He reports that when he accesses a font from the font drop-down list on the Formatting toolbar, all of the fonts are listed, but he cannot tell what the font looks like by looking at it in the list. He would like the list of fonts to appear using the font that each item in the list represents. For instance, Arial uses Arial font, Century uses Century font, Lucida Sans uses Lucida Sans font, and so on. Is this possible, and if so, what needs to be done?

   A. It is not possible.

   B. It is possible only if the Microsoft Advanced Font Add-In is downloaded and installed.

   C. It is an option in the Customize dialog box on the Options tab.

   D. It is an option on the Fonts toolbar.

3. A user reports that each time she opens Word 2003, the Startup Pane appears, and each time she clicks the X in the upper right corner of the pane to close it. She wants to avoid this extra step each time she opens Word and wants to configure the pane so that it does not open every time she opens the program. What do you tell her to do? (Select all correct procedures.)

   A. With Word open, click View, and clear the Task Pane command.

   B. With Word open, click View, point to Toolbars, and clear the Task Pane command.

   C. In the Task pane, click the X in the upper right corner. Click View, point to Toolbars, and verify that Task Pane is cleared.

   D. Click Tools, click Options, and on the View tab, clear the Startup Task Pane check box.

Lesson Summary

- To personalize Office applications, add, remove, or customize toolbars, the Menu bar, and the menu lists.

- To further personalize Office applications, configure options in the Options dialog box, including print, view, save, edit, and security options.

Lesson 4: Configuring Proofing Tools

Proofing tools are components of Microsoft Word and other applications that allow users to check their spelling and grammar in different languages; create and use Auto-Correct, AutoSummarize, AutoFormat, and AutoText; use configured dictionaries; and work with fonts and localized templates. In this lesson, you will learn how to configure these tools for end users.

> **After this lesson, you will be able to**
> - Resolve language-related proofing problems.
> - Troubleshoot problems caused by templates.
> - Resolve issues with spelling and grammar tools.
>
> **Estimated lesson time: 25 minutes**

Proofing in Other Languages

The Office System offers users the ability to edit documents in multiple languages. Word 2003 can automatically detect many languages, including (but not limited to) Chinese, French, German, Italian, Japanese, Russian, and Spanish. Editing documents in various languages requires that you install the spelling and language tools for the language from the Office System Language Settings, turn on Automatic Language Detection, and set spelling and grammar options.

To install the spelling and grammar tools for a specific language, follow these steps:

1. From the Start menu, point to All Programs, point to Microsoft Office, point to Microsoft Office Tools, and select Microsoft Office 2003 Language Settings.
2. Select the Enabled Languages tab.
3. In the Available Languages dialog box, select the language to enable. Click Add.
4. If any Office programs are running, you must quit and restart all open Office applications to apply the changes. Click OK and click Yes if prompted.

> **Note**   Depending on the operating system and languages selected, you might have only limited functionality of the editing tools. If this is the case, you will be prompted on how to gain full functionality in these languages.

After you have installed the spelling and grammar tools, you need to turn on Automatic Language Detection by following these steps:

1. Open Word 2003, and from the Tools menu, point to Language, and then select Set Language.

2. Select the Detect Language Automatically check box, as shown in Figure 6-17, and click OK.

Figure 6-17   Detecting language automatically by configuring preferences in the Language dialog box.

To set the spelling and grammar options for the new language, follow these steps:

1. In Word 2003, from the Tools menu, select Options.

2. On the Spelling & Grammar tab, configure the language options as desired. Click OK.

To edit a document in the new language, open the document in Word 2003. Word automatically scans the document for spelling errors and denotes them as necessary. If additional proofing tools are required, you will be prompted with a dialog box.

> **Note**   Microsoft Office System Proofing Tools is an add-in package that contains the proofing tools that Microsoft makes for more than 30 languages. It includes fonts, spelling and grammar checkers, AutoCorrect lists, AutoSummarize rules, translation dictionaries, and for Asian languages, **Input Method Editors (IMEs)**. These proofing tools are available at *http: // www.shop.microsoft.com*.

Troubleshooting Automatic Language Detection

Several things can go wrong when using automatic language detection, including common problems that occur when the language is not supported by Microsoft or when Word does not correctly detect the language (which are addressed in the Microsoft

Office Word Help files) and other, less common, problems (which are detailed in various Microsoft Knowledge Base articles). For most issues, a DST's best resources are the Microsoft Word Help files and the Knowledge Base. Almost any problem you will encounter while using automatic language detection is addressed in these two areas.

Some of the Word Help files that you might be interested in reading include the following:

- Troubleshoot Automatic Language Detection
- Languages Word Can Detect Automatically
- Automatically Switch Keyboard Languages
- Automatically Correct Text As You Type In Another Language
- Install System Support For Multiple Languages
- Enable Editing Of Multiple Languages

Some Knowledge Base articles that you might be interested in reading include:

- Changes to The Default Language Settings Are Not Retained—Knowledge Base article 292106.
- Cannot Install German Language MUI Files—Knowledge Base article 831030.
- "The Dictionary For This Language Was Not Found" Error Message When You Try to Use Handwriting on the Language Bar—Knowledge Base article 831591.

Familiarize yourself with these articles and other common problems so that you can resolve service calls that revolve around these problems quickly and effectively.

AutoSummarize

Word 2003 can be used to automatically summarize a document. Users can choose to have Word 2003 highlight the important aspects and main points of the document in the document itself, insert a summary at the beginning of the document, create a new document and put the summary there, or create a summary in the document and hide everything else.

To automatically summarize a document, follow these steps:

1. Open the document in Word 2003.
2. From the Tools menu, select AutoSummarize.
3. Select the type of summary you want. There are four options:
   - ❑ Highlight Key Points
   - ❑ Insert An Executive Summary Or Abstract At The Top Of The Document

❑ Create A New Document And Put The Summary There

❑ Hide Everything But The Summary Without Leaving The Original Document

4. In the Percent Of Original box, type or select the level of detail to include in the summary. Using higher numbers includes more detail; lower numbers include less. There are several preconfigured options: 10 Sentences, 20 Sentences, 100 Words Or Less, 500 Words Or Less, 10%, 25%, 50%, and 75%. After you make a selection, the Summary and Original Document figures change to reflect your selection.

5. If you do not want AutoSummarize to replace the existing keywords and comments in the document's Properties dialog box (available by selecting Properties on the File menu), clear the Update Document Statistics check box.

6. Click OK.

AutoSummarize is an extremely powerful tool that allows users to create summaries of their work quickly. In addition, users who receive long documents can use AutoSummarize to view the key points before reading it, review key points before a meeting, or create notes for study. When visiting a new user's desk, ask if he or she is familiar with this feature.

Understanding Templates

When you create documents, they contain specific fonts, font styles, and font sizes so that headings, paragraphs, notes, tips, numbered and bulleted lists, summaries, and other components of the document are easily recognizable. Templates can also contain AutoText entries, page layout information, and **macros**. All documents created in Word 2003 use Word's Normal template by default. Templates define what a document, publication, website, e-mail message, or fax looks like when published, printed, or viewed. Templates also define the options that are available to the creator of the document (macros, font sizes and styles, and so on).

You can access and configure templates in the Templates And Add-Ins dialog box. (Click Tools, and then click Templates And Add-Ins.) Templates created specifically for a type of publication can be attached to any working document. You can also modify templates by opening the template, making changes, and resaving the template.

▶ **Attaching a Template**

To attach a localized or global template, follow these steps:

1. In Word 2003, from the Tools menu, select Templates And Add-Ins.

2. On the Templates tab, select Attach to attach a document template. The template listed is the template currently attached to the active document.

3. In the Attach Template dialog box, select the template to add. You might have to browse for the template. Click Open.

4. To automatically update the document styles, select the Automatically Update Document Styles check box. Click OK.

When you modify a template, the template is changed permanently (or until it is changed again). These changes affect any new documents that are created using the template.

With this in mind, to modify an existing template, follow these steps:

1. From the File menu, select Open, and locate the template to modify.

2. Make any changes desired to the template's text and graphics, styles, formatting, and so on.

3. From the File menu, select Save.

Spelling and Grammar

Any user can tell you that creating documents involves much more than typing words on a page, just as editing documents involves much more than checking spelling and grammar. As a DST, you will be called on to help end users work smarter and faster by teaching them to use the available editing tools. These tools can make both creating and editing documents easier, and there are many tools available.

AutoCorrect is one such tool. It can be used to automatically correct spelling errors as a user types, capitalize days of the week, capitalize the first letter in sentences, and more. You can use AutoFormat to automatically apply styles such as bulleted lists, fractions, and hyperlinks. AutoText lets you automatically complete text entries such as Dear Madam or Sir, Special Delivery, To Whom It May Concern, and even personal entries created by the user.

In addition to these tools, users can add words to the dictionaries and configure spelling and grammar options. Users can even add words to the AutoCorrect list so that the dictionary recognizes them. (These can include symbols, too.)

AutoCorrect

You can configure AutoCorrect options from the AutoCorrect dialog box or by right-clicking on the misspelled word. Adding an entry to the AutoCorrect list by using either procedure places the misspelled word in the AutoCorrect list in case the word is ever misspelled again. When a misspelling occurs, the word is automatically corrected while the user types. Figure 6-18 shows an example of adding a misspelled word to the AutoCorrect list by right-clicking it.

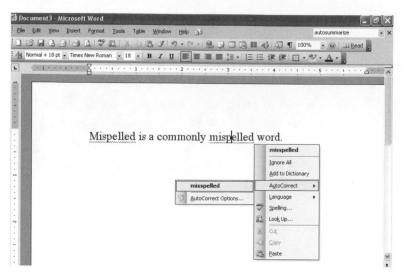

Figure 6-18   Adding AutoCorrect entries by right-clicking.

You can also add AutoCorrect entries by using the AutoCorrect dialog box. To add words in this manner, follow these steps:

1. From the Tools menu, select AutoCorrect Options.

2. In the Replace box, type the word that is commonly misspelled.

3. In the With box, type the desired replacement.

4. Click OK.

> **Note**   Most people have words they commonly misspell. Take a few minutes to teach your users how to add their troublesome words to the AutoCorrect list. They will work faster and smarter, which has several benefits, one being a happier end user.

AutoFormat

AutoFormat options allow text to be formatted while the user types and creates documents. For instance, when you use bullets or numbered lists, Word 2003 automatically adds the next bullet or the proper number in the list. Straight quotes can be replaced with smart quotes (the quotes point in the right direction), and Internet or network paths can automatically be configured as hyperlinks in the documents. All of these formatting options and more can be selected or cleared in the AutoCorrect dialog box on the AutoFormat and AutoFormat As You Type tabs.

AutoText

AutoText is a feature of Microsoft Office that allows a user to type the first few letters of a common word or entry, such as Best Regards, Attention, or Dear Mom and Dad, and have the rest of the word or phrase offered so that the user does not have to type the entire entry. Figure 6-19 shows an example. To add the word or complete the entry, the user simply presses ENTER.

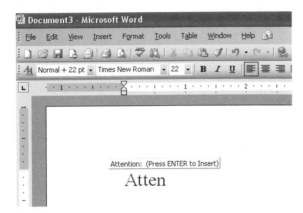

Figure 6-19   AutoText offers the entire word or phrase when applicable.

Users can add their own entries to the AutoText entry list by following these steps:

1. From the Tools menu, select AutoCorrect Options, and select the AutoText tab.

2. In the Enter AutoText Entries Here text box, type the entry to add. This might be a company name, a user name, a website, or a word or words the user types often.

3. Click Add to add the entry to the AutoText database, and then click OK to close the AutoCorrect dialog box.

AutoText entries are perfect for long words, phrases, or titles that a user types often. Consider adding a user's job title, department name, Web address, company name, or address.

Adding Words to the Dictionary

You access the dictionary from the Options dialog box on the Spelling & Grammar tab. You can add entries to the glossary for words that Microsoft Office applications think are misspelled. For instance, user names; postal codes; company names; acronyms such as DVDs, CDs, ISBN, and ASAP; and Web addresses are often underlined as misspelled words. Adding these entries to the dictionary not only causes them not to be underlined in a document the next time they are used but also keeps them from being marked as misspellings in Outlook, Excel, PowerPoint, or other Microsoft Office applications.

To add an entry to the default dictionary, follow these steps:

1. In Word 2003, from the Tools menu, select Options, and select the Spelling & Grammar tab.

2. Choose Custom Dictionaries.

3. In the Custom Dictionaries dialog box, select the dictionary to which you want to add the entry, and select Modify.

4. In the dictionary's dialog box, in the Word box, type the word to add. Click Add to add the word to the dictionary. Click OK to close the dictionary's dialog box, click OK to close the Custom Dictionaries dialog box, and click OK to close the Options dialog box.

It is easier to tell users to add words to the dictionary by right-clicking them in their documents. If the user knows that a word in a document is a real word and wants to add it to the dictionary, he or she can right-click the word and select Add To Dictionary. The word is then added.

Spelling and Grammar Options

There are several spelling and grammar options, and these are set in the Options dialog box on the Spelling & Grammar tab, shown in Figure 6-20. End users might want you to change the default options to suit their personal needs.

Figure 6-20   Configuring spelling and grammar options from the Spelling & Grammar tab.

Table 6-3 lists some common end-user requests and the best way to resolve them. Each solution is achieved by using the spelling and grammar options in the Options dialog box. Make sure you are familiar with all of the options.

Table 6-3   Common Spelling and Grammar Requests and Solutions

Request	Resolution
I do not want to see my spelling errors as I type. It is distracting; I will check the document when I am finished with it.	Select the Hide Spelling Errors In This Document check box.
I type using a lot of uppercase letters, but the spelling checker never checks them.	Clear the Ignore Words In Uppercase check box.
I do not want to see grammatical errors as I type. It is distracting; I will check the document when I am finished with it.	Clear the Check Grammar As You Type check box.
I need to see the readability statistics for my documents once a grammar check is complete, including the average number of sentences per paragraph, the number of passive sentences, and the grade level the document is written for.	Select the Show Readability Statistics check box.

Practice: Configure Proofing Tools

In this practice, you will configure proofing tools and AutoCorrect options.

Exercise 1: Configure Proofing Tools

1. Log on to Windows XP.

2. On the Start menu, point to All Programs and then to Microsoft Office, and select Microsoft Office Word 2003.

3. On the Tools menu, select Options.

4. On the Spelling & Grammar tab of the Options dialog box, under Spelling, clear the Check Spelling As You Type check box. Under Grammar, clear the Check Grammar As You Type check box.

5. Under Spelling, click Custom Dictionaries.

6. In the Custom Dictionaries dialog box, in the Dictionary list, ensure that Custom.dic is selected, and click Modify.

7. In the Custom.dic dialog box, in the Word text box, type **Contoso** and click Add.

8. In the Custom.dic dialog box, click OK.

9. In the Custom Dictionaries dialog box, click OK.

10. In the Options dialog box, under Grammar, click Settings.

11. In the Grammar Settings dialog box, ensure that the Writing Style drop-down list has Grammar Only selected.

12. In the Grammar And Style Options list, under Style, select the Clichés, Colloquial-isms, And Jargon check box. Also select the Sentence Length (More Than Sixty Words) and Use Of First Person check boxes. Click OK.

Exercise 2: Configure AutoCorrect Options

1. Log on to Windows XP.

2. On the Start menu, point to All Programs and then to Microsoft Office, and select Microsoft Office Word 2003.

3. On the Tools menu, select AutoCorrect Options.

4. In the AutoCorrect dialog box, on the AutoFormat tab, under Replace, clear the Internet And Network Paths With Hyperlinks check box.

5. On the AutoCorrect tab, clear the Correct Two Initial Capitals and Replace Text As You Type check boxes. Click OK.

6. In the AutoFormat dialog box, click OK.

7. Close Word, and do not save changes.

Lesson Review

The following question is intended to reinforce key information presented in this lesson. If you are unable to answer the question, review the lesson materials and try the question again. You can find answers to the question in the "Questions and Answers" section at the end of this chapter.

You support end users who create documents in Word 2003 on computers running Windows XP Professional. They often call with problems relating to proofing, editing, and summarizing documents. Common service calls are listed on the left; match them with the appropriate solution on the right.

---

1. A user is late for a meeting and needs to create a cheat sheet containing the main points in the document he received last week. What should he do?

A. Configure AutoCorrect.

2. A user confides in you that she is not a good speller and that she always misspells the same words over and over. Instead of right-clicking and choosing the correct spelling of these words time after time, she would like to know if she can set Word 2003 to automatically correct these words each time she misspells them. What should she do?

B. Configure AutoFormat.

3. A user creates documents that contain hyperlinks to network resources. These documents are posted on the company's internal website, and users access them when they need help and support. The user complains that he has to manually create the hyperlinks and wants Word to create them automatically. What should he do?

C. Use AutoSummarize, and create a summary that highlights the key points.

4. A user is writing a children's book, and several of the words she is using are not real words. She wants to add these words to the dictionary because the underlining throughout the document makes it hard to concentrate. What should she do?

D. Configure spelling options on the Spelling & Grammar tab.

Lesson Summary

- Office 2003 lets users edit and proof documents in multiple languages. Editing documents in various languages requires that you install the spelling and language tools for the language from the Office System Language Settings, turn on Automatic Language Detection, and set spelling and grammar options.

- Templates define what a document, publication, website, e-mail message, or fax looks like when published, printed, or viewed. Templates also define which options are available to the creator of the document (macros, font sizes and styles, and so on).

- Office 2003 offers many tools to help with spelling and grammar, from traditional spelling checkers to automatic tools such as AutoCorrect and AutoText.

Case Scenario Exercises

In the following scenarios, you must use what you have learned throughout the lessons in this chapter to answer questions based on a real-world scenario. Read each scenario, and answer the questions. If you have trouble, review the chapter and try again. You can find answers in the "Questions and Answers" section at the end of this chapter.

Scenario 6.1

The company you work for is named Contoso Pharmaceuticals. Users complain that every time they create a document in Word, PowerPoint, Excel, or another Microsoft Office application, the company name is underlined because it is believed to be misspelled. Users want this behavior to stop. In addition, users want the entire company name typed automatically each time they type in the first few letters of it. They are tired of typing the words *Contoso Pharmaceuticals* every time they want to type the company name. What should you tell each user in the company to do?

A. Add the word *Contoso* to the dictionary. Add *Contoso Pharmaceuticals* to the AutoText list.

B. Add the word *Contoso* to the AutoText list. Add *Contoso Pharmaceuticals* to the AutoCorrect list.

C. Add both *Contoso* and *Pharmaceuticals* to the AutoCorrect list.

D. Add both *Contoso* and *Pharmaceuticals* to the AutoText list.

Scenario 6.2

A small business owner wants you to install Microsoft Office Professional Edition 2003 on the computers in his office. He reports that he has 10 computers, 3 of which use Windows 98, 2 of which use Windows Me, and 5 that use Windows XP Professional. They are configured as a workgroup. Each of these computers runs Microsoft Office 2000. He purchased five Microsoft Office CDs because a friend told him that he installed his Microsoft Office CD on his desktop PC and his laptop, and they both run like a charm. He figures he will just use the five CDs to install Office Professional Edition 2003 on the 10 computers. Where is the flaw in his logic? (Pick two.)

A. There is a problem with the licensing requirements. Although a user can install Office Professional Edition 2003 on a desktop PC and a laptop, it cannot be installed on two different computers for two different users.

B. Office Professional Edition 2003 can only be installed on computers running Windows XP.

C. Office Professional Edition 2003 cannot be installed on the computers running Windows 98 or Windows Me.

D. Office Professional Edition 2003 cannot be installed on workgroup computers, only on computers in a domain. He will need to purchase Microsoft Office Standard Edition 2003.

Troubleshooting Lab

The accounting group at a company named Contoso often has to collaborate on documents created in Excel. The documents are financial and laden with XY scatter charts, line graphs, and flow charts. One of your users wants to create a custom menu named Charting to assist with creating and editing these items and has asked for your help.

Furthermore, accounting group members collaborate in groups on the documents. They need to be able to save and load documents from a network share. To keep strict track of what document is being worked on by whom and when, they check the documents in and out. The user would like your help creating a custom toolbar named Collaboration that contains the Check In and Check Out, Send For Review, and Reply With Changes commands.

Chapter Summary

- To install an application successfully, verify that the application is compatible with the operating system and the computer hardware and that the computer meets minimum or recommended requirements. Verify that the proper licenses are readily available.

- To personalize Office applications, add, remove, or customize toolbars, the Menu bar, and the menu lists.

- To further personalize Office applications, configure options in the Options dialog box, including print, view, save, edit, and security options.

- To create an Office application that works for the user, configure proofing tools, including spelling and grammar, templates, and AutoSummarize options.

Exam Highlights

Before taking the exam, review the key topics and terms that are presented in this chapter. You need to know this information.

Key Points

■ Windows XP offers compatibility features for running older programs. You can run a program in one of four compatibility modes—Windows 95, Windows 98/Me, Windows NT (Service Pack 5), and Windows 2000. You can also configure particular compatibility settings, such as running in 256 colors or in 640 × 480 resolution.

■ In Windows XP, you must have administrative permissions to install most programs. Some programs, such as Office 2003, are good about warning you of this fact before you start the installation; some programs are not.

Key Terms

AutoRecover files   Files that are saved automatically when an application shuts down unexpectedly. AutoRecover files can help a user recover a document when the power goes out or when a computer shuts down unexpectedly.

encryption   A process for converting plain text to code for the purpose of security. Encrypted files use scrambled data that makes the file unreadable to everyone except the person who created it. Secure websites use encryption to secure transactions.

macro   A set of actions used to automate tasks. Macros are recorded by the end user and are then performed when a specific keystroke or menu selection is made.

personalized menu   A menu that shows most recently viewed or used commands. Hidden commands appear after a few seconds. Full menus can be configured if personalized menus are not desired.

Questions and Answers

Lesson 1 Review

Page
6-11

1. A user wants you to install Office Professional Edition 2003 on his computer. He uses Windows XP Home Edition and has a Pentium III processor, 512 MB of RAM, 40 GB of free hard disk space, and a generic plug-and-play Super VGA monitor capable of 800 x 600 resolution. Which of the following upgrades (if any) will be needed so that the program will run well (thus meeting recommended requirements)? (Choose all that apply.)

   A. Upgrade from Windows XP Home Edition to Windows XP Professional Edition.

   B. Upgrade to a Pentium 4 or equivalent.

   C. Add more RAM.

   D. Partition the hard disk into two 20-GB sections. Office cannot work with large disk drives.

   E. Install Service Packs 1 and 2.

   F. Upgrade to a flat-screen monitor or a monitor with resolution that can be configured at 1024 x 768.

   G. Nothing needs to be upgraded.

   G is the correct answer. A, B, C, D, E, and F all meet recommended requirements.

2. Which of the following types of software would it be safe to run under Windows XP, using an application compatibility mode?

   A. A game that was written for Windows 95

   B. Backup software that was written for Windows 98

   C. Disk partitioning software that was written for Windows 2000

   D. Antivirus software that was written for Windows 2000

   A is the only correct answer. B, C, and D are incorrect because you should never use a program compatibility mode to force system tools (such as antivirus or CD-burning software) that are written for another operating system to work under Windows XP.

Lesson 2 Review

Page 6-21 The following table lists some common installation problems and their causes. To answer this question, match the installation problem on the left with the likely cause on the right.

1. The program installed correctly but fails online activation.	A. The program was probably downloaded from the Internet, and the download was not successful.
2. The error Can't Copy File To Disk prevents installation from starting or completing.	B. The computer does not meet minimum hardware requirements.
3. The installation of the program stops, and an error message appears that states that some of the downloaded files are missing or corrupt.	C. An antivirus program is running.
4. Installation stops, hangs, or quits.	D. There might be a typographical error created by the user.
5. The validation code will not validate the software.	E. The program has already been installed on another computer, and licensing restrictions and requirements are preventing the successful installation of the program.

1. E is correct. Programs that have been installed on another computer can sometimes be installed on a second computer, but activation will fail if licensing restrictions are imposed. 2. C is correct. Running antivirus programs while installing programs can cause these errors. 3. A is correct. Missing or corrupt file errors are usually caused by bad CDs or problematic downloads. 4. B is correct. When an installation hangs or quits, it is generally because of problems with the computer's hardware, especially RAM or processors. 5. D is correct. Many validation code or product ID errors are caused because the user did not type the correct code.

Lesson 3 Review

Page 6-35 **1.** An employee in the marketing department of your company works in Excel most of the day, but she spends an equal amount of time on the Internet. There she obtains product information and competitor prices from websites to create quotes. She is also pretty new to Excel and often has to access the Help and Support files. You want to help her work faster and smarter. What can you suggest? (Choose all that apply.)

   A. Add the Web toolbar to Excel.

   B. Customize the toolbars, and reset the menu and toolbar usage data.

   C. Add the Task pane to the Excel interface.

   D. Add the Formula Auditing toolbar to Excel.

A and C are correct. Adding the Web toolbar to Excel will allow the employee to access Favorites, the home page, previously visited sites, and hyperlinks within Excel. Adding the Task pane will offer a place for the employee to get help quickly from Microsoft Office Online. B will only reset the toolbars to their defaults and will not show the Web toolbar or offer help and support faster than before. D provides a toolbar used to circle invalid data and evaluate formulas, and it is not appropriate here.

2. An employee in the graphics department of your company uses Microsoft Office PowerPoint Professional Edition 2003 to create documentation for company meetings with prospective clients. He reports that when he accesses a font from the font drop-down list on the Formatting toolbar, all of the fonts are listed, but he cannot tell what the font looks like by looking at it in the list. He would like the list of fonts to appear using the font that each item in the list represents. For instance, Arial uses Arial font, Century uses Century font, Lucida Sans uses Lucida Sans font, and so on. Is this possible, and if so, what needs to be done?

   A. It is not possible.

   B. It is possible only if the Microsoft Advanced Font Add-In is downloaded and installed.

   C. It is an option in the Customize dialog box on the Options tab.

   D. It is an option on the Fonts toolbar.

   C is correct. Fonts can be shown in the fonts list. A is incorrect because C is correct. B is not a valid downloadable application. D is not correct because there is no Fonts toolbar.

3. A user reports that each time she opens Word 2003, the Startup Pane appears, and each time she clicks the X in the upper right corner of the pane to close it. She wants to avoid this extra step each time she opens Word and wants to configure the pane so that it does not open every time she opens the program. What do you tell her to do? (Select all correct procedures.)

   A. With Word open, click View, and clear the Task Pane command.

   B. With Word open, click View, point to Toolbars, and clear Task Pane.

   C. In the Task pane, click the X in the upper right corner. Click View, point to Toolbars, and verify that Task Pane is cleared.

   D. Click Tools, click Options, and on the View tab, clear the Startup Task Pane check box.

   D is the correct answer. A and B will close the Task pane only temporarily, but the Task pane will open again when Word is restarted. C is incorrect because this will close the Task pane only during the current session.

Lesson 4 Review

Page
6-46
You support end users who create documents in Word 2003 on computers running Windows XP Professional. They often call with problems relating to proofing, editing, and summarizing documents. Common service calls are listed on the left; match them with the appropriate solution on the right.

---

1. A user is late for a meeting and needs to create a cheat sheet containing the main points in the document he received last week. What should he do?	A. Configure AutoCorrect.
2. A user confides in you that she is not a good speller and that she always misspells the same words over and over. Instead of right-clicking and choosing the correct spelling of these words time after time, she would like to know if she can set Word 2003 to automatically correct these words each time she misspells them. What should she do?	B. Configure AutoFormat.
3. A user creates documents that contain hyperlinks to network resources. These documents are posted on the company's internal website, and users access them when they need help and support. The user complains that he has to manually create the hyperlinks and wants Word to create them automatically. What should he do?	C. Use AutoSummarize, and create a summary that highlights the key points.
4. A user is writing a children's book, and several of the words she is using are not real words. She wants to add these words to the dictionary because the underlining throughout the document makes it hard to concentrate. What should she do?	D. Configure spelling options on the Spelling & Grammar tab.

---

1. C is correct. AutoSummarize can be used to highlight and list the main points in a document. 2. A is correct. AutoCorrect can be configured so that misspelled words (when repeatedly misspelled) are corrected automatically. 3. B is correct. AutoFormat options can be set so that hyperlinks are automatically created. 4. D is correct. One of the spelling options is Hide Spelling Errors In This Document.

Case Scenario Exercises: Scenario 6.1

Page
6-47 The company you work for is named Contoso Pharmaceuticals. Users complain that every time they create a document in Word, PowerPoint, Excel, or another Microsoft Office application, the company name is underlined because it is believed to be misspelled. Users want this behavior to stop. In addition, users want the entire company name typed automatically each time they type in the first few letters of it. They are tired of typing the words *Contoso Pharmaceuticals* every time they want to type the company name. What should you tell each user in the company to do?

A. Add the word *Contoso* to the dictionary. Add *Contoso Pharmaceuticals* to the AutoText list.

B. Add the word *Contoso* to the AutoText list. Add *Contoso Pharmaceuticals* to the AutoCorrect list.

C. Add both *Contoso* and *Pharmaceuticals* to the AutoCorrect list.

D. Add both *Contoso* and *Pharmaceuticals* to the AutoText list.

> A is the only correct answer. Adding Contoso to the dictionary will prevent the word from appearing misspelled in documents. Adding Contoso Pharmaceuticals to the AutoText list will cause it to be automatically offered after the first few letters of the company name are typed. The others are incorrect because AutoCorrect is used to correct misspelled words as a user types, and AutoText is used to automatically offer suggestions for the text typed.

Case Scenario Exercises: Scenario 6.2

Page
6-48 A small business owner wants you to install Microsoft Office Professional Edition 2003 on the computers in his office. He reports that he has 10 computers, 3 of which use Windows 98, 2 of which use Windows Me, and 5 that use Windows XP Professional. They are configured as a workgroup. Each of these computers runs Microsoft Office 2000. He purchased five Microsoft Office CDs because a friend told him that he installed his Microsoft Office CD on his desktop PC and his laptop, and they both run like a charm. He figures he will just use the five CDs to install Office Professional Edition 2003 on the 10 computers. Where is the flaw in his logic? (Pick two.)

A. There is a problem with the licensing requirements. Although a user can install Office Professional Edition 2003 on a desktop PC and a laptop, it cannot be installed on two different computers for two different users.

B. Office Professional Edition 2003 can only be installed on computers running Windows XP.

C. Office Professional Edition 2003 cannot be installed on the computers running Windows 98 or Windows Me.

D. Office Professional Edition 2003 cannot be installed on workgroup computers, only on computers in a domain. He will need to purchase Microsoft Office Standard Edition 2003.

A and C are correct. A correctly describes the licensing agreement, and C correctly describes the operating systems on which the Office System can be installed. B is incorrect because the Office System can be installed on a computer running Windows 2000 (Service Pack 3). D is incorrect because all Microsoft Office editions can be installed on computers, no matter their network configuration.

Troubleshooting Lab

Page 6-49

The accounting group at a company named Contoso often has to collaborate on documents created in Excel. The documents are financial and laden with XY scatter charts, line graphs, and flow charts. One of your users wants to create a custom menu named Charting to assist with creating and editing these items and has asked for your help.

Furthermore, accounting group members collaborate in groups on the documents. They need to be able to save and load documents from a network share. To keep strict track of what document is being worked on by whom and when, they check the documents in and out. The user would like your help creating a custom toolbar named Collaboration that contains the Check In and Check Out, Send For Review, and Reply With Changes commands.

> **Note**   The answer that follows is just a sample; the answer can vary.

In this sample answer, a Charting menu was created with the graphing and flow chart functions that are commonly used. Figure 6-21 shows this menu with Flowchart selected.

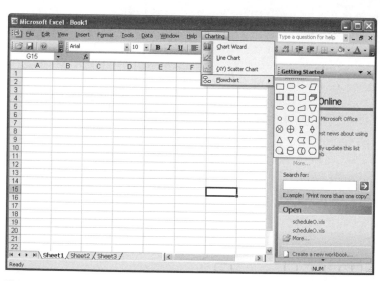

Figure 6-21   Use the Charting custom menu with Flowchart selected.

Also, a custom toolbar was created with the Check In, Check Out, Send For Review, and Reply With Changes commands, as shown in Figure 6-22.

Figure 6-22   The custom Collaboration toolbar is a sample solution.

7 Troubleshooting Office Applications

Exam Objectives in this Chapter:

- Configure and troubleshoot Office applications
- Answer end-user questions related to configuring Office applications
- Resolve issues related to Office application support features
- Resolve issues related to Outlook Express features

Why This Chapter Matters

The goal of this chapter is to teach you to resolve end-user requests regarding Microsoft Office applications, including Word 2003, Excel 2003, PowerPoint 2003, and Outlook 2003. You will learn ways, including using Microsoft Office Online, to resolve issues with these applications. You will also learn how to perform ordinary tasks in each application and resolve common end-user requests. In addition to these Office applications, Microsoft Outlook Express is covered.

Although it would be impossible to detail all aspects of the Office applications effectively in the space provided in this chapter, be aware that you must be familiar with each application's toolbars, features, and components; know how to recover lost files; and be able to use and troubleshoot the main components of each application. You should also know how to use the available online tools to resolve issues that you are not familiar with and to learn new skills.

Lessons in this Chapter:

Before You Begin

Before you begin this chapter, you should have Office 2003 installed on your computer. You should also be familiar with the concepts discussed in Chapter 4, "Microsoft Outlook and Outlook Express," and Chapter 6, "Installing and Configuring Office Applications."

Lesson 1: Supporting Word 2003

In Chapter 6, "Installing and Configuring Office Applications," you learned to install and configure Word 2003. After users begin using Word 2003 and perform configuration tasks on their own, create documents with sounds and images, use macros, and access the advanced features in the application, they might encounter problems using them. In this lesson, you will learn how to resolve some of the more common troubleshooting tasks in Word 2003.

After this lesson, you will be able to

- Troubleshoot missing toolbars, features, and components.
- Resolve issues related to text formatting.
- Resolve issues with embedded and linked objects.
- Recover lost files.

Estimated lesson time: 45 minutes

Missing Toolbars, Features, and Components

As users start customizing the user interface in Word 2003, you will start receiving calls about missing toolbars, features, and components. Users might accidentally hide or customize a toolbar so that the default options are absent, move or resize toolbars, or remove components and features, thus making them unavailable. You will need to be able to resolve these types of calls and locate missing interface items.

Restoring the Defaults

When users request that the changes they have made be removed or when a computer is transferred to another user, you will need to restore the defaults to the menus, buttons, menu choices, and default toolbars. These changes can affect both menus and toolbars. Table 7-1 details how to reset the default arrangements for a single menu, for a single toolbar, and for all menus and toolbars.

Table 7-1   Restore Defaults

To Restore Original Settings For	Perform These Steps
A menu	1. From the Tools menu, choose Customize, and select the Commands tab.
	2. Click Rearrange Commands.
	3. In the Rearrange Commands dialog box, select Toolbar, select Menu Bar, and in the Controls list, select the menu to reset.
	4. Click Reset.
	5. In the Reset Changes Made To 'File' Menu For drop-down list, select Normal and click OK. Click Close, and click Close again to exit.
A built-in toolbar	1. From the Tools menu, choose Customize, and select the Toolbars tab.
	2. In the Toolbars list box, select the toolbar to restore. Click Reset.
	3. In the Reset Changes Made To 'Control Toolbox' Toolbar For drop-down list, select Normal and click OK. Click Close to exit.
All default toolbars and menu commands	1. From the Tools menu, choose Customize, and select the Options tab.
	2. Click the Reset Menu And Toolbar Usage Data button.
	3. Click Yes to configure the menu and toolbar reset, and then click Close to close the Customize dialog box.

You can also restore original settings for a built-in toolbar button or menu command by using similar techniques. Remember, you can show or hide any toolbar by right-clicking an empty area of the Menu bar and selecting or deselecting it, or you can resize or move a toolbar by dragging it.

Creating a Custom Toolbar

When users report that the default toolbars that they use and access do not suit their purposes, you can guide the users through creating a custom toolbar. Custom toolbars allow users to add their own buttons, add various built-in menus, and even create a custom name for the new toolbar. This is the perfect solution for those users who are constantly tweaking the default toolbars and menus. To create a custom toolbar for an end user, follow these steps:

1. From the Tools menu, choose Customize, and select the Toolbars tab.

2. Click New.

3. In the New Toolbar dialog box, in the Toolbar Name text box, type a name for the new toolbar.

4. From the Make Toolbar Available To drop-down list, select the template or document in which you want to make the toolbar available. Click OK.

5. Select the Commands tab.

6. To add a button, select a category in the Categories list box, and drag the command you want to the new toolbar.

7. To add a built-in menu, select Built-In Menus in the Categories list box, and drag the menu you want to the new toolbar. Figure 7-1 shows an example of a customized toolbar.

Figure 7-1 This customized toolbar has several formatting options.

8. Click Close when finished, and drag the new toolbar to an area of the interface to dock it.

Adding or Removing Components

When you originally install Office, certain components are installed with it. If components are missing or are no longer needed, you will have to locate the original source files (they might be on a network server, CD, or mapped drive) and use the Windows Add Or Remove Programs feature in Control Panel to add or remove them.

Some of the components for Word 2003 include the following:

- **.NET Programmability Support** Allows for programmability with **Microsoft .NET Framework** version 1.1

- **Help** Help for Microsoft Word

- **Repair Broken Text** Repairs documents that display text incorrectly (Eastern European and complex script languages only)

- **Wizards And Templates** Includes various wizards and templates for Word

- **Address Book** Provides tools for integrating the Microsoft Exchange Personal Address Book and Microsoft Office Outlook Address Book

- **Page Border Art** Includes page borders to enhance documents

When components are missing or not needed, you will need to add or remove them from Control Panel by following these steps:

1. Open Control Panel, and open Add Or Remove Programs.

2. Select Microsoft Office Professional Edition 2003, and click Change.

3. On the Microsoft Office 2003 Setup page, select Add Or Remove Features. Click Next.

4. On the Custom Setup page, clear the check boxes for any applications you would like to remove (if applicable), select the check boxes for any applications you would like to install, leave the other components in their current state, select the Choose Advanced Customization Of Applications check box, and click Next.

5. Expand the tree for Microsoft Office Word. (You can use this same technique for components of other Office applications.) Components not installed will have a red X beside them. Figure 7-2 shows an example.

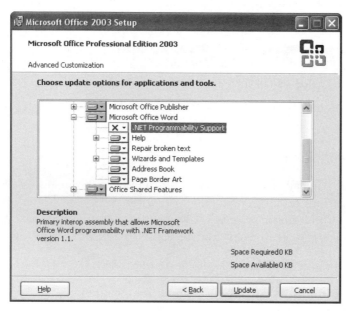

Figure 7-2   Add missing components by using Add Or Remove Programs in Control Panel.

6. To add a component, click the down arrow beside it, and select Run All From My Computer. That option will be added. To remove a component, click the down arrow beside it and select Not Available. Figure 7-3 shows an example.

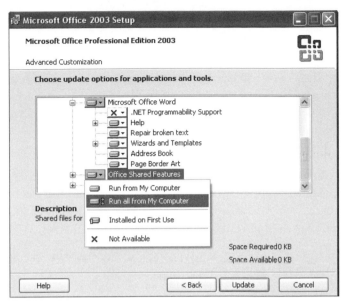

Figure 7-3   Select a component to add or remove from the component's drop-down list.

7. Click Update, and click OK when finished. Click Close to close Add Or Remove Programs.

Exam Tip   If a user feels that something is missing from the interface, there are three common reasons: personalized menus are enabled and the user is not seeing all the commands available, a user has customized the interface and certain commands are missing, or the feature was not installed.

You might also need to add Office Tools components such as Microsoft Office Picture Manager, Equation Editor, Office Binder Support, Research Explorer Bar, or others. You can view these components and information about them by expanding the Office Tools tree on the Advanced Customization page. When you select a component, you will see a description listed in the Description area.

See Also   There is a wealth of free information about Office 2003 in the Help files. Just type any query in the task pane. For example, you could type the query *formatting*, and look through the search results for items that start with *Training*. (For example, the previous example, *formatting*, returns a training article titled, "Format your document with styles.") Selecting a Training link takes you to Microsoft Office Online, where a free course automatically starts. There is even a friendly voice to guide you through it. Work through these free training courses in your spare time, and urge your end users to do the same.

Text Formatting

Formatting queries are fairly common in an office environment. Although most users are able to format their own text, you might be called on to resolve advanced text formatting issues when they arise. These calls might be for you to teach an end user to perform a task, which might require you to search for the procedure by using the task pane and Microsoft Office Online. The queries might also be for you to resolve known issues, which will require you to visit the Knowledge Base or TechNet. As a desktop support technician (DST), you should be prepared for anything.

Because queries relating to formatting will be varied, it is far easier to detail where to find answers than how to resolve specific issues. In the following section, you will learn a little about both.

> **Note**   The Microsoft Office Online Help and Support files work only if the user is connected to the Internet. The rest of this section makes this assumption.

Customizing Bulleted and Numbered Lists

Most users know how to create bulleted and numbered lists, but they may need help customizing the number format, number style, or even the number's position in the list to meet a company's style requirements for Web pages, publications, or documents. Although *you* might have an idea about how to do this, walking the user through finding the answer and following a written procedure will be the best solution in the long run. You will not only resolve the call but most likely will prevent future calls from the same user.

To customize a bulleted or numbered list, and to teach the end user to use Microsoft Office Online Help and Support at the same time, follow this procedure:

1. Open Word 2003 and the working document.
2. From the View menu, verify that the task pane is selected.
3. In the task pane, click the down arrow and select Help. The task pane with Help selected is shown in Figure 7-4.

Figure 7-4   The Word Help task pane offers a wealth of information.

4. Under Assistance, in the Search For text box, type **Customize bullets and numbering** and press ENTER on the keyboard, or click the green arrow beside the text box.

5. From the search results offered, select Modify Bulleted Or Numbered List Formats.

> **Note**   Notice that you can also choose Troubleshoot Bulleted And Numbered Lists, Restore A Customized List Format To Its Original Setting, Create A Multiple-Level Picture Bullet List, and Convert Bullets To Numbers And Vice Versa.

6. From the Microsoft Office Word Help window, follow the directions offered for modifying any bulleted or numbered list. These procedures cover using a unique symbol or picture bullet, customizing numbered list formats, and formatting bullets and numbers differently.

Changing the Language Format

As with customizing bulleted and numbered lists, you can get help from Microsoft Office Online to change the language format of a document. Again, walking the user through this procedure reduces further service calls for that user, helps you learn new tasks and skills, and resolves the problem quickly for the user.

To resolve problems with the language format of a document, follow these steps:

1. Open Word 2003 and the working document.

2. From the View menu, verify that Task Pane is selected.

3. In the task pane, click the down arrow and select Help.

4. Under Assistance, in the Search For text box, type **Language format**. Press ENTER on the keyboard, or click the green arrow next to the text box.

5. From the search results offered, select Change The Language Format Of Text.

> **Note**   Notice that you can also choose Install System Support For Multiple Languages, Troubleshoot Automatic Language Detection, Enable Editing Of Multiple Languages, and Change The Language Of The User Interface Or Help In Office Programs.

6. From the Microsoft Office Word Help window, follow the directions offered for changing the language format of the text.

AutoFormat

AutoFormat quickly applies formatting, including headings, bullets, numbered lists, borders, numbers, fractions, and similar items, with little effort from the end user either while the document is being created or afterward. Users typically have problems with AutoFormat when it is configured to format text as they create a document, usually because they dislike the formatting Word applies. They typically have problems when applying formatting to a document after it is created for the same reason.

AutoFormat has several listings in the Microsoft Office Online Help and Support files, including:

- Review AutoFormat Changes.
- Turn On Or Off Automatic Formatting.
- Troubleshoot Automatic Formatting.
- About Automatic Formatting.

These Help files, like others associated with Word, guide you through resolving various AutoFormat issues. For instance, to learn how to review and accept or decline Auto-Format changes, follow these steps:

1. Open Word 2003 and the working document.

2. From the View menu, verify that Task Pane is selected.

3. In the task pane, click the down arrow and select Help.

4. Under Assistance, in the Search For text box, type **AutoFormat**. Click the green arrow.

5. From the search results offered, select Review AutoFormat Changes.

6. From the Microsoft Office Word Help window, follow the directions offered for reviewing, accepting, and rejecting changes.

Embedded and Linked Objects

You can insert objects, which can include files, tables, charts, spreadsheets, images, and sounds, into a working document (a destination file) when you want to include additional information from other sources (source files). For instance, you might insert into a Word document an Excel file that contains sales data that is updated daily, a Publisher file that contains a table that is updated weekly, a Microsoft Access file that contains an employee phone list that is updated monthly, or a simple sound or image that is stored on a network server that is never updated. These inserted objects come from various sources and are thus referred to as *source files*. Items that you insert into a Word document can be either embedded or linked.

When you embed an object, the information in the destination file does not change if you modify the source file. An embedded object is like a snapshot of the object. These objects become part of the destination file, making this type of insertion useful for distributing multiple files in a single document. When embedded objects are edited, they are double-clicked in the destination file and edited in the source file's native program. Files with embedded data can be quite large.

When you link an object, the information in the destination file is updated when you modify the source file. Linked data is stored in the source file, not the destination file. The destination file stores only information about where the source file is located. With linked files, you can maintain data in a separate program, and when you open the destination file, Word automatically accesses the most up-to-date information. When you edit linked objects, you use the Links command from the Edit menu, and you edit the data in the source file's native application. Files with linked data are generally smaller than those with embedded data.

Embedding and Linking Objects

You embed and link objects by using the Insert and Edit menus, and sometimes by using the Copy and Paste Special commands. The easiest type of object you can add to a document is a new embedded Microsoft Excel file: All you have to do is click the Insert Microsoft Excel Worksheet icon on the Standard toolbar and select the size of the worksheet to embed. Figure 7-5 shows an example. After the worksheet is embedded, you edit it as you would in Excel, using Excel's toolbars. After you have completed the Excel worksheet, click outside the worksheet area, and Word's toolbars reappear.

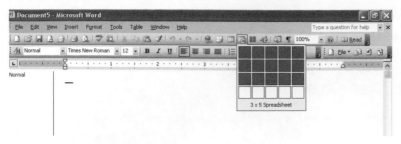

Figure 7-5   Embed a new Excel worksheet.

You can also embed preexisting objects or files that have already been created by using the Insert menu and the Object command, as follows:

1. Open Word 2003, and click where the embedded object should be inserted.
2. From the Insert menu, choose Object, and then select the Create New tab.
3. In the Object Type list box, select the type of object you want to create.
4. Select the Display As Icon check box.
5. Click OK.
6. In the application that opens, open or create and save the file you want to embed. Minimize or close the file's application. The file will be embedded.

> **Note**   You can also choose not to select Display As Icon, but failing to make this selection changes the default process of embedding a file. For instance, if you embed an Excel file but do not choose Display As Icon, an actual Excel document will be added to the existing document, not an existing Excel file. If you choose to embed a wave sound using this same technique, you will have to create the sound before it can be embedded. You will not be given the option of opening an existing wave file.

Here is an example of how to embed or link cells from an Excel file:

1. Open both Word and Excel.
2. In Excel, copy the cells you want to embed or link.
3. In Word, position the mouse pointer on the page where you want the data, and then choose Paste Special from the Edit menu.
4. Select Paste from the Paste Special dialog box to embed the file; select Paste Link to link the file.

5. If you want to link the object, select the Display As Icon check box to display the linked file as an icon.

6. In the As list, select the format that you want to use to embed or link the file. Click OK to save your changes.

After you have embedded or linked an object, you can edit it by right-clicking and selecting from the options. Links can be updated, edited, opened, and more. Embedded objects can be opened, edited, formatted, and converted; hyperlinks can be added; and more. Experiment with the different options for both.

Troubleshooting Linked and Embedded Files

Users will have problems with both embedded and linked files, but problems with linked files can be a little more difficult to diagnose. Table 7-2 lists some common issues with linked files and their solutions. You can find these and other tips and tricks in the Microsoft Office Online Help and Support files.

Table 7-2   Troubleshooting Linked Files

Problem	Solution
The error message "Cannot Edit" appears when a linked or embedded object is double-clicked.	Verify that the program that is used to create or open the file is installed on the computer and is running. If the object is linked, verify that the file has not been moved. If the linked object is on another computer on the network, verify that you can connect to that computer.
The linked or embedded object cannot be opened because the program used to create it is not installed on the computer.	Convert the object to the file format of a program that is installed by choosing Edit, Linked Worksheet Object, Video Clip Object, Slide Object, or a similar option and then clicking Convert.
The linked or embedded object is cropped around the edges.	In the source program, reduce the size of the data. You can do this by choosing a smaller font, resizing an image, or reducing the column size in a worksheet.
Excel objects do not open in Word.	Open Excel. On the Tools menu, choose Options, and on the General tab, clear the Ignore Other Applications check box.

These and other troubleshooting problems and solutions are available from Microsoft Office Online Help and Support, from the Knowledge Base, and from TechNet. You can also get help from newsgroups and third-party Internet sites. A good DST accesses these sites and resources not only to solve problems but also to learn about common issues before they happen.

Recovering Lost Files

The most disastrous problem from an end user's point of view has to be dealing with lost files. A user can lose a file for many reasons, including a power outage, a computer problem, or a user error. Other times, files are lost because the document is damaged or the data is corrupt. When the file is lost because of a power outage, power surge, or computer problem, chances are good that you can find the file on the hard disk as long as the computer can be rebooted.

> **Note**   Configure Word to always keep a backup copy of open files. On the Tools menu, choose Options, and select the Save tab. Select the Always Create Backup Copy check box. In addition, select the Allow Background Saves and Save AutoRecover Info Every __ Minutes check boxes.

Using Microsoft Office Application Recovery

If an end user reports that Word 2003 is not responding, you can recover the program. This causes Word to attempt to recover the files the end user was working on and restart the application. To access this recovery feature, follow these steps:

1. From the Start menu, choose All Programs, Microsoft Office, Microsoft Office Tools, and Microsoft Office Application Recovery.

2. In the Microsoft Application Recovery dialog box, select the program that is not responding, and click Recover Application or Restart Application (only one will be available), or choose End Application if you want to close the application. The latter option causes you to lose recent changes.

3. If you want to report the problem to Microsoft, click Report Problem; otherwise, click Don't Report Problem.

4. Reopen the application if necessary. In the Document Recovery task pane, click the arrow next to the file name and either select Open or Save As. Click Yes if prompted to replace the existing file.

Using AutoRecover

AutoRecover files are the files that Word automatically creates in the background every few minutes as specified by the end user. By default, AutoRecover saves files every 10 minutes. If a user encounters a problem with an application, the application offers the last saved version of the file to the user the next time he or she starts the application. Word stores the AutoRecover files in the folder specified in the Options dialog box (accessed from the File Locations tab). You can change both the file location and AutoRecover default behavior quite easily by following these steps:

1. Open Word 2003. From the Tools menu, choose Options.

2. On the Save tab, verify that the Save AutoRecover Info Every __ Minutes check box is selected and that a number between 1 and 120 is configured in the box. You can disable AutoRecover by clearing the check box.

3. On the File Locations tab, select AutoRecover Files, and click Modify to change the location of the recovered files. Browse to a new location, and click OK.

4. Click OK to close the Options dialog box.

Note   You can also manually recover files by browsing to the AutoRecover file location.

Using Open And Repair

Additionally, you can help end users recover text from a damaged or corrupt document by using the Open And Repair option. To open and repair documents, follow these steps:

1. Open Word. From the File menu, choose Open.

2. In the Look In drop-down list, browse to the location of the file you want to open. Select the file, but do not click Open.

3. Click the arrow next to the Open button, and then select Open And Repair.

There are other options for recovering lost data, so if none of these options work, you might have to restore the data from backup; contact a network administrator; or, if the user created the lost file since the last backup, accept that the file is lost. Encourage users to create backup copies, schedule regular backups, and allow background saves.

Note   These recovery options are also available in other Microsoft applications.

Dealing with User Errors

If a user forgets where he or she saved a file, you can search for it by using the Search Results window that is available on the Start menu. You can search by the date the file was created or modified, by its name, or using other options. In addition, all Microsoft applications offer a list of most recently opened documents from the File menu. Finally, clicking Start, pointing to My Recent Documents, and accessing a document shown there is also helpful in finding missing files.

Practice: Configure and Troubleshoot Word 2003

In this practice, you will restore the default menu settings in Word 2003, remove unneeded components from Office 2003, use the Open and Repair feature, and use Microsoft Office Application Recovery.

> **Note**   Exercise 4 and Exercise 5 each require files from the Tools folder on the CD that is included with this book. Exercise 4 requires a file named Disclaimer. Exercise 5 requires a file named Bad Macro. You should copy these files from the Practice folder on the CD into your My Documents folder before starting these exercises.

Exercise 1: Restore Default Menu Settings in Word 2003

1. Log on to Windows XP.

2. From the Start menu, select All Programs, select Microsoft Office, and then select Microsoft Office Word 2003.

3. In Word, from the Tools menu, select Customize.

4. In the Customize dialog box, on the Commands tab, in the Categories list, select File.

5. In the Commands list, drag Web Page Preview into the File menu and drop it under Close.

6. In the Customize dialog box, click Close.

7. From the Tools menu, select Customize.

8. In the Customize dialog box, on the Commands tab, click Rearrange Commands.

9. In the Rearrange Commands dialog box, under Choose A Menu Or Toolbar To Rearrange, verify that Menu Bar is selected. In the drop-down list adjacent to Menu Bar, verify that File is selected. Click Reset.

10. In the Reset Toolbar message box, click OK. Note that the Preview Web Page command has been removed from the File menu.

11. Close all open windows and programs. Do not save changes.

Exercise 2: Remove Unneeded Components from Office

1. Log on to Windows XP using an account with administrator privileges.

2. From the Start menu, select Control Panel.

3. In Control Panel, click Add Or Remove Programs.

4. In the Add Or Remove Programs window, in the Currently Installed Programs scroll window, select Microsoft Office Professional Edition 2003. Click Change.

5. In the Microsoft Office 2003 Setup Wizard, on the Maintenance Mode Options page, verify that Add Or Remove Features is selected and click Next.

6. On the Custom Setup page, select the Choose Advanced Customization Of Applications check box. Click Next.

7. On the Advanced Customization page, click the Microsoft Office Publisher node drop-down list. Select Installed On First Use. Click Update.

8. The Now Updating Office page measures the progress of uninstalling the component. When it is finished, a Microsoft Office 2003 Setup message box appears. Click OK.

9. Close the Add Or Remove Programs window and Control Panel.

Exercise 3: Use the Open and Repair Feature

1. Log on to Windows XP.

2. From the Start menu, select All Programs, select Microsoft Office, and then select Microsoft Office Word 2003.

3. In Word, from the File menu, select Open.

4. In the Open dialog box, ensure that All Word Documents is selected in the Files Of Type drop-down list. Navigate to your My Documents folder.

5. Select the document named Disclaimer, but do not click Open. Instead, click the down arrow on the Open button. Select Open And Repair.

6. Close Word.

Exercise 4: Use Microsoft Office Application Recovery

1. Log on to Windows XP.

2. From the Start menu, select All Programs, select Microsoft Office, and then select Microsoft Office Word 2003.

3. From the Tools menu, select Options.

4. In the Options dialog box, on the Security tab, in the Macro Security section, click Macro Security.

5. In the Security dialog box, on the Security Level tab, select Medium. Click OK.

6. In the Options dialog box, click OK.

7. From the File menu, select Open.

8. In the Open dialog box, navigate to your My Documents folder. Select the document named Bad Macro, and click Open.

9. In the Security Warning message box, click Enable Macros.

10. In the Bad Macro document, after *Text:*, type two lines of text and press ENTER.

11. From the Tools menu, point to Macro and select Macros.

12. In the Macros dialog box, ensure that *BadMacro* appears in the Macro Name text box, and click Run.

13. Microsoft Word will stop responding.

14. Press CTRL+ESC to open the Start menu. Point to All Programs, point to Microsoft Office, point to Microsoft Office Tools, and select Microsoft Office Application Recovery.

15. In the Microsoft Office Application Recovery dialog box, ensure that in the Application section Microsoft Office Word is selected, and click Recover Application.

16. In the Microsoft Office Word message box, click Don't Send.

17. A Microsoft Office Word message box appears and indicates the progress of recovering your document. When you are asked whether you want to load the normal document template, click Yes. After this, Word is launched automatically.

18. In the Security Warning dialog box, click Disable Macros.

19. The Bad Macro document should appear with the text you added plus the line, "Microsoft Word will now stop responding." On the left, the Document Recovery task pane has automatically opened.

20. In the Document Recovery task pane, in the Available Files section, click the down arrow on the Bad Macro [Recovered] button and select Save As.

21. In the Save As dialog box, in the File Name text box, type **Lab7-Recovered**. Click Save.

22. Close Word.

Lesson Review

The following questions are intended to reinforce key information presented in this lesson. If you are unable to answer a question, review the lesson materials and try the question again. You can find answers to the questions in the "Questions and Answers" section at the end of this chapter.

1. A user needs to insert a table into her Word document that a colleague created by using Access. The table is updated daily with the latest company statistics and is stored on a network server. The user wants her Word file to always offer the most up-to-date information each time the file is opened. Unfortunately, each time she opens the document, she gets the same information, and the table is never updated. What is the problem?

   A. The user embedded the table instead of linking it.

   B. The user linked the table instead of embedding it.

   C. The user needs to choose Package For CD to package the Word file with the table so that both are available when the file is opened.

   D. The user needs to be made a member of the Domain Power Users group so that she can have automatic access to domain resources.

2. A user complains to you that she cannot find the command for inserting a text box into a Word document. What is most likely the problem?

   _____

   _____

   _____

   _____

   _____

   _____

Lesson Summary

- To restore missing toolbars and to customize features in any Office application, use the View menu and choose Customize.

- Embedded objects become a permanent part of the document into which they are embedded. Linked objects are still attached to the source document from which they are generated. If you change the source document, linked objects are updated, whereas embedded objects are not.

- You can normally recover lost files just by restarting an application after it crashes. Office applications use saved files called AutoRecover files to safeguard against data loss. You can also use the Microsoft Office Application Recovery tool when a program crashes.

Lesson 2: Supporting Excel 2003

After end users begin using Excel 2003 and start performing configuration tasks on their own, creating spreadsheets, performing calculations, using macros, and accessing some of the more advanced features available in the application, they might encounter problems using them. In this lesson, you examine some of the common troubleshooting tasks in Excel 2003.

After this lesson, you will be able to

- Resolve issues related to calculations.
- Work with Excel macros.
- Recover lost Excel files.

Estimated lesson time: 30 minutes

Calculations

Word 2003 end users do a lot of text formatting; Excel 2003 end users perform a lot of calculations. After calculations are complete, users also sort, filter, validate, consolidate, and group data. You need to have functional familiarity with each of these tasks and be able to troubleshoot various issues with Excel as they arise. In addition to performing calculations and working with their results, Excel users also create tables and charts; format text, cells, rows, and columns; and use AutoFormat in ways similar to Word users. You need to make sure that you are versed in these tasks also.

As in the last section, in this section you will learn how to resolve end-user problems by using Microsoft Office Online Help and Support. It is the best way to resolve problems, get to know the applications, and learn new skills all at the same time.

Using the Formula Bar

The Formula bar is where you enter formulas, and these formulas determine how calculations are created for cells. You must start a formula with an equal sign (=), followed by the formula itself. For instance:

- =100+200 adds 100 and 200.
- =15+2*4 adds 15 to 8 (2 times 4).
- =AVERAGE(A1:B6) averages the numbers between cells A1 and B6.

The plus sign (+), multiplication sign (*), and similar elements of formulas are called *operators*. Users often require help entering or troubleshooting formulas using these operators. To be able to help them resolve calculation queries, you need to know in what order Excel performs operations, which operators perform which calculations, and how to enter the most commonly used formulas.

Users can create a formula from scratch or use one of Excel's functions (such as Sum or Average) to enter a simple formula into the Formula bar. To use a function to create a simple formula and create a calculation, follow these steps:

1. Open Excel 2003, and open a new workbook.

2. Type random numbers in cells A1 through A10.

3. Select cell A11.

4. On the Formula bar, click FX. The Insert Function dialog box opens. Both the spreadsheet and the dialog box are shown in Figure 7-6.

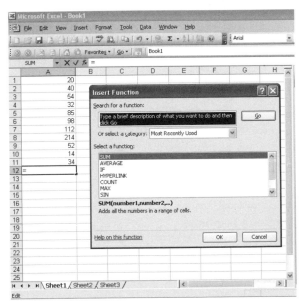

Figure 7-6   Create a simple formula using one of Excel's functions.

5. Double-click Sum in the Insert Function dialog box. In the Function Arguments dialog box, shown in Figure 7-7, notice that the numbers to be added include cells A1 through A11. In this example, the value is 755. Click OK to insert the formula.

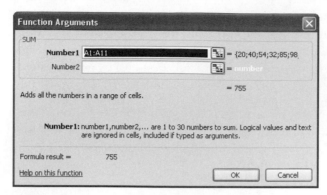

Figure 7-7   The Function Arguments dialog box.

The cell now contains the sum of the cells and a related formula. To view the formula, click the cell and you can view the formula in the Formula bar. You can add various types of formulas in the same manner, or you can type them in manually. As you become more adept with the program, you can decide what you are most comfortable with.

Common Formulas

As you can probably surmise, formulas can be quite complex and can be used to do much more than just add a list of numbers. Users can create Excel formulas to perform calculations on dates and times, keep a running balance, calculate the median of a group of numbers, average a set of numbers, round numbers, convert measurements (Celsius to Fahrenheit, for example), and more. Table 7-3 lists several common types of formulas that you will be called on to troubleshoot; the procedure following this table guides you through learning how to create and enter any or all of them.

Table 7-3   Common Formulas

Formula Type	Common Formulas
Dates and times	Add dates, add times, calculate the difference between two dates or two times, convert times, count down days until a date, and insert the date and time in any cell.
Basic math	Add, subtract, multiply, divide, round, and average lists of numbers.
Advanced math	Calculate a percentage of the difference between two numbers, raise a number to a power, calculate the median of a group of numbers, and convert measurements.
Conditional	Calculate based on a previous calculation. For instance, if a number is larger than x, perform some other calculation.
Financial	Calculate various interest rates, annuity payments, annual yields, depreciation rates, and accrued interest.
Statistical	Calculate probabilities, deviations, frequency distributions, trends, slope, and variance.

These and many additional formulas are already created and ready to use from Microsoft Office Online Help and Support files. To learn how to create and enter any of the formulas listed in Table 7-3 (and many others), follow these steps:

1. Open Excel 2003 and a working document.

2. From the View menu, verify that Task Pane is selected.

3. In the task pane, click the down arrow and select Help.

4. Under Assistance, in the Search For text box, type **List of worksheet functions**, and from the list choose About Functions. Press ENTER on the keyboard, or click the green arrow.

5. Read About The Syntax Of Functions, and then click See Also. In the See Also list, select List Of Worksheet Functions (By Category).

6. Browse through the worksheet functions. To see an example of how you use any worksheet function, select it. A new page appears with information about entering the formula.

7. Return to the About Functions page by using the Back button, and from the See Also options, select Examples Of Commonly Used Formulas. Browse through those options. Figure 7-8 shows instructions for creating a formula to raise a number to a power. These and similar tutorials are available from these Help files.

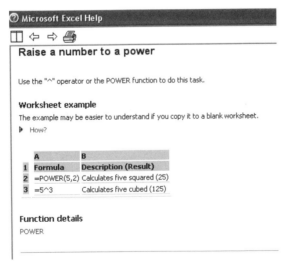

Figure 7-8   Learn about functions and formulas from the Microsoft Office Help files.

Understanding the Operators

To use a formula, create a formula, or troubleshoot a formula created by an end user, you must understand the operators used in the formula. These can include signs such as plus (+), minus (–), multiply (*), divide (/), less than (<), greater than (>), and raise to a power (^), as well as text operators such as SUM, IF, AVERAGE, POWER, CON-VERT, and similar arguments. Although there is no simple way to learn all of the uses of these operators, plenty of help is available from Microsoft Office Online.

In addition to becoming familiar with operators, you must also understand in which order operators are calculated. For instance, when parentheses are involved, Excel performs the calculations within them first. Multiplication and division are always performed before addition and subtraction. Successful troubleshooting of calculations includes knowing the basic order of operations. From left to right, calculations are performed in the following order:

1. Parentheses

2. Exponents

3. Multiply and divide

4. Add and subtract

5. Equal to, less than, greater than, or comparisons

Note   To troubleshoot Excel for end users, you need to have a good understanding of basic math, algebra, and formulas. To be the best DST that you can be might mean taking an additional math class to brush up on your skills.

Real World   Saying "I Don't Know"

Here's a simple phrase that, believe it or not, can earn you a lot of respect in the desktop support world: "I don't know, but I'll find out." As a DST, you may often feel as though you are expected to know everything that relates to computers—even concepts such as advanced financial calculations in Excel. Obviously, it is an unreasonable expectation, but that does not make the pressure any less real.

When you come upon something you do not know, regardless of whether you feel it is something you should know, do not be afraid to admit it. And do not be afraid to do some work finding out the answer. You have a wealth of information at your disposal in the form of books, the Internet, newsgroups, Microsoft Tech-Net and Microsoft Knowledge Base, and other users. A good DST is one who can isolate a problem and figure out the answer—even if you do not know the answer off the top of your head.

Troubleshooting Calculations

When a calculation has a logical error or an error with its syntax, the end user is alerted to it with the error message #VALUE! in the cell box instead of a numeric value. If it is your job to troubleshoot this error, you have to understand what calculation the user is trying to make, look up the correct formula in the Help files or create your own, or rewrite the formula that the user has already written. Excel offers some help as well, and sometimes that help is sufficient.

Figure 7-9 shows an example of an error message. Notice that there is a box next to the error, and clicking the arrow in this box opens the drop-down menu shown. It is an error in value, and there are options to get help for the error, show calculation steps, edit the formula in the Formula bar, and more. Generally, selecting Help On This Error is the best choice for beginners.

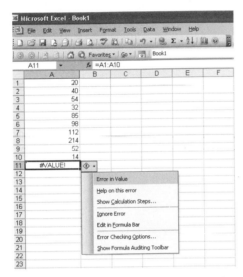

Figure 7-9   Automatic help with errors is available from the drop-down menu.

You will have to practice creating formulas and performing calculations to get a feel for how Excel works and to troubleshoot problems for end users. If your end users use Excel to perform their daily tasks, you might consider taking a short course in the subject or working through the Microsoft Office Online Excel tutorials.

Working with Macros

Another component of Excel (and other Office applications) that many users employ is the **macro**. A macro is a short program that a user can create to automate tasks. When a user creates a macro, keystrokes and mouse movements are recorded, and the user can play those movements back at any time with only a few quick clicks of the mouse. For instance, if calculating the company's payroll each month requires the user to repeat the same steps—perhaps selecting a range of cells, selecting various menus and menu options, and creating the same print configurations—the user can automate those steps by recording a macro for them. The next time the user needs to perform that task, he or she simply runs the macro.

Your role as a DST might require you to create and troubleshoot macros. In the next three sections, you learn to do both.

Creating Macros

To create a simple macro for an end user in Excel 2003 (the procedure is similar in other applications), follow these steps:

1. From the Tools menu, choose Macro and then Record New Macro.

2. In the Macro Name text box, enter a name for the macro. The name of the macro must start with a letter and must not contain any spaces. It cannot be a name used as a cell reference.

3. To create a **shortcut key** for running a macro, type a letter in the Shortcut Key box.

4. In the Store Macro In drop-down list, select the location in which to store the macro. If you want the macro to be available each time you use Excel, select Personal Macro Workbook. If you want the macro to be available only to this workbook, select This Workbook. If you want the macro to be available for a new workbook, select New Workbook. See Figure 7-10.

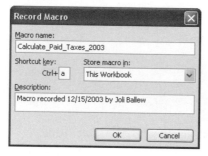

Figure 7-10   Configure the macro by using the Record Macro dialog box.

5. In the Description text box, type a description if desired. Click OK.

6. If the macro is to run relative to the position of the active cell (the selected cell), click Relative Reference on the Stop Recording toolbar. Relative reference means that the macro will run based on which cell is chosen when the macro is run. When Relative Reference is not selected, the macro runs using the cells chosen in the initial creation of the macro each time, no matter which cell is chosen and active.

7. Perform the steps involved in the procedure to record the macro. Click Stop Recording when finished.

To run the macro, on the Tools menu, choose Macro and then Macros, select the macro you want to run, and then click Run. If the macro does not work properly, you will either have to rerecord the macro or troubleshoot it.

Macros and Security

Because macros are **Visual Basic** programs, they can contain viruses or pose security risks. Microsoft Excel offers several choices for dealing with this risk. Four security levels can be set for macros:

- **Very High**   When this is selected, only macros installed from trusted locations can be run. All other macros are disabled.

- **High**   Unsigned macros are disabled, and signed macros are dealt with depending on their source.

- **Medium**   Unsigned macros are disabled, and signed macros are dealt with depending on their source. This setting is similar to but more lenient than the High security setting.

- **Low**   Almost all macros can be run. This is not a recommended setting.

> **Exam Tip**   Remember the levels of macro security and what they mean.

To use macros in Excel or any other Office program effectively, you must set the macro security level to Medium or Low. To set the security level, follow these steps:

1. On the Tools menu, choose Options, and select the Security tab.

2. Select Macro Security.

3. On the Security Level tab, select Medium or Low, as shown in Figure 7-11.

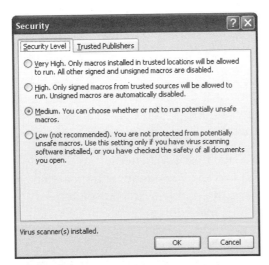

Figure 7-11   Set a macro security level to control which macros are allowed to run.

4. Click OK to save your changes, and then click OK again to close the Options dialog box.

Note   To disable macros installed from all sources, even trusted sources, click Tools, point to Macro, and select Security. From the Trusted Publisher tab, deselect the Trust All Installed Add-Ins And Templates option.

Troubleshooting Macros

There are several reasons why a macro might not run properly or be available, including a user selecting the wrong macro from the list or typing the wrong shortcut key, having the macro security level set too high, or having the macro assigned to a specific workbook that the user does not currently have open. Changing the security setting to Low or Medium solves the security issue. The other issues can be resolved by using the Macro dialog box, as follows:

1. From the Tools menu, choose Macro and then Macros.

2. In the Macro dialog box are several options:

   ❑ **Run**   Runs the macro.

   ❑ **Cancel**   Closes the dialog box.

   ❑ **Step Into**   Opens the Visual Basic Editor, which you can use to manually debug the macro using its Visual Basic code.

   ❑ **Edit**   Opens the Visual Basic Editor, which you can use to manually edit the macro using its Visual Basic code.

   ❑ **Delete**   Deletes the macro.

   ❑ **Options**   Opens the Macro Options dialog box, where you can view or change the macro's description and shortcut key.

   ❑ **Macros In**   Use this list to sort the macros by All Open Workbooks, by This Workbook, or by a file name.

Excel might also encounter problems if the macro was recorded incorrectly, if the macro looks for a specific cell that is no longer there, if a cell is formatted incorrectly, or if the macro needs to access data that is no longer available.

If the macro is a fairly simple one, sometimes it is better just to re-create it. If the macro produces an error message, which it often does under these circumstances, the message usually offers some insight into the problem. If you see an error message when you run a recorded macro, follow this procedure:

1. Copy the macro error and error number.

2. From the Tools menu, choose Macro, and then choose Visual Basic Editor.

3. In the new Visual Basic Editor window, select Help, and choose Microsoft Visual Basic Help. Verify that you are connected to the Internet.

4. In the task pane, type the error number and press ENTER.

5. In the Microsoft Visual Basic Help results, locate the error and the solution.

Some errors are because of known issues with Excel, and you can find their solutions in the Microsoft Knowledge Base. If your search using the Visual Basic Editor Help files does not produce a solution, try the Knowledge Base articles.

Recovering Lost Files

The first section of this chapter on Word 2003 detailed options for recovering lost files. The same options that are available for Word are also available for Excel 2003. When a user reports that a file has been lost because of a computer problem, power outage, or user error, you should work through those options, which include the following:

- **Using Microsoft Office Application Recovery**   From the Start menu, choose All Programs, Microsoft Office, Microsoft Office Tools, and Microsoft Office Application Recovery. In the Microsoft Office Application Recovery dialog box, select Microsoft Office Excel. Select either Recover Application or End Application.

- **Using AutoRecover**   Restart or recover the application by using Microsoft Office Application Recovery or by restarting the computer. In the Document Recovery task pane, shown in Figure 7-12, select the document to recover. You can configure AutoRecover on the Tools menu by choosing Options and selecting the Save tab.

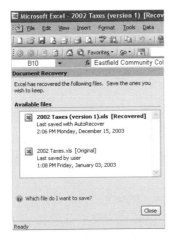

Figure 7-12   The Document Recovery task pane offers several options.

- **Using Open and Repair**   From the File menu, choose Open, and select the file to recover. Click the arrow next to the Open button, and select Open And Repair.

- **Dealing with User Errors**   From the File menu, locate the lost file, or on the Start menu, choose My Recent Documents and select the file to reopen.

Practice: Configuring and Supporting Excel 2003

In this practice, you will create a chart in Excel, and then you will create and modify an Excel macro.

Note   These exercises require a file named Lilliputian500 that is found in the Tools folder on the CD included with this book. You should copy this file from the Tools folder on the CD to your My Documents folder before starting these exercises.

Exercise 1: Create a Chart in Excel

1. Log on to Windows XP.

2. From the Start menu, point to All Programs and then to Microsoft Office, and select Microsoft Office Excel 2003.

3. From the File menu, select Open.

4. Navigate to your My Documents folder, and open the Excel spreadsheet named Lilliputian500.

5. In Microsoft Office Excel 2003, in the Lilliputian500 worksheet, click cell A4: 31-Dec-69.

6. Scroll down to row 413, and while holding down the SHIFT key, click cell B413: 1,252.33. The block of cells from A4 to B413 should now be selected.

7. From the Insert menu, select Chart.

8. In the Chart Wizard — Step 1 Of 4 — Chart Type dialog box, in the Chart Type list, select Line. In the Chart sub-type section, select the upper left option: Line. (The chart type is described below the Chart sub-type section.) Click Finish.

Note   Do not close Excel. The next exercise continues from this point.

Exercise 2: Create an Excel Macro

1. Select the plot line in the chart by clicking it.

2. From the Tools menu, select Macro, and then select Record New Macro.

3. In the Record Macro dialog box, in the Macro Name text box, type **Trendliner**. In the Shortcut Key text box, type **t**. Click OK.

4. Right-click the plot line, and select Add Trendline.

5. In the Add Trendline dialog box, on the Type tab, under Trend/Regression Type, verify that Linear is selected and click OK.

6. Right-click the plot line, and select Add Trendline.

7. In the Add Trendline dialog box, on the Type tab, under Trend/Regression Type, select Moving Average. In the Period text box, type **180**. Click OK.

8. Right-click the plot line and select Add Trendline.

9. In the Add Trendline dialog box, on the Type tab, under Trend/Regression Type, select Moving Average. In the Period text box, type **130**. Click OK.

10. Right-click the plot line and select Add Trendline.

11. In the Add Trendline dialog box, on the Type tab, under Trend/Regression Type, select Moving Average. In the Period text box, type **60**. Click OK.

12. On the Stop Recording toolbar, click the Stop Recording button (the small square).

13. Click a blank area in the chart, and press DELETE. This deletes the chart.

14. Re-create the chart according to steps 5 through 8 in Exercise 1.

 Note   Do not close Excel. The next exercise continues from this point.

Exercise 3: Edit an Excel Macro

1. From the Tools menu, select Macro and select Macros.

2. In the Macro dialog box, verify that in the Macro Name text box Trendliner appears and click Edit.

3. In the Microsoft Visual Basic — Lilliputian500.xls window, verify that the Lilliputian500.xls — Module1 (Code) window is the active window.

4. From the Edit menu, select Find.

5. In the Find dialog box, in the Find What text box, type **130** and click Find Next.

6. Change the found instance of 130 to 120. Click Cancel to close the Find dialog box.

7. From the File menu, select Save Lilliputian500. Close Microsoft Visual Basic.

8. In Microsoft Excel, select the plot line in the line chart. Press CTRL+T.

9. Close Microsoft Excel, saving changes to the Lilliputian500 file.

Lesson Review

The following questions are intended to reinforce key information presented in this lesson. If you are unable to answer a question, review the lesson materials and try the question again. You can find answers to the questions in the "Questions and Answers" section at the end of this chapter.

1. An Excel 2003 user needs to create a formula for calculating the average of 10 numbers in cells A1 through A11. Which of the following formulas is best?

    A. =AVERAGE(A1:A11)

    B. AVERAGE(A1:A11)

    C. =SUM(A1:A11)\10

    D. =AVERAGE(A1;A11)

2. An Excel 2003 user reports that he needs to build his own equations by picking symbols from a toolbar, as well as by typing numbers and variables. You determine that he needs the Equation Editor, which is not currently installed on his computer. What should you do?

    A. Download and install the Equation Editor from the Microsoft Office Online website.

    B. Install the Equation Editor from the Microsoft Office 2003 CD, under Office Tools on the Advanced Customization page.

    C. Open Excel 2003, click Tools, click Options, and from the Calculation tab, enable the Equation Editor.

    D. Open Excel 2003, click View, and click Equation Editor.

Lesson Summary

■ After calculations are complete, users also sort, filter, validate, consolidate, and group data. You need to have functional familiarity with each of these tasks and be able to troubleshoot various issues with Excel as they arise.

■ A macro is a short program that a user can create to automate tasks. When a user creates a macro, keystrokes and mouse movements are recorded, and the user can play those movements back at any time with only a few quick clicks of the mouse. Macros also carry security risks, so you should be aware of the macro security offered by Office applications.

■ Recovering lost files in Excel 2003 is a lot like recovering lost files in Word 2003. Tools for recovering lost files include Microsoft Office Application Recovery, AutoRecover, and Open and Repair.

Lesson 3: Supporting PowerPoint 2003

After end users begin using PowerPoint 2003 and start performing configuration tasks on their own, creating presentations, using macros, and accessing some of the more advanced features available in the application, they might encounter problems using them. Although troubleshooting tasks will vary, in this lesson you will learn how to resolve some of the more common ones.

After this lesson, you will be able to

- Resolve issues related to sharing presentations.
- Recover lost PowerPoint files.

Estimated lesson time: 10 minutes

Sharing Presentations

PowerPoint users' common tasks include creating, moving, and deleting slides; adding and editing text; embedding and linking music and sounds; viewing slide shows; and inserting charts and tables. You should have functional knowledge of these things, too.

PowerPoint users do much more than create presentations, though. They share these presentations. Sharing a presentation, whether it is sent over a network, shown using a laptop and a projector, or burned onto a CD, is often a source of difficulty for the user. This is especially true when additional files are involved, such as a music file that plays in the background, a linked graph or chart, or an image. Users often call for help on these issues.

> **Note**   Formatting text, creating macros, and troubleshooting missing toolbars and components can also be a part of resolving PowerPoint calls. These tasks were detailed in the Word 2003 and Excel 2003 sections of this chapter, and procedures for them are similar in PowerPoint.

Packaging and Sharing

When a user is ready to send a completed presentation to a CD, a network file server, or a colleague, that presentation must be packaged so that all of the files included in the presentation (music, graphics, fonts, charts, and so on) are incorporated. The Package for CD feature in PowerPoint 2003 simplifies this process. The Package for CD feature can be used to burn the presentation and all of its included files onto a CD, save them to a folder, copy them to a network file server, or even copy them to a floppy disk. In addition (excluding when the presentation is saved to a floppy disk), a PowerPoint Viewer is also added, so that any person using almost any computer can view the presentation.

These steps are required to successfully package a completed presentation:

1. Open a completed and saved PowerPoint presentation.

2. From the File menu, choose Package For CD.

3. In the Package For CD dialog box, type a name for the CD (or file).

4. Linked files, embedded TrueType fonts, and the PowerPoint Viewer are included by default. To make any changes to the defaults or to apply a password to any of the files, click Options. Make the appropriate changes, and click OK.

5. To add files, select Add Files. Browse to the location of the files to add, select them, and click Add.

6. To copy the file to a folder or a network file server, click Copy To Folder. Browse to the location in which to save the files. Click Select, and click OK.

7. To burn the entire presentation onto a CD, click Copy To CD.

8. Wait while the files are packaged and copied. Click Close when finished.

The saved and packaged presentation is now ready for viewing. The folder contains all of the files needed for the presentation, including copies of music, images, charts, graphs, a PowerPoint Viewer, an AutoRun file, and more. Showing the presentation involves only starting it or putting the CD into the CD-ROM drive.

Note   Embedding and linking sounds and images is an important part of creating Power-Point presentations. Embedding and linking were detailed in the Word 2003 portion of this chapter, and procedures for embedding and linking objects are similar in PowerPoint.

Recovering Lost Files

The first section of this chapter on Word 2003 detailed options for recovering lost files. The options available for that application are also available for PowerPoint 2003. When a user reports that a file has been lost due to a computer glitch, power outage, or user error, you should work through those options, which include the following:

■ **Using Microsoft Office Application Recovery**   From the Start menu, choose All Programs, Microsoft Office, Microsoft Office Tools, and Microsoft Office Application Recovery. In the Microsoft Office Application Recovery dialog box, select Microsoft Office PowerPoint. Select either Recover Application or End Application.

■ **Using AutoRecover**   Restart or recover the application by using Microsoft Office Application Recovery or by restarting the computer. In the Document Recovery task pane, select the document to recover. You can configure AutoRecover on the Tools menu by choosing Options and selecting the Save tab.

- **Using Open and Repair**   From the File menu, choose Open, and select the file to recover. Click the arrow next to the Open button, and select Open And Repair.

- **Dealing with User Errors**   From the File menu, locate the lost file in the File menu, or on the Start menu, choose My Recent Documents and select the file to reopen.

Lesson Review

The following question is intended to reinforce key information presented in this lesson. If you are unable to answer this question, review the lesson materials and try the question again. You can find answer to the question in the "Questions and Answers" section at the end of this chapter.

Lost files can be recovered in a number of ways, including using Microsoft Office Application Recovery, AutoRecover, Open and Repair, and more. To demonstrate your familiarity with these options and others, match the situation on the left with the best file recovery method on the right.

1. PowerPoint has locked up and is not responding. The user has not saved the presentation he is working on in quite some time and does not want to lose his work. What should you try first?	A. Open and Repair
2. A user deleted an e-mail and needs to retrieve it. She has not emptied her Deleted Items folder, although it is configured to delete items in that folder when she exits Outlook. What should you tell the user to do?	B. The File menu
3. A user reports that his Excel file will not open, and he thinks it is corrupt. The computer shut down from a power failure, and when he rebooted and started Excel again, nothing happened. He was not offered any recovered files. What should he try now?	C. Microsoft Office Application Recovery
4. A user saved a file yesterday but cannot remember where she saved it. She needs to access the file quickly. Where can she look?	D. Open the folder, locate the file, and drag it to a different folder.

Lesson Summary

- The Package for CD feature in PowerPoint 2003 simplifies the process of saving a complete presentation to a CD, including music, graphics, fonts, charts, and so on.

- Recovering lost files in PowerPoint 2003 is a lot like recovering lost files in Word 2003 or Excel 2003. Tools for recovering lost files include Microsoft Office Application Recovery, AutoRecover, and Open and Repair.

Lesson 4: Troubleshooting Outlook Express

In Chapter 4, "Microsoft Outlook and Outlook Express," you were introduced to Outlook Express, and you learned how to create and troubleshoot e-mail and newsgroup accounts. Although some configuration tasks were included, customizing the toolbars, menus, and their commands; setting personalization options; and configuring the available tools are quite similar to configuring the full version of the application, Outlook 2003, which was also covered in that chapter. This lesson focuses on Outlook Express and introduces you to some of the more common issues end users encounter.

After this lesson, you will be able to

- Resolve attachment issues.
- Resolve issues with international settings and encoding.
- Identify and resolve other common issues.
- Recover lost e-mail.

Estimated lesson time: 25 minutes

Attachments

Service calls regarding attachments can be varied, but they likely revolve around attachments that cannot be opened or attachments that cannot be sent. Sometimes an attachment is unavailable or does not have a program associated with it. Sometimes e-mail with attachments remains in the Outbox or causes error messages on sending. The first problem is the most common; almost all service calls regarding the inability to open attachments can be resolved by clearing a single check box. When a user reports that attachments are unavailable and cannot be opened, follow these steps:

1. From the Tools menu, choose Options, and select the Security tab.

2. Clear the Do Not Allow Attachments To Be Saved Or Opened That Could Potentially Be A Virus check box. Click OK.

3. Close and reopen Outlook Express.

If this does not solve the problem, or if the problem is one of the others mentioned, you have to delve a little deeper. If the user is a member of a domain, check domain policies for dealing with attachments. In some instances, network policies will not allow attachments to be opened. This policy is not common, however, as attachments are a large part of corporate life; but if the preceding procedure does not resolve the problem, you need to check on this.

No Associated Program

A user will not be able to open an attachment if no program is associated with it. For instance, if a user tries to open a proprietary file type such as .pdd (Photoshop) or .ged (Arts and Letters), and the file's respective programs are not installed on the user's computer, opening the attachment fails and an error message similar to the one shown in Figure 7-13 appears.

Figure 7-13   The "Windows cannot open this file" error message.

When this happens, instruct the end user to choose the Use The Web Service To Find The Appropriate Program option. The Microsoft Windows File Associations website automatically opens, and information regarding the programs that can be used to open the file is listed. Sometimes this information includes a link that you can use to download and install a viewer to open the file, or you might need to download and install a trial version of a program. Figure 7-14 shows this website; notice that you can use Adobe Photoshop, CorelDRAW, and Microsoft Office PhotoDraw to open the .pdd file.

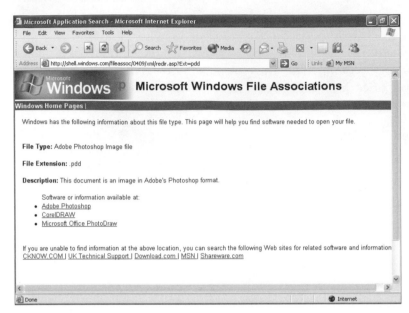

Figure 7-14 Microsoft Windows File Associations Web page.

If the user does not have Web access, instruct the user to choose the Select The Program From A List option to see whether any compatible programs are available on the computer. In some instances, the user might have a compatible program installed but Windows does not recognize it as a compatible file type. The .pdd file shown in Figure 7-13 was opened easily by using Photoshop, even though the error message appeared.

See Also To learn more about which types of files can be opened with which programs, visit *http://www.oktec.com/help/file_types.htm* and similar sites. To learn more about working with file associations in Windows XP, see Chapter 3, "Troubleshooting the Operating System."

E-Mail with Attachment Remains in Outbox

Problems sending attachments usually have to do with third-party software that is installed on the computer. If an e-mail with an attachment cannot be sent even after you click Send/Receive but instead remains in the Outbox, check for Internet filtering programs (such as Net Nanny). Either uninstall the program or reconfigure it to allow attachments to be sent. Check the Microsoft Knowledge Base for information regarding various third-party software and known issues.

E-Mail with Attachments Produces Errors When Sending

Problems that produce error messages when attachments are sent are usually caused by hardware configuration or compatibility problems. Hardware problems can be caused by incompatible or incorrectly configured modems, firewalls, or similar hardware. These error messages might include references to the server unexpectedly terminating the connection, the Simple Mail Transfer Protocol (SMTP) server not responding, the server timing out, or other problems. If the only connectivity problems are associated with sending attachments, visit the Knowledge Base or the hardware manufacturers' websites for help.

International Settings and Encoding

Users who send and receive e-mail in more than one language might need you to troubleshoot these tasks. A user in the United States who has been successful in sending e-mail to her colleague in France might report that she has been unable to do that lately and ask you to figure out why. A home user who is Italian might want you to teach him to send e-mail to his mother in their own language.

Sending and receiving e-mail in multiple languages by using Outlook Express has a few requirements. When checking for problems or setting up Outlook Express for the first time, verify that these items are in working order:

- Set Regional Options for the language to be used from Control Panel as detailed in Chapter 3.

- Configure Text Services and Input Languages to include the language to be used, also detailed in Chapter 3.

- Verify that the user knows how to switch between languages from the taskbar (next to the notification area).

- Verify that any appropriate keyboards are installed if applicable.

To configure Outlook Express to send and receive e-mail in other languages, follow these steps:

1. From the Tools menu, choose Options, and select the Send tab.
2. Under Sending, click International Settings, and make sure that the second language is the default.
3. If prompted, install the necessary language pack.
4. Click OK to close the International Send Settings dialog box. Click OK to close the Options dialog box.

When creating the message, make sure the user has selected the correct language, click Format, and point to Encoding to verify that the correct encoding option is selected.

Other Common Issues

There are some other issues that Outlook Express end users might encounter, and you should try to become familiar with them. You can usually resolve these problems by changing the configuration options in Outlook Express, so you should familiarize yourself with all aspects of the program. Table 7-4 lists some of these problems and their solutions.

Table 7-4   Other Common Issues

Problem	Solution
Newsgroup messages automatically download, but the user wants to download messages only after reading the header.	1. From the Tools menu, choose Options and select the Read tab. 2. Clear the Automatically Download Messages When Viewing In The Preview Pane check box.
The user wants to automatically hide messages in the Inbox that have already been read.	1. From the View menu, choose Current View. 2. Select Hide Read Messages.
The user's e-mail folder is quite large. He or she wants to reduce the amount of space it takes up without deleting any old messages.	1. Select an e-mail folder. 2. From the File menu, choose Folder, and then choose Compact.
A user is distracted by the new mail notification sound each time a new e-mail arrives.	1. From the Tools menu, choose Options, and select the General tab. 2. Clear the Play Sound When New Messages Arrive check box.

Make sure you can resolve these problems and others related to Outlook Express.

Recovering Lost E-Mail

If a user has accidentally deleted an e-mail that he or she needs, there are a few ways to try to locate and restore it. First you can see whether the message can be located in the Deleted Items folder. If the e-mail is found there, restoring it is as simple as dragging the deleted item to another folder, such as the Inbox. If the e-mail is no longer in the Deleted Items folder, you can try to restore it from the Recycle Bin or by using a third party's restoration tool.

Another option is recovering the missing files from a backup. For a home user, this might be a stretch because many home users do not know how to back up Outlook Express e-mail messages, so no backup exists. Network users generally have a backup of each day's files on a network server, but obtaining those files might require contacting a network administrator.

> **Note**   If messages have been recently exported as a means of backup, those messages can be imported as a way to recover lost data. You can import messages by using the File menu and the Import And Export command as detailed in Chapter 4.

Keep in mind that although an end user calls to report that all of the e-mail messages are missing, they might not be. Consider these errors in user logic:

- The user might have changed or does not understand the interface. The wrong folder might be selected in the Local Folders list.

- The user might be looking for items in the Deleted Items folder, and those items might be configured to be deleted on exit.

- The folder where the e-mail is stored by default might have been changed. Outlook Express might not be able to find the folder.

- The user might be using two or more e-mail clients, and the missing incoming and outgoing e-mail might be in another e-mail–handling program.

- An expected e-mail might have been caught by a spam filter. Check any folders configured to hold messages that are blocked by rules or by filtering programs.

For the most part, you need to teach your Outlook Express users how to back up their messages. Outlook Express has no automatic recovery, and there is no Microsoft Windows or Microsoft Office tool for Outlook Express application recovery.

> **Note**   Damaged e-mail folders can be repaired by copying the folder's contents to a temporary folder, deleting the damaged folder, closing and reopening Outlook Express (the folder will be re-created), and then copying the messages back to the newly created folder.

Practice: Troubleshooting Outlook Express

In this practice, you will back up Outlook Express data. Although there are several ways to do this, the way detailed next has been outlined in previous Knowledge Base articles and is generally regarded as the most straightforward.

1. Open Outlook Express, and from the Tools menu, select Options.
2. On the Maintenance tab, select Store Folder.

3. Using your pointer, select the entire path for the folder location, right-click the selection, and choose Copy.

4. Click Cancel to close this dialog box, and click Cancel again to close the Options dialog box.

5. From the Start menu, select Run.

6. Place the cursor in the Open text box, right-click, and choose Paste. Click OK.

7. In the resultant window, select the Edit menu, and choose Select All.

8. Choose Edit again, and select Copy. Close the window.

9. Right-click the Desktop or any other area to store the data, point to New, and select Folder. Name the new folder Mail Folder, followed by the date.

10. Open that folder, right-click in the resultant window, and select Paste. Wait while the data is added. Close the Mail Folder window.

Lesson Review

The following question is intended to reinforce key information presented in this lesson. If you are unable to answer the question, review the lesson materials and try the question again. You can find answers to the question in the "Questions and Answers" section at the end of this chapter.

A user reports that he cannot open any attachments because the paper clip is unavailable. After questioning the user, you find out that the problem started yesterday after he installed Windows XP Home Edition Service Pack 1 on his computer. What do you tell the user to do?

A. Choose the Use The Web Service To Find The Appropriate Program option, locate a program to open the attachment with, and install it.

B. Uninstall Service Pack 1.

C. Restart the computer.

D. From the Tools menu, choose Options, and select the Security tab. Clear the Do Not Allow Attachments To Be Saved Or Opened That Could Potentially Be A Virus check box. Click OK.

Lesson Summary

- Service calls regarding attachments usually involve attachments that cannot be opened or attachments that cannot be sent. Sometimes an attachment is unavailable or does not have a program associated with it. Sometimes e-mail with attachments remains in the Outbox or causes error messages on sending.

- Sending and receiving e-mail in multiple languages requires that you set Regional Options properly in Control Panel, that you configure Text Services and Input Languages to include the language to be used, that you know how to switch between languages, and that appropriate keyboards be installed.

- After a deleted e-mail is removed from the Deleted Items folder, it is difficult to recover without a third-party tool or without restoring a backup.

Lesson 5: Troubleshooting Outlook 2003

In Chapter 4, you learned quite a bit about Outlook 2003. In Chapter 6, you learned how to install and configure it. In this lesson, you will learn how to troubleshoot Outlook 2003.

After this lesson, you will be able to

- Resolve issues with the Calendar.
- Resolve issues with Contacts.
- Resolve issues with Tasks.
- Resolve issues with the Journal.

Estimated lesson time: 25 minutes

Resolving Issues with the Calendar

The Calendar is an organizational tool for keeping track of meetings, appointments, and reminders. End users are reminded of events before they occur, thus offering them a type of virtual secretary. End users who rely on the Calendar to keep track of events often have questions regarding its use. Although service calls will vary, most can be resolved by using Microsoft Office Online, the Knowledge Base, or TechNet.

Receiving Reminders for Past Meetings

If a user reports that he or she is receiving reminders for meetings that have already occurred, follow these steps:

1. In Outlook 2003, choose Microsoft Office Outlook Help from the Help menu (or press F1).

2. In the Outlook Help task pane, type **Troubleshoot Calendar Reminders** and press ENTER.

3. In the Search Results pane, click Troubleshoot Calendar if it is available, or open another appropriate Help file.

Note   In the Troubleshoot Calendar Help file, there are lots of Help topics, including I Opened Another Person's Calendar, And I Can't Find A Way To Close It; Other People See My Schedule As Busy When I Don't Have Any Appointments Or Meetings; and I Can't See The Little Calendar.

4. Follow the instructions in the Help file to resolve the problem. This might include dismissing the meeting, removing a duplicate entry, removing a recurrence setting, or modifying the date or time field, depending on the circumstance.

Appointments and Meetings Are Missing

If a user reports that appointments and meetings are missing from the Calendar, follow these steps:

1. In Outlook 2003, choose Microsoft Office Outlook Help from the Help menu (or press F1).

2. In the Outlook Help task pane, type **Troubleshoot Calendar Appointments** and press ENTER.

3. In the Search Results pane, scroll through the available articles and Help files. Select one that has to do with appointments, that you feel will most likely offer a solution to missed appointments.

4. Follow the instructions in the Help file to resolve the problem. This might include changing the view of the Calendar or filtering the Calendar entries, depending on the circumstance.

It is up to you to become familiar with all of the components of Outlook 2003, including the Calendar. There are a lot of Help files and books on this subject, and you should try to become well versed in using this component (as well as others).

Resolving Issues with Contacts

As with the Outlook Calendar, you can use Microsoft Office Online to resolve issues with the Contacts feature as well. The Contacts folder is used to organize all of the user's e-mail contacts. The options in the Troubleshoot Contacts Help file include detailed instructions on how to resolve many problems, including the following:

■ I cannot see my contacts.

■ Information is missing from my contacts.

■ My contacts do not sort in the order that I expect.

■ The text in the contact card is cut off.

■ When I sort, filter, or mail merge my contacts, the address or name field is not displayed correctly.

■ I added a custom field to my contacts, but I do not see it.

As with other Outlook components, searching for answers to questions here is generally the best choice. If a user reports problems with Outlook Contacts, follow these steps:

1. In Outlook 2003, choose Microsoft Office Outlook Help from the Help menu (or press F1).

2. In the Outlook Help task pane, type **Troubleshoot Contacts** and press ENTER.

3. In the Search Results pane, scroll through the list and find the link named "Troubleshoot Contacts." Click the link to open a new window with troubleshooting suggestions.

Resolving Issues with Tasks

You can use Microsoft Office Online to resolve issues with the Tasks feature as well. The Tasks feature allows the user to keep track of tasks that need to be done on a "to do" list. The options in the Troubleshoot Tasks Help file include detailed instructions on how to resolve many problems, including the following:

- I cannot see my tasks.
- I assigned a task, and it disappeared.
- I received a task update message in my Inbox, but it disappeared.
- I cannot skip a recurring task.
- The TaskPad is missing.

If a user reports problems with Outlook Tasks, follow these steps:

1. In Outlook 2003, choose Microsoft Office Outlook Help from the Help menu (or press F1).

2. In the Outlook Help task pane, type **Troubleshoot Tasks** and press ENTER.

3. In the Search Results pane, scroll through the list and find the link named "Troubleshoot Tasks." Click the link to open a new window with troubleshooting suggestions.

Resolving Issues with the Journal

You can also use Microsoft Office Online to resolve issues with the Journal feature. The Journal allows users to keep notes and keep track of long-term and short-term goals, as well as phone calls, letters, meetings, and more. The options in the Troubleshoot Journal Help file include detailed instructions on how to resolve many problems, including the following:

- When I open a Journal item, I want the item to open to the Journal entry.

- I do not see the Journal button in the Navigation pane.

- The contact I want to automatically record items for does not appear in the For These Contacts list in the Journal Options dialog box.

If a user reports problems with the Outlook Journal, follow these steps:

1. In Outlook 2003, choose Microsoft Office Outlook Help from the Help menu (or press F1).

2. In the Outlook Help task pane, type **Troubleshoot Journal** and press ENTER.

3. In the Search Results pane, scroll through the list and find the link named "Troubleshoot Journal." Click the link to open a new window with troubleshooting suggestions.

Real World   Be Careful Using the Outlook Journal

The automatic journaling feature in Outlook 2003 can be useful, but it can also cause problems if it is not configured properly. Outlook can record an amazing number of things in the journal automatically, including every time you send an e-mail message or have other interactions with contacts; or when Office documents are created, modified, or saved. It is tempting when configuring journaling to just turn on automatic journaling for everything, but this causes two problems. The first is that recording entries in the journal takes a bit of time and can decrease the perceived performance of a system. The other problem is that journal entries take up space, and if you do a lot of work in Outlook, journal entries can quickly grow to consume a good bit of your hard disk.

You can gain the most control over journaling by turning off automatic journaling and creating entries manually. If you decide to use automatic journaling, start by enabling automated entries for only the most important contacts, and limit the activities that are recorded.

Recovering Lost E-Mail

Outlook 2003 offers several options for recovering lost e-mail. Users can retrieve e-mail from the Deleted Items folder if it is still there. If the item is gone from the Deleted Items folder, the user might be able to recover the e-mail from the Recycle Bin or from a Microsoft Exchange server (if it is configured to keep deleted items for a period of time after they have originally been deleted). Users might also be able to restore deleted items from Internet Message Access Protocol (IMAP) folders or search for missing e-mail in the Junk E-Mail folder.

Using the Deleted Items Folder

To restore a deleted e-mail that has not been removed from the Deleted Items folder, follow these steps:

1. From the Go menu, choose Folder List, and then in the Navigation pane, select Deleted Items.

2. Select the items to retrieve; you can select multiple items by holding down the CTRL key while selecting.

3. Right-click the selected items and choose Move To Folder, and in the Move Items dialog box, select Inbox (or any other folder). Click OK to move the items.

You can also drag e-mail items to any folder from the Deleted Items folder.

Restoring from a Microsoft Exchange Server

If the client is looking for e-mail that has been previously deleted, the Deleted Items folder has been emptied, *and* the client is using a Microsoft Exchange Server e-mail account on a Microsoft Exchange server (running version 5.5 or later), you can try to restore the deleted e-mail from the server. An Exchange server can be configured to save deleted items for a period of time after deletion from the user's computer. If this is the case and the foregoing requirements have been met, follow these steps:

1. From the Go menu, choose Folder List, and then in the Navigation pane, click Deleted Items.

2. Select the items to retrieve; you can select multiple items by holding down the CTRL key while selecting.

3. From the Tools menu, choose Recover Deleted Items.

Restoring IMAP E-Mail

If the user has an IMAP e-mail account, you can restore messages that have been marked for deletion by selecting the deleted item, clicking Edit, and clicking Undelete. Items marked for deletion can be viewed by clicking View, pointing to Arrange By, pointing to Current View, and clicking Group Message Marked For Deletion.

Checking the Junk E-Mail Folder

When the junk e-mail filtering options are set too high, some legitimate e-mail might get sent to the Junk E-Mail folder. If a user reports that e-mail that should have arrived never did, and the sender verifies that the e-mail was sent, check the Junk E-Mail folder. If the missing e-mail is found, lower the Junk E-Mail settings, create a rule for safe recipients, or configure no automatic filtering in the Junk E-Mail options.

Real World Reports and Updates

Occasionally when a problem occurs with an Office application, the application will shut down and you or the user will have a chance to report the error to Microsoft and view a Microsoft Online Crash Analysis report. Good DSTs will always report the error and read the analysis. Reporting the error helps Microsoft determine what errors are occurring and why, and allows them to create patches and fixes for those problems. Reading the report offers insight into what caused it.

An analysis report can offer different types of information. It might include specific information regarding the cause of the problem, such as an incompatible driver; it might offer only generic advice about drivers and approved hardware and software; or it might include a link to an update that has already been released to fix the problem. Figure 7-15 shows the latter.

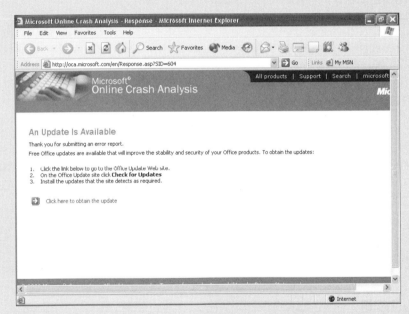

Figure 7-15 Microsoft Online Crash Analysis report offers information about the problem and offers available updates.

When an update is available and an Online Crash Analysis offers one, the update should be installed immediately. As a preemptive strike against these types of errors, updates should be manually sought out weekly.

Lesson Review

The following question is intended to reinforce key information presented in this lesson. If you are unable to answer the question, review the lesson materials and try the question again. You can find answers to the question in the "Questions and Answers" section at the end of this chapter.

A user reports that several messages sent by a colleague never showed up in her Inbox. She spoke with the colleague on the phone and verified that he was using the correct e-mail address. Her colleague also reports that he did not receive any error messages telling him the message could not be delivered. The user is receiving messages from other people just fine. What could be the problem?

A. The user's outgoing mail server is incorrectly configured.

B. The user's incoming mail server is incorrectly configured.

C. Outlook is incorrectly flagging the colleague's messages as junk e-mail.

D. The user should configure her account as a Post Office Protocol version 3 (POP3) account rather than an IMAP account.

Lesson Summary

- Take the time to learn the major functions of Outlook 2003, including Calendar, Contacts, Tasks, and Journal. Understanding how these features work is your best bet when helping users. You can also use Help and Support and Microsoft TechNet for answers to questions you are not familiar with.

- Outlook 2003 users can retrieve e-mail from the Deleted Items folder if it is still there. If e-mail is not still there, it might be recoverable from the Recycle Bin (or from a Microsoft Exchange server if it is configured to keep deleted items for a period of time).

Case Scenario Exercises

In the following scenarios, you must use what you have learned throughout the lessons in this chapter to answer questions based on a real-world scenario. Read each scenario, and answer the questions. If you have trouble, review the chapter and try again. You can find answers in the "Questions and Answers" section at the end of this chapter.

Scenario 7.1

John, the owner of a small company, travels quite a bit and has purchased a laptop. He wants his wife to use his old computer because she will take over the duties involved in running the company while he is away. She will use the same applications, data, and network John used, so there are not too many changes to make. You have created a new user account; transferred all of John's personal files to his laptop; reset the Taskbar, Start menu, background, and screen saver; and made other personal configuration changes. Now you need to restore the defaults to the menus, buttons, menu choices, and default toolbars in each of the Office applications installed on the computer.

How do you restore all of the default toolbars and menu commands in Word 2003, Excel 2003, Access 2003, Outlook 2003, and PowerPoint 2003?

  A. In each Office application, choose Customize from the Tools menu, and select the Options tab. Then click Reset Menu And Toolbar Usage Data.

  B. In any one of the Office applications, choose Customize from the Tools menu, and select the Options tab. Then click Reset Menu And Toolbar Usage Data.

  C. In each Office application, choose Customize from the Tools menu, and select the Toolbars tab. In the Toolbars box, select the toolbar to restore. Click Reset. In the Reset Toolbar dialog box, select Normal and click OK. Click Close to exit.

  D. In any one of the Office applications, choose Customize from the Tools menu, and select the Toolbars tab. In the Toolbars box, select the toolbar to restore. Click Reset. In the Reset Toolbar dialog box, select Normal and click OK. Click Close to exit.

Scenario 7.2

Theresa, a PowerPoint user, has created a presentation that is almost finalized. All of the slides are created, the transitions have been selected, and a graph and image have been embedded. To finish the presentation, she needs only to add a song that will act as background music for the presentation. She has the song on a CD and has the appropriate licenses to use it. After the song has been added to the presentation, she wants to burn the final presentation onto a CD that can be played on her instructor's computer. The steps involved are listed here. Put the steps in order.

1. From the File menu, choose Package For CD.

2. Insert the song into the completed PowerPoint presentation.

3. Select Copy To CD.

4. Copy the song to use in the presentation from the CD to the hard disk.

5. Test the presentation to verify that it is correct.

6. Open the Custom Animation task pane, and set Effect Options so that the song starts playing at the first slide and stops playing at the last slide.

_____

_____

_____

_____

Troubleshooting Lab

One of your customers has come to you with a problem. He was working in Microsoft Word 2003 recently and had several documents open on which he had been working for some time. Without warning, Word shut down and closed all of his documents in the process. When he restarted Word, he noticed that many of the toolbar buttons and menu commands were missing. When he opened the documents that he had been working on, none of his recent work had been saved. Later that day, one of your customer's colleagues called to warn him that a document he had sent your customer contained a macro virus. Another person to whom the colleague sent the document had detected it and alerted him.

Your customer installed antivirus software, updated the software via the Internet, and scanned his system. The software detected a virus in several files (including the document sent by the colleague) and removed them from the system. The customer would now like to have the Word interface back the way it was originally. He would also like Word to better protect him against macros and to let him recover documents in the event of a crash.

What suggestions would you have for this user?

_____

_____

_____

_____

_____

_____

_____

_____

_____

_____

Chapter Summary

- To restore missing toolbars and to customize features in any Office application, use the View menu and choose Customize.

- To add or remove Office components, use the Microsoft Office CD and Add Or Remove Programs in Control Panel.

- To learn to format bulleted and numbered lists, embed and link objects, create and edit formulas, package and share presentations, and resolve issues with other Office components or tasks, visit Microsoft Office Online.

- To recover lost files, use Microsoft Office Application Recovery, AutoRecover, and the Open and Repair options.

Exam Highlights

Before taking the exam, review the key topics and terms that are presented in this chapter. You need to know this information.

Key Points

- If a user feels that something is missing from the interface, there are three common reasons: Personalized menus are enabled and the user is not seeing all of the commands available, a user has customized the interface and certain commands are missing, or the feature was not installed.

- Most Office applications support macros, but you must weigh the usefulness of macros against the security risk they carry. There are four levels of macro security in Office applications: Very High, High, Medium, and Low. Learn the settings for each level.

Key Terms

Microsoft .NET Framework   Microsoft .NET Framework is a platform for building, deploying, and running Web services and applications.

shortcut key   A key combination associated with a macro for the purpose of running the macro. Common shortcut keys include CTRL+A, SHIFT+Z, and CTRL+V.

Visual Basic   A programming language used for websites and applications. Macros created in Excel, Word, and other Office programs can be edited with the Visual Basic Editor, included with the applications.

Questions and Answers

Lesson 1 Review

Page
7-18
1. A user needs to insert a table into her Word document that a colleague created by using Access. The table is updated daily with the latest company statistics and is stored on a network server. The user wants her Word file to always offer the most up-to-date information each time the file is opened. Unfortunately, each time she opens the document, she gets the same information, and the table is never updated. What is the problem?

   A. The user embedded the table instead of linking it.

   B. The user linked the table instead of embedding it.

   C. The user needs to choose Package For CD to package the Word file with the table so that both are available when the file is opened.

   D. The user needs to be made a member of the Domain Power Users group so that she can have automatic access to domain resources.

   A is correct. The user must link the table, not embed it. B is wrong for this reason. C is an option in PowerPoint, not Word, and D is an unnecessary step and would give the user unnecessary permissions within the domain.

2. A user complains to you that she cannot find the command for inserting a text box into a Word document. What is most likely the problem?

   The command for inserting text boxes is found on Word's Insert menu. If the user does not see it, there are two possibilities. The most likely cause is that the user has personalized menus turned on, so all commands are not shown. Instruct the user to look for a double arrow at the bottom of the Insert menu that causes the whole menu to be shown. To turn off personalized menus altogether, have the user select Customize from the Tools menu, switch to the Options tab, and select the Always Show Full Menus check box. Another possible cause is that the user has accidentally removed the Text Box command from the Insert menu. You can add the command back to the menu or reset the menu.

Lesson 2 Review

Page
7-32
1. An Excel 2003 user needs to create a formula for calculating the average of 10 numbers in cells A1 through A11. Which of the following formulas is best?

   A. =AVERAGE(A1:A11)

   B. AVERAGE(A1:A11)

   C. =SUM(A1:A11)\10

   D. =AVERAGE(A1;A11)

A is correct. In a formula, = always comes first, followed by the cells to be added separated by a colon. B is incorrect because there is no =. C is incorrect because the division sign is backward, and D is incorrect because it contains a semicolon instead of a colon.

2. An Excel 2003 user reports that he needs to build his own equations by picking symbols from a toolbar, as well as by typing numbers and variables. You determine that he needs the Equation Editor, which is not currently installed on his computer. What should you do?

   A. Download and install the Equation Editor from the Microsoft Office Online website.

   B. Install the Equation Editor from the Microsoft Office 2003 CD, under Office Tools on the Advanced Customization page.

   C. Open Excel 2003, click Tools, click Options, and from the Calculation tab, enable the Equation Editor.

   D. Open Excel 2003, click View, and click Equation Editor.

B is the correct answer. The Equation Editor is available in the Office Tools tree on the Office System CD and must be installed. A is incorrect because it is not a downloadable component, C is incorrect because there is no such option, and D is incorrect because there is no Equation Editor toolbar on the View menu.

Lesson 3 Review

Page 7-36

Lost files can be recovered in a number of ways, including using Microsoft Office Application Recovery, AutoRecover, Open and Repair, and more. To demonstrate your familiarity with these options and others, match the situation on the left with the best file recovery method on the right.

1. PowerPoint has locked up and is not responding. The user has not saved the presentation he is working on in quite some time and does not want to lose his work. What should you try first?	A. Open and Repair
2. A user deleted an e-mail and needs to retrieve it. She has not emptied her Deleted Items folder, although it is configured to delete items in that folder when she exits Outlook. What should you tell the user to do?	B. The File menu

3. A user reports that his Excel file will not open, and he thinks it is corrupt. The computer shut down from a power failure, and when he rebooted and started Excel again, nothing happened. He was not offered any recovered files. What should he try now?

C. Microsoft Office Application Recovery

4. A user saved a file yesterday but cannot remember where she saved it. She needs to access the file quickly. Where can she look?

D. Open the folder, locate the file, and drag it to a different folder.

The answer to 1 is C. Microsoft Office Application Recovery gives the Recover Application and Restart Application options. Both will work in this instance. 2 is D. The user should not restart the application but should instead locate the missing e-mail in the Deleted Items folder and restore it to another folder. 3 is A. When a file is corrupt, and because no recovered file was offered, the user should try to open the file by using Open and Repair. 4 is B. Most recently opened files are located at the bottom of the File menu.

Lesson 4 Review

Page 7-44

A user reports that he cannot open any attachments because the paper clip is unavailable. After questioning the user, you find out that the problem started yesterday after he installed Windows XP Home Edition Service Pack 1 on his computer. What do you tell the user to do?

A. Choose the Use The Web Service To Find The Appropriate Program option, locate a program to open the attachment with, and install it.

B. Uninstall Service Pack 1.

C. Restart the computer.

D. From the Tools menu, choose Options, and select the Security tab. Clear the Do Not Allow Attachments To Be Saved Or Opened That Could Potentially Be A Virus check box. Click OK.

D is correct. After you install Service Pack 1, defaults are set for Outlook Express regarding attachments, and this needs to be changed. A is incorrect because a user receives this error message after an attachment has been opened, not before. B is unnecessary, and C will not solve the problem.

Lesson 5 Review

Page
7-52

A user reports that several messages sent by a colleague never showed up in her Inbox. She spoke with the colleague on the phone and verified that he was using the correct e-mail address. Her colleague also reports that he did not receive any error messages telling him the message could not be delivered. The user is receiving messages from other people just fine. What could be the problem?

   A. The user's outgoing mail server is incorrectly configured.

   B. The user's incoming mail server is incorrectly configured.

   C. Outlook is incorrectly flagging the colleague's messages as junk e-mail.

   D. The user should configure her account as a POP3 account rather than an IMAP account.

> C is correct. If Outlook is incorrectly flagging the colleague's messages as junk e-mail, they are likely being moved to the Junk E-Mail folder. The user never sees them in the Inbox. A is incorrect because the outgoing mail server would not affect incoming messages. B is incorrect because the incoming mail server is undoubtedly set up correctly; the user is receiving other messages without any problem. D is incorrect because neither type of account would prevent messages from one person from showing up in the Inbox.

Case Scenario Exercises: Scenario 7.1

Page
7-53

John, the owner of a small company, travels quite a bit and has purchased a laptop. He wants his wife to use his old computer because she will take over the duties involved in running the company while he is away. She will use the same applications, data, and network John used, so there are not too many changes to make. You have created a new user account; transferred all of John's personal files to his laptop; reset the Taskbar, Start menu, background, and screen saver; and made other personal configuration changes. Now you need to restore the defaults to the menus, buttons, menu choices, and default toolbars in each of the Office applications installed on the computer.

How do you restore all of the default toolbars and menu commands in Word 2003, Excel 2003, Access 2003, Outlook 2003, and PowerPoint 2003?

   A. In each Office application, choose Customize from the Tools menu, and select the Options tab. Then click Reset Menu And Toolbar Usage Data.

   B. In any one of the Office applications, choose Customize from the Tools menu, and select the Options tab. Then click Reset Menu And Toolbar Usage Data.

   C. In each Office application, choose Customize from the Tools menu, and select the Toolbars tab. In the Toolbars box, select the toolbar to restore. Click Reset. In the Reset Toolbar dialog box, select Normal and click OK. Click Close to exit.

D. In any one of the Office applications, choose Customize from the Tools menu, and select the Toolbars tab. In the Toolbars box, select the toolbar to restore. Click Reset. In the Reset Toolbar dialog box, select Normal and click OK. Click Close to exit.

A is correct. The change must be made in each application, and this details the correct procedure. B is incorrect for this reason. C and D describe how to reset a built-in toolbar, not all default toolbars and menu commands.

Case Scenario Exercises: Scenario 7.2

Page
7-53
Theresa, a PowerPoint user, has created a presentation that is almost finalized. All of the slides are created, the transitions have been selected, and a graph and image have been embedded. To finish the presentation, she needs only to add a song that will act as background music for the presentation. She has the song on a CD and has the appropriate licenses to use it. After the song has been added to the presentation, she wants to burn the final presentation onto a CD that can be played on her instructor's computer. The steps involved are listed here. Put the steps in order.

1. From the File menu, choose Package For CD.

2. Insert the song into the completed PowerPoint presentation.

3. Select Copy To CD.

4. Copy the song to use in the presentation from the CD to the hard disk.

5. Test the presentation to verify that it is correct.

6. Open the Custom Animation task pane, and set Effect Options so that the song starts playing at the first slide and stops playing at the last slide.

4, 2, 6, 5, 1, and 3. The song must first be copied to the hard disk and then inserted into the presentation. The song must be configured to play from the first slide to the last, and next the presentation must be tested and then packaged for a CD. Packaging for a CD adds the PowerPoint Viewer to the presentation, so any user on any computer can view it. Finally, the CD must be burned.

Troubleshooting Lab

Page
7-54
One of your customers has come to you with a problem. He was working in Microsoft Word 2003 recently and had several documents open on which he had been working for some time. Without warning, Word shut down and closed all of his documents in the process. When he restarted Word, he noticed that many of the toolbar buttons and menu commands were missing. When he opened the documents that he had been working on, none of his recent work had been saved. Later that day, one of your customer's colleagues called to warn him that a document he had sent your customer contained a macro virus. Another person to whom the colleague sent the document had detected it and alerted him.

Your customer installed antivirus software, updated the software via the Internet, and scanned his system. The software detected a virus in several files (including the document sent by the colleague) and removed them from the system. The customer would now like to have the Word interface back the way it was originally. He would also like Word to better protect him against macros and to let him recover documents in the event of a crash.

What suggestions would you have for this user?

There are several possible answers to this question. To restore the Word interface, you can use any of the following methods:

• Use the Toolbars tab of the Customize dialog box to reset the affected toolbars and the menu bar to their default state. This restoration technique will have a minimal impact on the environment and will take the least amount of time. However, it will be difficult to be certain that everything has been restored correctly and that all damage has been fixed.

• Use the Detect And Repair command on the Help menu. This feature scans the Office installation files and replaces any that have changed since the installation. Used in combination with resetting the toolbars, this will be a fairly effective way of restoring the Word interface.

• Rename or delete the Normal.dot template, and restart Word. This technique will force Word to create a new Normal.dot template, in turn restoring the toolbars and menus to their default state. The downside of using this technique is that other customizations made by the customer might also be lost.

• Remove and reinstall Microsoft Office. This is the most drastic solution, but you can be pretty certain that all damage will be repaired and the interface will be restored. This technique will also require the most time and care because you will need to be certain that all important data (for example, the Outlook data file) is backed up.

After you implement a solution for restoring the Word interface, your next step should be to set the macro security level for the customer. You should set the level to at least Medium so that the user is warned of unsafe macros and has the option of enabling or disabling them.

Finally, you should teach the user about Word's AutoRecover feature. Enable AutoRecover, discuss an appropriate AutoRecover save interval with the customer, and then walk him through the process of recovering a document.

8 Common Connectivity Problems

Exam Objectives in this Chapter:

- Identify and troubleshoot name-resolution problems
- Identify and troubleshoot network adapter configuration problems
- Identify and troubleshoot LAN, Routing, and Remote Access configuration problems

Why This Chapter Matters

The purpose of this chapter is to teach you to recognize and resolve common connectivity problems that end users encounter in small home office workgroups, larger local area networks (LANs), and corporate domains. Resolving connectivity problems at the tier-1 level involves testing the physical connections, testing the hardware, and verifying that the servers are online (if applicable), followed by testing and troubleshooting configured connections at the end user's computer. An end user might have several connections configured, including a direct or shared Internet connection; a connection to another computer through a hub, switch, or router; a connection to a larger LAN through the Internet; or a connection to a domain or a domain server.

In addition to calls that involve physical and configured connections, you might be asked to resolve more advanced connectivity issues. At the end of this chapter, you will learn about these advanced issues and how to use command-line utilities such as Ping, Ipconfig, and PathPing to determine the problem; how to configure **Domain Name System** (DNS) and **Windows Internet Naming Service** (WINS) addresses; and how to troubleshoot files such as HOSTS and LMHOSTS.

Lessons in this Chapter:

Before You Begin

Before you begin this chapter, you should have basic familiarity with the Microsoft Windows XP interface. You should also have access to a computer running Windows XP on which you can experiment with changing various settings. To complete some of the practices in this chapter, you will also need a network adapter installed in your computer, and you will need to be connected to the Internet.

Lesson 1: Resolving Physical Connectivity Issues

Many connectivity problems occur because the physical connection between the end user's computer and the hub, router, switch, phone jack, or server, or between the user's computer and the Internet is not working properly. These connectivity problems are virtually the same for both home users and network domain users. Connection problems can be the result of malfunctioning cables, network interface cards (NICs), modems, hubs, or **wireless access points**, or they can be caused by the incorrect configuration of these devices. In this lesson, you learn some basic troubleshooting techniques that can be used to diagnose physical connectivity problems. If you determine that the physical connections are good, you can move on to checking the configurations of the network connections.

After this lesson, you will be able to

- Check physical network connections.
- Troubleshoot installed networking hardware.
- Troubleshoot modem hardware.

Estimated lesson time: 25 minutes

Checking Connections

Many of the service calls you will be asked to handle as a tier-1 desktop support technician (DST) are resolved by simply reconnecting the Ethernet cable or phone line to the computer, modem, or hub. This is especially true in an office or corporate environment where the furniture is moved or relocated often, or when a cleaning crew comes in each night and works around users' computers. When a user reports that he or she cannot access the workgroup computers, the LAN, the domain, or the Internet, check these physical connections first.

Note   A workgroup or domain client cannot access workgroup or domain resources if his or her network server is down or the workgroup computer he or she is trying to reach is not turned on or is otherwise unavailable. Before getting too far into the troubleshooting procedure, verify that network computers are functional.

In addition to the physical connection of the cable or phone line to the NIC or modem, verify that these other items are properly connected (if applicable):

- The Ethernet cable to the hub
- The Ethernet cables from the hub to other computers

- The physical connections to and from routers and firewalls

- The phone line to the phone jack

- The modem, hub, and other devices that need power to the wall jack

- The universal serial bus (USB) or FireWire cable to and from the personal digital assistant (PDA), handheld PC, or other device

- Any other connection to and from any other device on the user's computer

In addition, if a wireless access point is configured, make sure that it is within the range that is listed in its documentation. The wireless access point might have been moved or might have fallen behind a user's desk. A wireless user will not be able to connect if the wireless access point is not within the required range.

 Note   If you notice that a desk, chair, or other piece of furniture is positioned on top of an Ethernet cable, or that the Ethernet cable is crimped, try replacing the cable with a new one. The cable could be damaged.

Troubleshooting Installed Hardware

If the physical network connections look OK, your next step is to check the networking hardware that is installed on the computer so that you can rule out malfunctioning hardware as the cause of the problem. Checking physical hardware connections includes verifying through Device Manager that the connectivity devices are working properly. If they are not, you must troubleshoot those devices. If problems persist, you also need to verify that the hardware is installed properly.

Using Device Manager

Device Manager details the hardware components that are on the computer and denotes any malfunctioning hardware with either a red X or a yellow exclamation point. You should check Device Manager if physical connectivity is not the problem, and before you attempt other troubleshooting techniques. If you find a problem with a modem or NIC, the hardware can be repaired or replaced quickly, and the user can be connected to the network again promptly.

To use Device Manager to locate and troubleshoot hardware devices installed on the computer, follow these steps:

1. Open Control Panel, open Performance And Maintenance, open System, and in the System Properties dialog box, select the Hardware tab.

2. Select Device Manager.

3. Check for red X's or yellow exclamation points. Expand any tree to see the name of the device. Figure 8-1 shows Device Manager with the Modems and Network Adapters trees expanded. In this figure, each component is functioning correctly.

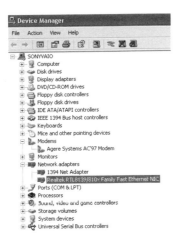

Figure 8-1   Device Manager shows installed hardware, including modems and NICs.

If problems are denoted in Device Manager, the component most likely has a device driver issue, is disabled, or has malfunctioned. You can troubleshoot the device in the device's Properties dialog box by using the General tab. Figure 8-2 shows the General tab for a modem that appears to be working correctly. Notice that the device is enabled in the Device Usage list box.

Figure 8-2   The General tab details the device status.

If you believe that a device is the cause of the problem, if the device is disabled, or if it has a red X or a yellow exclamation point beside it, you can use Device Manager to troubleshoot it by following these steps:

1. Open Device Manager.

2. Expand the tree for the component to troubleshoot. Double-click the device name.

3. In the Properties dialog box, select the General tab.

4. Verify that the Device Usage option is set to Use This Device (Enable). If it is not, use the drop-down list to select it. (This might solve the problem.)

5. Select Troubleshoot.

6. Work through the Help and Support Center's Troubleshooting Wizard to resolve the problem.

The Help and Support troubleshooting wizards are a great way to troubleshoot a piece of hardware because they walk you through current, reliable techniques for solving common problems with hardware. In addition, they offer exceptional learning tools for beginning DSTs.

> **Note**   To learn more about Device Manager, read Microsoft Knowledge Base (KB) article 314747.

Checking Physical Connections

If Device Manager finds a problem and you cannot resolve it by using the troubleshooting wizards, or if the device that you are looking for is missing from the Device Manager list (no modem listed, no NIC listed), check the physical connection of the networking hardware.

Occasionally, especially after a computer has been moved or bumped, a component inside the computer slips out of place just enough to cause the component to fail. When a modem or NIC is not **seated** properly, it cannot work properly. If you have the proper credentials (A+ certification or approval from your superiors, for instance), you should open the case and check these connections.

To check for the proper connections inside a computer case, follow these steps:

1. Turn off the computer and unplug it.

2. Remove the cover from the computer case.

3. Ground yourself to the computer by using an antistatic wrist strap.

4. Locate the modem or NIC, and press lightly on the card to verify that it is seated properly. If the card is not properly seated, remove the card from the computer chassis and remove and reseat the card.

5. Replace the cover, plug in the computer, and turn it on.

If the connection still does not work or if there were no obvious problems with the hardware, continue working through the troubleshooting techniques listed in the following sections.

Using the Modem Troubleshooter

The Microsoft Windows Help and Support files offer a modem troubleshooter (among others). If you believe that the modem is the cause of the connectivity problem, if it is configured correctly and enabled in Device Manager, and if you know it is seated correctly or connected properly at the computer, you can try the Modem Troubleshooter in Help and Support.

This troubleshooter guides you through what to do if users have problems connecting to the Internet by using the modem, if Windows does not detect the modem, or if the Network Setup and New Connection Wizards are not working properly. In this case, you would choose to follow the wizard through the options for solving a problem using the modem to connect to the Internet.

To use the Modem Troubleshooter, follow these steps:

1. From the Start menu, select Help And Support.

2. Under Pick A Help Topic, select Fixing A Problem.

3. Under Fixing A Problem, select Networking Problems, and from the right pane, select Modem Troubleshooter.

4. On the What Problem Are You Having page, select I Have Problems Using My Modem To Connect To The Internet. Click Next.

5. Work through the various troubleshooting pages to do the following:

   a. Verify that the **COM port** is turned on.

   b. Verify that the modem is functional.

   c. Verify that the physical connection is configured properly.

   d. Verify that the modem is turned on.

   e. Verify that the COM port settings are correct.

   f. Verify that the modem is on the Microsoft Hardware Compatibility List (HCL).

   g. Verify that the COM port, modem, or cable is not faulty.

h. Upgrade the basic input/output system (BIOS) of the internal modem if necessary.

i. Locate conflicting devices.

j. Upgrade the modem's .inf file (a file that lists commands that the modem supports) or driver.

k. Verify that the modem is installed correctly.

l. Re-create dial-up connections.

m. Visit the Windows Update website or the manufacturer's website.

As you can see from this list, the Windows Help and Support troubleshooting wizards are quite thorough. Whenever possible, access these wizards to help you to resolve end-user problems. In your spare time, work through the wizards to learn new techniques for resolving problems.

Note   If you believe that the NIC is not functioning properly, work through Help and Support's Drives And Network Adapters Troubleshooter.

Lesson Review

The following questions are intended to reinforce key information presented in this lesson. If you are unable to answer a question, review the lesson materials and try the question again. You can find answers to the questions in the "Questions and Answers" section at the end of this chapter.

1. What is the name of the Windows utility that lists the current state of the hardware installed on the system?

    A. msconfig

    B. System Information

    C. Device Manager

    D. Computer Management

2. You are troubleshooting a networking problem for a user. The user was having no problems connecting to her network when she left the office yesterday afternoon. This morning, when she came to work, she could not connect to the network. You know that other users on the network are not having the same problems. What is the first thing you should check?

    _____

    _____

Lesson Summary

■ To resolve connectivity problems on a workgroup or a domain, check all physical connections, including cables, hubs, switches, routers, and network computers first.

■ Use Device Manager to ensure that connectivity devices installed on the computer are working properly.

■ Use the Windows troubleshooters to help when troubleshooting network connectivity and hardware issues.

Lesson 2: Resolving Network Configuration Issues

If the physical connections are not the cause of connectivity problems, the configuration of those connections might be. For instance, although the modem might be working properly, the user will not be able to connect to the Internet if the phone number that is used to dial the Internet service provider (ISP) is configured incorrectly. If a DSL line is used but the connection is configured incorrectly or is unavailable, the user will not be able to connect either. Configuration problems such as these are quite common. In this lesson, you learn how to troubleshoot configuration settings for these types of Internet connections, plus two other types: workgroup connections and domain connections.

After this lesson, you will be able to

- Troubleshoot modem connections.
- Troubleshoot cable and DSL connections.
- Troubleshoot workgroup connections.
- Troubleshoot domain connections.

Estimated lesson time: 50 minutes

Troubleshooting Modem Connections

Internet connectivity problems involving modems occur for a variety of reasons. A problem can be caused by something as simple as dialing an incorrect phone number or having the connection automatically disconnect after a period of time or something as complicated as an improperly configured name server address. In this section, you learn about the most common problems with configured Internet connections; later, you will learn about more complicated name-resolution problems.

Users often report connectivity problems that are fairly common. These include:

- My modem will not connect to my ISP.
- I get an error message when the modem dials, stating that the number is not in service.
- I cannot hear my modem when it dials.
- I hear my modem when it dials.
- I keep getting disconnected from the Internet after 20 minutes of inactivity.
- When I get disconnected from the Internet, the connection is not redialed automatically.

- When I disconnect from my ISP at night, the computer redials and connects even though I do not want it to.

- I keep getting prompted for my name and password, phone number, and other information.

- Sometimes my ISP's phone number is busy. I have an alternative number. How do I change the number that the computer dials?

Each of these problems can be resolved in the same place: the Properties dialog box of the Internet connection.

Resolving Tier-1 Internet Connectivity Calls

You can resolve the problems listed in the preceding list from the Internet connection's Properties dialog box, shown in Figure 8-3. To access this dialog box, open Control Panel, click Network And Internet Connections, click Network Connections, right-click the Internet connection, and then click Properties.

Figure 8-3   The Internet Properties dialog box is the place to configure the modem.

Table 8-1 details how to resolve each of the calls in the preceding list by using the Internet Properties dialog box.

Table 8-1   Resolving Common Internet Connectivity Calls

Complaint/Report	Possible Solution
My modem will not connect to my ISP.	Call the ISP, and verify or obtain a phone number. On the General tab, retype the phone number.
I get an error message when the modem dials, indicating that the number is not in service.	Call the ISP, and obtain a new phone number. On the General tab, insert the phone number.
I cannot hear my modem when it dials.	On the General tab, click Configure. Select the Enable Modem Speaker check box. In Device Manager, double-click the modem, and on the Modem tab, configure the speaker volume.
I hear my modem when it dials.	On the General tab, select Configure. Clear the Enable Modem Speaker check box.
I keep getting disconnected from the Internet after 20 minutes of inactivity.	On the Options tab, change the setting for Idle Time Before Hanging Up to Never, 24 Hours, 8 Hours, 4 Hours, or any other setting.
When I get disconnected from the Internet, the connection is not redialed automatically.	On the Options tab, select the Redial If Line Is Dropped check box.
When I disconnect from my ISP at night, the computer redials and connects even though I do not want it to.	On the Options tab, change the value for Redial Attempts to 0. Clear the Redial If Line Is Dropped check box.
I keep getting prompted for my name and password, phone number, and other information.	On the Options tab, clear the Prompt For Name And Password, Certificate, Etc.; Include Windows Logon Domain; and Prompt For Phone Number check boxes as applicable to the network.
Sometimes my ISP's phone number is busy. I have an alternative number. How do I change the number that the computer dials?	On the General tab, click Alternates. In the Alternate Phone Numbers dialog box, click Add. Add the new number, and click OK to exit the dialog boxes.

When you are finished making changes, click OK in the Internet Properties dialog box and disconnect and redial the number to activate the changes.

Troubleshooting Cable and DSL Connections

Internet connectivity problems involving cable and DSL modems occur for a variety of reasons. A problem can be caused by something as simple as a disconnected cable or a dial-up modem that is not disabled or something as complicated as troubleshooting a slow connection or identifying the source of DSL interference. In this section, you learn about the most common problems with these types of configured Internet connections; later, you will learn about more name-resolution problems and problems with DNS and WINS servers.

Users often report connectivity problems that are fairly common. These include:

- My dial-up modem keeps trying to dial out.

- My Internet connection is unavailable.

- I try to connect, but nothing happens at all.

- My Internet connection is slow.

- I think I am getting interference. Could something be causing that?

Resolving Tier-1 Internet Connectivity Calls

You can resolve the problems listed in the preceding list by using common sense and familiar troubleshooting techniques. Table 8-2 details how to resolve these calls.

Table 8-2   Resolving Common Internet Connectivity Calls

Complaint/Report	Possible Solution
My dial-up modem keeps trying to dial out.	Open Control Panel, open Network And Connections, and then open Internet Options. Choose the Connections tab, and select LAN Settings. Clear all selected settings. Click OK twice to close the two open dialog boxes. Open Internet Explorer, and from the Tools menu, select Internet Options. On the Connections tab, select Never Dial A Connection. Click OK.
My Internet connection is unavailable.	Check all physical connections to and from modems, routers, and the computer. Swap out questionable cables for new ones. If problems still exist, right-click the connection in Network Connections, choose Properties, select Internet Protocol (TCP/IP), and click Properties. Note that if you are using a dial-up connection, the Internet Protocol (TCP/IP) information is on the Networking tab of the network connection's Properties dialog box. Verify with the ISP that the settings are correct. A common setting is Obtain An IP Address Automatically. Click OK to work out of the dialog boxes.
I try to connect, but nothing happens at all.	Verify that all power supplies to modems or routers are plugged in and that all hardware is turned on. Verify that the NIC and all hardware are functional by using Device Manager as detailed earlier.
My Internet connection is slow.	Contact the ISP first. The problem could lie in the ISP's capabilities. It is possible that the servers are overloaded. A newer modem might also be available.

Table 8-2   Resolving Common Internet Connectivity Calls

Complaint/Report	Possible Solution
I think I am getting interference. Could something be causing that?	Yes. Interference can be caused by lighting dimmer switches, AM radio stations, and other sources.

For more information about troubleshooting cable modems, read Knowledge Base article 310089, "Troubleshooting Cable Modems."

Troubleshooting Workgroup Connections

A workgroup is a common network configuration. Generally, a workgroup consists of a few computers, each of which is connected to a hub, router, or switch through an Ethernet cable or wirelessly, for the purpose of sharing files in a small office or a home. Problems in this type of network occur for many reasons. When troubleshooting a user's access to another workgroup computer or resource on the network, check the physical connections first, check the status of the hub and NIC, verify the workgroup name in My Computer, and try repairing or disabling and enabling the connection from Network Connections. If the problem cannot be resolved by using any of these techniques, you might have to re-create the network connection.

> **Note**   Before performing any of the following troubleshooting techniques, verify that the user is logged on to the computer appropriately, that physical connections are solid, that the NIC has a green light indicating that it is functional (if the NIC has diagnostic LEDs), and that the hub, switch, or other device is working properly.

Resolving Tier-1 Workgroup Connectivity Calls

If the physical connections and hardware are all functional and connected properly, you can begin troubleshooting the connection's properties. These properties might have been changed because the user ran the Network Connections Wizard, the Network Setup Wizard, or the New Connection Wizard; because the user changed the name of the workgroup or the name of the computer in the System Properties dialog box; or for a number of other reasons. You should first verify that the workgroup name and computer name are correct in the System Properties dialog box by following these steps:

1. Open Control Panel, open Performance And Maintenance, and then open System.

2. On the Computer Name tab, verify that the computer is a member of a workgroup and that the workgroup name is correct. If these settings are correct, click OK.

3. If the workgroup name is incorrect, click Change, and in the Computer Name Changes dialog box, shown in Figure 8-4, type the correct workgroup name and click OK.

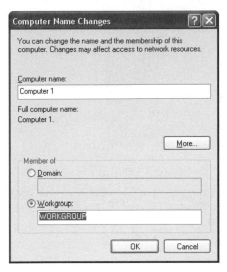

Figure 8-4   Verify the workgroup name from System in Control Panel.

4. If the computer name is incorrect, click Change, and in the Computer Name Changes dialog box, shown in Figure 8-4, type the correct computer name and click OK.

5. If the information on the Computer Name tab states that the computer is a member of a domain instead of a workgroup, click Change, and in the Computer Name Changes dialog box, select Workgroup and type the correct workgroup name. Click OK.

6. Click OK to close the System Properties dialog box, and reboot the computer if prompted.

You can also check the computer name, user name, workstation domain, and other information by using the command-line utility net config workstation. The information provided can be quite useful when troubleshooting tier-1 connectivity calls. To see what information can be obtained, follow these steps:

1. From the Start menu, point to All Programs, point to Accessories, and select Command Prompt.

2. At the prompt, type **net config workstation**, and press Enter on the keyboard. Figure 8-5 shows a sample result.

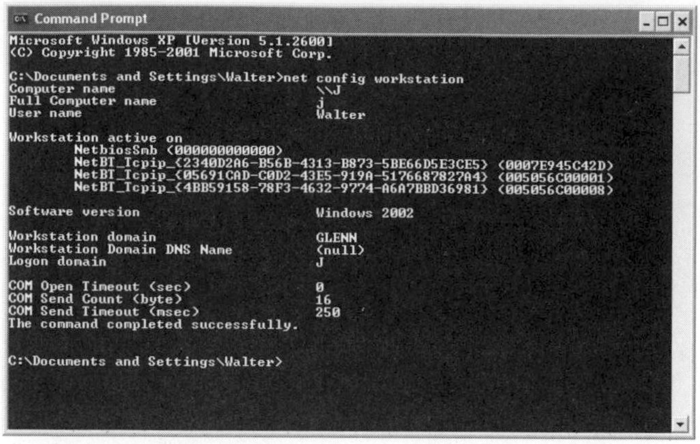

Figure 8-5 The command-line utility net config workstation offers plenty of information.

Notice in Figure 8-5 that the following pertinent information is offered (among other items):

■ Computer name

■ User name

■ Workstation domain

■ Logon domain

This command-line utility thus offers another way to locate and obtain information about the computer, and this information can prove quite helpful in troubleshooting connectivity problems.

If the workgroup name and the computer name are correct, try repairing and then disabling and enabling the connection by following these steps:

1. Open Control Panel, open Network And Internet Connections, and open Network Connections. Verify that the local area connection is enabled. If it is not, right-click the connection and choose Enable. Check to see whether this resolves the problem.

2. Right-click Local Area Connection, and choose Repair. Choosing this option forces a network adapter to acquire a new IP address and thus resets the network connection for that computer. Wait to see the status of the attempted repair.

3. If the repair is successful, double-click the Local Area Connection icon. Verify that **packets** are being sent and received, as shown in Figure 8-6. This denotes a healthy network connection. Click Close.

Figure 8-6   A working network connection shows packets being sent and received.

4. If the repair procedure fails, right-click Local Area Connection and choose Disable. Right-click again, and choose Enable.

5. If enabling is successful, double-click the Local Area Connection icon. Verify that packets are being sent and received, as shown in Figure 8-6. This denotes a healthy network connection. Click Close.

If the local area connection is still not working properly, clear all network connections by clicking an empty area of the Network Connections window. In the left pane, under See Also, click Network Troubleshooter. Next, follow these steps:

1. From the Help And Support Center Networking Problems page, select Home And Small Office Networking Troubleshooter.

2. On the first page, under What Problem Are You Having?, select I'm Having Problems Sharing Files Or Printers. Click Next.

3. On the following wizard pages, make sure that I Want The Troubleshooter To Investigate Settings On This Computer is selected as you work through the options.

If the problem cannot be resolved by using any of these techniques, you might have to re-create the network connection.

Re-Creating the Network Connection

As a last resort before tackling advanced command-line utility troubleshooting techniques, and prior to making complicated changes to DNS or WINS server addresses, re-create the network connection and reintroduce the computer to the network. This often works to bring the computer back online.

Because there are many ways in which a network can be configured, and because a computer in a network can be configured in multiple ways as well, the steps that are involved in re-creating a network connection can take many different forms. For instance, a computer configured to provide (or host) a shared dial-up Internet connection has a much different configuration from a computer that connects to the Internet through a **router.** Therefore, the following procedure details how to re-create the connection for a computer that connects directly to the Internet and provides shared Internet access to the other computers on the network. Procedures for other configurations are performed similarly.

To re-create a LAN connection and reintroduce the computer to the network, follow these steps:

1. From the Start menu, point to All Programs, point to Accessories, point to Communications, and select Network Setup Wizard. Click Next to start the wizard.

2. Read the information on the Before You Continue page, and click Next.

3. On the Select A Connection Method page, shown in Figure 8-7, select the statement that best describes the computer you are troubleshooting:

   ❏ This Computer Connects Directly To The Internet. The Other Computers On My Network Connect To The Internet Through This Computer. (The rest of the steps in this example show the procedure when this option is selected.)

   ❏ This Computer Connects To The Internet Through Another Computer On My Network Or Through A Residential Gateway.

   ❏ Other. (If you select this option, the Network Setup Wizard offers you additional choices, and you need to make the appropriate choice depending on the circumstances.)

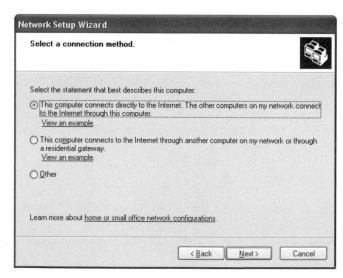

Figure 8-7   Select the statement that best describes the computer.

4. When prompted to select an Internet connection, select the connection that the client uses to connect to the Internet from the list offered. Click Next.

5. If prompted that the computer has multiple connections, choose Let Me Choose The Connections To My Network. On the resulting wizard page, make the appropriate selections for your network. Click Next.

6. On the Give This Computer A Description And Name page, type a computer description (this is optional), and type the computer name. Click Next.

7. On the Name Your Network page, in the Workgroup Name box, type the name of the existing workgroup. Click Next.

8. On the Ready To Apply Network Settings page, verify that the settings are correct and click Next. (Click Back if they are not, and make any necessary changes.)

9. Wait while the Network Setup Wizard completes. When prompted to add other computers to the network, select Just Finish The Wizard; I Don't Need To Run The Wizard On Other Computers. Click Next, and then click Finish.

The user should now be able to access network resources on the computers running Microsoft Windows XP on the network and should have access to the Internet. Open My Network Places to verify this.

If problems still exist after you work through the troubleshooting techniques in this section, you need to apply some advanced techniques. These advanced procedures are detailed in the following sections of this chapter.

> **Note**   Workgroups can use Automatic Private IP Addressing (APIPA) to connect workgroup resources, and this type of addressing can cause connectivity issues. APIPA can also be used in domains. For more information about APIPA, see the section "APIPA Connections" later in this chapter.

Troubleshooting Domain Connections

A domain is another type of network configuration. Generally, a domain consists of many computers (10, 100, 1000, or more), each of which can be connected to a server (or servers) on the network through an Ethernet cable, wirelessly, through fiber-optic cable, through a T1 line, over the Internet, or by using a combination of these or other connectivity options. A server called a domain controller authenticates the user onto the domain for the purpose of sharing files and folders, hardware, and other network resources. Those resources can be in the same office or anywhere in the world.

> **Note**   A computer running Windows XP Home Edition cannot join a domain.

Problems can occur with this type of network for many reasons. When troubleshooting a user's access to a domain server or resource on the network, you must verify that the user is logged on to the domain with the correct credentials and password, check the status of the servers and the physical connections, and check the status of the NIC. As with a workgroup connection, you can also try repairing and disabling and then enabling the connection from Network Connections. If you cannot resolve the problem by using any of these techniques, you will have to use more advanced troubleshooting techniques, including troubleshooting Transmission Control Protocol/Internet Protocol (TCP/IP) settings.

> **Note**   Before performing any of the following troubleshooting techniques, verify that physical connections are solid, that the NIC has a green light indicating that it is functional (if the NIC has diagnostic LEDs), and that switches, routers, and other devices are working properly and are available.

Resolving Tier-1 Domain Connectivity Calls

If the physical connections and hardware (including servers) are all in working order and connected properly, you can begin troubleshooting the connection's properties. You should first verify that the connection is functional and that packets are being sent and received. As with a workgroup, try repairing and then disabling and enabling the connection by following these steps:

1. Open Control Panel, and open Network Connections. Verify that the local area connection to the server is enabled, if such a connection exists. If it is not enabled, right-click the connection and choose Enable. Check to see whether this resolves the problem.

2. Right-click the local area connection for the domain if it exists, and choose Repair. (See Figure 8-8.) This connection might be a network bridge, a wireless connection, or another type of local area connection. Wait to see the status of the attempted repair.

Figure 8-8   Repair network connections as a first step in troubleshooting.

3. If the repair is successful, double-click the connection's icon. Verify that packets are being sent and received. Click Close.

4. If the repair procedure fails, right-click the connection and choose Disable. Right-click again, and choose Enable. Repeat this with the network bridge if one exists.

5. If enabling is successful, double-click the Local Area Connection icon. Verify that packets are being sent and received. This denotes a healthy network connection. Click Close.

6. If the user connects to the domain over the Internet, verify that the user's Internet connection is active. If it is not, connect to the Internet before continuing. Double-click that connection to verify that data is being sent and received. Additionally, verify the speed, errors, and compression numbers. These might produce significant hints as to the source of the connectivity problem. For instance, if the user's Internet connection speed is 28.8 Kbps, the user's requests for data will probably **time out** before they ever reach the server.

Note   If a user's Internet connection is the source of the problem, you might have to troubleshoot the modem or contact the ISP for information about the problem.

If the physical connection to the server or domain is functional and packets are being sent and received or an Internet connection is working properly, verify that the user is logging on to the domain and not the computer. When a computer running Windows XP Professional is a member of a domain, users can log on to either the domain or the local computer. If a user has logged on to the computer instead of the domain, that user might not be able to access domain resources. To verify that the user is logging on to the domain, follow these steps:

1. Log off Windows XP by clicking Start, selecting Log Off, and then selecting Log Off again.

2. When you see the Welcome To Windows dialog box, press CTRL+ALT+DELETE to open the Log On To Windows dialog box.

3. In the Log On To drop-down list, make sure you select the name of the domain to which you want to log on. This list also holds an option for logging on to the local computer.

4. Enter the user's user name and password, and click OK.

If the user is logging on to an incorrect domain (for instance, if the user is trying to log on using a laptop normally used for accessing the corporate domain and is now trying to use that same computer to log on to a different local domain), you have to change the computer's domain or workgroup membership on the Computer Name tab. Note that in order to do this, you must have a user account in the domain with administrative rights to create new computer accounts in the domain. If you do not, you must have a domain administrator add the computer for you. To change the computer's domain membership, follow these steps:

1. Right-click My Computer and select Properties, or open System from Control Panel.

2. Select the Computer Name tab, and choose Change.

3. In the Computer Name Changes dialog box, shown in Figure 8-9, select Domain and type the name of the new domain. Click OK.

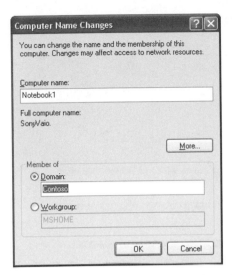

Figure 8-9   Make domain changes from the Computer Name Changes dialog box.

4. You are prompted for the user name and password of an account with permission to create a new computer account in the domain. Enter the proper credentials, and click OK.

5. Reboot as prompted, and have the user log on to the new domain.

Caution   If the computer is not configured with the correct DNS server addresses (or cannot contact the DNS servers), you will not be able to change the computer's membership. There will be more on DNS servers later in this chapter.

If the user has logged on to the domain correctly and the connection is functioning properly, open Network Connections, and clear all network connections by clicking an empty area of the Network Connections window. In the left pane, under See Also, click Network Troubleshooter, and then follow these steps:

1. On the Help And Support Center Networking Problems page, select Diagnose Network Configuration And Run Automated Networking Tasks.

2. Select Set Scanning Options, and select each item in the list. Click Save Options when you are done.

3. Click Scan Your System. The results will help you diagnose the problem, and this is a good first step. Figure 8-10 shows a sample report.

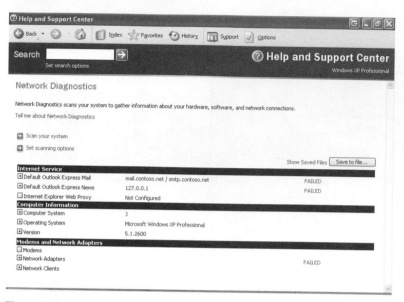

Figure 8-10   A system scan using the Network Troubleshooter can offer assistance.

Notice that this report produces a few failures, including contacting the mail server configured in Outlook Express, a problem with the wide area network (WAN) Miniport (IP) network adapter, and issues with the connection to a DNS server. Expanding each tree offers more information, including how the error was discovered (such as a ping failure or a server timeout).

In this case, each failure revolved around accessing the same IP address. All other network components, including modems, are functioning properly. IP addressing information and other networking configurations on the local computer are set up properly. The problem thus lies with that particular resource. Sometimes the information here is just enough to get you started on the right track when troubleshooting domain access.

DHCP Connections

On a domain, most computers are configured to get their TCP/IP addresses automatically from a **Dynamic Host Configuration Protocol** (DHCP) server. These unique TCP/IP addresses allow computers to communicate with other computers and resources on the network and, in many cases, on the Internet. The DHCP server is responsible for automatically configuring IP addresses for computers and other resources on both local and remote networks. DHCP prevents an administrator from having to manually configure **static IP addresses** for individual resources.

When a problem occurs with users' TCP/IP configurations, the users will not be able to access the network's resources. For example, if the DHCP server is offline, users cannot obtain the necessary addresses from the DHCP server, and without a valid TCP/IP address from the DHCP server, the user will not be able to communicate with anyone on the network or access network resources.

When a DHCP server is unavailable, APIPA takes over. APIPA offers a temporary TCP/IP addressing scheme so that computers that are on the local network can communicate with each other until a DHCP server becomes available again. However, because APIPA uses a different addressing scheme from all other networks (the addresses are reserved for this purpose), it also causes problems on networks that use DHCP because the two schemes cannot communicate. Even though APIPA causes some problems, it still allows communication between computers on the local network until the issue causing the problem is resolved. APIPA is detailed further next.

APIPA Connections

APIPA is a feature of Windows XP TCP/IP that automatically configures a unique IP address for each computer on a network when the TCP/IP protocol is configured for dynamic addressing and a DHCP server is not available. APIPA thus automates the IP configuration of all network resources and connections. These addresses are always in the range 169.254.0.1 through 169.254.255.254 and use a **subnet mask** of 255.255.0.0. The purpose of APIPA is to allow a network to be easily and quickly configured for both workgroups and domains and to allow resources to be available even if the DHCP server is offline.

> **Exam Tip** On the exam, you will often be shown IP addressing information for use in troubleshooting a networking problem. Remember the range of IP addresses used by APIPA. If you see that a computer has an IP address starting with 169.254, it is a dead giveaway that a DHCP server is not being reached. This could happen because of a networking problem or a DHCP issue.

When you configure a TCP/IP connection to obtain an IP address automatically, by default the computer attempts to contact a DHCP server for that address. If the server is available, a user is given an address from the **scope of addresses** on the DHCP server. If a DHCP server is not configured or not available, the computer uses the alternate configuration to determine whether to use APIPA.

> **Note** APIPA addresses are never used on the Internet. In addition, because APIPA does not offer a **gateway address,** APIPA clients cannot access anything outside the local subnet. APIPA is useful only in emergencies in domain subnets and on small LANs that have only a single subnet and do not access outside resources.

To configure a computer to use automatic TCP/IP addressing and APIPA when neces-sary, follow these steps:

1. Open Network Connections.

2. Right-click the configured network connection, and then choose Properties.

3. On the General tab for a local area connection or on the Networking tab for all other connections, select Internet Protocol (TCP/IP), and then click Properties.

4. Verify that Obtain An IP Address Automatically is selected, and click OK. Click OK again to close the Local Area Connection Properties dialog box.

You can easily find out whether a computer is using an APIPA address and whether APIPA is enabled by typing **ipconfig /all** at the command prompt and proceeding as follows:

1. From the Start menu, choose All Programs, Accessories, and Command Prompt.

2. Type **ipconfig /all** and press ENTER.

> **Note**   You can also use **ipconfig** without the /all switch if you need less information. Ipcon-fig with no switch offers the IP address, subnet mask, and default gateway of each connec-tion, including any local area networks and the Internet connections.

3. Under Windows IP Configuration, locate the Autoconfiguration IP Address. If the IP address is in the range 169.254.0.1 through 169.254.255.254, the computer is configured with an APIPA address, and APIPA is active.

4. To see whether APIPA is enabled, check the Autoconfiguration Enabled parame-ter. If the parameter is set to Yes, APIPA is enabled.

If APIPA is active, it automatically checks every five minutes for an available DHCP server, just in case one comes back online.

Practice: Resolve Network Configuration Issues

In this practice, you will configure an Internet connection, install a modem, and change workgroup names.

> **Note**   In Exercise 1, you will configure a nonfunctioning Internet connection using a modem that does not exist. In Exercise 2, you will install a nonfunctioning modem. When you are done with these exercises, delete the items that you have created.

Exercise 1: Configure an Internet Connection

1. Log on to Windows XP using an account with administrator privileges.

2. From the Start menu, select My Computer.

3. In the Other Places section in the left pane, select My Network Places.

4. In the My Network Places window, in the Network Tasks section, click View Network Connections.

5. In the Network Connections window, in the Network Tasks section, click Create A New Connection.

6. In the New Connection Wizard, on the Welcome To The New Connection Wizard page, click Next.

7. On the Network Connection Type page, verify that Connect To The Internet is selected, and click Next.

8. On the Getting Ready page, select Set Up My Connection Manually, and click Next.

9. On the Internet Connection page, verify that Connect Using A Dial-Up Modem is selected, and click Next.

10. On the Connection Name page, in the ISP Name text box, type **Contoso**, and click Next.

11. On the Phone Number To Dial page, in the Phone Number text box, type **1-000-000-0000**. Click Next.

12. On the Connection Availability page, click Next.

13. On the Internet Account Information page, in the User Name text box, type your name. In the Password and Confirm Password text boxes, type **password**. Click Next.

14. On the Completing The New Connection Wizard page, click Finish.

Exercise 2: Install a Modem

1. Log on to Windows XP using an account with administrator privileges.

2. From the Start menu, select Control Panel.

3. In Control Panel, click Printers And Other Hardware.

4. In the task pane, under See Also, click Add Hardware.

5. In the Add Hardware Wizard, on the Welcome To The Add Hardware Wizard page, click Next.

6. On the Is The Hardware Connected? page, select Yes, I Have Already Connected The Hardware and click Next.

7. On the The Following Hardware Is Already Installed On Your Computer page, in the Installed Hardware list, scroll to the bottom and select Add A New Hardware Device. Click Next.

8. On the The Wizard Can Help You Install Other Hardware page, select Install The Hardware That I Manually Select From A List (Advanced), and click Next.

9. On the From The List Below, Select The Type Of Hardware You Are Installing page, in the Common Hardware Types list, select Modems. Click Next.

10. On the Install New Modem page, select the Don't Detect My Modem; I Will Select It From A List check box, and click Next.

11. On the Install New Modem page, in the Manufacturer list, ensure that (Standard Modem Types) is selected. In the Models list, select Standard 56000 bps Modem, and click Next.

12. On the Install New Modem page, in the Ports window, select COM1. Click Next.

13. The Install New Modem page appears. Click Finish when it becomes active.

14. Close all open windows.

Exercise 3: Change Workgroups

1. Log on to Windows XP using an account with administrator privileges.

2. From the Start menu, right-click My Computer and select Properties.

3. In the System Properties dialog box, on the Computer Name tab, click Change.

4. In the Computer Name Changes dialog box, under Member Of, in the Workgroup text box, enter a new workgroup name.

5. Click OK.

6. In the Computer Name Changes message box welcoming you to the new workgroup, click OK.

7. In the Computer Name Changes message box instructing you to restart to activate changes, click OK.

8. In the System Properties dialog box, click OK.

9. In the System Settings Changes message box asking whether you want to restart your computer, click Yes.

Lesson Review

The following questions are intended to reinforce key information presented in this lesson. If you are unable to answer a question, review the lesson materials and try the question again. You can find answers to the questions in the "Questions and Answers" section at the end of this chapter.

1. You are troubleshooting a network connectivity problem for a workgroup containing 12 computers. One of the computers cannot access network resources. After verifying that the physical connections are good, that the NIC light is on and the NIC produces no errors in Device Manager, and that the computer name and workgroup name are correct in System Properties, you still cannot solve the problem. What should you try next?

   A. Remove two of the computers from the workgroup; workgroups can have only 10 or fewer computers connected.

   B. Open Network Connections, and try to repair the connection.

   C. Re-create the network connection.

   D. Configure the workgroup to use APIPA.

2. A user complains to you that he is not able to connect to any network resources after installing a new networking card. You open the Command Prompt window on the user's computer and type **ipconfig /all**. You get the following results:

```
Ethernet adapter Local Area Connection:
        Connection-specific DNS Suffix
        Description . . . . . . . . . . . : Intel(R) PRO/1000 CT
        Physical Address. . . . . . . . . : 00-05-E8-45-B4-2E
        DHCP Enabled. . . . . . . . . . . : Yes
        IP Address. . . . . . . . . . . . : 169.254.011.202
        Subnet Mask . . . . . . . . . . . : 255.255.0.0
        Default Gateway . . . . . . . . . :
        DNS Servers . . . . . . . . . . . :
```

What do these results tell you? (Choose all that apply.)

   A. The computer is configured to connect to a DHCP server.

   B. The computer is not configured to connect to a DHCP server.

   C. The computer is successfully connecting to a DHCP server.

   D. The computer is not successfully connecting to a DHCP server.

Lesson Summary

- Home and small business users are likely to connect to the Internet by using a modem or by a broadband connection such as cable or DSL. Troubleshooting problems for these users involves ensuring that the user has the correct information from his or her ISP and that Windows is configured correctly for the user's type of connection.

- Users on networks will be members of one of two types of networks: a workgroup or a domain. Workgroups are small collections of computers that do not rely on a server for authentication. Domains are larger networks wherein servers called domain controllers authenticate users and provide network security and administration.

Lesson 3: Resolving Complex Networking Issues

If a domain or workgroup user is still unable to access a network resource on a domain or workgroup; if you have checked that the user has logged on correctly, that the physical connections are good, that the network connections are working properly, and that an IP address problem (because of APIPA) is not causing the problem; and if the Network Troubleshooter did not help you solve the problem or gave you only a few hints, you have a more serious issue on your hands. Complex problems generally require troubleshooting from the command line. In this lesson, you learn some common commands, what type of information each of these commands offers, and how to work with the information you find.

After this lesson, you will be able to

- Use the ping command to test TCP/IP connections.
- Use the ipconfig /all command to display TCP/IP configuration information.
- Use the net view command to view networking information.
- Use the tracert and pathping commands for advanced connection testing.

Estimated lesson time: 20 minutes

Using ping

When the problem appears to have to do with TCP/IP, either because you have ruled out problems with NICs, physical connections, and the other causes detailed in this chapter or because the Network Troubleshooter pointed out a TCP/IP address problem, you need to start the troubleshooting process with the ping command. The ping command allows you to check for connectivity between devices, including the local computer's NIC, the network's DNS server, the DHCP server, the gateway, and other resources.

When you use the ping command, you will ping from the inside out. You want to find out where the communication and connection fail. For example, you will ping the **loopback address** first, then a local computer on the same **subnet** (basically, a subnet is the equivalent of a LAN), then a DNS or DHCP server on the local subnet if one exists, then the default gateway, then a remote computer on another subnet (a network outside the local area network), and finally a resource on the Internet. You should be able to find out where the breakdown occurs by compiling the results of these checks.

Note   When using the ping command, you can use either the computer name or the computer's IP address.

The Loopback Address

The loopback address (127.0.0.1) is the first thing you should check when a TCP/IP problem appears. If this check fails, the TCP/IP configuration for the local machine is not correct. To ping the loopback address, follow these steps:

1. From the Start menu, point to All Programs, point to Accessories, and select Command Prompt.

2. Type **ping 127.0.0.1**. A successful ping to a loopback address is shown in Figure 8-11.

```
Command Prompt                                              _ □ x
Microsoft Windows XP [Version 5.1.2600]
(C) Copyright 1985-2001 Microsoft Corp.

C:\Documents and Settings\Walter>ping 127.0.0.1

Pinging 127.0.0.1 with 32 bytes of data:

Reply from 127.0.0.1: bytes=32 time<1ms TTL=128
Reply from 127.0.0.1: bytes=32 time<1ms TTL=128
Reply from 127.0.0.1: bytes=32 time<1ms TTL=128
Reply from 127.0.0.1: bytes=32 time<1ms TTL=128

Ping statistics for 127.0.0.1:
    Packets: Sent = 4, Received = 4, Lost = 0 (0% loss),
Approximate round trip times in milli-seconds:
    Minimum = 0ms, Maximum = 0ms, Average = 0ms

C:\Documents and Settings\Walter>
```

Figure 8-11   Ping the loopback address to verify that TCP/IP is configured correctly.

If pinging the loopback address fails, check the configuration of TCP/IP by following these steps:

1. Open Network Connections, right-click the configured connection, and choose Properties.

2. Select Internet Protocol (TCP/IP), and click Properties to view the configuration. If a static address is configured and a DHCP server is available, select Obtain An IP Address Automatically. If Obtain An IP Address Automatically is selected but a static IP address is necessary, select Use The Following IP Address, and then enter the address, subnet mask, and gateway to use. If the configuration is correct, you might have to reset TCP/IP.

3. Click OK in the Properties dialog box and OK in the connection's Properties dialog box. Reboot the computer if prompted.

See Also   If reconfiguring the TCP/IP settings did not help solve the loopback problem, you can try resetting TCP/IP. Knowledge Base article 299357 details how.

Pinging Other Resources

To ping any other computer on the network, simply replace the loopback address with the TCP/IP address of the resource on the network. Ping a local computer on the same subnet first, and then ping the gateway address. If you can ping the loopback address, a local computer on the same subnet, but the ping command to the gateway fails, you have probably found the problem. In this case, check the configuration on the local computer for the gateway address and verify that the gateway (or router) is operational. To check a computer's configured gateway address, follow these steps:

1. Open Network Connections, right-click on the configured connection, and choose Properties.
2. Select Internet Protocol (TCP/IP), and select Properties to view the configuration.
3. In the connection's Properties dialog box, select Advanced.
4. In the Advanced TCP/IP Settings dialog box, check the address for the default gateway. If the address is incorrect, choose Edit. If no gateway is configured and one should be, choose Add. To remove an address, choose Remove.
5. If Edit or Add was selected in step 4, in the TCP/IP Gateway Address dialog box, shown in Figure 8-12, type the correct address. Click OK.

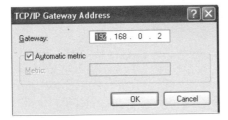

Figure 8-12   Configure a gateway address.

6. Click OK twice to close the remaining dialog boxes, and click Close to apply the change.

If the ping to the gateway address is successful, however, continue to ping outward until you find the problem. For instance, ping a computer on a remote subnet next, and verify that the DNS server is operational.

Note   For more information about troubleshooting using ping and similar commands, read Knowledge Base article 314067, located at the following website. *http://support.microsoft.com/ kb/314067/.*

Using ipconfig /all

The ipconfig /all command displays statistics about the local computer's IP address, subnet mask, and default gateway; the physical address or addresses of the NIC or NICs; whether the computer is DHCP enabled; the addresses of the DNS servers; and more. This information can be quite useful in troubleshooting IP address problems, including improperly configured default gateways, subnet masks, and DNS server addresses.

Figure 8-13 shows an example of an ipconfig /all report. There are two sections on this particular report. (Configurations and reports will vary.)

```
Command Prompt                                                      _ □ ×
Microsoft Windows XP [Version 5.1.2600]
(C) Copyright 1985-2001 Microsoft Corp.

C:\Documents and Settings\Walter>ipconfig /all

Windows IP Configuration

        Host Name . . . . . . . . . . . . : j
        Primary Dns Suffix . . . . . . . :
        Node Type . . . . . . . . . . . . : Unknown
        IP Routing Enabled. . . . . . . . : No
        WINS Proxy Enabled. . . . . . . . : No

Ethernet adapter Local Area Connection:

        Connection-specific DNS Suffix  . :
        Description . . . . . . . . . . . : Intel(R) PRO/1000 CT Network Connect
ion
        Physical Address. . . . . . . . . : 00-07-E9-45-C4-2D
        Dhcp Enabled. . . . . . . . . . . : No
        IP Address. . . . . . . . . . . . : 192.168.1.2
        Subnet Mask . . . . . . . . . . . : 255.255.255.0
        Default Gateway . . . . . . . . . : 192.168.1.1
        DNS Servers . . . . . . . . . . . : 69.1.30.43
                                            69.1.30.42

C:\Documents and Settings\Walter>_
```

Figure 8-13   The ipconfig /all report offers a myriad of information.

- **Windows IP Configuration**   This section details the host name (computer name), the DNS suffix (domain name), the node type (details how NetBIOS name queries are resolved), whether IP routing is enabled, and whether WINS Proxy is enabled.

- **Ethernet Adapter Local Area Connection**   This section details the physical address of the network adapter, whether DHCP and autoconfiguration (APIPA) are enabled, the IP address, the subnet mask, and the default gateway.

The information here can be especially useful when you need to verify that the IP address, subnet mask, and default gateway address are correct.

Rules About TCP/IP Addressing

When checking for problems using ipconfig /all, you should verify that the IP address, subnet mask, and gateway address are what you expect. To do that, you need to know something about TCP/IP addressing.

There are five classes of IP addresses, but for the most part, you will be concerned with only three. Table 8-3 details the various TCP/IP address classes that you are likely to see on a home or corporate network and their start and end addresses. An address in that range must have an associated subnet mask that agrees with the IP address. Subnet masks enable computers to determine when to send packets to the gateway in order to communicate with computers on remote subnets. When checking for TCP/IP configuration problems, verify that the IP address is using the correct subnet mask.

Table 8-3   Addresses and Related Subnet Masks

Class	Beginning IP Address	Ending IP Address	Default Subnet Mask
A	1.0.0.1	127.255.255.254	255.0.0.0
B	128.0.0.1	191.255.255.254	255.255.0.0
C	192.0.0.1	223.255.255.254	255.255.255.0

In addition to IP addresses and subnet masks, gateways and routers are used to connect users of the subnet to outside resources such as the Internet or other subnets on the network. The gateway or router must have an IP address also, and that IP address must be accessible from the user's local subnet. A router that connects a Class A network to a Class C network will need two IP addresses—one that is a Class A address and one that is a Class C address—so that the computers on each subnet can access it.

Finally, certain rules apply to all TCP/IP address schemes:

- IP addresses that start or end with 0 are not allowed, so 0.208.254.121 is invalid, as is 10.1.10.0. However, addresses with 0 in the middle are allowed.

- The IP address 127.x.y.z is reserved as the loopback address and cannot be used.

- Each computer in each subnet must have a unique TCP/IP address. If two computers have the same IP address, problems will result.

- When you assign an IP address, you must also assign a subnet mask.

- Routers must be available from the subnet on which they reside. A Class C network with clients that use the IP addresses 192.168.1.2 through 192.168.1.14 might have a router configured at 192.168.1.1 or 192.168.1.15.

Using net view

The net view command is another command that you can use to test TCP/IP connections. To use the command, log on with the proper credentials that are required to view shares on a remote or local computer, open a command prompt, and type **net view *ComputerName*** or **net view *IPAddress***. The resulting report lists the file and print shares on the computer. If there are no file or print shares on the computer, you see the message There Are No Entries In The List.

If the NetView command fails, check the following:

- The computer name in the System Properties dialog box.

- The gateway or router address in the TCP/IP Properties dialog box.

- The gateway or router's status.

- The remote computer is running the File and Printer Sharing for Microsoft Networks Service. (This service can be added in the TCP/IP Properties dialog box.)

Using tracert

When a connection on a route breaks down on the way from the destination computer to the target computer, communication fails. The tracert command-line utility can help you figure out exactly where along the route this happened. Sometimes the connection breaks down at the gateway on the local network and sometimes at a router on an external network.

To use tracert, type **tracert** followed by the IP address of the remote computer. The resulting report shows where the packets were lost. You can use this information to uncover the source of the problem.

Using pathping

The ping command is used to test communication between one computer and another; tracert is used to follow a particular route from one computer to another. The pathping command is a combination of both ping and tracert, displaying information about packet loss at every router between the host computer and the remote one. The pathping command provides information about data loss between the source and the destination, allowing you to determine which particular router or subnet might be having network problems. To use the pathping command, type **pathping** followed by the target name or IP address.

Note   The Windows Help and Support files offer a list of all of the commands that can be performed at the command line. Search for Command-Line Reference A-Z. Each command reference includes a description of the command and how to use it.

Practice: Use Network Troubleshooting Tools

In this practice, you will use ping, tracert, and pathping. To complete this practice, you will need a network adapter installed in your computer, and you will need to be connected to the Internet.

Exercise 1: Use ping

1. Log on to Windows XP using an account with administrator privileges.

2. From the Start menu, select Run. In the Run dialog box, in the Open text box, type **cmd** and press ENTER.

3. At the command prompt, type **ping 127.0.0.1** and press ENTER. You should see four replies showing response times, followed by statistics for the ping attempts. This response indicates a successful ping of the local computer, meaning that TCP/IP is installed and working correctly.

4. Type **ping www.microsoft.com**. You should see information similar to that in step 3, but this time showing response times for Microsoft's server.

5. Minimize the command prompt window.

6. From the Start menu, select My Computer.

7. In the My Computer window, in the Other Places section, select My Network Places.

8. In the My Network Places window, in the Network Tasks section, click View Network Connections.

9. In the Network Connections window, under LAN Or High-Speed Internet, right-click Local Area Connection and select Properties.

10. In the Local Area Connection Properties dialog box, on the General tab, in the This Connection Uses The Following Items section, clear the Internet Protocol (TCP/IP) check box and click OK.

11. In the Network Connections message box, click Yes. This step disables the TCP/IP protocol on the local computer.

12. Minimize the Network Connections window, and restore the command prompt window.

13. At the command prompt, type **ping www.example.com** and press ENTER. This time, the ping command should respond with the text "Ping request could not find host www.microsoft.com. Please check the name and try again.", indicating that the ping attempt was unsuccessful. (This happens because you have disabled the TCP/IP protocol.)

14. Minimize the command prompt window, and restore the Network Connections window.

15. In the Network Connections window, under LAN Or High-Speed Internet, right-click Local Area Connection and select Properties.

16. In the Local Area Connection Properties dialog box, on the General tab, in the This Connection Uses The Following Items section, select the Internet Protocol (TCP/IP) check box and click OK.

17. Close the Network Connections window, and restore the Command Prompt window.

18. Type ping **www.example.com** and press ENTER. You should now see the proper ping response again.

19. Close the Command Prompt window.

Exercise 2: Use pathping

1. Log on to Windows XP using an account with administrator privileges.

2. From the Start menu, select Run. In the Run dialog box, in the Open text box, type **cmd** and press ENTER.

3. In the command prompt window, type **pathping www.example.com** and press ENTER.

4. Take a few moments to note what statistics pathping gathers.

Exercise 3: Use tracert

1. Log on to Windows XP using an account with administrator privileges.

2. From the Start menu, select Run. In the Run dialog box, in the Open text box, type **cmd** and press ENTER.

3. At the command prompt, type **tracert www.microsoft.com** and press ENTER.

4. Compare the information relayed by tracert with that of pathping.

Lesson Review

The following questions are intended to reinforce key information presented in this lesson. If you are unable to answer a question, review the lesson materials and try the question again. You can find answers to the questions in the "Questions and Answers" section at the end of this chapter.

1. Match the troubleshooting scenarios on the left with the appropriate command on the right.

1. You need to check to see whether TCP/IP is installed correctly on a user's computer.	A. ipconfig
2. You need to find out the IP address, subnet mask, and default gateway of the user's computer.	B. pathping IPAddress

3. You are unable to communicate with a remote com-   C. ping 127.0.0.1
puter. You suspect that data loss is occurring at a remote
router, but you are not sure which one. You want to test
the route that the packets take from your computer to the
remote one, and you want to view information about
packet loss at every router along the way.

4. You need to list the file shares on a remote computer   D. net view \\ComputerName
running Windows XP.

2. After the command ipconfig /all is used, the following results are given:

    A. IP Address.........192.168.0.5

    B. Subnet Mask.......255.255.255.255

    C. Default Gateway............192.168.0.7

Which of these is most likely configured incorrectly?

Lesson Summary

- Use the ping, tracert, and pathping commands to test TCP/IP connectivity.

- Use the ipconfig /all command to show detailed information about the TCP/IP configuration of a computer, including the IP address, subnet mask, default gateway, DNS servers, and DHCP information about every network connection on a system.

- There are five classes of IP address, A through E. Classes A, B, and C are the ones you will need to be familiar with. Each class is identified by a particular IP address range.

Lesson 4: Resolving Name-Resolution Issues

Name resolution is the process that allows network and Internet users to access resources by their names instead of their IP addresses. Names used might be (among other things) computer names, server names, printer names, or **fully qualified domain names** (FQDNs). Without name resolution, users would be forced to remember the IP addresses of each resource on the network or on the Internet. Thus, name resolution makes accessing resources much simpler. When problems occur with accessing network resources, often the solution involves troubleshooting these components.

After this lesson, you will be able to

■ Understand and resolve basic issues related to the Domain Name System.

■ Understand and resolve basic issues related to Windows Internet Naming Service.

■ Understand and resolve basic issues related to HOSTS files.

■ Understand and resolve basic issues related to LMHOSTS files.

Estimated lesson time: 15 minutes

Understanding DNS Issues

DNS servers resolve the names of network resources to their respective IP addresses. In a LAN, an administrator installs a DNS server and configures the information regarding the IP addresses of resources on the network. When something is wrong with the DNS configuration on a computer or the DNS server on a network, users will not be able to resolve computer names or FQDNs to their IP addresses, and connectivity to those resources will fail.

If you believe (because of results of ping, ipconfig /all, tracert, or other command-line tests) that an incorrect DNS configuration is preventing a user or users from resolving names to IP addresses, and you have verified the IP address of the DNS server and that the server is online, you should check the DNS settings on the local computer. You can view and reconfigure the DNS configuration on a computer running Windows XP quite easily by following these steps:

1. Open Network Connections, right-click the active local area connection, and choose Properties.

2. On the General tab of the Properties dialog box, select Internet Protocol (TCP/IP), and select Properties.

3. In the Internet Protocol (TCP/IP) Properties dialog box, shown in Figure 8-14, select Obtain DNS Server Address Automatically, or select Use The Following DNS Server Addresses and type the IP address of the DNS server.

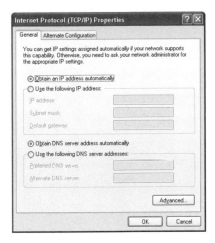

Figure 8-14   Set DNS properties.

4. If you need to configure an alternate DNS server address and you have configured the computer to obtain its IP and DNS server addresses automatically, on the Alternate Configuration tab, click User Configured, and type a preferred and alternate DNS server address. Click OK when you are done. (The Alternate Configuration tab appears only if you have configured the computer to obtain its IP address and DNS server addresses automatically.)

5. To configure advanced DNS settings, on the General tab, select Advanced.

6. In the Advanced TCP/IP Settings dialog box, select the DNS tab.

7. In the DNS Server Addresses, In Order Of Use list, note the configured DNS server addresses. Use Add, Edit, or Remove to make configuration changes to the DNS servers listed. Use the arrows to move a DNS server up or down the list. See Figure 8-15.

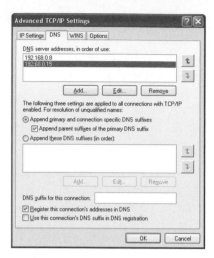

Figure 8-15   Configure advanced DNS settings.

8. Click OK or Close to close the dialog boxes.

WINS

In addition to DNS, WINS is sometimes employed on a network. WINS servers resolve **NetBIOS names** to their associated IP addresses. NetBIOS names allow computers with older operating systems, such as Windows NT, Windows Me, and Windows 98, to participate in a network and to access resources. NetBIOS names are unique, and the name is generally a "friendly" name such as Server01 or Computer22.

> **Note**   Not all networks use WINS servers. WINS integration is necessary only if the network includes computers running older operating systems.

If the network includes a WINS server, if you believe (because of results of ping, ipconfig /all, tracert, or other command-line tests) that an incorrect WINS configuration is preventing a user or users from resolving NetBIOS names to IP addresses, and if you have verified the IP address of the WINS server and that it is online, you should check the WINS settings on the local computer. You can view and reconfigure the WINS configuration on a computer running Windows XP quite easily by following these steps:

1. Open Network Connections, right-click the active local area connection, and choose Properties.

2. On the General tab of the Properties dialog box, select Internet Protocol (TCP/IP), and select Properties.

3. In the Internet Protocol (TCP/IP) Properties dialog box, shown in Figure 8-14, click Advanced.

4. In the Advanced TCP/IP Settings dialog box, select the WINS tab. Use Add, Edit, or Remove to make configuration changes to the WINS servers listed. Use the arrows to move a WINS server up or down the list. Leave the NetBIOS default settings, as shown in Figure 8-16. Click OK.

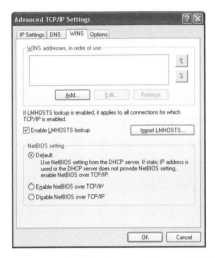

Figure 8-16   Configure advanced WINS settings by using the Advanced TCP/IP Settings Properties dialog box.

5. If you have configured the computer to obtain its IP address and DNS server address automatically and you need to configure an alternate WINS address, on the Alternate Configuration tab in the Internet Protocol (TCP/IP) Properties dialog box, click User Configured, and type a preferred and an alternate WINS server address. Click OK. Click Close.

> **Exam Tip**   For the exam, make sure you understand how to enable automatic configuration of DNS servers and where you would go to specify particular DNS servers. Also make sure you know how to enable WINS.

LMHOSTS

An LMHOSTS file is a text file located on the local computer that maps NetBIOS names to their IP addresses for hosts that are not located on the local subnet. In Windows XP Professional, that file is located in the %SystemRoot%\System32\Drivers\Etc folder.

LMHOSTS files can be manually updated and are useful in small networks where IP addresses change infrequently, or for networks with resources that have static IP addresses. When configuring WINS servers, make sure the Enable LMHOSTS Lookup check box is selected. LMHOSTS files serve as a backup for WINS servers.

HOSTS

HOSTS files are local text files that map host names and FQDNs to IP addresses. They are also located in the %SystemRoot%\System32\Drivers\Etc folder. Figure 8-17 shows a sample HOSTS file.

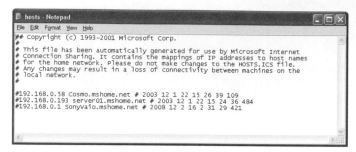

Figure 8-17   A HOSTS file maps host names and FQDNs to IP addresses.

Computers on the network are identified with their IP addresses. If a computer using a HOSTS file cannot connect to another using its host name, check this file for a bad entry.

Lesson Review

The following questions are intended to reinforce key information presented in this lesson. If you are unable to answer a question, review the lesson materials and try the question again. You can find answers to the questions in the "Questions and Answers" section at the end of this chapter.

1. You are troubleshooting a connectivity problem on a small home office work-group that includes four computers connected through an Ethernet hub. Each computer is connected directly to the Internet, and all computers should retrieve all TCP/IP addressing information automatically. One of the users complains that she can access other computers on the network but cannot access any websites. The other three computers are working just fine. You verify that the computer in question does not reach any websites when you type in the URL. However, you can get to websites when you type the actual IP address. You use the ipconfig /all command on each computer and determine that the computer that cannot access websites has different DNS servers listed than the other three computers. What is the likely problem?

   _____

   _____

2. You ping the other computers by IP address. The user at Computer1 cannot access any workgroup resources but is able to access the shared printer connected

directly to her computer; the other three computers can access all workgroup resources except for resources on Computer1, including the shared printer. What is most likely the problem?

   A. APIPA is in use.

   B. The network bridge is corrupt.

   C. The configured DNS server is not available.

   D. The Ethernet cable on Computer1 is disconnected from the NIC or the hub.

Lesson Summary

- DNS and WINS are automatic name-resolution services that resolve computer names to IP addresses. DNS is the native name-resolution mechanism used on the Internet and on Windows Server 2003–based networks. WINS is used on networks that support previous operating systems.

- HOSTS files are local text files that map host names and FQDNs to IP addresses. You can think of them as the manual equivalent of DNS.

- LMHOSTS files are local text files that map NetBIOS names to their IP addresses. You can think of them as the manual equivalent of WINS.

Lesson 5: Troubleshooting Internet Connection Sharing

Internet Connection Sharing (ICS) offers a simple way to configure computers in a small home office network to share a single Internet connection. For small networks, ICS offers a cost-effective way to provide Internet access to multiple computers.

After this lesson, you will be able to

- Configure Internet Connection Sharing.
- Identify the limitations of ICS.
- Enable ICS on a computer running Windows XP.

Estimated lesson time: 10 minutes

Configuring Internet Connection Sharing

When you set up ICS on a network, the computer with the physical connection to the Internet (whether that be a modem, cable, or other type of connection) is designated as the ICS computer. Other computers on the network connect to the Internet through the ICS. In addition to providing Internet access, the ICS host computer also dynamically allocates IP addresses to the clients on the network, provides name resolution, and serves as the gateway for the other computers.

Setting up ICS on a small network consists of the following general steps:

1. Make sure that the computer that will become the ICS computer is properly connected to the Internet.

2. Make sure that the ICS computer and the other computers are properly connected to one another by means of a local network.

3. On the ICS computer, enable Internet Connection Sharing on the Internet network connection. This is done by selecting the Allow Other Network Users To Connect Through This Computer's Internet Connection option on the Advanced tab of the network connection's Properties dialog box. When you enable ICS, the ICS computer configures itself with the IP address 192.168.0.1 and also becomes a DHCP server for the network so that it can provide IP addressing information to other computers.

4. Configure the remaining computers to obtain their IP address and DNS server information automatically, and restart the computers. When each computer restarts, it will obtain addressing information from the ICS computer and should be able to connect to the Internet. IP addresses of the computers will fall in the range 192.168.0.2 through 192.168.0.254.

ICS Limitations

Because of what ICS does for a network (IP address allocation, name resolution, and acting as the network's gateway), and because the IP address the host computer uses is always 192.168.0.1 with a subnet mask of 255.255.255.0, several conditions must be met while ICS is used:

- The IP addresses of the computers on the network must also be in the 192.168.x.y range, and the subnet mask must always be 255.255.255.0. If network computers cannot use these addresses, ICS will not work properly.

- Computers running Microsoft Windows 2000 Server or Windows Server 2003 configured as domain controllers, DNS servers, gateways, and DHCP servers cannot be used on the network.

- Computers with static IP addresses that do not fall in the ICS range will not work with ICS.

- If more than one network adapter is available, and if two or more local area connections are configured and all of them connect to computers on the network, those connections will need to be bridged. Bridging a connection is as simple as right-clicking the connection and selecting Bridge Connections.

- ICS must be enabled from the dial-up, virtual private network (VPN), broadband, or other connection to the Internet.

- You should not use this feature in a network with other domain controllers, DNS servers, gateways, or DHCP servers.

Problems can also occur with ICS if the host computer originally had a static IP address on the network or if the address 192.168.0.1 is being used by another computer on the network. (You can use ipconfig to find out.)

> **Note**   If you are having a problem with an ICS configuration, check the items in the preceding bulleted list. Make the appropriate changes to the network to resolve the problem.

Troubleshooting ICS

Although you can troubleshoot ICS by using many of the connectivity troubleshooting methods already covered in this chapter, if the network is small (10 or fewer computers), it is generally easiest to start over with ICS than to troubleshoot it. Once you know you have removed any offending DHCP or DNS servers or any computers with static IP addresses, simply reconfigure ICS on the host computer, and then reconfigure and restart the other computers on the network.

Lesson Review

The following question is intended to reinforce key information presented in this lesson. If you are unable to answer this question, review the lesson materials and try the question again. You can find the answer to the question in the "Questions and Answers" section at the end of this chapter.

A user has set up Internet Connection Sharing on a host computer that runs Windows XP but is experiencing problems with his clients being able to connect to both the Internet and other computers on the network. Which of the following items could be the cause of the problems? (Select all that apply.)

   A. There is a DHCP server on the network.

   B. There is a DNS server on the network.

   C. There are computers on the network with static IP addresses.

   D. There is a Windows 2000 server on the network.

Lesson Summary

- Internet Connection Sharing lets one computer with an Internet connection share that connection with other computers on the network. It is a good option for sharing a single Internet connection among a small number of computers.

- The computer running ICS always configures itself with the IP address 192.168.0.1. That computer also acts as a DHCP server and gives other computers on the network addresses in the 192.168 range.

- Troubleshooting ICS is fairly tricky, and the best option is almost always to reconfigure ICS on the network.

Case Scenario Exercises

Scenario 8.1

An owner of a small business purchased Windows Server 2003, installed it on his best computer, and configured it to be the domain controller on his network. He has eight other computers in his office, and he was able to successfully connect all of them to the domain except for two. Of the following choices, which would cause the two computers not to be installed?

   A. The two computers are running Microsoft Windows 98.

   B. The two computers are running Microsoft Windows Me.

C. The two computers are running Windows XP Home Edition.

D. The two computers are running Windows 2000 Server.

Scenario 8.2

A user of a small office workgroup has returned from a weeklong vacation. She boots her computer, and everything seems to be functional. As the day progresses, she accesses data from a workgroup file server, and she prints to a network printer. Later she tries to access another workgroup resource, a printer that is attached to a user's computer in the office upstairs, but she receives an error that the printer cannot be found. She reports that the Ethernet cable is connected and the NIC has a green light, and that she can access other resources on the network. What is the first thing you should do?

A. Check the status of the network router.

B. Check the status of the computer upstairs.

C. Ping the computer's loopback address.

D. Use the tracert command at a command prompt to view the route and possible packet losses.

Troubleshooting Lab

You are a technical support agent at Contoso.com. A user complains that she cannot access websites on the Internet. In investigating the problem, you ask her several questions:

■ Are there any sites on the Internet that you can access? No.

■ Have you ever been able to access websites on this computer before? Yes.

■ Was the computer on the same network, or on a different network when you were able to access websites before? It was at home.

■ Have you made any changes recently to Microsoft Internet Explorer or your computer? No.

■ What type of Internet connection do you have? Cable modem.

Using everything you have learned in this chapter, what would be your first steps in troubleshooting this problem?

_____

_____

_____

Chapter Summary

- To resolve connectivity problems on a workgroup or a domain, check all physical connections, including cables, hubs, switches, routers, servers, and network computers first.

- To resolve connectivity problems that do not involve physical connectivity problems, troubleshoot the network connection in Network Connections.

- To resolve connectivity issues that have to do with TCP/IP, check for APIPA use, and use command-line utilities such as ping, ipconfig, pathping, and others.

- To resolve name-resolution problems, verify that DNS and WINS are properly configured and in working order and that HOSTS and LMHOSTS files are correctly configured.

- To resolve problems with ICS, remove offending hardware such as DHCP and DNS servers, domain controllers, or computers with static IP addresses. Then run the Network Setup Wizard again.

Exam Highlights

Before taking the exam, review the key topics and terms that are presented in this chapter. You need to know this information.

Key Points

- Remember the range of IP addresses used by APIPA. If you see that a computer has an IP address starting with 169.254, it means that the computer is not pulling an IP address from a DHCP server. This could be the result of a networking problem or a DHCP issue.

- Make sure you know where in the Windows XP interface you configure DNS and WINS settings. Also make sure you understand what information resulting from the ipconfig / all command can show you about DNS and WINS servers.

Key Terms

Domain Name System (DNS)   A service that resolves host names to IP addresses for clients on a network. This service allows users to type a name such as www.microsoft.com instead of an IP address.

Dynamic Host Configuration Protocol (DHCP)   A service that assigns TCP/IP addresses automatically to clients on a network. DHCP servers provide this service.

gateway address   A network point that allows access into and out of a network. Gateways can be routers, firewalls, or proxy servers, and gateways decide whether a data packet belongs on the local network or on a remote one.

subnet   A separate and distinct part of a network, generally represented by one geographic location, such as an office or a building. Subnets use gateways to access the Internet, thus allowing all users to access the Internet through one shared network address.

subnet mask   Subnet masks enable computers to determine when to send packets to the gateway in order to communicate with computers on remote subnets.

Questions and Answers

Lesson 1 Review

Page 8-8 **1.** What is the name of the Windows utility that lists the current state of the hardware installed on the system?

  A. msconfig

  B. System Information

  C. Device Manager

  D. Computer Management

Answer C is correct. Device Manager lists the hardware installed on a system and each device's current operational state, and it offers tools for working with and troubleshooting the device. Answer A is incorrect because msconfig is used to configure the Windows startup environment. Answer B is incorrect because although System Information does show much of the hardware installed on a system, it gives no information about its current state. Answer D is incorrect because Computer Management is an administrative collection of tools for working with various aspects of Windows XP.

2. You are troubleshooting a networking problem for a user. The user was having no problems connecting to her network when she left the office yesterday afternoon. This morning, when she came to work, she could not connect to the network. You know that other users on the network are not having the same problems. What is the first thing you should check?

You should make sure that the network cable is seated properly in the jack on the back of the user's computer and in the jack on the wall. It is likely that something happened overnight, such as when the office was cleaned, that caused the connection to loosen.

Lesson 2 Review

Page 8-29 **1.** You are troubleshooting a network connectivity problem for a workgroup containing 12 computers. One of the computers cannot access network resources. After verifying that the physical connections are good, that the NIC light is on and the NIC produces no errors in Device Manager, and that the computer name and workgroup name are correct in System Properties, you still cannot solve the problem. What should you try next?

  A. Remove two of the computers from the workgroup; workgroups can have only 10 or fewer computers connected.

  B. Open Network Connections, and try to repair the connection.

  C. Re-create the network connection.

  D. Configure the workgroup to use APIPA.

Answer B is correct. The next logical step is to try to repair the connection. Answer A is not correct because a workgroup can have more than 10 computers; Answer C is incorrect because that is a process to try if the repair step fails. Answer D is incorrect because APIPA might disrupt the rest of the network.

2. A user complains to you that he is not able to connect to any network resources after installing a new networking card. You open the Command Prompt window on the user's computer and type **ipconfig /all**. You get the following results:

```
Ethernet adapter Local Area Connection:
        Connection-specific DNS Suffix
        Description . . . . . . . . . . . : Intel(R) PRO/1000 CT
        Physical Address. . . . . . . . . : 00-05-E8-45-B4-2E
        DHCP Enabled. . . . . . . . . . . : Yes
        IP Address. . . . . . . . . . . . : 169.254.011.202
        Subnet Mask . . . . . . . . . . . : 255.255.0.0
        Default Gateway . . . . . . . . . :
        DNS Servers . . . . . . . . . . . :
```

What do these results tell you? (Choose all that apply.)

A. The computer is configured to connect to a DHCP server.

B. The computer is not configured to connect to a DHCP server.

C. The computer is successfully connecting to a DHCP server.

D. The computer is not successfully connecting to a DHCP server.

Answers A and D are correct. The computer is configured to connect to a DHCP server. However, it is not getting an IP address from a DHCP server successfully. You can tell this because the IP address is in the range assigned by APIPA.

Lesson 3 Review

Page
8-38

1. Match the troubleshooting scenarios on the left with the appropriate command on the right.

1. You need to check to see whether TCP/IP is installed correctly on a user's computer.	A. ipconfig
2. You need to find out the IP address, subnet mask, and default gateway of the user's computer.	B. pathping IPAddress
3. You are unable to communicate with a remote computer. You suspect that data loss is occurring at a remote router, but you are not sure which one. You want to test the route that the packets take from your computer to the remote one, and you want to view information about packet loss at every router along the way.	C. ping 127.0.0.1.
4. You need to list the file shares on a remote computer running Windows XP.	D. net view \\ComputerName

1-C. Pinging the loopback address is useful in determining whether TCP/IP is installed correctly on a computer. 2-A. ipconfig offers the IP address, default gateway, and subnet mask. 3-B. pathping offers this information. 4-D. Net view lists shares on local and remote computers.

2. After the command ipconfig /all is used, the following results are given:

   A. IP Address.........192.168.0.5

   B. Subnet Mask.......255.255.255.255

   C. Default Gateway............192.168.0.7

   Which of these is most likely configured incorrectly?

   Answer B is correct because the IP address is a Class C address (as is the gateway); the subnet mask should be 255.255.255.0.

Lesson 4 Review

Page
8-44

1. You are troubleshooting a connectivity problem on a small home office workgroup that includes four computers connected through an Ethernet hub. Each computer is connected directly to the Internet, and all computers should retrieve all TCP/IP addressing information automatically. One of the users complains that she can access other computers on the network but cannot access any websites. The other three computers are working just fine. You verify that the computer in question does not reach any websites when you type in the URL. However, you can get to websites when you type the actual IP address. You use the ipconfig /all command on each computer and determine that the computer that cannot access websites has different DNS servers listed than the other three computers. What is the likely problem?

   The most likely problem is that the computer with the problem is not configured to obtain DNS server information automatically.

2. You ping the other computers by IP address. The user at Computer1 cannot access any workgroup resources but is able to access the shared printer connected directly to her computer; the other three computers can access all workgroup resources except for resources on Computer1, including the shared printer. What is most likely the problem?

   A. APIPA is in use.

   B. The network bridge is corrupt.

   C. The configured DNS server is not available.

   D. The Ethernet cable on Computer1 is disconnected from the NIC or the hub.

   Answer D is correct. Because Computer1 is functional, and because all of the other computers in the workgroup are communicating, the problem is likely with the computer itself and its connection to the workgroup hub. Answer A is incorrect because APIPA addresses would be used by each computer on the network, and thus all would be able to communicate. Answer B is incorrect because there is only one network segment, and no bridge is necessary. Answer C is incorrect because no DNS server is mentioned in the scenario, and DNS servers are configured for domains, not workgroups.

Lesson 5 Review

Page 8-48

A user has set up Internet Connection Sharing on a host computer that runs Windows XP but is experiencing problems with his clients being able to connect to both the Internet and other computers on the network. Which of the following items could be the cause of the problems? (Select all that apply.)

A. There is a DHCP server on the network.

B. There is a DNS server on the network.

C. There are computers on the network with static IP addresses.

D. There is a Windows 2000 server on the network.

Answers A, B, and C are correct. DHCP and DNS servers, as well as computers with static IP addresses, will all cause problems for ICS. Answer D is incorrect because Windows 2000 servers can be members of workgroups and work with ICS as long as they are not also domain controllers that provide DHCP or DNS services.

Case Scenario Exercises: Scenario 8.1

Page 8-48

An owner of a small business purchased Windows Server 2003, installed it on his best computer, and configured it to be the domain controller on his network. He has eight other computers in his office, and he was able to successfully connect all of them to the domain except for two. Of the following choices, which would cause the two computers not to be installed?

A. The two computers are running Microsoft Windows 98.

B. The two computers are running Microsoft Windows Me.

C. The two computers are running Windows XP Home Edition.

D. The two computers are running Windows 2000 Server.

Answer C is correct. Computers running Windows XP Home Edition cannot join a domain. The other choices are incorrect because computers running Windows 98, Windows Millennium Edition (Me), and Windows 2000 Server can all participate in a domain.

Case Scenario Exercises: Scenario 8.2

Page 8-49

A user of a small office workgroup has returned from a weeklong vacation. She boots her computer, and everything seems to be functional. As the day progresses, she accesses data from a workgroup file server, and she prints to a network printer. Later, she tries to access another workgroup resource, a printer that is attached to a user's computer in the office upstairs, but she receives an error that the printer cannot be found. She reports that the Ethernet cable is connected and the NIC has a green light, and that she can access other resources on the network. What is the first thing you should do?

A. Check the status of the network router.

B. Check the status of the computer upstairs.

C. Ping the computer's loopback address.

D. Use the tracert command at a command prompt to view the route and possible packet losses.

> Answer B is correct. Because the user can access other network resources, the problem is probably with the resource itself. The other answers are not likely correct because the user is able to access other network resources.

Troubleshooting Lab

Page 8-49

You are a technical support agent at Contoso.com. A user complains that she cannot access websites on the Internet. In investigating the problem, you ask her several questions:

- Are there any sites on the Internet that you can access? No.

- Have you ever been able to access websites on this computer before? Yes.

- Was the computer on the same network or on a different network when you were able to access websites before? It was at home.

- Have you made any changes recently to Microsoft Internet Explorer or your computer? No.

- What type of Internet connection do you have? Cable modem.

Using everything you have learned in this chapter, what would be your first steps in troubleshooting this problem?

> Because this is a home connection on a cable modem, you can be pretty sure that the computer should be set to obtain an IP address automatically from the ISP. Your first step, therefore, should be to open the command prompt and type **ipconfig /all**. Look for any problems with the IP addressing information. If you see an IP address in the 169.254 range, for example, you know that the computer is set to obtain an IP address automatically but cannot reach the DHCP server. This probably points to a loose cable or a malfunctioning network adapter or cable modem. If you rule out these problems, there is likely a problem at the ISP.

9 Security and Security Permissions

Exam Objectives in this Chapter:

- Identify and troubleshoot problems related to security issues
- Answer end-user questions related to application security
- Troubleshoot access to local resources
- Troubleshoot access to network resources
- Troubleshoot insufficient user permissions and rights

Why This Chapter Matters

The purpose of this chapter is to teach you to troubleshoot issues with end users' access to network or workgroup resources that are caused by permissions restrictions, multiple permissions, group membership, or local or group security policy settings. To troubleshoot these types of access problems, you need to be familiar with each, including how to create different types of shares, view and change settings for a local security policy, view and change settings for a group security policy, and more. The topics in this chapter revolve around working with share permissions, NTFS permissions, local security policies, and Group Policy.

Lessons in this Chapter:

Lesson 1: Understanding Security Permissions

You assign permissions to files, folders, printers, and other network resources to protect them from unauthorized access. In a workgroup, the owner of the resource determines the level of access (if any) and assigns the permissions; in a domain, network administrators set permissions, and resources are accessed through the network servers. As a tier 1 desktop support technician (DST), you will work with Simple File Sharing permissions on a Windows XP workgroup, as well as shared folders and NTFS permissions on workgroups and domains.

After this lesson, you will be able to

- Configure and troubleshoot Simple File Sharing.
- Configure and troubleshoot shared folders.
- Configure and troubleshoot NTFS permissions.

Estimated lesson time: 50 minutes

Working with Windows XP Simple File Sharing

When you create a home office network with Windows XP, Simple File Sharing is enabled by default. This is exactly what it sounds like: a simple way for home users to share files on a network. When Simple File Sharing is enabled, users can share files easily, and in just one step.

With Simple File Sharing, users can do the following:

- Share folders with everyone on the network
- Allow users who access the folder to view the files, edit the files, or both
- Make folders in his or her user profile private

Simple File Sharing does not permit users to do the following:

- Prevent specific users and groups from accessing folders
- Assign folder permissions to specific users and groups
- View the Security tab of a shared folder's Properties dialog box

To enable or disable Simple File Sharing or to see whether Simple File Sharing is in use, follow these steps:

1. Open Control Panel, select Appearance And Themes, and then select Folder Options.

2. Select the View tab and, under Advanced Settings, scroll down the list of choices to the last option.

3. Simple File Sharing is enabled if the Use Simple File Sharing (Recommended) check box is selected. To disable it, clear the check box. For the purposes of this section, verify that it is selected. Click OK.

Sharing a Folder on the Network

Once you have verified that Simple File Sharing is enabled, sharing a folder on the network is easy. Just follow these steps:

1. Right-click the Start menu and choose Explore.

2. Locate the folder you want to share, right-click it, and choose Sharing And Security.

3. In the Properties dialog box, select the Share This Folder On The Network check box. This is shown in Figure 9-1. Notice that a share name is automatically assigned. This is the name that the users will see when they browse the network for this shared folder. Change the name if desired; if the share must be readable to older operating systems such as MS-DOS and Windows 3.1, the share name must be 12 characters or fewer.

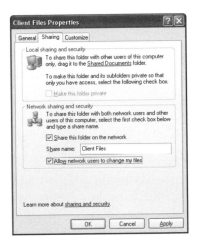

Figure 9-1   Simple File Sharing.

4. To allow others to make changes to the files in the shared folder, also select the Allow Network Users To Change My Files check box. Click OK.

When sharing a folder on a network in this manner, you give permission for everyone on the network to access and read the files in the folder. With Simple File Sharing, you cannot choose who can and cannot access a folder. When you also choose to allow users to make changes to the files in the shared folder, you allow them to write to (or make changes to) those files.

Two other options on the Sharing tab were not discussed. Under Local Sharing And Security, you can share a folder with other users of the same computer by dragging it to the Shared Documents folder. Anyone logged on to the workgroup or the computer can access the Shared Documents folder. The folder is accessed at C:\Documents And Settings\All Users\Documents, as shown in Figure 9-2. Sharing a folder in this manner works only for workgroups, though, not for domains.

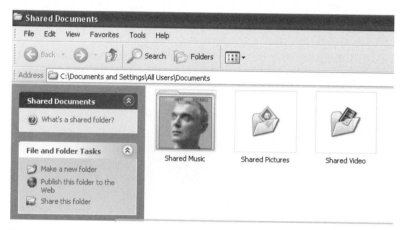

Figure 9-2   The Shared Documents folder can be used to share files on a computer or in a workgroup.

There is also the option to make a folder private. When you make a folder private, only the owner of the folder can access its contents. You can make folders private only if they are in the user's personal user profile (and only if the disk is formatted with NTFS, the native file system for Windows XP; you will learn more about NTFS in Chapter 11). A personal user profile defines customized desktop environments, display settings, and network and printer connections, among other things. Personal user profile folders include My Documents and its subfolders, Desktop, Start Menu, Cookies, and Favorites.

To locate the list of local user profiles, right-click My Computer, select Properties, and, from the Advanced tab, in the User Profiles section, select Settings. To view a personal user profile, browse to C:\Documents And Settings*User Name*, as shown in Figure 9-3.

Note   To learn more about user profiles, read Microsoft Knowledge Base articles 314478 and 294887.

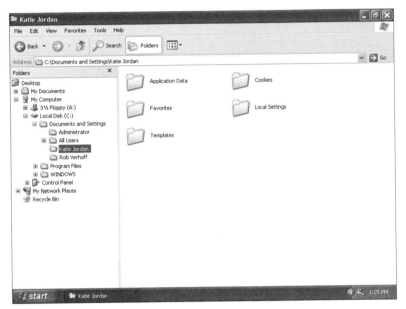

Figure 9-3   The Guest account's personal profile folders are located under Documents And Settings.

Note   Simple File Sharing works for all computers running Windows XP, whether they are formatted to use the **FAT** or **NTFS** file system.

Troubleshooting Simple File Sharing

There are only a few problems that you will run into when troubleshooting shares that are configured with Simple File Sharing, and they deal with user access to the shared resource. Assuming all network connections are functional, all computers and hubs are working properly, and Simple File Sharing is in use, Table 9-1 details some common problems and their solutions.

Table 9-1   Troubleshooting Simple File Sharing

Scenario/Report	Cause/Solution
A Microsoft Windows Me user reports that he cannot access a shared folder named Working Files On Computer 01.	If the share name is longer than 12 characters, computers running Microsoft Windows 98, Windows Me, Windows NT 4.0, or earlier operating systems cannot access the folder. Rename the share.

Table 9-1   Troubleshooting Simple File Sharing

Scenario/Report	Cause/Solution
An owner of a file reports that users can access the file but cannot make changes. She wants users to be able to make changes.	On the Sharing tab of the shared folder, select the Allow Network Users To Change My Files check box.
The owner of a file dragged the file to the Shared Documents folder and logged off the computer. When others log on, no one can access or even view the Shared Documents folder.	Users are logging on to a domain. Users will need to log on to the workgroup to access the file.
A user wants to share a file and assign specific permissions from the Security tab. However, the Security tab is not available.	With Simple File Sharing, the Security tab is not available. This is by design.

Working with Shared Folders

You can use share permissions with both file allocation table (FAT) and NTFS file systems, and share permissions offer more configuration options than Simple File Sharing. Compare the Sharing tab in Figure 9-1, which uses Simple File Sharing, with the Sharing tab in Figure 9-4, which has Simple File Sharing disabled. On the Sharing tab in Figure 9-4, notice the Permissions button. This opens the Permissions dialog box, which allows the user to configure specific share permissions.

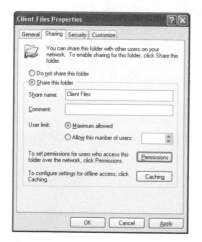

Figure 9-4   Share permissions.

There are three share permissions: Full Control, Read, and Change. You can configure these permissions only when Simple File Sharing is disabled, and you can use them to restrict who can access a particular resource and to what degree. You apply share per-missions to folders, not files, and they are often adequate for securing a small home network. These three share permissions are as follows:

- **Read**   The Read permission is the most restrictive and allows the user to only view file names and subfolder names in a folder, view data in the folder, and run any program in the folder.

- **Change**   This permission is less restrictive than the Read permission and allows a user to perform all Read tasks, add files or subfolders, change data in the files and save those changes, and delete any files or subfolders in the folder.

- **Full Control**   This permission is the least restrictive and allows a user to perform all Change tasks and change the permissions of the folder or take ownership of the share.

When applying permissions, you choose Allow or Deny for each permission that is available. Allow applies that permission to the group that is selected; Deny denies that permission. Deny always means deny and overrides any other permissions that are applied to the folder. To keep troubleshooting minimal, it is best to use the Deny option sparingly.

Caution   Share permissions apply only if the user is accessing the resource over a network. The permissions do no good if the user is sitting at the computer that contains the shares. In addition, share permissions apply to all subfolders in the folder.

Sharing a Folder

To share a folder and apply share permissions, verify that Simple File Sharing is dis-abled on the View tab of the Folder Options dialog box, and then follow these steps:

1. Use Windows Explorer to browse to the folder to share, or locate it by other means.

2. Right-click the folder to share and choose Sharing And Security.

3. On the Sharing tab, select Share This Folder.

4. In the Share Name area, type a name for the share. Keep the name under 12 char-acters. (You will be prompted if you use an invalid character.)

5. Type a comment if desired.

6. Next to User Limit, select Maximum Allowed or Allow This Number Of Users. If setting a user limit, enter the number of users to allow. By default, 10 is the max-imum.

7. Click Permissions.

8. To add a group, click Add. To remove a group, select the group and click Remove. If applicable, in the Select Users Or Groups dialog box, add or remove any group. Separate multiple groups with semicolons. (You will learn more about groups later in this chapter.) Click OK.

9. In the Group Or User Names list, select a group for which you want to configure permissions. In the Permissions For <*group name*> area, make changes to the permissions as desired. Figure 9-5 shows this dialog box. Click OK, and click OK again to close the Properties dialog box.

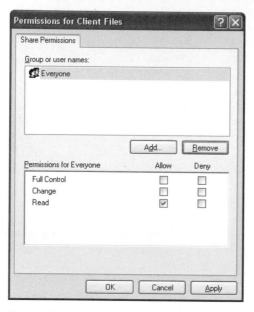

Figure 9-5   Set share permissions.

Troubleshooting Share Permissions

Problems can occur with share permissions just as they can with Simple File Sharing. Assuming that all network connections are functional, all computers and hubs are working properly, and Simple File Sharing is not in use, Table 9-2 details some common problems with share permissions and their solutions.

Table 9-2   Troubleshooting Share Permissions

Scenario/Report	Cause/Solution
All network users report that when they access a particular shared folder on the network, they get a message that access is denied. This does not happen with any other share.	The share permissions for that resource might be set to Deny for the Everyone group. Also, the computer that is hosting the share might be turned off or not available, or the owner might have changed the share permissions recently.

Table 9-2 Troubleshooting Share Permissions

Scenario/Report	Cause/Solution
An owner of a file reports that users can access the file but cannot make changes. He wants all users to be able to make changes.	On the Sharing tab of the shared folder, click Permissions. In the Share Permissions dialog box, select the Everyone group and select the Read and Change check boxes.
The owner of a share reports that she opened her shared folder this morning to find that some of the items in the folder had been deleted. She states that she did not assign the Full Control permission but did assign the Read and Change permissions to the Everyone group. She wants to know why users can delete her files.	By default, users with the Change permission for a folder can delete files in the folder. The user needs to reconfigure which files are in which shares, and who has access.
A user wants to share a file and assign specific permissions from the Security tab. However, the Security tab is not available.	The file system used is FAT, not NTFS.

Working with NTFS Permissions

NTFS file and folder permissions are available on drives that are formatted with the NTFS file system, and the permissions include Full Control, Modify, Read And Execute, List Folder Contents, Read, Write, and several special permissions. As with share permissions, these are assigned by selecting Allow or Deny. NTFS permissions are applied when a user is sitting at the computer or accessing the file or folder over the network, making NTFS permissions a better choice for offices and corporations.

Without including every aspect of each permission, the six basic NTFS folder permissions that you should be familiar with are as follows:

- **Read** This permission allows a user to view the files and subfolders.

- **Write** This permission allows a user to create files and folders and write data to files and subfolders.

- **List Folder Contents** This permission allows a user to traverse the folder, execute files, and view files and subfolders.

- **Read And Execute** This permission allows a user to view the files and subfolders, traverse folders, and execute files.

- **Modify** This permission allows a user to view files and subfolders, traverse folders, execute files, create files, write data, create folders, and append data.

■ **Full Control**   This permission allows a user to have complete control over the folder, including deleting files and subfolders, taking ownership, and all other tasks.

Sharing a File or Folder

To apply NTFS permissions, verify that Simple File Sharing is disabled on the View tab of the Folder Properties dialog box and that the drive that contains the folder on which you want to configure permissions is formatted using NTFS, and then follow these steps:

1. Right-click the folder to assign NTFS permissions to, and select Sharing And Security.

2. On the Security tab, in the Group Or User Names list, select the group or user for which you want to set NTFS permissions. To add a user or group that is not listed, click Add and in the Select Users Or Groups dialog box, enter the object names to select and click OK.

3. To change permissions for a group, select that group from the Security tab under Group Or User Names and select or clear the permissions to apply or deny. Figure 9-6 shows the default NTFS permissions given to the Power Users group when the group is added to the Group Or User Names list.

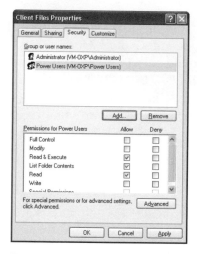

Figure 9-6   Set NTFS permissions.

4. To access the advanced settings and to set special permissions, click Advanced.

5. In the Advanced Security Settings dialog box, notice the four tabs: Permissions, Auditing, Owner, and Effective Permissions. Select the Permissions tab.

6. From the Permissions tab, the default selection is Inherit From Parent The Permission Entries That Apply To Child Objects. Include These With Entries Explicitly Defined Here. When this check box is selected, the file, folder, or object will inherit the permission entries from the parent folder (or object). When this selection is cleared, the object will not inherit the permission entries. For more information about inheritance, see the Windows Help file "Changing Inherited Permissions."

7. From the Permissions tab, the option to Replace Permission Entries On All Child Objects With Entries Shown Here That Apply To Child Objects is not selected. When selected, the permission entries on the child objects are reset so that they are identical to the current parent object. Click OK.

Optionally, you can create share permissions at the same time that you create NTFS permissions. Simply make the appropriate changes from the Sharing tab. Keep in mind that share and NTFS permissions are independent of each other, and when you give a user NTFS permissions for a folder, that user cannot access the folder across the network unless you have also shared the folder and given the user share permissions.

Troubleshooting NTFS Permissions

Issues can occur with NTFS permissions just as they can with Simple File Sharing and share permissions. Assuming that all network connections are functional, all computers and hubs are working properly, and Simple File Sharing is not in use, Table 9-3 details some common problems and their solutions.

Table 9-3 Troubleshooting NTFS Permissions

Scenario/Report	Cause/Solution
A user reports that he applied the NTFS permissions Read and Write for the group that will access a folder. However, when a member of the group opens the folder, she cannot run the programs in it. He needs the users to be able to run the programs without giving them excess privileges.	The user can add the Read And Execute permission to the group. This gives users who access the folder the ability to execute files in the folder without adding any other privileges.
A user wants to apply NTFS permissions, but all of the options on the Security tab under Allow are unavailable and cannot be set.	The permissions for this folder have been inherited from the parent folder. To make the permissions accessible for this file, select the This Folder Only check box in Apply Onto when setting the permissions on the parent folder.

Table 9-3   Troubleshooting NTFS Permissions

Scenario/Report	Cause/Solution
Although a network user is a member of the Power Users group, and this group has the Read NTFS permissions for a folder, the user cannot read the documents in the folder.	The user has been assigned a permission of Deny by another administrator or he or she is a member of another group that has been assigned the Deny permission for the folder. The user might also have the Deny share permission.
NTFS permissions cannot be applied because the Security tab is missing.	The file system used is FAT, not NTFS.

When Both Share and NTFS Permissions Exist

When a user is assigned multiple share permissions, the combination of the permissions is referred to as the user's **effective permissions** for the share. For instance, if the share permissions that are applied to a folder are Change and Read, the user can change and read the folder's contents. Likewise, when a user is assigned multiple NTFS permissions, the user's effective permissions for a folder are the combination of all NTFS permissions. For example, if the NTFS permissions Read, Write, and Modify exist, the user can read, write to, and modify the contents of the folder.

If a user is assigned both share and NTFS permissions for a folder, the user's effective permissions get a little more complicated. First, you must determine the user's effective shared permissions, and then determine the effective NTFS permissions. The final permissions on the folder are the more restrictive of the two.

Here is an example: A network user, Brenda Diaz, has access to a folder that has both share and NTFS permissions applied. The share permissions are Read and Change, and the NTFS permissions are Read and Read And Execute. Thus, Brenda's cumulative share permission is Change, and her cumulative NTFS permission is Read And Execute. To calculate Brenda's effective permissions, take the more restrictive of the two, which is Read And Execute. Brenda will not be able to change any data in the folder.

In all cases, if Deny is selected for a user, that user will not have access. Deny can be a share permission or an NTFS permission.

> ### Real World   Share Permissions on Large Networks
>
> If you are working on home and small business networks, you are likely to find either Simple File Sharing or share permissions used to control access to files and folders on the network. Even when drives are formatted with the NTFS file system, most people on small networks just do not bother with NTFS permissions.
>
> On large company networks, you find just the opposite. Administrators typically rely on NTFS permissions and leave the default share permissions (where Everyone has full access) in place. The reason for this is that NTFS permissions do a much better job of securing data. Because of the way share permissions and NTFS permissions interact, NTFS permissions secure data for both local and network access. Adding share permissions is really unnecessary and in fact complicates the web of permissions administrators must deal with. The exception to this is on systems running older versions of Windows (for example, Windows 98/Me) that do not support the NTFS file system; these systems must use share permissions if their data is to be shared on the network.
>
> Here are some rules to follow when you are working with different kinds of networks. If you are working on a home network, the users are probably using Simple File Sharing. If you are working on a small business network, users might be using Simple File Sharing or share permissions. If all of the computers on the network are running Windows 2000 or Windows XP, you might suggest moving over to the security of NTFS permissions and not worrying about share permissions. If you are working on a large network, NTFS permissions are likely used and share permissions are not. Make sure you understand the policies of the network before you make any changes.

Built-In Local Groups and Their Privileges

Windows XP has several built-in local groups: Administrators, Power Users, Users, and Backup Operators. Network administrators add end users to these groups manually. Each group (and each member of it) has specific user rights and privileges, and default permissions for file and folder access. Adding users to a group makes managing those users much easier because instead of managing users separately, the administrator can manage the users as a single group.

To troubleshoot end-user access to shares in a workgroup or a domain, you will need to understand what each group's default rights and permissions are. The four default user groups are covered in the next four sections.

Administrators

The Administrators group is the least restrictive group available. Administrators have full control of the computer, the files and folders on it, the local area network (if it exists), and the configured user accounts. Only a few users should be members of this group.

Besides being able to perform all of the tasks of any other group member, members of the Administrators group can also do the following:

- Take ownership of files and folders
- Back up and restore system data
- Set local policies
- Install service packs and Windows updates
- Perform upgrades
- Perform system repairs such as installing device drivers and system services
- Audit the network and manage logs

Power Users

The Power Users group is the next least restrictive group. Power Users have more control over the computer than members of the Users group do but less than administrators. Only users who are trusted employees and competent computer users should be members of this group.

Besides being able to perform all of the tasks a member of the Users group can, Power Users can also do the following:

- Modify computer-wide settings such as date, time, and power options
- Run older and noncertified Microsoft applications
- Install programs that do not modify operating system files or install system services
- Create local user accounts and local groups
- Manage local user accounts and local groups
- Stop and start system services that are not started by default
- Customize network printers
- Take ownership of files
- Back up and restore directories
- Install device drivers

Users

The Users group is the most secure group and is much more restrictive than the Administrators and Power Users groups. The Users group is the most secure because members of this group cannot compromise the integrity of the operating system by modifying registry settings, operating system files, or application files. Most users should be members of this group.

Members of the Users group can do the following:

■ Shut down their own workstations

■ Lock the workstation

■ Create local groups

■ Manage the local groups they have created

■ Run programs that are certified by Microsoft as compatible and that have been previously installed by administrators

■ Retain ownership of files and folders that they create

Members of the Users group cannot do the following:

■ Modify systemwide registry settings, operating system files, or program files

■ Shut down servers

■ Manage local groups that they did not create

■ Run older applications or applications that are not certified by Microsoft

■ Share directories

■ Share printers

Backup Operators

The Backup Operators group can back up and restore files on the computer, regardless of the permissions on those files. Those files can include users' files and folders, system state files, and other critical operating system files. They can also log on to the computer and shut it down, but they cannot change security settings.

Practice: Configure Security Permissions

In this practice, you will share a document locally and make a folder private. You will also share a document on the network using Simple File Sharing and using share permissions. Finally, you will also set NTFS permissions on a shared network folder.

Exercise 1: Share a Document by Using the Shared Documents Folder

1. Log on to Windows XP.

2. Right-click the desktop, point to New, and select Text Document. Type **Shared Document** for the name of the document, and press ENTER.

3. Right-click Shared Document on the desktop, and select Cut.

4. From the Start menu, select My Computer.

5. In the My Computer window, open the Shared Documents folder.

6. In the Shared Documents folder, from the Edit menu, select Paste.

Exercise 2: Make a Folder Private

1. Log on to Windows XP.

2. From the Start menu, select My Documents.

3. In My Documents, on the File Menu, select New, and then select Folder. Type **Private** for the name of the new folder.

4. Right-click the Private folder and select Properties.

5. In the Private Properties dialog box, on the Sharing tab, in the Local Sharing And Security section, select the Make This Folder Private check box. Click OK.

Exercise 3: Share Folders in a Workgroup by Using Simple File Sharing

1. Log on to Windows XP using an account with administrator permissions.

2. From the Start menu, select My Documents.

3. In My Documents, from the File menu, point to New and select Folder.

4. Type **Documents for Network** as the name of the folder and press ENTER.

5. Right-click the new folder and select Sharing And Security.

6. In the Documents For Network Properties dialog box, on the Sharing tab, in the Network Sharing And Security section, select the Share This Folder On The Network check box. Also select the Allow Network Users To Change My Files check box. Click OK.

7. If you see a Sharing message box, click Yes.

Exercise 4: Share Folders in a Workgroup Without Simple File Sharing

1. Log on to Windows XP using an account with administrator privileges.

2. From the Start menu, select My Computer.

3. In My Computer, from the Tools menu, select Folder Options.

4. In the Folder Options dialog box, on the View tab, in the Advanced Settings window, scroll to the end and clear the Use Simple File Sharing (Recommended) check box. Click OK.

5. Close the My Computer window.

6. From the Start menu, select My Documents.

7. In My Documents, from the File menu, point to New and select Folder.

8. Type **Documents for Administrators** for the name of the folder and press ENTER.

9. Right-click the new folder and select Sharing And Security.

10. In the Documents For Administrators Properties dialog box, on the Sharing tab, select Share This Folder. Click Permissions.

11. In the Permissions For Documents For Administrators dialog box, ensure that Everyone is selected in the Group Or User Names window. Click Remove. Click Add.

12. In the Select Users Or Groups dialog box, click Advanced.

13. In the second Select Users Or Groups dialog box, click Find Now.

14. In the search pane, select Administrators and click OK. (Make sure you select the Administrators group and not the Administrator user.)

15. In the first Select Users Or Groups dialog box, click OK.

16. In the Permissions For Documents For Administrators dialog box, under Permissions For Administrators, select the Change check box in the Allow column. Click OK.

17. In the Documents For Administrators Properties dialog box, click OK.

Exercise 5: Set NTFS Permissions on a Shared Network Folder

1. Log on to Windows XP using an account with administrator privileges.

2. From the Start menu, select My Documents.

3. In My Documents, on the File Menu, select New, and then select Folder. Type **Power Users Documents** for the name of the new folder.

4. Right-click the new folder and select Properties.

5. In the Power Users Documents Properties dialog box, on the Sharing tab, select Share This Folder, and then click Permissions.

6. In the Permissions For Power User Documents dialog box, ensure that Everyone is selected in the Group Or User Names window. In the Permissions For Everyone pane, select the Full Control check box in the Allow column. Click OK.

7. In the Power User Documents Properties dialog box, switch to the Security tab, and then click Add.

8. In the Select Users Or Groups dialog box, in the Enter The Object Name To Select (Examples) text box, type **Power Users**. Click Check Names. Click OK.

9. In the Power User Documents Properties dialog box, on the Security tab, in the Group Or User Names window, make sure Power Users is selected.

10. In the Permissions For Power Users window, select the Write check box in the Allow Column, and then click OK.

Lesson Review

The following questions are intended to reinforce key information presented in this lesson. If you are unable to answer a question, review the lesson materials and try the question again. You can find answers to the questions in the "Questions and Answers" section at the end of this chapter.

1. The company you work for hires quite a few temporary workers, and those workers need access to workgroup computers to perform their jobs. These employees are added to the default Users group when they are hired. Because they are members of the Users group, they have Read And Execute, List Folder Contents, and Read permissions by default. However, these users also need to be able to write data to the folders to which they have access. What is the best way to make this change without giving the users too much access?

   A. Add all new users to the Power Users group.

   B. Stop assigning NTFS permissions and assign the Read and Change share permissions.

   C. For the Users group on each share, assign the NTFS permission Write.

   D. For the Users group on each share, assign the NTFS permission Full Control.

2. A user's computer running Windows 2000 Professional was recently upgraded to Windows XP Professional. A member of the Users group reports that he can no longer run the older applications necessary to perform his job. You have looked for a newer version of the application but cannot find one. The user is a Microsoft Certified Desktop Technician and a Microsoft Certified Professional and has been

with the company for many years, so you feel he is competent and will pose no threat if given extra leniency. You need to allow this user to run his older application. What is the best course of action?

A. Move this end user from the Users group to the Power Users group.

B. Decrease the default security settings for all members of the Users group.

C. Purchase a new program that is Microsoft certified and train the users in the company to use it. Uninstall the older application.

D. Move this end user from the Users group to the Administrators group.

Lesson Summary

- There are several ways to configure sharing on a network, including using Simple File Sharing, setting share permissions, and setting NTFS permissions.

- When share and NTFS permissions are applied, the cumulative permissions of both are determined, and the most restrictive of those create the user's effective permission.

Lesson 2: Troubleshooting Group Membership

When resources are protected by both share and NTFS permissions, calculating effective permissions can be a little tricky. When a user cannot access a particular resource, you have to take into account the share permissions that are applied and the NTFS permissions that are applied, and then take the more restrictive of the cumulative permissions for both. When a user is a member of more than one group, or if group membership has been recently changed, the problem of calculating effective permissions is exacerbated.

After this lesson, you will be able to

- Explain what happens when users are members of more than one group.
- Troubleshoot problems related to group membership.

Estimated lesson time: 10 minutes

When Users Are Members of More than One Group

When users are members of multiple groups, they will have multiple permissions on the files and folders that they have access to. When calculating effective permissions for a specific folder, do the following:

1. List the folder's assigned share permissions for each group the user is a member of and calculate the effective share permissions. List the most lenient permission.

2. List the folder's assigned NTFS permissions for each group the user is a member of and calculate the effective NTFS permissions. List the most lenient permission.

3. Compare the most lenient permissions in step 1 and step 2. Choose the more restrictive permission. This is the effective permission.

Exam Tip Although you will not see too many questions about combining permissions on the exam, you may see a few, so it is worth knowing how it works. First figure out the NTFS permissions that a user has by combining the permissions of all the groups in which the user is a member and taking the least restrictive combination. Remember, though, that if any group is denied permission to the object, the user is denied permission. Next, figure out the share permissions on the object in the same way—by combining the share permissions of the groups in which the user is a member and taking the least restrictive combination. (Again, a Deny permission for any group yields a Deny permission for the user.) Finally, combine the NTFS and share permissions and take the most restrictive combination of those two.

Changes in Group Membership

Other problems occur when a user's group membership changes. This is especially true if a user was a member of the Power Users group and has been downgraded to the Users group or if a worker has been demoted and given more restrictive permissions to resources. When troubleshooting resource access, be sure you note any changes to the user's group status.

Practice: Add a User to the Backup Operators Group

In this practice, you will create a local user and then add that user to the Backup Operators local group.

1. Log on to Windows XP using an account with administrator privileges.

2. From the Start menu, right-click My Computer and select Manage.

3. In the Computer Management console, in the console tree, expand System Tools, and then expand Local Users And Groups.

4. Right-click the Users folder and select New User.

5. In the New User dialog box, type the following information:

    ❑ User Name: **ksanchez**

    ❑ Full Name: **Ken Sanchez**

    ❑ Password and Confirm Password: **lion54dunk**!

6. In the New User dialog box, clear the User Must Change Password At Next Logon check box, and then click Create. Click Close.

7. In the right-hand pane of the Computer Management console, right-click ksanchez and select Properties.

8. In the ksanchez Properties dialog box, on the Member Of tab, click Add.

9. In the Select Groups dialog box, click Advanced.

10. In the second Select Groups dialog box, click Find Now.

11. In the search pane, select Backup Operators and click OK.

12. In the Select Groups dialog box, click OK.

13. In the ksanchez Properties dialog box, click OK.

14. Close the Computer Management console.

Lesson Review

The following question is intended to reinforce key information presented in this lesson. If you are unable to answer the question, review the lesson materials and try the question again. You can find answers to the question in the "Questions and Answers" section at the end of this chapter.

1. A user named John is a member of several groups in a domain: the Research Group, the Marketing Group, and the Support Group. Each group he belongs to has access to a different set of folders and data. However, one folder named Help And Support is shared so that all users in the company can access it, although some users have more access than others. John's group membership and the permissions assigned to the Help And Support folder for each group are listed here. What is John's effective permission for the folder?

Group	Share Permissions	NTFS Permissions
Research	Read and Change	Read, Write, List Folder Contents, Read And Execute
Marketing	Read	Read, Read And Execute
Support	Full Control	Modify, Read And Execute, List Folder Contents, Read, Write

   A. Read

   B. Write

   C. Modify

   D. Full Control

Lesson Summary

- A user's group membership determines the level of access to the computer and its files and folders.

- When a user is a member of multiple groups, the permissions for all groups are combined and the least restrictive permission is applied.

- Changes in group membership affect users' access to resources. Take membership into account when troubleshooting access.

Lesson 3: Troubleshooting Local Security Settings

Local security settings are configured on the local computer, and they affect everyone who logs on to it. In this lesson, you learn to work with two types of security settings—account policies and local policies.

After this lesson, you will be able to

- Explain the types of local security settings.
- Troubleshoot issues with account policies.
- Troubleshoot issues with local security policies.

Estimated lesson time: 25 minutes

Understanding Local Security Settings

The local security settings that you will be concerned with as a DST are account policies and local security policies. Account policies control how people log on to the computer.

There are two kinds of account policies:

- Password policies
- Account lockout policies

There are three kinds of local security policies:

- Audit policies
- User rights assignments
- Security options

Together these security policies define the rules for who can log on to the computer, what they can do once logged on, and more. These policies are configured to protect the computer and limit a user's access. Local security policies are generally configured for computers that are in workgroups, especially in situations in which multiple users access the same computer. Local security policies are also applied to computers that are accessed by people in kiosks or other public places. Local policies can be applied to computers in domains, too, but the local security policy is overridden by any site policies, domain policies, and organizational unit policies (in that order) that are in place. If conflicts arise, the local security policy is ignored and the other policies in the hierarchy are applied. Therefore, local security policies in a domain are not very powerful. Local policies are set from the Local Security Policy administrative tool, available in Control Panel and shown in Figure 9-7.

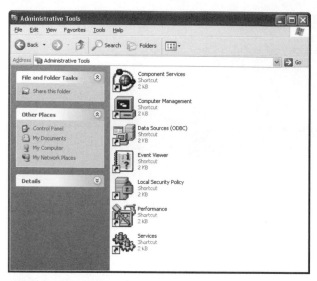

Figure 9-7   Local security policies protect the computer from harm.

Account Policies

There are two types of account policies, and, in this section, you will learn about each of them. It is important to understand the policies that can and might be set so that you can recognize and troubleshoot problems that occur because of policies that are put in place by administrators. For instance, one configurable account policy is to lock out a user when a specific number of failed logon attempts is met. This prevents someone from trying unlimited name and password combinations. Therefore, if a user reports that he forgot his password and he tried four different ones and is now locked out, you should be able to recognize that this has to do with a local security policy put in place by administrators and have a fair understanding of how to resolve the problem. With this in mind, we will look at the available options for account policies.

Password Policies

To view the available password policies, open Control Panel, open Performance And Maintenance, open Administrative Tools, open Local Security Policy, and expand Account Policies. Click Password Policy. Figure 9-8 shows the options that you can set.

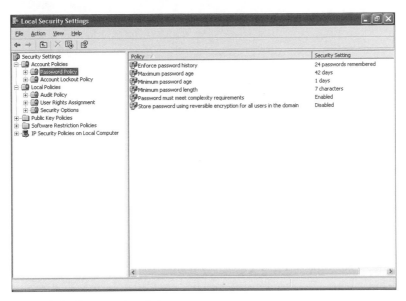

Figure 9-8 Password policies.

If password policies have been set by local security policy or another policy on the network, an end user's password problem might be directly related to the policies configured. The policies shown in Figure 9-8 allow an administrator to enable or enforce the following actions:

- **Enforce Password History** Determines the number of unique new passwords that a user must create before he or she can reuse an old password. This prevents a user from reusing the same two passwords over and over, thereby forcing the user to continually create new ones.

- **Maximum Password Age** Determines the period of time (in days) that a user can use a password before the system requires the user to change it. This forces users to change their passwords every so often. If users do not change their passwords, they will not be able to log on and will need the assistance of a network administrator.

- **Minimum Password Age** Determines the period of time (in days) that a user must use a password before he or she can change it. If a user reports that he or she cannot change a password, this might be the issue.

- **Minimum Password Length** Determines the least number of characters that a password must contain.

- **Password Must Meet Complexity Requirements** Requires passwords to contain at least six characters, not contain a part of the user's name, and have three of the following four items: uppercase letters, lowercase letters, digits, and non-alphanumeric characters.

- **Store Password Using Reversible Encryption For All Users In The Domain**   Determines whether Microsoft Windows 2000 Server, Windows 2000 Professional, and Windows XP Professional store passwords by using **reversible encryption**.

If a user has a problem with one of these items, logging on might require the assistance of a workgroup or network administrator. This is detailed shortly.

Account Lockout Policies

If account lockout policies have been set by local security policy or another policy on the network, an end user's logon problem might be directly related to the configured policies. The three account lockout policies allow an administrator to enable or enforce the following:

- **Account Lockout Duration**   Determines the number of minutes a locked-out account remains locked before it automatically becomes unlocked. A user who has entered too many incorrect passwords might become locked out and either has to wait for the duration set here or ask an administrator for help.

- **Account Lockout Threshold**   Determines the number of failed logon attempts that causes an account to be locked out.

- **Reset Account Lockout Counter After**   Determines the number of minutes that must elapse before the failed logon attempt counter is reset to 0.

If a user is locked out and you have administrator privileges on the computer, you can unlock the user's account. This is detailed next.

Troubleshooting User Account Problems

If you are the administrator of a workgroup and need to unlock an account, reset a user's password because he or she has forgotten it, force the user to change his or her password for security reasons, or perform similar tasks, you do that from the Administrative Tools option, Computer Management.

▶ **Unlock a User Account**

To unlock an account, follow these steps:

1. Log on to the computer by using your Administrator account.

2. Open Control Panel, open Performance And Maintenance, open Administrative Tools, and open Computer Management.

3. In the Computer Management window, expand System Tools and expand Local Users And Groups. Select Users.

4. In the right pane, locate the user whose account needs unlocking, right-click on that account, and choose Properties.

5. To unlock the account, clear the Account Is Locked Out check box. (If the account is disabled, clear the Account Is Disabled check box.) Click OK.

▶ **Reset a User's Password**

To reset a user's password because he or she has forgotten it, follow these steps:

1. Log on to the computer using your Administrator account.

2. Open Control Panel, open Performance And Maintenance, open Administrative Tools, and open Computer Management.

3. In the Computer Management window, expand System Tools and expand Local Users And Groups. Select Users.

4. In the right pane, locate the user whose account needs the password to be reset. Right-click on that account and choose Set Password.

5. Read the information in the Set Password dialog box. If a password reset disk is available, use it as suggested. If a password reset disk is not available, click Proceed.

6. In the Set Password dialog box, type the new password and confirm it. Click OK. The Set Password dialog box is shown in Figure 9-9.

Figure 9-9 The Set Password dialog box allows an administrator to reset a user's password if he or she has forgotten it.

7. Click OK to confirm that the password has been set.

▶ **Force a User to Change a Password at Next Logon**

To force the user to change his or her password at the next logon, follow these steps:

1. Log on to the computer using your Administrator account.

2. Open Control Panel, open Performance And Maintenance, open Administrative Tools, and open Computer Management.

3. In the Computer Management window, expand System Tools and expand Local Users And Groups. Select Users.

4. In the right pane, locate the user whose password needs to be changed, right-click on that account, and choose Properties.

5. Select the User Must Change Password At Next Logon check box. Figure 9-10 shows an example. Click OK.

Figure 9-10   Reset an account from Computer Management.

Local Security Policies

You can configure three types of local security policies and, in this section, you will learn about each of them. You should understand the policies that can and might be set so that you can recognize and troubleshoot problems that occur because of policies put in place by administrators. For instance, one configurable security policy prevents the installation of unsigned device drivers. Therefore, if a user reports that on her own computer she can install unsigned device drivers but on the computer in the lobby she cannot, you should be able to recognize that the computer in the lobby has a stricter local security policy than the user's computer does. With that in mind, we will look at the three available configurable local security policy options.

Audit Policies

Administrators can set audit policies to log the success or failure of various events. This auditing helps an administrator determine whether there are too many logon failures (implying that someone might be trying to hack into the system), whether someone has successfully changed a user rights assignment policy or audit policy, or a number of other events. As a tier 1 DST, you will not be in charge of setting audit policies. However, because they are a configurable local security policy option, they bear a brief introduction.

To view the available audit policies and learn the purpose of setting each, follow these steps:

1. Open Control Panel, open Performance And Maintenance, open Administrative Tools, and open Local Security Policy.

2. Expand Local Policies, if necessary, and select Audit Policies. Double-click any audit policy to change its properties and to enable or disable auditing.

3. To learn more about audit policies, click Help and click Help Topics. In the Microsoft Management Console help files, expand Local Security Policy, expand Concepts, expand Understanding Local Security Policy, and click Account And Local Policies. In the right pane, select Audit Policy.

User Rights Assignment

User rights assignment options are likely to be set on shared computers, computers in kiosks and public places, and workgroup computers. Setting a user rights assignment is the same as setting an audit policy: Open Local Security Settings, expand Local Policies, select User Rights Assignment, and double-click the policy to change or set. Some user rights assignment policies that might be set on a computer include who or what might or might not be able to do the following:

- Access the computer from the network
- Add workstations to a domain
- Back up files and directories
- Change the system time
- Create permanent shared objects
- Load and unload device drivers
- Log on locally
- Manage auditing and the security log
- Remove a computer from a docking station
- Shut down the system
- Take ownership of objects

Therefore, if a user reports that he or she cannot perform a required function such as change the system time, shut down the system, or another task listed here, you might need to check the local security policy (and the user's group membership).

Security Options

Finally, security options are likely to be set by administrators on computers in a domain, although you sometimes find them set on workgroups. Setting a security option is the same as setting any policy: Open Local Security Settings, expand Local Policies, select Security Options, and double-click the policy to change or set. Some security options that might be set on a computer include the following, and these can be enabled or disabled:

- Administrator account status
- Guest account status
- Renaming the Administrator or Guest account
- Shutting down the system if security audits cannot be logged
- Preventing users from installing printer drivers
- Unsigned device driver installation behavior
- Displaying the last user name
- Requiring CTRL+ALT+DEL when logging on
- If message text is to appear when users log on
- If logoff is forced when users' logon hours expire
- If the virtual memory pagefile should be cleared when the computer is shut down

Because of the number of options that are available, it is important to view and understand what each option does or does not allow. This way, when a user reports an obscure problem, asks that you disable CTRL+ALT+DEL for logon, asks that you rename the Guest account, or wants you to configure message text that users must read when logging on, you know exactly where to look and how to configure the changes.

Practice: Configure Local Security Settings

In this practice, you will set password and account lockout policies, assign user rights, and configure security options.

Exercise 1: Set Password Policies

1. Log on to Windows XP using an account with administrator privileges.
2. From the Start menu, select Control Panel.
3. In Control Panel, select Performance And Maintenance.
4. In the Performance And Maintenance window, select Administrative Tools.
5. In the Administrative Tools window, double-click Local Security Policy.

6. In the Local Security Settings console, expand Account Policies and select Password Policy.

7. In the right-hand pane, double-click Maximum Password Age.

8. In the Maximum Password Age Properties dialog box, in the Password Will Expire In text box, enter **90**. Click OK.

9. In the Suggested Value Changes dialog box, click OK.

Exercise 2: Set Account Lockout Policies

1. Log on to Windows XP using an account with administrator privileges.

2. From the Start menu, select Control Panel.

3. In Control Panel, select Performance And Maintenance.

4. In the Performance And Maintenance window, select Administrative Tools.

5. In the Administrative Tools window, double-click Local Security Policy.

6. In the Local Security Settings console, expand Account Policies and select Account Lockout Policy.

7. In the details pane, double-click Account Lockout Threshold.

8. In the Account Lockout Threshold Properties dialog box, in the Account Will Not Lock Out text box, enter **5**. Click OK.

9. In the Suggested Value Changes dialog box, click OK.

Exercise 3: Assign User Rights

1. Log on to Windows XP using an account with administrator privileges.

2. From the Start menu, select Control Panel.

3. In Control Panel, select Performance And Maintenance.

4. In the Performance And Maintenance window, select Administrative Tools.

5. In the Administrative Tools window, double-click Local Security Policy.

6. In the Local Security Settings console, expand Local Policies and select User Rights Assignment.

7. In the right-hand pane, right-click Change The System Time and select Properties.

8. In the Change The System Time Properties dialog box, click Add User Or Group.

9. In the Select Users Or Groups dialog box, in the Enter The Object Names To Select (Examples) text box, type **ksanchez**. Click Check Names, and then click OK.

10. In the Change The System Time Properties dialog box, click OK.

Exercise 4: Configure Security Options

1. Log on to Windows XP using an account with administrator privileges.

2. From the Start menu, select Control Panel.

3. In Control Panel, select Performance And Maintenance.

4. In the Performance And Maintenance window, select Administrative Tools.

5. In the Administrative Tools window, double-click Local Security Policy.

6. In the Local Security Settings console, expand Local Policies and select Security Options.

7. In the right-hand pane, right-click Interactive Logon: Do Not Require CTRL+ALT+DEL and select Properties.

8. In the Interactive Logon: Do Not Require CTRL+ALT+DEL Properties dialog box, select Enable and click OK.

Lesson Review

The following question is intended to reinforce key information presented in this lesson. If you are unable to answer this question, review the lesson materials and try the question again. You can find answers to the question in the "Questions and Answers" section at the end of this chapter.

1. In the following table, match the policy on the left with the appropriate security setting folder on the right.

Policy	Local Security Setting Folder
1. Audit Logon Events	A. Local Policies, User Rights Assignment
2. Maximum Password Age	B. Group Policy, User Configuration, Administrative Templates, Control Panel
3. Interactive Logon: Do Not Require CTRL+ALT+DEL	C. Local Policies, Security Options
4. Shut Down The System	D. Account Policies, Account Lockout Policy
5. Account Lockout Threshold	E. Local Policies, Audit Policy
6. Hide Specific Control Panel Tools	F. Account Policies, Password Policy

Lesson Summary

- Account policies include password policies, which govern how passwords are configured and controlled, and account lockout policies, which control what happens when a user tries to log on using an invalid password.

- Local policies include audit policies, user rights assignments, and security options.

Lesson 4: Understanding Group Policy

Group Policy can be set for a single computer with multiple users, for computers in workgroups, or for computers in domains. Group Policy provides a way for administrators to customize or standardize how users' computers look and what can be accessed.

After this lesson, you will be able to

- Explain the use of Group Policy locally, in workgroups, and in domains.
- Identify the Group Policy settings in effect on a workstation.
- Troubleshoot Group Policy settings.

Estimated lesson time: 25 minutes

Understanding Group Policy

Administrators use Group Policy settings to customize and standardize many things, including but not limited to the following:

- Which programs can be accessed by users
- What is shown on the desktop
- What the Start menu and taskbar look like
- Which screen saver or wallpaper is used
- Where data is saved (which can be on a network server, not the local computer)
- Which Control Panel tools can be accessed

To understand how Group Policy settings might affect an end user or cause an end user's problem, you must understand what kinds of Group Policy settings can be used, how those settings will affect the end user, and how Group Policy is configured on the local computer.

Group Policy Settings in a Workgroup

In a workgroup, administrators can configure Group Policy for computers, users, or both. The options for each are listed under the Computer Configuration option and the User Configuration option, respectively, in the Group Policy console (which you can access by selecting Run on the Start menu, and then typing **gpedit.msc** in the Run dialog box). The Computer Configuration options, shown in Figure 9-11, include several policies covered earlier (account policies and local policies). There is also a Software Settings option and an Administrative Templates option.

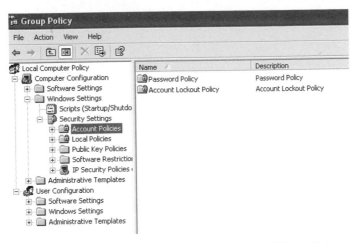

Figure 9-11   Computer Configuration options and Group Policy.

To reinforce the power of configured Group Policy, consider this: A user reports that he cannot add or delete sites from the Security Zones when using Microsoft Internet Explorer. The user would like to add a website to the Trusted Sites zone. The reason he cannot is that Group Policy has been configured in the Computer Configuration option with a setting that disallows this. Policies for Internet Explorer and other components can be set under Computer Configuration, Administrative Templates. Some of these options are fairly complex, and you should work through each of them separately.

The User Configuration options are the ones that we will be most concerned with here, although you should familiarize yourself with all aspects of Group Policy. User configurations offer a myriad of customization and standardization options. To understand the ways in which Group Policy can be configured, open the Group Policy console on a local computer in a workgroup by following these steps:

1. From the Start menu, choose Run and type **gpedit.msc**. Click OK.

2. Expand User Configuration (if necessary).

3. Expand Administrative Templates.

4. Notice that there are several options. Select Start Menu And Taskbar. Within the Start Menu And Taskbar options alone, there are 32 configurable options.

5. To configure any option, double-click it. As an example, double-click Prevent Changes To Taskbar And Start Menu Settings. To enable this setting, in the Prevent Changes To Taskbar And Start Menu Settings dialog box, shown in Figure 9-12, select Enabled. Select the Explain tab to see an explanation of the setting.

6. Click OK when finished, or click Previous Setting or Next Setting to make other changes.

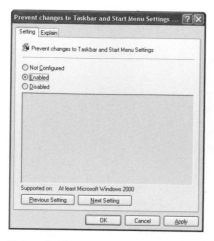

Figure 9-12   Enabling a Group Policy setting.

Click and explore each item in the Administrative Templates options, including all of the items in Windows Components, Desktop, Control Panel, Shared Folders, Network, and System. You must become familiar with what can and might be set on an end user's computer so that you can successfully troubleshoot end-user issues.

> **Note**   Some extremely strong restrictions can be placed on users of a computer by using Group Policy. Access to Control Panel can be disabled, Windows Messenger can be disabled, and items on the desktop or Start menu can be hidden.

Group Policy Settings in a Domain

If your end users are members of a domain, chances are good that domain Group Policy has been set. Domain Group Policy settings take precedence over any local Group Policy settings on a local computer. Users might ask why specific group or local policies that they configured sometimes work and sometimes do not work; the answer to that is simple. If the user is logged on to the workgroup, the local Group Policy settings are applied; when the user logs on to the domain, those local policy settings are overridden by domain Group Policy settings.

Troubleshooting Group Policy

When problems arise that you suspect are related to Group Policy, either because both local Group Policy and domain Group Policy settings exist, because local Group Policy is configured and you are not sure which settings are applied, or because you can see that unusual restrictions are in place, you can view the policy information set for the computer from the Help and Support Center by following these steps:

1. From the Start menu, choose Help And Support.

2. Below Pick A Task, select Use Tools To View Your Computer Information And Diagnose Problems.

3. In the Tools pane on the left, select Advanced System Information.

4. Click View Group Policy Settings Applied.

You can save, print, and e-mail the report for troubleshooting purposes. There are sections in the report for the last time Group Policy settings were applied, and a listing of all of the Group Policy and local policy configurations. This list can help you decide what, if any, Group Policy settings are causing the end user's problem. The Help and Support Center will most likely give you some insight into the problem at hand, and as you work with Group Policy, you will begin to understand that Group Policy settings can have a huge impact on end users.

To help you understand the types of calls you will respond to that involve Group Policy settings, Table 9-4 lists some common reports from end users and the Group Policy settings associated with them.

Table 9-4 Common Group Policy Restrictions

Report/Scenario	Associated Group Policy Setting
A user cannot enable AutoComplete for forms or passwords in Internet Explorer.	User Configuration, Administrative Templates, Windows Components, Internet Explorer, Disable AutoComplete For Forms
The user cannot access My Documents from the Start menu.	User Configuration, Administrative Templates, Windows Components, Start Menu And Taskbar, Remove My Documents Icon From Start Menu
A user cannot access Control Panel.	User Configuration, Administrative Templates, Windows Components, Control Panel, Prohibit Access To The Control Panel
When a user inserts a CD, AutoPlay never works and cannot be used.	Computer Configuration, Administrative Templates, System, Turn Off AutoPlay
A user does not want to be prompted to send a report each time an error occurs with a program.	Computer Configuration, Administrative Templates, System, Internet Communication Management, Internet Communication Settings, Turn Off Windows Error Reporting
A user does not have the Lock Computer option available when using CTRL+ALT+DEL.	User Configuration, Administrative Tools, Windows Components, System, CTRL+ALT+DEL Options, Remove Lock Computer

Of course, hundreds of other configurations can be made by administrators. You should take the time to browse through the available configurations and see what is available.

> **Note** Administrators who configure and use Group Policy to manage computers on a domain can also use the software installation and maintenance feature of IntelliMirror to install applications on computers. This is done in conjunction with **Active Directory directory service** and **Windows Installer**. For more information on application deployment, visit Microsoft TechNet.

Practice: Configure Group Policy in a Workgroup

In this practice, you will configure Group Policy to prevent users in a workgroup from accessing the Properties option on the Recycle Bin's shortcut menu.

1. Log on to Windows XP using an account with administrator privileges.

2. From the Start menu, select Run.

3. In the Run dialog box, in the Open text box, type **gpedit.msc** and press ENTER.

4. In the Group Policy console, in the console tree, expand User Configuration, expand Administrative Templates, and select Desktop.

5. In the right-hand pane, right-click Remove Properties From The Recycle Bin Context Menu and click Properties.

6. In the Remove Properties From The Recycle Bin Context Menu Properties dialog box, select Enabled and click OK.

7. Close all open windows and right-click the Recycle Bin. Note that Properties is no longer an option on the shortcut menu.

Lesson Review

The following questions are intended to reinforce key information presented in this lesson. If you are unable to answer a question, review the lesson materials and try the question again. You can find answers to the questions in the "Questions and Answers" section at the end of this chapter.

1. A Windows XP Professional user reports that she is unable to access the Add/Remove Programs icon in Control Panel. What is most likely the problem?

   A. The Windows XP installation is corrupt.

   B. A Group Policy setting is in place that prevents access.

   C. The antivirus program is restricting access.

> **D.** There are no programs to add or remove.
>
> **E.** The user is not logged on as an administrator.

2. Select all of the ways in which the Group Policy console can be accessed.

   A. Type **gpedit.msc** at the Run line.

   B. Open the Group Policy console from Administrative Tools.

   C. Open Group Policy from Control Panel, using the Group Policy icon.

   D. Open Group Policy by choosing Start, pointing to All Programs, pointing to Accessories, pointing to System Tools, and selecting Group Policy.

Lesson Summary

- Group Policy settings can restrict the user's desktop, Start menu, and taskbar and what the user can access and change after logging on to the computer.

- When multiple Group Policy configurations exist, domain policies always override local policies.

Case Scenario Exercises

Scenario 9.1

A small office user with three employees has just purchased a new computer running Windows XP and has set up a network using a four-port hub. She connected her three existing computers running Windows 98 and her new computer running Windows XP, and then she used the Network Setup Wizard on the computer running Windows XP to create the network. She reports that she made no other changes. After sharing a few folders, she reports that everyone on the network can view and make changes to her shared files. She wants the users on her network to be able to view the files only, not edit or change them. What should you tell the user to do? (Select all that apply.)

A. Disable Simple File Sharing.

B. Convert the file system of the computer running Windows XP to NTFS.

C. Clear the Allow Users To Change My Files check box on the Sharing tab of each shared folder.

D. Drag the shared folders to the Shared Documents folder.

E. Upgrade all of the computers to Windows XP.

Scenario 9.2

The company you work for has its users separated into four user groups: the Administrators group, the Power Users group, the Users group, and the Temporary Workers group. The company's network is configured as a workgroup. The first three groups are built-in groups, and a network administrator created the last group. A user at your company who has previously been a member of the Administrators group has recently been demoted and placed in the Power Users group. He reports several problems:

- He cannot back up or restore files and folders on the network.
- He cannot manage auditing and security logs.
- He cannot take ownership of files and folders.
- He cannot force shutdown of a remote system.

What is the cause of this?

A. This is the expected behavior based on the user's new group membership.

B. Local policies are preventing access.

C. Group Policy settings are preventing access.

D. Public key policies are preventing access.

Troubleshooting Lab

You are working as a DST. A small business owner calls and tells you that he has a small network on which he is the sole administrator. One of his employees recently requested that she be able to take ownership of files and other objects on a computer that she shares with other employees. The owner made the user a member of the Power Users group on the computer. However, the user still does not have the ability to take ownership of resources.

1. Using the Local Security Settings console, determine whether the Power Users group has the right to take ownership of files and other objects.

_____

_____

_____

_____

2. What would you suggest the owner do to give the user the necessary rights?

_____

_____

_____

_____

3. Using the Local Security Settings console, list the user rights assigned by default to the Administrators group that are not assigned by default to the Power Users group.

_____

_____

_____

_____

_____

_____

_____

Chapter Summary

- There are several ways to configure sharing on a network, including using Simple File Sharing, setting share permissions, and setting NTFS permissions.

- Multiple permissions affect a user's access level. When share and NTFS permissions are applied, the cumulative permissions of both are determined, and the most restrictive of those create the user's effective permission.

- A user's group membership can determine the level of access to the computer and its files and folders. When a user is a member of multiple groups, the permissions of the groups are compared and the least restrictive set of permissions is applied.

- Local policies can restrict how users log on, what their passwords must consist of, and what they can access and change after they have logged on to the computer.

- Group Policy settings can restrict the user's desktop, Start menu, and taskbar and what the user can access and change after she is logged on to the computer.

- When multiple Group Policy configurations exist, domain policies always override local policies.

Exam Highlights

Before taking the exam, review the key topics and terms that are presented in this chapter. You need to know this information.

Key Points

- When sharing a folder on a network with Simple File Sharing enabled, you cannot choose who can and cannot access a folder. When you share a folder with Simple File Sharing disabled, you give permission for everyone on the network to access and read the files in the folder.

- Combining permissions can be confusing. First, figure out the NTFS permissions that a user has by combining the permissions of all the groups in which the user is a member and taking the least restrictive combination. Next, figure out the share permissions on the object in the same way—by combining the share permissions of the groups in which the user is a member and taking the least restrictive combination. (Again, a Deny permission for any group yields a Deny permission for the user.) Finally, combine the NTFS and share permissions and take the most restrictive combination of those two. And remember, being denied access at any level or from any group means that the user is denied access in the end.

Key Terms

Active Directory   A centralized database that contains information about a network's users, workstations, servers, printers, and other resources. Active Directory (found on a domain controller) determines who can access what and to what degree. Active Directory is essential to maintaining, organizing, and securing the resources on a larger network; it allows network administrators to centrally manage resources; and it is extensible, meaning that it can be configured to grow and to be personalized for any company.

FAT   See file allocation table.

file allocation table (FAT)   A type of file system used by older computers to organize the files and folders on the computer. FAT organizes the files on the computer so that they can be accessed when they are needed.

NTFS   A type of file system used by newer computers that is much more advanced than the FAT file system. NTFS provides advanced file and folder permissions, encryption, disk quotas, and compression. NTFS is supported by Windows NT, Windows 2000, and Windows XP.

Windows Installer   A core component of IntelliMirror, which is used to deploy applications across a domain. Windows Installer is used to install applications and to manage user installation options.

Questions and Answers

Lesson 1 Review

Page
9-18

1. The company you work for hires quite a few temporary workers, and those workers need access to workgroup computers to perform their jobs. These employees are added to the default Users group when they are hired. Because they are members of the Users group, they have Read And Execute, List Folder Contents, and Read permissions by default. However, these users also need to be able to write data to the folders to which they have access. What is the best way to make this change without giving the users too much access?

   A. Add all new users to the Power Users group.

   B. Stop assigning NTFS permissions and assign the Read and Change share permissions.

   C. For the Users group on each share, assign the NTFS permission Write.

   D. For the Users group on each share, assign the NTFS permission Full Control.

   C is the best answer. Adding the Write permission adds only that option for the user and no more. A and D would give more access than necessary, and B would reduce the security of the shares.

2. A user's Windows 2000 Professional computer was recently upgraded to Windows XP Professional. A member of the Users group reports that he can no longer run the older applications necessary to perform his job. You have looked for a newer version of the application but cannot find one. The user is a Microsoft Certified Desktop Technician and a Microsoft Certified Professional and has been with the company for many years, so you feel he is competent and will pose no threat if given extra leniency. You need to allow this user to run his older application. What is the best course of action?

   A. Move this end user from the Users group to the Power Users group.

   B. Decrease the default security settings for all members of the Users group.

   C. Purchase a new program that is Microsoft certified and train the users in the company to use it. Uninstall the older application.

   D. Move this end user from the Users group to the Administrators group.

   A is correct. Members of the Power Users group can run older applications. Making this user a member of this group will likely pose no threat to the computer or the network. B would work but is not the best course of action because not all users need this capability. C is incorrect because it would require too much time and money, and it is unnecessary. D is incorrect because only a few employees should be given administrator status.

Lesson 2 Review

Page
9-22
1. A user named John is a member of several groups in a domain: the Research Group, the Marketing Group, and the Support Group. Each group he belongs to has access to a different set of folders and data. However, one folder named Help And Support is shared so that all users in the company can access it, although some users have more access than others. John's group membership and the permissions assigned to the Help And Support folder for each group are listed here. What is John's effective permission for the folder?

Group	Share Permissions	NTFS Permissions
Research	Read and Change	Read, Write, List Folder Contents, Read And Execute
Marketing	Read	Read, Read And Execute
Support	Full Control	Modify, Read And Execute, List Folder Contents, Read, Write

    A. Read

    B. Write

    C. Modify

    D. Full Control

C is the correct answer. The cumulative share permissions are Full Control. The cumulative NTFS permissions are Modify. The more restrictive of those two is Modify. The other answers are incorrect for this reason.

Lesson 3 Review

Page
9-32
1. In the following table, match the policy on the left with the appropriate security setting folder on the right.

Policy	Local Security Setting Folder
1. Audit Logon Events	A. Local Policies, User Rights Assignment
2. Maximum Password Age	B. Group Policy, User Configuration, Administrative Templates, Control Panel
3. Interactive Logon: Do Not Require CTRL+ALT+DEL	C. Local Policies, Security Options
4. Shut Down The System	D. Account Policies, Account Lockout Policy

Policy	Local Security Setting Folder
5. Account Lockout Threshold	E. Local Policies, Audit Policy
6. Hide Specific Control Panel Tools	F. Account Policies, Password Policy

The following answers are correct because they represent the only place the policies can be set for each item: 1-E. 2-F. 3-C. 4-A. 5-D. 6-B.

Lesson 4 Review

Page
9-38

1. A Windows XP Professional user reports that she is unable to access the Add/Remove Programs icon in Control Panel. What is most likely the problem?

   A. The Windows XP installation is corrupt.

   B. A Group Policy setting is in place that prevents access.

   C. The antivirus program is restricting access.

   D. There are no programs to add or remove.

   E. The user is not logged on as an administrator.

   B is correct. Group Policy can be set to disable access to specific Control Panel tools. A is not correct because a corrupt installation would cause various other problems; C is incorrect because antivirus programs do not generally restrict access to Control Panel; D is incorrect because there are always programs that can be added or removed; and E is not correct because you do not have to be an administrator to access Add/Remove Programs.

2. Select all of the ways in which the Group Policy console can be accessed.

   A. Type **gpedit.msc** at the Run line.

   B. Open the Group Policy console from Administrative Tools.

   C. Open Group Policy from Control Panel, using the Group Policy icon.

   D. Open Group Policy by choosing Start, pointing to All Programs, pointing to Accessories, pointing to System Tools, and selecting Group Policy.

   A is correct. B and C are incorrect because Group Policy is not an option from Administrative Tools or from Control Panel. D is incorrect because Group Policy is not an option from System Tools.

Case Scenario Exercises: Scenario 9.1

Page
9-39

A small office user with three employees has just purchased a new computer running Windows XP and has set up a network using a four-port hub. She connected her three existing computers running Windows 98 and her new computer running Windows XP, and then she used the Network Setup Wizard on the computer running Windows XP to create the network. She reports that she made no other changes. After sharing a few folders, she reports that everyone on the network can view and make changes to her shared files. She wants the users on her network to be able to view the files only, not edit or change them. What should you tell the user to do? (Select all that apply.)

A. Disable Simple File Sharing.

B. Convert the file system of the computer running Windows XP to NTFS.

C. Clear the Allow Users To Change My Files check box on the Sharing tab of each shared folder.

D. Drag the shared folders to the Shared Documents folder.

E. Upgrade all of the computers to Windows XP.

> C is the only correct answer because by default, new networks created with the Network Setup Wizard use Simple File Sharing. Clearing this option from the shared folders will solve the problem. A is incorrect because although disabling Simple File Sharing would allow the user to configure other options, disabling it will not solve the problems at hand. B is incorrect because Simple File Sharing works with both FAT and NTFS. D is incorrect because this technique is used to share folders with other users of the same computer. E is incorrect because the computers do not need to be running Windows XP to participate in and follow the rules of a network.

Case Scenario Exercises: Scenario 9.2

Page 9-40 The company you work for has its users separated into four user groups: the Administrators group, the Power Users group, the Users group, and the Temporary Workers group. The company's network is configured as a workgroup. The first three groups are built-in groups, and a network administrator created the last group. A user at your company who has previously been a member of the Administrators group has recently been demoted and placed in the Power Users group. He reports several problems:

- He cannot back up or restore files and folders on the network.
- He cannot manage auditing and security logs.
- He cannot take ownership of files and folders.
- He cannot force shutdown of a remote system.

What is the cause of this?

A. This is the expected behavior based on the user's new group membership.

B. Local policies are preventing access.

C. Group Policy settings are preventing access.

D. Public key policies are preventing access.

A is correct. By default, only members of the Administrators group can perform these tasks, and because he is no longer a member, he no longer has those privileges. B is incorrect, even though policies can be changed and set here. C is incorrect because Group Policy settings are used to customize and standardize other settings. D is incorrect because public key policies have to do with encryption, not rights and privileges.

Troubleshooting Lab

Page 9-40 You are working as a DST. A small business owner calls and tells you that he has a small network on which he is the sole administrator. One of his employees recently requested that she be able to take ownership of files and other objects on a computer that she shares with other employees. The owner made the user a member of the Power Users group on the computer. However, the user still does not have the ability to take ownership of resources.

1. Using the Local Security Settings console, determine whether the Power Users group has the right to take ownership of files and other objects.

   The Power Users group is not assigned this right by default; only the Administrators group has this right. However, you can use the Local Security Settings console to assign the right to the Power Users group or to the individual user.

2. What would you suggest the owner do to give the user the necessary rights?

   The owner could add the user to the Administrators group, but this option would likely give more permissions to the user than the owner wants her to have. The owner could also give the Power Users group the right to take ownership of files and other objects. However, if there are other members of the Power Users group, they also would be given this right. The best course of action is to assign the right directly to the user.

3. Using the Local Security Settings console, list the user rights assigned by default to the Administrators group that are not assigned by default to the Power Users group.

   By default, the rights assigned to the Administrators group that are not assigned to the Power Users group include the following:

   - Adjust memory quotas for a process.
   - Allow logon through Terminal Services.
   - Back up files and directories.
   - Create a pagefile.
   - Debug programs.
   - Force shutdown from a remote system.
   - Increase scheduling priority.

- Load and unload device drivers.
- Manage auditing and security logs.
- Modify firmware environment values.
- Perform volume maintenance tasks.
- Profile system performance.
- Restore files and directories.
- Take ownership of files or other objects.

10 Protecting the Computer

Exam Objectives in this Chapter:

- Identify and troubleshoot network connectivity problems caused by the firewall configuration
- Identify and respond to security incidents
    - Answer end-user questions related to security incidents
    - Identify a virus attack
    - Apply critical updates

Why This Chapter Matters

The goal of this chapter is to teach you how to protect computers by using a variety of methods and techniques. Applying critical Microsoft updates, configuring Windows Firewall, and protecting the computer from viruses are all extremely important to the overall dependability and stability of a computer or network.

Lessons in this Chapter:

Before You Begin

Before you begin this chapter, you should have basic familiarity with the Microsoft Windows XP interface. You should also have access to a computer running Windows XP, on which you can experiment with changing various settings. Your computer must be connected to the Internet in order to complete tasks related to using the Microsoft Update website.

Lesson 1: Updating Windows and Microsoft Office

Critical updates and security updates help keep computers protected from new vulner-abilities that are discovered (and threats that are created) after the initial shipping of an operating system or application. The Automatic Updates feature in Windows XP auto-matically downloads and installs critical and security updates for Windows XP and select other Microsoft products, such as Microsoft Office. Microsoft provides a website named Microsoft Update that can scan a computer, determine what is already installed, and list available updates. In addition to the critical and security updates available through Automatic Updates, Microsoft Update also offers optional hardware and soft-ware updates.

After this lesson, you will be able to

■ Configure Automatic Updates in Windows XP.

■ Explain the differences between critical, software optional, and hardware optional updates.

Estimated lesson time: 25 minutes

Configuring Automatic Updates in Windows XP

Microsoft Update is an online update website provided by Microsoft to keep users' computers up-to-date and protected from the latest security threats. Microsoft Update provides and distributes security fixes, critical updates, updated help files, newly released and signed drivers, and various other updates for Microsoft products. Anyone with valid administrator credentials on the computer and a genuine, licensed copy of the operating system can download and install these updates for free.

While users can use the Microsoft Update site to download updates, encourage users instead to configure the Automatic Updates feature in Windows XP so that it routinely automatically downloads and installs new critical updates. The first time a computer starts after Windows XP is installed (or after Windows XP Service Pack 2 is installed if it is installed separately), Windows displays a dialog box that allows you to turn on Automatic Updates. If a user reports problems acquiring updates on a regular basis, verify that Automatic Updates is enabled and configured appropriately by following these steps:

1. From the Start menu, click Control Panel.

2. In Control Panel (in Category View), click Performance And Maintenance.

3. In the Performance And Maintenance window, click System.

4. On the Automatic Updates tab, click Automatic (Recommended), as shown in Figure 10-1. This setting configures Windows XP to download and install updates automatically at the configured time (3:00 A.M., by default).

5. You can also specify whether the user should be notified before downloading and installation, have downloads happen automatically and be notified before installation, or download and install automatically according to a schedule. For the highest level of security (and the least intervention required by users), use the fully automatic option and configure a time when the computer will not be used. Click OK.

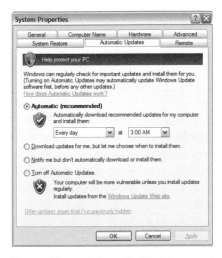

Figure 10-1   Automatic Updates can be configured in a variety of ways.

Using the Microsoft Update Site

The Microsoft Update site offers a more hands-on approach to updating Microsoft products than using Automatic Updates. If a user resists using the Automatic Updates feature, teach the user to frequently visit the Microsoft Update site and let it scan the computer and suggest updates. Even if Automatic Updates is enabled, an occasional visit to the Microsoft Update site is still a good idea because it offers other updates in addition to the critical updates managed by Automatic Updates.

There are actually three updates types: High Priority updates, Software Optional (non-critical updates for Windows and other products), and Hardware Optional (hardware driver updates). Automatic Updates handles only critical updates. To download Software Optional and Hardware Optional updates, you must use the Microsoft Update website. Each type of update is discussed in the next few sections. However, downloading and installing updates is the same for each type, so the installation of updates is covered only in the first section.

High Priority Updates

High Priority updates are crucial to the operation of the computer and should always be installed. These updates provide solutions to known issues, include patches for security vulnerabilities, and might contain updates to the operating system or the applications installed on it, among other things.

To obtain updates manually from the Microsoft Update site, follow these steps:

1. Click the Start menu, point to All Programs, and then click Windows Update.

   The Microsoft Update site determines whether you have the latest version of the software required to scan your computer for recommended updates. If it does not, Microsoft Update must install the software before you can continue. After the latest software is installed, Microsoft Update provides two choices: Express and Custom.

2. Click Express to scan the computer for critical and security updates only, and then automatically download and install the available updates of these types. Usually, you will not need to restart the computer after an Express install. However, some updates may require a restart, particularly if a critical system file or driver is replaced. If you choose Express, this is the last step you need to perform. Clicking Custom allows you to select the updates you want to install. The remainder of this procedure details the steps of a custom installation.

3. After clicking Custom, Microsoft Update scans your computer. After the scan is complete (a process that is performed locally—no information is sent to Microsoft's servers), select a category under Select By Type, and then select the check box for each update you want to install. After the updates have been selected, click Review And Install Updates. The following categories are available:

   ❑ **High Priority**   High Priority updates include critical and security updates. These updates are crucial to the operation of the computer, so you should *always* install them. These updates provide solutions to known issues, include patches for security vulnerabilities, and might contain updates to the operating system or other applications. Service packs are also included as critical updates.

   ❑ **Software Optional**   Software Optional updates are less critical than the previously detailed updates and range from application updates for Microsoft software to updates for previously applied operating system service packs. Not everyone needs all of these updates, however, so you should read the descriptions prior to adding them to the installation list and add only necessary updates.

   ❑ **Hardware Optional**   Hardware Optional updates include new and updated drivers for a user's particular computer and setup. When Microsoft

Update scans the computer, it acquires information about the modem, network card, printer, and similar hardware; and then offers any available driver updates. Users often find that driver updates enhance the performance of the computer.

4. The Microsoft Update site selects all high priority updates and service packs for you automatically. You must add optional updates to the installation manually.

> **Important**   Pay attention to the updates that you select; some updates must be installed independently of other updates.

5. After selecting the updates you want to install, click Review And Install Updates.

6. Review the updates you have selected, and then click Install Updates.

7. If Windows displays a license agreement, read it and then click Accept. Wait while the updates are installed and then restart the computer if prompted.

It is imperative that you install all critical updates. Figure 10-2 shows a healthy system report from the Microsoft Update site.

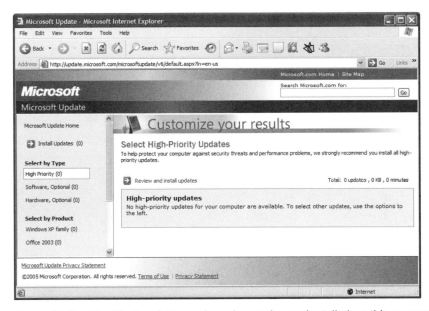

Figure 10-2   All critical updates and service packs are installed on this computer.

Software Optional Updates

Software Optional updates, which are less critical than the previously detailed updates, range from application updates for Microsoft programs to updates for previously applied operating system service packs. Not everyone needs all updates, however, so a description of each is given with the update itself. You should read the descriptions prior to adding them to the installation list and add only necessary updates.

You download and install Software Optional updates in the same manner as High Priority updates; however, in most instances you can download and install multiple updates simultaneously.

Hardware Optional Updates

Hardware Optional updates offer new and updated drivers for a user's particular computer system and peripherals. When Microsoft Update scans the computer, it acquires information about the modem, network card, printer, and similar hardware; and if an updated driver is available for any component, it is offered. End users often find that driver updates enhance the performance of the computer.

Configuring automatic updates or obtaining the updates manually helps make sure that a computer is protected from attacks on discovered security weaknesses and that the best possible compatibility with applications is maintained.

> **Real World** **Driver Updates**
>
> The driver updates that are on the Microsoft Update site are versions of drivers that have been tested by Microsoft and certified as being compatible with Windows XP. This means that the drivers you download from Microsoft Update are safe to use.
>
> However, having only certified drivers on the site also means that the drivers on Microsoft Update are rarely the most recent drivers available for a hardware device. It also means that Microsoft Update probably will not have driver updates for the majority of devices because the majority of hardware manufacturers submitted drivers for certification when Windows XP was first released and have not submitted newer drivers since the release.
>
> When you see that new drivers are available on the Microsoft Update site, check the version of the drivers and then compare it with the version that is already installed on the computer (you can do this using Device Manager). Often, the drivers already installed on your system are more recent than the certified drivers available on the Microsoft Update site, even if the Microsoft Update site suggests that it has newer drivers. Also, if you are thinking of installing drivers as a means of troubleshooting a device, trying to increase performance, or using new features, you should check the device manufacturer's website to determine whether newer drivers than those available at the Microsoft Update site are available.

Practice: Updating Windows XP

In this practice, you will use the Microsoft Update site to manually update Windows XP.

1. Log onto Windows XP using an account with administrator permissions.

2. From the Start menu, point to All Programs, and then click Windows Update.

3. If you see a Security Warning dialog box, click Yes.

4. The Microsoft Update site spends some time checking for updates to the scanning software that the site uses to scan your computer. When this scan finishes, on the Welcome To Microsoft Update page, click Express.

5. If you see a dialog box asking whether you accept the End-User License Agreement, click I Agree or Accept (whichever is displayed).

6. A Microsoft Update dialog box appears and displays progress. After installation is complete, you may receive a dialog box prompting you to restart the computer. If so, click OK.

Lesson Review

The following question is intended to reinforce key information presented in this lesson. If you are unable to answer the question, review the lesson materials and try the question again. You can find the answer to the question in the "Questions and Answers" section at the end of this chapter.

1. An end user reports that although he was able to install Microsoft Update files when he first purchased his computer two years ago, he now cannot install Service Pack 2. After a quick check, you discover that Automatic Updates is enabled in System Properties, and is configured to automatically download updates. You verify that the user can download Service Pack 2 but cannot install it. What is most likely the problem?

   A. The user has an unlicensed copy of Windows XP.

   B. The user is running Windows XP Home Edition and needs to upgrade to Windows XP Professional Edition.

   C. The user needs to register Windows XP with Microsoft.

   D. The user needs to activate Windows XP with Microsoft.

   E. Microsoft Update determined after scanning the computer that the user does not need to install the service packs.

Lesson Summary

- You can download and apply critical updates for Windows XP automatically using the Automatic Updates feature.

- You can use the Microsoft Update site to manually download High Priority updates, Software Optional updates, and Hardware Optional updates.

Lesson 2: Configuring Windows Firewall

A firewall protects a computer from the outside world (specifically, the Internet) by blocking all network traffic except that which you specifically configure the firewall to allow through. This lesson introduces firewalls and looks at the local firewall software included with Windows XP—Windows Firewall.

After this lesson, you will be able to

- Explain how firewalls protect computers.
- Configure Windows Firewall.
- Troubleshoot connectivity problems associated with Windows Firewall.

Estimated lesson time: 40 minutes

Understanding Windows Firewall

A firewall acts as a security system that creates a border between the computer or network and the Internet. This border determines what traffic is allowed in or out of the local network or computer. Firewalls help keep hackers, viruses, and other evils from infiltrating the computer and network.

There are two basic types of firewalls:

- **Perimeter firewalls**   Perimeter firewalls help protect an entire network. Most of the time, especially on small networks, perimeter firewalls are dedicated hardware devices that connect directly to the network between the Internet connection device (such as a modem) and the computers on the network. There are also software-based perimeter firewalls that run on a computer connected to the network.

- **Local firewalls**   Local firewalls are always software-based and help protect a single computer. Windows Firewall is a local firewall program that is included with Windows XP with Service Pack 2.

Any computer connected directly to the Internet, whether it is a standalone computer or a computer that provides Internet Connection Sharing (ICS) services for other computers on a network, should have a local firewall like Windows Firewall enabled.

Windows Firewall is installed when you install Windows XP Service Pack 2, and is an updated version of the Internet Connection Firewall found on versions of Windows XP with Service Pack 1 and previous. Windows Firewall is a stateful, host-based firewall that drops all incoming traffic that does not meet one of the following conditions:

- Solicited traffic (valid traffic that is sent in response to a request by the computer) is allowed through the firewall.

- Expected traffic (valid traffic that you have specifically configured the firewall to accept) is allowed through the firewall.

Windows Firewall has the following characteristics:

- Is enabled by default for all network connections.

- Limits the network traffic that comes into a computer by blocking transmission over all ports except those specifically configured to allow traffic to reach the computer. When you allow a specific type of traffic into a computer through Windows Firewall, this is called creating an exception. You can create exceptions by specifying the file name of an application or by configuring specified ports for which to allow traffic. Windows Firewall lets you create separate exceptions for each network connection.

- Restricts traffic by IP address (or IP address range), meaning that only traffic from computers with valid IP addresses is allowed through the firewall.

- Allows you to enable or disable Windows Firewall on each connection configured on a computer running Windows XP Professional, whether that connection is a LAN, dial-up, or wireless connection. You can also set global configurations that affect all connections.

- Allows you to keep a security log of blocked traffic so that you can view firewall activity.

- Performs stateful packet filtering during startup so that the computer can perform basic network tasks (such as contacting DHCP and DNS servers) and still be protected.

How to Enable or Disable Windows Firewall for all Network Connections

The only users who can make changes to Windows Firewall settings are those who log on to the computer with a user account that is a member of the local Administrators group. To enable or disable Windows Firewall for all network connections, use these steps:

1. Click Start, and then click Control Panel.

2. In Control Panel (in Category View), click Network And Internet Connections.

3. In the Network And Internet Connections window, click Windows Firewall.

4. On the General tab of the Windows Firewall dialog box, shown in Figure 10-3, click On (Recommended) to enable the firewall for all connections. Click Off (Not Recommended) to disable the firewall for all connections.

5. Click OK.

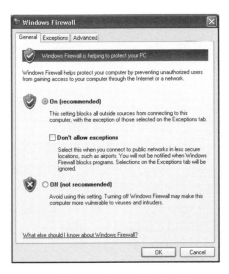

Figure 10-3   Enable or disable Windows Firewall for all network connections.

How to Enable or Disable Windows Firewall for a Specific Network Connection

In addition to being able to enable or disable Windows Firewall for all connections, you can control whether Windows Firewall is enabled on each connection on a computer. To enable or disable Windows Firewall for a specific network connection, use these steps:

1. Click Start, and then click Control Panel.

2. In Control Panel (in Category View), click Network And Internet Connections.

3. In the Network And Internet Connections window, click Windows Firewall.

4. In the Windows Firewall dialog box, click the Advanced tab, shown in Figure 10-4.

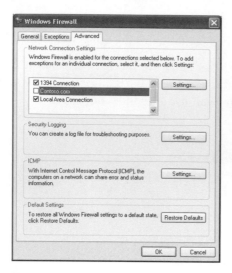

Figure 10-4   Enable or disable Windows Firewall for specific network connections.

5. To enable Windows Firewall for a connection, select the check box for that connection. To disable Windows Firewall for a connection, clear the check box for that connection.

6. Click OK to close the Windows Firewall dialog box.

Windows Firewall Advanced Options

After enabling Windows Firewall, you might need to configure it for a specific situation. You have several options for configuring Windows Firewall options, including the following:

- Enabling Windows Firewall logging to log network activity

- Creating an exception for a service or application to allow traffic through the firewall

- Creating a custom service definition when a built-in exception does not suit your needs

- Creating an Internet Control Message Protocol (ICMP) exception so that the computer responds to traffic from certain network utilities

How to Enable Windows Firewall Logging

You can configure Windows Firewall to log network activity, including any dropped packets or successful connections to the computer. Security logging is not enabled by default for Windows Firewall. To enable security logging for Windows Firewall, use these steps:

1. Click Start, and then click Control Panel.

2. In Control Panel (in Category View), click Network And Internet Connections.

3. In the Network And Internet Connections window, click Windows Firewall.

4. In the Windows Firewall dialog box, on the Advanced tab, in the Security Logging section, click Settings.

   Windows displays the Log Settings dialog box, shown in Figure 10-5.

Figure 10-5   Enable security logging for Windows Firewall.

5. In the Logging Options section, select one or both of the following check boxes:

   ❏ **Log Dropped Packets** Logs all dropped packets originating from the local network or the Internet.

   ❏ **Log Successful Connections** Logs all successful connections originating from the network or the Internet.

6. Note the location of the security log. By default, the log file is named pfirewall.log and is located in the %SystemRoot% folder. Click OK to close the Log Settings dialog box. Click OK again to close the Windows Firewall dialog box.

How to Access the Windows Firewall Log File

After you enable logging, you can access the log file by browsing to its location and opening the file. Log entries provide insight about which packets have been successful in getting into the network and which have been rejected. There are two sections of the log: the header and the body. The header includes information about the version of Windows Firewall, the full name of the Windows Firewall, where the time stamp on the log learned of the time, and the field names used by the body of the log entry to display data. The body details the log data.

There are 16 data entries per logged item, which include information about the date and time the log was written and information about the data that passed. This information tells which types of packets were opened, closed, dropped, and lost; which **protocol** was used in the data transmission; the destination IP address of the data; the **port** used by the sending computer; the port of the destination computer; and the size of the packet logged.

To locate and open the Windows Firewall log file, use these steps:

1. Click Start, and then click Control Panel.

2. In Control Panel (in Category View), click Network And Internet Connections.

3. In the Network And Internet Connections window, click Windows Firewall.

4. In the Windows Firewall dialog box, on the Advanced tab, in the Security Logging section, click Settings.

5. In the Log Settings dialog box, in the Log File Options section, click Save As.

6. In the Save As dialog box, right-click the pfirewall.txt file, and then click Open.

7. After reviewing the firewall log, close the Notepad window and the Save As dialog box, click OK to exit the Log Settings dialog box, and then click OK again to close the Windows Firewall dialog box.

 Exam Tip   You should know where Windows Firewall log files are stored, whether logging is available, and what kind of information you can learn from log files.

▶ How to Create an Exception for a Service or Application

By default, Windows Firewall blocks all unsolicited traffic by default. You can create exceptions so that particular types of unsolicited traffic are allowed through the firewall. For example, if you want to allow sharing of files and printers on a local computer, you must enable the File And Printer Sharing exception in Windows Firewall so that requests for the shared resources are allowed to reach the computer.

Windows Firewall includes a number of common exceptions, such as Remote Assistance, Remote Desktop, File And Printer Sharing, and Windows Messenger. Windows Firewall also automatically extends the exceptions available for you to enable according to the programs installed on a computer. You can manually add exceptions to the list by browsing for program files.

To create a global exception that applies to all network connections for which Windows Firewall is enabled, use these steps:

1. Click Start, and then click Control Panel.

2. In Control Panel (in Category View), click Network And Internet Connections.

3. In the Network And Internet Connections window, click Windows Firewall.

4. In the Windows Firewall dialog box, click the Exceptions tab, shown in Figure 10-6.

Figure 10-6   Create a global exception for all connections in Windows Firewall.

5. In the Programs And Services list, select the check box for the service you want to allow. If you need to add an exception for an installed program that does not appear on the list, click Add Program to locate the executable file for the program, and then enable the exception after the program is added to the list.

6. Click OK to close the Windows Firewall dialog box.

▶   **How to Create an Exception for a Particular Port**

If Windows Firewall does not include an exception for the traffic you need to allow, and adding an executable file to the list does not produce the results you need, you can also create an exception by unblocking traffic for a particular port.

To create a global exception for a port that applies to all network connections for which Windows Firewall is enabled, use these steps:

1. Click Start, and then click Control Panel.

2. In Control Panel (in Category View), click Network And Internet Connections.

3. In the Network And Internet Connections window, click Windows Firewall.

4. In the Windows Firewall dialog box, on the Exceptions tab, click Add Port.

   Windows displays the Add A Port dialog box. To create an exception based on a Transmission Control Protocol (TCP) or User Datagram Protocol (UDP) port number, you must know the proper port number used by an application of service to use this option.

5. Type a name for the exception, type the port number you want to allow access for, and then select whether the port is a TCP or UDP port.

   You can also change the scope to which the exception applies. Your options are to have the exception apply to any computer (including computers on the Internet), the local network only, or a custom list of IP addresses.

6. To change the scope of the exception, click Change Scope to open the Change Scope dialog box, where you can configure the scope options. Click OK to return to the Add A Port dialog box.

7. Click OK again to add the exception and return to the Windows Firewall dialog box.

   After you have added the exception, it appears in the Programs And Services list on the Exceptions tab of the Windows Firewall dialog box.

8. Select the check box for the exception to enable it.

9. Click OK to close the Windows Firewall dialog box.

To create a service exception for a particular network connection for which Windows Firewall is enabled, use these steps:

1. Click Start, and then click Control Panel.

2. In Control Panel (in Category View), click Network And Internet Connections.

3. In the Network And Internet Connections window, click Windows Firewall.

4. In the Windows Firewall dialog box, on the Advanced tab, in the Network Connection Settings section, click the connection for which you want to configure an exception, and then click Settings.

   Windows displays the Advanced Settings dialog box, shown in Figure 10-7.

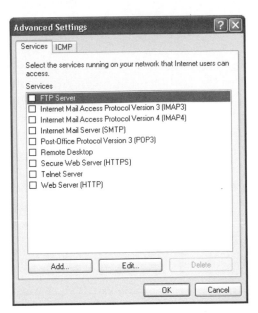

Figure 10-7   Create an exception for a particular network connection in Windows Firewall.

5. On the Services tab, click Add.

   Windows displays the Service Settings dialog box.

6. Type a description of the service.

7. If the computer on which you are configuring Windows Firewall is an ICS host, you can configure Windows Firewall to forward traffic for the port to a particular computer on the network by typing that computer's IP address. If the computer is not an ICS host, you should enter the IP address for the local computer.

Tip   Instead of entering the IP address for the local computer, you can also use the loopback address 127.0.0.1, which always refers to the local computer. This is useful should the IP address of the local computer change.

8. Enter the port information for the service.

9. Click OK to close the Service Settings dialog box. Click OK to close the Advanced Settings dialog box. Click OK again to close the Windows Firewall dialog box.

▶ **ICMP Exceptions**

ICMP allows routers and host computers to swap basic error and configuration information. The information includes whether or not the data sent reaches its final destination, whether it can or cannot be forwarded by a specific router, and what the best route for the data is. ICMP tools such as Pathping, Ping, and Tracert are often used to troubleshoot network connectivity.

ICMP troubleshooting tools and their resulting messages are helpful when used by a network administrator, but harmful when used by an attacker. For instance, a network administrator sends a ping request in the form of an ICMP packet that contains an echo request message to the IP address that is being tested. The reply to that echo request message allows the administrator to verify that the computer is reachable. An attacker, on the other hand, can send a **storm** of specially formed pings that can overload a computer so that it cannot respond to legitimate traffic. Attackers can also use ping commands to determine the IP addresses of computers on a network. By configuring ICMP, you can control how a system responds (or does not respond) to such ping requests. By default, Windows Firewall blocks all ICMP messages.

Table 10-1 provides details about ICMP exceptions you can enable in Windows Firewall.

Table 10-1   ICMP Options

ICMP Option	Description
Allow Incoming Echo Request	Controls whether a remote computer can ask for and receive a response from the computer. Ping is a command that requires you to enable this option. When enabled (as with other options), attackers can see and contact the host computer.
Allow Incoming Timestamp Request	Sends a reply to another computer, stating that an incoming message was received and includes time and date data.
Allow Incoming Mask Request	Provides the sender with the subnet mask for the network of which the computer is a member. The sender already has the IP address; giving the subnet mask is all an administrator (or attacker) needs to obtain the remaining network information about the computer's network.
Allow Incoming Router Request	Provides information about the routes the computer recognizes and passes on information it has about any routers to which it is connected.
Allow Outgoing Destination Unreachable	The computer sends a Destination Unreachable error message to clients who attempt to send packets through the computer to a remote network for which there is no route.
Allow Outgoing Source Quench	Offers information to routers about the rate at which data is received; tells routers to slow down if too much data is being sent and it cannot be received fast enough to keep up.

Table 10-1   ICMP Options

ICMP Option	Description
Allow Outgoing Parameter Problem	The computer sends a Bad Header error message when the computer discards data it has received that has a problematic header. This message allows the sender to understand that the host exists, but that there were unknown problems with the message itself.
Allow Outgoing Time Exceeded	The computer sends the sender a Time Expired message when the computer must discard messages because the messages timed out.
Allow Redirect	Data that is sent from this computer will be rerouted if the path changes.
Allow Outgoing Packet Too Big	When data blocks are too big for the computer to forward, the computer replies to the sender with a "packet too big" message. Note that this option applies only to networks using the IPv6 protocol.

Security Alert   Generally, you should enable ICMP exceptions only when you need them for troubleshooting, and then disable them after you have completed troubleshooting. Make sure that you do not allow or enable these options without a full understanding of the consequences and risks involved.

How to Enable ICMP Exceptions

To enable a global ICMP exception for all connections on a computer, use these steps:

1. Click Start, and then click Control Panel.

2. In Control Panel (in Category View), click Network And Internet Connections.

3. In the Network And Internet Connections window, click Windows Firewall.

4. In the Windows Firewall dialog box, click the Advanced tab.

5. In the ICMP section, click Settings.

6. In the ICMP Settings dialog box, select the check boxes for the exceptions you want to enable.

7. Click OK to close the ICMP Settings dialog box. Click OK again to close the Windows Firewall dialog box.

To enable an ICMP exception for a network connection, use these steps:

1. Click Start, and then click Control Panel.

2. In Control Panel (in Category View), click Network And Internet Connections.

3. In the Network And Internet Connections window, click Windows Firewall.

4. In the Windows Firewall dialog box, click the Advanced tab.

5. In the Network Connection Settings section, click the connection for which you want to configure an exception, and then click Settings.

6. In the Advanced Settings dialog box, click the ICMP tab, shown in Figure 10-8.

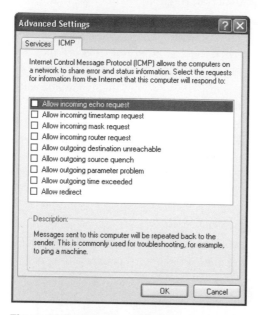

Figure 10-8   Create an ICMP exception for a connection.

7. In the ICMP Settings dialog box, select the check boxes for the exceptions you want to enable.

8. Click OK to close the Advanced Settings dialog box. Click OK again to close the Windows Firewall dialog box.

Troubleshooting Windows Firewall

There are a few common problems that end users encounter when using Windows Firewall, including the inability to enable or disable Windows Firewall on a connection, problems with file and print sharing, a network user's inability to access a server on the network (such as a Web server), problems with Remote Assistance, and problems running Internet programs.

When troubleshooting Windows Firewall, make sure that you remember to check the obvious first. The following are some basic rules that you should follow, and any deviation from them may cause many of the common problems that are encountered when using Windows Firewall:

- Windows Firewall can be enabled or disabled only by administrators. It can be enabled or disabled by a Local Security Policy or Group Policy, as well—sometimes preventing access even by a local administrator.

- To share printers and files on a local computer that is running Windows Firewall, you must enable the File And Printer Sharing exception.

- If the local computer is running a service, such as a Web server, FTP server, or other service, network users cannot connect to these services unless you create the proper exceptions in Windows Firewall.

- Windows Firewall blocks Remote Assistance and Remote Desktop traffic by default. You must enable the Remote Desktop exception for remote users to be able to connect to a local computer with Remote Desktop or Remote Assistance.

Practice: Configure Windows Firewall

In this practice, you will ensure that Windows Firewall is enabled on all connections on your computer. You will disable and then re-enable Windows Firewall on your LAN connection only. You will then enable an exception in Windows Firewall for all connections. The practices in this exercise require that you have a properly configured LAN connection.

Exercise 1: Ensure that Windows Firewall is Enabled For All Network Connections

1. Click Start, and then click Control Panel.

2. In Control Panel (in Category View), click Network And Internet Connections, and then click Network Connections.

3. In the Network Connections window, right-click your LAN connection, and then click Properties.

4. In the Local Area Connection Properties dialog box, on the Advanced tab, in the Windows Firewall section, click Settings.

5. In the Windows Firewall dialog box, ensure that On (Recommended) is selected. Also ensure that the Don't Allow Exceptions check box is cleared.

   Leave both the Windows Firewall dialog box and the Local Area Connection Properties dialog box open for the next exercise.

Exercise 2: Disable and Re-enable Windows Firewall on Your Local Area Connection Only

1. In the Windows Firewall dialog box, click the Advanced tab.

2. In the Network Connection Settings section, in the list of connections, clear the check box next to Local Area Connection, and then click OK.

   Windows Firewall is now disabled for the local area connection. A message appears in the notification area informing you that your computer is at risk because the firewall is disabled.

3. In the Network Connections window, right-click Local Area Connection, and then click Properties. In the Local Area Connection Properties dialog box, click the Advanced tab. In the Windows Firewall section, click Settings.

4. In the Windows Firewall dialog box, on the Advanced tab, select the check box next to Local Area Connection, and then click OK.

   Windows Firewall is now enabled for the local area connection. Leave the Local Area Connection Properties dialog box open for the next exercise.

Exercise 3: Enable an Exception in Windows Firewall for All Connections

1. In the Local Area Connection Properties dialog box, on the Advanced tab, in the Windows Firewall section, click Settings.

2. In the Windows Firewall dialog box, on the Exceptions tab, select the File And Printer Sharing check box.

3. Click OK.

   Windows Firewall is now configured to allow file and printer sharing traffic into your computer.

4. Click OK again to close the Local Area Connection Properties dialog box.

Lesson Review

The following questions are intended to reinforce key information presented in this lesson. If you are unable to answer a question, review the lesson materials and try the question again. You can find answers to the questions in the "Questions and Answers" section at the end of this chapter.

1. A small office user has a network that consists of four computers. One computer running Windows XP Professional Edition acts as the host and provides ICS services, and the other three computers access the Internet through this

host computer's Internet connection. The administrator of the network wants to protect the network by using Windows Firewall. What must the administrator do?

    A. Purchase and install a router that is compatible with Windows XP and Windows Firewall.

    B. Upgrade to DSL or a cable modem; Windows Firewall does not work with a dial-up connection.

    C. Enable Windows Firewall on the host computer.

    D. Enable Windows Firewall on all four network computers.

2. You are troubleshooting a network connection and need to use the Ping command to see if a host is reachable. Which ICMP option should you enable on the host computer?

    A. Allow Incoming Router Request

    B. Allow Incoming Echo Request

    C. Allow Outgoing Source Quench

    D. Allow Redirect

Lesson Summary

■ Windows Firewall is a software-based firewall built into Windows XP. Windows Firewall is enabled by default for all network connections. You can enable or disable Windows Firewall for any particular network connection and configure what types of traffic it allows to enter or leave the computer.

■ Internet Control Message Protocol allows routers and host computers to swap basic control information when data is sent from one computer to another. ICMP tools such as Ping and Tracert are often used to troubleshoot network connectivity.

■ Most of the problems you will encounter with Windows Firewall involve users not being able to enable Windows Firewall for a particular connection and users having connectivity problems resulting from having Windows Firewall turned on and blocking necessary traffic.

Lesson 3: Troubleshooting Virus Attacks

With Windows Update and Windows Firewall configured and enabled, it is time to turn your attention away from configuring operating system components and toward protecting the computer by using third-party software. Protecting the computer from viruses and dealing with viruses that infiltrate the computer or the network can be a big part of a DST's job. In this lesson you learn about installing, configuring, and using virus scanning software, and how and when you should apply **signature updates**. You will also learn how to determine if a virus attack has occurred and where to go for help when a virus has been detected.

After this lesson, you will be able to

- Explain the use of virus scanning software.
- Apply virus signature updates.
- Manage antivirus programs with Security Center.
- Explain common signs of virus activity.

Estimated lesson time: 20 minutes

Virus Scanning Software

Virus scanning software, also called antivirus software, protects the computer or network from virus attacks. All your end users should have antivirus software installed on their computers, but as a DST, you will find many (especially home users) who do not. If you discover that a user does not have virus scanning software, you should encourage him or her to get some type of protection immediately. Viruses can cause significant damage to unprotected computers, and after they are infected, those computers are much more difficult to recover than those with antivirus software installed. In addition, users need to be told how and why to keep the software updated because antivirus manufacturers continually release definitions for newly discovered viruses.

Installing and Configuring Virus Scanning Software

You install virus scanning software like any other software, generally by inserting a product CD and following the prompts provided, or by opening the executable file downloaded from a manufacturer's website. Configuring the software is an important part of the installation procedure, too, because improper configuration of the software can leave the computer vulnerable to attacks, even if you have installed the software.

> **Note**   Larger companies and corporations will most likely have a combination of hardware and software already in place to protect the network. If you are a tier 1 network technician in a large company, you will probably be involved only in applying updates or recovering from virus attacks.

After you have installed virus scanning software, browse through the software options and verify or enable the following settings:

- The software should start automatically when Windows is booted, and protection should be continuous. This prevents lapses in protection.

- Incoming and outgoing e-mail for POP3 and IMAP accounts should be scanned for viruses every time, although this is not recommended for Exchange Server accounts. This prevents viruses from being propagated throughout the network through e-mail.

- Scripts should be blocked, if possible. Scripts could contain viruses and cause harm to the computer or network.

- System scans should be configured to run daily or weekly to locate any previously undetected viruses.

- Virus definitions or signature updates should be configured to update themselves daily at a specified time. These definitions should be configured to install automatically when appropriate for the network. This confirms that the protection will always be current.

- The software should be renewed when the subscription expires to prevent a lapse in protection.

- The software should be configured to protect instant messaging software and prevent **spyware** or **adware** from being installed on the computer.

- When viruses are detected, the files should be automatically repaired when possible. If a file with a virus cannot be repaired, it should be quarantined or deleted.

With these configurations in place, the computer should be protected, and the user can feel confident that his or her data and network are safe. However, it is extremely important that signature updates be installed regularly; manually installing these updates is detailed next.

Note   During the installation of many applications, the setup software advises that you disable antivirus software during the installation, and you should follow this advice. However, be sure you remember to enable the antivirus software following the installation.

Updating Virus Scanning Software

Virus signature updates are similar to the critical updates that Windows Automatic Updates downloads and installs. Virus signature updates contain the latest virus definitions and provide the best protection possible from the latest known security threats.

Most antivirus software can be configured to download and install updates automatically or manually. When possible, you should configure the updates to occur automatically. If this is not possible due to network restrictions or group or domain policies, updates must be obtained manually. For most virus scanning software, obtaining updates manually is achieved as follows:

1. From the Start menu, choose All Programs, and then choose the software scanning program name in the All Programs list.

2. From the options, locate the option to obtain updates.

3. If the updates do not run automatically, work through the wizard that is offered, click Start, or otherwise follow the instructions on the screen.

Depending on the sensitivity of the system and of the data, automatic updates should be applied daily or weekly.

Security Alert   By far, the most important action a user can take to prevent viruses is to install antivirus software and keep it updated.

Managing Antivirus Programs with Security Center

Windows XP with Service Pack 2 includes a tool named Security Center (shown in Figure 10-9) for centrally managing the three most important aspects of protecting a computer: firewall settings, automatic updates, and virus protection. Security Center shows the status of each of these security tools and also provides centralized security alerts to users, letting them know when updates are available, and when programs are out of date. You can open Security Center by clicking Start, pointing to All Programs, pointing to Accessories, pointing to System Tools, and then clicking Security Center.

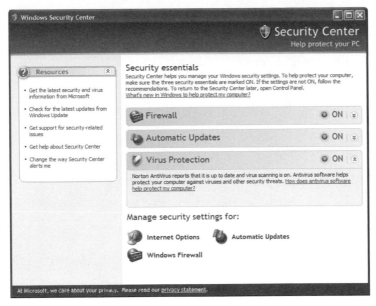

Figure 10-9   Security Center shows the status of Windows Firewall, Automatic Updates, and virus protection.

A green light on the header for each section (Firewall, Automatic Updates, and Virus Protection) indicates that it is properly configured and working. A red light indicates that the feature is disabled or needs your attention. You can click the down arrow at the right side of each section to view more information about that section.

Most modern antivirus programs work well with Security Center and properly report their status. When virus software is out of date, Security Center displays a red light and provides recommendations for what to do. Windows also displays an alert in the notification area letting you know that the program needs to be updated, whether or not Security Center is open.

If you have an antivirus program that does not report its status to Security Center properly, the Virus Protection section will display a button named Recommendations. Clicking this button opens a dialog box that provides recommendations for antivirus software that works with Security Center and also allows you to disable Security Center virus notifications, so that you can manage your antivirus program yourself instead.

Taking Notice of Common Signs

No matter how secure a computer or network is, there is always a chance that a virus can infect your computer anyway. Viruses can come through e-mail, a floppy disk, or a downloaded application or network program, just to name a few ways. There are many kinds of viruses, too, including simple viruses that replicate themselves and are passed on without causing actual harm to the computer; Trojan horse viruses that steal sensitive data; worms that infect computers even when the user has not opened any e-mail attachments, programs, or other infected components; and combinations of these that cause an assortment of effects.

Symptoms of virus infection for which you should be on the lookout include the following:

- The computer system or network slows down.

- Network users all report similar problems almost simultaneously.

- Activity occurs on the computer, including messages, music, or pop-ups.

- A network e-mail server slows down or stops responding.

- Data files become corrupt or are missing.

- Files and folders are changed.

- Programs do not run or they run chaotically.

- Computer partitions become unavailable.

- E-mail is sent from a computer automatically and to everyone in the user's address book.

Recovering from a Virus

Recovering from a virus might require a multifaceted approach. It likely will involve running the antivirus software installed on the computer first. If that is not possible, it can involve booting the computer using the virus scanning software recovery disk, if one exists. You can also access many third-party sites on the Internet for information, including the virus scanning software manufacturer's website. Many of these sites offer online tools to detect and remove a virus even if the end user does not own a copy of the software.

If the computer is so severely infected that you cannot access the online options and the computer will not boot to the recovery disk (or if one is not available), you can use an uninfected computer to make a scan and install repair tools from most of the major antivirus manufacturers' websites. There are many options from these types of websites, and they can be extremely helpful for resolving problems.

Finally, if you know the name of the virus (perhaps you have seen it on the news, or it offers a name during infection), or if you have researched the symptoms and have narrowed down the virus to a single one, you can search the Internet for removal options. This information can be located in newsgroups or on third-party sites, but reliable information is also available from the Microsoft support pages. Figure 10-10 shows the Web page at *http://www.microsoft.com/security/antivirus*, which currently details the Swen worm, the Sobig virus and its variants, the Blaster worm, and other viruses.

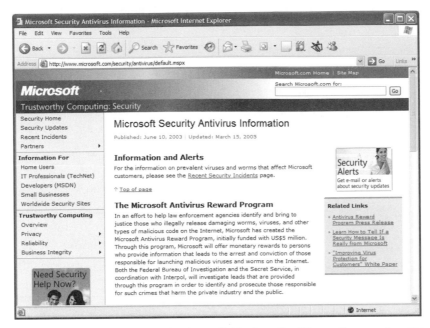

Figure 10-10 Virus information is available from the Microsoft support pages.

Using the information here, network technicians and home users alike can locate information that details how to get rid of a virus after it has been detected and stay up to date on other security issues.

See Also End users and desktop technicians can get more information about protecting a computer from *http://www.microsoft.com/security/protect/windowsxp/firewall.asp*.

Lesson Review

The following questions are intended to reinforce key information presented in this lesson. If you are unable to answer a question, review the lesson materials and try the question again. You can find answers to the questions in the "Questions and Answers" section at the end of this chapter.

1. An end user reports that she has noticed some bizarre behavior on her computer all morning, and she believes it is getting worse. She reports that the computer is displaying odd messages, that she cannot open her JPEG files, and that some programs will not run. She says she has not opened any e-mail attachments all

morning and that no one except her has accessed the computer. What is most likely the problem?

A. The user has a virus on her computer and it is most likely a simple replicating virus.

B. The user has a virus on her computer and it is most likely a worm.

C. The user has an internal problem that cannot be a virus because the user states that she did not open any e-mail attachments recently.

D. The user's operating system needs to be reinstalled; these are common signs of a corrupt installation.

2. You work for an Internet service provider (ISP). An end user calls and reports that he has a virus on his computer. He has discovered through his friends and from watching the national news that he has the Blaster worm. He does not have any antivirus software installed. Although it is not your job to assist the user in ridding the computer of the virus, you want to assist in some way in the time you are allotted. List four ways the user can get help in ridding the computer of the virus.

_____

_____

_____

_____

Lesson Summary

■ To get the best protection possible, install and properly configure virus scanning software to download signature updates automatically, automatically protect the computer, and scan incoming and outgoing e-mail.

■ Microsoft and other companies make virus information freely available and often offer removal tools for specific viruses.

Lesson 4: Using Microsoft Baseline Security Analyzer

Microsoft Baseline Security Analyzer (MBSA) is one more tool that helps you protect a computer. MBSA scans computers for common security lapses and then generates individual security reports for each computer it scans. You can use these reports to determine what steps you should take to further secure the computer or computers on the network.

After this lesson, you will be able to

■ Download MBSA.

■ Use MBSA to scan a system for vulnerabilities.

Estimated lesson time: 15 minutes

Downloading MBSA

You can run MBSA on computers running Microsoft Windows 2000 and Windows XP, as well as Microsoft Windows Server 2003. MBSA can scan the local computer or remote computers. You must download the MBSA tool before you can use it; it does not come with any computer operating system. You can find MBSA version 2.0 in the Tools folder on the CD that is included with this book; the filename is MBSASetup-en.msi. Install it by double-clicking the file and following the prompts in the setup wizard. After you install MBSA, you can use it to check for security vulnerabilities by following these steps:

1. Click Start, point to All Programs, and select Microsoft Baseline Security Analyzer 2.0.

2. When prompted by MBSA, select Scan A Computer or Scan More Than One Computer.

3. Select the computer or computers to scan, and set the options for scanning. Options include the following:

   ❑ Windows administrative vulnerabilities

   ❑ Weak passwords

   ❑ IIS administrative vulnerabilities

   ❑ SQL administrative vulnerabilities

   ❑ Security updates

4. Click Start Scan.

5. Wait while the computer is scanned, and then view the report. Part of a sample report is shown in Figure 10-11.

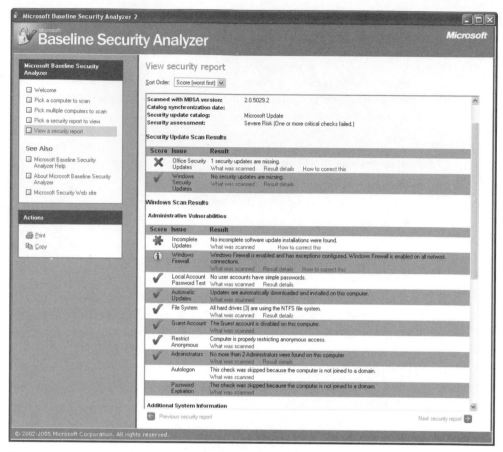

Figure 10-11   The MBSA report lists security lapses and vulnerabilities.

In this example, an available Office security update has not been applied to the computer. In addition, Windows Firewall has some exceptions configured, but these exceptions may be necessary. These are security vulnerabilities that can be easily corrected. Notice that for each security issue listed, options are given for resolution. To resolve any issue, select the How To Correct This link shown next to the issue description.

Practice: Install and Run MBSA

In this practice, you will install and configure MBSA. This practice requires that you install the MBSASetup-en.msi file that is in the Tools folder on the CD that comes with this book.

Exercise 1: Install MBSA

1. Log on to Windows XP using an account with administrator privileges.

2. Locate the MBSASetup-en.msi file in the Tools folder on the CD that comes with the book. Double-click the file to start the installation.

3. In the Microsoft Baseline Security Analyzer Setup Wizard, on the Welcome To The Microsoft Baseline Security Analyzer Wizard page, click Next.

4. On the License Agreement page, select I Accept The License Agreement and click Next.

5. On the Destination Folder page, click Next to accept the default installation location and proceed.

6. On the Start Installation page, click Install.

7. The Installation Progress page displays the installation progress.

8. On the MBSA Setup page, click OK.

Exercise 2: Run MBSA

1. From the Start menu, point to All Programs and select Microsoft Baseline Security Analyzer 2.0.

2. In the Microsoft Baseline Security Analyzer Wizard, click Scan A Computer.

3. Ensure that the computer selected is the local computer, and then click Start Scan.

4. The Scanning page appears and indicates progress.

5. On the Pick A Security Report To Review page, in the Computer Name column, select the name of your computer.

6. On the View Security Report screen, take a moment to browse the results.

Lesson Review

The following question is intended to reinforce key information presented in this lesson. If you are unable to answer the question, review the lesson materials and try the question again. You can find the answer to the question in the "Questions and Answers" section at the end of this chapter.

1. List the types of vulnerabilities for which MBSA can scan.

_____

_____

Lesson Summary

- MBSA runs on Windows 2000, Windows XP, and Windows Server 2003.

- MBSA scans for several types of vulnerabilities, including missing updates, weak passwords, and insecure operating system configurations.

Case Scenario Exercises

Scenario 10.1

An end user is setting up a server that he will host himself using his small office network, and he wants Internet users to be able to connect to the Web pages stored on it. He is also setting up an additional server that will permit users to upload and download files using the Internet instead of the local network. Which two services must he enable to permit the required traffic to flow through the Windows Firewall he currently has configured on this connection? (Choose two.)

A. Web Server (HTTP)

B. FTP Server

C. Telnet Server

D. POP3

Scenario 10.2

As a desktop technician for a small office network, it is your job to make sure all the computers on the network are as secure and protected as possible. You have configured Automatic Updates to obtain and install updates automatically, you have Windows Firewall configured on all of the computers that need it, you have antivirus software installed on each computer, you incorporate a router for extra protection, and you enforce password policies that require users to create strong passwords on their computers. You now want to be able to test the computers on the network regularly from your desktop computer and check for additional vulnerabilities as they arise. The computers are all in the IP range of 192.168.0.1 to 192.168.0.12. You want to check the following:

- Whether the most recent security updates have been installed

- Whether password requirements are configured

- Whether the file systems are all configured as NTFS

- Whether the Guest account is enabled on any of the computers

- How many shares are present on each computer

- Whether Microsoft Internet Explorer security zones have security issues

Is there a single free program available to do this? Select the best answer.

A. There is no program like this available, but one is not needed; the computers are amply protected.

B. There is no program like this available, but MBSA offers some of these options.

C. MBSA offers all of these options and can be used from the administrator's desktop.

D. There is no free program available, but several applications can be purchased that will perform these tasks.

Troubleshooting Lab

On your own computer, perform the following actions so that you understand how they work:

1. Visit the Microsoft Update website. Install all available High Priority updates on your computer. Scan through the list of Software Optional and Hardware Optional updates available and install any that you think are necessary.

2. After you are confident that your computer is updated, configure Automatic Updates so that Windows XP downloads and installs critical updates automatically each day at a time that is appropriate for you.

3. Enable the Windows Firewall on your Internet connection, if it isn't already enabled. Make sure that you allow traffic for any services you require.

4. If you are running antivirus software, ensure that it is updated with the latest virus definitions. Scan your system for viruses and make sure that the antivirus software is configured to protect your system automatically. (If you do not have antivirus software, visit *http://www.microsoft.com/athome/security/protect/windowsxp/ antivirus.mspx* for a list of recommended software.) Check Security Center to make sure that your antivirus program is reporting properly.

5. Run Microsoft Baseline Security Analyzer (MBSA) if you have not already. You can find the tool in the Tools folder on the CD-ROM accompanying this book or download the tool from the following website, *http://www.microsoft.com/technet/ security/tools/mbsahome.mspx,* and follow its recommendations for increasing the security on your computer.

Chapter Summary

- To install Windows updates as they become available, configure Automatic Updates to check for the updates regularly or set a schedule to obtain updates manually. Always install critical updates and service packs.

- To use Windows Firewall, verify that the computer connects directly to the Internet, and then use the Advanced tab of the Internet Connections Properties dialog box to enable it.

- To troubleshoot network and connectivity problems, enable ICMP options for the network connection configured to provide Windows Firewall.

- When adding servers and services to a local area network, add its respective service to Windows Firewall so that the required traffic for the service can pass.

- To get the best protection possible, install and properly configure virus scanning software to download signature updates automatically, automatically protect the computer, and scan incoming and outgoing e-mail on POP3 and IMAP accounts.

- To use MBSA, download it from the Microsoft support pages, and then run it to obtain a detailed report listing the security vulnerabilities on the computer.

Exam Highlights

Before taking the exam, review the key topics and terms that are presented in this chapter. You need to know this information.

Key Points

- Enabling Automatic Updates and configuring it to download and install updates automatically according to a preset schedule is the recommended way for handling critical updates for Windows XP and select Microsoft products.

- Understand how to turn on log files for Windows Firewall and what kinds of information the logs can show you.

- Install antivirus software on all computers and keep the software up to date.

Key Terms

port   An entry point or exit point for data on a computer. Printers use printer ports, universal serial bus (USB) devices use USB ports, and modems typically use serial ports. In addition, data that is sent or received from the Internet or a network also enters and exits using a port, defined by a number. For instance, HTTP traffic uses port 80, FTP traffic uses port 21, and Telnet traffic uses port 23.

protocol   A set of rules for sending information over a network, such as the Internet. These rules and conventions allow computers, networks, routers, and other hardware to communicate with one another all over the world.

signature updates   Virus definition updates. Signature updates contain files that protect the computer from the latest security threats and are part of virus scanning software's options.

Questions and Answers

Lesson 1 Review

Page
10-7

1. An end user reports that although he was able to install Microsoft Update files when he first purchased his computer two years ago, he now cannot install Service Pack 1. After a quick check, you discover that Microsoft Update is enabled in System Properties, and is configured to automatically download updates. You verify that the user can download Service Pack 2 but cannot install it. What is most likely the problem?

    A. The user has an unlicensed copy of Windows XP.

    B. The user is running Windows XP Home Edition and needs to upgrade to Windows XP Professional Edition.

    C. The user needs to register Windows XP with Microsoft.

    D. The user needs to activate Windows XP with Microsoft.

    E. Windows Update determined after scanning the computer that the user does not need to install the service packs.

Answer A is correct. End users must have a licensed copy of Windows XP (any version) to install service packs. Answer B is incorrect because both Home and Professional Editions can be used to obtain and install Windows Update files. Answer C is incorrect because registration is optional. Answer D is incorrect because the computer would not function after two years if the product had never been activated. Answer E is incorrect because everyone should install distributed service packs.

Lesson 2 Review

Page
10-22

1. A small office user has a network that consists of four computers. One computer running Windows XP Professional Edition acts as the host and provides ICS services, and the other three computers access the Internet through this host computer's Internet connection. The administrator of the network wants to protect the network by using Windows Firewall. What must the administrator do?

    A. Purchase and install a router that is compatible with Windows XP and Windows Firewall.

    B. Upgrade to DSL or a cable modem; Windows Firewall does not work with a dial-up connection.

    C. Enable Windows Firewall on the host computer.

    D. Enable Windows Firewall on all four network computers.

Answer C is correct. Enabling Windows Firewall on the host computer is all the administrator needs to do on a network that is already configured and running properly. Answers A and B are incorrect because routers, DSL, and cable modems are not requirements of Windows Firewall. Answer D is incorrect because Windows Firewall should not be installed on computers that are not directly connected to the Internet.

2. You are troubleshooting a network connection and need to use the Ping command to see if a host is reachable. Which ICMP option should you enable on the host computer?

   A. Allow Incoming Router Request

   B. Allow Incoming Echo Request

   C. Allow Outgoing Source Quench

   D. Allow Redirect

   Answer B is correct because it allows the host computer to respond to ping requests. Answer A is incorrect because this option passes on information about connected routers and the flow of traffic from the computer. Answer C is incorrect because this option allows the computer to send a message to slow the flow of data. Answer D is incorrect because this option allows routers to redirect data to more favorable routes.

Lesson 3 Review

Page 10-29

1. An end user reports that she has noticed some bizarre behavior on her computer all morning, and she believes it is getting worse. She reports that the computer is displaying odd messages, that she cannot open her JPEG files, and that some programs will not run. She says she has not opened any e-mail attachments all morning and that no one except her has accessed the computer. What is most likely the problem?

   A. The user has a virus on her computer and it is most likely a simple replicating virus.

   B. The user has a virus on her computer and it is most likely a worm.

   C. The user has an internal problem that cannot be a virus because the user states that she did not open any e-mail attachments recently.

   D. The user's operating system needs to be reinstalled; these are common signs of a corrupt installation.

   Answer B is correct. These symptoms are common signs of a virus that is a worm. Answer A is incorrect because simple replicating viruses usually replicate only through e-mail and the network. Answer C is incorrect because viruses can travel in ways other than e-mail. Answer D is incorrect because these are not common signs of a corrupt installation; they are common signs of a virus.

2. You work for an Internet service provider (ISP). An end user calls and reports that he has a virus on his computer. He has discovered through his friends and from watching the national news that he has the Blaster worm. He does not have any antivirus software installed. Although it is not your job to assist the user in ridding

the computer of the virus, you want to assist in some way in the time you are allotted. List four ways the user can get help in ridding the computer of the virus.

Answers may vary, but the following list shows the common ways of helping get rid of viruses:

- Visit *http://www.microsoft.com/security/antivirus*.
- Visit *http://www.microsoft.com/athome/security/protect/windowsxp/firewall.mspx*.
- Visit the website of a manufacturer that produces antivirus software.
- Purchase antivirus software, install it, and run the virus removal tools.
- Visit a virus removal newsgroup.
- Visit the Microsoft Knowledge Base, *http://support.microsoft.com/search/*.

Lesson 4 Review

Page
10-33

1. List the types of vulnerabilities for which MBSA can scan.

The vulnerabilities for which MBSA can scan include the following:

- Windows administrative vulnerabilities
- Weak passwords
- IIS administrative vulnerabilities
- SQL administrative vulnerabilities
- Windows and Office software updates

Case Scenario Exercises: Scenario 10.1

Page
10-34

An end user is setting up a server that he will host himself using his small office network, and he wants Internet users to be able to connect to the Web pages stored on it. He is also setting up an additional server that will permit users to upload and download files using the Internet instead of the local network. Which two services must he enable to permit the required traffic to flow through the Windows Firewall he currently has configured on this connection? (Choose two.)

A. Web Server (HTTP)

B. FTP Server

C. Telnet Server

D. POP3

Answers A and B are correct. The Web Server (HTTP) service allows users to access the Web pages stored on the Web server, and the FTP Server service allows users to upload and download files stored on the additional server. Answer C is incorrect because Telnet servers are used to log on to network computers from remote locations. Answer D is incorrect because POP3 servers are used to receive e-mail.

Case Scenario Exercises: Scenario 10.2

Page
10-34
As a desktop technician for a small office network, it is your job to make sure all the computers on the network are as secure and protected as possible. You have configured Windows Update to obtain and install updates automatically, you have Windows Firewall configured on all of the computers that need it, you have antivirus software installed on each computer, you incorporate a router for extra protection, and you enforce password policies that require users to create strong passwords on their computers. You now want to be able to test the computers on the network regularly from your desktop computer and check for additional vulnerabilities as they arise. The computers are all in the IP range of 192.168.0.1 to 192.168.0.12. You want to check the following:

- Whether the most recent security updates have been installed

- Whether password requirements are configured

- Whether the file systems are all configured as NTFS

- Whether the Guest account is enabled on any of the computers

- How many shares are present on each computer

- Whether Microsoft Internet Explorer security zones have security issues

Is there a single free program available to do this? Select the best answer.

A. There is no program like this available, but one is not needed; the computers are amply protected.

B. There is no program like this available, but MBSA offers some of these options.

C. MBSA offers all of these options and can be used from the administrator's desktop.

D. There is no free program available, but several applications can be purchased that will perform these tasks.

Answer C is correct. MBSA does all of these things. The other answers are incorrect for this reason.

11 Troubleshooting Application Access on Multiuser, Multiple Boot, and Networked Computers

Exam Objectives in this Chapter:

- Configure the operating system to support applications
    - ❑ Configure and troubleshoot file system access and file permission problems on multiboot computers
    - ❑ Configure access to applications on multiuser computers
    - ❑ Configure and troubleshoot application access on a multiple–user client computer

Why This Chapter Matters

This chapter teaches you to work with various types of computer setups, specifically those with multiuser or multiple boot configurations, and computers that participate on a network. For the most part, this chapter revolves around configuring applications and allowing access to them for each type of configuration. Other topics include understanding the three basic file system types—file allocation table (FAT) and file allocation table 32-bit (FAT32), and NTFS—and how applications should be configured when these file systems are used.

Lessons in this Chapter:

Before You Begin

Before you begin this chapter, you should have basic familiarity with the Microsoft Windows XP interface. You should also have access to a computer running Windows XP on which you can experiment with changing various settings.

Lesson 1: Working with Multiuser Computers

A multiuser computer is one that has multiple local user accounts that are configured to support different people logging on to the computer at different times to work, use e-mail, and perform other computing tasks. To resolve service calls involving multiuser computers, you must have a basic understanding of the types of user accounts that you will encounter. You also must have an understanding of how data and applications are shared among the users who log on to the computer. After you learn about user accounts and a little about how multiuser computers work, you will learn how to configure application access on multiuser computers so that all users who access the computer can also access the applications that are installed on it.

After this lesson, you will be able to

■ Explain how user accounts are used on a multiuser computer.

■ Explain how a multiuser computer is used.

■ Configure access to applications on a multiuser computer.

Estimated lesson time: 15 minutes

Understanding User Accounts

Users who share a computer running Microsoft Windows XP Home Edition or Windows XP Professional Edition are assigned a user account by the administrator of that computer. Each time the user logs on with this personal account, the computer retrieves the desktop settings, personal folders, passwords, Internet and e-mail configurations, and other information for this particular user so that the computer is personalized for the user. Configuring user accounts also serves as a way to keep users' personal data safe from and inaccessible to other users who log on to the same computer.

The user account type also defines the level of access that the user has while logged on to the computer, such as whether or not she can install software or hardware, create additional user accounts, make permanent changes to the computer, or change passwords. There are four types of user accounts that you will encounter:

■ **Computer Administrator**   This user account offers the user complete and unlimited authority to modify the computer in any way at all, including creating, changing, and deleting user accounts; making permanent changes to systemwide settings (such as setting local policies); and installing and uninstalling hardware and software. Local Administrator accounts are configured for stand–alone computers and computers that are in workgroups and domains.

- **Standard**   This type of user account allows the user to install and uninstall software and hardware, and to make changes to the account password and the picture that is associated with the account, which appears on the Windows Welcome screen and on the Start menu when a user is logged on. The standard account can be configured only for computers running Windows XP Professional in a domain environment.

- **Limited**   This type of user account allows the user to make changes to his account password and picture, but does not allow him to change computer settings, delete important files, install or uninstall hardware or software, or make changes to systemwide settings. These accounts are configured on stand-alone computers and computers that are running in workgroups and domains.

- **Guest**   This user account is a built-in account that can be enabled when needed, and allows a user to operate the computer in the same manner as a user with a limited account. Users can log on and check e-mail, browse the Internet, and use applications that are installed on the computer, but can cause no harm to the computer by installing programs or making permanent changes. The Guest account can be enabled on stand-alone computers and those that are running in workgroups and domains.

Using a Shared Computer

Users who share a computer log on by using their personal account. This account can be configured on a single, stand-alone local computer or on a computer that is part of a workgroup or a domain. If a shared computer is a stand-alone computer or a member of a workgroup, users can share data on the computer by moving the data to any of the Shared Documents folders. If the computer is a member of a domain, domain policies override any local settings, and the Shared Documents folders are not available. Figure 11-1 shows the Shared Documents folders on a computer running Windows XP Professional that is not a member of a domain.

Besides sharing data, applications can be shared among the users who log on to the computer. Applications do not need to be installed for each user who has access to the computer.

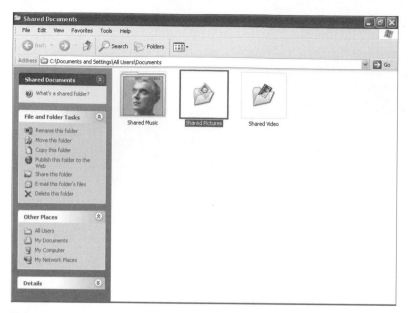

Figure 11-1   The Shared Documents folders offer an easy way to share files among multiple users.

Real World   Fast User Switching

Fast User Switching is a feature of Windows XP Professional Edition and Windows XP Home Edition. Fast User Switching is available on stand-alone computers or computers running in a workgroup, but not on computers running in a domain. Fast User Switching makes it possible for users to quickly switch between accounts without logging off or even exiting running applications. Suppose, for example, that one user is typing a letter in Microsoft Word and another user wants to check her e-mail. The second user could switch over to her account, check her e-mail, and then switch back to the original user's account—all without closing Word or any other running applications.

Fast User Switching provides enormous benefits in a multiuser environment, but it also comes with a disadvantage. People who use Fast User Switching often develop the habit of leaving programs running and leaving themselves logged on because it saves time. The problem with this is that every application that is running, even those running on a user account that you have "switched away" from, consumes system resources. If several users are logged on and have applications running, do not be surprised if the computer runs quite slowly. As a desktop support technician (DST), remember to ask if a computer is using Fast User Switching when users complain about the computer running very slowly.

Also, the habit of leaving applications running increases the risk of lost data in an application (if, for example, one person decides to shut the computer down without checking with everyone else first).

Configuring Access to Applications

When an administrator installs a program on the computer by using the default settings, other administrators, limited or standard users, and guests who access the computer can use the installed program. The user simply needs to select the program from the All Programs menu. The first time the user opens the application, it either configures itself automatically, as shown in Figure 11-2, or prompts the user to input additional information, such as her e-mail and Internet service provider (ISP) information. Virus scanning programs and other programs that are configured to protect the computer continue to work without additional configuration by users.

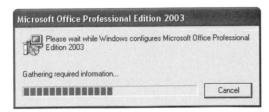

Figure 11-2   Application configuration in Microsoft Office.

If a program is not compatible with Windows XP or was not installed by using the installation defaults (for instance, if the program was installed to a private folder, recovered from the Recycle Bin, or otherwise modified so Windows does not recognize it as a shared application), you can place a shortcut to the application in the Shared Documents folder, and anyone who accesses the computer can then access the program. Other users can also copy that shortcut to their desktop, Start menu, or Quick Launch toolbar.

If users cannot access an application that is installed on a computer running Windows XP, follow these steps:

1. Log on as an administrator.

2. Right-click the Start button and choose Explore All Users.

3. Using Windows Explorer, browse to the application that should be shared.

4. In the left pane of Windows Explorer, expand the drive on which Windows XP is installed (possibly C), expand Documents And Settings, expand All Users, and locate Shared Documents.

5. Right-click the application to share in the right pane, and drag its icon to the Shared Documents folder. Click Create Shortcut Here.

Any user who can log on to the computer can access items in the Shared Documents folder. In addition, you can add shortcuts to any user's desktop by copying a shortcut to the Desktop folder in the user profile for each user who needs access.

> **Exam Tip**   You must be a computer administrator to install applications.

Practice: Add a User Account to a Computer

In this practice, you will add a user account to a computer running Windows XP.

1. Log on to Windows XP using an account with administrator privileges.

2. From the Start menu, right-click My Computer and select Manage.

3. In the Computer Management console, expand System Tools, expand Local Users And Groups, and select Users. From the Action menu, select New User.

4. In the New User dialog box, in the User Name text box, type **mbaker**. In the Full Name text box, type **Mary Baker**. In the Password and Confirm Password text boxes, type **password**.

5. Clear the User Must Change Password At Next Logon check box. Click Create. Click Close.

6. In the Computer Management console, in the right-hand pane, right-click the new mbaker account and select Properties.

7. In the mbaker Properties dialog box, on the Member Of tab, click Add.

8. In the Select Groups dialog box, in the Enter The Object Names To Select (Examples) text box, type **Power Users** and click Check Names. Click OK.

9. In the mbaker Properties dialog box, click OK.

Lesson Review

The following questions are intended to reinforce key information presented in this lesson. If you are unable to answer a question, review the lesson materials and try the question again. You can find answers to the questions in the "Questions and Answers" section at the end of this chapter.

1. A multiuser computer running Windows XP has four user accounts configured for the four users who access the computer. Bob has an Administrator account and is in charge of the computer, John and Mary have Standard accounts and access the computer during the day, and Bill has a limited user account and accesses the computer at night. Knowing this, which of the following must also be true? (Choose all that apply.)

A. The computer is a member of a domain.

B. The computer is running Windows XP Professional Edition.

C. All users can change or delete their account passwords.

D. The computer is running Windows XP Home Edition.

2. A client calls to report that she needs to share her single stand-alone computer with a guest who will be visiting next month. She stresses that the computer contains highly personal documents, files, Internet history, personalization settings, e-mail configuration, and more. Her guest will stay for two weeks and will need access to the computer for e-mailing, creating Microsoft Word documents, working on Microsoft Excel files, and creating Microsoft PowerPoint presentations. The client reports that she has Microsoft Office 2003 Professional Edition installed on the computer. What should you advise the user to do to protect the computer from harmful downloads or program installations by her guest and keep her own documents safe, while still allowing the guest access to the applications on the computer?

A. Create a limited user account for the guest and install Office 2003 under that account.

B. Create a standard user account for the user and drag Office 2003 to the Shared Documents folder.

C. Enable the Guest account for the user.

D. Create a limited user account for the guest and create a local computer policy that does not allow access to the Add Or Remove Programs tool in Control Panel and also does not allow downloading of programs.

Lesson Summary

■ When configuring a multiuser computer, configure a user account for each user who will log on to it and verify that each user has access to the applications that are installed.

■ There are four basic types of user account: computer administrator, standard, limited, and Guest.

■ Applications that are designed for Windows XP will be available automatically to all user accounts that are configured on the computer. Other applications are probably usable to all users, but you may need to create shortcuts for each user manually.

Lesson 2: Working with Multiple Boot Computers

Multiple boot computers run two or more operating systems, including Windows XP, Microsoft Windows 2000, Windows NT, Windows 95, Windows 98, or Windows Me, and, sometimes, even Windows 3.1, MS-DOS, or a third-party operating system. As you gain experience working as a DST, you will see various configurations.

To troubleshoot multiple boot computers, you must be familiar with the three basic file systems, how permissions play a role in users' access to resources, and how installed programs should be configured.

After this lesson, you will be able to

■ Identify the file systems that are supported by Windows XP and explain the differences between the file systems.

■ Troubleshoot file system access on multiple boot computers.

■ Troubleshoot permissions issues on multiple boot computers.

■ Configure applications on multiple boot computers.

Estimated lesson time: 25 minutes

Understanding Disk Partitions

Disk drives are among the most important resources on any computer. After all, there would not be much point to using a computer if you could not store what you create. A partition is a logical section of a hard disk on which data may be written. Every hard disk must be partitioned before it can be used. Most often, a disk is configured as one big partition that takes all the space on the disk, but you may also divide a disk into several partitions. When you partition a disk, you decide how much disk space to allocate to each partition.

Some people create separate partitions to help organize their files. For example, you might store the Windows system files and application files on one partition, user documents on another partition, and backup files on yet another partition. Another important reason to use multiple partitions is to be able to isolate operating systems from one another when a computer is configured to run multiple operating systems. Although it is technically possible to install some operating systems on the same partition as another operating system, it is never recommended. You should always create a separate partition for each operating system.

You can create three types of partitions on a disk:

- **Primary** A primary partition can be set as the bootable partition. A computer running a Windows operating system can have up to four primary drives (three if you also have an extended partition on the disk). Any primary partition may be configured as the active, or bootable, drive, but only one primary partition can be active at any time. When you are configuring a multiple boot computer, you will create a primary partition for each operating system and then install each operating system onto a different primary partition.

- **Extended** An extended partition provides a way to get around the four primary partition limits. You cannot format an extended partition with any file system. Rather, extended partitions serve as a shell in which you can create any number of logical partitions.

- **Logical** You can create any number of logical partitions inside an extended partition. You cannot set a logical partition as an active partition, so you cannot use logical partitions to hold most operating systems. Instead, logical partitions are normally used for organizing files. All logical partitions are visible, no matter what operating system is booted, so logical partitions provide a good method for making files available to any of the operating systems installed on a multiple boot computer.

You can create partitions in a number of ways, including the following:

- Prior to installing any operating systems, you can use the MS-DOS command fdisk to view and create partitions. Fdisk is useful because you can start a computer using an MS-DOS floppy boot disk and set up your partitions before installing any operating systems. You can learn more about using fdisk in Microsoft Knowledge Base article 255867.

- During the installation of Windows NT 4.0, Windows 2000, or Windows XP, you can use the setup program to create multiple partitions. For more information, see Knowledge Base articles 138364 (for Windows NT and 2000) and 313348 (for Windows XP).

- After installation of any version of Windows, you can create and manage partitions by using built-in disk management tools, including Disk Administrator in Windows NT 4.0, and Disk Management in Windows 2000 and Windows XP.

> **Note**   The terminology regarding computers with more than one operating system installed can be confusing. You will hear such computers referred to as "multiboot," "multiple boot," and "dual-boot." The objectives for this exam use the term "multiboot," but this chapter uses the term "multiple boot" for one important reason: the majority of articles you will find on TechNet and in the Knowledge Base also use the term "multiple boot" (though occasionally use "dual-boot," as well). When you are reading this chapter, and when taking the exam, know that the terms "multiboot," "multiple boot," and "dual-boot" all refer to the same basic setup—a computer running more than one operating system. When you are searching online for help on the subject, be sure to check for articles that mention both "multiple boot" and "dual-boot."

Understanding File Systems and File System Access

Setting up or troubleshooting file system access on a multiple boot computer requires that you understand why different file systems are required and some common issues that arise when different file systems are used in a multiple boot environment. The three types of file systems discussed here are FAT and FAT32 (which are earlier and simpler file systems) and NTFS (which is newer, more secure, and more complex).

On computers that contain multiple operating systems, compatibility and file access across operating systems becomes an issue because all operating systems do not support all file systems. File compatibility problems result in files on a particular partition being unavailable when using another operating system on the computer. Having an understanding of the three file system types helps you troubleshoot these access problems.

FAT and FAT32

FAT is a file system that is used by MS-DOS- and Windows-based operating systems to arrange and manage files that are stored on the computer. This type of file system organization allows information about the files to be accessed quickly and reliably. FAT is the only choice of file systems for MS-DOS, Windows 3.1, and the original release of Windows 95 because FAT is a 16-bit file system; FAT32 is a 32-bit file system that is compatible with newer operating systems, starting with Windows 95 OSR2.

FAT32 is an enhanced version of the FAT file system that supports larger **volumes** than FAT. FAT32 is a better choice than FAT when a larger hard disk is installed and when NTFS cannot be used. FAT32 can be used with all modern operating systems, as detailed later in Table 11-1. Windows XP can convert a partition formatted as FAT or FAT32 to NTFS without loss of data, and conversion is usually a good choice. However, converting back to FAT or FAT32 from NTFS without loss of data is not supported. The only way to change a drive from NTFS to FAT or FAT32 is to back up your data, reformat the disk as FAT or FAT32, reinstall Windows and any applications, and then restore your data.

NTFS

NTFS is a superior file system that provides organization, performance, security, reliability, and advanced features that the FAT and FAT32 file systems do not provide. NTFS offers encryption, file and folder permissions, **disk quotas**, and more. NTFS is supported only by the latest operating systems, as detailed in Table 11-1.

Supported File Systems

Table 11-1 shows the file systems that are supported in various Microsoft operating systems. Keep in mind that the support that is listed refers to the local file system only. Any operating system that can access network shares can do so regardless of the file system that is used on the computer sharing the data.

Table 11-1 Supported File Systems

Operating System	Supports FAT	Supports FAT32	Supports NTFS
MS-DOS	Yes	No	No
Windows 3.1	Yes	No	No
Windows NT Server and Workstation	Yes	No	Yes
Windows 95	Yes	No	No
Windows 95 OSR2	Yes	Yes	No
Windows 98	Yes	Yes	No
Windows Me	Yes	Yes	No
Windows 2000 Professional and Server	Yes	Yes	Yes
Windows XP	Yes	Yes	Yes
Windows Server 2003	No	Yes	Yes

Because of file system limitations, a multiple boot computer running Windows 98 and Windows XP needs to have one FAT or FAT32 partition for Windows 98, and a FAT, FAT32, or NTFS partition for Windows XP. However, although NTFS is the better choice for security, users will encounter file access problems when they boot to the Windows 98 partition because Windows 98 does not support NTFS. These problems and others are detailed in the next section.

> **Exam Tip** The *only* reason to use FAT32 on a system running Windows XP is if the system is also configured to run an operating system that cannot interpret NTFS. If a system runs only Windows XP, you should always use the NTFS format.

Troubleshooting File System Access

Table 11-1 detailed which operating systems provide support for which file systems. It is important to understand the significance of this data. As just mentioned, file system access problems can occur when a user is logged on to one operating system and tries to access a file or folder on another partition using a file system that the operating system does not support. An operating system that can access only a FAT partition does not recognize any files on a FAT32 or NTFS partition; an operating system that can access only FAT or FAT32 partitions does not recognize an NTFS partition.

When faced with problems that are caused by incompatible file systems, the only real solution is to **format** the partitions by using the correct file system configuration. For instance, if users need to dual boot between Windows 3.1 and Windows XP, and need to be able to access files on each partition regardless of which operating system they have booted to, the file systems for both partitions must be configured as FAT. This is because Windows 3.1 recognizes only FAT, so it cannot recognize the Windows XP partition unless it is formatted as FAT as well.

If file system configuration is not the problem, meaning that the configured file systems and operating systems are compatible, consider these other items that can cause problems on multiple boot computers:

- Each operating system must be installed on a separate volume or partition. Microsoft does not support installing multiple operating systems on the same partition or volume, nor is this encouraged.

- NTFS operating systems should not be installed on **compressed drives** that were not compressed by using the NTFS compression utility.

- You must install the operating systems in a specific order: MS-DOS, Windows 95, Windows 98, Windows Me, Windows NT, Windows 2000, and then Windows XP.

- If you are using Windows NT 4.0, apply Service Pack 5 or later. Windows automatically updates all NTFS partitions to the version of NTFS used in Windows 2000 and Windows XP. This resolves most file access problems among NTFS partitions.

- Multiple boot computers cannot be configured for Windows 95, Windows 98, and Windows Me; these operating systems all use the same boot file.

As with troubleshooting any problem you will encounter, there are plenty of articles available from the Knowledge Base, TechNet, the Windows XP Expert Zone, and various newsgroups. When faced with a problem with file access and multiple boot computers, access these sites and resources.

Real World **Better Solutions than Multiple Boot**

Although the ability to boot into various operating systems sounds like a good idea, making it work can be complicated, and the level of complication grows with the more operating systems you intend to run. The following are some alternative solutions to using a multiple boot computer:

- If you intend to keep a previous operating system to support older applications, do yourself a big favor and find out whether you can run those applications directly under Windows XP.

- If you intend to keep a previous operating system because it is configured the way you want it and you hate to give that up, consider that you will have to spend significant amounts of time getting applications to run in a multiple boot environment, and you will likely spend time getting Windows XP set up the way you like it anyway.

- If you want to be able to boot into multiple operating systems but do not need to share data between the operating systems, consider using a physical switch designed to switch between hard drives (or use an inexpensive removable hard drive tray system). You can install an operating system on each drive without worrying about partitions and file systems, and then boot using the hard drive you want.

- For a good software-based solution, consider using virtualization software such as Microsoft Virtual PC 2004. Virtual PC lets you run multiple, virtual, PC-based operating systems simultaneously on a single computer running Windows XP. For more information, see *http://www.microsoft.com/virtualpc*.

As a DST, you might also consider investing in a product such as Virtual PC for your own use. The ability to quickly start up different operating systems in different configurations and run different versions of software is a great tool when testing solutions for users.

Troubleshooting Permission Problems

Some users might encounter file permission problems when working with multiple boot computers, especially if those computers are also multiuser computers. Users must have the correct permissions to access files and folders and to perform specific tasks on a multiple boot computer. If proper permissions are not assigned to the user or the user's group, she receives a file permission error message, generally in the form of an Access Is Denied message, as shown in Figure 11-3.

Figure 11-3   Access denied messages appear when permissions are not assigned or are not assigned correctly.

When a user encounters access denied messages to a file or a folder, you will be called on to resolve those errors. If the user needs access and the owner of the file wants to grant it, you can offer access by changing the share and NTFS permissions on the file or program in question to include that user by following these steps:

1. Use Windows Explorer to locate the problem folder.

2. Right-click the folder and choose Properties.

3. On the Sharing tab, verify that the folder is shared, and then click Permissions.

4. In the Permissions for the folder dialog box, verify that the user has access to the folder. If the user does not have access, add the user or the user's group by clicking Add and selecting the user or group appropriately. If the user or group is already added, verify that the permissions are configured correctly. Click OK.

5. If NTFS permissions have been applied, select the Security tab. Verify that the user has access to the file or folder. If the user does not have access, add the user or the user's group by clicking Add and selecting the user or group appropriately. If the user or group is already added, verify that the permissions are configured correctly. Click OK.

Users might also receive errors when installing programs. Remember, only users with Standard or Administrator accounts can install programs. To resolve this issue, the user either has to be given additional advanced permissions or be assigned to a different group with the required permissions.

See Also   Chapter 9, "Security and Security Permissions," offers much more information on troubleshooting permissions. The topics covered there can be applied to multiple boot computers. Make sure that you review that chapter with multiple boot computers in mind.

Difficult-to-Diagnose Errors

Access and permissions errors that are hard to diagnose can occur, especially when errors appear and everything seems to be in order, including the user name and password, permissions, and group membership. These errors are best resolved using the Knowledge Base or TechNet.

For instance, Knowledge Base article 810881 discusses how an Access Is Denied message can be issued to the owner of a folder if the original folder was created on an NTFS file system volume by using a previous installation of Windows, and then Windows XP Professional was subsequently installed. The article goes on to state that the error occurs because the **security ID** for the user has changed. Even if the user offers the same user name and password, the security ID no longer matches; thus, the owner of the folder cannot open his or her own folder. (The resolution of this issue requires logging on as an administrator and taking ownership of the folder.)

Additional problems can occur when folders have been moved or if a partition has been reformatted. When you encounter access problems after an upgrade or after modifying a partition, check the Knowledge Base first for answers.

Installing and Accessing Applications

When configuring a multiple boot computer, many users incorrectly assume that they can install a program once under a single operating system and then run the program from any other installed operating system. They might get this idea because *multiuser* computers need to have their applications installed only once, but that is an incorrect assumption about *multiple boot* computers. When users' applications do not work, you will be called on to resolve the problem. For the most part, you will need to reinstall the required programs only on each operating system in which the user requires access.

As you begin installing the applications for each operating system, you might run into compatibility problems. An application that runs well on Windows 98 might not run properly on Windows XP. When this happens, you will need to install the program using program compatibility mode.

> **Note** You do not need to install an application under every operating system on a multiple boot computer. However, you do need to install an application under each operating system in which you want to use the application.

Multiple Installations

When a user complains that an application is not working properly and does not run on a multiple boot computer, verify that the application is installed for the correct operating system. If the user is simply browsing to the application's executable file and trying to run it from another operating system's partition, you have found the problem. To resolve the problem, reboot the computer and install the application on the operating system with which it is to be used.

To determine where a particular program is installed, follow these steps:

1. Locate the program by browsing to it using Windows Explorer, or ask the user from where he or she is accessing the file. You might find that he or she has created shortcuts on the desktop, added the program to the Start menu, or performed other creative tasks.

2. Right-click the icon and select Properties.

3. In the Properties dialog box, select the General tab. In the Location box, note the location of the installed file.

4. If necessary, reinstall the application under the correct operating system.

Using Program Compatibility Mode

When troubleshooting applications on multiple boot computers, you might find that the applications are installed correctly but are still not functioning correctly. If the applications are installed correctly for the operating system, the issue might lie with the program compatibility settings. Program compatibility settings allow older applications to work on newer operating systems, and newer applications to work on older ones.

In Chapter 6, "Installing and Configuring Office Applications," program compatibility mode was discussed in depth, but for the purpose of review, you can configure program compatibility mode settings as follows:

1. Use Windows Explorer to locate the executable file for the application that is not running properly.

2. Right-click the executable file and choose Properties.

3. In the file's Properties dialog box, select the Compatibility tab.

4. Select the Run This Program In Compatibility Mode For check box and, from the available drop-down list, select the appropriate operating system. This is shown in Figure 11-4.

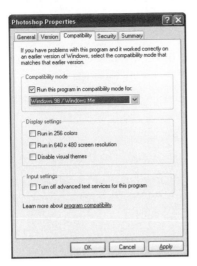

Figure 11-4   Configure compatibility settings from the application's Properties dialog box.

5. If necessary, select any or all of the following check boxes:

   ❑ **Run In 256 Colors**   This setting adjusts the color quality setting to 256 colors while the program is running. When the program is closed, the color quality settings return to the user's defaults.

   ❑ **Run In 640 × 480 Screen Resolution**   This setting adjusts the screen resolution to 640 × 480 while the program is running. When the program is closed, the screen resolution settings return to the user's defaults.

   ❑ **Disable Visual Themes**   This setting prevents visual themes from being applied to the program. This often works to resolve problems with menus or buttons in the program. When the program is closed, the theme setting returns to the user's default.

   ❑ **Turn Off Advanced Text Services For This Program**   This setting turns off any advanced text services while the program is running. When the program is closed, the text settings return to the user's defaults and are available in other programs.

6. Click OK to apply.

Practice: Configure Boot Options on a Multiple Boot Computer

In this practice, you will use the System Properties dialog box to configure the boot options that are displayed on a multiple boot computer.

1. Log on to Windows XP using an account with administrator privileges.

2. From the Start menu, right-click My Computer and select Properties.

3. In the System Properties dialog box, on the Advanced tab, in the Startup And Recovery section, click Settings.

4. In the Startup And Recovery dialog box, in the System Startup section, change the Time To Display List Of Operating Systems to 60 seconds.

5. Click OK to close the Startup And Recovery dialog box. Click OK again to close the System Properties dialog box.

Lesson Review

The following questions are intended to reinforce key information presented in this lesson. If you are unable to answer a question, review the lesson materials and try the question again. You can find answers to the questions in the "Questions and Answers" section at the end of this chapter.

1. A user has a multiple boot computer that is running both Windows 98 and Windows XP. The Windows 98 partition is configured to use FAT32, and the Windows XP partition is configured to use NTFS. The client reports that when running Windows 98, he cannot view files on the Windows XP partition. However, when he is running Windows XP, he can view files on the Windows 98 partition. How can he configure the computer so that he can view all the files no matter what operating system he is running? (Choose the best solution.)

   A. Convert the Windows 98 partition to NTFS using the convert /fs:NTFS command at the command prompt.

   B. Convert the Windows XP partition to FAT32 using the convert /fs:FAT32 command at the command prompt.

   C. Reformat the Windows XP volume so that it uses FAT32.

   D. Reformat and repartition both partitions to use FAT.

2. Which of the following operating systems are capable of recognizing a partition formatted with NTFS?

   A. Windows 95 (original release)

   B. Windows 95 OSR2

   C. Windows NT 4.0

   D. Windows 98

   E. Windows 98 Second Edition

   F. Windows Me

    G. Windows 2000

    H. Windows XP

Lesson Summary

- Windows XP supports three file systems: FAT, FAT32, and NTFS. FAT and FAT32 support is provided for compatibility with older operating systems. NTFS, which is the native file system of Windows XP, provides many advanced features.

- You should configure a partition on a computer running Windows XP with FAT32 only if you will be using a multiple boot configuration with a second operating system that does not recognize NTFS, such as Windows 98 or Windows Me. Otherwise, you should use NTFS.

- Applications must be installed in each operating system that is running on a computer. Installing an application in one operating system does not make it available for other operating systems.

Case Scenario Exercises

Scenario 11.1

A user has a multiple boot computer that has Windows 2000 Professional with Service Pack 3 and Windows XP Professional Edition installed. Windows 2000 Professional is installed on the first partition, Windows XP Professional is installed on the second partition, and both are formatted with NTFS. Office 2003 is installed on the Windows XP partition. The user complains that she encounters problems when running Office 2003 from the Windows 2000 Professional partition. She needs to be able to access and run the program from both partitions. What can you do to solve this problem?

    A. Install Office 2003 on the Windows 2000 Professional partition.

    B. Purchase Microsoft Office 2000 and install it on the Windows 2000 Professional partition. Office 2003 works properly only on computers running Windows XP and later.

    C. Reformat and reinstall the computer, and switch the order of the operating systems. Windows XP Professional should be on the first partition and Windows 2000 Professional on the second.

    D. Run Office 2003 in program compatibility mode for Windows 2000.

Scenario 11.2

A user has a computer with one hard disk partition that has been running Windows 98. He uses third-party software to resize his current partition so that it takes up only half of the hard disk and then creates another primary partition of the same size on the other half of the hard disk. The user installs Windows XP to the new partition by starting the computer using the Windows XP CD-ROM, following the prompts, and selecting the new partition when asked where he wants to install. After Windows XP is installed, the user finds that he can boot into either operating system successfully. He installed his applications under Windows XP and they run fine. He was also able to open documents from the Windows 98 partition while running Windows XP because Windows XP shows both partitions as hard drives in the My Computer window. However, when the user is running Windows 98, the My Computer window shows only one hard drive. The user is unable to see anything on the Windows XP partition. The user must be able to access both partitions from either operating system. What is the solution?

A. The user needs to upgrade from Windows 98 to Windows 98 Second Edition.

B. In Windows 98, the user must use the Disk Management tool to add the Windows XP partition.

C. The user should reformat the Windows XP partition, reinstall Windows XP, and be sure to format the drive using FAT32.

D. The user needs to configure a user account in Windows XP that exactly matches the user account configured in Windows 98.

Troubleshooting Lab

In this lab, you will examine a common problem with file access. If you are unable to answer the question, review the chapter and try the question again. You can find answers to the question in the "Questions and Answers" section at the end of this chapter.

Scenario

A user complains that she cannot access files on a computer that was upgraded from Microsoft Windows NT 4.0 to Windows XP.

All the data for the computer is stored on a separate partition from the operating system. When Windows XP was installed, the data partition was left alone. The user's access problems are occurring for a folder called Client Data located on the root of the data partition.

After doing some research, you find that the problem might be described in Microsoft Knowledge Base article 810881, "'Access is Denied' Error Message When You Try to Open a Folder."

Before you attempt to fix the user's problem, you have decided to try to re-create the folder on your own system to see how you will solve the problem on the user's system. Describe your solution.

_____

_____

_____

_____

_____

_____

Chapter Summary

- When configuring a multiuser computer, configure a user account for each user who will log on to it, and verify that each user has access to the applications installed.
- When troubleshooting multiple boot computers and file and folder access, verify that the file systems used are compatible with the operating systems installed.

Exam Highlights

Before taking the exam, review the key topics and terms that are presented in this chapter. You need to know this information.

Key Points

- In Windows XP, you must have an account with administrator privileges to install applications.
- The only reason to use FAT32 on a system running Windows XP is if the system is also configured to run an operating system that would not be able to interpret NTFS. If a system runs only Windows XP, you should always use the NTFS format.

Key Terms

compressed drive   A drive that has been condensed to take up less space on the hard disk by using a compression tool such as NTFS compression utilities.

disk quotas   A restriction that can be placed on users so that they can only use a pre-defined amount of a hard disk's available space.

partition   A smaller part of a larger hard disk. When a disk is partitioned, it is split into two or more smaller, virtual drives. Partitions can be created to hold data, hold applications, or create a multiple boot computer.

volume   An area of the hard disk used for storing data. See also partition.

Questions and Answers

Lesson 1 Review

Page
11-6

1. A multiuser computer running Windows XP has four user accounts configured for the four users who access the computer. Bob has an Administrator account and is in charge of the computer, John and Mary have standard accounts and access the computer during the day, and Bill has a limited user account and accesses the computer at night. Knowing this, which of the following must also be true? (Choose all that apply.)

   A. The computer is a member of a domain.

   B. The computer is running Windows XP Professional Edition.

   C. All users can change or delete their account passwords.

   D. The computer is running Windows XP Home Edition.

   A, B, and C are the correct answers. A is correct because standard accounts can be configured only on computers running Windows XP Professional that are members of a domain. B is correct because if the computer is a member of a domain, it must be running Windows XP Professional (computers running Windows XP Home Edition cannot join a domain). C is correct because each of these types of users can change or delete their passwords. D is incorrect because Windows XP Home Edition cannot be used to join a domain.

2. A client calls to report that she needs to share her single stand-alone computer with a guest who will be visiting next month. She stresses that the computer contains highly personal documents, files, Internet history, personalization settings, e-mail configuration, and more. Her guest will stay for two weeks and will need access to the computer for e-mailing, creating Microsoft Word documents, working on Microsoft Excel files, and creating Microsoft PowerPoint presentations. The client reports that she has Microsoft Office 2003 Professional Edition installed on the computer. What should you advise the user to do to protect the computer from harmful downloads or program installations by her guest and keep her own documents safe, while still allowing the guest access to the applications on the computer?

   A. Create a limited user account for the guest and install Office 2003 under that account.

   B. Create a standard user account for the user and install Office 2003 to the Shared Documents folder.

   C. Enable the Guest account for the user.

   D. Create a limited user account for the guest and create a local computer policy that does not allow access to the Add Or Remove Programs tool in Control Panel and does not allow downloading of programs.

C is correct. The Guest account allows access to installed applications; at the same time, it allows only limited access by the user. A is incorrect because applications do not need to be reinstalled under each account on a shared computer. B is incorrect because Office 2003 should already be automatically shared, and a standard user account is configured for domains only. D is incorrect because C is the better answer and because a local policy would affect all users on the computer.

Lesson 2 Review

Page
11-18

1. A user has a multiple boot computer that is running both Windows 98 and Windows XP. The Windows 98 partition is configured to use FAT32, and the Windows XP partition is configured to use NTFS. The client reports that when running Windows 98, he cannot view files on the Windows XP partition. However, when he is running Windows XP, he can view files on the Windows 98 partition. How can he configure the computer so that he can view all the files no matter what operating system he is running? (Choose the best solution.)

    A. Convert the Windows 98 partition to NTFS using the convert /fs:NTFS command at the command prompt.

    B. Convert the Windows XP partition to FAT32 using the convert /fs:FAT32 command at the command prompt.

    C. Reformat the Windows XP volume so that it uses FAT32.

    D. Reformat and repartition both partitions to use FAT.

    C is correct. Windows 98 supports only FAT and FAT32, so reformatting and repartitioning the Windows XP partition would make it compatible. A is incorrect because Windows 98 does not support NTFS and does not support this command. B is incorrect because no such command exists, and NTFS cannot be converted to FAT32 without formatting the drive. D is incorrect because, although it would work, it is not the best solution.

2. Which of the following operating systems are capable of recognizing a partition formatted with NTFS?

    A. Windows 95 (original release)

    B. Windows 95 OSR2

    C. Windows NT 4.0

    D. Windows 98

    E. Windows 98 Second Edition

    F. Windows Me

G. Windows 2000

H. Windows XP

C, G, and H are correct. Windows NT, Windows 2000, and Windows XP are capable of using the NTFS file system. They are also capable of using FAT/FAT32. A, B, D, E, and F are incorrect because each of these operating systems is capable of using only FAT or FAT32.

Case Scenario Exercises: Scenario 11.1

Page
11-19

A user has a multiple boot computer that has Windows 2000 Professional with Service Pack 3 and Windows XP Professional Edition installed. Windows 2000 Professional is installed on the first partition, Windows XP Professional is installed on the second partition, and both are formatted with NTFS. Office 2003 is installed on the Windows XP partition. The user complains that she encounters problems when running Office 2003 from the Windows 2000 Professional partition. She needs to be able to access and run the program from both partitions. What can you do to solve this problem?

A. Install Office 2003 on the Windows 2000 Professional partition.

B. Purchase Microsoft Office 2000 and install it on the Windows 2000 Professional partition. Office 2003 works properly only on computers running Windows XP computers and later.

C. Reformat and reinstall the computer, and switch the order of the operating systems. Windows XP Professional should be on the first partition and Windows 2000 Professional on the second.

D. Run Office 2003 in program compatibility mode for Windows 2000.

A is correct. Applications must be installed on all partitions that require access. B is incorrect because Office 2003 is compatible with Windows 2000 Professional, as long as it also has Service Pack 3 installed. C is incorrect; the operating systems were installed correctly, from earliest to latest. D is incorrect because the application would still need to be installed on the Windows 2000 partition.

Case Scenario Exercises: Scenario 11.2

Page
11-20

A user has a computer with one hard disk partition that has been running Windows 98. He uses third-party software to resize his current partition so that it takes up only half of the hard disk and then creates another primary partition of the same size on the other half of the hard disk. The user installs Windows XP to the new partition by starting the computer using the Windows XP CD-ROM, following the prompts, and selecting the new partition when asked where he wants to install. After Windows XP is installed, the user finds that he can boot into either operating system successfully. He installed his applications under Windows XP and they run fine. He was also able to open documents from the Windows 98 partition while running Windows XP because Windows XP shows both partitions as hard drives in the My Computer window.

However, when the user is running Windows 98, the My Computer window shows only one hard drive. The user is unable to see anything on the Windows XP partition. The user must be able to access both partitions from either operating system. What is the solution?

A. The user needs to upgrade from Windows 98 to Windows 98 Second Edition.

B. In Windows 98, the user must use the Disk Management tool to add the Windows XP partition.

C. The user should reformat the Windows XP partition, reinstall Windows XP, and be sure to format the drive using FAT32.

D. The user needs to configure a user account in Windows XP that exactly matches the user account configured in Windows 98.

C is correct. Windows 98 cannot recognize the partition formatted with NTFS. A is not correct because Windows 98 Second Edition also cannot recognize partitions formatted with NTFS. B is not correct because the Disk Management tool is only available in Windows 2000 and Windows XP, and the disk does not need to be added, anyway. D is not correct because user accounts have nothing to do with whether the running operating system can read local files on another partition.

Troubleshooting Lab

Page
11-20
In this lab, you will examine a common problem with file access. If you are unable to answer the question, review the chapter and try the question again. You can find answers to the question in the "Questions and Answers" section at the end of this chapter.

Scenario

A user complains that she cannot access files on a computer that was upgraded from Microsoft Windows NT 4.0 to Windows XP.

All the data for the computer is stored on a separate partition from the operating system. When Windows XP was installed, the data partition was left alone. The user's access problems are occurring for a folder called Client Data located on the root of the data partition.

After doing some research, you find that the problem might be described in Knowledge Base article 810881, "'Access is Denied' Error Message When You Try to Open a Folder."

Before you attempt to fix the user's problem, you have decided to try to re-create the folder on your own system to see how you will solve the problem on the user's system. Describe your solution.

Answer

Create a folder on the root of your C drive and open its Properties dialog box. On the Security tab, click Advanced, and then click the Owner tab. To fix the problem on the user's computer, you will need to reassign the ownership, which is attached to a security ID left over from the previous operating system.

Read Knowledge Base Article 810881, found on the Internet.

12 Resolving Issues with Locally Attached Devices

Exam Objectives in this Chapter:

- Identify and troubleshoot problems with locally attached devices

Why This Chapter Matters

The purpose of this chapter is to teach you to resolve basic end-user calls involving devices that are attached to a computer. The chapter explains the different types of ports on a computer and shows how to troubleshoot basic problems that users of applications might encounter. This chapter also covers handheld devices such as personal digital assistants (PDAs), handheld computers, smart displays, and tablet PCs. Making these connections requires an understanding of the devices themselves, available connection types, and the software required by the devices. Advanced skills include understanding basic input/output system (BIOS) requirements and port requirements and troubleshooting BIOS settings when the connection is not functioning properly.

Lessons in this Chapter:

Before You Begin

Before you begin this chapter, you should have basic familiarity with the Microsoft Windows XP interface. You should also have access to a computer running Windows XP on which you can experiment with changing various settings.

Lesson 1: Understanding Connection Types

As a desktop support technician (DST), you will often be approached by users who are having trouble with devices that are attached to their computer. From an application support standpoint, you may be faced with questions about why a user cannot print a document, scan in an image, or get a handheld device to work. To support locally attached devices, it is important that you first understand how they are attached. This lesson introduces you to the common connection types available on modern computers.

After this lesson, you will be able to

- Identify the common ports available on most computers.
- Explain the use of each port type and identify the peripherals that use the port types.
- Identify common problems associated with each type of port.

Estimated lesson time: 15 minutes

Understanding Ports and Connectors

Every computer has several different types of ports available. Typically, ports are accessed from the back of the computer, although some computers also have ports on the front. These ports offer a place to connect portable devices such as printers, scanners, keyboards, and mice. The following are the six common types of ports that you will work with:

- Serial
- Parallel
- Universal serial bus (USB)
- FireWire (IEEE 1394)
- Infrared Data Association (**IrDA**)
- Wireless

The next several sections discuss each type of port in detail.

Note   Obviously, there are more types of ports than those listed in this section. You are likely to see specialized ports such as network or modem ports for network cables and modems, display ports for monitors, and audio jacks for speakers and other audio devices. However, this section focuses on multifunction ports—those to which different types of devices can be connected.

Serial Port

Almost all computers come with a serial port. Serial ports were, at one time, the primary way in which data was transferred between the computer and its peripheral devices. Today, serial ports are still used to connect some mice and keyboards, but they can also be used to connect older modems, Global Positioning System (GPS) hardware, and musical synchronizers that offered only a serial connection when they were manufactured. A serial port transfers data between devices one **bit** at a time, which is quite slow; thus, serial ports are unlikely candidates for peripherals needing fast transfer rates.

The cables that are used with serial ports vary. When connecting a printer to a serial port, a special type of serial cable called a null modem cable is needed. Special conversion cables can be purchased, too, and these cables can connect a USB device (among other things) to an available serial port.

Many end users who have older computers have only serial ports, and these users must have a way to connect their newer devices to their older computers' serial ports. Because of this, manufacturers have created devices and converters that can connect to these ports for backward compatibility. These devices include (but are not limited to) the following:

- PDAs, Pocket PCs, and other personal organizers
- Synchronization cradles for PDAs and other personal organizers
- Card readers
- Digital converters
- Digitizer tablets
- Serial-to-USB adapters

When troubleshooting a device that connects by using a serial port, always verify that there is not another faster port available. If there is not, verify that the serial port is functional by plugging in another device (such as a mouse), that the connection to and from the peripheral and the computer is solid, and that the cable that connects the two is not worn or damaged.

Exam Tip   If you are working with a computer that has older serial-based devices such as modems, a common problem is that different serial devices may be configured to use the same system resources (resources such as interrupt request, or IRQ, numbers). If a mouse or modem is not recognized by Windows, or if the mouse pointer behaves erratically when using a modem, use the Input Devices And Modem troubleshooters available in the Help and Support Center.

Parallel Port

Almost all computers come with a parallel port. Parallel ports have 25 pins and may be referred to as parallel ports or Centronics ports (after the company that designed the original specification). You most often use parallel ports to connect print devices, and they are common ports for connecting print servers. You can also use parallel ports to connect Zip drives, but you probably will not find many PDAs or similar devices connected there. Parallel ports send data one **byte** at a time.

USB Port

Almost all newer computers come with two or more USB ports. USB 1.1, which supports 12–Mbps data transfer, is used to connect a myriad of devices. USB 2.0, which supports transfer rates up to 480 Mbps, is quickly becoming standard equipment on all new computers. Connecting a USB 2.0 device to a USB 1.1 port will generally produce problems and create error messages, but it also slows the transfer rate down to USB 1.1 levels. Devices can include printers, scanners, flash drives, external drives, digital cameras, PDAs, and handheld devices.

You can also use USB ports to connect these PDA peripherals:

- Synchronization kits
- Charger kits
- Cradles
- Adapter cables

When you troubleshoot a device that connects by using a USB port, always verify that there is not another, faster port available such as FireWire. If there is not, verify that the port is functional by plugging in another device (such as a printer, scanner, or flash drive), ensure that the connection to and from the peripheral and the computer is solid, and verify that the cable that connects the two is not worn or damaged.

FireWire Port

Many newer media centers and high-end computers now come with FireWire ports (often called IEEE 1394 ports, after the Institute of Electrical and Electronics Engineers standard that defines the technology). FireWire can transfer data at a rate of 400 Mbps or 800 Mbps. FireWire is used mainly for video transfer from digital movie cameras, but it will soon become a popular option for newer PDAs and handhelds, including cradles, chargers, and synchronizers.

When troubleshooting a device that connects by using a FireWire port, always verify that the port is functional by plugging in another device (such as a digital camera), ensure that the connection to and from the peripheral and the computer is solid, and verify that the cable that connects the two is not worn or damaged.

IrDA Ports

Many newer media centers and high-end computers now come with IrDA ports. IrDA is another type of port used to transfer data between devices. IrDA data transfer requires a clear line of sight between devices and that the devices should be in close proximity to each other. IrDA ports are found on many devices, including the following:

- Media centers
- PDAs, handhelds, and portable computers
- Printers
- Digital cameras
- Other devices that connect and share information and data

When you troubleshoot a device that connects by using an IrDA port, always verify that the port is functional and that it is transmitting and receiving data, that the connection to and from the peripheral and the computer is within the required proximity, and that the two devices have a clear line of sight. You might also need to verify that the connection is enabled by using the Network Connections window.

Wireless Access Points

Wireless local area networking is a technology that allows computers and other network devices (such as smart displays, PDAs, and handheld computers) to transfer data without cables or wires. A wireless access point is a device that allows users to connect to a network by using a wireless networking card that is installed in their computing device. The wireless access point functions as a bridge between wireless devices and allows those devices to communicate. Depending on the environment, one access point can offer up to 300 feet of wireless coverage.

Many devices have wireless networking cards and can communicate with a wireless access point, including the following:

- Media centers
- Smart displays
- Laptops
- Handheld computers, PDAs, and Tablet PCs
- Printers

When you troubleshoot devices that use a wireless access point, verify that the connection is enabled and functioning by using Network Connections, ping the access point's Internet Protocol (IP) address, verify the signal strength by hovering over the network connection icon in the notification area, try changing channels if applicable, ensure that the clients are in the required range, and verify that connectivity (if any exists to another network) is connected securely and properly.

Troubleshooting Ports and Connections

Every type of external device that is connected to your computer, from printers to scanners to digital cameras, is either connected to a port by a cable or connected wirelessly. When you troubleshoot locally attached devices, you must be able to isolate the problem before you can propose a solution. The following list shows some of the problems that can prevent a device from working properly within an application:

- The application is not properly configured to use the device. If a device seems to be working but is not providing the results that a user expects, the problem may well be in the application settings, not with the device itself. For example, a user might print a document from Microsoft Word and complain that certain parts of the document do not print (such as reviewer comments). In this case, you would need to configure Word to print comments.

- The device is connected and functions but is not properly configured in Windows. You can use Device Manager (from the Start menu, right-click My Computer and choose Properties, click the Hardware tab, and then click Device Manager) to determine whether a device is enabled in Windows XP, has drivers installed, and is working properly. For more information on using Device Manager, see Microsoft Knowledge Base article 314747.

- The device does not have a proper driver or other software installed. Without a driver installed, Windows cannot interact with a device. Windows XP ships with a large number of hardware drivers but may not have built-in drivers for hardware that was shipped after the release of Windows XP.

- The device is not turned on.

- The device is not properly connected to the computer, or the cable used for the connection is damaged.

- The device itself is malfunctioning.

The Windows XP Help and Support Center offers a number of troubleshooters that can help you isolate and resolve issues with connected devices. You can also work through the troubleshooters yourself to learn a lot about the process of troubleshooting connected devices. You can access a list of troubleshooters using the following steps:

1. From the Start menu, select Help And Support.

2. In the Help And Support Center window, select Fixing A Problem.

3. In the Fixing A Problem list on the left side of the window, select Troubleshooting Problems.

4. In the Troubleshooting Problems list on the right side of the page, select List Of Troubleshooters.

Exam Tip   When you come across a device that is not working as expected, start troubleshooting from the highest interface level (the application) and work your way to the lowest level (the device itself). Check application configuration, then Windows configuration, then the device driver or other software, then the port, then the cable, and then the device.

Real World   Configuring the Computer's BIOS

A computer's BIOS is built-in software that contains the code that is required to boot the computer and control the keyboard, display, disk drives, and serial communications on a computer. The BIOS is stored on a chip that is connected to the computer's motherboard, so it is not affected by disk drive failures.

Some products (often printers or imaging devices) require that specific ports be configured in the BIOS before the products can be used. Generally, configuring the BIOS involves booting the computer and pressing DEL or F1, F2, F3, or another function key before the operating system has started. The documentation that comes with the device will have specific directions if configuring these ports is required.

The BIOS also allows you to configure the hardware settings for both serial and parallel ports (the base I/O address and interrupt) in the BIOS setup utility. You can enable or disable bidirectional communication, Enhanced Capabilities Port (ECP), and Enhanced Parallel Port (EPP) for the parallel port, or enable or disable serial and parallel ports altogether. When troubleshooting devices that use serial or parallel connections, make sure that you verify that the ports are enabled in the BIOS.

Practice: Configure Ports

In this practice, you will change the port speed of a serial port. You will also disable and then re-enable a parallel port.

Exercise 1: Change the Port Speed on a Serial Port

1. Log on to Windows XP using an account with administrator privileges.

2. From the Start menu, select Control Panel.

3. In Control Panel, select Performance And Maintenance.

4. In the Performance And Maintenance window, select System.

5. On the Hardware tab, select Device Manager.

6. Expand Ports (COM & LPT), right-click Communications Port (COM1) and choose Properties, and then select the Port Settings tab.

7. On the Bits Per Second drop-down list, choose 128000.

8. Click OK and close all the open dialog boxes.

Exercise 2: Disable and Re-enable a Parallel Port

1. Log on to Windows XP using an account with administrator privileges.

2. From the Start menu, select Control Panel.

3. In Control Panel, select Performance And Maintenance.

4. In the Performance And Maintenance window, select System.

5. On the Hardware tab, select Device Manager.

6. Expand Ports (COM & LPT), right-click Printer Port (LPT1), and choose Properties.

7. On the General tab of the Printer Port (LPT1) Properties dialog box, in the Device Usage drop-down list, select Do Not Use This Device (Disable). Click OK.

8. In the Device Manager window, note that the icon for Printer Port (LPT1) has a red X on it, indicating that the device is disabled. Right-click Printer Port (LPT1) and choose Properties.

9. On the General tab of the Printer Port (LPT1) Properties dialog box, in the Device Usage drop-down list, select Use This Device (Enable). Click OK.

10. Close all open dialog boxes.

Lesson Review

The following question is intended to reinforce key information presented in this lesson. If you are unable to answer the question, review the lesson materials and try the question again. You can find answers to the question in the "Questions and Answers" section at the end of this chapter.

1. For each of the connection types listed, match its name on the left with its description on the right.

1. Serial	A. Sends data at 12 Mbps
2. Parallel	B. Sends data one bit at a time
3. USB 1.1	C. Sends data at 400 Mbps or 800 Mbps
4. FireWire	D. Can transmit data between wireless devices up to 300 feet apart
5. Wireless access point	E. Sends data one byte at a time

Lesson Summary

- Common port types that are available on most computers include serial, parallel, USB, FireWire, IrDA, and wireless.

- When you troubleshoot connections, ensure that the device is enabled and listed as working properly in Device Manager. If the device is enabled, the problem is most likely with the application. If the device is not listed as working properly in Device Manager, make sure that the device is turned on, that the port is configured properly, and that the cable is in working order. You can also use the Windows troubleshooters to help isolate the problem.

Lesson 2: Resolving Issues with Handheld Devices

In this lesson, you learn about the different types of handheld devices that you will encounter as a tier 1 DST. You should make a point to become familiar with handheld devices because you will be called on to connect them for end users or to troubleshoot existing connections.

Although there are different brands and types of peripheral devices, this chapter generically introduces the four main types of handheld devices that you are likely to encounter:

- Simple pocket organizers that generally do not connect to the computer

- PDAs, handheld computers, and Pocket PCs that combine computing, Internet access, telephone, fax, and networking features

- Smart displays that act as mobile monitors for existing computers

- Tablet PCs that are an extension of the notebook computer

> **After this lesson, you will be able to**
> - Identify the types of handheld devices.
> - Troubleshoot basic problems with handheld devices.
>
> **Estimated lesson time: 15 minutes**

Understanding Personal Digital Assistants

PDAs are extensions of the earliest personal organizers. They are also referred to as digital organizers, digital assistants, handheld computers, and Pocket PCs, and they offer features that were included with the earliest electronic handheld devices. Microsoft Pocket PC 2002 used a special operating system called Windows CE, which is a scaled-down version of its full operating system; Microsoft Windows Mobile 2003 software for Pocket PC is an upgrade to the Pocket PC platform.

PDAs generally include a calculator, notepad, and address book. They now also include other features such as e-mail and Internet access, a way to organize contacts, a task list, a memo pad, and a calendar for keeping track of appointments. They usually consist of a touch screen with handwriting-recognition capabilities, a processor and memory, and an operating system. PDAs can synchronize with desktop computers so that the information on both is always coordinated.

Users can add various applications to their PDAs, including the following:

- Streets and maps software

- Picture applications such as slide show software or photo editing software

- Database software

- Organizational software

- Language translation, currency converter, encyclopedia, dictionary, and thesaurus software

- Financial software

- Game software

For the most part, your job will consist of connecting these devices to a user's desktop computer, but that might extend to troubleshooting the device itself. Because this might be the case, you should become familiar with the most popular PDAs, the software that is used on them, and the ways they are used in your workplace.

Smart Displays

A smart display is an additional monitor that connects wirelessly to a user's desktop PC and allows a user to access his or her computer running Windows XP Professional (not Windows XP Home Edition) from anywhere in the home or office as long as the user is within a specified distance (usually about 100 feet). The smart display remotely displays the computer desktop, and the user can work while sitting on the couch, on the back porch, or from another office. This peripheral device allows a user to do any task remotely that can be done at the computer.

Smart displays work by connecting to the computer by using an **802.11b wireless connection**. The user uses a stylus to access the touch-sensitive screen and has available an on-screen keyboard. The smart display offers handwriting recognition and support for wireless mice and keyboards. Smart displays do not have an operating system installed; they simply provide remote access to a user's desktop computer.

Tablet PCs

Tablet PCs are powerful handheld computers that use a specialized version of the Microsoft Windows XP operating system called Windows XP Tablet PC Edition. Tablet PCs support handwriting recognition and can wirelessly share information with other computer users. With a Tablet PC, a user writes directly on the screen and notes are saved in his or her own handwriting, which can then be converted easily to text. Tablet PCs also offer the following features:

- The capability to work from anywhere, as with a laptop, except the Tablet PC is about the size of a legal pad

- Full computing capabilities, including available applications for word processing, database and spreadsheet work, graphic editing, and more

- Encryption, access control, and secure logon as with Windows XP Professional
- The capability to plug in keyboards and other peripherals
- Wireless connection to the Internet for e-mail, Web access, and more

Installing Software for Handheld Devices

As with any type of hardware, handheld devices require a working port of some type, as detailed in the previous lesson. In addition to connecting the hardware to the required port, a user might need help performing an initial setup when she connects the PDA to the computer for the first time. Generally, this consists of installing the client software, connecting the synchronization cradle, and doing an initial synchronization with the PDA. Because manufacturers differ, refer to the documentation that came with the hardware itself, or visit the manufacturer's website.

Note   Always verify that the software is compatible with Windows XP before installing. If the software does not list the operating system, visit the manufacturer's website. Also, many manufacturers of handheld devices have explicit instructions for connecting and configuring their devices, and these instructions often contradict the general instructions for attaching peripheral devices in Windows XP. Always check the manufacturer's setup instructions for any installation idiosyncrasies.

Troubleshooting Handheld Devices

Connectivity and synchronization generally occur between the PDA and the desktop PC by using a synchronization cradle, which is a docking station that stays connected to the computer. When troubleshooting these types of devices, check this connection first. For the most part, you connect these devices using the serial and USB ports. The user should be able to place the PDA in the cradle and establish a connection either automatically or by pressing a button on the cradle, so if this does not happen, check the connections. If hardware is not the issue, check the software. Make sure that it was installed properly, and if necessary, reinstall it. Also, verify that the connection speeds on the PDA and the port that is on the computer match. Finally, verify that the port is functional by connecting a device that is known to be functional and Plug and Play–compatible, like a flash drive or mouse.

Lesson Review

The following questions are intended to reinforce key information presented in this lesson. If you are unable to answer a question, review the lesson materials and try the question again. You can find answers to the questions in the "Questions and Answers" section at the end of this chapter.

1. For each of the items listed, match its name on the left with its description on the right.

1. PDA	A. The operating system used on the Pocket PC 2002 handheld computer.
2. Windows CE	B. A variation of the notebook computer on which a stylus is used to write on an LCD screen, and on which that handwriting is analyzed by the computer and stored as data. It has its own operating system and is a full-fledged computer.
3. Smart display	C. A handheld device that offers telephone and fax capabilities, Internet and e-mail access, and networking features. It can also have a Web browser and offer handwriting-recognition capabilities.
4. Tablet PC	D. A wireless handheld device that acts as an extension of the user's computer desktop, which allows the user to access the computer remotely when within a specified range.

2. A user has a new computer running Windows XP Home Edition and has recently purchased a smart display. The user cannot set up the device. Why?

   A. Smart displays require Windows XP Professional.

   B. The user has not installed the accompanying software.

   C. The smart display, the computer, and the wireless network adapter are not in a clear line of sight.

   D. The smart display is defective.

3. A user reports that she has owned the same Pocket PC for more than a year and that she has been using the same computer, cradle, synchronization software, and additional components without any problems. She recently returned to the office after a week away and reports that she cannot get her PDA and computer to connect. She reports that the PDA works fine and that she could connect to and synchronize with her laptop without problems while she was traveling. Which of the following is most likely the cause of this problem?

A. There is no data to synchronize.

B. The BIOS on the desktop computer needs to be updated.

C. The desktop computer needs to have its synchronization software updated.

D. The cradle or cable that connects the PDA to the desktop computer is not connected properly.

Lesson Summary

- Mobile and handheld devices vary in functionality and purpose. Some mobile devices act as remote terminals, some act as movable displays, and some hold data.

- Mobile and handheld devices connect to computers in a variety of ways, including wireless connections, by using a USB or FireWire port, or by slower methods such as a serial port.

- Connecting a handheld or mobile device to the computer requires that the proper port be available, and the BIOS must offer the required support. Software must be installed so the computer and the peripheral device can communicate.

Case Scenario Exercises

Scenario 12.1

John needs to purchase a handheld device so that he can make and track appointments while on the road, send e-mail to contacts and access the Internet, organize contacts, create a task list, and create a screen saver using pictures he has taken of his kids. He must also be able to synchronize the contact and appointment data with his desktop computer when he returns to the office. He does not need to have Microsoft Office applications installed. His desktop computer runs Windows XP Professional and has one available USB port. He wants to find something that is fairly inexpensive. What type of mobile device should he purchase?

A. Smart display

B. Tablet PC

C. PDA

D. Electronic organizer

Scenario 12.2

You are in charge of deciding what type of mobile device to purchase for the employees in your surveying department. They need to have the ability to send e-mail and connect to the office over the Internet, run corporate applications, and connect to the company's wireless network when at the office. This handheld device should also offer handwriting-recognition capabilities, secure logon to the company network, and the capability to encrypt sensitive data. What type of device should you purchase and why?

Troubleshooting Lab

In this lab, you will work within Device Manager to familiarize yourself with the devices that are attached to your own computer. Open Device Manager by following these steps:

1. Log on to Windows XP using an account with administrator privileges.
2. From the Start menu, select Control Panel.
3. In Control Panel, select Performance And Maintenance.
4. In the Performance And Maintenance window, select System.
5. On the Hardware tab, select Device Manager.

Using Device Manager, answer the following questions about your own computer.

1. What are the issue date and version of the drivers used for your mouse?

---

2. Which of the following types of ports does your computer have installed: serial, parallel, FireWire, USB? How are these ports listed in Device Manager?

---

3. How is your printer port configured to manage interrupts?

_____

_____

_____

Chapter Summary

- Common port types available on most computers include serial, parallel, USB, FireWire, IrDA, and wireless.

- When you troubleshoot connections, ensure that the device is enabled and listed as working properly in Device Manager. If Device Manager shows that the device is enabled and is working, the problem is most likely in the application. If the device is not listed as working properly when you view it in Device Manager, ensure that the device is turned on, that the port is configured properly, and that the cable is in working order. You can also use the Windows troubleshooters to help isolate the problem.

- Mobile and handheld devices vary in functionality and purpose. Some mobile devices act as remote terminals, some act as movable displays, and some simply hold data.

- Mobile and handheld devices connect to computers in a variety of ways, including wirelessly, by using a USB or FireWire port, or by slower methods such as a serial port.

- Connecting a handheld or mobile device to the computer requires the proper port to be available, and the BIOS must offer the required support. Software must be installed so the computer and the peripheral device can communicate.

Exam Highlights

Before taking the exam, review the key topics and terms that are presented in this chapter. You need to know this information.

Key Points

- If you are working with a computer that has older serial-based devices such as modems, a common problem is that different serial devices may be configured to use the same system resources (resources such as IRQ numbers). If a mouse or modem is not recognized by Windows, or if the mouse pointer behaves erratically when using a modem, use the Input Devices and Modem troubleshooters available in the Help and Support Center.

■ When faced with a device that is not working as expected, start troubleshooting from the highest interface level (the application) and work your way to the lowest level (the device itself). Check application configuration, then Windows configuration, then the device driver or other software, then the port, then the cable, and then the device.

Key Terms

802.11b wireless connection An industry standard for communicating through a wireless network. These network connections support a maximum bandwidth of 11 Mbps.

basic input/output system (BIOS) A computer's BIOS program determines in what order the computer searches for system files on boot up, manages communication between the operating system and the attached devices on boot up, and is an integral part of the computer.

IrDA Short for Infrared Data Association, a type of port installed on newer computers, printers, and other devices that allows them to communicate wirelessly. IrDA ports transmit data at about the same rate as a parallel port does, and the devices must be in close proximity and have a clear line of sight between them.

Questions and Answers

Lesson 1 Review

Page
12-9

1. For each of the connection types listed, match its name on the left with its description on the right.

1. Serial	A. Sends data at 12 Mbps
2. Parallel	B. Sends data one bit at a time
3. USB 1.1	C. Sends data at 400 Mbps or 800 Mbps
4. FireWire	D. Can transmit data between wireless devices up to 300 feet apart
5. Wireless access point	E. Sends data one byte at a time

1-B. 2-E. 3-A. 4-C. 5-D.

Lesson 2 Review

Page
12-13

1. For each of the items listed, match its name on the left with its description on the right.

1. PDA	A. The operating system used on the Pocket PC 2002 handheld computer.
2. Windows CE	B. A variation of the notebook computer on which a stylus is used to write on an LCD screen, and on which that handwriting is analyzed by the computer and stored as data. It has its own operating system and is a full-fledged computer.
3. Smart display	C. A handheld device that offers telephone and fax capabilities, Internet and e-mail access, and networking features. It can also have a Web browser and offer handwriting-recognition capabilities.
4. Tablet PC	D. A wireless handheld device that acts as an extension of the user's computer desktop, which allows the user to access the computer remotely when within a specified range.

1-C. 2-A. 3-D. 4-B.

2. A user has a new computer running Windows XP Home Edition and has recently purchased a smart display. The user cannot set up the device. Why?

A. Smart displays require Windows XP Professional.

B. The user has not installed the accompanying software.

C. The smart display, the computer, and the wireless network adapter are not in a clear line of sight.

D. The smart display is defective.

A is correct: Smart displays are supported only by Windows XP Professional. B is incorrect because accompanying software is not necessary. C is incorrect because smart displays do not have to be in direct line of sight of the wireless access point. D is incorrect because the smart display cannot be determined to be defective if it cannot be installed.

3. A user reports that she has owned the same Pocket PC for more than a year and that she has been using the same computer, cradle, synchronization software, and additional components without any problems. She recently returned to the office after a week away and reports that she cannot get her PDA and computer to connect. She reports that the PDA works fine and that she could connect to and synchronize with her laptop without problems while she was traveling. Which of the following is most likely the cause of this problem?

A. There is no data to synchronize.

B. The BIOS on the desktop computer needs to be updated.

C. The desktop computer needs to have its synchronization software updated.

D. The cradle or cable that connects the PDA to the desktop computer is not connected properly.

D is the correct answer. Because the PDA works fine with the laptop, and the desktop computer sat idle for a week, physical connectivity is likely the problem. The cable that connects the two devices has probably become disconnected. A is incorrect because the connection should be made even if there is no data to synchronize. B is incorrect because the PDA and the computer were working fine earlier, indicating that the BIOS is fine. C is incorrect for the same reason.

Case Scenario Exercises

Case Scenario Exercises: Scenario 12.1

Page 12-14 John needs to purchase a handheld device so that he can make and track appointments while on the road, send e-mail to contacts and access the Internet, organize contacts, create a task list, and create a screen saver using pictures he has taken of his kids. He must also be able to synchronize the contact and appointment data with his desktop computer when he returns to the office. He does not need to have Microsoft Office applications installed. His desktop computer runs Windows XP Professional and has one available USB port. He wants to find something that is fairly inexpensive. What type of mobile device should he purchase?

A. Smart display

B. Tablet PC

C. PDA

D. Electronic organizer

C is correct. A PDA offers all of these options and is the best choice. A is incorrect because smart displays simply extend the monitor of a computer and do not provide any computing capabilities on their own. B is incorrect because Tablet PCs are much more expensive than PDAs. D is incorrect because electronic organizers do not provide the capabilities needed.

Case Scenario Exercises: Scenario 12.2

Page 12-15 You are in charge of deciding what type of mobile device to purchase for the employees in your surveying department. They need to have the ability to send e-mail and connect to the office over the Internet, run corporate applications, and connect to the company's wireless network when at the office. This handheld device should also offer handwriting-recognition capabilities, secure logon to the company network, and the capability to encrypt sensitive data. What type of device should you purchase and why?

The correct answer is a Tablet PC. Tablet PCs offer all these things plus the necessary security components. Of all the devices outlined in this chapter, only the Tablet PC offers the capability to encrypt sensitive data and allow for secure network logons.

Troubleshooting Lab

Page 12-15 Using Device Manager, answer the following questions about your own computer.

1. What are the issue date and version of the drivers used for your mouse?

   In Device Manager, expand Mice And Other Pointing Devices, right-click the mouse, and select Properties. Look for the information on the Driver tab.

2. Which of the following types of ports does your computer have installed: serial, parallel, FireWire, USB? How are these ports listed in Device Manager?

   Serial and parallel ports are both listed under the Ports (COM & LPT) category. Serial ports are listed as communications ports, and parallel ports are listed as printer ports. FireWire ports have their own top-level category in Device Manager. Depending on your device, the ports may be listed as FireWire Controllers or as IEEE 1394 Bus Host Controllers. USB ports are listed as Universal Serial Bus Controllers.

3. How is your printer port configured to manage interrupts?

   In Device Manager, expand Ports (COM & LPT), right-click Printer Port (LPT1), and select Properties. Look for the information on the Port Settings tab in the Filter Resource Method section.

Part 2
Prepare for the Exam

13 Configuring and Troubleshooting Applications (1.0)

The Configuring and Troubleshooting Applications objective domain focuses on the configuration and troubleshooting of four main areas: Microsoft Office applications, Microsoft Internet Explorer, Microsoft Outlook Express, and the Microsoft Windows XP operating system. Windows XP provides a rich set of features for installing and configuring applications, as well as for working with them on a daily basis.

As a desktop support technician (DST), you must understand how to install Microsoft Office 2003 to suit user needs. You must be able to configure and troubleshoot each of the primary applications in Office, including Microsoft Word, Microsoft Excel, and Microsoft PowerPoint. In addition, you should be able to set up and troubleshoot various types of e-mail accounts in both Microsoft Outlook and Outlook Express. You should also be able to configure and troubleshoot Internet Explorer, and understand how Service Pack 2 changes the behavior of Internet Explorer.

Within the Windows XP operating system, you should be able to configure the desktop, Start menu, and taskbar to provide an environment suitable for users' needs when running applications. You should also be able to troubleshoot these operating system features when problems occur. Finally, you should understand how to configure compatibility in Windows XP for older applications.

Tested Skills and Suggested Practices

The skills that you need to successfully master the Configuring and Troubleshooting Applications objective domain on the Supporting Users and Troubleshooting Desktop Applications on a Microsoft Windows XP Operating System exam include:

- Configuring and troubleshooting Office applications.
  - ❏ Practice 1: Install Office 2003.
  - ❏ Practice 2: Install an older application using the Program Compatibility Wizard in Windows XP.
  - ❏ Practice 3: Configure Post Office Protocol version 3 (POP3) and Internet Message Access Protocol version 4 (IMAP4) accounts in Outlook.

- Configuring and troubleshooting Internet Explorer.

  ❑ Practice 1: Change the current home page in Internet Explorer. Also, spend time working with the available toolbars. Customize the Standard toolbar by changing the buttons that appear.

  ❑ Practice 2: Change how much disk space can be used by Internet Explorer to save temporary files.

  ❑ Practice 3: Change the security level for the Internet zone in Internet Explorer and note the differences in the available security levels.

  ❑ Practice 4: Change the privacy level in Internet Explorer and note the differences in the available privacy levels.

  ❑ Practice 5: Create a profile using Internet Explorer's Profile Assistant to store personal information.

- Configuring and troubleshooting Outlook Express.

  ❑ Practice 1: Set up POP3 and IMAP4 e-mail accounts in Outlook Express.

  ❑ Practice 2: Configure an account so that copies of e-mail messages are left on a server.

  ❑ Practice 3: Configure Outlook Express so that it does not play a sound when new messages arrive.

  ❑ Practice 4: Change the Outlook Express layout so that the Preview pane is shown to the right of the message pane and the Outlook Bar is displayed.

  ❑ Practice 5: Download an HTML e-mail with embedded pictures. Note that Outlook Express does not display the embedded images by default.

  ❑ Practice 6: Open Outlook Express options, and examine each setting on every tab. If you do not understand an option, refer to the Outlook Express help files.

- Configuring the operating system to support applications.

  ❑ Practice 1: Add a shortcut for a folder to the All Programs menu on the Start menu. Pin the shortcut to the Start menu.

  ❑ Practice 2: Clear the recently used program list on the Start menu and configure it so that the eight most recently used programs are displayed.

  ❑ Practice 3: Configure a program to start with Windows by placing it in the Startup folder.

  ❑ Practice 4: Turn on the Quick Launch toolbar and add a shortcut to it.

  ❑ Practice 5: Configure the taskbar so that it appears on the right edge of the display and so that it automatically hides when not in use.

Further Reading

This section lists supplemental readings by objective. Study these sources thoroughly before taking exam 70-272.

Objective 1.1   "Office 2003 Resource Kit." (Available online at *http://www.microsoft.com/office/ork/2003/.*) This site provides a wealth of information for IT professionals about supporting Office 2003, including the full text of the resource kit.

Microsoft Office System Inside Out, 2003 Edition, by Michael J. Young and Michael Halvorson. This book, which is designed for advanced users, includes information on configuring, supporting, and troubleshooting all the Office applications.

"Windows XP Application Compatibility Technologies." (Available online at *http://www.microsoft.com/technet/prodtechnol/winxppro/plan/appcmpxp.mspx.*)

Microsoft Office Outlook 2003 Inside Out, by Jim Boyce. This book, which is designed for advanced users, includes information on configuring, supporting, and troubleshooting Outlook 2003.

Objective 1.2   "Microsoft Internet Explorer 6 Resource Kit." (Available online at *http://www.microsoft.com/resources/documentation/ie/6/all/reskit/en-us/default.mspx.*)

"Description of the Internet Explorer Information Bar in Windows XP SP2," Microsoft Knowledge Base article 843017. (Available online at *http://support.microsoft.com/kb/843017/.*)

"Changes to Functionality in Microsoft Windows XP Service Pack 2, Part 5: Enhanced Browsing Security." (Available online at *http://www.microsoft.com/technet/prodtechnol/winxppro/maintain/sp2brows.mspx.*)

Objective 1.3   "How to Configure Outlook Express for Internet News," Microsoft Knowledge Base article 171164. (Available online at *http://support.microsoft.com/kb/171164/.*)

"How to Configure Outlook Express to Use a Hotmail Account," Microsoft Knowledge Base article 220852. (Available online at *http://support.microsoft.com/kb/220852/.*)

"How to Upgrade from Outlook Express to Outlook 2002 or to Outlook 2003," Microsoft Knowledge Base article 287073. (Available online at *http://support.microsoft.com/kb/287073/.*) This article applies to both Outlook 2002 and Outlook 2003.

"Changes to Functionality in Microsoft Windows XP Service Pack 2, Part 4: E-mail Handling Technologies." (Available online at *http://www.microsoft.com/technet/prodtechnol/winxppro/maintain/sp2email.mspx.*)

Objective 1.4   "Microsoft Windows XP Professional Resource Kit Documentation," by Microsoft Corporation. (Available online at *http://www.microsoft.com/resources/ documentation/Windows/XP/all/reskit/en-us/prork_overview.asp*.) In particular, look through Chapter 5, "Managing Desktops."

"Description of the Microsoft Windows Registry," Microsoft Knowledge Base article 256986. (Available online at *http://support.microsoft.com/kb/256986/*.)

"How To Prevent a Program from Being Displayed in the Most Frequently Used Programs List in Windows XP," Microsoft Knowledge Base article 284198. (Available online at *http://support.microsoft.com/kb/284198/*.)

"How to Change the Behavior of Taskbar Grouping," Microsoft Knowledge Base article 281628. (Available online at *http://support.microsoft.com/kb/281628/*.)

Configure and Troubleshoot Office Applications

As a DST, you should be able to install and support the various applications that make up Office, including Word, Excel, PowerPoint, and Outlook. You should be familiar with how to install, configure, and customize these applications, as well as how to troubleshoot common errors.

To answer the questions in this objective, you should know how to configure the basic options for each of the Office applications, including default save locations and user information. You should also know how to create and manage e-mail accounts using Outlook.

Objective 1.1 Questions

1.   One of your customers has Outlook installed on her home computer. She has also just purchased a notebook computer with Outlook. She has a new job that requires her to travel two weeks out of each month. She needs to be able to check e-mail from both her home and notebook computers, and she wants to read e-mail in Outlook. You explain to her that you can set up a POP3 account on both computers and then configure one of the computers to leave a copy of messages on the server. She does not like this idea because it means she would see duplicate messages in one location. What else can you suggest?

    A.   She can set up Outlook to retrieve messages as an HTTP account.

    B.   She can set up Outlook to retrieve messages as an IMAP account.

    C.   She can set up Outlook to retrieve messages as an SMTP account.

    D.   The proposed solution is the only one that works.

2.   Which of the following are valid minimum hardware requirements for running Office Professional Edition 2003? (Choose all that apply.)

    A.   233-megahertz (MHz) processor

    B.   256 MB of RAM

    C.   400 MB of hard disk space

    D.   Super VGA display (800 × 600 dots per inch, or dpi)

3.   One of your customers has four computers, named Client1, Client2, Client3, and Client4. These computers are running the following operating systems:

Client1: Microsoft Windows 2000 (with Service Pack 1)

Client2: Windows 2000 (with Service Pack 2)

Client3: Windows Millennium Edition (Me)

Client4: Windows XP (Service Pack 1)

On which of these computers does the customer need to install additional service packs or upgrade the operating system before being able to install Office Professional Edition 2003? (Choose all that apply.)

    A.   Client1

    B.   Client2

    C. Client3

    D. Client4

4. Which of the following protocols is used to send messages from a mail client (such as Outlook) to a mail server?

    A. POP3

    B. IMAP

    C. SMTP

    D. HTML

5. You receive a call from a customer who tells you that she is trying to install her son's favorite game, Microsoft Flight Simulator 2000. When she tries to install it, it gives her the following error: "Please insert the correct CD-ROM, select OK, and restart the program." She has inserted the CD, but the error still happens. What is the likely problem?

    A. She needs to right-click the Setup.exe program on the CD and use the program's Properties dialog box to set compatibility options.

    B. She needs to start the installation from the command prompt.

    C. She needs to configure her desktop resolution for 640 × 480 dpi and use a color depth of 256 colors.

    D. She needs to install the program by using the Program Compatibility Wizard.

6. One of your customers has a computer running Windows XP Professional. He tells you that he has several applications that he wants to install, but they are older versions. The customer knows that Windows XP features an application compatibility mode, but he wanted to check with you before installing any of the programs. Which of the following applications should you tell the customer to purchase a new version of rather than installing by using an application compatibility mode?

    A. Two games, belonging to his son, which were designed for Windows 98.

    B. A diagnostics program designed for Windows 2000 that includes disk scanning and defragmenting software.

    C. Antivirus software designed for Windows 2000.

    D. The software that came with a scanner the customer bought when he was using Microsoft Windows Me.

7.   One of your customers has recently upgraded to Office Professional Edition 2003. Now, whenever someone sends him a Word document as an attachment via e-mail and he opens the attachment, the document opens in Word in something called Reading Layout view. The customer has to constantly change the view to Normal, so he wants Word to open documents without using the Reading Layout view. What should you do?

   A. Tell the user to save the attachment to hard disk and then open the Word document.

   B. In Word, on the General tab of the Options dialog box, clear the Allow Starting In Reading Layout check box.

   C. In Word, on the Options tab of the Customize dialog box, clear the Allow Starting In Reading Layout check box.

   D. The customer cannot disable automatic starting in Reading Layout view.

8.   Which of the following applications creates files by default using the .doc extension?

   A. Notepad

   B. Word

   C. Excel

   D. PowerPoint

Objective 1.1 Answers

1.   Correct Answers: B

    A. Incorrect: You can configure Outlook on both of her computers to use IMAP to retrieve messages.

    B. Correct: You can configure Outlook on both of her computers to use IMAP to retrieve messages. The messages are stored on the server and only read and are manipulated using the Outlook interface.

    C. Incorrect: You can configure Outlook on both of her computers to use IMAP to retrieve messages.

    D. Incorrect: You can configure Outlook on both of her computers to use IMAP to retrieve messages.

2.   Correct Answers: A, C, and D

    A. Correct: A 233-MHz processor is the minimum requirement. However, a Pentium III or better processor is recommended.

    B. Incorrect: The minimum required amount of RAM is 128 MB.

    C. Correct: 400 MB of hard disk space is the minimum requirement. However, an additional 290 MB of space is recommended for extra options and an installation files cache.

    D. Correct: Office Professional Edition 2003 requires a Super VGA or higher display.

3.   Correct Answers: A, B, and C

    A. Correct: Office Professional Edition 2003 requires Windows XP or Windows 2000 (with Service Pack 3 or later).

    B. Correct: Office Professional Edition 2003 requires Windows XP or Windows 2000 (with Service Pack 3 or later).

    C. Correct: Office Professional Edition 2003 requires Windows XP or Windows 2000 (with Service Pack 3 or later).

    D. Incorrect: Of the computers listed, only the one running Windows XP is capable of supporting Office Professional Edition 2003.

4.   Correct Answers: C

    A. Incorrect: POP3 is a message retrieval protocol used to download messages from a mail server.

    B. Incorrect: IMAP is a message retrieval protocol used to download messages from a mail server.

    C. Correct: SMTP is used to send e-mail messages. Clients use SMTP to send messages to a mail server. Mail servers also use SMTP to send messages to other mail servers.

    D. Incorrect: HTML is a markup language used to format and display web pages. HTML mail is a browser-based e-mail system.

5.   Correct Answers: D

    A. Incorrect: She cannot set compatibility options in a program on the CD. Also, she needs to configure compatibility for the program that is to be installed, not for the setup program itself.

    B. Incorrect: Starting the installation from the Command Prompt would not be any different than starting the installation from Microsoft Windows Explorer.

    C. Incorrect: Although these settings occasionally help older, graphically-based programs to run, they do not make a difference in letting a setup program recognize the CD-ROM drive.

    D. Correct: The Program Compatibility Wizard lets the user specify the program on the CD and test various compatibility settings.

6.   Correct Answers: B

    A. Incorrect: While there is no guarantee they will work, the games are safe to install using an application compatibility mode.

    B. Correct: You should not use an application compatibility mode to force system tools to work—particularly those that interface with the hard disk or CD-ROM drive.

    C. Incorrect: Unless the software manufacturer specifically states that the product functions with Windows XP, you should not use antivirus software designed for previous versions of Windows.

    D. Incorrect: If the software includes drivers for the scanner, is not likely that the Windows Me drivers will work under Windows XP. However, the software is safe to install. If the scanner does not function, you may need to download drivers written for Windows XP.

7.   Correct Answers: B

    A. Incorrect: This will not solve the user's problem. By default, Word opens some documents in Reading Layout view.

    B. Correct: You can prevent Word from opening documents in Reading Layout view by clearing the Allow Starting In Reading Layout check box on the General tab of the Options dialog box.

    C. Incorrect: The Options tab of the Customize dialog box does not contain the option for preventing Word from starting in Reading Layout view.

    D. Incorrect: You can prevent Word from opening documents in Reading Layout view.

8.   Correct Answers: B

    A. Incorrect: Notepad is used to create .txt files.

    B. Correct: Word documents have the file extension .doc.

    C. Incorrect: Excel documents have the file extension .xls.

    D. Incorrect: PowerPoint documents have the file extension .ppt.

Configure and Troubleshoot Internet Explorer

This objective focuses on configuring connectivity for Internet Explorer, configuring security and privacy settings, and troubleshooting problems within the program. As a DST, you need to understand the different configuration options available in Internet Explorer to support your users effectively. Service Pack 2 changes many aspects of Internet Explorer. You must understand these changes, and know how to configure and troubleshoot Internet Explorer on systems with or without Service Pack 2 installed.

You configure and customize Internet Explorer by using the Internet Options dialog box, which includes a variety of tabs related to specific categories of settings. To answer the questions in this objective, you should know how to configure general Internet Explorer settings, configure security and privacy settings, and resolve connectivity issues.

Objective 1.2 Questions

1.   One of your customers manages a small business office with six computers running Windows XP Professional. She was at a colleague's office lately and noticed that whenever she started Internet Explorer, it opened to a blank Web page. She wants to do this on the computers in her office, too. She also wants to ensure that users cannot change to a different home page. What should you do? (Choose all that apply.)

   A. On the General tab of the Internet Options dialog box, click Use Blank to have Internet Explorer open to a blank home page.

   B. On the General tab of the Internet Options dialog box, configure the settings for Temporary Internet Files so that Internet Explorer never checks for a new version of pages.

   C. Use the Local Security Policy tool to create a local policy enforcing the Disable Changing Home Page Settings option.

   D. Use gpedit.msc to create a policy enforcing the Disable Changing Home Page Settings option.

2.   One of your customers uses a notebook computer running Windows XP Professional. She has a large number of news-related websites that she reads daily. Frequently, she disconnects her notebook computer from the Internet to take it to a more comfortable location. She wants to be able to read her news sites while she is disconnected. How can she configure Internet Explorer to allow her to do this?

   A. Increase the size of the cache for temporary Internet files to its maximum.

   B. Add the sites to her Favorites menu and then use the Organize Favorites dialog box to make the sites available offline.

   C. On the Connections tab of the Internet Options dialog box, use the LAN Settings button to configure offline access to the websites she wants to read.

   D. She cannot configure Internet Explorer in this manner. You should suggest that she set up a wireless connection to the Internet.

3.   One of your customers recently had a nephew stay at his house for the weekend. The nephew used the customer's computer and changed the search engine used by Internet Explorer. The customer wants to change the search engine back but cannot remember what the default was. What should you do?

   A. Use the General tab of the Internet Options dialog box to clear the Internet Explorer history.

    B. Use the Content tab of the Internet Options dialog box to change the AutoComplete information.

    C. On the Programs tab of the Internet Options dialog box, use the Reset Web Settings button.

    D. Reinstall Internet Explorer.

4. One of your customers has enabled Content Advisor on her home computer to protect her child from questionable content on the Internet. However, there are a number of sites with acceptable content that the child cannot access, probably because Content Advisor is not letting Internet Explorer display sites that have not been rated. Your customer wants to let the child view the acceptable sites, yet still maintain control of the sites the child visits. What is the best solution?

    A. Disable Content Advisor and instead set the Privacy setting in Internet Explorer to High.

    B. Configure Content Advisor so that users can see sites that have no rating.

    C. Enter the sites the child needs to access into Content Advisor's list of approved sites.

    D. You cannot configure this by using Content Advisor. The customer should purchase a third-party filtering program.

5. Which of the following privacy settings in Internet Explorer blocks third-party cookies that do not have a compact privacy policy and third-party cookies that use personal information without a user's explicit consent?

    A. Low

    B. Medium

    C. High

    D. Block All Cookies

6. Which of the following types of resources can you view from Internet Explorer without launching a separate application? (Choose all that apply.)

    A. Websites

    B. HTML files stored on the local computer

    C. FTP sites

    D. Telnet sites

7.   One of your customers has recently upgraded his computer from Windows 98 to Windows XP Professional. The computer is connected to the Internet using a cable modem. The upgrade went fine, but the customer noticed that the Web pages he sees in Internet Explorer do not always seem up to date. What do you suspect is the problem?

   A. The temporary Internet files folder is full.

   B. The temporary Internet files settings are not configured to check for newer versions of stored pages.

   C. Internet Explorer is configured to use a dial-up connection instead of a LAN connection.

   D. The network adapter or cable modem is malfunctioning.

8.   One of your customers frequently accesses a financial site using Internet Explorer. The site uses custom controls to allow the user to obtain and chart stock quotes. After upgrading to Windows XP, the customer gets an error message whenever he visits the site. Which of the following solutions can solve the user's problem while keeping him the most secure when visiting other sites?

   A. Use the Security tab of the Internet Options dialog box to place the financial site into the Trusted Sites zone.

   B. Use the Security tab of the Internet Options dialog box to change the settings for the Internet zone to allow custom controls.

   C. Use the Privacy tab of the Internet Options dialog box to set the user's Privacy setting to Medium.

   D. Use the Privacy tab of the Internet Options dialog box to set the user's Privacy setting to Low.

9.   An administrative assistant uses a travel agent's website to book flights for her manager. Unfortunately, she can no longer use the website. When she attempts to access the site, Internet Explorer shows the Information Bar with the message: "Your security settings do not allow ActiveX controls to run on this page. This page may not display correctly. Click here for more options." Recently, the IT department deployed new security settings; however, you have been directed to adjust security settings as necessary so that users can do their jobs. How would you allow the administrative assistant to use the website?

   A. Open Internet Options, and click the Security tab. Click the Internet zone, and then click Custom Level. Change Download Signed ActiveX Controls to Enable.

   B. Open Internet Options, and click the Security tab. Click the Internet zone, and then click Custom Level. Change Download Unsigned ActiveX Controls to Enable.

C. Open Internet Options, and click the Security tab. Click the Local Intranet zone, and then click Custom Level. Change Run ActiveX Controls And Plug-ins to Prompt.

D. Open Internet Options, and click the Security tab. Click the Internet zone, and then click Custom Level. Change Run ActiveX Controls And Plug-ins to Prompt.

Objective 1.2 Answers

1.   Correct Answers: A and D

   A.   Correct: This option causes Internet Explorer to open to a blank page.

   B.   Incorrect: This option prevents Internet Explorer from refreshing any Web pages automatically. It does not cause Internet Explorer to use a blank home page.

   C.   Incorrect: You cannot create software restrictions using the Local Security Policy tool.

   D.   Correct: A group policy enforcing this setting will prevent users from changing their Internet Explorer home page.

2.   Correct Answers: B

   A.   Incorrect: Increasing the temporary Internet files cache does not make sites available while she is disconnected.

   B.   Correct: You can configure any site in your Favorites folder to be available offline. The site is downloaded to a cache on the local hard drive at scheduled times.

   C.   Incorrect: The LAN Settings button is used to configure a connection to the Internet or a network – not to enable offline files.

   D.   Incorrect: Although a wireless connection does provide the customer the access she wants, you can also configure Internet Explorer to make sites available offline.

3.   Correct Answers: C

   A.   Incorrect: Clearing the history from Internet Explorer does not reset the search engine.

   B.   Incorrect: AutoComplete fills in certain forms and text fields automatically. It has nothing to do with the search engine used in Internet Explorer.

   C.   Correct: The Reset Web Settings button lets you reset the home page and/or search engine in Internet Explorer to their default settings.

   D.   Incorrect: You do not need to reinstall Internet Explorer to reset the search engine and home page.

4.   Correct Answers: C

   A.   Incorrect: Privacy settings control what cookies are allowed, and do not prevent access to any sites.

B. Incorrect: Although this choice lets the child access the acceptable sites currently being blocked, it also gives the child access to any questionable sites that have not been rated.

C. Correct: You can create a list of websites that Content Advisor should allow access to, regardless of whether or how they are rated.

D. Incorrect: You can solve this problem by using Content Advisor.

5. **Correct Answers: A**

A. Correct: This setting blocks third-party cookies that do not have a compact privacy policy or that use personally identifiable information without a user's implicit consent.

B. Incorrect: This setting blocks third-party and first-party cookies that do not have a compact privacy policy or that use personally identifiable information without a user's implicit consent.

C. Incorrect: This setting blocks all cookies that do not have a compact privacy policy and all cookies that use personally identifiable information without a user's explicit consent.

D. Incorrect: This setting blocks all cookies, and the existing cookies on the computer cannot be read by the websites that created them.

6. **Correct Answers: A, B, and C**

A. Correct: Internet Explorer is designed to display websites.

B. Correct: Internet Explorer can display local HTML files just as easily as those found on websites.

C. Correct: Internet Explorer does provide a limited FTP interface so that you can access and manipulate files on an FTP site.

D. Incorrect: Internet Explorer does not allow you to access telnet sites. You need a separate telnet client.

7. **Correct Answers: B**

A. Incorrect: A full temporary Internet files folder does not cause this problem.

B. Correct: On the General tab of the Internet Options dialog box, click Settings. On the Settings dialog box that opens, configure Internet Explorer to check for newer versions of pages more often.

C. **Incorrect:** This does not cause the described problem. Instead, it prevents Internet Explorer from accessing the Internet at all.

D. **Incorrect:** This does not cause the described problem. Instead, it prevents Internet Explorer from accessing the Internet at all.

8.   Correct Answers: A

A. **Correct:** Placing the site into the Trusted Sites zone allows the site's custom controls to run on the user's computer. This solution does not affect the security level at other sites.

B. **Incorrect:** Although this solution does allow the user to access the financial site properly, it also allows other sites to install custom controls on the user's computer.

C. **Incorrect:** The Privacy setting controls what types of cookies can be stored on the user's computer, not what types of custom controls can be installed.

D. **Incorrect:** The Privacy setting controls what types of cookies can be stored on the user's computer, not what types of custom controls can be installed.

9.   Correct Answers: D

A. **Incorrect:** Changing this setting would cause Internet Explorer to automatically download signed ActiveX controls. However, the message provided by the Information Bar indicates a different problem: namely, that Internet Explorer has been configured to not run ActiveX controls. Therefore, you must adjust the Run ActiveX Controls And Plug-ins setting.

B. **Incorrect:** Changing this setting would cause Internet Explorer to automatically download unsigned ActiveX controls. However, the message provided by the Information Bar indicates a different problem: namely, that Internet Explorer has been configured to not run ActiveX controls. Therefore, you must adjust the Run ActiveX Controls And Plug-ins setting.

C. **Incorrect:** The Local Intranet zone includes only websites on your organization's internal network. To adjust settings for public websites, you must change security for the Internet zone.

D. **Correct:** If the security level for a zone is set to High, Internet Explorer, by default, will prevent all ActiveX controls from running. To enable users to selectively run ActiveX controls, change the Run ActiveX Controls And Plug-ins from Disabled to Prompt.

Objective 1.3

Configure and Troubleshoot Outlook Express

Outlook Express is e-mail client software that comes with Windows XP, although it is considered part of Internet Explorer. You can configure Outlook Express to access three different e-mail server types: POP3, IMAP, and HTTP servers. In addition to supporting these three types of e-mail servers, Outlook Express also acts as a newsreader client, allowing you to access the wealth of information in online newsgroups.

To answer the questions in this objective, you should know how to set up and test e-mail and news accounts in Outlook Express. You should also understand how to troubleshoot problems that can occur in Outlook Express.

Objective 1.3 Questions

1.   One of your customers works at a small business that has 10 computers running Windows XP. These computers are on a network and are members of the same workgroup. The customer is using Outlook Express configured with a POP3 account to retrieve messages from a mail server at the company's Internet Service Provider. The user complains that whenever she creates a new message and clicks Send, the message is sent right away. She uses Outlook 2003 at home and is used to having messages go to an Outbox when she clicks Send. She wants to set Outlook Express up to behave in this manner. What should you do?

   A. On the General tab of the Options dialog box in Outlook Express, select the Save Copy Of Sent Messages In The Outbox Folder check box.

   B. On the Send tab of the Options dialog box in Outlook Express, clear the Send Messages Immediately check box.

   C. On the General tab of the Options dialog box in Outlook Express, clear the Check For New Messages Every ____ Minutes check box.

   D. This feature is not available in Outlook Express.

2.   Which of the following account types does Outlook Express support for retrieving messages? (Choose all that apply.)

   A. POP3

   B. IMAP

   C. SMTP

   D. HTTP

3.   One of your customers has just purchased a new computer for her home. The computer runs Windows XP Home Edition. She has used the instructions from her ISP to configure Outlook Express to send and receive messages. She wants to copy her address book from her old computer to her new one, but she does not need to copy all the messages from her old computer. She does not have the computers networked and must use a floppy disk for the transfer. What should you tell her? (Choose all that apply.)

   A. On the old computer, in Outlook Express, use the Export Address Book command to export the address book to a comma-separated-values file.

   B. On the old computer, in Outlook Express, use the Export Address Book command to export the address book to an .iaf file.

    C. On the new computer, in Outlook Express, use the Import Address Book command to import the .iaf file.

    D. On the new computer, in Outlook Express, use the Import Address Book command to import the comma-separated-values file.

4. You have a customer who recently decided to give up his rented office and move his business to his home. He has three computers running Windows XP Professional. The computers are networked together using a router attached to a cable modem. The customer uses a hosting company separate from his ISP to host his Web server and mail server. Each of the computers is configured to retrieve messages from a different account on the hosted mail server. When the customer moves his computers to his home, he is forced to change to a different ISP. He hooks the same router up to his new cable modem at home, and hooks his computers up the same way they were connected at the office. The computers can connect to one another on the network, and all three computers can access the Internet. When the customer opens Outlook Express on each computer, Outlook Express can receive messages but returns an error when the customer tries to send messages. This is true on all three computers. What do you suspect is the problem?

    A. The customer needs to use a different router.

    B. The customer needs to change the outgoing mail server configured in Outlook Express.

    C. The customer forgot to notify his separate hosting company that he was moving his computers.

    D. The customer needs to configure his router to allow outgoing messages.

5. One of your customers has a computer at home running Windows XP Home Edition. She also has Office Professional Edition 2003 installed. She recently used Windows Update to upgrade to the latest version of Internet Explorer and Outlook Express and to install Windows XP Service Pack 1. Colleagues often send her Word and Excel documents as attachments to e-mail messages. She has always been able to open these attachments in the past, but following the upgrade, she finds that Outlook Express does not let her open any of these attachments. In fact, Outlook Express does not even show her that attachments are present. What should you do?

    A. On the Security tab of the Options dialog box in Outlook Express, clear the Do Not Allow Attachments To Be Saved Or Opened That Could Potentially Be A Virus check box.

    B. On the Security tab of the Options dialog box in Outlook Express, set the Internet Explorer security zone used to Internet Zone.

    C. Uninstall the latest version of Outlook Express.

    D. Uninstall Windows XP Service Pack 1.

6.   You have a customer who has several accounts configured in Outlook Express for several different e-mail addresses that she uses regularly. However, she wants only one e-mail address to be used to reply to any messages that she sends. Which of the following solutions requires the least effort each time the user sends a message?

   A. On the General tab of each account's Properties dialog box, configure the reply address that she wants to use.

   B. On the General tab of the account for the address she wants to use as a reply address, select the Use This Account For All Replies check box.

   C. On the Send tab of the Options dialog box in Outlook Express, select the account to use as a reply address from the Use This Account For All Replies drop-down list.

   D. There is no built-in way to do this. The customer should add a signature to all outgoing messages that asks recipients to use a specific reply address.

7.   One of your customers has a computer at home that runs Windows XP Home Edition, and the computer has a user account set up for each family member. Until yesterday, all members of the family used Outlook Express for e-mail. Your customer's husband installed Office Professional Edition 2003 on the computer and when he ran Outlook 2003 for the first time, he configured Outlook as the default mail program. Now, Outlook is the default mail program for every user. The customer wants to change the default mail program for all users except her husband back to Outlook Express. What should you do? (Choose all that apply.)

   A. Log in to each of the other users' accounts, and use the Customize Start Menu dialog box to change the e-mail program used.

   B. Log in to each of the other users' accounts, start Internet Explorer, and use the Programs tab of the Internet Options dialog box to select Outlook Express as the e-mail program.

   C. Log in to each of the other users' accounts, start Outlook Express, and use the General tab of the Options dialog box to make Outlook Express the default mail program for that user.

   D. Nothing. There can only be one default mail program for all users.

8.   You have a customer who routinely sends confidential messages. He sends messages in plain text, not HTML, because he communicates with many users of older mail clients. Although he does not want to go through the trouble of setting up encrypted messages, he wants to add a disclaimer to the bottom of every message he sends. What should you do?

   A. In Outlook Express, use the Signatures tab of the Options dialog box to create a signature, and specify that it be added to all outgoing messages.

    B. In Outlook Express, use the Compose tab of the Options dialog box to create mail stationery with the disclaimer at the bottom of the message.

    C. Configure Outlook Express to use Word as its default mail editor, and create an AutoText entry in Word with the text of the disclaimer.

    D. Create a message with the text of the disclaimer and save it as a draft. When the customer creates a message, he should copy the draft message.

9. A customer reports that he configured specific fonts to use when using stationery. However, each time he composes a message (or replies or forwards one), the standard 12-point Courier New font that he configured for composing and reading plain text is used. When he closes the Fonts dialog box, he selects the Always Use My Fonts check box, but he still can only compose e-mail using 12-point Courier New. What is the cause of the problem?

    A. The fonts chosen for new mail, for replying, and for forwarding are not installed on the computer or are corrupt. Reinstall the fonts.

    B. The screen resolution on the computer is set too low to display the proper font.

    C. The customer must send messages using the HTML format.

    D. Outlook Express offers only one font when using stationery.

10. One of your customers uses Outlook Express as her newsreader. Often, Outlook Express presents an error message stating that the connection to the news server has timed out. Your customer spoke to a friend who recommended that she increase the server timeout value. How can you do this?

    A. In Internet Explorer, use the Server Timeouts slider on the Advanced tab of the Internet Options dialog box.

    B. In Outlook Express, use the Server Timeouts slider on the Advanced tab of the news account's Properties dialog box.

    C. In Outlook Express, change the value for the Check For New Messages Every ___ Minutes option on the General tab of the Options dialog box.

    D. In Outlook Express, on the Connection tab of the Options dialog box, adjust the Server Timeouts slider.

11. You recently upgraded a user's computer to Windows XP Service Pack 2. The user complains that many e-mails do not display properly. Specifically, e-mails that contain images do not show the images by default. The user asks you why this is. What do you reply?

    A. Service Pack 2 contains a bug that causes Outlook Express to display HTML e-mail messages incorrectly.

    B. Service Pack 2 improves the performance of Outlook Express by not displaying images.

    C. Service Pack 2 updates Outlook Express to not download images by default in order to reduce the risk of spam and to protect your privacy.

    D. Service Pack 2 reduces the amount of storage space Outlook Express uses. By not downloading images, Outlook Express will not consume as much disk space.

12. A user is extremely concerned that a malicious e-mail might infect his computer with a virus. You explain that Service Pack 2, which is installed on his computer, updates Outlook Express to minimize security risks. However, the user is interested in maximizing the level of security while reading e-mail, even if he has to sacrifice formatting information in messages. What additional configuration can you provide to further improve e-mail security?

    A. Click the Tools menu, and then click Options. Click the Security tab. Deselect the Block Images And Other External Content In HTML E-mail check box.

    B. Click the Tools menu, and then click Options. Click the Security tab. Select Encrypt Contents And Attachments For All Outgoing Messages.

    C. Click the Tools menu, and then click Options. Click the Send tab. Under Mail Sending Format, click Plain Text.

    D. Click the Tools menu, and then click Options. Click the Read tab. Select Read All Messages In Plain Text.

Objective 1.3 Answers

1.   Correct Answers: B

   A. Incorrect: This option does not exist on the General tab of the Options dialog box.

   B. Correct: Clearing this option causes Outlook Express to store messages in the Outbox until a full Send/Receive is performed.

   C. Incorrect: This solution does not achieve the desired result.

   D. Incorrect: This feature is available in Outlook Express.

2.   Correct Answers: A, B, and D

   A. Correct: Outlook supports POP3, IMAP, and HTTP accounts for retrieving messages.

   B. Correct: Outlook supports POP3, IMAP, and HTTP accounts for retrieving messages.

   C. Incorrect: The SMTP protocol is used for sending messages, not retrieving them.

   D. Correct: Outlook supports POP3, IMAP, and HTTP accounts for retrieving messages.

3.   Correct Answers: A and D

   A. Correct: A comma-separated-value file is the easiest way to export and import an address book. Because it is a text file, it should easily fit on a floppy disk.

   B. Incorrect: The .iaf, or Internet Accounts File, is used to export information about mail and news accounts—not address books.

   C. Incorrect: The .iaf, or Internet Accounts File, is used to export information about mail and news accounts—not address books.

   D. Correct: A comma-separated-value file is the easiest way to export and import an address book. Because it is a text file, it should easily fit on a floppy disk.

4.   Correct Answers: B

   A. Incorrect: Because the computers can connect to one another and to the Internet, the router is working.

   B. Correct: The customer most likely had to use the outgoing mail server of the previous ISP because most mail providers do not allow customers to send messages using their servers unless they are connected directly to their system. The customer needs to configure Outlook Express on each computer to use the outgoing mail server of the new ISP.

    C. Incorrect: The hosting company does not need to be notified of the move.

    D. Incorrect: Routers do not block outgoing messages. Also, outgoing messages were successfully sent at the previous location using the same router.

5.   **Correct Answers: A**

    A. Correct: After Service Pack 1 is installed, the Do Not Allow Attachments To Be Saved Or Opened That Could Potentially Be A Virus check box is selected by default. In order to access these types of attachments, the customer must clear this setting. Note that clearing this setting increases the risk of the user accidentally running malicious software, such as a virus.

    B. Incorrect: Changing the security zone setting affects how messages in HTML format are displayed, but does not affect attachments.

    C. Incorrect: This is not necessary.

    D. Incorrect: This is not necessary and does not correct the problem.

6.   **Correct Answers: A**

    A. Correct: For each account, you can specify a reply address that is different from the address for the account itself.

    B. Incorrect: This check box does not exist.

    C. Incorrect: This drop-down list does not exist.

    D. Incorrect: You can set specific reply addresses for accounts in Outlook Express.

7.   **Correct Answers: B and C**

    A. Incorrect: This option controls the e-mail program that appears on the Start menu, but does not make the program the default mail handler.

    B. Correct: You can use the Programs tab of the Internet Options dialog box to configure the default for several Internet programs.

    C. Correct: You can use the Default Messaging Programs section of the General tab to make Outlook Express the default mail and/or news program for the current user.

    D. Incorrect: This is not true; each user can have a separate default mail program.

8.   **Correct Answers: A**

    A. Correct: You can use the Signature feature to add text to all outgoing messages.

    B. Incorrect: Although this method does include the text with outgoing messages, stationery requires that you use messages formatted in HTML, not in plain text.

    C. Incorrect: Outlook Express cannot use Word as its default mail editor (although Outlook 2003 can). Also, using an AutoText entry requires that the user insert the disclaimer manually; it does not happen automatically.

    D. Incorrect: Draft messages cannot be used this way.

9.   **Correct Answers: C**

    A. Incorrect: The customer could not select the font if it were not installed.

    B. Incorrect: The screen resolution has nothing to do with what fonts can be displayed.

    C. Correct: Stationery requires the use of HTML.

    D. Incorrect: You can use any available font when using stationery.

10.   **Correct Answers: B**

    A. Incorrect: You cannot set new server timeout values within Internet Explorer.

    B. Correct: By adjusting the Server Timeouts slider, you can increase the amount of time Outlook Express will wait for a server response.

    C. Incorrect: This value affects how frequently Outlook Express checks for new messages on mail servers.

    D. Incorrect: The Server Timeouts slider is not available on the Connection tab of the Options dialog box.

11.   **Correct Answers: C**

    A. Incorrect: This is not a bug, but rather an intentional security feature designed to improve the user's privacy and to reduce spam.

    B. Incorrect: Although a side-effect of not displaying images is to improve performance slightly and to decrease bandwidth utilization, the primary goal is to improve privacy and to reduce spam.

    C. Correct: Spam messages often have embedded images that the senders use to track who reads their e-mails. By not automatically downloading these embedded images, Outlook Express protects user privacy and can reduce the amount of spam the user receives.

    D. Incorrect: The primary goal of the feature is to improve privacy and reduce spam.

12.   Correct Answers: D

A. Incorrect: Clearing this check box would actually increase security and privacy risks because it causes Outlooks Express to process and display images in inbound e-mail messages.

B. Incorrect: Encryption can be used to improve the confidentiality of outbound e-mail messages. However, it would not reduce the security risks on the user's computer because it does not affect how Outlook Express processes or displays inbound messages.

C. Incorrect: While plain text e-mail does have slightly less security risk than HTML e-mail, changing this setting would only affect outbound e-mail messages. Therefore, it would not improve the security of the user's computer.

D. Correct: Reading all messages in plain text reduces the security risks associated with rendering HTML e-mails. Note that the risks associated with rendering HTML e-mails are not necessarily severe. However, users who are very security-conscious may want to use this setting.

Objective 1.4

Configure the Operating System to Support Applications

Windows XP provides a configurable platform with which to organize, launch, and switch between applications. In addition to providing the overall interface that you use for managing applications, Windows XP also provides services to the applications themselves—services such as file access and security, printing, and network connectivity.

As a DST, you should know how to configure Windows XP to support the use of applications. This knowledge includes configuring Windows XP elements, such as the desktop, Start menu, taskbar, and notification to best suit the way a user works with applications. From a troubleshooting standpoint, you must be able to isolate operating system problems from application problems, and also understand how each affects the other.

To answer the questions in this objective, you should know how to configure the Windows desktop, especially with regard to launching and managing running applications. You should also be able to solve basic operating system issues involving the major desktop features.

Objective 1.4 Questions

1. In which of the following ways can you open Task Manager? (Choose all that apply.)

    A. Right-click an open area on the taskbar and choose Task Manager.

    B. Right-click an open area on the desktop and choose Task Manager.

    C. In any open folder, on the Tools menu, choose Task Manager.

    D. Press CTRL+ALT+DEL.

2. After letting her daughter use her computer for an afternoon, one of your customers reports that the clock no longer shows up at the bottom right of her display. What should you do?

    A. Right-click the notification area and choose the Show The Clock command.

    B. On the General tab of the System Properties dialog box, select the Show The Clock check box.

    C. On the Taskbar tab of the Taskbar And Start Menu Properties dialog box, select the Show The Clock check box.

    D. You must re-enable the system clock in the computer's BIOS setup.

3. What is the correct name for the toolbar on the Windows XP taskbar that contains shortcuts for launching various programs?

    A. System Tray

    B. Task Manager

    C. Notification area

    D. Quick Launch

4. One of your customers has recently upgraded from Windows 2000 to Windows XP. She does not like the new interface for the Windows XP Start menu and would prefer to see the Start menu the way it was in Windows 2000. What should you tell the customer?

    A. Right-click the Start button and choose the Classic View command.

    B. Right-click any open area of the taskbar and choose the Classic View command.

    C. On the Start menu tab of the Taskbar And Start Menu Properties dialog box, select the Classic Start Menu option.

    D. The customer must use the new Windows XP Start menu.

5. One of your customers tells you that he wants to have quicker access to some of the folders he uses most frequently. He likes the Quick Launch bar but wants to use it only for shortcuts to applications. He would rather have a different toolbar named Folders. What should you tell the customer? (Choose all that apply.)

     A. Create a folder, name it Folders, and create the desired shortcuts in the folder. Right-click the taskbar and choose New Toolbar from the Toolbars submenu. Select the Folders folder.

     B. Create a folder, name it Folders, and create the desired shortcuts in the folder. Using the right mouse button, drag the Folders folder to the taskbar and choose Create Toolbar from the shortcut menu that appears.

     C. Right-click the taskbar and choose New Toolbar from the Toolbars submenu. Using the New Toolbar dialog box, create a new folder named Folders. Drag the desired shortcuts onto the new Folders toolbar.

     D. Windows XP does not allow you to create custom toolbars on the taskbar.

6. A user calls and says that she has just upgraded her computer from Windows Me to Windows XP Home Edition. She frequently accesses documents in her My Documents folder. She seems to remember that when a friend opened the Start menu on her own computer, the My Documents folder appeared as a menu. Her friend could access anything in the My Documents folder right from the Start menu. Your customer wants to set this up on her computer. What should you tell her?

     A. On the Advanced tab of the Customize Start Menu dialog box, in the Start menu items list, select the Display As A Menu option under My Documents.

     B. On the Start menu, right-click the My Documents folder and choose the Display As Menu Command.

     C. You must upgrade to Windows XP Professional for this feature to work.

     D. She is mistaken. You cannot do this in Windows XP.

7. One of your customers has a computer running Windows XP Professional, and she uses Outlook 2003 for e-mail. She recently used Windows Update to upgrade to the latest versions of Internet Explorer and Outlook. Now, the icon for Outlook Express appears on her Start menu instead of the icon for Outlook 2003. How can you change the icon?

     A. Use the Customize Start Menu dialog box to change the e-mail program used.

     B. Right-click the E-Mail icon on the Start menu and select the Choose Default Mail Handler command.

     C. Start Internet Explorer and use the Programs tab of the Internet Options dialog box to select Outlook as the default e-mail program.

    D. Start Outlook and use the Other tab of the Options dialog box to make Outlook the default mail program for that user.

8. A customer complains to you that when she runs an application, the application's window always covers up her taskbar. She has to press the Windows key or minimize all her windows to access the taskbar. What should you do?

    A. Right-click any open area of the taskbar and choose the Always On Top command.

    B. On the Taskbar tab of the Taskbar And Start Menu Properties dialog box, select the Keep The Taskbar On Top Of Other Windows check box.

    C. On the Taskbar tab of the Taskbar And Start Menu Properties dialog box, clear the Auto-Hide The Taskbar check box.

    D. On the Taskbar tab of the Taskbar And Start Menu Properties dialog box, select the Lock The Taskbar check box.

9. One of your customers works at a small business, where she shares a computer with another person. She would rather not have the list of recent documents shown on the Start menu. However, the other user of the computer does want to have his recent documents listed. What is the best option for the customer?

    A. The user must go to the Advanced tab of the Customize Start Menu dialog box whenever she leaves the computer, and then click Clear List to clear the list of documents.

    B. On the Advanced tab of the Customize Start Menu dialog box, clear the List My Most Recently Opened Documents check box.

    C. Create separate user accounts. Configure the customer's account to not show recent documents, and configure the other user's account to show recent documents.

    D. There is no way to meet all the requirements. Only one list of recent documents is used for all users on a computer.

10. A customer tells you that her Start menu is too crowded and that Windows cannot display all the icons without her having to scroll. She keeps a long list of recent programs and also pins a number of shortcuts to the Start menu, and she really doesn't want to change either practice. She tells you that she has not made any changes to the Start menu interface other than pinning shortcuts to it. How can you help her?

    A. Right-click the Start button and choose the Do Not Scroll command.

    B. Right-click the Start button and choose the Display Small Icons command.

    C. On the General tab of the Customize Start Menu dialog box, select the Do Not Scroll check box.

    D. On the General tab of the Customize Start Menu dialog box, select the Small Icons option.

11. One of your customers reports to you that she always has difficulties in Windows Explorer determining the type of any given file because it is hard to remember what all the icons mean. Upon questioning, you determine that she cannot see the file extensions of files. How can you force Windows to display file extensions?

    A. Open Control Panel. Click Appearance And Themes. Click Folder Options. Select the View tab. Clear the Hide Extensions For Known File Types check box.

    B. Open Control Panel. Click Appearance And Themes. Click Folder Options. Select the File Types tab. Clear the Hide Extensions For Known File Types check box.

    C. Open Control Panel. Click Appearance And Themes. Click Display. Select the Appearance tab. Clear the Hide Extensions For Known File Types check box.

    D. Open Control Panel. Click Performance And Maintenance. Click System. Select the Advanced tab. Clear the Hide Extensions For Known File Types check box.

12. A customer tells you that her Quick Launch bar has become too crowded because she has installed several programs that added shortcuts to it. She wants to remove some that she does not use. How can she do this?

    A. Click Start, point to All Programs, point to the Quick Launch folder, right-click any undesired shortcut in that folder, and choose the Delete command.

    B. Right-click any undesired shortcut on the Quick Launch bar and choose the Delete command.

    C. Hold down the ALT key while dragging an undesired shortcut away from the Quick Launch bar.

    D. Disable the Quick Launch bar and re-create it.

13. One of your customers complains that there are too many icons in the notification area. She does not think that many of the programs represented there need to be running in the background anyway. What can you do to prevent the programs from starting up with Windows?

    A. Right-click the icon in the notification area and choose the Do Not Start With Windows command.

    B. On the Taskbar tab of the Taskbar And Start Menu Properties dialog box, click Customize. Use the Customize Notifications dialog box that opens to configure programs not to start with Windows.

    C. Use the msconfig.exe command to disable particular programs from starting with Windows.

    D. Use the gpedit.msc tool to disable particular programs from starting with Windows.

14. Which of the following commands can you use to open a troubleshooting tool that lets you find detailed information about the graphics adapter installed on a computer?

    A. msconfig.exe

    B. msinfo32

    C. SFC /Scannow

    D. ipconfig

Objective 1.4 Answers

1.   **Correct Answers: A and D**

   A. Correct: You can open Task Manager by right-clicking an open area on the taskbar.

   B. Incorrect: You cannot open Task Manager this way.

   C. Incorrect: You cannot open Task Manager this way.

   D. Correct: In Windows XP, pressing CTRL+ALT+DEL opens the Windows Security dialog box, and from there you can open Task Manager.

2.   **Correct Answers: C**

   A. Incorrect: There is no Show The Clock command on the shortcut menu for the notification area.

   B. Incorrect: The Show The Clock check box does not appear on the General tab of the System Properties dialog box.

   C. Correct: You can enable or disable the clock using the Show The Clock check box.

   D. Incorrect: There is no way to disable the system clock in a computer's BIOS setup.

3.   **Correct Answers: D**

   A. Incorrect: The term System Tray was used in previous versions of Windows. System Tray is now named notification area.

   B. Incorrect: Task Manager is a multitabbed dialog box that shows running applications, running process, and performance information.

   C. Incorrect: Notification area, which appears at the right side of the taskbar, contains icons for programs running in the background.

   D. Correct: The Quick Launch toolbar is an optional toolbar that can be displayed on the Taskbar. Quick Launch contains shortcuts for launching programs.

4.   **Correct Answers: C**

   A. Incorrect: There is no Classic View command on the shortcut menu for the Start button.

   B. Incorrect: There is no Classic View command on the shortcut menu for the taskbar.

C. Correct: Windows XP lets you choose between using the Windows XP Start menu and a classic Start menu.

D. Incorrect: Windows XP does let you choose between using the Windows XP Start menu and a classic Start menu.

5. Correct Answers: A and C

A. Correct: You can create a new toolbar out of an existing folder in this manner.

B. Incorrect: There is no Create Toolbar command on the shortcut menu that appears when you drag a folder to the taskbar.

C. Correct: You can create a new toolbar and then populate it with shortcuts in this manner.

D. Incorrect: Windows XP does allow you to create custom toolbars on the taskbar.

6. Correct Answers: A

A. Correct: This option causes the My Documents icon on the Start menu to work as a menu.

B. Incorrect: There is no Display As Menu command on the shortcut menu for the My Documents folder.

C. Incorrect: You can use this feature in both Windows XP Professional and Home Editions.

D. Incorrect: This feature is supported in Windows XP.

7. Correct Answers: A

A. Correct: This option controls the e-mail program that appears on the Start menu.

B. Incorrect: This command does not exist on the shortcut menu for the E-Mail icon.

C. Incorrect: This method does change the default mail handler, but does not change the icon that appears on the Start menu.

D. Incorrect: This method does change the default mail handler, but does not change the icon that appears on the Start menu.

8. Correct Answers: B

A. Incorrect: There is no Always On Top command on the shortcut menu for the taskbar.

B. Correct: Selecting the Keep The Taskbar On Top Of Other Windows check box causes the taskbar to be shown at all times.

    C. Incorrect: The Auto-Hide The Taskbar check box controls whether the taskbar slides out of view when not in use.

    D. Incorrect: This setting does not affect whether the taskbar appears on top of other windows.

9. **Correct Answers: C**

    A. Incorrect: Although this method does prevent her recent documents from showing up after she leaves the computer, it is not the best solution. Also, this process clears the other user's recent documents.

    B. Incorrect: This method prevents the other user's recent documents from showing up on the list.

    C. Correct: Each user can specify whether recent documents are shown.

    D. Incorrect: You can configure separate user accounts. Then, each user can specify whether recent documents are shown.

10. **Correct Answers: D**

    A. Incorrect: There is no Do Not Scroll command on the shortcut menu for the Start button.

    B. Incorrect: There is no Display Small Icons command on the shortcut menu for the Start button.

    C. Incorrect: There is no Do Not Scroll check box on the General tab of the Customize Start menu dialog box.

    D. Correct: By default, Windows XP uses large icons on the Start menu. Changing this to display small icons provides considerably more room.

11. **Correct Answers: A**

    A. Correct: Clearing the Hide Extensions For Known File Types check box causes Windows to show file extensions for all files.

    B. Incorrect: The Hide Extensions For Known File Types check box does not appear on the File Types tab.

    C. Incorrect: The Display Properties dialog box is used to control display settings, themes, and desktop backgrounds, and it does not offer options for controlling file and folder views.

    D. Incorrect: The Advanced tab of the System Properties dialog box is used to control performance settings, user profiles, and startup and recovery features.

12.   Correct Answers: B

A. Incorrect: There is no Quick Launch folder in the All Programs folder.

B. Correct: You can delete a shortcut from the Quick Launch bar by simply right-clicking the shortcut and choosing the Delete command.

C. Incorrect: This method does not remove a shortcut from the Quick Launch bar.

D. Incorrect: When you disable a custom toolbar, you must re-create it. This is not true for the Quick Launch bar (or other built-in toolbars). When you turn the Quick Launch bar back on, the shortcuts will still be there.

13.   Correct Answers: C

A. Incorrect: This command does not appear on the shortcut menus of icons in the notification area.

B. Incorrect: You cannot configure programs not to start with Windows using the Customize Notifications dialog box. You can specify only whether the program icon is shown or hidden in the notification area.

C. Correct: The msconfig.exe command opens the System Configuration Utility, which lists all the programs that start with Windows and lets you selectively disable them from starting up.

D. Incorrect: The gpedit.msc command opens the Group Policy console, which is used to create Group Policy objects.

14.   Correct Answers: B

A. Incorrect: msconfig.exe opens the System Configuration Utility, which is used to control the Windows startup environment.

B. Correct: Msinfo32 opens the System Information tool, which provides detailed information about a local or remote computer's hardware configuration, computer components, installed software, drivers (signed or unsigned), BIOS version, memory configuration, product activation status, and more.

C. Incorrect: SFC opens the System File Checker, which is used to determine whether any protected system files are missing. The /Scannow parameter causes SFC to scan the computer immediately.

D. Incorrect: Ipconfig is used to display TCP/IP network configuration information.

14 Resolving Issues Related to Usability (2.0)

The Resolving Issues Related to Usability objective domain focuses mainly on configuring Microsoft Office applications, Microsoft Internet Explorer, Microsoft Outlook Express, and the Microsoft Windows XP operating system. You might be making configuration changes to implement connectivity or usability, or just to satisfy a user request. You will be expected to be able to resolve application errors, as well as operating system errors related to running applications.

Windows XP provides a more stable and secure environment for running applications than any previous version of Windows. Great strides have been taken in designing the Windows XP interface to make applications easier to configure and to use. Since no system is perfect, though, two of your primary responsibilities as a desktop support technician will be to set up Windows XP and other applications the way a user prefers, and to resolve errors when they occur.

Tested Skills and Suggested Practices

The skills that you need to successfully master the Resolving Issues Related to Usability objective domain on the Supporting Users and Troubleshooting Desktop Applications on a Microsoft Windows XP Operating System exam include:

- Resolving issues related to Office application support features.
    - ❏ Practice 1: Remove several of the default commands from one of the toolbars in an Office application. (The method is the same in all of them.) Add some new commands to that same toolbar. Finally restore the toolbar to its default settings.
    - ❏ Practice 2: Create a custom menu in an Office application (the method is the same in all of them), and add commands to that menu. Further customize the menu by renaming the commands you have added and grouping them by function.
    - ❏ Practice 3: In Microsoft Word, change the AutoFormat As You Type options so that Word does not automatically format numbered and bulleted lists. Change the spelling and grammar options so that Word does not check spelling and grammar in the background as you work.

■   Resolving issues related to Internet Explorer support features.

  ❏   Practice 1: Set a new home page in Internet Explorer. Also, change the size of the toolbar buttons to make them smaller, and try adding some buttons to the toolbar.

  ❏   Practice 2: Use Internet Explorer's History feature to visit a site that you visited two weeks ago. Configure the History feature so that it saves pages for three weeks.

  ❏   Practice 3: From within Internet Explorer, delete your temporary Internet files. Also, run the Disk Cleanup tool.

  ❏   Practice 4: Open the Internet Options dialog, and browse the settings on the Security tab. Pay particular attention to settings that might restrict content and cause problems for users. Note which types of objects are disabled by default when Service Pack 2 is installed.

  ❏   Practice 5: After installing Windows XP Service Pack 2, visit a website that uses pop-up windows. Note how Internet Explorer blocks the pop-ups, and how users can use the Information Bar to force Internet Explorer to show a single pop-up or all pop-ups for a site.

■   Resolving issues related to Outlook Express features.

  ❏   Practice 1: Export your Outlook Express Address Book to a text file as a backup.

  ❏   Practice 2: Create an Internet Accounts file in Outlook Express to back up information about mail folders and accounts for the current Outlook Express identity.

  ❏   Practice 3: Configure Outlook Express so that attachments that might be viruses cannot be opened or saved.

  ❏   Practice 4: After installing Service Pack 2, use Outlook Express to download an HTML e-mail message with embedded images. Notice that the images are hidden by default, but that you can force Outlook Express to display the images.

■   Resolving issues related to operating system features.

  ❏   Practice 1: Configure the Windows XP notification area so that inactive icons are not hidden, and then change this setting back. Configure a particular icon so that it is always hidden.

  ❏   Practice 2: Use the msconfig.exe tool to identify the programs that start with Windows. If you see any that you would rather did not start, disable them.

  ❏   Practice 3: Turn on the Quick Launch toolbar, and add a shortcut to it. Create a custom toolbar for the Taskbar by using your My Documents folder.

❏ Practice 4: Configure Windows XP to use the classic Start menu instead of the Windows XP Start menu.

❏ Practice 5: Change the file association for files with the .txt extension so that they open with Microsoft Word.

❏ Practice 6: After installing Service Pack 2, notice that the Security Center warns you if you do not have antivirus software installed. Use Security Center to disable the warning without installing antivirus software.

Further Reading

This section lists supplemental readings by objective. Study these sources thoroughly before taking exam 70-272.

Objective 2.1   "Office 2003 Resource Kit." (Available online at *http://office.microsoft.com/ en-us/FX011511471033.aspx.*) This site provides a wealth of information for IT professionals about supporting Office 2003, including the full text of the Resource Kit.

"Office 2003 Security Enhancements." (Available online at *http://www.microsoft.com/ technet/prodtechnol/office/office2003/deploy/secdesn.mspx.*)

Microsoft Office System Inside Out, 2003 Edition, by Michael J. Young and Michael Halvorson. This book is designed for advanced users and includes information about configuring, supporting, and troubleshooting all of the Microsoft Office applications.

Objective 2.2   "How to Manage Cookies in Internet Explorer 6," Microsoft Knowledge Base Article 283185. (Available online at *http://support.microsoft.com/kb/ 283185/.*)

"Microsoft Internet Explorer 6 Resource Kit." (Available online at *http:// www.microsoft.com/resources/documentation/ie/6/all/reskit/en-us/default.mspx.*) Review Part 2, "Privacy and Security Features"; Part 5, "Customization and Installation"; and Part 6, "Maintenance and Support."

"Using Microsoft Windows XP Professional with Service Pack 1 in a Managed Environment: Controlling Communication with the Internet." (Available online at *http://www.microsoft.com/technet/prodtechnol/winxppro/maintain/xpmanaged/ 11_xp_ie.mspx.*) This document contains good information about supporting Internet Explorer in a corporate environment.

"Description of the Internet Explorer Information Bar in Windows XP SP2," Microsoft Knowledge Base article 843017. (Available online at *http:// support.microsoft.com/kb/843017/.*)

"Changes to Functionality in Microsoft Windows XP Service Pack 2, Part 5: Enhanced Browsing Security." (Available online at *http://www.microsoft.com/technet/prodtechnol/winxppro/maintain/sp2brows.mspx.*)

Objective 2.3   "How to Back Up and Recover Outlook Express Data," Microsoft Knowledge Base article 270670. (Available online at *http://support.microsoft.com/kb/270670/.*)

"Changes to Functionality in Microsoft Windows XP Service Pack 2, Part 4: E-mail Handling Technologies." (Available online at *http://www.microsoft.com/technet/prodtechnol/winxppro/maintain/sp2email.mspx.*)

Objective 2.4   "Description of the Microsoft Windows Registry," Microsoft Knowledge Base article 256986. (Available online at *http://support.microsoft.com/kb/256986/.*)

"Windows XP Events and Errors Database." (Available online at *http://www.microsoft.com/technet/prodtechnol/winxppro/support/xpevnt.mspx.*) This page describes how to search for the error and event messages generated by Windows XP.

"Windows XP System Restore," by Melissa Wise. (Available online at *http://www.microsoft.com/technet/prodtechnol/winxppro/maintain/xpsysrst.mspx.*) This article provides a detailed look at using the System Restore tool in Windows XP.

"Microsoft Windows XP Professional Resource Kit Documentation," by Microsoft Corporation. (Available online at *http://www.microsoft.com/resources/documentation/Windows/XP/all/reskit/en-us/prork_overview.asp.*) In particular, look through Chapter 5, "Managing Desktops"; Chapter 6, "Managing Files and Folders"; and Chapter 9, "Managing Devices."

"Understanding Windows Firewall." (Available online at *http://www.microsoft.com/windowsxp/using/security/internet/sp2_wfintro.mspx.*)

"Changes to Functionality in Microsoft Windows XP Service Pack 2, Part 3: Memory Protection Technologies." (Available online at *http://www.microsoft.com/technet/prodtechnol/winxppro/maintain/sp2mempr.mspx.*)

Objective 2.1

Resolve Issues Related to Office Application Support Features

As a DST, you should be able to support a wide variety of applications in Windows XP, ranging from MS-DOS–based applications to modern 32-bit applications. Fortunately, Windows XP provides a wealth of support tools for doing just this.

In particular, you should be able to support the various applications that make up Microsoft Office, including Microsoft Word, Microsoft Excel, Microsoft PowerPoint, and Microsoft Outlook. You should be familiar with how to install, configure, and customize these applications, as well as how to troubleshoot common errors.

To answer the questions in this objective, you should know how to configure the options for each of the Microsoft Office applications, including default save locations and user information. You should also know how to customize each application's interface, including adding and removing toolbars, creating custom toolbars and menus, and adding and removing commands from the interface.

Objective 2.1 Questions

1. You get a call from a user who has deleted several buttons from the Standard toolbar in Word 2003. She wants to know the best way to reset the toolbar to the way it was when Word was first installed. Where would you go in Word 2003 to do this?

    A. The Customization tab of the Options dialog box

    B. The Defaults tab of the Options dialog box

    C. The Toolbars tab of the Customize dialog box

    D. There is no way to reset a toolbar automatically. You will have to restore each command in turn.

2. You receive a call from a customer who tells you that he received a Word document from one of his co-workers that contains unsigned macros the co-worker has created. Your customer needs to be able to use these macros, but they are always disabled. What is the highest macro security level you can set that will let the customer use the macros in the document?

    A. Very High

    B. High

    C. Medium

    D. Low

3. A customer tells you that she works on important documents in Word 2003 and saves them every few minutes to avoid losing work. She asks whether there is a way to have Word do this automatically. What do you tell her?

    A. She can enable Word's AutoRecover feature and configure how often it saves a copy that Word can restore should the program crash.

    B. She can enable Word's AutoSave feature and configure how often it saves a copy that Word can restore should the program crash.

    C. She can use Word's Version feature to configure how often Word saves a new version of the document.

    D. She cannot configure Word to automatically save documents.

4. A customer needs to insert a Word document into her Excel spreadsheet. The Word document is updated regularly with the latest company contact and disclaimer information and is stored on a network server. The user wants her spreadsheet to always

show the most up-to-date information each time the file is opened. Unfortunately, each time she opens the document, she gets the same information, and the information from the Word document is never updated. What is likely the problem?

A. This customer needs to choose Package For CD to package the spreadsheet with the document so that both are available when the file is opened.

B. The customer needs to be made a member of the Domain Power Users group so that she can have automatic access to domain resources.

C. The customer embedded the document instead of linking to it.

D. The customer linked to the document instead of embedding it.

5. A customer calls and tells you that while he was working on a presentation in Power-Point, the application froze. He can still move his mouse pointer, and other applications are working, but the PowerPoint window has the words "Not Responding" in the title bar. The user cannot remember when he last saved his document, but he needs to recover his work. What should you tell him to do?

A. Close all applications except for PowerPoint, and then press the reset button on his computer.

B. Close all applications except for PowerPoint, and use the Microsoft Office Application Recovery tool.

C. Use the Processes tab of Task Manager to end the POWERPNT.EXE process.

D. Use the Applications tab of Task Manager to end the Microsoft PowerPoint application, and then start PowerPoint again to activate the AutoRecover function.

Objective 2.1 Answers

1.   **Correct Answers: C**

   A. Incorrect: There is no Customization tab on the Options dialog box.

   B. Incorrect: There is no Defaults tab on the Options dialog box.

   C. Correct: On the Toolbars tab of the Customize dialog box, select the toolbar you want to reset, and click Reset.

   D. Incorrect: Although you can restore a toolbar to its default state by manually returning each button, there is no need to.

2.   **Correct Answers: C**

   A. Incorrect: At this level, Word automatically disables all macros (signed or unsigned) that are not in a trusted location, meaning that the macros in the document will not work.

   B. Incorrect: At this level, Word automatically disables unsigned macros, meaning that the macros in the document will not work.

   C. Correct: This setting prompts the user when an unsigned macro is detected. The user can then enable or disable macros for that session.

   D. Incorrect: While this setting would allow the macros in the document to run, it would offer no protection at all against macros in other documents.

3.   **Correct Answers: A**

   A. Correct: Word's AutoRecover feature automatically saves a copy of all open documents based on the number of minutes you configure on the Save tab of the Options dialog box. Should Word crash, Word automatically opens the last saved AutoRecover file when Word is reopened.

   B. Incorrect: Word does not have an AutoSave feature.

   C. Incorrect: Word's Version feature does not work in this way. The Version feature is used to save multiple versions of a document in the same file but does not offer automated saves.

   D. Incorrect: Word's AutoRecover feature does provide a way to save documents automatically in case of a program crash.

4.   Correct Answers: C

    A. Incorrect: Package For CD is an option in PowerPoint, not in Word or Excel.

    B. Incorrect: This is not necessary and would give the user more permissions than she likely needs.

    C. Correct: For the spreadsheet to always display information from the current Word document, the customer must insert the Word document as a link.

    D. Incorrect: The customer should link the document. Embedding the document breaks all ties with the original document.

5.   Correct Answers: B

    A. Incorrect: This will not solve the user's problem and might corrupt important files. You should always use the Shut Down or Restart command.

    B. Correct: The Microsoft Office Application Recovery tool is intended for use when an Office application is not responding. The user should start this tool and, when prompted, choose Recover Application.

    C. Incorrect: This action will not recover the user's document and may actually prevent PowerPoint's AutoRecover feature from being able to recover the document as well.

    D. Incorrect: While this might work, it might not be as successful as using the Microsoft Office Application Recovery tool.

Objective 2.2

Resolve Issues Related to Internet Explorer Support Features

The Resolve Issues Related To Internet Explorer Support Features objective focuses on supporting Microsoft Internet Explorer. As a DST, you need to understand the different configuration and customization options available in Internet Explorer to support your users effectively. Most of these settings can be configured by using the Internet Options dialog box, which includes a variety of tabs related to specific categories of settings. For example, the Internet Options dialog box includes a Security tab and a Content tab.

Service Pack 2 changes some of the default security settings, and adds several important features. These changes can cause usability problems after installing Service Pack 2, because they change how Internet Explorer behaves.

To answer the questions in this objective, you should know how to configure general Internet Explorer settings, configure security and privacy settings, resolve connectivity issues, and customize the Internet Explorer interface.

Objective 2.2 Questions

1. A customer calls and tells you that she recently got a new cable modem connection to the Internet. When the service person came to hook it up, everything was working fine. However, whenever she opens Internet Explorer, it attempts to dial into her old ISP using her modem. She would like to keep the modem and the dial-up networking connection to her old ISP as a backup for when her cable modem is not working. However, she would like Internet Explorer to automatically use her cable modem connection when she starts it. What is the best solution?

    A. On the Connections tab of the Internet Options dialog box, select the Never Dial A Connection option. Tell the user that when she needs to use her modem, she'll have to go to the Dial-Up Networking folder to manually start the connection.

    B. On the Connections tab of the Internet Options dialog box, select the Always Use LAN Connection option. Tell the user that when she needs to use her modem, she'll have to go to the Dial-Up Networking folder to manually start the connection.

    C. On the Connections tab of the Internet Options dialog box, select the Dial Whenever a Network Connection Is Not Present option. Tell the user that when her cable modem connection is not functioning, Internet Explorer will automatically start her modem connection to her old ISP.

    D. Tell the user that she must delete the dial-up connection to the old ISP and manually re-create it when she needs to use it.

2. A customer calls and tells you that she is having a problem with Internet Explorer. Her brother recently gave her his old notebook computer, and she says that her Internet Explorer toolbar is filled with tiny buttons that she can barely see and that they have no names. She says that on her desktop computer, the buttons are big and most of them have names. She wants to make it the same way on her notebook computer. What should you do?

    A. Open the Customize Toolbar dialog box, and click Reset.

    B. On the View menu, point to Text Size, and then select a larger text size.

    C. Open the Internet Options dialog box, and use the settings on the Content tab to change the toolbar appearance.

    D. Open the Customize Toolbar dialog box. Set the Icon Options setting to Large Icons, and set the Text Options setting to Show Text Labels.

3. You get a call from the owner of a small business who runs Internet Explorer on her employees' computers. The owner would like to personalize the Internet Explorer title bar so that it shows the company's name. She also wants to customize the home page, default search page, and online support page that Internet Explorer uses and to prevent her employees from changing these settings. What tool can she use to do this?

    A. These options are all available on the Content tab of the Internet Options dialog box.

    B. She needs to run cmd.exe using the Run dialog box.

    C. She needs to run gpedit.msc using the Run dialog box.

    D. She needs to run the Local Security Policy tool, available in the Administrative Tools folder.

4. Which of the following Internet Explorer features would you use if a parent wanted to configure Internet Explorer so that her child could browse the Web safely?

    A. Security Zones

    B. Content Advisor

    C. Privacy Settings

    D. Certificates

5. Which of the following privacy settings in Internet Explorer blocks all cookies that do not have a compact privacy policy and all cookies that use personally identifiable information without a user's explicit consent?

    A. Low

    B. Medium

    C. High

    D. Block All Cookies

6. Which of the following methods can you use to delete temporary Internet files? (Choose all that apply.)

    A. Disk Cleanup

    B. Disk Defragmenter

    C. General tab of the Internet Options dialog box

    D. Security tab of the Internet Options dialog box

7. Recently, a user bought a computer that had Windows XP Professional with Service Pack 2 installed. The user of that computer complains that a Web application does not work properly. You investigate the application, and discover that the application uses ActiveX. What should you ask the user to do to resolve the problem?

    A. Click the Tools menu, and then click Internet Options. Click the Security tab. Adjust the security settings for the Internet zone to Low.

    B. Look for the Information Bar. When it appears, click it, and then click Install ActiveX Control.

    C. Log on to the computer as a member of the local Administrators group.

    D. Uninstall Service Pack 2.

8. A user complains that she needs to use a website, but the pop-up window that normally appears does not appear. After further questioning, you discover that the user recently installed Windows XP Service Pack 2 and is using Internet Explorer. What is the best way to resolve the problem? (Choose all that apply.)

    A. Click the Tools menu, click Pop-up Blocker, and then click Pop-up Blocker Settings. Clear the Show Information Bar When A Pop-up Is Blocked check box.

    B. Contact the website administrators and have them update their website to not use pop-ups.

    C. Click the Tools menu, and then click Manage Add-ons. Select the Pop-up Blocker add-on, click Disable, and then click OK.

    D. Visit the website. When the Information Bar appears, click it, and then click Always Allow Pop-ups From This Site.

Objective 2.2 Answers

1.   Correct Answers: C

A. Incorrect: When configured this way, Internet Explorer will not dial a connection automatically, even if the cable modem connection is not functioning. While this method will achieve the desired results, it is not the best method available.

B. Incorrect: There is not an Always Use LAN Connection option on the Connections tab of the Internet Options dialog box.

C. Correct: While other responses might produce the desired results, this is the best answer since it handles dialing the backup Internet connection via modem automatically for the customer.

D. Incorrect: While this might work, it is unnecessarily cumbersome.

2.   Correct Answers: D

A. Incorrect: The Reset command resets the commands shown on the toolbar, replacing any that the user has removed and restoring any that the user has placed there. The Reset command does not change the size of the buttons or the text options.

B. Incorrect: The text sizes available on the Text Size submenu affect the size of the font shown on Web pages and not the size of buttons on toolbars.

C. Incorrect: The Content tab of the Internet Options dialog box is used to enable the Content Advisor, work with certificates, and configure personal information.

D. Correct: Internet Explorer can display large or small icons on the toolbar. Whichever size icons are displayed, Internet Explorer can also display no text labels with the buttons, text labels with all buttons, or text labels with select buttons.

3.   Correct Answers: C

A. Incorrect: The Content tab of the Internet Options dialog box is used to enable the Content Advisor, work with certificates, and configure personal information.

B. Incorrect: cmd.exe simply opens a Command Prompt window.

C. Correct: gpedit.msc opens the Group Policy console, which she can use to make the required changes.

D. Incorrect: The Local Security Policy tool cannot be used to set software restrictions.

4. **Correct Answers: B**

    A. **Incorrect:** Security Zones are used to specify the security settings for different websites. These security settings control the downloading of ActiveX, Java, and other downloadable content.

    B. **Correct:** Content Advisor lets you control what sites and content are accessed on the Internet. The parent assigns a password and configures settings for what Internet Explorer is and is not allowed to display without that password.

    C. **Incorrect:** Privacy settings affect how Internet Explorer downloads and uses cookies.

    D. **Incorrect:** Certificates are used to verify your identity or the identity of a Web publisher or certification authority.

5. **Correct Answers: C**

    A. **Incorrect:** This setting blocks third-party cookies that do not have a compact privacy policy or that use personally identifiable information without a user's implicit consent.

    B. **Incorrect:** This setting blocks third-party and first-party cookies that do not have a compact privacy policy or that use personally identifiable information without a user's implicit consent.

    C. **Correct:** This setting blocks all cookies that do not have a compact privacy policy and all cookies that use personally identifiable information without a user's explicit consent.

    D. **Incorrect:** This setting blocks all cookies, and existing cookies on the computer cannot be read by the websites that created them.

6. **Correct Answers: A and C**

    A. **Correct:** Disk Cleanup deletes files in the Downloaded Program Files folder, the Temporary Internet Files folder, the Temporary Files folder, the Recycle Bin, and more. Deleting these files regularly helps keep the computer running smoothly.

    B. **Incorrect:** Disk Defragmenter is used to clean up the fragmentation of files that happens over time as they are stored on hard disks. Disk Defragmenter does not delete temporary Internet files.

    C. **Correct:** You can click Delete Files on the General tab of the Internet Options dialog box to delete temporary Internet files.

    D. **Incorrect:** The Security tab of the Internet Options dialog box handles Security Zones and does not provide a way to delete temporary Internet files.

7.   Correct Answers: B

    A. Incorrect: This would reduce the security of the user's computer, and make the user vulnerable to potentially malicious websites. Instead, the user should click the Information Bar when it appears to install the ActiveX control.

    B. Correct: After Service Pack 2 is installed, Internet Explorer shows an Information Bar instead of prompting the user to install an ActiveX control. However, the Information Bar is easy for users to overlook, so they may not understand why Web applications do not work correctly.

    C. Incorrect: User permissions do not affect how Internet Explorer installs ActiveX controls. Instead, the user should click the Information Bar when it appears to install the ActiveX control.

    D. Incorrect: Uninstalling Service Pack 2 would probably resolve the problem. However, Service Pack 2 includes many new features and other significant improvements, and uninstalling Service Pack 2 should be avoided whenever possible. Therefore, it is better to selectively enable ActiveX objects by clicking the Information Bar.

8.   Correct Answers: D

    A. Incorrect: Changing this setting would only hide the fact that Internet Explorer was blocking pop-ups, and not allow the user to click the Information Bar to selectively enable pop-ups.

    B. Incorrect: Although websites should avoid using pop-ups, Internet Explorer with Service Pack 2 can selectively allow pop-ups to support sites that use them. This approach is valid, therefore, but it is not the best way to resolve the problem.

    C. Incorrect: The Internet Explorer Pop-up Blocker is not an add-on, and cannot be configured by using the Manage Add-ons tool.

    D. Correct: By default, Service Pack 2 updates Internet Explorer to block all pop-ups. However, you can use the Information Bar to open a single pop-up or to enable pop-ups for an entire site.

Objective 2.3

Resolve Issues Related to Outlook Express Features

Outlook Express is a messaging tool that many people use for e-mail transactions and newsgroup communications. Understanding how to configure and troubleshoot Outlook Express settings is vital to guiding your user in making the most of this application. You can configure Outlook Express to access three different e-mail server types: POP3, IMAP, and HTTP servers. In addition to supporting these three types of e-mail servers, Outlook Express also acts as a newsreader client, allowing you to access the wealth of information in online newsgroups.

Both Service Pack 1 and Service Pack 2 made substantial improvements to Outlook Express security. However, some of these changes can cause usability problems. Be aware of these potential problems so that you can assist users after they install a service pack.

To answer the questions in this objective, you should know how to set up and test e-mail and news accounts in Outlook Express. You should also understand how to customize the Outlook Express interface, how to import and export information, and how to resolve common errors that occur.

Objective 2.3 Questions

1.   A customer calls and tells you that Outlook Express will not let her open Word documents that her sister sends her. When you ask her further questions, she verifies that Word is installed but says that in Outlook Express the paper clip icon indicating an attachment is not there. You also determine that she updated her computer recently with Service Pack 1 for Windows XP. What should you tell her to do?

   A. Restart the computer.

   B. On the Security tab of the Options dialog box in Outlook Express, set the Internet Explorer Security Zone that is used to Internet Zone.

   C. On the Security tab of the Options dialog box in Outlook Express, clear the Do Not Allow Attachments To Be Saved Or Opened That Could Potentially Be A Virus check box.

   D. Uninstall Service Pack 1.

2.   You are speaking with a customer who is using Outlook Express as his newsreader. He tells you that newsgroup messages are automatically downloaded when he selects a newsgroup. Instead, he would prefer it if only the headers were downloaded rather than the entire message. What should you tell him?

   A. On the Read tab of the Options dialog box in Outlook Express, the customer should clear the Automatically Download Messages When Viewing In The Preview Pane check box.

   B. On the General tab of the Options dialog box in Outlook Express, the customer should clear the Check For New Messages Every ____ check box.

   C. On the Read tab of the Options dialog box in Outlook Express, the customer should clear the Get ____ Headers At A Time check box.

   D. You should tell the customer that this cannot be done in Outlook Express.

3.   You have a customer who has recently purchased a notebook computer and would like to copy the Outlook Express e-mail addresses from his desktop computer to the new notebook computer. What is the best solution?

   A. Use the Send Address Book feature in Outlook Express to mail the Address Book as an attachment to the e-mail account used on the notebook computer.

   B. Connect the notebook and desktop computers to the same network, and then use the Export command in Outlook Express to export the address book from the desktop computer to the notebook computer.

C. Use the Export command in Outlook Express on the desktop computer to export the Address Book to a comma-separated text file. Use the Import command in Outlook Express on the notebook computer to import from the comma-separated text file.

D. Copy the contents of the Program Files\Outlook Express folder on the desktop computer to the same folder on the notebook computer.

4. A user complains that he doesn't see images in HTML e-mail messages. Which are valid ways for the user to view the images? (Choose all that apply.)

A. Click the Some Pictures Have Been Blocked To Help Prevent The Sender From Identifying Your Computer link.

B. Double-click the message to open it in a separate window.

C. Click the Tools menu, and then click Options. Click the Security tab. Then clear the Block Images And Other External Content In HTML E-mail check box.

D. Click the Tools menu, and then click Options. Click the Read tab. Clear the Read All Messages In Plain Text check box.

Objective 2.3 Answers

1.   Correct Answers: C

A. Incorrect: Restarting the computer will not solve this problem.

B. Incorrect: Changing the Security Zone setting affects how messages in HTML format are displayed but does not affect attachments.

C. Correct: After Service Pack 1 or later is installed, the Do Not Allow Attachments To Be Saved Or Opened That Could Potentially Be A Virus check box is selected by default. To access these types of attachments, the customer must clear this setting.

D. Incorrect: This is not necessary and will not correct the problem.

2.   Correct Answers: A

A. Correct: This setting causes Outlook not to download message bodies automatically.

B. Incorrect: This setting affects whether Outlook Express should periodically check for new e-mail messages and does not affect newsgroups.

C. Incorrect: This setting controls whether Outlook Express downloads all available headers (when the option is disabled) or downloads only the specified number of headers (when the option is enabled).

D. Incorrect: You can configure Outlook Express not to download messages automatically.

3.   Correct Answers: C

A. Incorrect: There is not a Send Address Book feature in Outlook Express.

B. Incorrect: The Export command in Outlook Express does not provide this functionality.

C. Correct: This is the preferred method for transferring the contents of an Address Book. Exporting to a text file is also a good way to back up an Address Book.

D. Incorrect: This folder holds only program files and does not contain the Address Book.

4.   Correct Answers: A and C

    A. Correct: Clicking this link, located at the top of an HTML e-mail message, will cause Outlook Express to download and display the images for that individual message.

    B. Incorrect: When you double-click a message to open it in a separate window, Outlook Express does not automatically download HTML images. You still need to click Some Pictures Have Been Blocked To Help Prevent The Sender From Identifying Your Computer.

    C. Correct: Clearing this check box causes Outlook Express to automatically download images for all messages. Note that this sacrifices some user privacy, however, and should be avoided.

    D. Incorrect: Clearing this check box will not cause Outlook Express to display images embedded in an HTML message. Additionally, this check box is not selected by default so it will rarely cause user problems.

Objective 2.4

Resolve Issues Related to Operating System Features

From a troubleshooting standpoint, operating system issues are generally separated quite clearly from application issues because Windows XP protects the operating system from most application errors. If an application is a suspected cause of an issue, it has little to no chance of interfering directly with the operating system and its services. This concept is useful in helping a DST know where to look and what steps to take to troubleshoot a specific issue.

Windows XP is a powerful, highly customizable operating system that supports powerful, highly customizable applications. As a DST, part of your responsibility will be helping users customize their environments to suit their needs. It is up to you to understand whether configurations are required in an application or in the operating system itself and to be able to make (or instruct the user how to make) those changes.

Operating system updates, especially Windows XP Service Pack 2, can introduce new types of issues that users have not previously experienced. You must understand the types of operating system issues that Service Pack 2 can cause, and how to troubleshoot these issues. In particular, Service Pack 2 adds Security Center and Data Execution Prevention (DEP), both of which might display error messages that users need your assistance with.

To answer the questions in this objective, you should know how to customize and troubleshoot the Windows XP desktop, especially with regard to running applications. This includes working with files and folders, customizing the Start menu, and customizing the Taskbar.

Objective 2.4 Questions

1. A user calls and says that her operating system was recently upgraded to Windows XP from Windows 98. She frequently connects to resources on other computers on the network and used to do that using the Network Neighborhood icon on her desktop. She does not see any icon for accessing the network now that she is using Windows XP. You also find out that the My Network Places icon does not show up on her Start menu. How would you place the My Network Places icon on her Start menu and on her Desktop? (Two answers form the two parts of the solution.)

    A. On the Advanced tab of the Customize Start Menu dialog box, in the Start menu items list, select the My Network Places check box.

    B. On the Start Menu, point to All Programs and then to Accessories, right-click the My Network Places icon, and click Pin To Start Menu.

    C. On the Advanced tab of the Customize Start Menu dialog box, in the Desktop items list, select the My Network Places check box.

    D. On the Start menu, right-click the My Network Places icon and click Show On Desktop.

2. A customer using Windows XP Home Edition calls and complains that he doesn't have enough room on his taskbar to show all of his open programs. He says he has to scroll to see the additional programs, and wants to know whether there is there some way of grouping the programs together. He says he has seen it done on a friend's computer. What should you do?

    A. On the Taskbar tab of the Taskbar And Start Menu Properties dialog box, select the Group Similar Taskbar Buttons check box.

    B. On the Taskbar tab of the Taskbar And Start Menu Properties dialog box, select the Hide Inactive Icons check box.

    C. Right-click the taskbar, and choose Group Taskbar Buttons.

    D. You must tell the customer that this is a feature of Office 2003 and not Windows XP.

3. What is the correct name for the area at the bottom right of the Windows XP desktop that contains the system clock?

    A. System Tray

    B. Task Manager

    C. Notification Area

    D. Quick Launch

4.   A customer has recently installed the latest version of Microsoft Windows Media Player on her computer. The first time the program ran, she says it asked whether she wanted to make Windows Media Player the default program for opening media files and she told it no. She would now like to make Windows Media Player the default program for playing certain media files, including files ending in .avi and .mpg. What should you do?

A. Use the File Types tab of the Folder Options dialog box to change the program that opens .mpg and .avi files to Windows Media Player.

B. Reinstall Windows Media Player, launch, it, and then set it to be the default program for media files.

C. On the General tab of the Folder Options dialog box, click Restore Defaults.

D. Start Windows Media Player, and then drag a file of each type onto the Windows Media Player window.

5.   A customer tells you that a colleague recently e-mailed several files with the .xls extension. However, the customer cannot open the files. Which program does the customer need to open these files?

A. Microsoft Word

B. Microsoft Excel

C. Microsoft PowerPoint

D. Windows Media Player

6.   A customer tells you that he recently installed some new software that added an icon to the Quick Launch area of his Taskbar. However, the Quick Launch bar is not big enough to display the additional icon, and he has to press a button with two "right arrows" to access the additional icon. He would like to enlarge the Quick Launch bar but cannot seem to do so by dragging its right edge. In fact, he says he cannot even see the right edge. What should you tell the customer? (Choose all that apply.)

A. He will need to remove an icon from the Quick Launch bar because it cannot be resized.

B. The taskbar is locked. He needs to log in using an account with Administrator privileges to unlock it.

C. The taskbar is locked. He should clear the Lock The Taskbar check box on the Taskbar tab of the Taskbar And Start Menu Properties dialog box.

D. The taskbar is locked. He should right-click the taskbar and select Lock The Taskbar. He should then be able to make the Quick Launch bar larger.

7. You get a call from a customer who has just recently installed antivirus software on his computer. When he first installed the software, he says that a picture for the software showed up near the clock on the taskbar. Recently he has not seen the picture and wants to know whether his antivirus software is still running. What should you tell the user?

    A. The software is probably still running. He should click the arrow to the left of the notification area to expand it and see whether the icon is present.

    B. The software is probably still running. He should press Ctrl+Alt+Del to activate the Task Manager and look at the list of running processes on the Process tab for something that looks like his antivirus software.

    C. The user should reinstall the antivirus software.

    D. The user should open the antivirus software by using the shortcut on the Start menu and search for an option that displays the icon in the notification area.

8. A customer complains to you that now, after she let a friend use her computer, the taskbar is missing. There is a thin blue line at the bottom of the display, but when she moves her pointer there, nothing happens. What should you tell the user?

    A. Her friend probably resized the taskbar to its smallest state. She should right-click the taskbar, choose Properties, and then clear the Auto-Hide The Taskbar check box.

    B. Her friend probably resized the taskbar to its smallest state. She should move her pointer over it until the pointer turns to a double arrow and then click and drag to make the taskbar bigger.

    C. She should restart her computer.

    D. She should right-click the taskbar, choose Properties, and then clear the Hide Inactive Icons check box.

9. A customer tells you that she uses a few accessories all the time, including Calculator and Notepad. She is tired of having to navigate all the way to the Accessories folder each time she wants to use them. How can you help her? (Choose all that apply.)

    A. Go to the Accessories folder, right-click the icon for each of these programs in turn, and select Pin To Start Menu.

    B. Go to the Accessories folder, right-click the icon for each of these programs in turn, and select Show On Desktop.

    C. On the Advanced tab of the Customize Start Menu dialog box, in the Start Menu Items list, select the Calculator and Notepad check boxes.

D. Go to the Accessories folder, and using the right mouse button, drag the icons for the Calculator and Notepad in turn to the Quick Launch bar. Click Copy Here from the menu that opens.

10. A customer tells you that when she logs on every morning, she always starts Microsoft Outlook and Internet Explorer. It would be nice if she could have these programs automatically start whenever she logs on. How can you help her? (Choose all that apply.)

A. Configure a scheduled task that launches these programs at the same time she usually gets in each morning.

B. Configure a scheduled task that launches these programs whenever the computer starts.

C. Configure a scheduled task that launches these programs shortly before the user arrives every morning. Tell her to leave her workstation running and not to log off when leaving for the evening.

D. Add shortcuts to these programs to the user's Startup folder.

11. A user complains about a message that appears regularly on her computer: "Your Computer Might Be At Risk. Antivirus Software Might Not Be Installed." You discuss the importance of having antivirus software installed, but the user simply wants the warnings turned off. How can you eliminate the warnings?

A. Open Control Panel, and then open Security Center. Click Windows Firewall, and then click Off to disable Windows Firewall.

B. Open Control Panel, and then open Security Center. In the Virus Protection area, click the Recommendations button. Select the I Have An Antivirus Solution That I'll Monitor Myself check box.

C. When a warning appears, select the Do Not Show This Warning Again check box, and then click OK.

D. Security Center antivirus warnings cannot be disabled.

12. A user complains that an important application is causing Data Execution Prevention (DEP) problems. The user is not concerned about security risks with the application and would like to disable DEP for that application. How should you disable DEP?

A. Open the System Properties dialog box, and click the Advanced tab. Under Performance, click Settings. Click the Data Execution Prevention tab, and then click Turn On DEP For All Programs And Services Except Those I Select. Click the Add button, and select the application that is causing problems.

B. Open Control Panel, and then open Security Center. Click Windows Firewall, and then click Off to disable Windows Firewall.

C. Open Control Panel, and then open Security Center. Click Windows Firewall, and then click the Exceptions tab. Add the application that is causing problems.

D. Open Control Panel, and then Open Security Center. Click Data Execution Prevention. Click Disable DEP For The Following Programs And Services. Click the Add button, and select the application that is causing problems.

Objective 2.4 Answers

1. **Correct Answers: A and D**

    A. **Correct:** This option places the My Network Places icon on the Start menu.

    B. **Incorrect:** A My Network Places icon is not found in the Accessories folder.

    C. **Incorrect:** There is no Desktop items list on the Advanced tab of the Customize Start Menu dialog box.

    D. **Correct:** After the My Network Places icon appears on the Start menu, you can use this option to display it on the Desktop as well.

2. **Correct Answers: A**

    A. **Correct:** This option causes Windows XP to group multiple taskbar buttons for a single program (for example, Internet Explorer) under a single button.

    B. **Incorrect:** The Hide Inactive Icons option affects whether the Notification Area collapses to hide icons not used frequently.

    C. **Incorrect:** There is no Group Taskbar Buttons option on the Taskbar's shortcut menu.

    D. **Incorrect:** Grouping similar taskbar buttons is a Windows XP feature.

3. **Correct Answers: C**

    A. **Incorrect:** The term System Tray was used in previous versions of Windows.

    B. **Incorrect:** The Task Manager is a multitabbed dialog box that shows running applications, running processes, and performance information.

    C. **Correct:** This area is called the Notification Area.

    D. **Incorrect:** The Quick Launch toolbar is an optional toolbar that can be displayed on the taskbar. Quick Launch contains shortcuts for launching programs.

4. **Correct Answers: A**

    A. **Correct:** The File Types tab contains tools for controlling how Windows XP associates programs with file extensions.

    B. **Incorrect:** This method would associate Windows Media Player with .avi and .mpg files. However, it is a burdensome solution and would also associate all other media files with Windows Media Player—something the user did not ask for.

C. Incorrect: This option restores the settings on the General tab to their default values and has nothing to do with file extensions.

D. Incorrect: This method would cause Windows Media Player to play the files but would not change the default program used to open files of those types.

5.   Correct Answers: B

A. Incorrect: xls is a Microsoft Excel file format.

B. Correct: xls is a Microsoft Excel file format.

C. Incorrect: xls is a Microsoft Excel file format.

D. Incorrect: xls is a Microsoft Excel file format.

6.   Correct Answers: C and D

A. Incorrect: Like other elements of the taskbar, the Quick Launch bar can be resized.

B. Incorrect: You do not need to be an administrator to unlock and lock the taskbar.

C. Correct: When the taskbar is locked, you cannot resize or move its components.

D. Correct: When the taskbar is locked, you cannot resize or move its components.

7.   Correct Answers: A

A. Correct: By default, the notification area hides inactive icons. You should explain to the user why this happens. If the user would feel more comfortable, you should explain to him how to make the antivirus software always show up in the notification area.

B. Incorrect: While it might be possible to find a process indicating that the antivirus software is running, this is certainly not the easiest way to find out. You are likely to confuse the user and show him a tool that without proper explanation could get him in trouble, and you might not be able to identify the correct process anyway.

C. Incorrect: This is unnecessary.

D. Incorrect: Although such an option might be available, it is likely already selected since the user noted seeing the icon previously. If expanding the notification area does not reveal the icon, this would be a logical subsequent step.

8.   Correct Answers: B

   A. Incorrect: If the Auto-Hide setting were turned on, the Taskbar would appear when she moved her pointer to the bottom of the display.

   B. Correct: Unlike a hidden taskbar, which pops up automatically when you move your pointer to the bottom of the display, a resized taskbar can be hard to find. If she cannot resize the taskbar, she may need to unlock it first.

   C. Incorrect: Restarting her computer would not restore the taskbar to its default state.

   D. Incorrect: This setting controls whether the notification area shows all icons or only active icons.

9.   Correct Answers: A and D

   A. Correct: This method will cause the icons for Calculator and Notepad to show up on the first level of the Start menu, directly under the Internet and Email icons.

   B. Incorrect: The Show On Desktop option is not available for these programs; it is available only for certain system folders, such as My Computer and My Documents.

   C. Incorrect: These items are not available on the Start Menu Items list. The Start Menu Items list contains only select system folders and special Start menu items.

   D. Correct: You can copy any shortcut from the Start menu or Windows Explorer to the Quick Launch bar for easy access.

10.   Correct Answers: B and D

   A. Incorrect: Although you can schedule these programs to open at a certain time, this is not a good way to address the user's request. There is no guarantee that she will arrive and log on at exactly the same time every morning.

   B. Correct: Although not as easy as just adding shortcuts to the programs to the Startup folder, this method will achieve the desired result.

   C. Incorrect: This is bad advice. Although the user might arrive to find her programs running each morning, leaving herself logged on to the computer when she is away is a significant security risk.

   D. Correct: This is the simplest way to achieve the desired results. Shortcuts in the Startup folder run each time Windows is started.

11.   Correct Answers: B

   A. Incorrect: Windows Firewall is not directly related to the antivirus software warnings. Additionally, disabling Windows Firewall would make the user's computer less secure.

   B. Correct: You can disable warnings about antivirus software by selecting the I Have An Antivirus Solution That I'll Monitor Myself check box.

   C. Incorrect: Security Center warnings do not give you the option to directly disable future warnings.

   D. Incorrect: Security Center antivirus warnings can be disabled by opening Security Center, clicking the Recommendations button in the Virus Protection area, and then selecting the I Have An Antivirus Solution That I'll Monitor Myself check box.

12.   Correct Answers: A

   A. Correct: If an application is causing DEP errors and the root cause of the problem cannot be fixed, you can prevent the error messages from appearing by disabling DEP for that specific application by using System Properties.

   B. Incorrect: Windows Firewall is not related to DEP.

   C. Incorrect: Windows Firewall is not related to DEP.

   D. Incorrect: You cannot configure DEP from Security Center. Instead, you must use System Properties.

15 Resolving Issues Related to Application Customization (3.0)

The Resolving Issues Related to Application Customization objective domain focuses on customizing Microsoft Office applications, Microsoft Internet Explorer, and Microsoft Outlook Express. The objective domain also covers customizing the Microsoft Windows XP operating system in support of running applications. You will make these customizations mostly to satisfy user requests for helping make applications work best to suit user needs.

The various applications that make up Microsoft Office 2003, including Word 2003, Outlook 2003, Excel 2003, and PowerPoint 2003, are highly customizable. Aside from setting standard program options that control how the programs themselves behave, you can also control which menus and toolbars are displayed and even which commands appear on those menus and toolbars. You can even create custom toolbars and menus and then populate them with just the right commands and macros to help users get their jobs done quickly and easily.

Internet Explorer also provides a high degree of customizability. You can control which buttons appear on the toolbars, the size of those buttons, and whether names of buttons are displayed. You can customize the Internet Explorer home page, control how temporary Internet files are stored and used, set up additional languages, and even control the way text appears on Web pages. You can also configure content, privacy, and security options to suit the user.

Outlook Express also provides a number of ways to customize its interface. As with Internet Explorer, you can control which buttons appear on the Outlook Express toolbar and how those buttons look. You can change text sizes and other formatting options for viewing messages, change the basic layout of elements in the Outlook Express window, and configure many options that control how e-mail and newsgroup information is downloaded and presented.

Finally, the Windows XP interface provides a greater degree of customization than any version of Windows to date. You can control many options concerning the Start menu, taskbar, and notification area that make finding, running, and switching between applications easy.

Tested Skills and Suggested Practices

The skills that you need to successfully master the Resolving Issues Related to Application Customization objective domain on the Supporting Users and Troubleshooting Desktop Applications on a Microsoft Windows XP Operating System exam include:

- Resolving issues related to customizing an Office application.
    - ❏ Practice 1: Add the Work menu to Word 2003, and add several favorite documents to it.
    - ❏ Practice 2: Create a custom menu in Excel 2003 named Web. Move the Web-related commands from the File menu to the new menu. Add any other Web-related commands you can find to that menu.
    - ❏ Practice 3: Configure Microsoft Outlook 2003 so that messages are composed in plaintext by default and so that Microsoft Word 2003 is used as the default editor for composing messages.
    - ❏ Practice 4: Configure Outlook 2003 so that messages are always spell-checked before they are sent.
- Resolving issues related to customizing Internet Explorer.
    - ❏ Practice 1: Set the text size for viewing Web pages in Internet Explorer to its largest settings. Configure Internet Explorer so that your settings override any settings configured for the websites you visit.
    - ❏ Practice 2: Add the Full Screen and Related buttons to your Internet Explorer toolbar.
    - ❏ Practice 3: Configure Internet Explorer so that temporary Internet files are allowed to use only up to 100 MB.
    - ❏ Practice 4: After installing Service Pack 2, use the Manage Add-ons tool to enable, disable, and update add-ons.
- Resolving issues related to customizing Outlook Express.
    - ❏ Practice 1: Add the Folder List button to the Outlook Express toolbar, and move it to the far left side of the toolbar.
    - ❏ Practice 2: Configure Outlook Express so that the Preview pane is shown to the right side of messages.
    - ❏ Practice 3: Configure Outlook Express so that the Contacts area and the status bar are not shown.
    - ❏ Practice 4: Configure Outlook Express so that it automatically checks for new messages every 10 minutes.

■ Resolving issues related to customizing the operating system to support applications.

❑ Practice 1: Configure the Windows XP taskbar so that similar taskbar buttons are grouped.

❑ Practice 2: Create a new folder named Shortcuts. In the new folder, create shortcuts to a number of your favorite programs, folders, and files. Create a new toolbar on the taskbar using the Shortcuts folder.

❑ Practice 3: Clear the list of recently used programs from the Start menu, and configure the Start menu so that only the four most recently used programs are shown on the list.

❑ Practice 4: Configure the Start menu to use small icons.

❑ Practice 5: Change to the classic Start menu instead of the default Windows XP Start menu.

Further Reading

This section lists supplemental readings by objective. Study these sources thoroughly before taking exam 70-272.

Objective 3.1   "Office 2003 Resource Kit." (Available online at *http://office.microsoft.com/en-us/FX011511471033.aspx*.) This site provides a wealth of information for IT professionals about supporting Office 2003, including the full text of the resource kit.

Microsoft Office System Inside Out, 2003 Edition, by Michael J. Young and Michael Halvorson. This book is designed for advanced users and includes information about configuring, supporting, and troubleshooting all of the Microsoft Office applications.

Microsoft Office System Inside Out, by Mary Millhollon and Katherine Murray.

Microsoft Office System Inside Out, by Craig Stinson and Mark Dodge.

Microsoft Office Outlook 2003 Inside Out, by Jim Boyce.

Objective 3.2   "Customize Your Web Browsing Layout." (Available online at *http://www.microsoft.com/windows/ie/using/howto/customizing/custombrowser.asp*.)

"Microsoft Internet Explorer 6 Resource Kit." (Available online at *http://www.microsoft.com/resources/documentation/ie/6/all/reskit/en-us/default.mspx*.) Review Part 5, "Customization and Installation."

"Control Internet Explorer Add-ons with Add-on Manager." (Available online at *http://www.microsoft.com/windowsxp/using/web/sp2_addonmanager.mspx*.)

Objective 3.3   "Organize Outlook Express E-Mail Messages." (Available online at *http://www.microsoft.com/windows/ie/using/howto/oe/organize.asp.*)

"Personalize Your E-Mail Messages." (Available online at *http://www.microsoft.com/windows/ie/using/howto/oe/personalize.asp.*)

Objective 3.4   *Microsoft Windows XP Inside Out, Deluxe Edition*, by Ed Bott, Carl Siechert, and Craig Stinson.

"How to Customize the Windows Explorer Views in Windows XP," Microsoft Knowledge Base article 307856. (Available online at http://support.microsoft.com/kb/307856/.)

"Microsoft Windows XP Professional Resource Kit Documentation," by Microsoft Corporation. (Available online at *http://www.microsoft.com/resources/documentation/Windows/XP/all/reskit/en-us/prork_overview.asp.*)

Objective 3.1

Resolve Issues Related to Customizing an Office Application

As a desktop support technician (DST), you should be able to customize the appearance and function of Microsoft Office applications to suit users' needs. You should be familiar with the options you can set using the Options dialog box in Microsoft Word, Microsoft Excel, Microsoft Outlook, and Microsoft PowerPoint. This includes configuring program functions, default file storage locations, and user information.

You should also know how to customize each application's interface, including adding and removing toolbars, creating custom toolbars and menus, and adding and removing commands from the interface.

Objective 3.1 Questions

1. A customer using Outlook 2003 tells you that he often sends messages to clients. He would like to be able to send copies of these messages to his boss without the customer being able to tell that the boss was copied on the message. How can you help the user?

    A. Use Outlook's View menu to turn on the BCC field.

    B. Use Outlook's View menu to turn on the CC field.

    C. Turn on the BCC field from within any new message window.

    D. Turn on the CC field from within any new message window.

2. A customer calls and tells you that she has recently upgraded from Excel 2000 to Excel 2003. Now, when she is working with a spreadsheet, she says that many of her menu commands are missing. What should you tell her to do? Choose all that apply.

    A. On the View menu, point to Toolbars, and select Show Full Menus.

    B. On the Options tab of the Customize dialog box, select Always Show Full Menus.

    C. On the Customize tab of the Options dialog box, select Always Show Full Menus.

    D. Use the Commands tab of the Customize dialog box to add each necessary command to the menus.

3. A user would like to add a menu to Microsoft Word that works like the Favorites menu in Internet Explorer. What should you do?

    A. Use the Customize dialog box to add Word's built-in Work menu.

    B. Use the Customize dialog box to add Word's built-in Favorites menu.

    C. Use the Customize dialog box to add Word's built-in Recent menu.

    D. Use the Customize dialog box to add Word's built-in Documents menu.

4. Which Office applications allow you to customize the shortcut menus that are available when you right-click elements in a document? (Choose all the apply.)

    A. Word

    B. Excel

    C. Outlook

    D. PowerPoint

5.   Which of the following actions is it possible to take in Office applications without having the Customize dialog box open?

    A. Hold down the ALT key and right-click a toolbar button or command to change its name.

    B. Hold down the ALT key and drag a toolbar button into a new position on the toolbar.

    C. Hold down the ALT key and drag a button or command away from a toolbar or menu to remove it.

    D. Hold down the ALT key and click a button or command to open its Properties dialog box.

6.   What is the name of the files created by Office applications so that documents can be restored in the event of an error or a crash?

    A. AutoSave files

    B. AutoRecover files

    C. AutoRestore files

    D. AutoRepair files

7.   A customer tells you that she has always had trouble spelling certain words. She has noticed that Microsoft Word fixes the spelling of some words when she types them and wants to know whether she can add her own common misspellings. What should you tell her?

    A. Use Word's AutoFormat As You Type feature to add new words to the list.

    B. Use Word's AutoCorrect feature to add new words to the list.

    C. Use Word's AutoText feature to add new words to the list.

    D. Word does not support adding new words for automatic spelling correction.

8.   A customer tells you that he has a separate hard drive installed on his system that Windows has assigned the letter D. He stores all of his documents in folders on that drive. In Word and Excel, when he uses the Open or Save As command, the applications always default to his My Documents folder. He wants to know whether he can change this so that Word and Excel open to his D drive instead. What do you tell the user?

    A. Use the Save tab of the Options dialog box in both programs to set the Documents location to the D drive.

B. Use the General tab of the Options dialog box in both programs to set the Documents location to the D drive.

C. Use the Save tab of the Options dialog box in both programs to set the Documents location to the D drive.

D. You cannot make this change in Word or Excel. The best option is to create a shortcut to the D drive in the My Documents folder.

Objective 3.1 Answers

1. **Correct Answers: C**

    A. **Incorrect:** There is no way to turn on the Blind Carbon Copy (BCC) field from Outlook's view menu.

    B. **Incorrect:** Recipients listed in the Carbon Copy (CC) field are visible to all recipients.

    C. **Correct:** The Blind Carbon Copy (BCC) field is used to send copies of a message to recipients and have those recipients be hidden from view. Activate the field from within any new message window, and the field will stay active for all new messages.

    D. **Incorrect:** Recipients listed in the CC field are visible to all recipients.

2. **Correct Answers: B**

    A. **Incorrect:** There is no Show Full Menus selection on the Toolbars submenu.

    B. **Correct:** By default, all Office 2003 applications use a feature named Personalized Menus that shows only common and recently used commands. Use the Always Show Full Menus check box to turn this feature on and off.

    C. **Incorrect:** There is no Customize tab on the Options dialog box.

    D. **Incorrect:** This is unnecessary. The commands are already present, just hidden.

3. **Correct Answers: A**

    A. **Correct:** Word's Work menu works much like the Favorites menu in Internet Explorer. Add it using the Commands tab of Word's Customize dialog box.

    B. **Incorrect:** Word does not have a built-in Favorites menu. The menu is named Work.

    C. **Incorrect:** Word does not have a built-in Recent menu. The menu is named Work.

    D. **Incorrect:** Word does not have a built-in Documents menu. The menu is named Work.

4. **Correct Answers: A and D**

    A. **Correct:** Using the Toolbars tab of the Customize dialog box, turn on the Shortcuts toolbar. Switch to the Commands tab to add commands to specific shortcut menus that are available on the Shortcuts toolbar.

    B. **Incorrect:** Excel does not allow customization of shortcut menus.

    C. Incorrect: Outlook does not allow customization of shortcut menus.

    D. Correct: Using the Toolbars tab of the Customize dialog box, turn on the Shortcuts toolbar. Switch to the Commands tab to add commands to specific shortcut menus that are available on the Shortcuts toolbar.

5.   **Correct Answers: C**

    A. Incorrect: You cannot do this in an Office application.

    B. Incorrect: You cannot do this in an Office application.

    C. Correct: This is the only toolbar and menu customization you can make without the Customization dialog box open.

    D. Incorrect: You cannot do this in an Office application.

6.   **Correct Answers: B**

    A. Incorrect: There are no AutoSave files in Microsoft Office.

    B. Correct: AutoRecover files are created periodically and are used in the event of a crash. You can use the Save tab of the Options dialog box in Word, Excel, and PowerPoint to control how often AutoRecover files are generated.

    C. Incorrect: There are no AutoRestore files in Microsoft Office.

    D. Incorrect: There are no AutoRepair files in Microsoft Office.

7.   **Correct Answers: B**

    A. Incorrect: AutoFormat As You Type does not automatically correct misspelled words.

    B. Correct: The AutoCorrect feature is available by selecting AutoCorrect Options on Word's Tools menu. Using the AutoCorrect tab, the user can add as many words to the list as she likes. Depending on the word, the user may also be able to right-click a misspelled word, click AutoCorrect, and then click the proper spelling.

    C. Incorrect: AutoText does not automatically correct misspelled words.

    D. Incorrect: This is not true. The user can use the AutoCorrect feature.

8.   **Correct Answers: C**

    A. Incorrect: You cannot set the Documents location on the Save tab.

    B. Incorrect: You cannot set the Documents location on the General tab.

    C. Correct: Use the File Locations tab to set the default Documents location as well as other file locations.

    D. Incorrect: This is not true. You can change the location in Word and Excel.

Objective 3.2

Resolve Issues Related to Customizing Internet Explorer

This section of the exam focuses on customizing the Microsoft Internet Explorer interface. As a DST, you need to know how to customize toolbars and other window elements. You should also understand how to configure the text size and colors used to display Web pages. Because many user problems are caused by Internet Explorer add-ons, you must understand how to enable, disable, and update add-ons by using the Manage Add-ons tool, which is included with Service Pack 2.

You should also understand how to configure and customize Internet Explorer by using the Internet Options dialog box, which includes a variety of tabs related to specific categories of settings.

To answer the questions in this objective, you should know how to configure general Internet Explorer settings, as well as security and privacy settings, resolve connectivity issues, and customize the Internet Explorer interface.

Objective 3.2 Questions

1.   A customer calls and tells you that the bottom part of her Internet Explorer window seems to be cut off. She used to see a picture of a lock at the bottom of the window when she was on a secure site, as well as text and other pictures. She wants to bring the bottom part of the window back and make it stay this time. What should you tell her? (Two answers form two parts to the correct solution.)

    A.   On the View menu, select the Status Bar command.

    B.   On the General tab of the Internet Options dialog box, select the Status Bar check box.

    C.   On the View menu, point to Toolbars, and then select Lock The Toolbars.

    D.   On the File menu, select Save Current View.

2.   A customer tells you that she recently set the text size in Internet Explorer to its largest size because she has trouble reading small text. However, most of the websites she visits are still displayed in smaller text. What should the customer do?

    A.   Use the Accessibility options on the General tab of the Internet Options dialog box to ignore the settings specified on Web pages.

    B.   Use the Advanced tab of the Internet Options dialog box to ignore the settings specified on Web pages.

    C.   These options must be configured using the Group Policy console.

    D.   There is no way to override the options set on Web pages.

3.   You get a call from a customer who complains that he likes using large buttons on the Internet Explorer toolbar, but the toolbar is not big enough to show all the buttons. He says that there are several buttons that he does not use and wants to know whether he can remove them. What do you tell him?

    A.   Use the General tab of the Internet Options dialog box to remove buttons from the toolbar.

    B.   Right-click any toolbar, and choose Customize. Use the Customize Toolbar dialog box to remove buttons from the current toolbar.

    C.   Hold down the ALT key while dragging the button away from the toolbar.

    D.   Run the Local Security Policy tool, and use it to remove the buttons.

4. Which of the following Internet Explorer features would you use if you wanted to keep from having to enter the same personal information every time you registered for a different site?

    A. Profile Assistant

    B. Content Advisor

    C. AutoComplete

    D. Certificates

5. One of your customers tells you that she often would like to view Web pages that are similar to a Web page she is viewing. She understands that she can use a search engine, but she often has trouble coming up with terms that properly describe the page; when she does come up with relevant terms, the number of search results is usually too large to deal with. How can you help her?

    A. Add the Related button to the Internet Explorer toolbar.

    B. Add the Similar button to the Internet Explorer toolbar.

    C. In the Address bar of Internet Explorer, type the word related followed by the URL of the page, and then click Go.

    D. In the Address bar of Internet Explorer, type the word similar followed by the URL of the page, and then click Go.

6. Recently, a Windows XP Service Pack 2 user installed an Internet Explorer add-on toolbar to help him search the Web. Since then, the user has noticed more advertisements and pop-up windows, and suspects the add-on toolbar might be the cause. The toolbar does not seem to be listed in Add Or Remove Programs. How should you prevent the add-on toolbar from responding to generated advertisements and pop-up windows?

    A. Click the Tools menu, and then click Manage Add-ons. Select the unwanted add-on, click Disable, and then click OK.

    B. Click the Tools menu, and then click Internet Options. Click the Security tab, and then click the Add-ons button. Click the unwanted add-on, click Uninstall, and then click OK.

    C. Click the Tools menu, and then click Internet Options. Click the Programs tab, and then click the Manage Add-ons button. Select the unwanted add-on, click Uninstall, and then click OK.

    D. Uninstall and then reinstall Internet Explorer.

7.   Which is the most efficient way to update an ActiveX Control Internet Explorer add-on?

    A. Visit the add-on developer's website to download and install an update.

    B. Enable Automatic Updates.

    C. Click the Tools menu, and then click Manage Add-ons. Select the add-on, and then click Update ActiveX.

    D. Click the Tools menu, and then click Manage Add-ons. Select the add-on. Click Disable, and then click Enable.

8.   Which is the most efficient way to update a non-ActiveX Internet Explorer add-on?

    A. Visit the add-on developer's website, and download and install an update.

    B. Enable Automatic Updates.

    C. Click the Tools menu, and then click Manage Add-ons. Select the add-on, and then click Update ActiveX.

    D. Click the Tools menu, and then click Manage Add-ons. Select the add-on. Click Disable, and then click Enable.

Objective 3.2 Answers

1. **Correct Answers: A and C**

   A. **Correct:** The status bar contains the lock icon denoting a secure site and other information. You can turn it on and off using the Status Bar command on the View menu.

   B. **Incorrect:** You cannot enable the status bar in this way.

   C. **Correct:** Locking the toolbars in Internet Explorer also locks the status bar, which will prevent it from being turned off in the future.

   D. **Incorrect:** There is no Save Current View command in Internet Explorer.

2. **Correct Answers: A**

   A. **Correct:** You can specify that colors, font styles, and font sizes specified on Web pages be ignored. Note, however, that this may cause some Web pages to be improperly formatted.

   B. **Incorrect:** You cannot use the Advanced tab to set these options.

   C. **Incorrect:** This is not true. The options are configured within Internet Explorer.

   D. **Incorrect:** This is not true. The options are configured within Internet Explorer.

3. **Correct Answers: B**

   A. **Incorrect:** You cannot remove buttons from the toolbar in this way.

   B. **Correct:** You can use the Customize Toolbar dialog box to add and remove buttons, as well as to change the size of the buttons.

   C. **Incorrect:** You cannot remove a button this way in Internet Explorer.

   D. **Incorrect:** The Local Security Policy tool cannot be used to control software interfaces.

4. **Correct Answers: A**

   A. **Correct:** The Profile Assistant stores personal information. You can access it from the Content tab of the Internet Options dialog box.

   B. **Incorrect:** Content Advisor lets you control which sites and content are accessed on the Internet. The parent assigns a password and configures settings for the content that Internet Explorer is and is not allowed to display without that password.

C. Incorrect: AutoComplete stores previous entries in the Address bar and some form fields, but you cannot rely on it to supply personal information every time.

D. Incorrect: Certificates are used to verify your identity or the identity of a Web publisher or certification authority.

5. **Correct Answers: A**

A. Correct: The Related button performs a search for similar Web pages. You can add it by right-clicking any toolbar and selecting Customize.

B. Incorrect: No similar button is available in Internet Explorer.

C. Incorrect: This technique will not return similar pages.

D. Incorrect: This technique will not return similar pages.

6. **Correct Answers: A**

A. Correct: Use the Manage Add-ons tool to enable and disable Internet Explorer add-ons.

B. Incorrect: You cannot use the Security tab of the Internet Options dialog box to uninstall add-ons. Instead, you should disable them with the Manage Add-ons tool.

C. Incorrect: You cannot use the Programs tab of the Internet Options dialog to directly uninstall add-ons. However, you can launch the Manage Add-ons tool from this tab. A more direct way is to open the Manage Add-ons tool directly from the Tools menu.

D. Incorrect: Reinstalling Internet Explorer would be overly complex. Instead, you should disable the add-on by using the Manage Add-ons tool.

7. **Correct Answers: C**

A. Incorrect: While add-on developers may offer updates on their websites, you must first find the developer's website. It is easier to use the Update ActiveX button from the Manage Add-ons dialog box.

B. Incorrect: Automatic Updates cannot be used to update ActiveX Control add-ons.

C. Correct: You can use the Manage Add-ons dialog box to update ActiveX Control add-ons.

D. Incorrect: Disabling and re-enabling an add-on does not cause it to be updated. Instead, you should click the Update ActiveX button.

8.   Correct Answers: A

A. Correct: Internet Explorer does not offer a tool to automatically update non-ActiveX add-ons. Therefore, the best way to update the add-ons is to visit the developer's website.

B. Incorrect: Automatic Updates cannot be used to update any type of Internet Explorer add-on.

C. Incorrect: While this is a very efficient way to update ActiveX Control add-ons, the button is disabled if you select a non-ActiveX add-on.

D. Incorrect: Disabling and re-enabling an add-on does not cause it to be updated. Instead, you should visit the add-on developer's website.

Objective 3.3

Resolve Issues Related to Customizing Outlook Express

Outlook Express is a popular messaging client, and many of your customers will expect you to know how to help them customize it to suit their needs, both as an e-mail client and as a newsreader.

To answer the questions in this objective, you should know how to customize the Outlook Express toolbar by changing the button size and text display and by adding new buttons. You should know how to customize the display of the Preview pane and other window elements. You should also know how to customize the display of e-mail messages, including the text size and format. Finally, you should be familiar with the program options in the Options dialog box.

Objective 3.3 Questions

1. A customer calls and tells you that she would like to be able to insert pictures into the bodies of messages she sends using Outlook Express. However, when she tries to insert a picture, she finds that the Picture command on the Insert menu of the message window is not available. What is likely the problem?

    A. The customer needs to configure Outlook Express to use Microsoft Word as the e-mail editor.

    B. The customer needs to change the format of the messages to plaintext.

    C. The customer needs to change the format of the messages to Rich Text (HTML).

    D. Outlook Express does not support images in the bodies of messages.

2. A customer using Outlook Express would like to include her name, her address, and a short disclaimer at the bottom of all outgoing messages. She would like this to be automatic. What should you do?

    A. Use the Mail Format tab of the Options dialog box to configure a signature for the user.

    B. Use the Mail Format tab of the Options dialog box to configure stationery for the user.

    C. Configure Microsoft Word as the e-mail editor, and then configure an AutoText entry with the desired text.

    D. Create a draft e-mail message with the required text, and copy it each time the user needs to type a new message.

3. You have a customer who shares her computer running Windows XP with her husband. They each have their own user account. Her husband uses Outlook 2003 for e-mail, and she uses Outlook Express. After she installed Outlook 2003, her default mail handler changed to Outlook 2003. She would like to change it back to Outlook Express. What is the best solution?

    A. Reinstall Outlook Express, and choose to make it the default mail handler the first time it runs.

    B. Use the General tab of the Options dialog box in Outlook Express to make it the default mail handler.

    C. Use the Maintenance tab of the Options dialog box in Outlook Express to make it the default mail handler.

    D. Use the Folder Options tool in the Windows Control Panel window to change the file association for message files to Outlook Express instead of Outlook.

4.   You have a customer who has a colleague who always requests read receipts on messages sent to the customer. The customer wants to know if there is a way to turn off the notifications. What should you tell him?

    A. You cannot turn off read receipt notifications in Outlook Express.

    B. Use the Never Send A Read Receipt option on the Receipts tab of the Options dialog box in Outlook Express.

    C. Use the Never Send A Read Receipt option on the Send tab of the Options dialog box in Outlook Express.

    D. Use the Never Send A Read Receipt option on the Connections tab of the Options dialog box in Outlook Express.

5.   One of your customers uses Outlook Express and has two separate accounts configured. She would like for her Inbox view to display a column that identifies the account for each message. She is sure she has seen this configured in a friend's Outlook Express. What should the customer do?

    A. Use the Columns command on the View menu to add the desired column.

    B. Use the Layout command on the View menu to add the desired column.

    C. Use the Customize Current View command on the View menu to add the desired column.

    D. Right-click any toolbar, and click Customize to add the desired column.

6.   You have a customer who uses Outlook Express. When the customer views a message in the Preview pane for more than a few seconds, the message is marked as read. The customer would like for messages not to be marked as read automatically. What should you tell the customer?

    A. Use the Layout command on the View menu, and clear the Mark Message Read After Displaying For ____ check box.

    B. Use the Read tab of the Options dialog box to clear the Mark Message Read After Displaying For ____ check box.

    C. Use the Compose tab of the Options dialog box to clear the Mark Message Read After Displaying For ____ check box.

    D. Use the General tab of the Options dialog box to clear the Mark Message Read After Displaying For ____ check box.

Objective 3.3 Answers

1.   Correct Answers: C

    A. Incorrect: You cannot configure Outlook Express to use Microsoft Word as an editor. This option is available in Microsoft Outlook.

    B. Incorrect: The customer needs to change the format to HTML to allow images to be included in the message body.

    C. Correct: Images can be inserted into the bodies of messages formatted in HTML only. If the Insert Picture command is unavailable, the message is probably formatted in plaintext.

    D. Incorrect: This is not true. Outlook Express does support images in message bodies that are in HTML format.

2.   Correct Answers: A

    A. Correct: A signature is text that is appended to all new messages created in Outlook Express.

    B. Incorrect: Stationery controls the background image and font settings of messages.

    C. Incorrect: You cannot configure Outlook Express to use Microsoft Word as an editor. This option is available in Microsoft Outlook.

    D. Incorrect: Although you can save drafts of messages in Outlook Express, you cannot copy them in this way.

3.   Correct Answers: B

    A. Incorrect: Reinstalling Outlook Express is not really an option. Also, this would be an unnecessarily cumbersome solution.

    B. Correct: The General tab has options for making Outlook Express the default mail handler and default news handler.

    C. Incorrect: This option is found on the General tab of the Options dialog box.

    D. Incorrect: While this change is possible to make, it would cause saved Outlook messages to open in Outlook Express and would not make Outlook Express the default mail handler.

4.   Correct Answers: B

    A. Incorrect: You can turn off read receipt notifications in Outlook Express by using the Receipts tab of the Options dialog box.

B. **Correct:** You can use this option to disable notifications and have Outlook Express never send a receipt.

C. **Incorrect:** This option is found on the Receipts tab of the Options dialog box.

D. **Incorrect:** This option is found on the Receipts tab of the Options dialog box.

5.   Correct Answers: C

A. **Correct:** A number of columns are available that are not displayed by default in Outlook Express.

B. **Incorrect:** The Layout dialog box lets you configure the window elements shown in Outlook Express as well as set Preview pane options.

C. **Correct:** The Customize Current View command lets you select whether specified messages are shown or hidden in a folder.

D. **Incorrect:** This opens the Customize Toolbar dialog box, which lets you add, remove, and customize toolbar buttons.

6.   Correct Answers: B

A. **Incorrect:** The Layout dialog box lets you change where the Preview appears, but not how messages are handled.

B. **Correct:** This command lets you turn off this feature or set the time limit before messages are marked as read.

C. **Incorrect:** The Mark Message Read After Displaying For ____ check box is found on the Read tab of the Options dialog box.

D. **Incorrect:** The Mark Message Read After Displaying For ____ check box is found on the Read tab of the Options dialog box.

Resolve Issues Related to Customizing the Operating System to Support Applications

Windows XP provides a highly customizable interface, offering more than one method for achieving almost any task. As a DST, you will be responsible for helping users customize their Windows XP desktops so that they can run applications more efficiently.

To answer the questions in this objective, you should know how to customize the Windows XP desktop. You should know how to configure options governing the Start menu and know how to add, remove, and arrange the items on the menu. You should also know how to set taskbar options and how to add custom toolbars and arrange them on the taskbar. Finally, you should understand how the notification area works and how to customize its interface.

Objective 3.4 Questions

1.   A user calls and says that when she is working in Microsoft Word, she is constantly interrupted by a dialog box asking whether she wants to use Sticky Keys. She always clicks Cancel to get out of the dialog box but would like it to stop appearing. What should she do?

    A. Turn off the shortcut by using the Accessibility Options tool in Windows Control Panel.

    B. Turn off the shortcut by using the Display tool in Windows Control Panel.

    C. Use the Customize dialog box in Word to dissociate the Shift key shortcut from the Sticky Keys option.

    D. Use the Customize dialog box in Word to assign a different function to the Shift key.

2.   Which of the following applications can be used to open files with the .avi extension?

    A. Microsoft Word

    B. Microsoft Excel

    C. Notepad

    D. Windows Media Player

3.   What is the name for the built-in taskbar toolbar that contains shortcuts to commonly used applications?

    A. System Tray

    B. Task Manager

    C. Notification Area

    D. Quick Launch

4.   One of your customers has resized her taskbar, making it larger so that it can accommodate the toolbars she uses and still show taskbar buttons. However, she would like it to disappear when she is not using it but appear automatically when she moves her pointer to the bottom of the display. What should you tell her to do?

    A. Right-click the taskbar, and turn off the Lock Taskbar option.

    B. Use the Taskbar And Start Menu Properties dialog box to clear the Keep The Taskbar On Top Of Other Windows check box.

    C. Use the Taskbar And Start Menu Properties page to select the Auto-Hide The Taskbar check box.

    D. Right-click the taskbar, and choose AutoHide.

5. From which of the following can you create a new toolbar on the Windows XP taskbar?

    A. A folder

    B. A document

    C. An Internet URL

    D. A picture file

6. A customer tells you that after letting his son use his computer, he came back to find the Windows taskbar on the right edge of his display. It is very narrow, and he cannot see anything on it well. He cannot seem to resize it or move it. What should he do? (Two answers make up two parts to the solution.)

    A. Right-click the taskbar, and clear the Lock Taskbar option.

    B. Drag the taskbar to the bottom edge of the display.

    C. Open the Taskbar And Start Menu Properties dialog box, and select the Bottom check box.

    D. Open the Taskbar And Start Menu Properties dialog box, and click Reset.

Objective 3.4 Answers

1.   Correct Answers: A and D

   A. Correct: By default, this dialog box opens when you press the Shift key five times in a row. Use the Accessibility Options tool to disable the shortcut key sequence for this and other accessibility options.

   B. Incorrect: The Display tool is used to control desktop display settings, not accessibility settings.

   C. Incorrect: You cannot control this setting from within Word.

   D. Correct: You cannot assign a function directly to the Shift key in Word.

2.   Correct Answers: D

   A. Incorrect: AVI is a movie format and cannot be opened with Word.

   B. Incorrect: AVI is a movie format and cannot be opened with Excel.

   C. Incorrect: AVI is a movie format and cannot be opened with Notepad.

   D. Correct: AVI is one of several movie formats that Windows Media Player can play.

3.   Correct Answers: D

   A. Incorrect: The term System Tray was used in previous versions of Windows.

   B. Incorrect: The Task Manager is a multitabbed dialog box that shows running applications, running processes, and performance information.

   C. Incorrect: The Notification Area contains the system clock and icons for background applications.

   D. Correct: The Quick Launch toolbar is an optional toolbar that can be displayed on the taskbar. Quick Launch contains shortcuts for launching programs.

4.   Correct Answers: C

   A. Incorrect: The Lock Taskbar option prevents the taskbar from being modified but does not automatically hide it when not in use.

   B. Incorrect: Clearing the Keep The Taskbar On Top Of Other Windows check box causes other windows to show up on top of the taskbar but does not make the taskbar appear when you move your pointer to the bottom of the display.

   C. Correct: This option causes the taskbar to disappear when not in use and reappear when you move your pointer to the bottom of the display.

   D. Incorrect: No AutoHide option is available on the taskbar's shortcut menu.

5. **Correct Answers: A and C**

    A. **Correct:** If you create a toolbar using a folder, all items in the folder appear as shortcuts on the toolbar—much like the Quick Launch toolbar.

    B. **Incorrect:** You cannot create a toolbar from a document.

    C. **Correct:** If you create a toolbar by using a URL, the actual Web page appears on the taskbar.

    D. **Incorrect:** You cannot create a toolbar from a picture file.

6. **Correct Answers: A and B**

    A. **Correct:** Before you can resize or move the taskbar, you must first make sure it is unlocked.

    B. **Correct:** Once the taskbar is unlocked, you can drag it to its original position at the bottom of the display.

    C. **Incorrect:** No Bottom check box is available on this dialog box.

    D. **Incorrect:** There is no Reset command in this dialog box.

16 Configuring and Troubleshooting Connectivity for Applications (4.0)

The Configuring and Troubleshooting Connectivity for Applications objective domain focuses on configuring and troubleshooting network connections in Microsoft Windows XP. Users of applications often require connectivity so that they can access documents located on a network, share documents with colleagues, and use e-mail. As a desktop support technician (DST), you should be able to isolate the cause of the problem when a user reports a loss of connectivity. Specifically, you should be able to configure network connectivity in Windows XP, as well as troubleshoot problems related to network adapter cards, network configuration, firewalls, and name resolution. In addition, you should be able to determine the best course of action to take when users report that they cannot access locally attached devices such as printers, scanners, mice, and so on.

Tested Skills and Suggested Practices

The skills that you need to successfully master the Configuring and Troubleshooting Connectivity for Applications objective domain on the Supporting Users and Troubleshooting Desktop Applications on a Microsoft Windows XP Operating System exam include:

- Identifying and troubleshooting name-resolution problems.
  - ❏ Practice 1: Use the ipconfig /all command to determine the Domain Name System (DNS) servers used by your computer.
  - ❏ Practice 2: Use the Properties dialog box for a network connection to determine whether the connection is configured to obtain DNS server addresses automatically.
- Identifying and troubleshooting network adapter configuration problems.
  - ❏ Practice 1: Use Device Manager to find out what kind of network adapter is used on your computer.

❑ Practice 2: Using Device Manager, disable the network adapter and restart your computer. Try to establish a network connection. Re-enable the network adapter.

❑ Practice 3: In Device Manager, open the Properties dialog box for your network adapter. On the Power Management tab, configure Windows XP so that the computer is not allowed to turn off the device to save power.

■ Identifying and troubleshooting LAN and Routing and Remote Access configuration problems.

❑ Practice 1: Configure a network connection in the Network Connections window to obtain an Internet Protocol (IP) address and DNS server addresses automatically.

❑ Practice 2: Configure a network connection in the Network Connections window to use a static IP address.

❑ Practice 3: Use the ipconfig /all command to determine the current Transmission Control Protocol/Internet Protocol (TCP/IP) settings for a computer.

❑ Practice 4: Familiarize yourself with the other tools available for troubleshooting network connections, including ping.exe, pathping.exe, and tracert.exe.

■ Identifying and troubleshooting network connectivity problems caused by the firewall configuration.

❑ Practice 1: On a computer running Windows XP with Service Pack 1 installed, enable Internet Connection Firewall (ICF) on a connection using the default settings.

❑ Practice 2: Upgrade a Windows XP computer to Service Pack 2. Notice that ICF is replaced by Windows Firewall, and that Windows Firewall is enabled by default.

❑ Practice 3: Configure Windows Firewall so that it allows inbound Web traffic on TCP port 80. Afterward, remove the unnecessary exception to reduce security risks.

❑ Practice 3: Turn on security logging for Windows Firewall. After using the Internet for a period of time, look through the log and become familiar with the entries.

❑ Practice 4: Configure Windows Firewall so that it allows incoming Internet Control Message Protocol (ICMP) ping requests.

■ Identifying and troubleshooting problems with locally attached devices.

❑ Practice 1: Install a Plug and Play device such as a digital camera or scanner into a computer running Windows XP.

❑ Practice 2: Determine the version of the driver software used by your display adapter. Determine whether a more recent version of the driver is available from the manufacturer.

❑ Practice 3: Determine whether there are any FireWire ports available on your computer.

❑ Practice 4: Determine the number of serial and parallel ports available on your computer.

Further Reading

This section lists supplemental readings by objective. Study these sources thoroughly before taking exam 70-272.

Objective 4.1 "Choosing a Name-Resolution Method." (Available online at *http:// www.microsoft.com/resources/documentation/Windows/XP/all/reskit/en-us/ prjj_ipa_lnia.asp*.) This site provides an overview of the name-resolution methods available in Windows XP.

Objective 4.2 "Troubleshooting Network and Other Internal Adapters." (Available online at *http://www.microsoft.com/resources/documentation/Windows/XP/all/ reskit/en-us/prdh_dmt_hdrj.asp*.)

"Microsoft Windows XP Professional Resource Kit Documentation." (Available online at *http://www.microsoft.com/resources/documentation/Windows/XP/all/ reskit/en-us/*.) Review Part IV, "Networking."

Microsoft Windows XP Professional Resource Kit, Third Edition, by The Microsoft Windows Team, with Charlie Russel and Sharon Crawford (Microsoft Press, 2005). Review Chapter 9, "Managing Devices."

Objective 4.3 "Understanding Routing." (Available online at *http://www.microsoft.com/ technet/prodtechnol/windowsserver2003/library/ServerHelp/e353ed05-da4d-411a-abd9- 41018224c1dc.mspx*.) Provides a good description of network routing in a corporate environment.

"Home Network Hardware Requirements." (Available online at *http://www.microsoft.com/ resources/documentation/Windows/XP/all/reskit/en-us/prcg_cnd_pnaf.asp*.) Explains the components involved in home networking.

Objective 4.4   "Internet Connection Firewall Feature Overview." (Available online at *http://www.microsoft.com/technet/prodtechnol/winxppro/plan/icf.mspx.*) Remember that ICF is replaced by Windows Firewall after installing Service Pack 2. However, you should understand ICF because some computers will not have Service Pack 2 installed.

"Understanding   Windows   Firewall."   (Available   online   at   *http:// www.microsoft.com/windowsxp/using/security/internet/sp2_wfintro.mspx.*)

"Windows XP Baseline Security Checklists." (Available online at *http://www.microsoft.com/ technet/security/chklist/xpcl.mspx.*)

Objective 4.5   "Windows Marketplace Tested Products List." (Available online at *http://testedproducts.windowsmarketplace.com.*) Shows products that have earned the "Designed for Windows" or the "Compatible with Windows" designation.

"Managing   Devices."   (Available   online   at   *http://www.microsoft.com/resources/ documentation/Windows/XP/all/reskit/en-us/prdh_dmt_zehg.asp.*) Review Chapter 9.

Identify and Troubleshoot Name-Resolution Problems

Name resolution is the process that allows network and Internet users to access resources by their names instead of their Internet Protocol (IP) addresses. The name used might be (among other things) a computer name, server name, printer name, or fully qualified domain name (FQDN). Without name resolution, users would be forced to remember the IP addresses of each resource on the network or on the Internet.

As a DST, you must be able to determine when an apparent lack of connectivity is the result of name-resolution issues. You should be able to use the tools in Windows XP to configure and troubleshoot name-resolution problems with client computers.

Objective 4.1 Questions

1. Which of the following name-resolution methods is the most common name-resolution method used on the Internet and on Windows Server 2003–based networks?

   A. Domain Name System

   B. Windows Internet Naming Service

   C. HOSTS files

   D. LMHOSTS files

2. Which of the following commands can you use to determine the IP addresses of the DNS servers configured for a computer running Windows XP?

   A. ipconfig

   B. ipconfig /all

   C. ipconfig /dns

   D. ipconfig /servers

3. You are troubleshooting a connectivity problem on the network of a small business. The business has eight computers that are connected together through a combination Ethernet router and switch, which also acts as a Dynamic Host Configuration Protocol (DHCP) server and provides access to the Internet. Each computer is connected directly to the Internet through the router, and all computers should retrieve all TCP/IP addressing information automatically. One of the users complains that although he can access other computers on the network, he cannot access any Internet websites or retrieve e-mail from an Internet server. The other computers on the network can access Internet websites and retrieve e-mail. You verify that the computer in question does not reach any websites when you type in the URL. However, you can get to websites when you type in the actual IP address. Also, you can successfully retrieve e-mail from the mail server if you configure Outlook Express to use the IP address of the mail server instead of its name. You use the ipconfig /all command on each computer and determine that the computer that cannot access websites has different DNS servers listed than the other computers. What is the likely problem?

   A. The computer should be configured to obtain DNS server addresses automatically.

   B. The DNS service is not installed on the computer.

   C. The computer should be configured to run Internet Connection Sharing (ICS).

   D. The computer should be configured to use WINS.

Objective 4.1 Answers

1.   Correct Answers: A

   A. Correct: DNS is the most widely used name-resolution method for the TCP/IP protocol. DNS is used on the Internet and on Windows Server 2003–based networks.

   B. Incorrect: WINS is supported only on Windows-based networks. It has been supplanted by DNS as the default name-resolution mechanism on modern Windows networks.

   C. Incorrect: HOSTS files are local text files that map host names and FQDNs to IP addresses. While they can be used to complement DNS naming, they are not commonly used.

   D. Incorrect: LMHOSTS files are text files located on the local computer that maps NetBIOS names to their IP addresses for hosts that are not located on a local subnet. Although they can be used to complement WINS naming, they are not commonly used.

2.   Correct Answers: B

   A. Incorrect: Typing ipconfig at the command prompt displays basic TCP/IP information that shows the IP address, subnet mask, and default gateway for each connection. However, it does not display DNS server information.

   B. Correct: Typing ipconfig /all at the command prompt displays detailed TCP/IP information, including the DNS servers configured for all connections.

   C. Incorrect: There is no /dns switch available for the ipconfig command.

   D. Incorrect: There is no /servers switch available for the ipconfig command.

3.   Correct Answers: A

   A. Correct: Because the router is acting as a DHCP server, computers should be configured to obtain IP addressing information and DNS server information automatically.

   B. Incorrect: The DNS service is installed automatically on computers running Windows XP. The problem at hand does not suggest a problem with the DNS service itself.

C. **Incorrect:** Internet Connection Sharing is a service that allows one computer to share its Internet connection with other computers on a network. Because all computers connect to the Internet directly through a router, ICS should not be used.

D. **Incorrect:** WINS is not used for Internet name resolution.

Identify and Troubleshoot Network Adapter Configuration Problems

A network adapter is a device, usually a card inserted into a computer, that provides network connectivity and features one or more jacks for plugging in a network cable. As a DST, you must be able to troubleshoot physical problems that might affect network connectivity, such as an unplugged or malfunctioning modem, an unplugged or bad cable, or even a damaged network adapter. You must also be able to troubleshoot the configuration of network adapters in Windows XP.

Question 4.2 Questions

1. You are working as a DST for a help desk. A user calls because he is having problems accessing his company network from home. He installed Windows XP Professional on his home computer earlier that day. He purchased a do-it-yourself kit from the local cable company and installed the cable modem and the network adapter supplied with the kit. After verifying that the cable modem is powered on and is physically connected to the computer, you have the user open Device Manager. He tells you that there is no device listed under the Network Adapters category. However, he tells you that he does see a device with a yellow exclamation point listed in the Unknown Devices category that is named PCI Network Adapter. What do you suspect is the problem?

   A. TCP/IP is not properly installed on the computer.

   B. The network adapter is not compatible with Windows XP.

   C. The driver is not installed for the device, or an improper driver is installed.

   D. The network adapter is not compatible with the cable modem.

2. Which of the following would you use to determine whether a network adapter was properly configured and working in Windows XP?

   A. Properties dialog box of a network connection

   B. Networking tab of the System Properties dialog box

   C. Device Manager

   D. Services

3. You are working as a DST for a help desk. You get a call from a user who has just changed offices. Instead of waiting for a technician, she had one of her coworkers help her move her computer to the new office. She can start the computer but cannot access the company network. Your company uses DHCP servers to provide IP addressing information to client computers automatically. What is the first thing you should have the user do?

   A. Type **ipconfig /all** at the command prompt and then tell you the IP address displayed.

   B. Make sure that she has connected a networking cable to her network adapter.

   C. Check Device Manager to see whether the network adapter is working properly.

   D. Check the Properties dialog box of the network connection to make sure that TCP/IP is installed.

Objective 4.2 Answers

1. **Correct Answers: C**

    A. Incorrect: The problem is with the configuration of the device itself, not with the TCP/IP protocol configuration.

    B. Incorrect: The information listed in the question does not suggest an incompatibility with Windows XP. Although it may turn out that the device is incompatible, it is too early to declare incompatibility to be the cause of this problem.

    C. Correct: The driver is not included by default in Windows XP. Were the correct driver installed, the device would be listed by name and would appear under the Network Adapters category in Device Manager, even if the device were disabled or not working properly.

    D. Incorrect: The information in the question does not suggest an incompatibility. Also, it is not likely that an incompatible network adapter would be included in a kit with the cable modem.

2. **Correct Answers: C**

    A. Incorrect: The Properties dialog box of a network connection is used to configure the clients and protocols associated with the connection—not the network adapter.

    B. Incorrect: There is no Networking tab on the System Properties dialog box.

    C. Correct: Device Manager lists the hardware devices on a computer, identifies the working status of each device, lets you to configure settings for the device, and enables you to identify and work with device drivers.

    D. Incorrect: The Services utility lets you view and configure all program services installed on Windows. Services does not let you configure hardware devices.

3. **Correct Answers: B**

    A. Incorrect: This is not the first step you should take. If it turns out that the networking cable is connected, using ipconfig /all should be your second troubleshooting step.

    B. Correct: Because the computer was working properly prior to the move, and because the computer is likely already configured to obtain an IP address automatically, it will most likely work following the move if it is connected properly.

C. Incorrect: This is not the first step you should take. If it turns out that the networking cable is connected, and after checking the IP addressing information, you may end up using this step later in the troubleshooting process.

D. Incorrect: Because the computer was working before the move, you can be pretty sure that TCP/IP is installed.

Identify and Troubleshoot LAN and Routing and Remote Access Configuration Problems

Windows XP includes a number of advanced networking features—more than any other client operating system. Windows XP includes stronger support than ever for the TCP/IP protocol and also includes advanced networking features such as ICS, Windows Firewall, and Remote Desktop. Windows XP also makes it easier than ever to connect to a local area network or to the Internet. Windows XP Service Pack 2 adds robust, user-friendly tools for connecting to wireless networks.

As a DST, you should know how to configure local area network connections, wireless network connections, and dial-up connections in Windows XP. You should understand how TCP/IP connections work and how to troubleshoot them when they do not work. Each device on a TCP/IP network is assigned one or more unique IP addresses that identify it on the network. Computers running Windows XP can be assigned a static (unchanging) IP address or can be configured to obtain IP addresses automatically from a DHCP server on the network. In addition to IP addresses, DHCP servers provide other TCP/IP information, such as subnet masks, default gateways, and DNS server addresses. Should a computer running Windows XP not be able to obtain an address automatically from a DHCP server, the computer will, by default, assign itself an address using Automatic Private IP Addressing (APIPA).

Objective 4.3 Questions

1.   You are working as a DST for a help desk. A user in your company is having problems connecting to the Internet and tells you that he tried to troubleshoot the problem himself using the Properties dialog box for the network connection. You have the user open the command prompt and type **ping 127.0.0.1**. The user receives an error message. What does this suggest to you?

    A. TCP/IP is not properly installed on the computer.

    B. The user should configure 127.0.0.1 as the static IP address for the connection.

    C. The computer is having trouble resolving names using the configured DNS servers.

    D. The 127.0.0.1 address is assigned by the Windows APIPA feature because a DHCP server cannot be located.

2.   One of your customers complains that he can connect to some network resources with no problem, but connections to some resources in remote offices seem particularly slow. You suspect that there may be problems with routing on the network. Which of the following tools is best for examining these issues?

    A. ipconfig

    B. ping

    C. pathping

    D. msconfig

3.   A user complains to you that he cannot connect to any network resources after installing a new networking card. You open the Command Prompt window on the user's computer and type **ipconfig /all**. You get the following results:

Ethernet adapter Local Area Connection:

```
        Connection-specific DNS Suffix. :
        Description . . . . . . . . . . . : Intel(R) PRO/1000 CT
        Physical Address. . . . . . . . . : 00-02-F4-32-04-2C
        Dhcp Enabled. . . . . . . . . . . : Yes
        IP Address. . . . . . . . . . . . : 169.254.102.111
        Subnet Mask . . . . . . . . . . . : 255.255.0.0
        Default Gateway . . . . . . . . . :
        DNS Servers . . . . . . . . . . . :
```

What do these results suggest? (Choose all that apply.)

    A. The computer is configured to connect to a DHCP server.

    B. The computer is not configured to connect to a DHCP server.

    C. The computer successfully connected to a DHCP server.

    D. The computer did not successfully connect to a DHCP server.

4.   You get a call from a home user. She tells you that she has two computers in her home: one is the main family computer, and one is her son's computer. Both computers are running Windows XP Home Edition. Her husband networked the two computers together so that the son could access the printer on the main computer. The main computer is connected to the Internet using a cable modem. She wants the other computer to be able to access the Internet as well, but does not want to pay for a separate Internet connection. What should you tell her?

    A. She can use ICS to share the connection.

    B. She can use ICS to share the connection, but both computers must be upgraded to Windows XP Professional Edition.

    C. She can use ICS to share the connection, but the main computer sharing the connection must be upgraded to Windows XP Professional Edition.

    D. She can use ICS to share the connection, but the son's computer must be upgraded to Windows XP Professional Edition.

5.   One of your customers owns a small business with six computers running Windows XP. The business has a single Internet connection—a cable modem connected to one of the computers. The owner configured ICS on the computer connected to the Internet and then restarted the other computers on the network. All computers except one could connect to the Internet. You ask her to type **ipconfig** at the command prompt of the computer that does not connect, and she gets the following result:

Ethernet adapter Local Area Connection:

```
    Connection-specific DNS Suffix. :
    IP Address. . . . . . . . . . . : 10.5.23.102
    Subnet Mask . . . . . . . . . . : 255.255.255.0
    Default Gateway . . . . . . . . : 10.5.23.1
```

What is the likely problem?

    A. The default gateway information is incorrect.

    B. The subnet mask is incorrect.

    C. The computer is configured with a static IP address.

    D. There are no DNS servers configured.

6. One of your customers has three computers on a home network, and each is running Windows XP Home Edition. The computers are named Client1, Client2, and Client3. The customer configured each computer with a static IP address. Client1 and Client2 can communicate successfully with one another. Client3 cannot establish a connection with the other computers on the network. The IP addresses assigned to the computers are as follows:

```
Client1: 192.168.0.1
Client2: 192.168.0.100
Client3: 192.168.0.254
```

Assuming that the networking adapter is configured and working properly, and that the network cable is plugged in, which of the following is probably the problem?

A. APIPA is enabled on Client3.

B. The address 192.168.0.254 is out of the acceptable range.

C. The subnet mask is incorrectly configured on Client3.

D. The default gateway is incorrectly configured on Client3.

7. One of your customers uses a dial-up connection to the Internet on his home computer. Recently, his Internet service provider (ISP) added a new access telephone number, and the customer wants to use that number instead of the main number. How can you change this information?

A. Use the Dialing Rules tab of the Phone And Modem Options Properties dialog box, available in the Windows Control Panel.

B. Use the General tab of the dial-up connection's Properties dialog box.

C. Use the Remote tab of the System Properties dialog box, available in the Windows Control Panel.

D. You must delete the current dial-up connection and create a new one.

8. One of your customers uses a dial-up connection to the Internet on his home computer. He says that every time the computer dials in to the Internet, the noise the modem makes is very loud, and he would prefer not to hear it at all. What can you tell your customer?

A. Click Configure on the General tab of the dial-up connection's Properties dialog box and clear the Enable Modem Speaker check box in the Modem Configuration dialog box.

B. Use the Dialing Rules tab of the Phone And Modem Options Properties dialog box, which is available in the Windows Control Panel.

    C. You cannot disable the modem speaker using the Windows XP interface. The customer should check the software that came with the modem.

    D. You cannot disable the modem speaker, but you can silence it by muting the general volume in Windows XP.

9. You are working as a DST for a help desk. Recently, your organization deployed a wireless network. You get a call from a user who has just installed a wireless network adapter and would like to connect to the wireless network. The computer is running Windows XP with Service Pack 2. You check Device Manager and verify that Windows XP has detected and installed the wireless network adapter. You then use the Ipconfig command to verify that the network adapter has not successfully received an IP address assignment from your DHCP server. What is the best way to check whether the network adapter has connected to your wireless network?

    A. In the Notification Area, right-click the wireless network adapter icon, and then click View Available Wireless Networks.

    B. From a command prompt, run ipconfig /all.

    C. In Device Manager, right-click the wireless network adapter and click Properties.

    D. In the Services console, right-click the Wireless Zero Configuration service, and click Properties.

Objective 4.3 Answers

1. **Correct Answers: A**

   A. Correct: 127.0.0.1 is the local host's loopback address. Pinging 127.0.0.1 successfully means that TCP/IP is installed on the computer.

   B. Incorrect: 127.0.0.1 is a reserved address known as the local loopback address. It should never be assigned as an actual IP address.

   C. Incorrect: Receiving an error message when pinging the local loopback address does not indicate a name-resolution problem.

   D. Incorrect: APIPA assigns addresses in the 169.254.0.0–169.254.255.255 range.

2. **Correct Answers: C**

   A. Incorrect: Ipconfig displays information about the TCP/IP configuration on a computer, not information about the route used to reach network resources.

   B. Incorrect: Ping is a command-line tool used to verify a connection to another IP address on the network, but it does not display routing information.

   C. Correct: Pathping is a command-line tool that traces a route through a TCP/IP network. It combines the features of the tracert and ping commands.

   D. Incorrect: Msconfig is used to control the Windows XP startup environment.

3. **Correct Answers: A and D**

   A. Correct: DHCP is enabled for this computer.

   B. Incorrect: DHCP is enabled on this computer.

   C. Incorrect: The computer did not connect to a DHCP server. You can tell because the computer assigned itself an IP address in the APIPA range of 169.254.0.0–169.254.255.255.

   D. Correct: The computer did not connect to a DHCP server. You can tell because the computer assigned itself an IP address in the APIPA range of 169.254.0.0–169.254.255.255.

4. **Correct Answers: A**

   A. Correct: ICS is available in Windows XP Home Edition and can be used to share one computer's Internet connection with other computers on the network.

   B. Incorrect: ICS is available in Windows XP Home Edition.

   C. Incorrect: ICS is available in Windows XP Home Edition.

   D. Incorrect: ICS is available in Windows XP Home Edition.

5.   Correct Answers: C

  A. Incorrect: The default gateway information is incorrect, but that is not the cause of the current problem.

  B. Incorrect: The subnet mask is not the cause of the current problem.

  C. Correct: The computer is most likely configured with a static IP address. Were it configured to obtain an IP address automatically (which it should be), the ICS computer would supply the client computer with an address in the 192.168.0.2– 192.168.0.254 range.

  D. Incorrect: It is not possible to tell from this result whether there are DNS servers configured. You need to type **ipconfig /all** to see this information.

6.   Correct Answers: C

  A. Incorrect: Whether APIPA is enabled or not does not matter. The client is configured with a static IP address.

  B. Incorrect: The address 192.168.0.254 is within the acceptable range.

  C. Correct: All computers must be on the same subnet (and therefore have the same subnet mask) to communicate with one another. An incorrect subnet mask is the only possible problem of those listed.

  D. Incorrect: It does not matter which default gateway is used. The default gateway is used only to forward network traffic to computers that are not on the same subnet. The computers in this example should be on the same subnet.

7.   Correct Answers: B

  A. Incorrect: The Phone And Modem Options Properties dialog box is used to configure your location and general settings for the modem—not information for a particular dial-up connection.

  B. Correct: The General tab of the Properties dialog box for the dial-up connection lets you change the phone number, configure alternate phone numbers, and set dialing rules.

  C. Incorrect: The Remote tab of the System Properties dialog box is used to configure Remote Assistance and Remote Desktop.

  D. Incorrect: This is not necessary. You can use the General tab of the Properties dialog box for the dial-up connection to change the phone number.

8.   Correct Answers: A

  A. Correct: The Modem Configuration dialog box allows you to disable the modem speaker.

  B. Incorrect: You cannot disable the modem speaker on the Dialing Rules tab.

    C. Incorrect: You can disable the speaker in Windows XP. Also, most modems do not have separate applications.

    D. Incorrect: The computer volume does not affect the modem speaker. Also, you can disable the modem speaker in Windows XP.

9. Correct Answers: A

    A. Correct: This opens the Wireless Network Connections window, which shows you available wireless networks and their current status. You can also configure wireless network keys from this window.

    B. Incorrect: Ipconfig /all does not display any information about wireless networks.

    C. Incorrect: Device Manager does allow you to configure some aspects of a wireless network adapter, such as advanced wireless settings. However, it does not enable you to view current or available wireless connections.

    D. Incorrect: Windows XP uses the Wireless Zero Configuration service to automatically connect to available networks. However, you cannot use the Services console to configure wireless networks. Instead, you should use the View Wireless Connections dialog box.

Objective 4.4

Identify and Troubleshoot Network Connectivity Problems Caused by the Firewall Configuration

A firewall acts as a security system that creates a border between a computer and the Internet, or between a local network and the Internet. The firewall blocks all incoming traffic from the Internet, except those types of traffic that you explicitly allow. Firewalls help keep malicious attacks from infiltrating the computer and network.

Windows XP has a built-in software-based firewall named ICF. After installing Service Pack 2, ICF is updated to Windows Firewall. Windows Firewall offers many more capabilities than ICF and requires very different troubleshooting and configuration. Any computer connected directly to the Internet, whether it is a standalone computer or a computer that provides ICS services for other computers on a network, should have a firewall enabled.

As a DST, you should understand how to enable ICF or Windows Firewall for a network or dial-up connection. You should understand what kinds of traffic you can configure the firewall to allow and how to do so. You should know how to enable security logging for the firewall, how to locate the log file, and what kinds of information the log file contains. You should also know the purpose of the Internet Control Message Protocol (ICMP) and how to configure the firewall to allow particular ICMP messages to pass through the firewall.

1. One of your customers runs a small business network that consists of four computers running Windows XP Professional. One computer has a dial-up Internet connection and is configured with ICS. The other three computers access the Internet through the ICS computer. Your customer wants to protect the network by using Windows Firewall. What must the customer do?

    A. The customer should upgrade to a dedicated Internet connection. Windows Firewall is not available on dial-up connections.

    B. The customer should enable Windows Firewall on the ICS computer only.

    C. The customer should enable Windows Firewall on all computers on the network.

    D. Windows Firewall cannot protect a network in this manner. The customer should buy a router with a built-in firewall and install it on the network.

2. One of your customers has a home computer that runs Windows XP Professional with Service Pack 1 and has a dedicated Internet connection. The customer has ICF configured on the computer. The customer has just installed Internet Information Services on the computer so that she can host her own website. However, users from the Internet cannot view the website. What should the customer do?

    A. On the Services tab of the ICF's Advanced Settings dialog box, select the Web Server (HTTP) check box.

    B. On the ICMP tab of the ICF's Advanced Settings dialog box, select the Web Server (HTTP) check box.

    C. The customer should install ICS on the computer.

    D. The customer must disable ICF in order to allow access to the website.

3. What is the best way to configure Windows Firewall to allow incoming HTTP requests to IIS?

    A. Open Control Panel, and then open Security Center. Click Windows Firewall, and then click the Exceptions tab. Select the Internet Information Services check box.

    B. Open Control Panel, and then open Security Center. Click Windows Firewall, and then click the Exceptions tab. Click Add Port. In the Name box, type **IIS**. In the Port Number box, type **80**. Click TCP, and then click OK.

   C. Open Control Panel, and then open Security Center. Click Windows Firewall, and then click the Exceptions tab. Click Add Port. In the Name box, type **IIS**. In the Port Number box, type **80**. Click UDP, and then click OK.

   D. Open Control Panel, and then open Security Center. Click Windows Firewall, and then click Off.

4. One of your customers runs a database on her computer that allows applications to connect using TCP port 34562. The user prefers to keep Windows Firewall enabled on her Internet connection, but Windows Firewall prevents people from connecting to her database. Which of the following solutions would enable other users to connect to the database? (Choose all that apply.)

   A. Use the Add Port button on the Exceptions tab of the Windows Firewall dialog box to add the service and port number to those that Windows Firewall allows.

   B. On the Exceptions tab of the Windows Firewall dialog box, select the Allow Custom Services Above Port# 30000 check box.

   C. On the Advanced tab of the Windows Firewall dialog box, click the Settings button under ICMP to add the service and port number to those that Windows Firewall allows.

   D. Use the Add Program button on the Exceptions tab of the Windows Firewall dialog box to add the database program to those that Windows Firewall allows.

5. One of your customers runs a game server on his Windows XP Service Pack 2 computer. For game clients to detect whether the game server is full, the game client software must be able to ping the game server. When a game client tries to connect to the server, the game client software uses TCP port 8452 to connect to the game server. Your customer has Windows Firewall enabled, and he has already created an exception for TCP port 8452. What else must the customer do to allow the remote game client software to successfully ping his game server?

   A. On the Windows Firewall dialog box, click the Exceptions tab. Click the Add Port button, click Ping, and then click OK.

   B. On the Windows Firewall dialog box, click the Exceptions tab. Click the ICMP button, and then select the Allow Ping Requests check box.

   C. On the Windows Firewall dialog box, click the Advanced tab. Under ICMP, click Settings. Select the Allow Incoming Router Request check box, and then click OK.

   D. On the Windows Firewall dialog box, click the Advanced tab. Under ICMP, click Settings. Select the Allow Incoming Echo Request check box, and then click OK.

6. Which of the following types of information is collected in the Windows Firewall security log? (Choose all that apply.)

     A. Source IP

     B. Destination port

     C. Source DNS host name

     D. Source user name

Objective 4.4 Answers

1. **Correct Answers: C**

    A. Incorrect: Windows Firewall is available on dial-up connections.

    B. Incorrect: All computers should have Windows Firewall, ICF, or another host-based firewall enabled, even if there is another firewall protecting them from Internet attacks. The reason for this is that many attacks originate from the internal network. For example, if one of the user's four computers is a notebook, it might become infected with a worm while connected to an unprotected wireless network at a coffee shop. The next time the infected computer connected to the internal network, the worm could spread to the other computers if they do not have a firewall running.

    C. Correct: All computers should have Windows Firewall, ICF, or another host-based firewall enabled, even if there is another firewall protecting them from Internet attacks. The reason for this is that many attacks originate from the internal network. For example, if one of the user's four computers is a notebook, it might become infected with a worm while connected to an unprotected wireless network at a coffee shop. The next time the infected computer connected to the internal network, the worm could spread to the other computers if they do not have a firewall running.

    D. Incorrect: Windows Firewall can protect a network if it is enabled on the ICS computer that is directly connected to the Internet. However, all computers on the network should have a host-based firewall enabled to protect against attacks originating from the internal network.

2. **Correct Answers: A**

    A. Correct: Use the Services tab to select the services running on a computer that Internet users are allowed to access.

    B. Incorrect: The Web Server (HTTP) check box, as well as options for allowing other services, are located on the Services tab.

    C. Incorrect: ICS is used to share a computer's Internet connection with other computers on a local network.

    D. Incorrect: You can configure ICF to allow certain types of incoming traffic, including Web traffic.

3. **Correct Answers: B**

   A. **Incorrect:** There is no Internet Information Services check box on the Exceptions tab. Instead, you must manually add exceptions for the port number used by IIS, which is 80.

   B. **Correct:** IIS, by default, uses TCP port 80. To enable users to connect to IIS and view Web content, you must add an exception for that port number. While Windows Firewall automatically adds exceptions for many applications, it does not automatically add an exception for IIS.

   C. **Incorrect:** While this is the correct procedure for adding an exception for a port number, IIS uses TCP port 80, not UDP port 80.

   D. **Incorrect:** This disables Windows Firewall. While this would allow external users to view Web content, it would dramatically reduce the overall security of the computer. A more efficient method for allowing users to view Web content is to add an exception for TCP port 80.

4. **Correct Answers: A and D**

   A. **Correct:** You can add new services to those that Windows Firewall allows traffic for.

   B. **Incorrect:** There is no Allow Custom Services Above Port# 30000 check box.

   C. **Incorrect:** The Settings button under ICMP is used to create exceptions for ICMP messages only, not for applications.

   D. **Correct:** With Windows Firewall, you can create exceptions either for specific port numbers or for applications. Typically, it is more efficient and secure to configure exceptions by using the Add Program button.

5. **Correct Answers: D**

   A. **Incorrect:** Clicking the Add Port button does not give you the option to enable ping requests.

   B. **Incorrect:** There is no ICMP button on the Exceptions tab.

   C. **Incorrect:** To enable ping requests to succeed, you must select the Allow Incoming Echo Request check box. Selecting the Allow Incoming Router Request check box will not enable ping requests.

   D. **Correct:** The Allow Incoming Echo Request check box controls whether a remote computer can ask for and receive a response from the computer. Ping is a command that requires you to enable this option.

6. **Correct Answers: A and B**

A. **Correct:** The source IP (the IP address from which the traffic originated) is collected in the security log.

B. **Correct:** The destination port (the port number the traffic is configured to use) is collected in the security log.

C. **Incorrect:** The Source DNS host name is not collected by the security log.

D. **Incorrect:** The Source user name is not collected by the security log.

Objective 4.5

Identify and Troubleshoot Problems with Locally Attached Devices

As a DST, you will often be approached by users who are having trouble with devices attached to their computer. From an application support standpoint, you may be faced with questions about why a user cannot print a document, scan in an image, or get a handheld device to work.

All computers have different types of ports available, including serial ports, parallel ports, Universal Serial Bus (USB) ports, FireWire (or IEEE 1394) ports, infrared ports, and wireless ports. You should know the types of devices that use each type of port; how to configure ports in a computer's basic input/output system (BIOS) and in Windows XP; and how to determine whether a problem is caused by hardware, configuration, or application settings.

Objective 4.5 Questions

1. Which of the following types of ports is represented in Device Manager by the label Printer Port (LPT1)?

    A. A parallel port

    B. A serial port

    C. A FireWire port

    D. A USB port

2. A customer using Windows XP Home Edition calls and complains that he has connected an external 56-Kbps modem to his computer using a serial cable. However, the download speeds for the modem seem very slow to the user. What should you check first?

    A. You should download the latest firmware from the modem manufacturer's website and update the modem.

    B. You should tell the user that external modems are limited by the speed of the serial port, which is far less than 56 Kbps.

    C. You should configure a higher speed using the Properties dialog box for the network connection configured for the modem.

    D. You should use the modem's Properties dialog box in Device Manager to change the port speed for the serial port.

3. One of your users has just purchased a used printer with a parallel port connection and asks you to set it up. You connect the printer to the parallel port and install the software that came with the printer but cannot get Windows to recognize the printer. You check Device Manager, and you do not see a printer port listed in the Ports (COM & LPT) category. What is the likely problem?

    A. The parallel port is disabled in the computer's BIOS.

    B. The proper drivers are not installed for the port.

    C. The parallel cable you are using is bad.

    D. You should run Windows Update to locate more recent software for the printer.

4. Which of the following lists represents the correct order of each port type's maximum rated speed from slowest to fastest?

    A. Serial, FireWire, USB 1.1, USB 2.0

    B. Serial, USB 1.1, USB 2.0, FireWire

    C. USB 1.1, Serial, USB 2.0, FireWire

    D. USB 1.1, USB 2.0, Serial, FireWire

5. A customer calls and tells you that he recently installed a new driver for his scanner. Following the installation, his scanner stopped working. The customer has performed no other actions. The customer would like his scanner working as quickly as possible and no longer cares about updating the driver. What is the best action to take?

    A. Use the Driver tab of the scanner's Properties dialog box in Device Manager to roll back the driver to the previous version.

    B. Use the Add Or Remove Programs tool in Control Panel to uninstall the updated driver.

    C. Disconnect the scanner and then reconnect it.

    D. Disconnect the scanner, uninstall all software related to the scanner, and then reinstall the scanner using the original software.

Objective 4.5 Answers

1.   Correct Answers: A

A. Correct: Printer Port (LPT1) is a parallel port.

B. Incorrect: Printer Port (LPT1) represents a parallel port, not a serial port. Serial ports are represented in Device Manager with the label Communications Port (COM*x*), where *x* is the number of the port.

C. Incorrect: Printer Port (LPT1) represents a parallel port, not a FireWire port. FireWire ports are represented in Device Manager by the label FireWire Controllers or IEEE 1394 Bus Host Controllers.

D. Incorrect: Printer Port (LPT1) represents a parallel port, not a USB port. USB ports are grouped in a common category in Device Manager labeled Universal Serial Bus Controllers.

2.   Correct Answers: D

A. Incorrect: External modems are not typically upgradeable in this manner. This method does not solve the problem, anyway.

B. Incorrect: This is not true; serial ports are capable of speeds up to 128Kpbs.

C. Incorrect: You must use Device Manager to change the port speed.

D. Correct: You can use the modem's Properties dialog box to change the supported speed of the port to match or exceed the speed of the modem.

3.   Correct Answers: A

A. Correct: If you do not see a port listed in the Ports (COM & LPT), the chances are high that the port is disabled in the computer's BIOS.

B. Incorrect: Windows XP includes built-in drivers for serial and parallel ports. Were a port available, it would be configured automatically.

C. Incorrect: A bad parallel cable would not cause the printer port to not be listed in Device Manager.

D. Incorrect: Windows Update does not provide third-party software other than certain hardware drivers. This method does not solve the problem, anyway.

4.   **Correct Answers: B**

    A.   Incorrect: This is not the correct order.

    B.   Correct: This is the correct order. Serial ports have a maximum speed of 128Kpbs. USB 1.1 has a maximum speed of 12Mbps. USB 2.0 has a maximum speed of 480Mbps. FireWire has a maximum speed of 800Mbps.

    C.   Incorrect: This is not the correct order.

    D.   Incorrect: This is not the correct order.

5.   **Correct Answers: A**

    A.   Correct: Windows XP allows you to roll a driver back to a previous version if a new driver causes problems.

    B.   Incorrect: Hardware drivers do not usually display hardware drivers.

    C.   Incorrect: This does not solve a problem caused by a new driver.

    D.   Incorrect: Although this would probably achieve the desired result, it is an overly burdensome solution.

17 Configuring Application Security (5.0)

The Configuring Application Security objective domain focuses on four aspects of security in Microsoft Windows XP: configuring share and NTFS permissions, applying critical software updates to Windows XP and Microsoft Office, resolving virus issues, and configuring security within applications.

As a desktop support technician (DST), you should understand the difference between Simple File Sharing in Windows XP and the standard file sharing method. You should also understand how share permissions and NTFS permissions combine and interact, and how to configure both. Often, users' inability to access folders and documents is the result of security applied to those objects.

Microsoft supplies software updates for both the Windows XP operating system and for Office applications. You should understand how to configure Windows XP to download and install critical updates automatically. After installing Service Pack 2, Automatic Updates can download and install a wider variety of updates. You should understand the types of updates Automatic Updates can provide, as well as the types of updates that you will need to install manually.

You must also be aware of the damage that an unchecked virus infection can cause on a user's computer. You should be able to use Security Center (included with Service Pack 2) to determine if antivirus software is installed, and know how to configure antivirus software and keep it properly updated if antivirus software is missing.

Finally, you should be aware of the security offerings of the various applications in Office. You can configure how each application allows macros to run, as well as configure other document-specific protections.

Tested Skills and Suggested Practices

The skills that you need to successfully master the Configuring Application Security objective domain on the Supporting Users and Troubleshooting Desktop Applications on a Microsoft Windows XP Operating System exam include:

- Identifying and troubleshooting problems related to security permissions.
    - ❏ Practice 1: Share a folder using Simple File Sharing in Windows XP.
    - ❏ Practice 2: Create a new local user and a new local group on a computer running Windows XP. Make the new user a member of the new group.

❑ Practice 3: Turn off Simple File Sharing. Configure and test share permissions on a folder.

❑ Practice 4: Configure and test NTFS permissions on a folder. Note that the folder must be on a drive formatted with the NTFS file system in order to do this.

■ Identifying and responding to security incidents.

❑ Practice 1: Install antivirus software on a computer running Windows XP. Update the software with the latest virus definitions and run a virus scan on the computer.

❑ Practice 2: Configure the Automatic Updates feature in Windows XP to download and install critical updates automatically.

❑ Practice 3: Visit the Microsoft Update site at *http://windowsupdate.microsoft.com*. Perform both Express and Custom updates, and note the differences.

■ Managing application security settings.

❑ Practice 1: Set the macro security level to high in each of the Office applications. Examine the differences between the security levels.

❑ Practice 2: Configure Microsoft Word so that it does not save personal information with a document.

❑ Practice 3: Protect a Word document so that formatting is restricted. Protect a Microsoft Excel spreadsheet so that cells cannot be altered.

Further Reading

This section lists supplemental readings by objective. Study these sources thoroughly before taking exam 70-272.

Objective 5.1   "How to Set Security in Windows XP Professional That Is Installed in a Workgroup," Microsoft Knowledge Base article 290403. (Available online at *http://support.microsoft.com/kb/290403/)*

"How to Disable Simplified Sharing and Set Permissions on a Shared Folder in Windows XP," Microsoft Knowledge Base article 307874. (Available online at *http://support.microsoft.com/kb/307874/.)*

Microsoft Windows XP Inside Out, by Carl Siechert and Ed Bott. This book is designed for advanced users and includes information on configuring, supporting, and troubleshooting Windows XP.

Objective 5.2   "Securing Windows XP Desktops Resource Guide." (Available online at *http://www.microsoft.com/technet/security/chklist/winxpsrg.mspx.*)

"Changes to Functionality in Microsoft Windows XP Service Pack 2, Part 6: Computer Maintenance." (Available online at *http://www.microsoft.com/technet/prodtechnol/winxppro/maintain/sp2maint.mspx.*)

Objective 5.3   'Microsoft Office 2003 Editions Security Whitepaper." (Available online at *http://www.microsoft.com/technet/prodtechnol/office/office2003/operate/o3secdet.mspx.*)

Objective 5.1

Identify and Troubleshoot Problems Related to Security Permissions

Windows XP provides a feature named Simple File Sharing that is designed to make sharing files on small business and home networks easier for users. When you disable Simple File Sharing, more powerful security features become available. With Simple File Sharing disabled, you can configure specific permissions for users and groups when you share a resource. You can also configure NTFS permissions to provide powerful local security on disks formatted with the NTFS file system.

As a DST, you should be able to configure security permissions and determine when security permissions are preventing users' access to resources.

Objective 5.1 Questions

1. You get a call from a user who is trying to access a folder named Payroll. NTFS permissions are used to control access to the folder. The user is a member of a group named Sales, a group named Accounts, and a group named Executives. NTFS permissions are assigned to the Payroll folder as follows:

Sales group: Full Control permission denied to the folder

Accounts group: Full Control permission allowed to the folder

Executives group: Read permission allowed to the folder

The user's account: Modify permission allowed to the folder

What is the user's effective NTFS permission on the folder?

    A. The user cannot access the folder at all.

    B. The user has Full Control permission on the folder.

    C. The user has only Modify permission on the folder.

    D. The user has only Read permission on the folder.

2. You receive a call from a customer that manages a small business. The business has 10 computers on a network, all running Windows XP Professional Edition and members of the same workgroup. One of the computers has several folders on it that the manager wants to share on the network but control access to. The manager right-clicks the folder and chooses the Properties command. You ask her to switch to the Security tab, but she says she does not see one. Which of the following could be the reason? (Choose all that apply.)

    A. The user is not logged on using an account with administrator permissions

    B. Simple File Sharing is enabled on the computer

    C. The drive containing the folder is formatted with the FAT32 file system

    D. The computer must be part of a domain in order to assign NTFS permissions

3. What is the maximum number of users who can connect simultaneously to a single folder shared on a computer running Windows XP Professional?

    A. 1

    B. 5

    C. 10

    D. 15

Objective 5.1 Answers

1.   Correct Answers: A

    A. Correct: Being denied access overrides any access a user is allowed. Because the user is denied the Full Control permission, he is denied access to the folder entirely.

    B. Incorrect: Being denied access overrides any access a user is allowed. Because the user is denied the Full Control permission, he is denied access to the folder entirely.

    C. Incorrect: Being denied access overrides any access a user is allowed. Because the user is denied the Full Control permission, he is denied access to the folder entirely.

    D. Incorrect: Being denied access overrides any access a user is allowed. Because the user is denied the Full Control permission, he is denied access to the folder entirely.

2.   Correct Answers: B and C

    A. Incorrect: You do not need to be an administrator to assign permissions to a folder.

    B. Correct: When Simple File Sharing is enabled, the Security tab is not available. You can set NTFS permissions only when Simple File Sharing is disabled.

    C. Correct: The Security tab (and NTFS permissions) is available only on drives that are formatted with the NTFS file system.

    D. Incorrect: You can assign NTFS permissions on computers in a workgroup.

3.   Correct Answers: C

    A. Incorrect: Ten users can connect simultaneously to a single folder shared on a computer running Windows XP Professional.

    B. Incorrect: Ten users can connect simultaneously to a single folder shared on a computer running Windows XP Professional.

    C. Correct: Ten users can connect simultaneously to a single folder shared on a computer running Windows XP Professional.

    D. Incorrect: Ten users can connect simultaneously to a single folder shared on a computer running Windows XP Professional.

Identify and Respond to Security Incidents

As a DST, you need to be able to identify and respond to security incidents. You must be able to explain to users the importance of using antivirus software and keeping the software up to date. You should be able to configure antivirus software on a user's computer. You also must be able to configure Windows XP to automatically download and install critical updates. You should also be able to install updates manually using the Windows Update site.

Objective 5.2 Questions

1. After installing Service Pack 2, which of the following types of updates can you configure the Automatic Updates feature in Windows XP to download automatically?

    A. Critical updates for Windows

    B. Critical updates for non-Microsoft applications

    C. Driver updates for Windows

    D. Updates for Microsoft Office applications

2. A customer calls and tells you that she is having strange problems on her computer. She believes that her computer has a virus. She has antivirus software installed, and the software has not identified a problem. What should you have the user do?

    A. Reinstall the antivirus software.

    B. Boot Windows into Safe Mode and run a virus scan.

    C. Update the antivirus software with the latest virus definitions and run a virus scan.

    D. Run the Windows System File Checker.

3. You are configuring Automatic Updates for a user with Windows XP Service Pack 2. Which of the following are the recommended settings for running Automatic Updates?

    A. Automatic

    B. Download Updates For Me, But Let Me Choose When To Install Them

    C. Notify Me But Don't Automatically Download Or Install Them

    D. Turn Off Automatic Updates

4. Recently, a user's computer was infected by a virus. Unfortunately, the virus destroyed much of her data, and technical support had to reformat her hard disk and reinstall Windows XP and Service Pack 2 to ensure that the virus was removed. The user asks you what additional software, if any, she should install to reduce the risk from all types of malicious software. What is your reply? (Choose all that apply.)

    A. Antivirus software

    B. Antispyware software

    C. Personal firewall software

    D. Peer-to-peer software

Objective 5.2 Answers

1.   Correct Answers: A, C, and D

    A. Correct: Both before and after Service Pack 2, Automatic Updates can download and install critical updates automatically.

    B. Incorrect: Automatic Updates cannot download updates for non-Microsoft applications. You will need to identify alternative methods of keeping non-Microsoft applications updated.

    C. Correct: Automatic Updates can download driver updates automatically after installing Service Pack 2. Prior to Service Pack 2, Automatic Updates could not download driver updates.

    D. Correct: Automatic Updates can download Microsoft Office updates automatically. Prior to Service Pack 2, Automatic Updates could not download updates for Microsoft Office applications.

2.   Correct Answers: C

    A. Incorrect: This does not help the antivirus software catch a virus that it missed previously.

    B. Incorrect: Running the antivirus software from Safe Mode does not make a difference and might not be possible, anyway.

    C. Correct: The user should make sure that her virus software is up to date. After any virus issues are resolved, the user should also configure her antivirus software to keep itself updated automatically.

    D. Incorrect: The System File Checker checks the integrity of Windows system files; it does not detect viruses.

3.   Correct Answers: A

    A. Correct: The recommended practice is to configure Windows to automatically download and install updates.

    B. Incorrect: The recommended practice is to configure Windows to automatically download and install updates.

    C. Incorrect: You should configure Windows to automatically download and install updates.

    D. Incorrect: You should configure Windows to automatically download and install updates.

4.   Correct Answers: A and B

A. Correct: Windows XP does not have antivirus capabilities. Therefore, she will need to install antivirus software.

B. Correct: Windows XP does not have antispyware software. Therefore, she will need to install antispyware software.

C. Incorrect: Windows XP with Service Pack 2 includes Windows Firewall, which is personal firewall software. Although non-Microsoft personal firewall software might have additional features, Windows Firewall is sufficient for most users.

D. Incorrect: Peer-to-peer software does not offer any security protection. In fact, many viruses, worms, spyware, adware, and other malicious software infections occur because of peer-to-peer software.

Manage Application Security Settings

Each of the applications in Office offers the capability to configure how the application runs macros, which can often contain malicious code. In addition, some of the Office applications offer additional security settings. Word and Excel both offer ways to protect documents so that other users cannot modify them. Word, Excel, and Microsoft PowerPoint also offer a feature to keep the application from storing users' personal information with documents.

Objective 5.3 Questions

1.   Which of the following macro security levels prompts the user to choose whether potentially unsafe macros can be run?

    A. Very High

    B. High

    C. Medium

    D. Low

2.   One of your customers has created an Excel spreadsheet. The sheet has a number of cells in which data can be entered and several calculation cells that perform calculations on the entered data. The customer wants to protect only the cells that contain the formulas so that users of the spreadsheet can enter data but not alter the formulas. What should you tell him?

    A. The user must unlock all cells on the spreadsheet, lock only the formula cells, and then protect the document so that users cannot select locked cells.

    B. The user must lock the formula cells, and then protect the document so that users cannot select locked cells.

    C. The user must format the cells with formulas to be hidden.

    D. The user should lock the cells with formulas, and then enable the Read-Only attribute for the spreadsheet file.

Objective 5.3 Answers

1.   Correct Answers: C

   A. Incorrect: The Medium macro security level prompts the user to choose whether potentially unsafe macros can be run.

   B. Incorrect: The Medium macro security level prompts the user to choose whether potentially unsafe macros can be run.

   C. Correct: The Medium macro security level prompts the user to choose whether potentially unsafe macros can be run.

   D. Incorrect: The Medium macro security level prompts the user to choose whether potentially unsafe macros can be run.

2.   Correct Answers: A

   A. Correct: This method protects the cells with formulas while allowing users to enter data into the other cells.

   B. Incorrect: The user must first unlock all cells. By default, all cells in a spreadsheet are locked.

   C. Incorrect: If the user hides the formula cells, users cannot see the calculations.

   D. Incorrect: Enabling the Read-Only attribute does not protect locked cells.

Glossary

802.11b wireless connection   An industry standard for communicating through a wireless network. These network connections support a maximum bandwidth of 11 Mbps.

access violation error   Errors caused by corrupt files or low system resources. Access violation errors can occur because of inaccurate calculations, when launching programs, or when code is poorly written.

Active Directory directory service   A centralized database that contains information about a network's users, workstations, servers, printers, and other resources. Active Directory (found on a domain controller) determines who can access what and to what degree. Active Directory is essential for maintaining, organizing, and securing the resources on a larger network; it allows network administrators to centrally manage resources; and it is extensible—it can be configured to grow and to be personalized for any company.

ActiveX control   Small programs and animations on Web pages. ActiveX controls are downloaded to and run on a computer to enhance the Web experience.

adware   Software that shows ads that the program thinks the user would like to see. Adware is usually installed unknowingly and knows what a user likes because it watches what sites the user visits while online. Adware is a form of spyware.

AutoRecover files   Files that are saved automatically when an application shuts down unexpectedly. AutoRecover files can help a user recover a document when the power goes out or when a computer shuts down unexpectedly.

basic input/output system (BIOS)   A computer's BIOS program determines in what order the computer searches for system files on bootup, manages communication between the operating system and the attached devices on bootup, and is an integral part of the computer.

BIOS   See basic input/output system (BIOS).

bit   A binary digit, the smallest unit of information holding data on a computer. A single bit can hold only one of two values: 0 or 1.

broadcast storm   When a single message is sent to all hosts on a network or network segment. Broadcast storms can be used by attackers to disable a network by sending too many messages for the network to handle.

byte   A basic unit of computer storage. A byte contains 8 bits.

cache   An area of the hard disk that holds temporary files. In the context of Internet Explorer, temporary Internet files are cached so a user can use the Back and Forward buttons, access History, and use offline files and folders. Retrieving information from the cache is much faster than retrieving information from the Internet.

COM port   A computer's communication port. This port, which allows data to be sent one byte at a time, is often referred to as a serial port.

compact privacy policy   A website's privacy policy. The policy details what information is collected from visitors, whom the information is given to, and how the owners of the website use the information. It also conforms to the Platform for Privacy Preferences (P3P).

compressed drive   A drive that has been condensed to take up less space on the hard disk by using a compression tool such as NTFS compression utilities.

Conflicts folder   A folder in Outlook 2003 that holds multiple copies of conflicting items in the mailbox. If multiple changes have been made to an item, but the item is not updated correctly in the Navigation pane, check this folder.

cookie   A small text file that contains information about you and your computer. Websites place cookies on computers that visit them so that they can personalize the user's next visit. Generally, cookies are harmless.

device driver   Software that is used to allow a computer and a piece of hardware to communicate. Device drivers that are incompatible, corrupt, outdated, or of the wrong version for the hardware can cause errors that are difficult to diagnose.

DHCP   See Dynamic Host Configuration Protoco (DHCP).

disk quota   A restriction that can be placed on users so that they can only use a predefined amount of a hard disk's available space.

DLL   See dynamic-link library (DLL).

DNS   See Domain Name System (DNS).

Domain Name System (DNS)   A service that resolves host names to IP addresses for clients on a network. This service allows users to type in a name such as *www.microsoft.com* instead of its IP address.

Downloaded Program Files   A folder on a computer's hard disk that contains downloaded program files. These files can be ActiveX controls and Java applets, which are downloaded automatically from the Internet when you view certain pages.

Dynamic Host Configuration Protocol (DHCP) A service that assigns TCP/IP addresses automatically to clients on a network. DHCP servers provide this service.

dynamic-link library (DLL) DLL files, which are shared among multiple components of a computer and its applications, are used to run operating system components and applications. Missing DLL files cause multiple problems and usually generate an error message.

e-commerce Conducting business on the Internet. E-commerce allows business-to-business transactions and business-to-consumer transactions. In general end-user terms, it allows users to visit a website and purchase goods.

encryption A process for converting plaintext to code for the purpose of security. Encrypted files use scrambled data that makes the file unreadable to everyone except the person who created it. Secure websites use encryption to secure transactions.

Ethernet A type of cable that physically connects a computer to a network hub. This connection allows the computer and user to access network resources in a LAN.

Fast User Switching A feature of Windows XP Home and Professional Editions, available for users who are not members of domains, which makes it possible for users to switch quickly between user accounts without having to actually log off and on, or reboot the computer. Running programs do not need to be closed before switching users.

FAT See file allocation table (FAT).

file allocation table (FAT) A type of file system used by older computers to organize the files and folders on the computer. FAT organizes the files on the computer so they can be accessed when they are needed.

format The act of erasing all data on a computer drive, volume, or partition.

FQDN See fully qualified domain name (FQDN).

fully qualified domain name (FQDN) A name used to identify an entity on the Internet and part of a Uniform Resource Locator (URL). For example, *www.microsoft.com* is a fully qualified domain name.

gateway address A network point that allows access into and out of a network. Gateways can be routers, firewalls, or proxy servers; gateways decide if a data packet belongs on the local network or on a remote one.

Group Policy   A policy created by an administrator that affects all users on a computer or all users in a domain and is generally set by domain administrators on a domain level. Group policies are used to specify how a user's desktop looks, what wallpaper is used, and how the Internet Explorer title bar looks, to name only a few options.

HTTP e-mail account   An e-mail account that connects to an HTTP e-mail server, such as Hotmail. HTTP accounts, which can be added to Outlook 2003 or to Outlook Express, can download e-mail and synchronize mailbox folders.

IME   See Input Method Editor (IME).

Input Method Editor (IME)   A program that is used to enter different characters in Asian languages on a standard 101-key keyboard. As the user enters keystrokes, the program tries to identify the characters and convert them to phonetic and ideographic characters.

Internet cache files   A temporary copy of a Web page's text and graphics. These temporary files are stored in random access memory (RAM) on the hard disk and can be accessed more quickly than files retrieved fresh from the Internet for every visit to the page. Internet cache files make browsing the Internet faster because frequently visited pages can be loaded more quickly than they can if no cache files exist.

IrDA   Acronym for Infrared Data Association, a type of port installed on newer computers, printers, and other devices that allows them to communicate wirelessly. IrDA ports transmit data at about the same rate as a parallel port does, and the devices must be in close proximity and have a clear line of sight between them.

JavaScript   A programming language. JavaScript is used on websites to open pop-up windows when a link is clicked, to change the color of text when a mouse is rolled over it, or to change formatted information such as the time or date.

kernel mode   The computer mode that has direct access to hardware. Kernel mode maintains control over all resources and the system itself. Programs that run in kernel mode should not be run using program compatibility settings.

LAN   See local area network (LAN).

local area network (LAN)   A group of computers in a small geographic area such as a home, office, or floor of an office building. LANs can be workgroups or domains, can connect wirelessly or using Ethernet and a hub, or can connect by more complex connections such as fiber optic lines.

loopback address   A TCP/IP address reserved for testing internal TCP/IP settings on any computer. The loopback address is any address in the range 127.x.y.z, and a successful ping to a computer's loopback address verifies that TCP/IP is installed correctly.

macro   A series of program instructions in a Microsoft Office application that is grouped together as a single command to accomplish a task automatically.

Microsoft .NET Framework   Microsoft .NET Framework is a platform for building, deploying, and running Web services and applications.

.NET Programmability Support   Support for developers of .NET Framework applications. Microsoft .NET Framework is a platform for building, deploying, and running Web services and applications.

NetBIOS name   A friendly name used by computers on a network to distinguish them from other resources. WINS servers resolve NetBIOS names to their associated IP addresses. NetBIOS names allow computers with older operating systems such as Windows NT, Windows Me, and Windows 98 to participate in a network and to access resources.

NetMeeting   A real-time collaboration and conferencing application that combines application sharing, video and voice, and complete Internet conferencing.

NTFS   A type of file system used by newer computers that is much more advanced than the FAT file system. NTFS provides advanced file and folder permissions, encryption, disk quotas, and compression. NTFS is supported by Windows NT, Windows 2000, and Windows XP.

packets   Data sent over a network. Large messages and data are broken up into small pieces of data called packets. Although the individual packets might take different routes to the destination computer, once there, they are reassembled to form the original data.

page fault   An error that occurs when information cannot be found that the operating system needs to perform a task. This can occur due to lack of RAM or virtual memory; corrupt temporary files; a conflict between programs; or missing or corrupt cookies, Favorites, History, or other Internet Explorer data.

partition   A smaller part of a larger hard disk. When a disk is partitioned, it is split into two or more smaller virtual drives. Partitions can be created to hold data, hold applications, or create a multiboot computer.

post   A message sent to or read in a newsgroup.

protocol   A set of agreed-on rules for communicating among computers. Protocols are industry standards, and both the sending and receiving computers must agree on the protocols used for communication to take place.

retention policy   A company policy set by a network administrator. Retention policies are set to encourage users to keep e-mail and documents for a standard period of time and then delete or archive them. Retention policies override AutoArchive settings.

reversible encryption   A process used to camouflage a message or data. Encrypting data keeps data safe from access by intruders.

router   A device that forwards data packets between networks.

scope of addresses   The range of addresses a DHCP server can allocate to network clients.

ScreenTips   Reviewers' remarks. ScreenTips display comments in yellow pop-up boxes, and the comments appear when the user holds the mouse over the comment.

search engine   An application that can search through every page on every Web site on the Internet for the purpose of offering those pages when a user searches for information. Major search engines include Google and Yahoo!.

seated   A hardware card's connection to the motherboard. A modem, network interface card, or sound card is considered seated if it is properly connected to the motherboard.

security ID   A unique identification number called a security identifier that identifies each user in a network.

security policy   Policies configured by domain, workgroup, or system administrators. The policies keep the computer and the computing environment secure by limiting what users can and cannot do while logged on to the computer or network.

service level agreement (SLA)   SLAs are agreements between parties (such as a call center and the company that hires it) that define how long a call should take, how much time should be spent on each incident, and which reports and documents must be maintained. The SLA also defines penalties for not meeting requirements.

shortcut key   A key combination associated with a macro for the purpose of running the macro. Common shortcut keys include CTRL+A, SHIFT+Z, and CTRL+V.

SLA   See service level agreement (SLA).

spyware   Software that monitors a user's Web surfing activities. Spyware is often installed unwittingly on a computer when free software is downloaded from the Internet.

static IP address   An address configured for a computer that is not allocated by a DHCP server. The address never changes and must be manually input by a network administrator.

subnet   A separate and distinct part of a network, generally represented by one geographic location, such as an office or building. Subnets use gateways to access the Internet, thus enabling all users to access the Internet through one shared network address.

subnet mask   Subnet masks enable computers to determine when to send packets to the gateway to communicate with computers on remote subnets.

system partition   The physical area of the hard disk that holds the operating system files. The system partition is generally the C drive.

temporary files   Cached files. Temporary Internet files allow a user to use the Back and Forward buttons, access History, and use offline files and folders. Retrieving information from the Temporary Internet Files folder is much faster than retrieving information from the Internet.

temporary Internet files   See Internet cache files.

Terminal Services client software   Software used for client computers that access applications remotely on a network.

timeout   An error caused by an e-mail or news post that takes longer than the allotted time to download. Timeout errors can be eliminated by increasing how much time Outlook is allotted to download messages from a mail server.

Uniform Resource Locator (URL)   The URL of a website is its friendly name, for instance, *http://www.microsoft.com*.

URL   See Uniform Resource Locator (URL).

Visual Basic   A programming language used for websites and applications. Macros created in Excel, Word, and other Office programs can be edited with the Visual Basic Editor, which is included with the applications.

volume   An area of the hard disk used for storing data. See also partition.

Windows Installer   A core component of IntelliMirror, which is used to deploy applications across a domain. Windows Installer is used to install applications and to manage user installation options.

wireless access point   A device that provides wireless access to network resources. Users that have wireless networking cards in their computers can use this access point to wirelessly connect to the network.

XML tag   A data marker used to retrieve data from a document.

Index

H

I

Walter Glenn

Walter Glenn, Microsoft Certified System Engineer (MCSE), Microsoft Certified Desktop Support Technician (MCDST), and Microsoft Certified Trainer (MCT), has been a part of the computer industry for more than 17 years and currently works in Huntsville, Alabama, as a consultant, trainer, and writer. Walter is a regular columnist in Microsoft's TechNet Zone and is the author or coauthor of nearly 20 computer titles, including *Microsoft Exchange Server 2003 Administrator's Companion* (Microsoft Press, 2003), *Mike Meyers' MCSA Managing a Microsoft Windows Server 2003 Network Environment Certification Passport (Exam 70-291)* (Osborne, 2003), and *MCSE Self-Paced Training Kit (Exam 70-297): Designing a Microsoft Windows Server 2003 Active Directory and Network Infrastructure* (Microsoft Press, 2003). He has also written a number of Web-based courses that are geared toward Microsoft certification training.

Tony Northrup

Tony Northrup, CISSP, MCSE, and MVP, is a networking consultant and author living in the Boston, Massachusetts, area. During his seven years as Principal Systems Architect at BBN/Genuity, he was ultimately responsible for the reliability and security of hundreds of Windows servers and dozens of Windows domains—all directly connected to the Internet. Needless to say, Tony learned the hard way how to keep Windows systems safe and reliable in a hostile environment.

As a consultant, Tony has provided networking guidance to a wide variety of organizations, from Fortune 100 enterprises to nonprofit organizations and small businesses. Tony has authored or coauthored a dozen books on Windows and networking. When he is not consulting or writing, Tony enjoys cycling, hiking, and nature photography

For *Windows Server 2003* administrators

Microsoft® Windows® Server 2003 Administrator's Companion
ISBN 0-7356-1367-2

The comprehensive, daily operations guide to planning, deployment, and maintenance.
Here's the ideal one-volume guide for anyone who administers Windows Server 2003. It offers up-to-date information on core system-administration topics for Windows, including Active Directory® services, security, disaster planning and recovery, interoperability with NetWare and UNIX, plus all-new sections about Microsoft Internet Security and Acceleration (ISA) Server and scripting. Featuring easy-to-use procedures and handy workarounds, it provides ready answers for on-the-job results.

Microsoft Windows Server 2003 Administrator's Pocket Consultant
ISBN 0-7356-1354-0

The practical, portable guide to Windows Server 2003. Here's the practical, pocket-sized reference for IT professionals who support Windows Server 2003. Designed for quick referencing, it covers all the essentials for performing everyday system-administration tasks. Topics covered include managing workstations and servers, using Active Directory services, creating and administering user and group accounts, managing files and directories, data security and auditing, data back-up and recovery, administration with TCP/IP, WINS, and DNS, and more.

Microsoft IIS 6.0 Administrator's Pocket Consultant
ISBN 0-7356-1560-8

The practical, portable guide to IIS 6.0. Here's the eminently practical, pocket-sized reference for IT and Web professionals who work with Internet Information Services (IIS) 6.0. Designed for quick referencing and compulsively readable, this portable guide covers all the basics needed for everyday tasks. Topics include Web administration fundamentals, Web server administration, essential services administration, and performance, optimization, and maintenance. It's the fast-answers guide that helps users consistently save time and energy as they administer IIS 6.0.

To learn more about the full line of Microsoft Press® products for IT professionals, please visit:

microsoft.com/mspress/IT

Complete planning and migration information
for Microsoft Windows Server 2003

Introducing Microsoft® Windows Server™ 2003
ISBN 0-7356-1570-5

Get a detailed, official first look at the new features and improvements in Windows Server 2003. Windows Server 2003 provides significant improvements in performance, productivity, and security over previous versions. This official first-look guide shows you exactly what's new and improved in this powerful network operating system—including advanced technologies for XML Web services and components, security, networking, Active Directory® directory service, Microsoft Internet Information Services, support for IPv6, and more. It gives you all the information and tools you need to understand, evaluate, and begin deployment planning for Windows Server 2003, whether you're upgrading from Microsoft Windows NT® Server or Microsoft Windows® 2000 Server.

Migrating from Microsoft Windows NT Server 4.0 to Microsoft Windows Server 2003
ISBN 0-7356-1940-9

Get expert guidance, procedures, and solutions for a successful migration—direct from the Windows Server team. Get real-world guidance for planning and deploying an upgrade from Windows NT 4.0 to Windows Server 2003 for your small or medium-sized business. This book delivers straightforward, step-by-step instructions on how to upgrade to an Active Directory directory service environment; migrate your DHCP, WINS, file, print, remote access, and Web server roles; and implement Group Policy–based administration. Whether you support 10 or 1,000 users, you get the detailed information—plus evaluation software—you need to put Windows Server 2003 to work right away.

To learn more about the full line of Microsoft Press® products for IT professionals, please visit:

microsoft.com/mspress/IT

In-depth technical information and tools
for Microsoft Windows Server 2003

Microsoft® Windows Server™ 2003 Deployment Kit: A Microsoft Resource Kit
ISBN 0-7356-1486-5

Plan and deploy a Windows Server 2003 operating system environment with expertise from the team that develops and supports the technology—the Microsoft Windows® team. This multivolume kit delivers in-depth technical information and best practices to automate and customize your installation, configure servers and desktops, design and deploy network services, design and deploy directory and security services, implement Group Policy, create pilot and test plans, and more. You also get more than 125 timesaving tools, deployment job aids, Windows Server 2003 evaluation software, and the entire Windows Server 2003 Help on the CD-ROMs. It's everything you need to help ensure a smooth deployment—while minimizing maintenance and support costs.

Internet Information Services (IIS) 6.0 Resource Kit
ISBN 0-7356-1420-2

Deploy and support IIS 6.0, which is included with Windows Server 2003, with expertise direct from the Microsoft IIS product team. This official RESOURCE KIT packs 1200+ pages of in-depth deployment, operations, and technical information, including step-by-step instructions for common administrative tasks. Get critical details and guidance on security enhancements, the new IIS 6.0 architecture, migration strategies, performance tuning, logging, and troubleshooting—along with timesaving tools, IIS 6.0 product documentation, and a searchable eBook on CD. You get all the resources you need to help maximize the security, reliability, manageability, and performance of your Web server—while reducing system administration costs.

To learn more about the full line of Microsoft Press® products for IT professionals, please visit:

microsoft.com/mspress/IT

System Requirements

To follow the practices in this book, it is recommended that you use a computer that is not your primary workstation because you will make changes to the operating system and application configuration. The computer that you use must have the following minimum configuration.

Hardware Requirements

All hardware should be on the Microsoft Windows XP SP2 Hardware Compatibility List (HCL).

- Personal computer with a 233 MHz or higher processor; Intel Pentium/Celeron family, AMD K6/Athlon/Duron family, or compatible processor recommended
- 128 MB of RAM or greater
- 1.8 GB of available hard disk space; optional installation files cache requires an additional 300 MB of hard disk space
- CD-ROM drive or DVD-ROM drive
- Super VGA (800 x 600) or higher resolution monitor
- Keyboard and Microsoft Mouse, Microsoft IntelliMouse, or compatible pointing device

Additionally, several chapters have practices that require you to have an Internet connection.

Software Requirements

The following software is required to complete the procedures in this training kit. A 30-day evaluation edition of Microsoft Office Professional Edition 2003 is included on CD-ROM as well as a 120-day evaluation edition of Microsoft Windows XP Professional Edition with Service Pack 2.

- Microsoft Windows XP Professional Edition with SP2
- Microsoft Office Professional Edition 2003 (which you will install in Chapter 6, if you have not already)

 Caution   The evaluation edition software that is provided with this training kit is not the full retail product and is provided only for the purposes of training and evaluation. Microsoft Technical Support does not support evaluation editions.

What do you think of this book? We want to hear from you!

Do you have a few minutes to participate in a brief online survey? Microsoft is interested in hearing your feedback about this publication so that we can continually improve our books and learning resources for you.

To participate in our survey, please visit:

www.microsoft.com/learning/booksurvey

And enter this book's ISBN, 0-7356-2221-3. As a thank-you to survey participants in the United States and Canada, each month we'll randomly select five respondents to win one of five $100 gift certificates from a leading online merchant.* At the conclusion of the survey, you can enter the drawing by providing your e-mail address, which will be used for prize notification *only*.

Thanks in advance for your input. Your opinion counts!

Sincerely,

Microsoft Learning

Learn More. Go Further.

Save 15%
on your Microsoft® certification exam testing

Get certified

You invested in your future with the purchase of this book. Now, take the opportunity to get a full return on your investment and get the recognition your skills deserve. A Microsoft certification validates your technical expertise and provides industry recognition for your skills and experience with Microsoft products.

Test at any Microsoft Certified Exam Provider—worldwide!

Use this voucher to save 15% on one exam fee at any Microsoft Certified Exam Provider. Discount offer good on one exam in the Microsoft Certified Professional Program.

Redeem your discount voucher

Present the discount voucher on the back of this page in-person at a Microsoft Certified Exam Provider testing center, or use the voucher discount code to register online or via phone with the Microsoft Certified Exam Provider of your choice. For complete information on how to register for your exam, see the Microsoft Certified Exam Provider Web site:

www.microsoft.com/mcp/exams

Microsoft | Learning

15% off
your Microsoft certification exam

Turn this page to find your exam voucher discount code and for promotion details.

Redeemable at Microsoft Certified Exam Providers worldwide.
See **www.microsoft.com/mcp/exams** for complete list.

exam voucher

Microsoft

* See terms and conditions on reverse.

Present this discount voucher to any of 5,000 testing centers worldwide in 130 countries for 15% off your exam fee. Or, use the discount code on the voucher to register online or via phone with the Microsoft Certified Exam Provider of your choice.

Microsoft

Microsoft | Learning

This voucher good for 15% off one exam fee in the Microsoft Certified Professional Program

Offer expires 12/31/2010

Scratch off to find your discount voucher code.

Redeemable at Microsoft Certified Exam Providers worldwide.
See **www.microsoft.com/mcp/exams** for a complete list.

For more information or the location of a
Microsoft Certified Exam Provider near you, visit:

www.microsoft.com/mcp/exams

Promotion Terms and Conditions:

- Offer good for 15% off one exam fee in the Microsoft Certified Professional Program.
- Voucher can be redeemed online or at Microsoft Certified Exam Providers worldwide.
- Discounted exam must be taken on or before December 31, 2010.
- Promotion is limited to one discounted exam per candidate for each book purchased.
- Inform your Microsoft Certified Exam Provider that you want to use this voucher as payment for your exam at the time you register for the exam.

Voucher Terms and Conditions

- Expired voucher has no value and will not be replaced.
- Voucher code must be used at time of registration.
- This voucher may not be combined with other vouchers or discounts.
- This voucher is nontransferable and is void if altered or revised in any way. It may not be redeemed for cash, credit, or refund, and may not be used for any other exam.
- Any transfer or resale of this voucher is expressly prohibited.

X11-56768